NATASHA

Natasha

The Biography of Natalie Wood

By Suzanne Finstad

ARROW

Published by Arrow Books in 2002

1 3 5 7 9 10 8 6 4 2

First published in the US in a slightly different form by Harmony Books, a division of Random House, Inc.

First published in the United Kingdom in 2001 by Century
The Random House Group Limited, 20 Vauxhall Bridge Road, London SW1V 2SA

Random House Australia (Pty) Limited, 20 Alfred Street, Milsons Point, Sydney, New South Wales 2061, Australia

Random House New Zealand Limited, 18 Poland Road, Glenfield, Auckland 10, New Zealand

Random House South Africa (Pty) Limited, Endulini, 5a Jubilee Road, Parktown 2193, South Africa

The Random House Group Limited Reg. No. 954009

Grateful acknowledgment is made to the following for permission to reprint previously published material:

Criterion Music Corporation: Lyrics from "When the World Was Young," English lyrics by Johnny Mercer, French lyrics by Angele Vannier. Music by M. Philippe-Gerard. Copyright © 1950–1951, Copyright renewed 1978 by Enoch et Cie. Used by permission of Criterion Music Corporation.

Hobby-Catto Properties, L.L.C.: excerpt from "Natalie Wood: Hollywood's Number One Survivor" by Thomas Thompson, Look magazine, April 2, 1979.
Used with permission from Hobby-Catto Properties, L.L.C.

www.randomhouse.co.uk

A CIP catalogue record for this book is available from the British Library

Papers used by Random House UK Limited are natural, recyclable products made from wood grown in sustainable forests. The manufacturing processes conform to the environmental regulations of the country of origin.

ISBN 0 0994 31858

Typeset in Goudy by MATS, Southend-on-Sea, Essex
Printed and bound in Great Britain by Bookmarque Ltd, Croydon, Surrey

FRONTISPIECE: At the Sherry-Netherland in New York, spring 1963, during the filming of *Love with the Proper Stranger*. This was Natalie's favorite movie experience. Privately, her romance with Warren Beatty was unraveling and she was lonely. Photo used by permission of William Claxton.

OPPOSITE PAGE: Natasha at four, shortly after her parents changed the family name from Zakharenko to Gurdin and moved to Santa Rosa. Photo Courtesy of Ed Canevari.

For the three sisters:

Olga, the lucky one

Lana, the survivor

AND IN MEMORY OF

Natasha, the little girl lost inside

"Natalie Wood"

NOTE TO THE READER

THE SOURCE MATERIAL for *Natasha* is located at the back of the book, set forth in chapter order, by page number. If an individual or a publication is quoted without being named in the text, consult the notes section for identification.

For consistency and correctness, the Russian spellings of names are courtesy of Professor Olga T. Yokoyama, UCLA Department of Slavic Languages.

AUTHOR'S NOTE

FIVE YEARS AGO, I happened to see a documentary about Natalie Wood. As I watched the clips from some of the fifty movies in which she appeared from the age of four, I was moved by the vulnerability behind her hypnotic brown eyes, by a pathos in Natalie made more tragic by her mysterious disappearance at forty-three in the dark water she feared all her life. Her daughters, who were only eleven and eight when Natalie drowned in 1981, expressed their grief with such poignancy the sadness was overwhelming.

Natalie Wood haunted me afterward. When I discovered there had never been an authoritative biography about her, I felt compelled to write about Natalie's life, and her legacy, which has consumed the last four years of my life.

After interviewing close to four hundred people, watching her filmed performances, excavating ship's logs, articles, photographs, birth, death and marriage records dating from the 1800s, examining the sheriff's and coroner's official documents related to her drowning, making pilgrimages to every apartment, hospital, church, school, and house she lived in or attended, being taken by boat to the cove off Catalina where she was found in her nightgown that last, bizarre weekend, I am still moved by Natalie, who was as beautiful, and haunting, as those dark Russian eyes, and whose life is far more compelling than any of her movie roles.

Before she became Natalie Wood—Hollywood's child—

she was Natasha Zakharenko, the daughter of Russian immigrants who fled Bolsheviks. Her fame, and her drowning, had been foretold before she was born to her mother Maria, who claimed to be Russian royalty and who created the actress personality "Natalie Wood," a tale as rich, complex and mysterious as "Anastasia," the role Natalie was preparing to play before she was lost at sea twenty years ago. From the time she was a teenager to the night she disappeared off Catalina, Natalie was struggling to reclaim her lost identity as Natasha.

I am deeply grateful to the hundreds of people who contributed to this biography, including many who have never spoken publicly about Natalie before. My heartfelt thanks to her sisters Olga and Lana, who inspired the Chekhovian theme; to Natalie's cousins, the Liuzunies, for their treasury of photographs and Russian history; to Sue Russell for audiotapes of Natalie's mystic mother and alter ego, Maria Gurdin; to the Hyatts for invaluable confidences; to Natalie's close friends Ed Canevari, Maryann Brooks, Jacqueline Perry, Peggy Griffin, Scott Marlowe, and Jim Williams, who bared their souls to tell Natalie's powerfully moving story. It is a tribute to their affection for Natalie that this book is further enriched by the personal reminiscences of Robert Redford, Dennis Hopper, Tony Curtis, Maureen O'Hara, Sydney Pollack, Karl Malden, and countless other legendary stars and directors whose lives she touched. I have tried many times, in many different ways, over the last several years to meet with Robert Wagner. My intent, from the outset, was to present a sensitive, truthful account of this tender star as a legacy to her family and her legion of fans.

My gratitude is extended to Ned Comstock, the curator of Special Collections at USC, as well as to the staff at the

Academy of Motion Picture Arts and Sciences, and to JoAnne Grazzini, who spent countless hours researching or coordinating transcribers, including the exceptional Hillary Gordon. Thank you to my family, to Tony Costello, Phyllis Quinn, Duane Rasure, Louis Danoff, Marvin Eisenman, Charles Higham, Pat Broeske, Barry Redmond, Ed Jubert, Doug Bombard, Betty Batausa, Ariel Kochane, Diana Rico, and Henry Jaglom for further support, assistance, or insight; as well as to Bill Ogden, Gerry Abrams, and J. K. Selznick for guidance. Lastly, to my editor, Shaye Areheart, for her patience and for sharing my passion to honor Natalie with this book.

Suzanne Finstad
Los Angeles, March 2001

CONTENTS

ACT ONE

Star-Child

1908–1951

"She does her hair up in pigtails, like a little girl; then she talks with amazing archness . . ."

ANTON CHEKHOV
Three Sisters

1

"NATALIE WOOD" NEVER REALLY existed. The actress with that name was a fictional creation of her mother, a disturbed genius known by various first names, usually Maria. How Natalie was discovered, why she went into show business as a child, her background, were all part of a tapestry of lies woven by Maria that began before Natalie was even born. "God created her, but I invented her," her mother said once, after Natalie's body was discovered floating in the dark waters off Catalina Island the Sunday after Thanksgiving of 1981, when she was just forty-three. Natalie Wood, the celebrity, was an entwined alter ego of mother and daughter so powerfully macabre her drowning had been predicted by a gypsy, years before, to happen to *Maria*, not Natalie. The person inside the illusion of "Natalie Wood" was lost for years, even to herself.

Natalia Nikolaevna Zakharenko*, the real name of the actress known as Natalie Wood, was a child of Russia, once removed. Exactly where in Russia we may never know, for her mother, the source of the family history, was an unreliable witness, a feverishly imaginative woman who lived in a world of her own invention, only occasionally punctuated by the truth. Maria's friends characterized this as colorful; others considered her devious; her youngest child eventually concluded she was a pathological liar. There was intrigue to Maria no biographer could fully

---

*Spelled 'Zackharenko' on the birth certificate and by the family.

unravel. She would have three daughters—Olga, Natalia, and Svetlana—three sisters, as in the Chekhov play. For Maria, there was only and ever Natalia. Her consuming obsession with Natasha, Natalia's pet name, was the one thing no one questioned about Maria.

The rest of her life was a masquerade, with Maria assuming different disguises.

Natalie Wood's mother came into the world somewhere in Siberia. It was most likely the town of Barnaul, as her oldest child, Olga, believed and ship's records document, though she told a different daughter and a biographer that she was born in Tomsk. They are both close to Russia's border with Mongolia, near the Altai Mountains. Maria's early years were spent in this nethermost, Russian-Asian region of the more than four and a half million square miles known as Siberia, famous for its bitterly cold winters, romanticized for its forests primeval, and considered the ends of the earth.

Maria claimed, throughout her life, to have grown up in fantastical luxury on a palatial Siberian estate with a Chinese cook, three governesses, and a "nyanka" (nanny) per child. But her most cherished belief, or delusion, was that she was related, through her mother, to the Romanovs, Russia's royal family. Her stories—whether true or not, and most who heard them questioned their veracity—"kept you spellbound," according to a young actor who befriended Maria in the 1980s, after Natalie drowned. "She herself was quite the actress. She spoke in a very dramatic whisper, so you had to lean in, and pay close attention. She used her hands as she would describe in great detail her genealogy from Russia. She would whisper, '*We were descended from royalty . . .*' and you would just hang on every word."

What is known of Maria's family is that her father,

Stepan Zudilov, was married twice. He had four children—two boys, Mikhael and Semen, and two girls, Apollinaria (called Lilia) and Kallisfenia (or Kalia)—by his first wife, Anna. Anna died in childbirth with Kalia in 1905 in Barnaul, where the Zudilovs resided. Stepan took a second bride, who would likewise bear him two sons and two daughters in reverse order: a girl, Zoia, born in 1907, followed by Maria, then Boris and Gleb. Stepan Zudilov's youngest daughter, Maria Stepanovna Zudilova, would become the mother of Natalie Wood.*

According to Maria, her mother (also named Maria) was "close relations" to the Romanov family. It is believed her maiden name was Kulev. Whether she was an aristocrat is unknown. Kalia, Stepan's younger daughter by his first wife and the only Zudilov child other than Maria to immigrate to the United States, would later tell *her* children, "Somebody in the line was a countess." But as a Russian historian notes sardonically, "*Everyone* from Russia wants to be related to the Romanovs."

If Natalie Wood's grandmother had royal blood, her mother undermined her own credibility by the thousand-and-one variations on her lineage she offered, *Scheherazade*-style. "One story was that her parents took her to China when she was a little girl and she became a Chinese princess through some mysterious circumstances that were never explained," recalls a Hollywood friend. Another version that surfaced in studio biographies after Natalie became a child actress identified Maria as "being of French extraction." According to her eldest daughter, Olga, this

---

*An "a" is added in Russian to the surnames of female children. Middle names derive from the father's first name: in Maria's case, "Stepanovna" for Stepan.

was a prank on Maria's part. "When they would ask her if she's French, she'd say, 'Oh, yes . . .' She knew how to *speak* French, because she probably had French nannies." Even this was based solely on Maria's word, for Olga never heard her mother actually speak a word of French (nor did Maria's half-sister Kalia speak it). Maria's white lie sustained itself all the way to a 1983 television tribute to Natalie Wood, during which Orson Welles, her first costar, refers to Natalie being "not just of Russian but also of French descent." Maria, in the opinion of her daughter Lana (Americanized from Svetlana), was "frightening" in her ability to bend reality and convince others it was true, "because she did believe everything that came out of her mouth."

Maria told Lana that she was born to gypsy parents who left her on a hillside, where the Zudilovs found her and raised her as their own. "I heard that story my entire life." Maria would laugh about it with friends after Natalie became famous, muttering, in her heavy Slavic whisper, "They used to call me 'The Gypsy'! " She could easily create that impression as an adult, with her raven hair, magical tales and musical accent. "I could almost see her," remarked a Hollywood writer who spent hours with Maria, "waylaying me on a street with a bunch of heather, saying, 'Buy this or you'll be cursed for life.' "

The idea that Maria was the displaced child of gypsies is "hogwash" in the pronouncement of her closest traceable living relation—Kalia's son Constantine. No one in the family, including Lana, took this tale seriously. It originated, Maria's daughter Olga believes, as gossip among the family servants, for Maria was born, she told Olga, at the Zudilovs' "dacha," a country cottage, in the mountains. "And when my grandmother came back she had my mother, so the servants used to tell her, 'You were born by gypsies,' because she wasn't born right there where they could *see* her."

One clue exists to help decipher Maria's past. It is a photograph of the Zudilov family, retained separately by both Maria and Kalia, taken somewhere in Russia circa March 1919, according to the handwritten description. Maria's family, judged by their portrait, appears to be of means. They are dressed à la mode, the girls in shirtwaists and sailor dresses, posed regally, projecting a patrician mien. Stepan Zudilov, Natalie Wood's maternal grandfather, sits on a chair to the far left of the photograph, a stout but stately figure with a sweeping moustache, in a well-tailored three-piece woolen suit. At the center of the portrait, also seated, is his second wife, Maria, the putative Romanov. Maria evokes a gentle womanliness. She is possessed of a round face with soft features, girlishly pretty; her dark hair, contrasted by fair skin, is styled in marcelled waves. What distinguishes her as the grandmother of Natalie Wood are her liquid brown eyes: they hold the camera with their tender, slightly sad gaze.

Stepan and Maria occupy the front row with their four children—Natalie's mother, Maria, staring brazenly into the camera's eye; thirteen-year-old Zoia; and the two boys, Boris and Gleb, six and four, seated side-by-side in identical Lord Fauntleroy suits. (Maria would later bizarrely refer to them as "twins.") Standing behind Stepan's second family are his four grown children by his first wife, Anna; including Kalia, the corroborating witness to the family history. Anna's offspring are swarthier, with sharper features than Stepan's children by Natalie's grandmother. Everyone has captivating eyes.

The picture helps to solve the riddle of Maria's true age,

which would become the subject of whispered speculation once she came to Hollywood. From the time she was twenty or so, she gave her date of birth as February 8, 1912. On the back of the 1919 family photo, she is identified as "11 years, 1 month," which would mean she was born in 1908—the same year recorded in the ship's log when she immigrated to America. Both Maria and Kalia, Kalia's son cheerfully admits, "lied about their age."

The photograph of Maria's family, ironically, bears a resemblance to the romantic images of Russia's Tsar Nicholas II and his wife, Alexandra, in formal portraits with their children, taken in the last days of the Romanov monarchy. Maria kept this family photo beside a framed portrait of the Romanovs in similar pose, to the day she died, prizing them as jewels. Aside from Natalie, her link to Russian aristocracy is what defined Maria to *herself*, true *or* false, for as one companion remarked, "She believed every word of it. That's the mark of a good actress."

Musia or Marusia, as young Maria was affectionately called, was pampered from the time she was born because of her diminutive size. One of her stories was that she weighed only two pounds at birth, nearly dying. In the family portrait, she is nestled into her mother, cradled to her breast, as Marusia peers out with the smug self-possession of the favored child. She has an elfin quality, her dark hair pixie-short, with penetrating, birdlike eyes she compared to her father's as green, her daughter Olga describes as a changeable gray-blue, and those who considered her malevolent called "black and beady." Her expression, even at eleven, suggests cunning. She was a mischievous girl. Her German nanny was fired for making Marusia kneel; she learned to swear in Chinese from the cook. When she did so in front of her father, it was the cook—not Marusia—who "got a talking." The young Marusia adored jewelry (a bold bracelet leaps out from her tiny wrist in the family photo). She collected pictures and books depicting the royal family "because I worship them," she would say later, "almost like a god."*

Kalia, Maria/Marusia's older half-sister, supported her grandiose accounts of governesses and fur coats and seamstresses for their dolls, though Kalia identified the origin of the family's wealth as a factory that produced vodka and textiles, while Maria later said their father manufactured candles, ink and candy.† Kalia was not heard to repeat Maria's boast that the town where they kept their dacha was named after Natalie's grandfather. ("Because he was such a generous man. If a peasant is nice and he likes him, he'll give him house, he gives him horse, he gives him land.") According to Maria, her parents' marriage was arranged to merge Stepan Zudilov's fortune with Maria Zuleva's name. Neither Kalia nor Maria, once in America, had photos of the family's estate, or their dacha, to authenticate living such rarefied childhoods, though according to Kalia's son, they behaved like it. "Didn't cook, didn't clean, had other people do that."

This idyll, if it existed, came to a tragic end around 1919. A civil war erupted in Petrograd two years before, forcing Tsar Nicholas II to abdicate. Bolshevik workers seized the Winter Palace by October, naming Communist Vladimir Lenin as their leader. The summer of 1918, the Bolsheviks murdered Nicholas, his wife, Alexandra, and

---

*Grammar will remain uncorrected to reflect the speaker's personality.

†Maria's version made more sense, according to a Russian scholar: the textile industry was based near Moscow then, far from Barnaul, and vodka was controlled by the Russian state, prohibited by 1914.

their five young children, Grand Duke Alexei and the grand duchesses Olga, Tatiana, Maria, and presumably Anastasia.*

Natalie's grandparents kept an uneasy vigil at their home in Barnaul as the Bolshevik Revolution made its way toward Siberia. Sometime after March of 1919, the date they sat for their portrait, they were warned the Bolsheviks were coming. "They told us, '*Run!*' " said Maria, "because of Mother, the whole family would have been killed. They were killing aristocrats." They left so quickly, she recalled, there was no time to find her favorite brother, Semen.†

The Zudilovs, dressed as peasants, crossed the border into Manchuria, where they stayed a few days per Maria, a year by Kalia's version. "Then the Czechs came and chased the Communists away," Maria recounted, "so we came back."‡

Marusia and her family returned to Barnaul to find Semen hanging from the archway of their front door, a rope around his neck. Ten-year-old Marusia went into violent convulsions. "I was so little and I loved him so much—he was such a nice half-brother. When I saw him hanging there, with the tongue and everything, I start to have convulsions, starting with the neck, then with leg and hands, and then I just drop." The episode, a family legend, permanently affected Natalie's mother's nerves, leaving her subject to "the fits," she called it, damaging her psyche in ways unknowable.

Marusia and her family remained in Siberia until the Bolshevik Revolution reached their door, when they fled for China, "because the Reds were killing everybody." She

---

*A rumor, crystallizing into myth, would surface that Anastasia escaped.

†Kalia's descendants recall it as Mikhael.

‡Referring, most likely, to the Czech Army's march across Siberia.

and Kalia would provide essentially the same drama of the family's escape: how they packed what jewels and belongings they could onto a train their father bought from the Chinese. According to Maria, Natalie's grandfather buried "jewels and money and gold" worth "millions" in a waterproof box with a map of its location provided to everyone in the family "except me. I was young, they didn't give me the plan." A similar story surfaced from Kalia, though never, notably, the "plan." Whether the tale of their escape and the buried family treasure is true remains cryptic. "The problem with stories from Russians," one historian of the era observes, "is that they're *all* probable."

According to Natalie's mother, her parents changed everyone's names because they were afraid Communists would find them, exacting a promise from each child never to reveal the family's true identity—a reaction a Russian émigré friend considered extreme to the point of "demented." "Stepan Zudilov" is identified as Kalia's father on her 1905 birth certificate, *before* the alleged name change, and "Maria Kuleva" is the name documented as Marusia's mother on family possessions prior to the Revolution. These are also the names Natalie's mother would use to identify her parents on legal records once in the U.S., leaving little room for doubt that Natalie's grandparents were born Stepan Zudilov and Maria Kuleva; though Olga, Natalie's older sister, still expresses uncertainty those are their true names, "or if they changed them when they ran." Olga and Natalie's mother remained haunted all her life by the fear that Communists would come after her and "kill me like killed my brother."

Once in Manchuria, little Marusia and her family stayed at a hotel in Qiqihar, where Natalie's mother had the first of several alleged mystical experiences. As Maria later told the story, she "recognized" a house near their hotel as one she had lived in, remembering an outdoor playhouse and the ceiling of her bedroom, with "angels" on it. Her parents took her to the house, afraid she would have another seizure if they refused. Upstairs was a room with cherubim painted on the ceiling; in the backyard, concealed by spiders' webs, Marusia found a decaying playhouse. Natalie's mother believed in reincarnation ever after, despite the opposite position of the Russian Orthodox religion in which she was baptized, and to which she and her parents adhered. ("How can you explain that?" she would ask. "There was my angels!")

Natalie's grandparents settled in nearby Harbin, China, where so many Russians had fled, neighborhoods appeared to have been lifted out of Siberia. The family lived in such an enclave, in a "good" part of town. Stepan, Natalie's grandfather, is presumed to have managed a soap factory. Natalie's mother, Marusia, attended an all-Russian girls' school, though Marusia's eye was on "pretty young boys." She went to church so she could "look at the boys, and look at what the girls are wearing—is my dress better than theirs?" Marusia had thick, naturally curly, crow-black hair and was preternaturally tiny—just five feet—"But she carried herself as if she were seven foot tall," said an acquaintance from Maria's senior years. "She liked to talk about how she had been a great dancer, and how she had been a great beauty." Natalie's studio press releases would later describe her mother as a "professional ballerina" in China. "That was made up," admits daughter Olga. Teenage Marusia took *one* ballet class in Harbin. "For grace," she put it later, claiming her parents withdrew her, believing dancers and performers fell into a category with "prostitutes."

Marusia and her sisters placed absolute faith in Russian superstitions and "did gypsy stuff" using Romany magic, such as "looking in the mirror on a certain night between two candles and you can see the person you're supposed to marry." One day, the sisters had their fortunes read by a Harbin gypsy. The fortuneteller warned Marusia to "beware of dark water," for she was going to drown. The gypsy also predicted her second child "would be a great beauty, known throughout the world." Natalie Wood's life, and death, would be dictated by the gypsy's twin prophecies.

The fortuneteller's predictions held an immediate power over Natalie's mother. She refused to go near water, "especially if it's dark waters."

Marusia eloped in her teens, defying her parents by choosing a Russian-Armenian, the brawnily handsome Alexei Tatulov, originally "Tatulian," the son of an Armenian Cossack who, legend has it, led a regiment against the Turks astride a white horse. Marusia was fleeing a father too strict for her ambition; her choice of a "ladies' man" her girlfriends coveted revealed her vanity, and a competitive streak. (She told Olga, their daughter, she married Alexei "because he said he would kill himself if she didn't.") Natalie's mother was not a true beauty, as she imagined, but her vivid personality was a magnet.

She became pregnant in 1928; claiming, later, that she weighed only seventy-five pounds and doctors ordered her to abort. She would tell Natalie she had several abortions before this, because she was too tiny. By Maria's later account, her mother took her to a French doctor experienced with "narrow" Chinese women, who agreed to deliver her baby. Alexei brought a priest, she would recall, "because he thought I definitely was gonna die." Marusia gave birth to her first daughter, Olga, on October 28, 1928. She alleged that it was without anesthetic, that her labor lasted five days, and "it felt like my bones were cracking, they were stretching, it was horrible." "My mother," Olga would later sigh, "told so many stories."

Olga was originally called Ovsanna, christened in the Armenian Orthodox church. One morning, Stepan Zudilov took his infant granddaughter "for a walk," secretly bringing Ovsanna to a Russian Orthodox priest, who baptized her in the Zudilovs' religion, renaming her "Olga," a Russian name. Olga/Ovsanna had her part-Armenian father's dark eyes and gentle disposition.

When Olga was a little over a year old, Alexei and Marusia Tatulov made the bold decision to leave Harbin for America, Alexei's dream, according to Marusia, who saw America as "just this amazing land, and the Communists will never get there." Alexei boarded a ship called the *Taito Maru* in Kobe, Japan, on January 12, 1930. He arrived at the port of San Francisco, California, fifteen days later, identified in the ship's logs as an "auto mechanic." He had no job, no prospects, and fifty dollars in his pocket.

Marusia was rejected for the voyage, ostensibly underweight. She spent the next ten months in Harbin drinking a concoction of beer and milk to gain weight, a recipe she would one day give to actor Jack Lemmon, when Natalie starred in *The Great Race*. A Japanese nurse tended Olga while Marusia passed the time studying bookkeeping. She and Olga were issued their visas in November 1930, embarking on a grueling, month-long journey to the United States.

Dispossessed of her child's nurse, Marusia had no maternal instincts. She continued to breast-feed Olga, who was now two, and the little girl cried without ceasing as they traveled by train from China into Korea, then Tokyo, where they boarded a ship, the *Asama Maru*, sailing first to Hawaii, finally to San Francisco, sleeping on bamboo mats. Natalie Wood's mother's life of privilege, if it existed, existed no more.

2 MARUSIA AND OLGA'S SHIP, THE *Asama Maru*, arrived at San Francisco's Port of Angels on the eleventh of December 1930. Alexei met them at the pier, informing his wife he had a mistress. He still loved her, he told Marusia, but Armenians were "passionate" men who could not survive a year without a woman.

Marusia's next shock was her home, one room in a bungalow co-occupied by a crowd of Russian immigrants who worked with Alexei at the nearby shipyards. "I thought, 'What we gonna do?' " She had no money, a toddler, and spoke broken English. Marusia accepted the arrangement, consoled by the fact that she was further from Communists, about whom she was possessed by a terror bordering on the hallucinogenic.

Natalie's mother's escape from her demons, and her poverty, was the movies. She was "movie crazy," relates daughter Olga, who remembers how her father would give her mother money for food "and we'd go to the Temple Theater instead." Flights of fantasy transcended Marusia from the reality of having seen a brother hanged, or the squalor of her life in America. They infused her with the cheerfulness of the deranged. "She would say, 'Believe in the best, expect something good to happen, and it will.' "

Ballet was Marusia's secondary passion. She befriended

Nadia Ermolova, a model who taught ballet to children, enrolling Olga in her class. Marusia danced alongside the little girls, "doing it more than *we* would." Marusia left her toddler to her own devices. When she got a job as a church seamstress, lying that she knew how to sew, Marusia left Olga, then four, in the park while she went to work.

She was remembered as a "social climber" in the Russian community of San Francisco, which socialized at a Russian Center off Divisadero, where an Invalids Ball was held each year. Marusia was twice Queen and twice Princess, chosen on the basis of having collected the most money for Russian veterans. "Here we all were," recalls a neighbor, "not two pennies to rub together, and Marusia is standing around on the corners gathering money for the Invalidzi." A 1936 photo of Natalie's mother as Queen shows her sitting in a ballgown wearing her crown, a satin banner draped across her chest, trophy in one hand, a spray of flowers in the other, looking as if she had assumed her rightful place on the Russian throne. The gossip where Alex worked as a janitor was that he "took" the dress from the emporium where he worked as a janitor and returned it after the ball. Olga remembers her mother hiring a dressmaker a different year she was Queen, "using *all* her money for this one dress."

Marusia began acting in plays at the Russian Center, then at the Kolobok, a Russian club, where she danced onstage, dragging Olga, who would "fall asleep on pool tables." Marusia wanted to be an actress, in the opinion of her closest friend, Josephine Paulson, whose daughter Lois was Olga's playmate, giving Olga the lifelong nickname "Teddi," for Tatulov. Marusia read palms and threw tarot cards, "always into something." She looked at apartments full-time, moving the family at whim.

Though her husband continued to have affairs, Marusia

became pregnant in 1932. She collapsed on the street and was rushed to Mt. Zion Hospital, where her second reputed mystical episode occurred. She hemorrhaged during a blood transfusion, lost the baby, and was pronounced dead, regaining consciousness as a nurse prepared her to be embalmed. Marusia lay on the hospital bed, unable to speak or move to indicate she was alive. Alex arrived to accompany her body to the morgue, carrying dried flowers from a religious icon, sent by Marusia's mother. As he placed the flowers on Marusia's neck, she felt warmth. "I open my eyes and I start to scream. The nurse fainted, then she run out and said, '*She's alive!*' " Marusia's friend Josephine, Josephine's daughter, and Olga all confirm the incident, which Natalie's mother would consider a miracle, reinforcing both her religion and her belief in the mystic.

Marusia was still living with her husband, Alex, when she began dating a Russian sea captain, George Cetalopv, the "great passion" of her life. "My father had other interests," as Olga explained, "and she had this interest." One night Alex brought home for dinner a coworker from the sugar boats, a Russian immigrant named Nikolai Zakharenko. He was twenty-three; short, but well-built; with black hair, black eyes, and the refined face of a matinee idol. "God, he was so handsome," Maria would swoon in her later years of the man who would become Natalie's father. She continued to dally with her sea captain, but acquired Nick Zakharenko like a trophy. "All my girlfriends want him, and I thought, 'If they want him, I have to get him!' "

Nick and Musia, his pet name for Maria, made a dazzling couple on the dance floor, where they won prizes dancing together. He impressed Maria with his gentlemanly manners, for Nick had a poet's soul which expressed itself when he played the balalaika, a Russian string instrument. He was also possessed by a dark force that could explode after too much vodka. "Nick would get very moody and would hurt somebody," recalled Olga, who was seven when they met. "He would fight."

The underlying cause of Natalie's father's rage was not fully understood. His brother Dmitri believed it came from deep-seated hatred of Communists. The Zakharenko brothers—Nikolai, Dmitri and Vladimir—spent their childhoods in the eastern Siberian port of Vladivostok, where their father, Stepan, worked at a candy factory and their mother, the former Eudoxie Sauchenko, was known for her beauty. During the revolution, Stepan Zakharenko fought against the Bolsheviks. Nikolai, the eldest, was not quite ten when Communists killed his father. Eudoxie received financial aid from a brother who immigrated to California, enabling her to escape Vladivostok for Shanghai with her three handsome young sons. She remarried in China. Her new husband, a Russian naval engineer named Constantine Zavarin, determined to move the family to the U.S., far from Bolshevik forces. Their first stop was Vancouver, the end of 1927, when Nikolai was fifteen. By 1932 the family made their way south to Seattle, settling eventually in San Francisco. Dmitri and Vladimir Zakharenko survived their upbringing relatively unscathed; Nikolai emerged with psychic wounds even Dmitri considered an enigma. "He kept in touch with Russians that were in exile, and he read the Russian books—oh, and he was so proud of the Tsar's family. I didn't even *think* of them."

Nick struck out on his own when he was twenty, mining for gold in the Rockies. Dmitri, who briefly joined him, described a tortured artist playing balalaika part-time with an orchestra, railing against Communists during drunken binges on vodka. "He worried about and hated the Communists so much . . . it kills *you* instead of the other guy." Nick's anger came out in fistfights, when "he'd just lose his temper and threaten some guy. He'd never back down."

Alex Tatulov saved Nick's life in such a brawl before he brought him home to dinner. Natalie's mother, who thrilled to strong and handsome men, and to drama, may have found Nick Zakharenko's furies exciting at the start. They also shared a fanatical attachment to the royal family and a frenzied paranoia about Communists. Maria ended her "arrangement" with Alex and set up housekeeping with Nick, taking Olga. She filed for divorce in October 1935, identifying herself as Maria and as "Marie," a name she began to use arbitrarily. The new setup with Nick did nothing to deter Maria from carrying on her flirtation with George Cetalopv, the captain she considered her true love.

Maria became pregnant with Natalie in October 1937, six months after her divorce from Olga's father. She and Olga, who was nine, lived in a cubbyhole apartment in an alley with Nick, who was working as a janitor at Standard Oil. The conception was noteworthy, for Nick thought he could not have children, according to Maria, who was still romantically involved with George Cetalopv. The baby, from all accounts, was Nick's. He and Maria were married on February 8, 1938, in a small Russian Orthodox cathedral in the neighborhood, witnessed by Nick's artist brother, Vladimir. Why she waited until she was four months pregnant with Natalie to get married is one of Maria's mysteries. "George went on a trip because he was captain of the ship," recalls Olga. "When he came back, she was married to Nick." Olga wondered, then and later, why her mother married Nick and not George Cetalopv, the love of her life. "I asked her that once. She said she liked George *too* much, that she'd always be jealous of him. But who *knows* her story? Nick was *very* attractive . . . much more attractive than George."

Maria may have delayed marrying Nick because of his alcohol problem, which concerned her. "He drank a lot," she said later, "even when I married him. He was wonderful man—when he was not drinking."

Her choice of Nick Zakharenko over George Cetalopv would prove prophetic to Maria, despite its disturbing consequences. She was glad she married Nick, she said at the end of her life, because he gave her Natalie.

3

MARIA BELIEVED SHE WAS carrying destiny's child, the world-famous beauty the gypsy in Harbin had predicted as her second-born. She ingratiated herself to a rich, childless Russian couple, Theodore and Helen Loy (originally "Lopatin"), whom she met through friends in the immigrant community, asking them to be godparents, assuring wealthy patrons for the unborn child she was convinced fate had chosen for fame. Natalie, a childhood friend would observe, was stage-managed by her mother "from conception."

The Zakharenkos, who were struggling to pay the obstetrician's bills, managed to move out of the alley to a cheerful duplex nearby at 1690 Page Street by the time Maria went into labor the morning of July 20, 1938. True to the fortuneteller's prophecy, her baby, a girl, resembled "an exquisite, perfectly formed china doll," said a neighbor. Maria granted the wealthy Helen Loy, the fairy godmother, the manipulative privilege of naming her star-child. Loy chose "Natalia," for the pretty blond daughter of a friend in China. It was Americanized to "Natalie" on the birth certificate, which omitted the Russian patronymic "Nikolaevna" (daughter of Nikolai). The petite infant with flashing dark eyes carried the ponderous name Natalia Nikolaevna Zakharenko. She was called, simply, "Natasha."

"As soon as she was born, she brought us some luck," Maria boasted later. According to Maria, Nick placed a small bet on the Chinese lottery while she and Natasha were still in the hospital, winning "exactly the amount" owed the doctor. "She brought money, even when she was born!" her mother crowed.

Robert Wagner, the man Natalie would marry twice, said after her death that Natalie was born to be an actress, "as if she had the word 'movie star' written on her birth certificate." If so, the handwriting was Maria's. Maria *raised* Natasha to be a movie star, as she brazenly told a reporter later. She breast-fed Natasha at the movies, whispering in the darkness how she would be famous like the gypsy predicted; safeguarding her from imagined dangers as if she were the Lindbergh child. Maria would have crawled inside Natalia's skin if she could.

Nick simply adored Natasha. Astonished at having fathered a child, he treated her as if she were a fragile figment of his imagination, insisting that visitors wear masks so they wouldn't breathe on her. "He just went goofy over this little girl," an acquaintance noted. Natalie returned the affection in her eulogy to her "Fahd" years later: "I never knew anyone so brave," she said. There could be little doubt Natasha was Nick's daughter; she was a miniaturized version of him: tiny but perfectly proportioned, with his striking features. The quality uniquely Natasha's was in her eyes; deep, dark pools of sensitivity that seemed "to go way back to Russia or beyond."

Natasha's earliest memories were of the Romanovs, seen from her crib. She slept in Nick and Musia's bedroom, where the walls were a picture gallery of the Russian royal family, hung with care by Nick, a skilled artisan. Natasha, whom he called "Meelaya," Russian for "dearest," was his grand duchess Anastasia. "He went out and bought this absolutely ostentatiously beautiful carriage, and everybody in the Russian colony just thought he was totally googy to spend all that money," said an émigré friend, who wondered how Nick, then an elevator operator, could afford it. "They didn't have a penny to their name really." Natasha was baptized in the Holy Virgin Russian Orthodox Church on Fulton Street in a christening gown and gold cross provided by the Loys.

Maria paraded her in front of the other immigrant mothers in Golden Gate Park each morning in her royal carriage, "and everyone oohed and aahed" over adorable Natasha. "She was a Russian-American princess," younger sister Lana would say later. Maria's purpose in life was to promote Natasha; to the exclusion of her daughter Olga, who was ten when Natasha was born, "old enough to take care of herself," in Maria's pronouncement. Olga, who had the disposition of a saint, accepted it without complaint. Cast adrift by her mother at two, she had attached herself to her friend Lois and retreated into fantasy, cutting out pictures of movie stars. She was proud, later, she had been permitted even to babysit Natasha. "My mother didn't let anybody else."

Olga's affection for her favored half-sister was a credit to

Olga's generosity and to Natasha's endearing personality. Like young Maria, Natasha was a tiny bird of a child. Marusia, with her piercing eyes and blue-black hair, called to mind a raven; Natasha was a trusting sparrow. She connected emotionally with her "Fahd" or "Papa" or "Deda," her nicknames for her father (she called her mother "Mud"), snuggling beside him at night, enchanted, as Nick read to her from the Russian fairy books of his childhood—fanciful tales of firebirds and wild animals transformed into princes. Natalie would carry this romanticized image of her father, and of Russia, throughout life. "He loved to read," she said later. "Dostoevsky, Tolstoy, Pushkin and Turgenev . . . he was a scholar." Natasha, "a smart little thing," absorbed her papa's passion for language and for Russian novels. "She was such a brilliant child. It was amazing sometimes," said Maria. "My husband, he was so clever, you ask him any questions, he always knew every answers, and she was like him." Natasha learned to speak in Russian and in "American," as she called it. "We never talked baby talk to her," said Olga. Natasha, as a tiny child, was an old soul.

When Natasha was one, her father, weary of being at the end of the alphabetical cattle call of immigrant laborers, changed the family name from "Zakharenko" to "Gurdin," a friend's surname. "Nick thought Zakharenko was too Russian," explains Olga. "During the end of the Depression, there would be great big long lines for work and there was discrimination. The people with the most comfortable names to call were called out for jobs." The effect of living in near-poverty, forced by his immigrant circumstances to take menial jobs, took its toll on a man of Nick's sensibilities, contributing to his escape in vodka.

"Mud," not "Fahd," was the disciplinarian in the Gurdin

household, which Natalie would unhappily recall as "very strict European." She and Olga were instructed to curtsy, forbidden to use "foul language," forbidden to ask questions. "My parents felt children should be in the corner, sheltered from listening to or understanding what the grown-ups were talking about," she said as an adult. Maria was an austere taskmaster, seldom demonstrative or affectionate. Nick, when sober, was the tender parent. "He *loved* life," Natalie eulogized. "He loved music, singing, dancing—and he was never embarrassed to let his feelings show." Little Natasha listened delightedly as her Fahd played the balalaika; thrilled when he gathered the family for "an adventure." He was also violent. "I remember him getting very drunk one time and breaking the balalaika," recalls Olga. "I didn't know whether he was going to get a pistol. He would, periodically." No one knew when, if, or why Nick's demons would be unleashed by vodka. Olga believed he was tormented by witnessing his grandfather buried alive during the revolution. Natalie, after years in analysis, would characterize her beloved Fahd as "complicated," possessing a "Russian soul" she likened to "a volcano that just had to erupt from time to time." To the child Natasha, the extreme chiaroscuro of his personality—the shifts from his "soft and gentle underside" to drunken "Russian explosions"—was frightening.

Nick's "rampages," as Olga referred to them, were often provoked by Maria, who "knew how to get to him." The house was a battlefield, with Olga and Natasha in the crossfire. Natasha, from earliest childhood, hated confrontation.

Her favorite word was "pretend." Olga wrote and performed playlets with Lois, using the communal garage as a make-believe theater with sheets as curtains. Olga and

Lois occasionally cast toddler Natasha, whose sun-dappled brown hair formed curls not unlike Shirley Temple's. The sisters, twelve and two, performed together for family, including cousins by Maria's older half-sister Kalia, who had immigrated from China to San Francisco and was married with children by a Russian named Sergei Liuzunie. "At that time they didn't have television, so we would both be into the performing," recalls Olga. "Turn on the music and dance and stuff." Natasha obligingly played along with her big sister; whereas Olga had a *passion* to perform. She loved to sing, especially Russian music, and had an appealing voice, teaching her precocious baby sister hand movements to popular songs. Olga kept a scrapbook of her ninety-four favorite movie stars, collected over years of matinees with her movie-mad mother.

Maria ignored Olga, whispering to Natasha their secret: Natasha was going to be a famous star . . . a fortuneteller in China foretold it. "When we walked down the street, Mother would put coins on the sidewalk when I wasn't looking and when I found them, she'd tell me it was magic, and that I was destined to be someone magical. For years I believed in magic," Natalie said years later. "She *brainwashed* her that she was this special child," a friend confirms. When Mud took Natasha to the movies and the camera, at the end of the newsreel, pointed to the audience, she would whisper dramatically: "*Natasha! It's taking your picture!*" "I'd pose, and smile," recalled Natalie, who thought the camera was directed at her. "My mother told me all these things and I'd believe them." By three, Natasha sat through two-hour films without moving.

Natasha's personality—intelligent, eager to please, and "dutiful," the word she later used to describe herself as a child—formed the tragically ideal combination for Maria's manipulation. "It was easy with her," Maria once chillingly admitted. Mud patched Natasha's dresses to pay for a piano to prepare her for stardom, pushing Natasha into lessons at three. "The teacher didn't think she was old enough," Maria recalled once. "She did beautifully. Whatever she does, Natalie does to perfection. Always."

The irony in their mother's fixation on Natasha was that "she *was* different," her sister Lana concedes. "It's like when you watch a film, a TV show, a commercial, see someone walking down the street—and they have something special about them." Natasha had a touching orphan's quality in her brown eyes that communicated a hunger to be loved. What part of that was Natasha, or the result of witnessing her troubled home life, is impossible to know.

Maria kept the fortuneteller's prediction that Natasha was destined for stardom their secret. The other half of the prophecy—that Maria was going to drown—was family legend. "Mother thought that she would die drowning because the gypsy told her," confirms Olga. "She was terrified," concurs Lana. "She wouldn't get in the water." In her dramatic whisper and heavy Russian accent, Maria would hypnotize little Natasha, conjuring up visions of stardom and magic in one ear; warning, "Beware of dark water," in the other. "She really created an impression in her mind," relates Olga. Natasha was afraid to learn to swim; frightened even to have her hair washed, because her head would be submerged in the bath water. "She was always afraid of water, like I am, especially if it's dark waters," Maria said later. "My *mother* contributed to her fear of the water, because my *mother* was afraid of the water," corrects Olga. "My mother was afraid of swimming, and she was told that she'd drown. So this communicated itself to Natalie."

Natasha grew up in a house of paranoia—fear of Communists, gypsy curses, hysterical convulsions, drunken demons. Her mother was like a fictional character written in magic realism, with her accounts of mystical reincarnation and resurrection, guiding her life by superstitions and instilling them in her daughters. "Peacock feathers or pictures of peacocks are bad luck," recounts Olga. "You don't *pass* the salt, you put it down, otherwise you'll get into an argument. If you give somebody tablecloths or sheets, you're wishing for them to go away." As an adult, Natalie would remark that she "didn't like mystery" as a child, how Russian superstitions had created paranoia in her she did not want her children to have. Her mother trusted only Natasha's father and Olga to babysit her; Fahd refused to allow her in crowds because she was so tiny.

Fear was in the air Natasha breathed.

4 WHEN THE JAPANESE ATTACKED Pearl Harbor in December 1941, the paranoid Nick believed they would bomb San Francisco, so he moved the family to the outskirts of the city, in Sunnyvale. The Gurdins lived in the low-income projects, Natasha's fifth apartment by the age of three. Nick found work at the naval yard as a draftsman and Maria took a part-time job babysitting, entrusting Natasha to Olga.

Maria and her daughters' diversion from this charmless existence, apart from movies, were holidays near the Russian River in the picturesque wine country, a two-hour drive north. Families, most of them Russian, shared rental cottages the immigrants referred to nostalgically as "dachas." One such holiday, in September of 1942, Maria, Olga and Natasha took a scenic drive with a Russian friend through the nearby town of Santa Rosa. As the friend turned down a country road at the edge of town, Maria's eye seized on a new bungalow. She asked her friend to stop the car. "I want that house," Maria announced. She found a carpenter inside and engaged him in conversation, learning that the owner was in despair because his wife had run off with the contractor. Maria entreated the carpenter to phone the owner, who struck a deal with her that afternoon, selling his heartbreak house to Maria for a down payment of $100, all the money the Gurdins had. "She *conned* him into it," marvels Olga. "I think he even gave her money to buy furniture." Maria, who didn't drive, forged her absent husband's signature. "How she managed to get a loan, I don't know," said Olga. When Nick arrived to take Musia and the girls back to Sunnyvale, "I said, 'Nick, we're not gonna go back home. We have a home here,' " she recalled. Flummoxed by his wife's machinations, concerned about the long drive to the shipyard, Nick was no match for the formidable Maria. The Gurdins' deed to the property at 2160 Humboldt was recorded on September 28, 1942, at a purchase price of $5400, making the immigrants homeowners and establishing Maria as the business head of the family.

Maria's almost mystic acquisition of the bungalow in bucolic Santa Rosa proved, ironically, to be a determining factor in Natalie's Hollywood career. Director Alfred Hitchcock had discovered the charms of the Sonoma Valley just before Maria, selecting Santa Rosa to represent an idealized small town in his suspense thriller *Shadow of a Doubt*. Hitchcock began shooting in Santa Rosa in August, the month before the Gurdins moved to town. That

September, a second picture, *The Sullivans*, a drama about five Iowa brothers recruited in World War II, set up location shooting. The timing was either synchronistic or Maria knew the two movies were being filmed in Santa Rosa and maneuvered the house purchase to be in proximity. In either case, she took her four-year-old golden child by the hand and followed the film crews. "She went to all of the locations. I don't know *how* she found out," said Olga.

When Maria would later talk about Natasha at this age, she described her as "always acting," desperate to be in movies. According to Olga, four-year-old Natasha was a "natural" when she performed, but she was not movie-struck. Maria was the one stalking movie crews seeking parts for herself and Natasha; Natasha "just went along." Olga—who knew every star, studied drama in school, and got her Social Security card so she could work as an extra—was an afterthought. "I wouldn't even come home from school. I'd know that wherever they'd be shooting, my mother and Natasha would be. So I'd walk over to some of the houses." Olga was happy just to be included. "My mother made everything *fun*."

The Gurdins had been in town a few weeks when Maria heard about a ten-year-old Santa Rosa girl "discovered" by Hitchcock in July. Edna May Wonacott, the "Cinderella Girl," as she was dubbed in the *Santa Rosa Press Democrat*, was flown to Los Angeles for a screen test and given a part in *Shadow of a Doubt*. The end of October, Santa Rosa staged an "Edna May Day," with a parade in her honor. Maria Gurdin became obsessed with Edna May Wonacott, following every nuance of her Cinderella story. Edna May, the bespectacled daughter of a grocer, had been downtown with two cousins, unaware Hitchcock was across the street, scouting for locations. She remembers: "We were standing on a street corner waiting for a bus—and him and Jack Skirball, the producer, were looking at the courthouse for angles. And then they turned around and started looking at me." Maria read the front-page story in the newspaper, which reported that Hitchcock noticed Edna May because of her pigtails, asking her to sing a song for her screen test. Maria made mental notes, using Edna May as a role model for Natasha. The town went Edna May–mad. "People stopped by the market just to touch my dad." Maria accelerated her efforts to get Natasha noticed by film crews. "She was a stage mother," recalls a neighbor. "Push, push, push."

By Thanksgiving, Hitchcock and the crew from *The Sullivans* were gone. Natasha enjoyed simply being a child. She baked cookies outdoors in an electric play oven with her first and only friend, a neighborhood boy named Edwin Canevari. Edwin was small for his age, like Natasha, and fiercely loyal. "We played husband and wife," he recalls. Maria trusted no one else to play with Natasha. "She was watching her all the time, even when we were playing out in the driveway." Natasha was never a "physical" child, according to Maria: "She liked to play piano and do some artwork." This was, to a degree, Natasha's nature; the rest of her perceived delicacy came from being treated like a hothouse flower. The gypsy's warning continued to haunt Natasha, further restricting her from physical activities. "Never did she go in the water," pronounced Canevari. "She was deathly afraid of the water." Maria encouraged Natasha to play the piano, taught her to embroider, and bought her the oven for her to sculpt with clay, heeding advice from Olga's nurse in China, who told Musia that working with the hands "exercised" a child's brain.

Life in the Russian River Valley was an idyll for the two sisters, who played amid the apple orchards and redwood trees, gathering walnuts and sweet chestnuts. Nick made a swing for the backyard and the family acquired a puppy. Natasha, who loved animals, adored her German shepherd. Remembers Olga: "I used to climb the hills with our dog, and pick cherries on cherry trees. We had rabbits in the back, that later ran over to the Canevaris' because they had radishes."

Inside the cottage on Humboldt Street, the spectre of the Russian Revolution possessed the Gurdin household like a sinister spirit. Canevari, who lived across the street, "heard about" Nick's drinking problem, "but I never saw it." He remembered Natasha's father as a "nice guy, used to rub my head and call me Butch." Nick's drinking, violence, and disappearances were the family's dark secret. Maria claimed Nick never hurt her in Santa Rosa, though she conceded it was better if he was "someplace else" when he was drunk. As a child actress, Natalie would confide in juvenile actor Robert Blake, who was an abused child. "She had *a lot* to recover from. They use those catchphrases like 'dysfunctional family.' I *know* that to be the case. And I'm not gonna sit here and say, 'Well yeah, her father was a drunk that beat her up' or 'Her mother was an unloving rat,' because I'm not gonna give you any of those things." Who knows what Natasha experienced inside her netherworld?

Maria imagined the mother of a neighbor girl was conspiring to poison Natasha. "I don't know why, but she always had that in her head. It was just a superstition," recalls Canevari, who heard his mother and Mrs. Gurdin talk about Maria's escape from Bolsheviks. He linked that experience to Natasha's mother's paranoia. "I don't know what she went through in the revolution, but she was afraid

Natasha was going to get poisoned by this one and that one—just people in general." Maria was "overprotective" to the point of "smothering" Natasha.

Something about Natasha inspired others to want to take care of her. "Even the seventh- and eighth-grade kids loved her," recalls principal Ethel Polhemus. "I remember we were doing the Virginia reel, and she got started the wrong way. I just took her by the arm and turned her the other way—oh, the youngsters were disturbed at *me!*" Natasha had a winsomeness that was endearing. "I can still see that little girl. Her eyes were dark. She was such a *pretty* little thing, a darling girl. She was just a doll . . . kind of dancing all the time, very sprightly." Natasha was extremely tender-hearted, refusing to go fishing "out of pity for the fish."

That year, when Natasha was four, she and Olga took a walk for a root beer, their German shepherd puppy tagging along. On the way back from the store, the puppy and Natasha darted ahead of Olga to cross the highway. A truck suddenly appeared, crushing the puppy under its wheels as Natasha watched in horror. "I told her to look ahead and to never look back," relates Olga. Natasha never made a sound, too traumatized to cry. It was to become a significant event in her life.

In January, Santa Rosa's movie theater, the California, held a special premiere for *Shadow of a Doubt,* attended by Hitchcock's daughter and celebrating his discovery, Edna May Wonacott, who had signed a seven-year contract with producer Jack Skirball. Maria, a theater usherette, further fixated on Edna May as the precedent for Natasha's impending fame. The Wonacotts sold their grocery store, moving closer to Hollywood. When the story broke in the Santa Rosa paper, "girls started standing on street corners in pigtails and glasses." Maria was possessed that Natasha become the next Cinderella Girl, though how she hoped to accomplish that was unclear. Natasha was more excited about the kindergarten play than Hollywood. She came up with the idea of putting white powder on her hair to make herself look like her character, an old woman, saying later it helped her "get into the mood of the part."

That summer, as school let out, Maria Gurdin's moment announced itself in the *Santa Rosa Press Democrat*. "*Movie Stars to Arrive in S.R. Today*," read the June 13, 1943, headline. By serendipity—this time there could be no calculation on Maria's part—Irving Pichel, a Harvard-educated stage actor turned director, happened to see *Shadow of a Doubt*, concluding that Santa Rosa was the perfect backdrop for his next picture. The film was called *Happy Land*, a Capra-esque piece of Americana starring Don Ameche as a small-town pharmacist who realizes the value of his life through the loss of his son in World War II. The story came from a best-selling novel excerpted in the *Saturday Evening Post*. Fifty-two-year-old Pichel, known for his patriotic, anti-Nazi themes, had already cast a few Santa Rosans in bit roles in *Happy Land*, including Mayor E. A. Eymann, who was asked to play the mayor of the mythical Midwest town of Hartfield in a commencement scene. Mayor Eymann, the paper reported, was officially welcoming Pichel and actor Don Ameche, providing a schedule of the film crew's locations around Santa Rosa, with the advisory that some of the scenes would "use upwards of 300 extras." To Maria, the article was tantamount to a golden oracle.

Natasha stood perfectly still the next morning as her mother brushed her curly hair, instructing her how to create attention so the *Happy Land* director would notice her, coaching her what to say so he would like her, reminding her to curtsy—repeating hypnotically the incantation that Natasha would someday be the most famous actress in the world. Natasha took her mother's prophecy to heart, concentrating while Mud braided her gold-tipped hair into pigtails, observing herself in the mirror as she metamorphosed into a tiny Russian replica of Edna May Wonacott.

Mother and daughter walked downtown in search of the film's director, determined to create the fairy tale that had serendipitously occurred for Edna May. They spotted the *Happy Land* crew near the courthouse, surrounded by curious spectators. Maria, holding on to Natasha, asked whoever walked by, "How does this work? Which one's the director?" When actors in army uniform began to assemble for a parade scene, Maria thrust four-year-old Natasha into the lineup. As Natalie would later describe it, "My mother made me go march with the soldiers. I really didn't want to do all this. I was kind of scared. . . . Mother, of course, wanted me to attract attention."

After a few days, Irving Pichel began to notice a "quaintly pretty little child" with an "absorbed expression" who kept following the *Happy Land* company from location to location, watching them closely. The toddler seemed to be leading the wandering crowd. Natasha made such an impression on the director, he mentioned the tiny Santa Rosa girl with the "winsome smile" a few years later as a tragic example of children being pushed into movies.

Pichel would have been chagrined to learn that what he observed was merely the prelude to Maria Gurdin's plan to get Natasha a part in *Happy Land*. By the second week, when the film crew moved to the high school auditorium for the mayor's scene, Maria had gleaned what she needed to know. "When she figured out that Irving Pichel was the director," Natalie would later recall, "she said to me, 'Natasha, go over there and sit on that man's lap and sing him your songs.' " Pichel would remember the waif he had been feeling sorry for coming up to him one noon. "Mr. Pichel, can I be in the movies?" she asked plaintively. "You don't want to be in the movies," the grandfatherly-looking director advised. Natasha, unprepared for this reaction, reflected for a moment, according to Pichel. The moment was profound. If she had been capable of free will, Natasha's response to Irving Pichel, and thus her life, might have been different. Instead she continued robotically, programmed by Mud to perform her piece. "She changed the subject by telling me that her name was Natasha Gurdin, that her birthday was July twentieth, that her parents were Russian and that she would like to sing me a Russian song, if I would like to hear it."

"I remember singing 'In My Arms,' with gestures," said Natalie, years later. " '*Comes the dawn, I'll be gone. Ain't I never going to have a honey holding me tight . . .*' " The Jewish director by chance understood Russian, according to Olga, "and he just fell in *love* with her." Ironically, Olga had taught Natasha to sing "In My Arms," and created the hand movements that charmed Irving Pichel. But it was Natasha with whom he was smitten, taken by "those eyes . . . she looks at you and you can read her thoughts."

Pichel was so enchanted with Natasha he offered her a small, nonspeaking part in *Happy Land*. Mud's improbable scheme to create the kismet that happened to Edna May had succeeded, establishing a precedent: if a formula worked, Mud copied it. The lesson for Natasha, from her staged encounter on Pichel's lap, was more troubling. "I learned at an early age that if you are nice to men, you can get anything you want from them," she said at thirty-one.

After Natalie became famous, Maria would tell people Natasha was discovered by Pichel when he spotted her on the street, or that Natasha wandered away and impulsively jumped into Pichel's lap—creating the deception that Natasha's first part, like Edna May's, was an accident of fate. Natasha, Olga, Irving Pichel and Natasha's friend Edwin knew differently.

Nick, by Maria's and Natalie's later accounts, disapproved of his daughter being in the movie, though Olga recalls no such objection. Whether Nick objected to Natasha acting or not was of no real consequence, for as Maria baldly told a reporter in the mid-sixties, "I made all the decisions in the family."

Natasha's cameo appearance in *Happy Land* required her to drop an ice cream cone in front of Marsh's drugstore, where Don Ameche's character worked as a pharmacist. The scene was to be shot in nearby Healdsburg, where the director had chosen a street with storefronts resembling middle America. An actress was hired to play Natasha's screen mother, who was to pick her up after she dropped her cone.

Natasha did not seem excited about being in the movie, according to both Olga and her chum Edwin. Her sister thought "she kind of took it in stride, she didn't buck it or anything, she enjoyed acting." Edwin's impression was that Natasha was being pushed. "You could see it in her face when her mother would come out and say, 'Natasha, come over here,' or 'Sit here,' or do this, do that." As an adult, Natalie seemed unsure how she felt, at four, about appearing in *Happy Land*. "Obviously I wasn't shy, because I did what I was told."

It is perhaps revealing that she asked Edwin to go with her the day she was to shoot her scene. Pichel agreed to let Natasha's friend appear in the movie with her, "playing a brother or something," Canevari recalls:

> So my mother took me down to the set. When I got down there, there were all these big lights. And I was only about 5 years old—hell, I didn't know what was going on. And I saw all these lights and they had these big sheets of metal making thunder and stuff, shaking them—and I took off running. It scared the hell out of me and I took off running and that was the end of me.

Natasha, under pressure from Mud to do whatever the director asked, did not have the luxury of a child's reaction. Upon hearing Pichel describe where on the sidewalk in Healdsburg he wanted Natasha to drop her ice cream and how to make it look natural, Maria asked the director: "With tears or without?" Musia even managed to get herself insinuated into the scene, walking behind Natasha—portending her role in her daughter's life. "Like having a shadow following you around," as Canevari put it. The genial Pichel included Olga in the background, pairing her with a young man from Annapolis.

Maria made sure everyone would be looking at Natasha. She dressed her in a tiny frock, doing her hair in Shirley Temple ringlets with an enormous white bow, like Dainty June, the baby doll character in *Gypsy*, Natalie's future film. Olga remembers dressing in the trailer with Ann Rutherford, the actress playing Don Ameche's wife, who picked up Natasha and hugged her, one of the few memories Natalie would have of *Happy Land*. By the time she dropped her cone, precisely where she was asked, Pichel was beguiled by the little Russian girl who curtsied each time he appeared.

Maria kept Natasha deliberately underfoot the rest of the *Happy Land* shoot, hoping to further ingratiate her to Pichel, "and I fell, I must confess, violently in love with her," he wrote later. According to Maria, Pichel sent attorneys to the house with legal papers to adopt Natasha, a story that would become part of Natalie Wood lore. Natalie herself repeated it, as an adult:

> He said to my mother, "Oh, your daughter is so adorable, I'd love to adopt her. What would you think of that?" My mother thought he was joking. She speaks, still, with a heavy Russian accent and sometimes she doesn't quite understand or make herself understood. So she thought he was joking and he thought that she was serious. The lawyers arrived at our house one day while the "Happy Land" filming was still going on . . . there was a big upheaval in the household.

How much of the story is true, or Maria's tall tale, is open to question. Olga, who was fourteen that summer, recalls Pichel visiting once, but there were no attorneys at the house. Her impression was that Pichel wanted a daughter because he only had sons, and that Natasha had requested a bunk bed if she moved into his house. But Olga is uncertain whether she heard this conversation, or if her mother told her about it later. "He *wanted* to adopt her, that I *know*. And Mother agreed, but then she told him of course it was a joke." In a later, highly suspicious version, Maria told the author of a book on celebrity mothers that Pichel wanted to *buy* Natasha and offered his life savings. ("I said, 'No, I don't sell my children,' " she recounted with great drama.)

Pichel, who was married with sons fourteen, nineteen, and twenty-two at the time, never mentioned to his children the possibility that Natasha might be adopted into the family. Nor did their mother. "It was probably folklore," suggests the middle son, Dr. Julian Pichel, though he concedes his parents "did want a daughter—that's true. I think that's why I was called 'Julie.' " All three brothers doubt that their mother, who resented the movie industry, would have consented to the adoption. Marlowe Pichel, who was fourteen, speculates his father may have wanted to help Natasha. "I do remember he was kind of smitten with her," relates Julian. Pichel talked openly about his affection for Natasha in a magazine piece several years later, never mentioning wanting to adopt her. "I seriously believe it's a complete fabrication," declares Natalie's younger sister, Lana, who heard their mother spin the yarn over the years. Natasha's "memory," at four, of attorneys creating an upheaval may have been implanted by Maria. Whether or not he tried to adopt her, Pichel's fondness for Natasha was unique, according to Julian, who never knew his father to form an attachment to any other child actor. "There must have been something special about Natalie."

Pichel stopped at the Gurdins' to say goodbye to Natasha when he finished filming *Happy Land* around her fifth birthday, which was on July 20, 1943. The story that would appear throughout Natalie's later movie career is that Pichel promised, during this visit, to keep her in mind when the right part came along. This was a falsehood invented by her mother, for the truth would have too nakedly revealed Maria.

As Irving Pichel left the house, he pleaded with Maria Gurdin to keep Natasha *away* from Hollywood, warning her that a child in the limelight will never be a normal child again.

Mud immediately wrote to Pichel, in the guise of a letter from Natasha. Charmed to hear from his Russian pet, Pichel began what he considered to be an affectionate correspondence with Natasha, but was actually an exchange of letters with Maria, writing *for* Natasha, who was too young to read—a foreshadowing of Maria's intertwining of their personalities. "She read me his letters," Natalie would recall, describing it as "a big day" for Mud when a note arrived from Pichel. "Mother was excited," affirms Olga.

When Natasha was with Edwin, or her sister, she never talked about movies, or about Irving Pichel. Edwin remembered them starting school that fall, "just kids playing in the backyard on the swing and baking cookies." Olga, who had begun dating Edwin's teenage brother Gino, "could care less" about the letters from Hollywood.

The correspondence, fueled by Maria's ambition and Pichel's fondness for Natasha, grew "quite voluminous." The two began exchanging birthday and Christmas gifts, Pichel would recall, with Natasha receiving books, dolls and a record from the director. Maria followed closely through Pichel's letters his upcoming movie projects, searching the plotlines for possible parts for Natasha, while continuing the artifice of an innocent exchange of letters from a child.

Maria's movie fever peaked in January, when *Happy Land* premiered on the West Coast in a special midnight screening one Saturday at the California Theater in Santa Rosa. "She told about thirty neighbors—*everybody*—that the movie was coming to town, they all had to come see Natasha."

Natasha's film debut, though just a few seconds, was a showcase for her. *Happy Land* begins with a narrator folksily describing Hartfield as the camera sweeps Main Street, stopping at the storefront of Marsh's drugstore. The next image is a close-up of Natasha's dimpled legs, as an ice cream cone falls and splatters. The camera lingers in close-up on the sidewalk where the cone drops on the word "PHARMACY." Natasha can be seen reaching down into the camera's eye to pick up the cone, then hesitating. The camera stays on her legs and the fallen cone, as a pair of women's shoes approach Natasha, silhouetted by the shadow of someone else's legs walking by—the unseen Maria. Once Maria has passed, the camera returns to full body length, revealing Natasha being picked up by her screen mother. The image then widens to include several storefronts as Natasha's movie mother carries her down the sidewalk. Olga and her film beau can be observed approaching the drugstore as the scene ends.

Irving Pichel had managed to accomplish, through clever editing and camera angles, what Natalie would spend years in analysis attempting to achieve: extricating her mother. "All you saw was her legs—they cut her scene! Marie was so embarrassed." The experience may have served to reinforce Maria's role as starmaker as opposed to star, for she emerged from the theater singularly possessed with parlaying her daughter's walk-on part into movie stardom. Mud's obsession to make Natasha famous vicariously fulfilled her lost stardust dreams. As Lana would observe: "She was going to offer her daughter this incredible life, and she was going to get to live it with her as well."

If Natasha was excited about seeing herself on-screen, there is no evidence. Maria was the zealot. She walked two miles to work as an usherette, and on her days off she took her girls to watch the same movies all over again. Natasha may have been baptized Russian Orthodox, but movies were her religion, the cinema her place of worship. The Gurdins did attend an Orthodox church in Santa Rosa, but its influence on Natasha was minimal compared to movies. Before she was able to read, Natasha could identify all the stars in fan magazines the way other children might name characters in Bible storybooks. Maria filled Natasha's head with fantastic visions of the Hollywood studios, where she would be a great actress, as temples of gold. Natasha invented a game called "going to the studio," using the garage as an imaginary film studio. "I used to 'check in' every day and I would pretend to be Sonja Henie, Bette Davis, Ann Sheridan or some other star."

That spring, as Natasha was completing school, Maria Gurdin toyed with the idea of moving to Hollywood. "Maybe she knew Pichel was doing a picture," suggests Olga. Pichel *was* directing a movie in June, a war drama with Dorothy Lamour, called *A Medal for Benny*, as Maria almost certainly knew from his letters to Natasha. The story, by John Steinbeck, included the minor character of a young Mexican boy. The possibility that Natasha might be considered for the role, despite being Russian, female, and blond, was enough to lure Maria. Pichel, who opposed Natasha acting in movies, knew nothing about it, as evidenced by the fact that Maria turned to gypsy magic to divine whether to move to Hollywood. "My mother put little notes behind icons in the vespers everywhere in the house," recalls Olga. "And actually the note said *not* to go, but she went anyway!"

Ignoring the forebodings from Pichel and her own gypsy ritual, Maria did not even wait for the school year to end. "We just sold everything," relates Olga. Nick, as usual, was a silent partner to his wife's ambitious schemes. "Mother could work him," was Olga's appraisal of the dynamic between Nick and Maria. "This house gonna sell bee-*uuuu*-tifully," the wizardly Maria purred to Nick, bragging later that she "got three times worth of what I paid for it."

Edna May Wonacott was the deciding factor in Maria's brazen decision. "The Wonacotts sold their grocery store, they sold their house, they moved to Hollywood . . . and so Mother sold the house," relates Olga. The distinction was that Edna May had a seven-year movie contract. Maria was uprooting her family to Hollywood on the gossamer hope of her five-year-old daughter's friendship with a film director who disapproved of Natasha acting in the movies. "She decided to go, whatever her reasonings were then," recalls Olga, "and we all went together."

Nick and Maria Gurdin appeared before a Santa Rosa notary to sign the deed granting their house to a couple named Mason and Abbie Ware on May 26, 1944. Natasha and the family would arrive in Hollywood a month before Pichel began filming *A Medal for Benny*.

Before they left, Maria planted this item in the Santa Rosa newspaper:

SIX-YEAR-OLD S.R. GIRL GOING TO HOLLYWOOD FOR ROLE IN MOVIES*

Little Natasha Gurdin, 6-year-old daughter of Mr. and Mrs. Nicholas S. Gurdin of 2168 Humboldt Street, will leave shortly—probably about the first of the week—for Hollywood and her chance at a motion-picture career.

Selected by Director Irving Pichel for a possible part in *A Medal for Benny*, Paramount film story planned to be

*Natasha was five.

made here in the spring, the little blonde, dark-eyed girl, will probably be given a screen test upon her arrival in the film center.

If finally selected for the role her light tresses will be darkened, to fit into the proposed role of a Mexican child.

Pichel met Natasha while he was here last summer directing Don Ameche, Frances Dee and Harry Carey in *Happy Land*. While he was here last week viewing proposed "locations" for the production company, Pichel visited Natasha and proposed the part in the new picture.

The article was pure fantasy, a brash announcement of the shameless promotion of Natasha that soon would distinguish Maria within the ranks of Hollywood stage mothers.

5

NATASHA'S CHILDHOOD, IF SHE had one, ended when she left Santa Rosa in the spring of 1944. She felt an oppressive burden, at five, to be a success in Hollywood, thinking she was responsible for the family's upheaval.

The move was wrenching for her and fifteen-year-old Olga, who would remember standing near the swing Nick built for them in the backyard, watching wistfully as their mother piled everything they owned into the car. Six-year-old Edwin walked over to say goodbye. "That killed me when they moved. I told Natasha I was going to miss her. I even gave her a hug goodbye." Natasha's last, flickering image of her childhood was of Edwin, her only friend, waving a forlorn farewell in front of the first house she and her sister had known. "I'm sorry we moved from Santa Rosa," admits Olga, expressing the one regret she would convey from a childhood of injustices. "But even if we'd stayed, Natalie would have found her destiny, I guess."

So effectively had Maria subjugated the minds of both daughters and her husband, all departed for Hollywood convinced Natasha would be in the movies. Whether her eventual stardom was fated, or manipulated by Maria, is the existential mystery. "She was *destined* for this *life*, because of that mother," suggests a close friend. "And the father. He was as guilty, he just was silent."

Natasha slept through her pilgrimage to the promised land, squeezed between Olga and the family belongings in the back seat of the car. Nick drove straight through the night, stopping to pick up a hitchhiker, a whimsy of Maria's. Olga kept a picture, among her mementoes, of the hitchhiker, posed alongside Natasha and their mother.

The Gurdins pulled into Hollywood around the beginning of June, 1944. They arrived virtual peasants: Nick did not have a job, they had no money, no home, no resources. The family's hopes were pinned entirely on Natasha.

Maria arranged for the Gurdins to stay with Olga's former ballet teacher, Nadia Ermolova, who had a small apartment and dance studio on Fountain in the bowels of Hollywood. From there "she called Irving Pichel, and did some little sob act. That they were very poor in Santa Rosa, and Natasha *loved* him so much, and could they come see him?" Pichel was surprised, then dismayed, as he later wrote: "The family turned up in Hollywood, where, Mrs. Gurdin revealed to me, she was interested in a career for Natasha." The director guiltily likened himself to "a modern Pied Piper who had, however unwittingly, piped the child out of her Hamelin town." He had a long, sobering talk with Maria and Natasha about child stars, explaining how their families suffer and how child actors miss having normal childhoods. To do that to Natasha, Pichel advised Maria, would be a tragedy. "The mother, like the daughter, appeared to accept my judgment," he wrote later. Within a week, Pichel began filming *A Medal for Benny*. Natasha Gurdin was not among the cast.

The calculated kismet upon which Maria had gambled the house, the family's security and Natasha's mental health did not go as she had planned, or the gypsy foretold.

Contrary to the impression she gave Pichel, Maria was neither chastened, daunted, nor persuaded by his alarm at the prospect of Natasha getting into movies. She simply determined to find another entrée. To that end, the Gurdins remained in Nadia Ermolova's cramped apartment through the summer and into the fall. Olga wrote despairing letters from Hollywood to Lois, her childhood companion in San Francisco, who remembered it as "a hard move for my friend." Natasha, who turned six that July, sent frequent, heartfelt scrawls to Edwin, suggestive of how lonely she was. Hollywood was not the kingdom of palaces her mother conjured. "When I first saw a studio I was five and expected red velvet and gold," she later said.

In a letter to Edwin that September, Natasha enclosed two photographs of herself, taken the same day in the front yard. Both are of Natasha in a full-skirted Russian costume with a head kerchief. In one photo, her mouth is painted with red lipstick and she playfully strikes a Russian dancer's stance, mugging for the camera. The other shows Natasha without makeup, holding out the sides of her Russian dress in a stilted pose, a pained smile forced onto her desperately sad face. They illustrate the schism she was feeling about her life.

The haunted expression behind Natasha's eyes in the second photograph provides a glimpse into the pressures she was experiencing. Maria had discovered *The Hollywood Reporter*, and foraged it daily for a part for Natasha, assimilating industry gossip like an agent on the make. "She'd read all the trade news, and keep up with what movie was shooting and who was doing it," relates Olga, who recalls her sister "trying for different things." Natasha was competing for roles against experienced child actors with agents and show business connections while *she* was being led around town by her Russian mother on the lure of a thirty-second cameo in *Happy Land*. "When I would go on an interview for a part and not get it—to me it was a total rejection. I thought they were turning *me* down." Natasha was guilt-ridden, feeling responsible for the family's move from Santa Rosa, desperate to please her overbearing mother, mesmerized into believing she must have a magical life. When she said her prayers at night, Natasha asked God to please make her a movie star.

The family made ends meet through Maria's machinations. According to Olga, her mother got Nick a job as a carpenter at one of the studios, "maybe through Pichel or somebody, I'm not quite sure." They scraped together enough money to move out of Nadia's by the first of the year, relocating to a small stucco cottage at 9060 Harland, off Doheny in West Hollywood. Nick made a swing for the backyard, where Natasha could pretend, at least, that she was back in Santa Rosa.

—

Maria had been unsuccessfully making the rounds in Hollywood with Natasha from June of 1944 to February of 1945 when she read in the trades about a movie Irving Pichel was directing called *Tomorrow Is Forever*. It was adapted from a popular wartime novel condensed in the *Ladies Home Journal*, based on a tragic, operatic poem by Tennyson called "Enoch Arden." Orson Welles, a Hollywood wunderkind from his masterpiece of four years before, *Citizen Kane*, was cast as an Army lieutenant so disfigured in World War I he nobly chooses to let his wife think he has died. The wife, played by Claudette Colbert, discovers she is pregnant with her husband's child at the same time he is presumed dead; after giving birth to a son, she remarries. Pichel was looking for a little girl to play the difficult role of an English-and-German-speaking Austrian refugee from the Second World War whom Orson Welles' character adopts while recovering from his injuries in Vienna.

"My mother got all excited about this," recalls Olga, who participated in Maria's strategy to get Pichel to cast Natasha as the Austrian orphan. Maria chose not to contact the director, knowing he would discourage her. She somehow managed to get Natasha's name onto a list of six girls auditioning for Pichel at the end of February. "When I saw it there," Pichel said later, "I was depressed." The pressure on Natasha was mounting. Six years of Maria's incantations had her believing the only thing that mattered in life was to be a great actress. "Ever since I was knee high," she would say later, "I've been waiting for my break." For months she had been paraded by Mud in front of casting directors who barely looked up. This was her *friend*, Mr. Pichel. She *had* to get the part; her family was depending on her. However burdened she felt, Natasha did not confide in anyone. Her desperation was internalized, hidden beneath the façade of the good little girl. As an adult, Natalie would tell Lana that most of her anxieties were from the pressures she felt at six to succeed in Hollywood.

Prior to the casting call, Maria carefully assessed Natasha, as Olga, her forgotten daughter, would recall; plotting how she could present her so Natasha would stand out from the competition. The afternoon of the audition, five pretty, painted little girls sat in Pichel's office wearing frilly dresses and Sunday curls. Natasha walked in with braids in her hair, dressed "the way she plays in the backyard," giving her an air of naturalness. Maria claimed, later, Pichel had advised her to do this, but it was Mud. "She was very alert. If all the other mothers did one thing, she'd say let's pick something that's not gussied up." In this case, Maria was emulating Margaret O'Brien, the gifted child star known for her dark pigtails and solemn grace—as Natalie would admit to O'Brien years later. "We kind of laughed about that," confirms O'Brien, "pigtails and everything." Maria was returning to her Edna May axiom: if a formula works, steal it.

The role of Margaret Ludwig, the bilingual Austrian war refugee in *Tomorrow Is Forever*, demanded a child actress with the gifts of a Margaret O'Brien. The character has been traumatized by seeing both parents killed by Nazis and anguishes over the frail health of her guardian (Welles), who has spirited her out of Vienna to America. Little Margaret has several heartrending scenes. In one, she reacts hysterically when a toy makes a popping noise, reminding her of the gunshots that killed her mother and father. The other occurs at the end of the film, when Welles' character succumbs to pneumonia and Margaret sobs, "Everyone who belongs to me dies." Pichel had chosen one of these scenes for the screen test, which had to be spoken in a German accent.

According to Natalie's eventual mythology, studio publicity, and her mother, her screen test was flawless. This was not so. "She played the scene and it was not very good," recalled Pichel. It was frankly remarkable Natasha had not suffered a nervous breakdown, asked at six to perform an emotional scene using a German accent with no acting experience, believing her family's welfare hinged on her performance, enchanted by Mud to expect *magic*. "I remember proudly telling my mother afterward that I hadn't cried even though they asked me to," Natalie said years later. "My mother got mad and said, 'What do you mean, you didn't cry?' "

Pichel's reaction to Natasha's poor audition was relief. He explained to Maria that he needed a little girl who could cry at will. "I took her mother aside and advised her not to feel too badly but, on the contrary, to be happy about it, as I was." His parting words to Maria were, "Natasha is too nice a little girl to be anything but a normal little girl." There was no argument.

Privately, Maria was frantic, remembers Olga, a witness to the crisis at home. After a night of "great commotion," Mud commanded Natasha, anguished at her imperfection, to telephone Pichel and beg him for a second chance. Then Maria got on the phone. She told Pichel Natasha had been crying desperately because she lost the part, that she had been so happy to see him she could not play a sad scene, "but if you will give her another chance, she will, she knows, be good." Pichel, moved by Natasha, agreed to another screen test.

Maria hung up the phone, possessed with getting

Natasha to cry on cue. The task of preparing her for her screen test fell to Olga, a cruel irony lost on Mud. Maria's older daughter did as she was told though "it just seemed funny to me, because I was only what, sixteen?" While coaching Natasha, Olga remembered her drama teacher in Santa Rosa instructing the class to think of something sad when they needed to cry. She told Natasha to think about the day their dog was killed in Santa Rosa. Natasha looked stricken, reliving the nightmare of her puppy darting in front of a truck. "I got her to cry," recalls Olga. Maria, hovering nearby, made mental notes of the technique.

Outwardly Natasha "seemed to get through the scene pretty well," her sister thought, unaware Natasha had been emotionally scarred. "From that time on, whenever I did a movie, I always counted the crying scenes," Natalie said later. "That was a barometer of how difficult the part was going to be for me." The true horror of that stigma was yet to come.

Maria took Olga out of Hollywood High for Natasha's screen test. Pichel would recall Natasha stepping aside before her scene. In those moments, Olga whispered to her to think about their little dog, coaxing Natasha into tears. Then something else occurred Natalie would later confide to actor Robert Redford. Her mother pulled her to the side, where no one could see, "took a live butterfly out of a jar and tore the wings off it." Tender-hearted Natasha went into hysterics as her mother called out, "She's ready!" grabbing her by the hand and pushing her in front of the camera. Natasha cried so profoundly Pichel was moved to write about it later, describing her tears as "seeming to come from the depth of some divine despair." Her audition broke Pichel's heart, and with it his resolve to keep her from becoming a child actress.

Twenty years later, when Natalie told Redford the story, he wondered, "How can anyone survive this? But she did." She survived, but Natasha was never the same, in ways that would gradually reveal themselves.

Maria's ruthlessness with the butterfly and the dead puppy was a warning how far she would go to advance Natasha's career to the detriment of her daughter. Though she was still only a child, Natasha was beginning to understand that her mother was living through her. The narcissism and drive that put Marusia on street corners collecting coins to become Queen of the Ball had been redirected toward her daughter, where it would be commingled for the rest of their lives. Fahd was relegated to the sidelines, too ineffectual to be her advocate.

Pichel cast Natasha Gurdin in *Tomorrow Is Forever* that March, saying, "After that second test, there was never any question—Natasha was 'in the movies.'" It was a dream come true, Maria would later reminisce to a friend. "But it was Marie's dream, it wasn't Natasha's," as the friend would perceptively observe.

International Pictures, the studio producing the film, agreed to pay Natasha one hundred dollars a week, minimum Screen Actors Guild wages, to play the part of Margaret Ludwig. When the picture was completed, the studio had the option to extend her contract for up to seven years. Maria functioned as Natasha's de facto agent, using the bookkeeping skills her father suggested she learn in China and her own shrewd intelligence to evaluate the contract. "When there's a small print, I have to read it," she said once, "I always looking out for everything." Because Natasha was a minor, the contract with International had to be executed by a parent. Maria assumed the task, signing as "Mary" Gurdin, for reasons unknown. By using so many names—Maria, Marie, Musia, Marusia, now Mary—contriving the mystery that her real Russian name was a secret, in a strange way, Maria had no identity. She was merging with Natasha.

Natasha had her own identity crisis when the movie contract was executed. William Goetz and Leo Spitz, the producers who founded International Pictures, decided "Natasha Gurdin" was too ethnic for their child star. After discussing it, possibly with Pichel, they Americanized "Natasha" to "Natalie," and came up with "Wood" after a director they both knew named Sam Wood, who directed *A Night at the Opera* and *Pride of the Yankees*. The choice was either an homage to Wood, as Natalie generally told the story, or he happened to walk by at that moment, in a different version. In either case, Natasha had no say. Goetz simply walked up to her and declared, "From now on your name will be Natalie Wood." "I hated it," she said later. "It didn't conjure up a pretty image." "Couldn't we make it Woods instead of Wood?" she suggested. "Then I could think of trees and forests." "Don't fret," she would recall Goetz replying. "When you see 'Natalie Wood' up in lights, you'll love it." Maria ("Mary") promptly signed an amendment authorizing "Natalie Wood" as her daughter's professional name and screen credit, taking away Natasha's identity at six. The Gurdins did not *legally* change their daughter's name, probably because she was a minor. As she became famous as Natalie Wood, she would preserve her real name for legal purposes, remaining Natasha Gurdin all her life, the one vestige of the little girl she once was.

Natasha's hint of spirit concerning her name was the last time she would question an adult for seven years. Mud spent countless hours before *Tomorrow Is Forever* admonishing her to do anything Pichel or the producers asked, to be polite to the adults, be on time, never forget her lines, and curtsy when introduced to a grown-up. Small wonder that as an adult actress, Natalie was once compared to a wind-up doll. Mud's plan was to turn Natasha into the most cooperative child actress in town, so that her contract would be extended and studio heads, directors, and casting agents would want to hire her. "Be nice to the director," Natalie recalled Mud saying, over and over. "Even when I'd disagree, I'd have to smile and be sweet, and listen."

Since Natasha did not know how to read, Olga and Mud read the script of *Tomorrow Is Forever* aloud to her, telling her which lines were hers. She memorized her part as the Austrian orphan by hearing her mother and sister read it, a process Natalie would recall as extremely difficult, since "I had to do it with a German accent and I had to learn a bit of German." According to Olga, Natasha had no voice coach and learned the German phonetically, extraordinary for a six-year-old. Robert Blake, who befriended Natalie when they were child actors, estimated her IQ at 150 or 160, "Phi Beta Kappa smart." Natasha quite possibly had a photographic memory, something Musia discovered reading the script to her. "She had unusual memory. She will memorize not only her part, but all who's with her." An early boyfriend, while acknowledging Natalie's intellect, ascribed her childhood memorization of complete scripts to sheer terror. "That mother did something to her at night—she must have—in bed . . . getting her to remember all those lines as a kid."

Natasha approached playing a war orphan opposite Orson Welles much as she had appearing in the kindergarten play, as an exercise in make-believe. Just as she put white powder in her hair to transform into an old woman, the studio hairdresser bleached her Russian brown hair Austrian blond so she could become Margaret Ludwig—braiding it, ironically, into pigtails. "Acting to me was just like playing house or playing with dolls." Olga or Mud explained to Natasha who the characters in the film were "in language I could understand," and she "played pretend." How Natasha *felt* about acting is less clear; sadly, even to her. "My feelings were largely submerged. I'd been told to act, and I simply acted without questioning," she reflected in middle age, speculating "something in me obviously wanted to act. When I was told to do so, I cooperated and enjoyed it." Natalie's analysis was probably correct, for as Pichel observed from his experience as a director, "If a child doesn't want to act, you can't make him."

Natasha's first day on a movie set as "Natalie Wood" was March 30, 1945. Her first scene was with Orson Welles. She walked onto the International Pictures lot with her mother, wide-eyed, expecting "velvet curtains and tinsel," the way she imagined, from Mud's fantastical descriptions, when she played "going to the studio." "I couldn't understand these rundown buildings. I thought they would be divine, all glitter and gold, and here were these old barns." She was "terribly disillusioned."

The towering Welles—her first leading man, as he was to call himself—made a lasting impression on tiny Natasha. She was struck by the huge star's "booming voice" and found him instantly kind, "always very helpful. I remember he was quite temperamental also—but never towards me." Something about the Russian child with the quaint curtsy melted Welles' heart, as it had Pichel's. "I was just a little in love with Natalie, since the first time we met. I never stopped loving her. I never will," he said later. Their first scene together captured that chemistry, despite Welles' dismissive comments about the film years later. When Pichel called action, Natasha, by some supernatural process, *became* Margaret, haunted by her parents' murders, clinging to her guardian. Her accent and her German were eerily authentic; in her ice-blond braids she seemed reborn an Austrian. Welles, who had been a child prodigy, found her talent "terrifying," as he told *Life* magazine that fall in a quote that often would be repeated. "I've had a lot of experience with child actors," he later observed, "but Natalie was far and away the most memorable—even more so than Liz Taylor. She was a professional when I first saw her. I guess she was born a professional." Welles was more correct than he imagined, for Natasha had been prepared for this moment since conception. She responded with genius to match Welles (who would claim to a friend, years later, that he "discovered" Natalie Wood).

Maria shrewdly and uncharacteristically withdrew into the background when Natasha was performing, correctly intuiting that her lack of interference would please the director and everyone on the set, increasing her daughter's likelihood of being hired again. She stood off to the side, her sharp eyes darting everywhere, noticing the tiniest detail, reminding Natasha, by her dark presence, to be letter-perfect. Welles would recall shooting six or seven takes of a scene where he held Natalie in his lap. "Should have been just one take," remembered Welles, "but I kept blowing my lines. Not Natalie. She was six years old at the time, but she was already a perfect little pro." Mud's fanaticism to create the model child actor left Natasha no room to be a child, or to be anything less than perfect, fostering a perfectionism Natalie would struggle with all her life: "I always felt I had to know my lines perfectly and not keep anybody waiting."

Natasha's raw performance in *Tomorrow Is Forever* was nearly perfect. The role of a shattered war orphan suited the sadly beguiling quality she herself possessed. Pichel even incorporated Natasha's curtsy into her character. Years later Natalie would remark that she was best playing sad characters because she could use the dark experiences in her life. Natasha's demons bled through her portrayal of Margaret. Welles noticed it during filming, commenting later on "those two great dark, deep-looking eyes," remarking how "they could dance with fun . . . [yet] they were shadowed too by something else, some deep reflection of . . . tragedy."

The tenderness of Orson Welles' relationship with Natasha carried over to their scenes. When the hulking Welles, as the ailing guardian, starts to remove his heavy overcoat, tiny, wistful Margaret—Natasha—races to his side, helping him out of the sleeves, a poignant gesture that reveals her love for him but also her fear that if he died she would be lost. The gesture, and Natasha's sensitive performance, were instinctual. As Welles put it, "Natalie acts from her heart, not from the script," proving that the pathos in her extraordinary screen test was more than Maria's gimmickry with a butterfly.

Natasha missed the last half of first grade shooting *Tomorrow Is Forever*. According to child labor laws, child actors had to have three hours of schooling every day. Natalie studied on the set between scenes with a studio tutor. "The way it works," recalls a kid actor who later worked with her, "[is] when the kids show up in the morning they go straight into wardrobe and makeup so they're prepared. Then they go to the teacher. The teacher would have a time clock and you start doing your schooling. The assistant director's job is to get that schooling out of the way—so they do it in increments. In about twenty minutes they would say, 'Okay, we need Natalie.' So she would go out and rehearse. Then they would say, 'Okay, go back to school.' While the lighting and everything is being done, the kid would be in school. It was very rare to get the whole three hours in." "I had to take my lessons on the set during the times they were lighting the scene," Natalie recalled, "so I learned to concentrate. If a lamp fell down I probably wouldn't hear it." Because she was underage, Natasha was also required to have a welfare worker and one of her parents with her on the set at all times. She was surrounded by an entourage of adults—her tutor, Maria, the welfare worker—in the middle of a sea of activity all day, every day, on the movie set. At night, Mud hovered about her like a hummingbird. The only time Natasha was alone was when she went to bed at night. Solitude began to frighten her.

The emotional scene Natasha performed at her screen test was scheduled a month into filming. She anticipated it with "absolute terror," traumatized by Mud's pressure on her to cry on cue. Maria borrowed Olga's tactic while Pichel was setting up the scene, reminding Natasha of her dead dog. Then she took it a step further. "Her mother would drag her behind a flat and tell her some *horrendous* story about tearing the wings off birds to get her hysterical, and then drag her back." This would be the technique Maria used with Natasha from then on. "She would get me all worked up and say to the director, 'Start shooting.' " Mud's brutality was effective; Natasha sobbed on Welles' shoulder in perfect German. Crying would remain her bête noire forever after.

Natasha also had fun on *Tomorrow Is Forever*. Welles taught her magic tricks, "always pulling cards out of my pigtails." She discovered she "loved grown-ups," which was not surprising, for Mud had turned her into a miniature adult. Her best friend on the set was a dwarf named Shorty, Welles' valet. "We became great pals, Shorty and I, and we kind of hung out together between takes," she later recalled. "And I remember Claudette Colbert. She was always dieting. My mother used to be amazed that 'Miss Colbert doesn't seem to eat any food, she just drinks fruit juice and vegetable juice.' She was thin as a reed. She had a little atomizer that she used to spray something—air, I think—into her eyes. She wanted them to sparkle. She was very sweet to me." Natasha observed it all, noticing how Welles changed the lighting to suit him, studying Colbert, "learning how to be a better actress." Welles taught her, by example, to keep a sense of humor about being a star. Colbert, her first female Hollywood role model, impressed Natasha as "kind and maternal . . . you felt that about her, not just in her performances but in life." The same would be said, in the future, of Natalie Wood.

Colbert became a mother figure to Natasha, in the movie and on set. "I always felt it sad somehow that in real life, Claudette never became a mother, for she had so much to give that way." Natasha found her "exceptionally sensitive and understanding and empathetic," qualities noticeably absent in Mud. Colbert returned the compliment, describing Natasha as "smart" and "sensitive," an opinion shared by Pichel, who concluded with some regret after directing her that Natasha had "the sensitivity, the temperament, the understanding of that cross between child and adult—the *actress*." Natalie Wood was a child-woman at six.

Her mature behavior on the set earned her a reputation in Hollywood as "very easy to handle." "Like I taught her," said Maria, "to be courteous to the grown-ups." Natasha was akin to a marionette; Maria pulled the strings and Natalie Wood performed.

Mud's strategy, and Natasha's talent, achieved Maria's desired end. Goetz and Spitz exercised the option to extend "Natalie Wood's" contract with International Pictures before she had even completed looping her scenes. By the terms of the option, her weekly salary would increase in increments each year she was under contract, beginning at $125 per week and graduating to $750 a week by the final year. Within twelve months of arriving in Hollywood, Maria had secured a seven-year contract with a major movie studio for Natasha. She was not quite seven years old.

On May 22, a package arrived at the Canevaris' in Santa Rosa, addressed to Edwin. Inside was an 8½-by-11 glossy of Natasha, as Margaret, in *Tomorrow Is Forever*, dressed in a gingham pinafore with puffed sleeves, her peroxide hair in braids, tiny hands folded primly on her lap, smiling sweetly for the camera. On the back of the photo Musia had written a letter, purporting to be from Natasha:

> Dear Edwin!
>
> Sending you my picture, Studio changed my name, my screen name is Natalie Wood. Thank you for a lovely hankies. I am wearing them to studio. If you will see something about me in Santa Rosa paper (newspaper) please send it to me. I am collecting all my publicity, I have a scrap book. My best regards to your mama and papa,
>
> Love Natasha.
>
> -1945-HOLLYWOOD

Natasha, who was learning to read, signed the picture herself, copying her sister Olga's perfect penmanship. "To dear Edwin, My best friend," she wrote neatly, "love Natalie Wood," adding, in parentheses, "(Natasha)."

It was a psychologically complex correspondence, foreshadowing, among other things, the interweaving of Maria's persona with Natasha's; Natasha's identity complex; and Mud's total domination of her movie star daughter. "God *made* her," she would say years later, "but *I* invented her."

6 BEFORE FILMING WAS COMPLETED on her first movie, a fan magazine called *Motion Picture* had already interviewed "Natalie Wood" for a profile called "Six-Year-Old Siren." Pichel made immediate arrangements to borrow her from International for his new movie at Paramount, *The Bride Wore Boots*, to start in July, putting Natasha back to work within three weeks, over what would have been her summer holiday.

Mud's paranoid behavior blossomed into hysteria now that "Natalie" was on the cusp of fame. She never let Natasha out of her sight and would not allow her to play at other children's homes because she was afraid Natasha might be kidnapped, instilling a disturbing new element to her growing fear of being alone, "this feeling that it was somehow *dangerous*." Natasha put off bedtime until as late as possible, "babbling" for hours, populating her bedroom with storybook dolls—believing that Bo-Peep, Cinderella, and twenty-eight other doll characters kept her from being alone. "I talked to my dolls and toys and I thought they came alive at night," she told a writer when she was an adult. "Sometimes I stayed up all night to see what they would do."

Mud's restrictions, and the absence of school, isolated Natasha. Her sole companion, apart from Olga and a cat named Voska, was a three-year-old boy who lived next door. Natasha called him "Father," for reasons she didn't tell. She lived in her imagination, inventing stories, identifying with the dark Russian fairy tales in Fahd's books, envisioning when she would travel to the Russia of Mud's romantic description, cloaked in ermine, riding through snowdrifts on the trans-Siberian express. Her reality was a childhood so lonely she named "Mr. Pichel" as her best friend when asked by a reporter from *Motion Picture*, referring wistfully to Edwin, her "boyfriend" in Santa Rosa.

Natasha's first day on Pichel's new movie was July 20, her seventh birthday. Mud and Fahd gave her a party, inviting all the neighborhood children with whom she was forbidden to play. They wore colorful hats and ate cake, bringing presents and singing "Happy Birthday." Natasha, who had never been to a child's party, was so overcome she cried. She told Mud afterward when she grew up she wanted to be a mother and have a hundred and fifty kids, "and they're all going to have to give me presents on my birthday."

Natasha's kiddie party was a brief diversion from her real life, acting in movies. The war ended a few weeks after she turned seven, and Pichel's new picture reflected the changing times. *The Bride Wore Boots* was a daffy comedy starring Barbara Stanwyck as an equestrienne married to a citified writer comically inept around horses (Robert Cummings). Natalie Wood and a cherubic six-year-old named Gregory Muradian played their children, given little more to do in the film than provide background scenery and play appealingly with a goat. Off camera, Gregory was "quite enamored of" his movie sibling, Natasha, whose Aryan blond braids as Margaret Ludwig had been replaced by a halo of golden brown curls. Most of the children's scenes were shot on location at a horse ranch, where Natasha and Gregory romped. After her demanding bilingual performance opposite Welles, Natasha essentially had to show up and look adorable. Her enduring memory was of Stanwyck's perfume. *The Bride Wore Boots* also introduced Natasha to horses, a passion of Stanwyck's. The film itself was a pallid imitation of Cary Grant/Katharine Hepburn screwball comedies, though it was pleasant and Natasha was beguiling. Pichel, borrowing from Hitchcock, appeared briefly in a scene.

Natasha finished shooting her part in September and returned to school, where she continued to be shadowed. Olga walked her to class every day, under instruction from Maria, who was still convinced that kidnappers lurked around every corner.

Tomorrow Is Forever would not be out until after Christmas, but "Natalie Wood" was already getting attention. Her profile in *Motion Picture* hit the newsstands, predicting she would be a candidate for a child Oscar and proclaiming her a prodigy. Maria controlled every aspect of her daughter's emerging persona and Natasha followed orders like a good little soldier. "I want to be a movie star," she "bubbled" to *Motion Picture*, repeating the mantra Mud canted to her since birth.

In November, *Life* magazine sent a reporter and a photographer to the Gurdins' cottage in West Hollywood to prepare a story on the seven-year-old actress who had Orson Welles at her feet. They took pictures of Natasha, tanned and topless, on the backyard swing; lying on the grass stroking her cat. Mud, hoping to glamorize Natalie's image, lied to the reporter, telling him her husband Nick was an "engineer," constructing an intricate tissue of falsehoods about how "Natalie Wood" got into the movies. She told the reporter that *Pichel* stumbled onto Natasha shooting *Happy Land* and *sent* for her to star in *Tomorrow Is Forever*. Then she fabricated an elaborate story that Natasha's father disapproved, so she "tricked" him by pretending to visit a friend in Los Angeles and "sneaking" Natasha to a screen test. Natasha begged to do the movie, said Maria, so she returned to Santa Rosa, convinced her husband, and sold the house.

When the *Life* pictorial came out at Thanksgiving, Maria Gurdin's outlandish lies were printed as fact, creating a Hollywood myth concerning the discovery of Natalie Wood that would crystallize, with time, into legend. Even Lana, who was born after the *Life* article, believed her mother's propaganda that Pichel sent for her sister from Santa Rosa to star in *Tomorrow Is Forever*, repeating it over the years as "the story that I have been told my entire life." The image of a movie star is *illusion*, a concept Mud, the ultimate fantasist, instinctively grasped. "Marie Gurdin was a highly imaginative genius," an industry friend once observed. "She managed to form, to invent, to chisel this image of Natalie Wood." In an irony, *Life* pronounced Natalie "stiff competition" for Margaret O'Brien, whose look Mud had brazenly copied. *Life* also reported that three studios were trying to buy Natalie's contract from International. Whether this was true, or more of Maria's hyperbole, is unsubstantiated.

Mud would do anything to get a foot in the door for Natasha. She read and re-read the trades, enrolling Natasha in ballet and classical dance with Tamara Lepke, hiring a piano instructor so she would be prepared to play any role. "They put a *lot* into her—piano lessons, dancing lessons—always to further her." Olga, who sang in Hollywood High operettas, had her voice lessons suddenly discontinued by Maria, who was insensitively oblivious to her elder daughter's talent. "I just decided to work and pay for my own lessons," relates Olga. To earn money, she babysat after school, "and I would work at department stores on Hollywood Boulevard." The Gurdin household was like a miniature studio dedicated to the training of just one star: Natalie Wood. Recalled Natalie: "My mother used to tell me, 'No matter what they ask you—"Can you sing, dance, swim, ride?" always say yes. You can learn later.' "

For all her gurgling to magazines about wanting to be a movie star, Natasha didn't seem excited about being in movies, her sister remembers. What compelled Natasha to act was not the desire to perform; it was a compulsion to *please*. She defined "acting," at six, as "doing things for people." Natasha, by nature, took pleasure in bringing joy to others. When Maria was in her seventies, she told this story about Natalie:

> I remember when she was, I think, in first or second grade in school. And there was a teacher—very homely, nobody liked her, and she was kinda strict, too. And when Natalie see person like that she just *loved* them—and want to make them happy. And she was old maid, that teacher. Her name was Grace Loop. And when it was Valentine Day, Natalie said, "Mother, let's go and get the biggest Valentine box with the candy for my teacher." And the teacher start to cry. She say, "Nobody give me . . ." She loved Natalie.

> And then when Natalie go back to the studio school and she was not her teacher anymore, she would send Grace Loop present for Christmas. Present for her birthday, too. And then one time suddenly it was stopped. Was car thrown Grace Loop. To the end, she have contact with Natalie.

It was this innate sensitivity to other people's feelings that made Natasha such an affecting child actress, and explained how she remained unspoiled. Singer Lena Horne's daughter Gail attended grammar school with Natasha that year as fame struck, and she remembers her fondly as "tiny, pretty Natalie, our resident movie star." Olga, who had every reason to resent her, considered it a treat to take Natasha to the movies.

Maria's driving ambition and Natasha's urgency to please were a dangerous cocktail. "I saw my parents as gods whose every wish must be obeyed or I would suffer the penalty of anguish and guilt," she said later. Olga would observe her sister at ballet recitals "concentrating so hard she put her tongue out the left side, biting her cheek." At seven, Natasha was playing Chopin. She studied Olga's movie scrapbook like a textbook, memorizing details of the ninety-four stars' lives, repeating them in interviews. When she watched movies, Natasha got so emotionally involved, once at a cinema with Olga, "she was watching the movie and I guess had to go to the bathroom. I didn't know it, so she must have been letting it out very slowly . . . and I was just so proper, I took her home right away. But she wet her pants!" When she wasn't in a movie, taking ballet or piano to prepare for a movie, or going to the movies, Natasha played "making movies."

Nick, according to a brother, was proud of the fact that

his daughter was acting. If it bothered him, as Natalie and Maria later maintained, he was too passive within the marriage to exert any authority, or to buffer Natasha from Mud. The fact that his wife had gotten him a job through his six-year-old daughter's connections underscored his impotence; the word in the Gurdins' Russian circle in San Francisco was that Natalie was the breadwinner in the family. Nick was "miserably unhappy," according to his younger daughter, Lana, who was conceived that June, between Natasha's films for Pichel.

Maria consequently dominated Natasha, inflicting strange paranoias to sculpt her into stardom. She refused to let Natasha go "on toe" too soon in ballet class, concerned that her calves would look too large on the screen. "After each exercise, I rubbed her with oil—the whole body I rubbed, not just the legs, so she wouldn't get the bulging muscles ballerinas usually get." When Natasha told her mother she wanted to be a ballerina *and* a movie star, Maria "said no. Ballerinas don't live very long, and it's bad for the heart." Mud repeatedly told Natasha she was frail. Both parents refused to let her run or play outside, for if she got hurt, she wouldn't be able to work. "I was so overprotected, I used to think I was as delicate as people said I was." Natasha began to imagine she had various illnesses, acquiring new fears—fast cars and earthquakes—to supplement her existing ones, dark water and being alone. "Natalie had a lot of fear *in* her," states a childhood friend, "all *misplaced* fear." Natasha's refuge was animals. Besides her cat, she had three turtles. Mud and Fahd bought her a German shepherd that year, to replace the puppy she saw killed. Natasha called him Rusty.

She needed a haven. Her sister Olga remembers walking into the house that winter to find Nick, drunk, holding a knife to Maria's pregnant belly. Olga created a diversion so her stepfather would come after her, deciding it would be better if he stabbed *her* than her pregnant mother. Though no one was hurt, it was a harrowing incident; a signal, to Olga, she should leave Nick's house. She stayed, but warily, forming the opinion that her mother was partially responsible because she could provoke Nick. It was a strange, complex marriage. Maria was still in romantic contact with the sea captain from San Francisco's Russian colony, where the gossip was that she was pregnant by a Hollywood producer. She told Olga the reason she didn't leave Nick was that "she was always *afraid* of him."

Whether Natasha was present when her Fahd held the knife to Mud's stomach that winter is unclear, though she certainly experienced violence. "She had a very tough, troubled life," reveals Robert Blake, a confidant from their years as child actors. "The things that she told me about her childhood, which are nobody's business, but they were tough. In today's world, Natalie would have been in child abuse groups . . . the courage and the strength that it took for her every day to get out of bed and pursue her life—she spent her life rowing upstream." Lana, who was born late that winter, described her father as "a mean drunk. He wasn't actually an alcoholic. He didn't drink all day long. He would get drunk probably once a week. He was just a really unhappy man."

Because Mud was nearly eight months pregnant with Lana, she sent Nick with Natasha to New York for the January premiere of *Tomorrow Is Forever*, possibly the only occasion when Lana would come before Natalie for Maria. It was a medical necessity, or Mud would never have missed the public unveiling of her creation, Natalie Wood. It was the first time she and Natasha had been apart. Mud must have been histrionic, sending her star-child on an airplane, across the country, without her. One of Natalie's crippling fears, later in life, was flying on planes, a fear that probably originated with this trip. The stress of the separation from Mud was evident in Natasha in other ways. While she was in New York, the studio sent her to children's hospitals and F.A.O. Schwarz, the famous toy store, for publicity shots for *Tomorrow Is Forever*. A mob of people clamored around International's new child star, tugging at her pigtails, which Fahd did not know how to braid correctly. "Fans pulled the ribbons off my pigtails," she would remember. "I was terrified." Pictures from the event reveal Natasha clutching her "mama doll," Gabriella, like a life preserver, masking her terror with an overanimated smile, prattling manically about wanting to be a movie star when she grew up. "My goodness!" she exclaimed, between flashbulb pops. "That time I didn't blink!" As an adult, Natalie would seldom make a negative remark in public about her child acting experiences, not wanting people to think she didn't enjoy it, saying that it was "a bore to complain"—still the consummate trouper. She revealed her true feelings indirectly, telling interviewers she would not want *her* child to act, as she had.

Natasha did experience one genuine thrill while promoting her movie in New York that January: snow. Although *Tomorrow Is Forever* would not be released until the spring, Natalie Wood was praised by New York newspapers, whose critics had attended the celebrity premiere.

Svetlana Gurdin's birth, on March 1, coincided with Natalie's first flush of fame, where the spotlight would lopsidedly, at times cruelly, remain. Giving birth was Mud's first, and last, maternal act toward her third daughter. As soon as she got home from the hospital, she relinquished Svetlana to Olga so she could devote herself to Natasha. Olga had already dropped out of school to babysit Natasha while Mud was in the hospital, inciting rumors at Hollywood High that Svetlana was *her* baby. "Natalie was under contract to the studio, and it was the law that I had to be with her," rationalized Maria. In truth, Mud believed she had a calling. Years later, she happily cooperated with a fan magazine for an article called "I Neglected Lana So Natalie Could Be a Star." "I was a non-person," observes Lana. Maria, who hand-selected the wealthy Loys as Natasha's godparents, saw no reason to choose a godmother for Svetlana, nor would she bother to teach her to curtsy. "I *think* I lived there, I'm not sure," remarks Lana.

Olga, who was a conscientious student, began to worry about missing class and returned to high school. Maria hired a nanny for Svetlana and accompanied Natasha to San Francisco the middle of March. International arranged a luncheon at the St. Francis and a press conference at the Warfield to "present" Natalie Wood to reporters, certain that her performance in *Tomorrow Is Forever* would attract even more attention when the film was released. "Natalie," under Mud's scrutiny, performed with mechanical animation. Reporters remarked on her poise, dutifully noting the vital statistics of her young life as she "rattled off facts," including her mother's fabrication that Pichel brought her to Hollywood to star in the movie. The accompanying articles must have thrilled Mud, announcing Natalie Wood as "the Margaret O'Brien of tomorrow."

Natasha and Mud returned to West Hollywood to read her first major review. *Look* magazine was only mildly complimentary of *Tomorrow Is Forever*, calling it old-fashioned, but the magazine extolled Natalie as a "real prize" and a rival to Orson Welles, with whom she was pictured in a nearly full-page close-up. Inside the Gurdin home circumstances were less sanguine. When the nanny fed Svetlana a banana and she choked, Maria fired her and commandeered her husband to quit his job and stay home with the baby. Irving Pichel's warning—that a child star upset the family balance of power—had sprung disastrously to life. Becoming a babysitter to Svetlana was the final indignity for Nick. His days, Lana would recall, consisted of drinking, reading and playing the balalaika. "There was nobody for him to talk to, there was nobody who understood that he was leading a life that he detested."

The pressure on Natasha from this turn of events was overwhelming. At the age of seven, she was supporting the family. She also felt guilty that her mother was sacrificing her life and creativity for *her* career. "I think if she had been able to express herself in some way . . . she would have been much happier," Natalie would remark after giving birth to her own children. Lana believes their mother had to have been unhappy, "But I don't think she ever knew it. Not consciously. How can you live your life for one person and have nothing else in your life?" A companion of Maria's in the last years of her life posits that Maria had everything she ever wanted, "her dream of being an actress, her dream of having wealth—but she had it through Natalie." From the time Mud saw her cameo cut from *Happy Land*, she transferred her dream of stardom to Natasha, living the fantasy through her creation, "Natalie Wood," the composite of mother and daughter. When Natalie received an invitation that spring to the Hollywood premiere of *Tomorrow Is Forever*, Maria, her alter ego, was beside her, strolling down the red carpet under the spotlight, gaping at

Gary Cooper, Greer Garson, Gene Tierney, Jane Wyman and Ronald Reagan, the movie stars whose pictures she cut out of fan magazines. Natasha, who had memorized their faces and life stories, found it enjoyable; Mud *reveled* in it. Natalie did her acting when she was given a part to play; Maria was an actress in her everyday life. As Lana recalls, "You couldn't take her anywhere, go anywhere, with anybody, because she would sing and dance at the drop of a hat and drive you crazy."

Tomorrow Is Forever received mixed notices when it opened at the Pantages in early April, though it would become a box office success. Louella Parsons, the influential gossip columnist, singled out Natasha before the movie came out, writing in her column: "Little Natalie Wood, as a tiny refugee, gives a remarkable performance for a child. She eats your heart out." It was the official Hollywood seal of approval.

7

THE BRIDE WORE BOOTS, Natasha's third film for Pichel, was released the same spring. Though it didn't make much of an impression, it increased Natalie's visibility. Goetz and Spitz, who had merged their company with Universal Pictures to form Universal-International, exercised her second six-month option on May 1, 1946, approved by "Mary" Gurdin, increasing Natalie's salary to $150 a week. Actor George Brent, who played Colbert's second husband in *Tomorrow Is Forever*, advised Maria to get Natasha an agent, taking her by the hand to Famous Artists Group, where Natalie Wood was signed to a three-year contract on May 8, represented by a cadre of six agents.

A few weeks later, Mud filed an official document with the court to reflect her "true" name as "Maria S. Gurdin," not "Mary." The implication was that she had assumed the persona of Mary Gurdin to execute Natalie's contracts; now that Natalie had Famous Artists, "Mary Gurdin" could be laid to rest. Mud was intelligent enough to recognize that Natasha needed a powerful agent and shrewd enough to keep her vise grip on her daughter's career. "Even though Natalie had an agent, she would still read the trades and then she would ask them, 'How about *this* picture, or *that* picture?' She was very much *on* to things," recalls Olga. According to a family friend, Maria still negotiated Natalie's contracts; Famous Artists did "what she told them to do." "My mother ran my career and did it well—seeing that I got the right parts," Natalie later complimented. Mud, with Famous Artists, submitted her for virtually every child's role that summer, capitalizing on her momentum from *Tomorrow Is Forever*.

Natasha began to go by her screen name of "Natalie Wood" around this time, though she signed her letters to relatives and friends "Natasha," or she would write "Natasha" in parentheses underneath "Natalie," symbolizing the distinction in her mind between who she really was and her movie persona.

Other sweeping changes came into her life near Halloween. Her mother felt cramped with a new baby, so the Gurdins purchased a somewhat larger house in less expensive Burbank, using Natalie's studio salary. Maria gave no thought to Olga, who wanted to finish her senior year at Hollywood High. "I was in an operetta there, *Sweethearts*, and I really liked the people, liked my teachers. I didn't want to switch schools yet again." Olga chose to stay behind, renting a room from a Bulgarian neighbor which she paid for with her department store wages. Mud did not even bother to attend her operetta, claiming it was too far from Burbank. Olga, who was devoutly Russian Orthodox, accepted her mother's heartlessness with her usual grace. "My girlfriend's family came. It *felt* like my family."

Natalie had her own adjustment problems. She felt displaced transferring to public school in Burbank with other third-graders. "I didn't like it at all—in those days, I didn't like children. I didn't think of myself as a child, and I didn't like any of the things children were interested in. Also, studio school had been so far advanced I was way ahead of the kids in public school and I was bored."

With Olga out of the house, no one in the family had any friends. "My mother never got to know neighbors," recalls Lana. "She had no sense of community or anything like that. Natalie was *it*." Natalie's touchstone was the faithful Edwin, who would hear from her via occasional letters telling him what her next movie would be. Maria set aside thirty percent of her daughter's salary in a savings account as required by law and was conservative with the rest ("It was a little bitty house in Burbank," remarks Lana), but it was Natalie's money supporting the family. Six months had passed since she was seen on the screen, a lifetime to Maria. When she was rejected for a part, "I felt awful," Natalie said later, "as if I had let everybody down."

Sometime after Halloween, Natalie's agents placed her in contention for a small film at Twentieth Century Fox called *The Big Heart*. She was up for the part of a precocious six-year-old Manhattanite named Susan Walker, instructed by her divorced, disenchanted mother not to believe in Santa Claus. The picture, which would become the Christmas classic *Miracle on 34th Street*, "was actually being filmed as a low budget 'B' movie," recalls one of the actors. Director George Seaton, a former stage actor, wrote the screenplay, called *It's Only Human*, based on a story suggested by his friend Valentine Davies while they were vacationing with their wives. Darryl Zanuck, the head of Fox, read the script and sent Seaton a note saying he loved it. The title was changed to *The Big Heart* and Zanuck assigned Maureen O'Hara, who was under contract, to play Susan's mother, a Macy's personnel director who hires a replacement Santa for the Thanksgiving parade who believes he *is* Kris Kringle. To play Kringle, the producers hired English stage actor Edmund Gwenn. Zanuck suggested John Payne as the neighbor determined to restore both mother and daughter's faith in miracles. "I was only eight years old," said Natalie in later years, "but I remember very clearly that at that time, at Fox, they were doing many, many pictures. They had no high hopes for *Miracle* whatsoever. It was just a little extra picture that was sort of done on the sideline." O'Hara, who had left for Ireland to see her parents and introduce them to her young daughter, had not even read the script.

Mud, who *had*, noticed that Susan was a pivotal role, determined that her daughter would get the part. As if Natalie were not already confused playing different characters, changing her name from Natasha to Natalie, Mud now instructed her to watch Margaret O'Brien pictures and act like *Margaret* during her screen test for the role of Susan. Maria darkened Natalie's hair and resurrected her pigtails so she would physically resemble O'Brien. "Margaret was the top child star, and Marie was so eager for Natalie to make it," explains a confidant. "Marie said, 'We kind of imitated Margaret, the look and the performance.' " Once they were friends, Natalie confessed her secret to

Margaret. "There were a million little girls trying to do it," observes O'Brien. "Natalie just did it better, I think."

Natalie got the part of Susan in *The Big Heart* in November, just as Darryl Zanuck was making final notes on an unusual, ethereally romantic Philip Dunne script called *The Ghost and Mrs. Muir*, adapted from a 1945 novel, *The Ghost of Captain Gregg and Mrs. Muir*. The story, set at the turn of the century, was about a lonely young widow in London who moves with her small daughter to an English seaside cottage, where she falls in love with the spirit of a roguish sea captain. Zanuck had assigned the film to Fox producer Fred Kohlmar, who hired Dunne, admired for his tender characterization in *How Green Was My Valley*. Kohlmar convinced Joseph Mankiewicz, the literate screenwriter-director-producer, to direct. Mankiewicz was challenged by the idea of creating what he described as "essentially a 'mood' story," a love affair between a woman and a ghost. Spencer Tracy and Katharine Hepburn agreed to play the leads, according to Dunne's wife, Amanda, "and Tracy bowed out." The handsome, acerbic English actor Rex Harrison, who had just had a major success with his first American film, *Anna and the King of Siam*, was cast to replace Tracy as the captain. With Tracy gone, Hepburn departed and several other actresses were considered to play Lucy Muir: Norma Shearer, Claudette Colbert, Olivia De Havilland. Zanuck decided upon Gene Tierney, the delicately beautiful brunette best known as the mysterious *Laura* from the 1944 Otto Preminger film. Petite Natalie, with her hair darkened to call to mind Margaret O'Brien, bore an amazing resemblance to Tierney, making her an obvious contender for the part of Mrs. Muir's daughter, Anna. It was not a large role—young Anna is in a dozen or so small scenes and disappears when the film leaps forward in time—but it was a prestige film.

In the final few days before she was to start *The Big Heart*, Natalie auditioned in front of director Joseph Mankiewicz for the part of Anna Muir, the English child. Mud's punishing preparation and Natalie's obsessive perfectionism were in evidence at the audition. As Mankiewicz would remember: "I asked her, 'Did you read the whole script, or just your part?' She answered, 'The whole script.' I then asked her, 'How do you spell Mankiewicz?' and she spelled it right, all the way down to the 'cz.' I told her she had the part."

Director George Seaton had decided to incorporate the actual Macy's Thanksgiving Parade into *The Big Heart* and got permission to film inside the store, so Natalie and Mud flew to New York on November 17 to start location shooting. Fox sent Maureen O'Hara a telegram in Dublin, where she had just arrived, instructing her to cut short her family reunion. O'Hara was furious. "Because I didn't know what the script was, I didn't know what it was about, I didn't know anything except I was ordered by my boss to be back in New York." "It was a low-budget film," observes one of the actors. "The producers were saying, 'Let's hurry up. We don't have any money.' "

O'Hara read the script when she unpacked, "and I thought, 'I'm not so mad after all.' " *Miracle on 34th Street* was charmed from the beginning, according to O'Hara. "Every day, it was magic. We had a wonderful, happy, magical time making the movie. Edmund Gwenn *was* Santa Claus. I mean that literally. He believed he was Santa Claus." So did Natalie, who found New York thrilling this trip, perhaps because she had Maria along for security. "I fell madly in love with Louie, the headwaiter at the

Carlton, and had chicken salad for breakfast, lunch and dinner."

On the set of *The Big Heart*, One-Take Natalie, her new nickname, impressed everyone. If the adult actors forgot their lines, she cued them. Seaton, the director, was amazed at how businesslike she was. Her only coaching came from Mud whispering, "*Be Margaret O'Brien.*" (Mud's coaching was strictly at night; on set, she continued to let the director control Natalie: "Marie never interfered with the filming. Marie interfered with the *negotiations*, the *contracts*. Once she got what she wanted, then Natalie went to work.") Natalie was in effect playing two parts: Susan, and Margaret O'Brien *playing* Susan. She was so effective, states O'Brien, "a lot of people think it's *me* in the movie." Natalie's most vivid memory of the film, later, was "Edmund Gwenn teaching me how to act like a monkey," a scene where her O'Brien impersonation is evident: O'Brien had imitated a monkey in exactly the same way in *Meet Me in St. Louis* two years before.

Natalie may have mimicked O'Brien, but her talent was genuine. Seaton, her director on *Miracle*, said she had "an instinctive sense of timing and emotion" he had seen in only one other child. Natalie described her technique as a child actress, later, as instinctive. She first read the script; if she had any questions about her character or the story, she asked an adult. Then she re-read the script "many times." The night before a scene, she memorized the next day's lines, "visualizing the whole page." When she played the scene, she said the lines the way she instinctually felt her character would. Her performances, as a result, were natural.

The part of a skeptical child whose parent teaches her Santa Claus isn't real was a radical departure from Natalie's own life. Her mother took her to see a department store Santa that December. When Natalie jumped off Santa's lap, Mud jumped on, whispering in Santa's ear everything she wanted for Christmas. Olga, who was along, cringed with embarrassment. Playing Susan required Natalie to create a character different from herself. She drew on her intelligence to become Susan, as opposed to the waifish vulnerability she projected as Margaret.

Natalie's acting gifts were tested that month. While she was playing Susan, the cynical New Yorker, she flew back to California to perform her first scenes as Anna, the English child, then she returned to New York to finish location shots as Susan, switching back and forth between an American and British accent. She began each day on the set of *The Ghost and Mrs. Muir* walking up to Mankiewicz in his director's chair and spelling out "M-A-N-K-I-E-W-I-C-Z." Mankiewicz, who had never directed a child before, called Natalie "the smartest moppet" he knew. "I knew she would become an actress because she was always watching. She watched Edna Best,* she watched Rex Harrison." Word of her simultaneous performances in *Ghost* and *The Big Heart* started to circulate at Fox, where the publicity department was calling Natalie a "wonder-child." When she received the Box Office Blue Ribbon Award at the end of the year for *Tomorrow Is Forever*, Fox made overtures to Universal-International to buy her contract. Universal refused.

Natalie was too busy to notice the fuss being made over her. She spent the end of December back at home in California on the Fox soundstage where Seaton was directing interior scenes on *The Big Heart*, occasionally

---

*Best played the housekeeper.

racing over to the set of *The Ghost and Mrs. Muir*. The exterior scenes in *Ghost* were being shot in Palos Verdes, north of Long Beach, which Mankiewicz had chosen to portray the English seaside. Fox set designers had constructed a gated Victorian as Mrs. Muir's haunted cottage, where Natalie's character, Anna, carves her name on a plank near the sea, the first of numerous water scenes in her films. Natalie would have fond memories of that winter:

> What a wonderful time that was for me. I was so young, and making movies, going to the studio every morning at dawn was magic. I'd check in on the set, have my makeup done and my hair wound up in one of those "period" hairdos and get all dressed up in a hoop-skirted costume. Then I'd run around that house all day pretending to be frightened by Rex Harrison's ghost.
>
> If we weren't on location, my mother would take me to lunch, and I'd have a couple of hours of school in the middle of the day. Then I'd report to [*The Big Heart*] set and they'd give me a modern New York hairdo and change my makeup, give me rosy cheeks and all those wonderful Bonnie Cashin winter clothes, and I'd play another part [Susan] for the rest of the day.

Gene Tierney suffered a nervous breakdown several years after *The Ghost and Mrs. Muir*. Screenwriter Philip Dunne's wife, Amanda Duff, who was an actress herself, remembers, "Gene had to be sort of pampered" during filming. "She and I would both get upset about things very easily." Actress Anna Lee, who played George Sanders' screen wife in *Ghost* and had an emotional scene in the film with Tierney, "never detected anything too wrong in Gene until much later." Lee was "very fond of her," and of Natalie. Tierney tripped on a flight of stairs in February and broke a toe, suspending production for eleven days. She returned in a cast, which her costumes camouflaged.

Natalie spent more time around Maureen O'Hara, her screen mother in *The Big Heart*. "She called me 'Mama Maureen,' " recalls O'Hara, who felt that Natalie liked her "in a very happy, young girl's way. She used to make these little ceramics that she used to bring me." O'Hara's impressions of Natalie and her mother differed from others who knew them in this period. She felt Natalie "absolutely loved" acting and "was a very happy little girl" without the underlying darkness that Orson Welles had perceived. "I never felt I wanted to protect her, ever. She didn't have that vulnerability. You felt completely at home with her, she felt at home with you. There was never any feeling that she *needed* anybody." From O'Hara's point of view Maria was a wonderful mother. "Because she wouldn't let Natalie in any way show any nonsense . . . she encouraged her and stood behind her and she didn't interfere with any of the work." O'Hara describes Natalie on the set of *Miracle* as: "Polite, charming, serious. Did her job and did her work, didn't throw any tantrums, she didn't cause any problems . . . she did what she was told." Almost verbatim Maria's edict to her.

In middle age, Natalie remembered herself in this period as "trying to please everyone—my parents, the director, the stars, the electricians. I was a very good little girl." A boyfriend Natalie confided in at seventeen wondered if her mother beat her to instill such eerily perfect behavior. Maria told a Fox publicist that winter that she pulled Natalie aside and threatened her in Russian with extra piano practice if she made a mistake on the set. "Mama was always there," recalls Maureen O'Hara. Bobby Hyatt, who had a small but important scene in *Miracle on 34th Street* as a seven-year-old who testifies for Kris Kringle, saw Maria "tear Natalie to shreds" if she happened to miss a cue, forget a line, or didn't hit her marks.

Hyatt, who was the only other featured child actor in the movie, spent several weeks on the Fox lot accompanied by his mother, Jean, offering them a glimpse into Maria's stage-mother tactics. "She was out for nothing but stardom," states Jean Hyatt. Maria refused to associate with the Hyatts and "whisked Natalie away" when she approached Bobby, because he was not a child *star*. Mud only wanted Natalie to be around people with status so they could advance her career. "Her mother wouldn't even let her *talk* to the extras under pain of punishment. She could only talk to the adults, and then she was only allowed to talk to the directors, the writers and the producers."

Maria kept Natalie isolated and under surveillance even when she was at studio school, demanding a private tutor and a separate classroom. When Natalie and Bobby became friends as teenagers, Natalie revealed her mother's strategy to him. During classes, Jean Hyatt and the other mothers played canasta or talked. "Marie would stay right in the schoolroom with Natalie," relates Hyatt, to "intimidate the tutor into not daring to give her anything less than an A or B," a studio requirement for child actors. "So as any kid would do, Natalie did not bother to do her homework or study for a test. Marie was teaching her that the only thing that was important was the grade, not the knowledge. All Marie wanted was to make sure that Natalie could read well, so she could read scripts . . . Natalie couldn't add."

Bobby *liked* Mrs. Gurdin despite—or because of—her

outrageous behavior. "She was so funny! She talked like the cartoon character Natasha in *Rocky and Bullwinkle* with the heavy Russian accent, except everything was so *secret* and in code words. She would squint her eyes and get this sinister look, like she's telling you this deep secret, in these whispers—except her sentence structure, and her Russian accent, came across as comical. Natalie would look at me when her mother would do these sinister half-whispers and we would crack up. Then Marie would laugh. *She* thought we were laughing at her wisdom. It was a riot."

Hyatt's affection for Marie Gurdin did not alter his severe opinion of her as an immigrant who wanted to make a million dollars in America using her daughter as "the family's ticket to fame and fortune." Bobby Hyatt and his mother watched Maria scavenge for film roles at Fox while Natalie was on the lot shooting *The Big Heart* and *The Ghost and Mrs. Muir* that winter, as Hyatt recalls:

> In those days lunch was a social event at the studio commissary. Between twelve and two, there would be waves of people coming from different soundstages on other movies and you could meet up for lunch. The mothers would sit together and us kids would eat together and visit. Natalie was never allowed to do that. Her mother would read *Variety* and find out what movies were coming up, or she would go to the casting office and say, "Anything coming up for a kid?" Then she would find out who the director and producer were and she would go to the commissary and try to reserve a seat at their table, or if she wasn't able to do that she would manipulate the seating so that she would get the table right next to them so that Natalie was right there. Natalie was

supposed to smile and wave at them and look cute. And that's how she got jobs.

Mud's commissary politics probably led to Natalie being cast that February in a Fox picture called *Summer Lightning*, a leaden farm drama about two stepbrothers, one good, one evil, competing for a mule team and the local beauty, played by June Haver. It was based on a novel called *Scudda Hoo Scudda Hay*, a phrase used to drive mules, the eventual title of the film. Darryl Zanuck had been developing *Summer Lightning* for Fox with screenwriter and first-time director F. Hugh Herbert since the summer before, and had already recommended child actress Connie Marshall to play the part of Haver's spirited kid sister "Bean." Just before filming, Natalie edged out Connie Marshall for the role, her third Fox film in three months. Bobby Hyatt, whose mother was too polite to aggressively promote him, half-admired Marie Gurdin's naked, wily ambition, for as Jean Hyatt admits, "Natalie's mother saw to it that she got the parts."

Bean McGill, Natalie's character in *Summer Lightning*, her first color film, was a know-it-all tomboy who eavesdrops behind bushes, inside clotheslines, and around barns to meddle in her sister's love life, providing comic relief from the heavy-handed melodrama. To play Bean, Natalie wore overalls, braids, and worked with a dialogue coach to talk like Ma Kettle, displaying a clever, spunky charm and natural comic timing. (In one scene, cranky character actor Walter Brennan, who plays a neighboring farmer, catches Natalie's character spying and confronts her. "Don't you *know* what happens to little girls what snoops?" he asks menacingly. Natalie, as Bean, looks him square in the eye. "Sure!" she says brightly. "What?" barks

Brennan. Natalie/Bean cocks her head to the side and answers smartly, "They get *hep* to things!" Brennan, watching Natalie, barely suppresses a smile.) Most of Natalie's scenes were with actor Lon McCallister, the heroic brother, who wins Bean's sister (June Haver) and the mules with the help of Bean's practiced snooping. An unknown starlet named Marilyn Monroe appeared briefly in a scene with Natalie and Haver as a barely seen friend, Monroe's film debut.

Since the story took place on a farm, the exterior scenes for *Summer Lightning* were shot at a ranch owned by Twentieth Century Fox. Natalie was in animal heaven, feeding chickens and riding mules. In one scene, she got to milk a cow. Another required her to swing over a shallow part of the river from a rope attached to a tree branch and jump off at the river's edge. Though Natalie barely got wet, she had to learn to swim enough to paddle convincingly on-screen, the *only* motivation that would get her in water. She had such fun with the farm animals shooting *Summer Lightning* she told a Fox publicist in February it was her favorite movie so far.

When Oscar nominations were announced that month, Natalie was overlooked for her inspired, naturalistic performance as Margaret in *Tomorrow Is Forever*, probably because the film had not been embraced by critics. The oversight had little impact on her burgeoning career, due to Natalie's talent and Mud's canny exploitation. For a spell, in February 1947, Natalie was acting in three pictures at the same time—*The Big Heart*, *The Ghost and Mrs. Muir*, and *Summer Lightning*—shuttling back and forth between the Fox lot, Palos Verdes and Century Ranch, slipping in and out of so many accents, costumes, and characters she had a difficult time remembering whom she was playing.

One day she became disoriented making the transition from Anna Muir to Susan Walker. "In one I was a sweet kid, in the other a bratty kid. That can be very difficult for an eight-year-old to handle." Natalie's English accent faltered in her performance as Anna, the only tangible evidence of the identity crisis she was experiencing drifting in and out of three fictional personalities. Between Bean, the Missouri farmgirl, Victorian Anna Muir, and pretending to be Margaret O'Brien portraying sophisticated New Yorker Susan, "I was playing so many parts, I had a hard time finding *me*." Natasha, her true self, was submerging into the characters "Natalie" was impersonating. At times, she would remember, "I took on their characteristics, emotionally at least . . . I was young enough to be impressed by their personalities."

Natalie spent so much time playing movie characters, the movies she was in began to seem real. Occasionally she got confused, unable to distinguish fantasy from reality. In the signature scene in *Miracle on 34th Street*, Natalie (as Susan) tugged on Edmund Gwenn's beard and discovered it was real, concluding he must be Santa Claus. "I still vaguely believed in Santa Claus," she said later. "I guess I had an inkling that *maybe* it wasn't so, but I really did think that Edmund Gwenn was Santa. And I had never seen him without his beard—because he used to come in early in the morning and spend several hours putting on this wonderful beard and moustache. And at the end of the shoot, when we had a set party, I saw this strange man, without the beard, and I *just* couldn't get it together."

The pressure of being eight years old and playing three different characters in three movies, providing financially for her parents and two sisters, manifested itself that winter. Natalie awakened one morning paralyzed. She had overheard her parents whispering about a polio epidemic and was convinced she had been stricken with the disease. Her mother later told a magazine writer Natalie was "always frail and subject to small illnesses, and when she does not have a real illness, she imagines one." Mud dismissed the psychological implications of her daughter's hypochondria, which *she* had fostered by her paranoia and overprotectiveness. On a deeper level, Natalie's psychosomatic paralysis was a warning sign that she was overwhelmed, a distress signal her parents ignored. "It was terrible for that kid," observes one of Natalie's first loves. "I don't know how she survived it . . . being forced to cry, forced to laugh. Every night, the nightmare she would go through to learn lines, to have the mother on the edge of the bed, *pretending* to be nice—and all she cared about is that Natalie delivered the lines exactly, didn't screw up, and that everyone said, 'Oh, how wonderful!' and 'She's as good as Elizabeth!' or whatever they would say. For Natalie, that was such a big, big event: she would get her mother's approval—this ogre, this monster."

Natalie obediently returned to work after her polio false alarm. Robert Hyatt remembers her walking past the Fox soundstage with her mother, gazing wistfully as he and his mother played canasta with the studio teacher. Maria swiftly guided her to the dressing room. Natalie passed the time between scenes sequestered with her mother, knitting or drawing—following Mud's Chinese maxim to use her hands to exercise her brain. "She wanted to play," recalls Hyatt. "She would wait and smile at me when I would see her. Her mother would not allow her to mix and mingle with anybody." Natalie never complained, observed Hyatt. "She always did what her mother told her."

8 NATALIE'S CAREER SUDDENLY, unexpectedly skyrocketed in May, as she was completing, ironically, *Summer Lightning*. The modest little film she made over the Christmas season with Maureen O'Hara and Edmund Gwenn, now known as *Miracle on 34th Street*, was given a preview screening by Fox a month before its June release. Louella Parsons, who attended the preview, described the audience reaction as "unbelievable." Parsons gushed over *Miracle on 34th Street* in her column before the movie came out, pronouncing Natalie "just about perfect."

Twentieth Century Fox was desperate to sign Natalie Wood to a contract, offering substantially more than her salary at Universal-International, where she was still under contract for another six years. Maria asked Fox to keep the offer a secret and made an appointment for Natalie to see Bill Goetz, the head of Universal, coaching Natalie ahead of time what to say. Natalie, accompanied by her mother, told Goetz that she was tired of acting and didn't want to do it anymore. Maria feigned maternal concern. Could they, Maria pleaded, break their contract in a "friendly" way? Goetz, faced with the unpalatable possibility of forcing an eight-year-old to work—unaware Fox had made her a better offer—suggested they think about it for a week, according to Maria. "He thought in a week I gonna come back and cry and say I want it back. I play very naïve and stupid, and he thought I didn't know anything about law or anything." At the end of the week, Mud rescinded Natalie's contract with Universal and immediately instructed Famous Artists Agency to commence negotiations with Fox. "It was very dirty trick, you know?" she admitted later. "But with Lana born, we need[ed] the money."

Olga's commencement from Hollywood High was in June, offering Natalie a rare chance to see her older sister, who was still living on her own in a rented room. Natalie eagerly dressed up and pinned on a corsage, but Fahd was too drunk to drive them to the ceremony. Olga graduated from high school as she had spent most of her eighteen years, without family to support her.

Natalie's home life was nightmarish. "My earliest recollections of my mom and dad's relationship were frighteningly stormy," recalls Lana, who was a toddler then. She and Natalie played in the backyard in Burbank, where Nick built a swing for them; Svetlana splashed in an inflatable wading pool during the hot summer months in the San Fernando Valley. "The thing that always stayed with me was being in the pool, seeing my dad carrying a gun chasing my mom around the pool," Lana relates. She and Natalie would watch their parents' fights escalate until "Pop," as Svetlana called Nick, lost control and became violent. "We were usually right in the middle of it. My mom was busy grabbing us and pushing one of us out the door and one out the window and then climbing out and screaming at my dad and saying to us, 'You run back' and 'You hide' and 'You run' and 'You do . . .'—you know, it was bad."

Child actor Robert Blake, who had a brother/sister relationship with Natalie from the time she was ten, learned about her house of horrors from Natalie. Making movies, he believes, saved her. "Being in show business was never her problem. That was her solution. Her problem was *away* from the camera. Her problem was a thing called family, love, security. I think the camera became her parents. It was her security blanket." Blake suspected Natalie was a sexually abused child. "I never talked to her about it but I always got that feeling. Coming from that place myself, I can usually smell those kind of people." Natalie's first serious adult boyfriend, an actor named Scott Marlowe, had similar suspicions throughout their relationship. "All the signs were there. She would never never *say* anything about anybody. I've suspected her father. I've suspected a lot of people. I suspected Irving Pichel even. You just don't *know*, with that mother."

Maria filled Natalie's head with bizarre superstitions and medieval fears about sex from the time she was tiny, hissing when she tucked her into bed at night to "keep her hands outside the bedcovers" as if it were evil. She whispered gruesome stories in her low Russian growl about how her bones had cracked and stretched for a week when she gave birth to Olga, narrowing her eyes to slits and telling Natalie she would die if she had a baby because she was "too small." Natalie listened, terrified, assimilating her mother's sinister suggestions about sex and childbirth as she had her gypsy prophecies portending fame and warning of dark water.

Fahd was an enigmatic, tormented shadow figure. A childhood friend of Natalie's who visited the house in those years remembers him "in the background, as if he didn't exist." Outside the house, he would pretend, at times, not to understand English. Nick *wanted* to disappear, from an existence he deemed wretched and a wife who "drove him crazy." Vodka was another means of escape. "Until he'd finally get totally drunk and he would flip out. Then everything would calm down, Marie would run squawking around, fluffing her feathers, 'He's a bad man, he's a bad man,' and then she'd start in on him again. This was like a cycle." Their father's drinking and violent behavior was a sensitive topic as they were growing up for Natalie and Lana, who regarded Fahd tenderly, like a wounded wild animal; their mother, they believed, was the provocateur. Both sisters bore emotional scars from the domestic violence. "I still have an intolerance for people shouting," declares Lana. Natalie hated confrontation of any kind.

Olga, who had grown into a sweetly pretty eighteen-year-old, met with a producer acquaintance of Natalie's after graduation to see about getting into the movies. The experience left her disenchanted. Her father, Alexei, Maria's handsome ex-husband, now a doorman at a San Francisco hotel, surprised Olga with a high school graduation trip to the Russian River near Santa Rosa, where she had spent her happiest years. While she was there she met a tall, good-looking college student, Alexei Viripaeff, who knew at a glance he wanted to marry "Teddi," though she had her eye on someone else. At the end of the holiday, Olga made the choice to move in with her father in San Francisco and enroll in college, surrendering her fantasy of a Hollywood life. She reconnected with "Lexi" Viripaeff on campus and this time, it clicked. Lexi's Russian-American background appealed to Olga, whose first language was Russian, and who felt an affinity for the music and adhered to the rituals of the Russian Orthodox church. "I was more Russian than my sisters," she avers, "because I was more exposed to it."

Natalie was almost nine and Svetlana only a year old when Olga left the fold at eighteen. The three sisters were almost from different generations, growing up in disparate contexts of their mother's life. "Marie tried to encourage Natalie and Lana to speak Russian so they would be bilingual," a friend recalls, "but they were more like American kids. They wanted to speak English. They did know a few Russian words, especially Natalie. If her mother and father were yapping in Russian, she could decipher what they were saying." Once Natalie was born, Mud took an interest in cooking. Natalie's comfort foods were rich, traditional Russian delicacies her mother prepared from family recipes: *piroshki* (tiny meat pies filled with cream cheese), beef stroganoff with *kasha* (buckwheat kernels), *tvorojniki* (cheesecake pastry). Maria instilled a fairy-tale romanticism in Natalie about Russia, telling her stories about "dachas hidden in forests" and other wonders of her childhood in Siberia before the Revolution. The Gurdins' house in Burbank, where Natalie spent several years of her childhood, was a colorful, eccentric fusion of her mother's Russian-Chinese past. Mud dressed like an Oriental high priestess in floor-length kimonos and occasionally bought kimonos for Natalie. The house was an explosion of imitation Chinese furniture, Oriental bric-a-brac, exotic birds, three turtles, a Doberman, and a German shepherd.

For Natalie, home was just a place to sleep, learn her lines for the next day, and practice piano (she was playing Rachmaninoff now). Ballet class was her only activity outside the studio. Her goal was to be the best ballet dancer in the world. She didn't have a single friend.

While Famous Artists and Mud were negotiating Natalie's new contract with Fox, a director of legendary status named Allan Dwan selected her for the starring role in a picture he was making for Republic Studios in June. Screenwriters Mary Anita Loos and Richard Sale had written an unusual, mystical screenplay called *Driftwood*, about an eight-year-old orphan who drifts into a small town from the desert and disarms everyone by speaking only the truth, quoting passages from the Bible. The waif—dismissed as "driftwood"—is viewed with suspicion until the end of the film, when she almost dies from a virus and her genuine goodness is appreciated. The role of Jenny, the innocent-but-wise orphan, showcased Natalie's strengths as a child actress: her perceptive intelligence, sweet charm, and sadly beguiling quality. Allan Dwan, who had been making movies since the silent era and twice directed Shirley Temple, told an interviewer years later what "intrigued" him about *Driftwood* was the opportunity to direct little Natalie Wood. "She had a real talent for acting, an ability to characterize and interpret, and she was a natural."

Dwan shot the film in black and white using religious imagery, which gave it an apocalyptic quality. He presented Jenny as a Christ-like figure who suffers and then offers redemption. Dwan was so impressed with Natalie's subtle performance, he would later claim (like Orson Welles) that he had discovered her.

In fact, Natalie's child acting career was at its pinnacle when Dwan was directing her in *Driftwood*. *Miracle on 34th Street* came out in June, creating a sensation, just as Louella Parsons had predicted, making Natalie Wood a household name. "It was literally a sleeper," recalls costar Robert Hyatt. "*Nobody* thought that it was going to be a classic. *Nobody* thought that it would make Natalie a major star." As one reviewer noted, "*Miracle on 34th Street* is, in short, something of a miracle in picture-making. . . ." The prestigious *New Yorker* devoted a full paragraph to Natalie:

> The most appealing of the lot, it seems to me, is a girl named Natalie Wood, who turns in a remarkably accurate performance as a progressive-school product indoctrinated against the whole idea of Santa Claus. My guess is that you'll find yourself refreshed by this neat little lassy.

The Hollywood Reporter, Maria's Bible, praised her daughter as "a totally unactorish child . . . [who] will bring an honest lump to audiences' throats when she goes around muttering, 'I believe. It's silly, but I believe.' Strangely enough, you are likely to believe, too."

The Ghost and Mrs. Muir was released a few weeks after *Miracle*. Though eventually it would be regarded as a classic, the "delicate borderline between imagination and reality" Joe Mankiewicz attempted to achieve with Gene Tierney and Rex Harrison's ghostly romance was not fully appreciated by audiences or by critics, who recommended the movie as a "novelty." After Natalie's attention-getting role in *Miracle on 34th Street*, her smallish part as Mrs. Muir's English daughter seemed, one reviewer wrote, "rather lost to view."

The Ghost and Mrs. Muir nonetheless added to her allure. In the same month, June 1947, Natalie was in the most popular movie in America, she had a featured role in a Joe Mankiewicz picture, and she was playing the lead in *Driftwood*. Fox agreed to sign her to a rich seven-year contract on June 30, beginning at $800 a week, increasing to $3300 a week by the seventh year—four times her salary at Universal. Maria also negotiated what may have been a precedent: the studio agreed to pay *her* for her "services" answering Natalie's fan mail. Natalie herself had "no conception about money whatsoever. I just knew that whenever I got a part I would get a present." (Her "reward" for *Driftwood* was a typewriter.)

Three days before her ninth birthday, Natalie appeared before a Superior Court judge to have the contract approved, because she was a minor. Photographs taken of her that day are heart-wrenching: a forlorn Natalie, her hair in pigtails, sits on a bench in the courtroom, knitting, the strain of adult pressures etched into her fourth-grade face. "Even though she said she loved being a young girl on the back lot, she got joy out of all that, I think sometimes she would like to have been just—you know, just a little girl." Hedda Hopper, Louella Parsons' rival columnist, used to observe Natalie in the studios, "clinging" to her mother's hand. "This tiny, poised little girl . . . with solemn, dark eyes, and straight hair in long braids. She wore Levi's and sweaters, and stood out from other screen tots, many of them bleached, permanented, and beruffled."

Natalie was finally permitted to make a friend during *Driftwood*. Her mother began exchanging show-business gossip with another mother on the set, Rosalie Infuhr, whose son Teddy had a featured part in the movie as a "mean little kid" whose pants are torn off by Jenny's (Natalie) dog. Mrs. Infuhr stopped by the Gurdins' house to see Maria from time to time and brought her son with her, throwing Natalie and Teddy together over several years. Infuhr remembers playing tag outside the Gurdins' tract home in Burbank—a rare privilege for the overprotected Natalie, whose Doberman chased Teddy and tore off his shirt, in a case of life imitating the movies. Infuhr's memories of Natalie at nine are of a "pretty outgoing" girl who liked to act and was "sharp" at her lines. He found Natalie's mother pleasant and her father antisocial. "Nobody seemed to like that man. He seemed very quiet, and very sullen. When people were around he'd just disappear."

Unsurprisingly, Natalie bonded more significantly with the adults on *Driftwood*. She began a permanent friendship with screenwriters Mary Anita Loos (the niece of Anita Loos, famous for *Gentlemen Prefer Blondes*) and Richard Sale, who were courting at the time. She also got reacquainted with Walter Brennan, her costar from *Scudda*

Hoo Scudda Hay, who had a supporting role in *Driftwood*. Natalie's favorite scene as Jenny took place in a bathtub filled with bubbles, where Brennan's character, a crochety old bachelor, scrubs her ears and lectures her about women. She felt like a "glamour girl," Natalie said later. Frank Arrigo, the art director who set up the bubblebath scene, went home raving about what a delightful child Natalie Wood was, "so easy to manage."

Mud was having quite a different experience with Svetlana, whom she had decided to put into movies now that she was a toddler. Maria convinced the director, Dwan, to use Svetlana in a scene—calling her "Lana," claiming she had named her after Lana Turner. The newly rechristened "Lana" resisted her mother's efforts to control her from the beginning, crying throughout her debut scene, which had to be cut from the film. Mud had no tolerance for Lana, whom she described in a magazine as "a nervous child," comparing her unfavorably to Natalie. Lana would not bend to their mother's will, as Natalie did, nor was she selfless like Olga. "Lana was always very very jealous," Maria told a reporter late in life. "She wants *me* there. But Olga—she was never like that. She was very nice, she was very good." Natalie adored her little sister. She put Lana in a wheelbarrow and pulled her around the *Driftwood* set like one of her storybook dolls.

Natalie took a trip north with her family soon after *Driftwood*, her first break in eight months and four movies. They visited Olga and the Liuzunies (Maria's half-sister Kalia's family) in San Francisco and stayed at a resort along the Russian River near Santa Rosa. Friends and relatives observed the dangerous dynamics in the family now that Natalie was famous. "*Miracle on 34*th *Street* changed their life," avers Natalie's cousin Constantine Liuzunie. "[Aunt]

Musia lived for Natalie and that was her shining star—her *only* star—and all she could do was think about her and talk about her." Lana withdrew into shyness. Nick made a last-gasp effort to assert his manhood, suggesting to Musia they use their "nest egg" from Natalie's earnings and stay in northern California. "She said, 'No way,' " recalls a Russian friend. "And so that was that." His fate sealed, Fahd anesthetized himself with vodka and fantasized his escape, as Lana recalls. "His dream was that Communism would end and he would go back to Russia."

Natalie was the only one in the family who bore her celebrity with grace. She was the same Natasha on that visit as she was at four, relates her cousin Constantine. Natalie remained unaffected by fame twenty-three years later in 1970, at the pinnacle of stardom, when she thoughtfully wrote Constantine ("Kotick," as she addressed him in the Russian affectionate) to tell him how touched she was by a ring he made for her birthday. She recalled that long-ago trip, and him, in warm detail in her letter, saying that the ring he designed "brought back many happy memories of our childhood" and all the "clever and interesting things" he was always making. Natalie complimented her Russian cousin on the beauty of his work, but expressed it was his "thoughts and caring" that made his gift to her "truly precious." She signed the note as "Natasha."

Natalie played with her childhood pal Edwin at the Russian River camp that summer as if she had never left Santa Rosa or become a movie star. "It never went to her head," he declares. Bobby Hyatt, the child actor forbidden to associate with Natalie, said that she was "a wonderful person from the time she was a little kid all the way up," despite the way her mother aggrandized her. "Natalie became the queen, not because Natalie *wanted* to be the queen, but because Marie *made* her the queen."

When she and Edwin played by the Russian River that summer, Natalie was still "deathly afraid" of water, even though she had learned to dog paddle slightly for *Scudda Hoo Scudda Hay*. "I can remember her and I laying on the beach and I used to get up—and I'm not a terrific swimmer—but I used to go in the river, you know, waist high, or chest high, and she wouldn't get close." Natalie never talked to Edwin about *why* she was frightened of the water, or the gypsy's warning. "Never told me, never asked."

Canevari remembers Maria keeping Natalie, who was nine, under military-like surveillance with boys. "If I had a guy, a buddy of mine, go up the river with me, she'd give me the third degree on who was this guy. She trusted me with Natalie because me and Natalie were kids together. If I wanted to go uptown and go and have a malt or a milkshake or something with her, it was okay, but if I had somebody with me, no way." As a child, Natalie *preferred* boys, a trait she may have picked up from Mud, who used to say that all women were catty and all women were jealous of her.

Someone took a snapshot of Natalie with Edwin that long-ago summer, standing beside an orange tree in the Canevaris' yard. "I told her I would keep it forever. That picture is still in my wallet."

Natalie resumed her lonely Hollywood life in the fall. She started fifth grade on the Fox lot in a studio school that had become a ghost town. "By the time I got into the schoolroom at Twentieth Century Fox," she later mused, "most of the child stars were already past me—Linda Darnell, Peggy Ann Garner, Roddy McDowall were gone.

I was the only one in the class." Natalie advanced scholastically due to the individual attention, but she was completely isolated. Since she wasn't making a movie, there wasn't even a film crew around. "It was a great event if I had another student to keep me company."

She celebrated Halloween by reading reviews of *Driftwood*. As with *Tomorrow Is Forever*, Natalie's complex performance was lauded while the picture she was in was criticized as overly sentimentalized. A typical review had this to say about Natalie as the truth-telling orphan: "Young Miss Wood gives with everything in the book, with a skill comparable with the best in recent times." She was billed as "the delightful new child star" because of *Miracle on 34th Street*, which was still showing in theaters four months after its release and continued to play through Christmas and beyond. Natalie rode the crest of the *Miracle on 34th Street* wave, receiving her second Box Office Blue Ribbon Award for her performance as Susan. She ended the year with a life-sized trophy from *Parents* magazine naming her "Most Talented Juvenile Star of 1947." A pigtailed Natalie was pictured in newspapers standing on tiptoes, peering over the trophy in amazement. Magazines began to dub her "The Pigtail Kid."

Miracle on 34th Street received three Academy Awards the next spring, for Best Screenplay (George Seaton), Best Original Story (Valentine Davies) and Best Supporting Actor (Edmund Gwenn). Natalie wasn't nominated, but she was given a Critics Award in April for playing Bean, the eavesdropping tomboy in *Scudda Hoo Scudda Hay*, which came out that month. The film was backhandedly complimented as a "fascinating discourse on mules," and would be remembered, if at all, for introducing Marilyn Monroe. Hollywood took notice of Natalie's instinct for comedy, however, opening up a different range of characters for her to play beyond the sensitive waifs for which she was known.

Fox put Natalie in her first picture under contract in the summer of 1948, a full year since she had completed *Driftwood*. The movie was called *Chicken Every Sunday*, another sentimental family drama taken from a popular novel. Gene Tierney was suspended for turning down the lead, which briefly passed to Jeanne Crain and succeeded to blond character actress Celeste Holm. Holm played the sensible wife of a dreamer in 1910 Tucson who keeps her husband and family afloat by turning their home into a boarding house. Musical star Dan Dailey was cast as the impractical husband, with Natalie playing their younger daughter, her hair dyed blond to match Holm's.

Though her part was minuscule, Natalie received star treatment at Fox. The studio provided a limousine and a driver to take her to and from Carson City, Nevada, to shoot the exterior scenes. Ruth Sydes, whose seven-year-old son, Anthony, had a bit part, recalls riding home in the limo with Natalie and her mother at the end of a day's shoot in Carson City. "Natalie gets in the car and says, 'No no no, I'm hungry, I want to eat.' I was delighted, 'cause I was starving and so was Anthony, but Anthony was a secondary person, character, in the show and Natalie was the little princess. So we stopped immediately." According to Sydes, "If someone of her age was neglected or put upon in a movie and Natalie felt they were not being looked after, she'd go after them and make friends with them," including Sydes' son Anthony. "She took care of him if anybody tried to do anything, 'cause he was three years younger. She had a real tender spot for the underdog."

Natalie celebrated her tenth birthday during the shoot.

The studio "made a big hoop-de-la" over it, remembers Sydes. "But she wanted all the other kids on the lot to come to her little party . . . and so they all went over and sang 'Happy Birthday' to her. She was a very sweet girl . . . she had a certain kindness about her that you're born with."

Since Maria didn't drive, Sydes offered to carpool her to the Fox lot. "I kind of expected not to like her," she admits. To Ruth Sydes' surprise, Maria "adopted" her. "She would take me places and she'd always pay. And this made her feel big, made her feel important." Mud spent the long days on set with Sydes, spewing her shrewd wisdom about the studios, spinning yarns about how she had met director Irving Pichel on the boat from China, where he "discovered" Natalie. "I used to listen every hour to her telling me this one particular story." Maria's grandiosity began to surface in the Twentieth Century Fox biography of Natalie distributed to publicists, which identified her father as an "architectural designer" and her mother as a French former ballerina. Movie magazines described the Gurdins as "Franco-Russian." Maria told friends she was an actress and a dancer. "Marie—Maria—used to make up stories all the time," relates Robert Hyatt, who was later close to Natalie and her father. "Nobody knows where she came from, nobody knows exactly what her name is." According to Hyatt, *Nick* wasn't even sure of his wife's origins.

Natalie got a microscope from her parents for completing *Chicken Every Sunday* and went directly into her next picture. *The Green Promise* was a curiosity financed by a flamboyant Houston oilman named Glenn McCarthy, who wanted to make "wholesome entertainment" and formed an alliance with actor Robert Paige to produce a low-budget movie for RKO extolling heartland values and 4-H clubs. He enlisted the 4-H organization to promote the film and staged a nationwide contest for a 4-H girl to play a small part. Paige cast himself in the agricultural drama as a county agent who tries to help a mean-spirited widower manage his farm as he woos the farmer's eldest daughter. The story centered on the youngest daughter, Susie, Natalie's character, who desperately wants to join 4-H and raise a pair of baby lambs. It was a showy, demanding role for Natalie, who had several crying scenes and a climactic sequence where her character sneaks out of a children's costume party alone in a thunderstorm.

Fox loaned Natalie to RKO for the picture, which teamed her for a third time with Walter Brennan, as the cruel father mismanaging his farm. McCarthy and Paige wanted Marguerite Chapman, a glamorous brunette actress known for being "difficult," to play Paige's love interest. "The movie seemed so depressing to me, I was mad as hell that I had to do it," she recalled. "I was in New York, having a great time at the Waldorf-Astoria way up in the Starlight Room . . . Greg Bautzer called, and he was representing Glenn McCarthy of Houston Oil. He said he'd give me a $5000 bonus if I did it, which I knew I'd never get. Bullshitter." Two well-known juvenile actors, Ted Donaldson and Connie Marshall, both fifteen, completed the main cast as Natalie's on-screen brother and spiteful middle sister. Paige chose a journeyman director named William Russell.

Russell started filming around Feather River near Sacramento, since most of the scenes were outdoors on a farm. "I came back from New York and the very next day I had to go to wardrobe with those godawful clothes, and here I was, one of the best-dressed women in the world," complained Chapman. "God! I was depressed to begin with with the whole damn thing. I dragged myself out of bed every day." Natalie's other screen siblings and Jeanne LaDuke, an Indiana 4-H girl who won the contest for a bit part, had a ball on location, horseback riding or playing golf. Natalie socialized with them only once in three weeks, when she and Ted and Connie played a word game in Ted's trailer "to see who could read the fastest." Maria's exclusionary tactics were not as obvious as with Bobby Hyatt, but Ted and Jeanne suspected she was isolating Natalie. Chapman noticed "her mother was with her constantly. There wasn't any interaction personally, not at all. The moment she finished a scene, she was gone." Maria kept her distance from the other mothers. The only time she and Natalie were seen off the set was in the dining room at the Feather River Inn, where everyone was staying. "They had this little pet chihuahua and it ate at the dining table, and that was a bit off-putting to some of us. They'd put it up and it would be licking stuff off the plate."

Natalie shared a tutor with the 4-H girl, Jeanne LaDuke, who was also ten, her first company in many months. Jeanne, who came straight from her family's farm in Indiana to be in the movie, viewed Natalie with fascination. "There was concern about what she ate, and she had dancing lessons and singing lessons . . . I wasn't used to ten-year-olds who were that professional." Jeanne thought Natalie was nice, not at all aloof. "The person who tutored us used to do cat's cradles, taught us all kinds of wonderful string things," their only extracurricular activity together. "I was considered a bright little kid," relates LaDuke, who grew up to be a college math professor. "We seemed to be very much at the same level. I didn't think of her as being a whole lot smarter than I, and I certainly didn't think of her as being less smart than I, we were just good intellectual companions." Ted Donaldson, a veteran child actor at fifteen, regarded Natalie as gifted. "No question about it. She didn't 'act'—I mean 'acting' acting." Natalie got little guidance from her directors, including William Russell. "I don't remember him spending a lot of time with anybody," recalls Donaldson. "There was not a lot of time *to* spend with people—we got a small budget film, we got four weeks to do it." Ted, who observed her mother's control, felt Natalie "freed" herself when acting.

Marguerite Chapman clashed spectacularly with Maria. "I went around to talk to her one time, and it was 'Natalie, Natalie, Natalie.' And I wasn't used to that, quite frankly I resented it. I was used to 'Marguerite!' " Chapman was jealous that a child star had usurped her status on a movie set. "*Everything* was 'Natalie, Natalie, Natalie' . . . one scene I had with her, I was fitting the bunny rabbit costume on her and I accidentally pricked her with a pin. I could've died. Cut right in."

Ted's mother and Connie Marshall's mother talked about Maria privately, concerned that her behavior might cause permanent damage to Natalie, whom everybody liked, even Chapman, who said, "She was such a darling child, very polite and very professional." According to Donaldson, "She seemed to be—I don't want to say repressed, but I got the sense of things being held in, of being forlorn. It was a subject of talk among many people on that set. We thought she was a lonely kid, and we all ascribed this to the mother." Part of it was Natalie's fawn-like appearance. Jeanne LaDuke was struck by the difference in their sizes at ten. "I'm just a healthy farm kid . . . Natalie was very delicate and small." "She was adorable as a child because she looked so lonely and so waif-like," observes Donaldson, who perceived a "sadness" in Natalie. "I'm thinking now of a scene—we're on the back of a truck, in between shots or something—and we're singing songs and she's enjoying it, she's enjoying the camaraderie of making films and of being with people, even if these two [kids] that she's with are five years older than she." He caught glimpses of Natalie's spirit and a sense of fun "*when* she let herself go," which was rare with Maria around. In the film, Natalie's character has several scenes with her pet black lambs, which she is seen tenderly caressing. "That's probably the freest, most open, most Natalie expressing who she was, [was] at those moments," assesses Donaldson. "I remember a certain kind of glow, and giving over to the moment with them. That was a very genuine thing."

The climax of *The Green Promise* was a harrowing sequence that takes place at night, during a thunderstorm, when Susie, Natalie's character, sneaks away from a children's costume party at a neighbor's farm to go home and rescue her lambs. Natalie, wearing her bunny costume, has to cross a precarious wooden bridge over raging water through wind and rain. The instant she steps to the other side, the bridge is rigged to collapse. According to Chapman, who was in a separate thunderstorm scene, Russell shot the bridge scene the last week of filming, when they were back in Hollywood on stage A or B at the Goldwyn lot. "That's where we did that godawful scene. It was wet and damp with this rain. Stormy. Great big wind machines. What a godawful set."

Natalie was petrified to do the scene, knowing the bridge would crash and she had to cross dark water. Her mother promised her nothing would happen to the bridge until she was on the other side, assuring her that she was safe. "They had huge airplane propellers blowing rain onto the set . . . and there was a waterfall and rushing water underneath," she said later. Natalie started across the bridge in her bunny suit, covering her face with her hands as the wind machine whipped her back and forth, movie lightning streaked through the black sky, sound effect thunder rumbled, and manufactured rain blinded her. "They were telling her to hurry across, because the bridge is going to collapse," recalls Lana. "When I was halfway across," Natalie said later, "somebody pulled the lever prematurely and I was thrown into the water." She managed to catch hold of the collapsing bridge, clinging to the edge as the current pulled her in the direction of the waterfall. "My mother leaped forward crying, 'My child!' " Natalie later told a reporter, "and the director said, 'Keep the cameras rolling! Keep the mother back!' " Natalie's left wrist was broken and she nearly drowned. "I don't even remember them fishing me out." "It was *so* traumatic for her," observes her later confidant, Mart Crowley, " And then there she was, fearful of her life." Ted Donaldson, who was off-set, remembers, "Something happened. I do recall that she did seem to be hurt. It seemed to me they continued shooting." The incident was hushed. Marguerite Chapman, who was in her dressing room, never knew Natalie had been injured, or that a stunt had gone wrong. "Natalie told me . . . whoever was timing it thought she was on the other side and she wasn't," relates Lana. "It was an accident."

Mud concealed Natalie's broken wrist from the producers and Natalie finished the film. "Marie told me she was not going to tell the studio, [that] it was her secret," recalls a friend. "She should have taken Natalie right away to get the bone cast." Olga explains why: "She didn't complain and she didn't sue because if you sued the studio you were blacklisted." Mud still refused to take Natalie to a doctor when filming was completed, telling Natalie doctors were evil. "I never like doctors," she said once. "I cure myself with my own remedies." There were hidden motivations behind Maria's refusal to fix Natalie's left wrist, Olga reveals. "My mother was afraid the doctors were going to talk. She was worried about Natalie being blackballed. And Mother was just worried about having operations."

9 NATALIE WAS NEVER THE SAME after the bridge collapsed on her during *The Green Promise*. She had recurring nightmares in which she saw herself drown, so many they haunted her, commingling with the gypsy's warning to her mother. Her fear of water, especially water that was dark, turned phobic. "It was a combination of injuring herself and thinking she was going to drown that really put this major fear of water in her mind," suggests a friend from that period. "The most water she'd get in is in the bathtub. That was probably not a *full* bathtub." She added thunderstorms and heights to her litany of fears. Child actor Bobby Blake, who met Natalie about this time, found her riddled with demons.

She continued to seek solace in her menagerie of pets, including a new bird she named "Gregory Peckwood," after her favorite actor. She began to fantasize having her own horse, with a pasture where she could ride. Fahd (or "Deda," as Natalie sometimes called him) showed his tender, artistic side to his troubled daughter. "When I had nightmares, Deda would talk to me in the middle of the night and draw me pictures of the corral or box stall he would build for my dreamed of horse. And by his love and understanding he would fix my worries."

Natalie's relationship with Mud shifted, for the worse. In her view, her mother had forced her to do a terrifying movie scene, then lied to her that she could not get hurt, even though the bridge had collapsed too soon. The accident changed the way Natalie perceived Mud. She was no longer a "god" whose every wish must be obeyed or Natalie would suffer the torture of the damned. Maria had been exposed to her as a ruthless stage mother willing to risk her safety and then ignore her injury for the sake of a movie role. Natalie felt used by both her mother *and* the studio. As the bone on her broken left wrist began to grow into place unnaturally, "she blamed my mom for not having the wrist properly set, taken care of by a doctor . . . she was angry about that," relates Lana.

Mud's gypsy magic, Russian folklore and old wives' tales took on ominous connotations for Natalie because of her malformed wrist, though a part of her still believed. Maria's superstitions were the house rules, as Lana relates. If she or Natalie broke a mirror, "we would have to go out and throw it over our shoulder into a yard." There were dozens more. "You don't put hats on beds or shoes on tables. You don't walk around opposite sides of a pole with someone because you'll have a fight with that person. You don't give sharp objects as gifts. If you give a ring or slippers, you have to give somebody money, otherwise you'll split up. You don't give scarves as gifts—they're bad luck. If you sing before the sun comes up, then you'll cry before the sun goes down—which used to drive me crazy, because I love to sing. You can't let the moon shine on you at night—it'll cause bad dreams, moon madness, insanity. Old European superstitions. Natalie really didn't want to believe that any of these things held a grain of truth, ever." But she did believe. Her mother's mysticism was too imbedded in her subconscious. "Natalie was scared of peacock feathers," recalls Lana, "because those were [supposed to be] evil . . . and whistling in a dressing room—she never did that." Maria's gypsy influence was inescapable. She told her daughters' fortunes from cards she insisted remain untouched for twenty-four hours, which she sat on or held in her hands before reading. "She was always right, but she was only predicting things in the very near future—receiving letters, receiving news, becoming ill, taking a trip, things like that. Natalie didn't like it." Bobby Hyatt, who reentered Natalie's life a few years later, remembers Maria reading his and Natalie's palms at the studio "all the time," though he claims she wasn't accurate. "Natalie would never let her [mother] read the palm with her damaged wrist though, I noticed that. That was very interesting."

Natalie's feelings of bitterness and disillusionment toward Mud and the studio after her traumatic injury filtered into her feelings about acting, and about her life. She went through a kind of existential crisis at ten, wondering, suddenly, who she was. "I found it very difficult . . . to figure out if I was just responding to a situation as though it were a scene or whether it was how I really felt about something." She realized as an adult that "from ages ten through twelve or so, I barely remember anything."

Natalie spent seven months in the deserted studio school before starting her next picture. She became aware of how lonely she was, of "missing out." "I *did* feel more comfortable in the company of grown-ups, because I wasn't around little kids very much. So I went through a period feeling probably inordinately shy with kids my own age."

Ted Donaldson, who was fifteen, described her as "ten going on sixteen or thirty." She considered herself a child freak, creating new paranoias. The thought of returning to public school "terrified" Natalie, especially speaking in front of a class. "I could do a *scene*, in a movie, and learn dialogue and do that with a fair amount of confidence, but . . . if I had to stand up in front of my own peers, kids my own age, and deliver a poem or speech, I just died! I was mortified." After years in the studio with a tutor, in the constant company of adults, Natalie felt disconnected from children her age. She existed in a kind of twilight zone between fantasy and reality, movie life and real life.

Olga got married in February to Lexi Viripaeff. The formal Russian ceremony, which featured crowns for the bride and groom in an incensed Russian Orthodox church ablaze with candelabras, seemed fairy-tale romantic to ten-year-old Natalie, who wore her first long dress as her sister's bridesmaid. It was Olga's final disconnection from Hollywood, a bittersweet moment for Natalie's overshadowed older sister. Olga settled into domestic life in San Francisco with Lexi, near her father and Lexi's parents, whose house would eventually become theirs. Natalie sent her a black-and-white publicity picture when Olga returned from her honeymoon, inscribed "Dearest Teddi . . . from Natalie Wood." They were in different worlds now.

The fact that Natalie gave her sister an autographed picture of herself was disturbing proof of Natalie's confusion about who she was. Her constant nightmare, she said later, was that she *had* no identity—that her personality depended on the part she was playing. "I didn't really have a very clear perception of myself. I was always Maureen O'Hara's daughter or Claudette Colbert's daughter . . . I was sort of discombobulated." Fox assigned Natalie to play

O'Hara's daughter again in a picture called *Father Was a Fullback* in March, ending her half-year of lonely isolation at the studio school. The picture was like a family reunion for Natalie. She got to see "Mama Maureen" from *Miracle on 34th Street*, and spent time with her friends Richard Sale and Mary Loos from *Driftwood*, who cowrote the script and were now married. The set was homey, as O'Hara describes: "You'd just sit around and have a good time and enjoy each other and gossip and chat and tease. It was different than today."

The cast's bonhomie was evident in the film, an occasionally hilarious comedy with O'Hara as the wife of a small-town college football coach (Fred MacMurray) who is frustrated by his team's losing streak and unable to cope with his teenage daughter's budding sexuality. A Broadway ingenue named Betty Lynn played the lovestruck daughter; Natalie was her smart-alecky kid sister, a character similar to Bean. Though the part wasn't large, Natalie had the movie's funniest lines, which she delivered gleefully, a challenge according to O'Hara, who remembers the director, John Stahl, as "difficult to work with because he shot sometimes as many as fifty takes. You'd say, 'Mr. Stahl, is there something we should change?' and he'd say, 'No no no, do it again.' And then you'd be shocked because he might print take three and you'd think, 'What was he looking for?' He would be the same with Natalie as he was with me and Fred MacMurray." MacMurray later commented he'd "never seen a child of such energy and delightful innocence" as Natalie, "and yet she knew everything." Natalie's happiest memory of the movie was wearing Betty Lynn's false eyelashes and makeup.

While she was filming, Glenn McCarthy staged a celebrity extravaganza in Houston to jointly promote the opening of his grand hotel, the Shamrock, and his first film, *The Green Promise.* He entreated another Texas millionaire, Howard Hughes, who owned RKO, to persuade Darryl Zanuck at Fox to allow Natalie to participate. She and Maureen O'Hara were flown to the premiere and a torchlight parade "with more national known figures . . . than have been in Houston since the National Democratic Convention." Jeanne LaDuke, the 4-H child who had a small part in the movie, remembers a young Houston girl so overcome at the parade she had to be restrained. The Texas showman whipped civic organizations into a similar frenzy, eliciting raving endorsements for his farm movie from every institution from the PTA to the Girl Scouts to the Daughters of the American Revolution, in addition to 4-H clubs. Film critics disparaged McCarthy's publicity as "ballyhoo" and dismissed his movie as "schmalz." Natalie's superior work as a child actress was once more lost in a mediocre film. As one critic wrote, "She plays the role with rare sensitiveness, changing moods from blissful dreaminess to crushed disappointment at an instant." Her desperate struggle to keep from drowning as the bridge collapsed remained in the film, a memento of her lost innocence.

Natalie received positive notices again that summer when *Father Was a Fullback* was released, though the film failed to impress critics, the pattern of her child acting career. In August, Samuel Goldwyn hired her from Fox to play yet another busybody kid sister in an issue-oriented low-budget drama called *Our Very Own.* Ann Blyth, a popular star of twenty-one, was cast in the lead as Natalie's oldest sister, a high school senior who learns from a conniving middle sister that she's adopted. Goldwyn wanted actress Jane Wyatt, who had just turned thirty-eight, to play their understanding mother. "I was so thrilled to be in a Goldwyn picture, but I wasn't terribly thrilled with the script," she recalls. "I wanted to be in something that was a really really typical Goldwyn script." Wyatt's true concern was portraying a *mother*. "I'd just finished playing opposite Gary Cooper and Cary Grant! I remember Mr. Goldwyn telling me, 'Don't be so silly, little girl. This is just right for you.' " One day when Wyatt stepped off the set of *Our Very Own*, still in costume, a producer named Gene Rodney happened to stroll by, striking up a brief conversation. He contacted her out of the blue several years later, asking her to play the mother in a television series called *Father Knows Best*, for which Wyatt would win three successive Emmys. "So that's how I happened to be in *Father Knows Best*. He always remembered this little encounter."

Natalie took a day off filming *Our Very Own* to attend a televised ceremony in which California's Lieutenant Governor Goodwin Knight presented her with a silver cup as "Child Star of the Year" for 1949. The event was sponsored by an organization called the Children's Day Council to draw attention to a newly created "Children's Day." It was Natalie's last hurrah as a child star. *Driftwood* and *The Green Promise*, the two films in which she was the lead, had failed to ascend her to the rarefied ranks of Shirley Temple or Margaret O'Brien, despite her emotionally complex performances. She hadn't been in a genuine hit since *Miracle on 34th Street*. The reality was painfully evident as she accepted her silver cup as Child Star of 1949. Mud put Natalie in a frilly dress with puffed sleeves and braided her hair into pigtails as if she were still five. Natalie, who had turned eleven that summer, appeared gangly and uncomfortable, her face frozen into an expression of forced gaiety.

"I found myself surprised when I heard that Natalie was actually eleven, because she looked more like a really little nine-year-old," remembers Joan Evans, who played the jealous sister. "That was one of the things that Mrs. Gurdin did, was to make sure that the makeup and the hair and the clothes accentuated the little girl." Maria forced Natalie to dress like a child so she could continue to play children's parts, though she was years past her chronological age of eleven, as Jane Wyatt observed. "She was dignified. It was funny seeing a little kid dignified like that, but she was." Wyatt was startled when Natalie walked over to a piano on the set, "and she played a whole Beethoven sonata. I was so impressed—this little girl, whirling through this very complicated piece."

"She was definitely very solemn, very quiet," confirms Joan Evans, who was fifteen then. Evans was shocked when Natalie transformed into an annoying chatterbox in her first scene, pestering a TV repairman. "We were all surprised in that little opening scene at how funny and cute she could be. Because it wasn't the child that we saw." Natalie's acting had begun to seem forced at times, even manic, like a child overly desperate to please. Ann Blyth got the sense that Natalie "wanted to be good, she wanted to do the best work." Between scenes, Maria would only permit her to talk to the director. "Her mother would usually sit in the doorway of whatever she had in the way of a dressing room on the set. The minute the scene was over, that's where Natalie went. And her mother was standing there waiting. . . . I don't know what her mother felt was going to happen, but everybody thought her mother was very strange." Jane Wyatt and Ann Blyth felt there was something very touching about Natalie, an "endearing" quality the camera captured. As Blyth, who also had been a child actress, remarked, "You can't teach that to someone. That is something that owns you, and she had that ability."

Joan Evans remembers Natalie covering her left wrist, when she was off camera, with "a very small brace—maybe an Ace bandage, a small flesh-colored thing." She understood that Natalie had hurt her wrist and it was "problematic" for her. "She was *so* tiny, and the wrist bone was very prominent." Evans suspected "*anything* imperfect was threatening to her mother. At that age, only your mother or your father can give you that kind of psychological feeling about something as relatively unimportant as that."

Natalie went through the motions of life, drifting from *Our Very Own* into another smallish role as somebody else's daughter. With her child stardom fading, Twentieth Century Fox let her option contract lapse. Though Nick was employed at the time building miniature props for one of the studios, Mud was possessed that Natalie continue to act, keeping her in pigtails to perpetuate what was left of her child-star image. Columbia put her in a tearjerker called *No Sad Songs for Me*, as the only child of a housewife dying of cancer, another of the weepy "woman's films" of the forties. The picture was a showcase for stage actress Margaret Sullavan; Natalie was basically a backdrop. In later years, she would interpret the shift as a transition to "character" roles, but Mud's plan was simply to keep her working any way she could. Taking smaller parts, Natalie said later, saved her from the tragic denouement of many forgotten child stars. "I was never a great, important child star like Shirley Temple or Margaret O'Brien. I was a child *actress* working regularly in films. There's a difference. I was luckier than Shirley Temple. I did not have to carry the whole picture, and as I got older, I simply moved into older roles." By comparison to popular child stars like Elizabeth Taylor, whose childhoods were played out in fan magazines, Natalie's life was normal. "I never saw film stars at home. We had no maid, no cook, no swimming pool . . ." What she had was domestic violence, the Gurdins' black secret. Lana recalls the Burbank years as a blur of fights with Pop drunk and her mother grabbing her and Natalie, "spending the night in motels, and spending the night at neighbors' homes that you didn't know."

Natalie submerged into her idealized movie family, where she could pretend to be Polly, the cherished daughter of noble cancer victim Margaret Sullavan, who "was so into her character that it was a little hard to think of her as Margaret Sullavan." She made a friend of Ann Doran, a respected thirty-something character actress cast as a socialite, who by coincidence would appear in four of Natalie's next films. The hard-working Doran admired Natalie's work ethic, which she ascribed to her mother. Doran liked Maria. "She was teaching Natalie good manners, and she did it from the time she was a little girl. On the set, if somebody did something for her benefit, Natalie would say thank you. She was not one of those, 'I'm a star so you do it for me.' And she would accept anything. She'd say, 'If that's what you want me to do, that's what I'll do.' " Doran believed that Natalie's kindness was a result of her upbringing. "She was raised to be polite, and politeness means being kind to other people." Doran did not consider Maria Gurdin a stage mother. In Doran's view, a stage mother was one who coached her child, " 'Be sure and do this, this'll be cute . . .' Jesus, it used to drive me crazy. Natalie's mother was not, believe me, was never the Hollywood horrible mother. I'd worked with others that freely I would have smashed them flat. Her mother was very quiet. She never told Natalie how to act. She figured the director knew how he wanted her to act. Her mother never interfered. Never, never, never."

The self-supporting Doran was on the same treadmill workwise as Natalie, going from one supporting part to another with barely a breath between. She gave no thought to whether *No Sad Songs for Me* would be a success, or that it was the first motion picture about cancer. "What the story was didn't mean a hoot in hell to me. I was only thinking who I was as a character in relation to the other ones." She had the utmost respect for Natalie's ability, at eleven, to get into character, which she watched her do in five films as a juvenile. "It was just her inborn talent. There are actors that spend their entire lives and don't act at all, they're just themselves. But Natalie was a different person on every picture she did."

Maria revealed to Olga, in this period, her secret plan to leave Nick and live in San Francisco with her Russian sea captain. Olga approved. "He would have been very good for her. He didn't drink, was a quiet, nice guy, nice with her. They made arrangements to go off together to get married . . . he was going to build this house for her and they would go on trips." The next communication Olga received was a phone call from Nick's brother Dmitri telling her that Nick had suffered a heart attack and her mother was with him at the hospital. When Olga next spoke to her, Maria had dropped her plans to elope. "I asked her how come, if you don't like Nick, why did you go to the hospital? She used a Russian phrase that means 'You get used to a dog.' She wouldn't admit—I'm sure she liked Nick, and maybe George was just a flirtation." The true reason was apparent to Olga. "She couldn't leave the Hollywood stuff. Mother was very much in love with Hollywood stuff." Fahd might have died if Natalie hadn't been home. Mud fainted when he had his heart attack, as she had during any trauma since her childhood convulsions. When she revived, Natalie was the only one with the presence of mind to phone a doctor.

Fahd's slow recuperation placed excruciating pressure on eleven-year-old Natalie. "My father couldn't work and the family depended on me," she said simply in later years, as if that were normal. Since she wasn't under contract anymore, Natalie had to compete for roles to bring in an income as her career was waning, at the most difficult age for child actors to find work: the preteen years. "I discovered the heartbreak and frustration of not getting parts . . . I was told on various occasions, 'You're too short. You're too tall. You're too young. You're too old.' It's awfully difficult for an adult, much less a child, to accept rejection." The rejection was more than personal for Natalie; she needed the job to support her parents. Mud's ruthless ambition turned deadly. "They would do anything to get a part. Natalie and she both," recalls a movie mother from that period. Maria thrived on the drama, recalls Lana. "The more dramatic life was for my mom, the better she liked it . . . the ups and downs—that was her bread and butter." A child actress who competed against Natalie then remembers how, at auditions, Natalie would tell producers, " 'I'll do anything.' If they asked, 'Can you ride a horse?' she'd say yes, and 'Can you tap dance?' she'd say yes—and then be quick to learn. She just seemed to have no limits. I didn't see any insecurity as to what she could do."

She and Mud, with Famous Artists, managed to snare her a role in a Fred MacMurray/Irene Dunne screwball comedy at RKO called *Come Share My Love*, later changed to *Never a Dull Moment*, which started shooting around Thanksgiving. Dunne was cast as a sophisticated Broadway star who impulsively marries a handsome rodeo rider (MacMurray) with a ramshackle ranch and two rascally daughters. Natalie was one of the daughters; Andy Devine, the famous cowboy sidekick, played MacMurray's matchmaking pal. Dunne recommended Ann Doran for the part of her rival. "We had so much fun on that picture," Doran recalls. "Everything about it was fun. The director, George Marshall, liked to do silly things on the set and Fred was a nut! Irene went along with it, and she loved it."

Doran was blissfully ignorant of the battle Maria was staging behind the scenes between Natalie and child actress Gigi Perreau, who was playing Fred MacMurray's other daughter. Gigi (short for Ghislaine, with a hard "G") was a cute, freckle-faced nine-year-old at the height of her popularity; Natalie was a gawky, aging child star of eleven-plus, all arms and legs and new front teeth. Mud schemed to edge out Gigi from the first contract negotiations, when "I got billing above Natalie," recalls Perreau, "which just drove her mother crazy. Natalie, to her, was her little special jewel, and nobody could mess around with it." Maria insisted on a clause in the contract guaranteeing Natalie an equal number of lines as Gigi. Gigi and her mother watched in disbelief as Natalie and Maria counted lines aloud together to make sure Gigi's and Natalie's came out the same. "I remember we had to stop filming at one point," recalls Perreau, "because Mrs. Gurdin discovered I had two more words than Natalie did that day. She called the agent over and they had to do some re-writing to even things up."

There was constant rivalry, according to Perreau. "On

my side I think it was a very healthy normal competition. On Natalie's, it probably wasn't as much. She was very, very ambitious, almost to the point sometimes of being very obnoxious—because of her mother." Perreau noticed, even between scenes, how Natalie seemed to have "enormous energy . . . she was just all over the place," the same manic energy Natalie had demonstrated in her comedy scenes in *Our Very Own*. Her need to please, to keep pace with Mud's fanatical drive, had reached a level of desperation, particularly since she was responsible for supporting the family. "Natalie was a very good vehicle for her ambitious mother," Perreau analyzes. "Any other kid who didn't want to do what they were doing would have rebelled. They would have said 'No, I'm not going to do it anymore.' Natalie didn't fight it . . . her mother would say, 'Oh, there's Mr. So-and-So, go up and give him a hug.' But she didn't mind the pushing. I never saw her object to the pushing." Natalie made an important friend on the set just before Christmas. Gossip Louella Parsons, whose daughter Harriet produced the movie, stopped by one day. Mud made a point of introducing Natalie, who promptly got a mention in Parsons' column.

Three days a week, Natalie studied ballet at a studio in Hollywood, which she and Maria took far more seriously than her schooling on the lot. The instructor was an elegant Russian named Michael Panieff, who had been a featured performer with the Ballet Russe de Monte Carlo. "The star system was still around at the time, and he was grooming those kids for anything and everything." Natalie was the only one in the class of mostly preteen boys and girls who had acted professionally, a distinction Mud exploited by insisting she be the lead dancer at every recital. Natalie "-didn't flaunt it," according to Don Zoute, who was in the class. "She didn't put on airs by any means. She was just one of the kids." The class "starlet," in Zoute's opinion, was a younger girl with curly hair named Jill Oppenheimer. "Panieff was old Russian school, where everybody was equal, no fancy costumes for the kids in the class. *Jill's* mother dressed her in the little tutus with all the ribbons in her hair, and the jewelry and the makeup. He was gonna make a star out of her come hell or high water." Another of Natalie's classmates was a cute, slightly chubby redhead of seven nicknamed "Taffy." By an odd coincidence, all three girls—Natalie, Jill and Taffy—would form lasting relationships as adults with actor Robert Wagner. Natalie would marry him, divorce him, and marry him again. Taffy, whose real name was Stefanie Powers, eventually would play his wife in the series *Hart to Hart*. Jill Oppenheimer, or Jill St. John, as she would call herself, would become Wagner's wife after Natalie drowned. As ballet classmates, their only socializing was at Panieff's Christmas party, when they lined up for a group picture.

Natalie typically gravitated toward the boys in the class—Zoute and another teenager named Robert Banas, who was her dance partner. Maria took them all on a picnic in Griffith Park, inviting them to the house beforehand to watch Natalie's movie *Driftwood*. Natalie and Robert regularly went horseback riding together. "I remember her mother would give me some money so we could go to the drugstore and I could buy Natalie an ice cream, and then we'd come back and watch *Driftwood*. It was kind of a routine." Maria was like a shadow trailing Natalie, even in Panieff's dance class, recalls Banas. Lana, who was nearly four, "was pushed in the background. It was kind of pathetic." Both Natalie and her mother approached ballet with the same determinism as Natalie's movie career. "I think at one time she really wanted to compete as a dancer," relates Zoute, who became a professional dancer himself. "She was very dedicated. I think it came through the training and working in films, where you had to be prepared. She was very, very serious about it. And she had potential." Her dance partner, Robert Banas, thought Natalie "wasn't exceptional but she was good, she was on point." The dance phase of Natalie's life came to a sudden end when Maria and Panieff had a "falling-out," according to Zoute. "Panieff had quite a little performing group of children at the time, and her mother wanted him to change the name from Panieff to the Natalie Wood Dance Company, and I think that's where the falling-out came. Because she was a very pushy woman."

Mud's competitiveness was even more cutthroat on the set of *Never a Dull Moment.* Andy Devine, the veteran comic actor, noticed that whenever he was in a scene with little Gigi Perreau and Natalie, Natalie would shove Gigi out of camera or sabotage her. Devine got so annoyed he would stop filming and ask the director to reshoot the scene. "I later did a play with Andy," recalls Perreau, "and he said to me, 'How could you stand working with that little brat? Do you know that there'd be scenes where you would run in and the two of you were supposed to give me a hug, and she would deliberately put her hand over your face as she hugged me?' " Natalie invited her dance partner, Robert, to the set several times that winter. "It was very obvious what was happening," he recalls. "Natalie was really upstaging Gigi."

Gigi was certain Natalie's mother had put her up to it. "I really and truly feel it was mom. Natalie had already been taught tricks to upstage. She knew all of the little things that people do to get attention: like when other children are bouncing down, you be up, or you use your left foot instead of your right foot—because then all of a sudden your eyes go to that one." Gigi spent the rest of the shoot "on guard when we were doing scenes together. I had to be sure that I didn't allow her to—she'd push you aside a little bit, things like that, little things. I don't think those are things that an eleven-year-old does automatically on their own." Gigi was correct, confirms Lana. "My mom was always really nasty about other kids. Brutal."

Gigi felt sorry for Natalie, despite their rivalry. "I remember feeling that I was so glad I had my mom, that my mom was normal. That I didn't have *her* mom. I never thought her mother was mean . . . we just avoided her. She was just this little kind of witchlike creature." It was clear to Gigi that Natalie was unhappy. She told Gigi she hated her braids. "She wanted to grow up, even at eleven and a half she wanted to grow up. There was no question but that she'd done enough things at that point and she was just very eager to be a teenager." Natalie had a crush on actor Farley Granger, Ann Blyth's movie boyfriend from *Our Very Own*, two pictures before. Gigi "got the feeling that she was very interested in boys." Natalie's oddly distended left wristbone was a source of increasing self-consciousness for her. She covered it with a western-style leather bracelet or hid it inside her sleeve in her scenes in *Never a Dull Moment*, telling Gigi there was a "scar" on her wrist. She was sensitive about what really happened, though "everybody knew that she did not like water," relates Perreau.

Gigi, who attended a Catholic school and had a conservative upbringing, sensed a longing in Natalie for a family like Gigi's. "It would have been interesting to have been able to talk to her about it, because I'm sure she felt such warmth and love from my mother and my siblings . . . and then she saw the kind of strange relationship with her own mother. I'm sure there were all kinds of psychological things going on."

The director gave Natalie and Gigi western-style suede jackets when they finished filming. Natalie asked her co-stars to sign hers and started collecting autographs on the jacket. She related everything to Hollywood. She was her mother's daughter.

Natalie entered the fifties in gloomy confusion that contrasted with the sunny ambience of the new decade. She had spent the last six years as Orson Welles' ward, June Haver's sister, Fred MacMurray's daughter . . . or simply "driftwood." She looked her age, nearly twelve, pretended to be nine or ten onscreen, and felt thirty. "It's not only that child actors lose their childhood, it's that they *use up* their childhood," explains Natalie's movie brother from *The Green Promise*, Ted Donaldson. "You have acted out much of your childhood. You use up a lot of the stuff that children only fantasize about, or maybe act out in games . . . so when you hit a certain age, a lot of changes start happening—girls have it before boys—and they don't know who the hell they are."

Natalie's distress at being forced to look younger, the pressure she felt to compete, and her increasing ambivalence about acting all coalesced that summer on a movie she did for Fox called *The Jackpot*. The picture was an expression of the era, a family comedy starring Jimmy Stewart as a hard-working husband who wins a radio contest of prizes that turn his household upside down. The movie, which was taken from a piece in the *New Yorker*, was surprisingly biting, with subtle, intelligent performances, Natalie's included, though her part was too insignificant to be noticed. The screenwriters were the witty wife-and-husband team of Phoebe and Henry Ephron, who drew from an experience of their daughter Delia's to create a scene for Stewart's movie children, played by Natalie and child actor Tommy Rettig (who would become famous as Jeff on *Lassie*). "My mother used to say, 'Everything is copy,' " recalled the Ephrons' oldest daughter, Nora, a screenwriter-director, "and she meant it. One day my sister Delia got her head caught in the banister rails while peeking through them and had to be rescued by the fire brigade. Nine months later . . . my parents wrote it into *The Jackpot* for an eight-year-old Natalie Wood." Nora Ephron was mistaken on two counts: the head-stuck-in-the-banister scene was performed by Rettig, not Natalie; and Natalie was *twelve* by the end of filming. The age issue was one of Natalie's tribulations about *The Jackpot*. She was *playing* eight, which meant that she had to endure another movie in pigtails and pinafores, white anklets and saddle shoes, pretending to be four years younger than she was. To add to her discomfort, the makeup department put temporary braces on her teeth to give her character an even more awkward appearance. Without the western bracelet from her last movie, Natalie's protruding left wrist was exposed below childish puffed sleeves. She felt so homely and humiliated making *The Jackpot*, "I cried."

One day as she and Mud walked to the set, they encountered an exceptionally handsome young man with his hair combed to the side in a wave, dressed as a Marine for a Fox war movie called *The Halls of Montezuma*. As he passed, the actor said hello and smiled—a smile so blinding Natalie stopped to stare, in one of those moments, for a child, that crystallizes into permanent memory. For Natalie, an awkward eleven dressed to appear eight, the beautiful twenty-year-old with the dazzling smile represented all that was golden and glamorous and glorious, things that seemed unattainable to her in her braces and braids and ugly saddle shoes. "When I thought it was safe, I turned around and stared," she said later, watching as her dreamboat disappeared. She lingered on the image, sighing to Mud, "When I grow up, I wish that I could marry him." Natalie recognized the actor as a new Fox contract player named Robert Wagner. Wagner would have no recollection of his encounter with eleven-year-old Natalie Wood, his future wife. "I was just a staring kid as far as he was concerned." (Wagner had also just met his *second* wife, Marion Marshall, an older blond actress playing a nurse in their scene together.) Natalie and Mud went to the Fox publicity department, asking for a head shot of the bit player from *Halls of Montezuma*. Natalie taped the picture of Robert Wagner to her bedroom wall, where she could gaze at the face of her fantasy husband, keeping her company beside forty-seven storybook dolls.

Natalie's misery was the catalyst for the family's move to Northridge, a less populated area of the Valley where she could keep a horse. With dance class stricken from her schedule, she lavished her free time on her trick palomino, Powder, purchased from one of the studios. She wanted to be a veterinarian, grasping for things outside show business to satisfy the longing that Gigi, Ted Donaldson, and others had apprehended in her. Natalie yearned to be *normal*, pleading with her parents to let her enroll in junior high, an early example of the survival instinct that Natalie possessed. She was still afraid to go to public school, but "I wanted so much to be like the other kids, and have friends of my own. I guess my parents saw my point because they let me have my way."

Mud enrolled her in seventh grade at Sutter Junior High in Canoga Park, a Valley suburb, beginning September 11, 1950. Natalie spent the night before worrying that she wouldn't fit in, that no one would like her, that she would seem "too Hollywood." "I got the biggest shock of my life when I saw the other girls. They were dressed in pretty sweaters and straight skirts. When I looked down and saw my frilly dress and long pigtails, I felt like crying." Her movie image, frozen at seven, made twelve-year-old Natalie appear freakishly juvenile. "I noticed how much older the other kids looked, how much more sophisticated they were. They had lipstick and tight skirts." A few seventh graders wearing falsies laughed at her. The humiliation went deeper than adolescent angst for Natalie. She was so driven to be perfect, to *please*, her self-esteem derived entirely from the approval of others. She went home traumatized. "It took me one day to get a costume change, but it was years before I got over having made such a fool of myself. I think I was a senior in high school before I began to realize that every other girl in the school felt as much like an orphan in the storm as I did." Mud consented to the new clothes, but the Pigtail Kid's braids were money in the bank.

Even in straight skirts and sweaters, Natalie still felt she was "on the outside looking in." After a few days, the other girls seemed immature to her despite their padded bras. Natalie was accustomed to movie stars, in an adult world. "I made the earth-shaking discovery that I didn't belong."

One weekend shortly after Natalie started seventh grade, Rosalie Infuhr and her son Teddy stopped by the Gurdins' house in Northridge. While the movie mothers talked shop, Natalie and Teddy went outside to saddle Natalie's palomino. Lana, who was four and a half, tagged along. "We decided to put her little sister on the horse," recalls Infuhr. Natalie walked Powder through the neighborhood while Lana sat in the saddle, thrilled to be alone on a horse at four. As Lana was riding Powder down the street, with Natalie pulling the reins, some neighbor children tore past them on bicycles, shooting cap guns and screaming. The horse reared, throwing Lana onto the street. As she hit the pavement, a horrified Natalie watched as Powder kicked her baby sister in the head, knocking her unconscious. "Everybody was all upset," remembers Infuhr. Lana had multiple skull fractures and fell into a coma. The superstitious Mud refused to take her to a hospital, demanding that medical equipment be sent to the house. She canceled a trip to San Francisco to see Olga, who had just had her first child, a son named Lexi. Maria lied to Olga, telling her that Lana had measles, so she wouldn't have to implicate Natalie in the horseback riding accident. Natalie was tortured with guilt, blaming herself for Lana's concussion, sick with grief over her sister. She sold her horse and kept a vigil at Lana's bedside, holding her hand. When Lana regained consciousness after a week, "it was Natalie who was sitting beside me . . . tears streaming down her cheeks." Lana's concern was that she had distracted their mother from Natalie's career for seven days.

Natalie fell into further turmoil that October when she was transferred to a newly constructed junior high called Robert Fulton, less than a month after enrolling at Sutter. Paramount immediately put her in a movie called *Dear Brat*, though the part was so small she missed less than two weeks of class. *Dear Brat* was intended to be a sequel to a pair of successful family comedies called *Dear Ruth* and *Dear Wife*, starring William Holden and Joan Caulfield. But as screenwriter Devery Freeman recalls, "Paramount said, 'The only thing is, Dev, we can't get Bill Holden. Oh and another thing is, we can't get Joan Caulfield . . . but we want it to *feel* like they're still in it . . .' " (Norman Krasna, who wrote the play on which the characters were based, requested that his name be removed from the credits, even though the film made money for Paramount.) Natalie's character, described in the script as a "charming and earnest" girl of twelve, was so incidental she wore a dress from her own closet during filming. Her salary for six full days of work was $2333.

She was hoping her minor roles in mostly B pictures in recent years would allow her to assimilate at Fulton, but "everybody went gaga when Natalie showed up," recalls an eighth-grader from 1950–51. One of the girls in Natalie's class admits, "All of us were sort of in awe of her." "She was already an established star," as classmate Rochelle Donatoni explains, "and so it wasn't like you would approach her and say, 'Oh hi, I'm so and so . . .' " Other girls avoided Natalie because they were jealous. "They didn't understand that I was dying to do their things, but they never asked, presumably because they figured I would automatically turn them down." "I look back now and I realize how much she wanted to be accepted," remarks a classmate named Helen MacNeil, who sensed Natalie's longing by "her *look*. The way she looked at you." Natalie was too shy to strike up a conversation and fell out of rhythm with the class, going to and from auditions. When she was at school, another Fulton student relates, "she seemed warm and she'd always smile—but she was out a lot, so you never felt that she was quite as much a part of the school as the people that were there on a daily basis."

Natalie experienced a breakthrough when she met

eighth-grader Mary Ann Marinkovich, a big-boned, tall brunette who wore pixie pink lipstick and was fearlessly extroverted. Mary Ann's parents were immigrants from Croatia with a chicken farm in the Valley. "That was one of the common things we had going," she assesses. "People that don't come from foreign-born families sometimes don't understand a lot of the things that go on, but we both did." Mary Ann was brazenly confident and enough of a character to be unimpressed by Natalie's fame. "I never bugged her about things, I never asked her about things. If she was here today, good; if she wasn't, that's fine. There was no pressure on her, where kids at that age are very cliquish and they demand loyalty et cetera, and she *couldn't*. They didn't realize she went to work, she wasn't going to just play around. I had a little older attitude."

Mary Ann was with Natalie at times when other junior high girls whispered jealously as they passed her by. "Natalie was really a very tender soul, and when people would rebuff her—and young girls are just the worst, they're vicious—she would take this to heart and I would say to her, 'Honey, you just *can't* please everyone . . . the hell with it. Forget about that.' I was a little harder, and I think it helped her to get over worrying about, 'Gee, this one didn't even *smile* at me when I walked by.' She didn't have a mean bone in her body. *Believe* me. There were times I wish she *had* been a little stronger, but she just would never dream of offending anybody. And believe me, there were times when she *should* have, but it wasn't in her."

Mary Ann was the first girlfriend Natalie ever had, the first friend she was permitted since Edwin. "The moment I met her mother," recalls Mary Ann, "her mother said to me, 'Oh, I want you to be Natalie's friend because you're very pretty.' " Mrs. Gurdin continued to scrutinize her, adding, "And because you're strong, and you're always *thinking*." In Mud's Machiavellian mind, Natalie's life was a movie and she was the director. She cast Mary Ann as Best Friend, though Mud really didn't want Natalie socializing with *anyone* who couldn't advance her career. If she gave a party for Natalie, Mary Ann noticed, Maria only invited girls who were blond, so they weren't in competition with Natalie. Though Mary Ann was dark, "I was bigger, totally different looking, so in her mother's eyes, I wasn't a threat. That's why her mother fostered and really harbored the friendship." Mary Ann used to tease Natalie about her tiny, five-foot frame, saying, "You actresses all look alike. Little paper dolls. You've gotta get somebody that wears a size ten shoe!" Natalie was sensitive about her size, which she worried made her seem even more juvenile. "She seemed poised, which you might consider more mature," a classmate observes, "but because of her looks I did not get the feeling she was older. She had this really cute, darling face that made her seem if anything younger than her years—almost a baby face, like a doll."

Natalie's personality flowered under Mary Ann's gregarious influence. They both attended Friday-night sock hops at the junior high, where the girls who weren't too jealous to talk to Natalie found her "very down to earth. I don't think any of us would ever say that she acted like a star. She was very sweet." Natalie never mentioned the movies she was in unless "you asked her about it," observes a classmate. "She wanted to be part of the clique."

Natalie ("Nat" to her classmates) savored her first taste of freedom. She went to the beach with Mary Ann without mentioning her fear of the water, though as Mary Ann recalls, "We both got reactions to the sun, and sun lotion, and blew up like balloons, so we never went again." They created code names. Natalie called herself "Mac," and Mary Ann was "Boo Boo," for reasons no longer clear to Mary Ann. The friendship liberated Natalie for brief intervals from the tyranny of Mud, and Hollywood. "It was a little relief of pressure being with me. There was no having to be 'on.' We could just sit in jeans and talk. And I think we all need that, and especially in the situation she was in, because she really didn't have a chance to *have* girlfriends, or a lot of friends, so the time we had together was really very special."

The only slumber parties Natalie attended were in her living room, with girls who met her mother's casting requirements. Maria still wouldn't let her go to anyone else's house, for fear of kidnappers. Natalie had not been alone in the daytime since she became a child star at six. "I couldn't even go to the bathroom alone," she once told a friend. "My mother and a social worker always went with me." In bed at night, the only time she was by herself, Natalie was terrified someone would kidnap her, or that she would have another drowning nightmare. Her bedroom was a shrine to her paranoia, with storybook dolls atop the furniture, crowded onto the bed, spilling over to the floor, squeezed amid toy animals and her caged parakeet, Gregory Peckwood, helping her to pretend she was not alone. "All this stuff! Jesus Christ, nobody else could sit in there!" recalls Mary Ann. "She had all kinds of stuffed animals, and those *dolls* . . . it was just spooky." Natalie had names for every doll and still talked to them, at twelve, as if they were real. "They always had to be in order," remembers Mary Ann, "like they were taken care of. I thought about that every once in a while . . . because then it wasn't the thing to do, and we were really kind of beyond that. But it was *important* to her . . . they had to *be* there. They were her friends." Mary Ann was astute enough, even at thirteen, to understand the underlying cause of Natalie's neuroses. "That stupid mother of hers did that—goddamn her."

Mud's disturbing dominance over Natalie became apparent to Mary Ann as she gained further entrée to the Gurdins' inner sanctum. Mud ("Mother Superior") kept Natalie physically and emotionally cloistered. Athletic activities were off-limits because "she might break a fingernail or something." The obsession with Natalie's health, appearance, and acting was "all Mama. Natalie didn't care. She wanted to make babies and walk off into the sunset like all young girls do." The dangerous element, in Mary Ann's view, was Natalie's pleasing nature. "That was the mother's feeding ground. Natalie would never raise her voice to her mother or say no *ever*." Natalie, according to her friend, was unaware of what Mud was doing, or the damaging effect it was having on her. "She really didn't have the time to sit or think about it, because her head was going in so many directions—if it wasn't school, it was scripts. Her mother had that all manipulated to keep this kid's head really cranking, and it worked."

Natalie auditioned for casting directors and producers throughout the fall, winter and spring of seventh grade, doing everything she could to make herself appealing. Robert Banas, her former ballet partner, has a vague recollection of Nick working as a studio guard, but it was Natalie's acting that kept the family solvent during Fahd's convalescence. The rumor at Fulton Junior High—sadly true—was that *she* bought the family's house in Northridge. Natalie got good notices for *Never a Dull Moment* when it came out that winter, but the picture "wasn't a great success," admits costar Ann Doran. *The Jackpot* also under-performed, and Natalie got mixed reviews. When *Dear Brat* came out that spring, her bit performance wasn't even mentioned. The pressure on Natalie to find work was almost unbearable.

Gigi Perreau, who was several years younger than Natalie but kept encountering her at auditions, describes the tension between them while vying for the same child's parts as unnervingly intense, "Her mother was ruthless." If being a child performer had ever been fun for Natalie, it wasn't anymore. "I didn't like it all so much," she admitted later. Acting, which had come naturally for her as a little girl, seemed "very difficult" now that she was almost thirteen. "I suddenly became self-conscious. I felt awkward." Worse, she was imprisoned in her movie childhood, a captive of the braids the public associated with "Natalie Wood." "The point was that the studio wanted me to stay looking young. That was the image." Whatever the studio wanted, Mud made sure Natalie provided. When she started junior high, Natalie "looked exactly like she looked in *Miracle on 34th Street*," a classmate recalls, "except she was bigger. Same face, same pigtails." A producer from this period convinced an executive from one of the studios not to sign Natalie to another long-term contract "because he thought I was going to turn out very homely."

Her ungainly self-image was exacerbated by the fact that Natalie was being raised by a mother who worshipped glamour and the illusion of perfection as photographed in movie magazines. Maria had transferred her fascination with the Romanovs to *Hollywood* royalty. Making a star of Natalie became an alternative way for Maria to position herself as a member of aristocracy. Beauty was the key to this kingdom. "Looks were *everything*," asserts Mary Ann. When Mud saw an unattractive child, she would tell her daughters, "If that was my kid, I'd drown it." "My mom had to have a special child," declares Lana, "she really wouldn't accept anything else." The pressure to look beautiful *at all times* imbedded itself in Natalie, who wouldn't leave the house unless she was stylish enough for a magazine layout.

"Natalie was very concerned at how people would perceive her," remembers Lana, who had her own problems as a child dealing with their mother's perfectionism. "I was a mud fence. I didn't have that 'special' thing, I really didn't. I was incredibly introspective, very quiet and overly sensitive and I kept to myself." Gigi Perreau felt sorry for Lana during the filming of *Never a Dull Moment*, when Natalie and Gigi costarred as sisters. "Little Lana was dragged along and kind of given things to do by the studio teacher. She was kind of like this little waif that wandered around while Natalie was getting all the attention." *Natalie* was the star of the family, *Natalie* could do no wrong, was Maria's mantra to the press. If she talked about Lana, it was pejorative. *Lana* felt overshadowed by her sister, *Lana* was high-strung, *Lana* was shy. Mud even told one reporter Lana "has a tendency to stoop—we are trying to correct that." According to Mary Ann, Lana was cute, an opinion borne out by photos of her at five, revealing a spindly but appealing little girl. "It was sad," comments Mary Ann. "She was not even the *also*-ran. Natalie's mother structured her whole life around Natalie. It was almost like when anybody came into the house, she would put Lana in the back room—really, physically."

To Natalie, Lana was still a "twerp" sister she teased by locking her in the closet and other "stupid and fun things," though she was becoming aware that Lana "had a hard time of it because . . . our mother's attention was focused on me, because I was the one working." There was an unexpected blessing to Lana's neglect, one Lana would discover, much later, through years in therapy. "We're all shaped to a certain extent by our parents, and I'm sure a lot of that carried over for Natalie. It didn't for me, because I wasn't really raised by anybody. I wasn't around our parents as much, and my personality being the way it is, I don't think I really listened. Because I was left to my own devices I learned to rely upon myself, and what *I* believed was correct, and not what I was being told. Natalie was so coddled and watched over, that my mother had a much greater impact on her. Much greater."

Mud influenced Natalie in a newly harmful way that spring as she prepared to turn thirteen, for she had discovered boys. The object of her adolescent fantasies was a dairy farmer's son from her art class named Jimmy Williams, the archetypal rebel in a leather jacket. As Jackie Eastes, one of the lovestruck, recalls, "He was kind of dangerous, in a way that he was very—he was like a bad boy, but not really . . . Jimmy just had a charisma. He worked at a farm around the corner from me, and I used to go and sit there, hours, just to be with him." Natalie was erotically charged by the wiry Jimmy's aura of power. "There was a group of us, about eight or ten of us, that ran the school," Williams states matter-of-factly. "Not that we were better than anybody, it's just that we were the 'in' crowd." Williams, an eighth-grader, "wasn't really overly impressed" with seventh-grade Natalie. "She was just another kid. So what, she's in the movies." Jimmy's casual disinterest made him more provocative to Natalie, who "wanted what she couldn't have," according to a friend who met her then.

Mud took immediate action, forbidding Natalie to date anyone in junior high. She warned her that if she even sat in a boy's lap she would get pregnant, misinformation that alarmed Natalie, who was already terrified to have a baby, thinking she would die, Mud's earlier admonition. Maria's "sex education" of Natalie was partly ignorance ("She was all messed up," relates Lana), for she offered the same advice about a boy's lap to Olga, who "had to learn the facts of life going to city college and reading the physiology class book with my husband." In the case of Natalie, Mud was deliberately instilling fears about boys so her star-child would remain under her black wing. "Her mother didn't want to lose control," asserts a witness to the manipulation, Natalie's friend Mary Ann.

Mary Ann got a closer view of Maria's hypnotic power over Natalie that April when Natalie got a part in a Jane Wyman film, her first acting job since Mary Ann became her friend. Wyman had won the Academy Award two years earlier for *Johnny Belinda*, and would be nominated again for this picture. The movie was called *The Blue Veil*, an adaptation of a sentimental French film about a self-sacrificing spinster (Wyman) hired to take care of other people's children via an agency known by its blue-veiled uniforms. Natalie was featured in the third vignette as the sort of wistfully appealing girl she played so convincingly; in this case, the sweet young daughter of a blowsy showgirl (Joan Blondell) too self-absorbed to pay attention to her. Desperate for love, Natalie's character forms a deep attachment to her nanny (Wyman).

The film, and her sympathetic role, were superior to the bit parts she had been playing, but it was an onerous blessing for Natalie, who had fallen under the sexual spell of eighth-grade rogue Jimmy Williams and was cast as a little girl in braids. "It seemed as though I'd spent my whole life in pigtails," she later sighed. At the time, no one involved had any idea Natalie, nearly thirteen, was humiliated by the way she looked in the movie, a virtual re-creation of the seven-year-old she played in *The Ghost and Mrs. Muir*, dressed in old-fashioned English schoolgirl frocks with braids coiled to her head. Mary Ann, who visited the set, was amazed at her pal's professionalism at twelve. "Of course I'm sitting back and watching the whole scenario . . . she was like the old *pro*—not in years, but in experience. Usually when actors are working with a younger person, they're kind of 'Oh-oh,' but with *her* it was wonderful. She was very sensitive and aware of others. If somebody didn't feel well or somebody messed up their lines or something, she was just always there to be encouraging, so everybody just loved her." Natalie's genuine tenderness came through in her portrayal of the forlorn young girl. The *Los Angeles Times* would praise her performance for its "remarkable sincerity."

What impressed Mary Ann was her friend's intellect, which she became aware of as Natalie prepared for the part. "This girl had a *brain* in her head. She could sit and *memorize* a script. I'd help her and she would just start verbatim and she knew everybody's part, not just hers. She'd even prompt other people with their lines!" On set, Mary Ann was surprised to observe, the atmosphere was more technical than creative. "They would say, 'Here, you do this. You do that. You walk here and you walk there and you smile.' It was very structured. And she was a pretty young girl who could walk in a straight line, who could do this, do that. Very structured, very disciplined. And she was extremely good at this, and she would always do *whatever* to please the director, to fill the need."

The extent to which Natalie had been driven to this by Mud was revealing itself to Mary Ann: "Her mom wanted her to be a movie star from *conception*. And that was gonna happen, come hell or high water, at whatever cost." Fahd's ineffectualness had also become apparent:

> Natalie's mother was the push and her dad just would never stand up to her. He'd try every once in a while—like sleeping in. Natalie worked real late sometimes and she was tired. And if we were supposed to go someplace the next morning, I'd come over and she'd be dead asleep, just dead to the world. Her dad would always be up and having coffee and we'd chit-chat. Mama was still sleeping, too, so he'd say, "We'll let them sleep." That woman would get up and call out, "Why is she sleeping?!!!"

The dark, tragic triangle that had been created between Natalie and her parents laid itself bare to her first close friend. Mary Ann had great affection for Natalie's father, who drove them around and whom she considered quiet and gentle, "the strong, silent type" who "catered to her mother, like most men do." She had observed Maria "run over" Nick time and again while he shrugged it off, too weak and tormented to resist. During *The Blue Veil*, the family secret was exposed. "Every once in a while her father would get loaded and then he'd had it, and her mother would open her mouth and oh Christ, then it really hit the fan. It was horrible. When you sit there and take that kind of stuff for how long—when you blow, you blow." When Mary Ann observed their brawls, it was usually over Maria forcing Natalie to do something, such as get up at four A.M. to go to the studio. "That's why the father got into it with her all the time, and why he got so ugly and awful." Natalie tried to ignore her parents' fights, concealing how much it disturbed her. "That's why she had a lot of the problems she had. She kept it all quiet and close because she didn't want to show weakness . . . she would just brace herself and go on. Natalie was very good about that."

The feisty Mary Ann wasn't. She was infuriated by Mud's relentless pushing and the effect it was having on Natalie, who was a hypochondriac, frightened to be alone, talking to dolls, forbidden to go anywhere, miserable playing nine-year-olds, pressured by competing for parts, bored with acting, but "wouldn't make 'Mama' unhappy. It's hard to understand that, but 'Mother' preyed on this. She *knew* what was going on and *knew* how this kid was being torn apart. That, to me, was the sin." Mary Ann stood up to Maria and encouraged Natalie to do the same. "She was becoming aware of what was going on, of what her mother was doing. She didn't want to be *pushed* so hard."

Natalie returned to Fulton for the last few weeks of seventh grade after finishing *The Blue Veil*. One morning while she was in art class, Jimmy Williams, who sat at the desk behind her, reached over the inkwell and "started flipping her pigtail."

Natalie turned around to face her teenage crush. "Why are you doing that?" she asked.

Jimmy stared back at her and teased, " 'Cause I don't like pigtails."

"Well, cut 'em off," Natalie taunted.

Jimmy took a knife out of his pocket "and I cut that pigtail off."

It was a revelatory moment. "She wasn't upset," he declares. "I can remember that. And I know I didn't get in trouble, so something happened. I believe that she went out of class and cut the other one off, or got some of the other girls to cut the other one off, and I think she told her mother *she* did it. 'Cause she didn't like 'em. And I don't think she ever, never wore pigtails again. That was the end of it, right there."

Natalie had defied her mother for the first time, severing the braids that made her famous, choosing *her* needs over "Natalie Wood's." The gesture was also rife with sexual symbolism. Appearing on-screen without pigtails was a rite of passage from child actress to young womanhood. The fact that it was Jimmy Williams who performed the rite for Natalie would have its own significance.

ACT TWO

Rebel

1951–1957

"Remember the poem? 'And he the rebel, seeks the storm as if in storms resided peace . . .' "

Anton Chekhov
Three Sisters

10

CUTTING OFF HER PIGTAILS WAS the attention-getting first step in Natalie's journey to disengage from her mother and discover who *she* was inside "Natalie Wood," the actress alter ego Maria had created for them both.

The catalyst was Jimmy Williams. "She was *gaga* with him, like 'Ooh, isn't he wonderful?' " remembers Mary Ann. Jimmy was Natalie's antithesis, a hot-headed rebel who challenged authority, with a mystique at Fulton as the last one standing in any altercation, despite his slight stature. "Jimmy had a temper, and when he got mad, he got mad and I think he could be pretty volatile," relates a female admirer. Jimmy considered himself "a risk-taker," following in the proud tradition of his great-great-great grandfather, "the only person that fought in the Revolutionary War, the War of 1812 and the Texas Revolution," for which a monument was erected in his honor. "I wasn't afraid of anybody or anything. I never got in a lot of fights, but I would never back down from a fight. And I got a reputation that they just didn't want to mess with me." Jimmy's punk heroism sexually magnetized and emboldened Natalie, who was drawn to the qualities he embodied as ones that could release her from Mud's iron grip. "Honestly, she kind of chased me from the time I cut her pigtail off."

Natalie came home from school without braids,

demanding to wear lipstick, desperate to get Jimmy to notice her. "I couldn't stand it anymore," she later told a fan magazine. "I got my parents to sit down and . . . I told them how funny it felt to be different from the other kids. I tried to get over to them how really important it was to me. They didn't change their minds right then and there, but I could see their resistance was lowered." In fact, Natalie battled with Mud and won, appearing in the schoolyard the next day in a short bob with "gobs of makeup on, just horrible, overdone," recalls Williams. "It was more like movie makeup, because I think that's all she knew." When she paraded past Jimmy and his group, "I made the statement that I thought that girls that wore too much makeup looked like a slut." Natalie tattled on Jimmy to a classmate's mother, who "set me down and gave me a lecture that I'll never forget. I told her, 'Well I didn't call her a slut. I said girls that have a lot of makeup on *look* like sluts.' " Natalie never wore makeup after that, Jimmy noticed, "just enough to give her some sheen." He ignored her anyway. "I wasn't interested. She was younger than I was, and she wasn't in my grade."

Natalie's Max Factor face captured the eye of a college student, who asked her on a date. She accepted, leading to a war between her and Mud that revealed a willfulness beneath Natalie's gentle demeanor. "Nobody told me whom I should date when I was a teenager," she told a magazine in middle age. "It wouldn't have worked anyway because I was very rebellious in those days." Natalie was determined, according to Mary Ann. "She was just starting to stand up a little bit . . . between 'I don't want to hurt my mother, but I want to stop hurting.' " Natalie and her college swain "went down the street for a Coke and he let me drive his car," she said later. "I think that's about all it amounted to. I was small and skinny but I wore quite a bit of lipstick and tried to look much older and I don't think the boy knew how old I really was." Mud subjected Natalie to painful humiliations when she got home, holding her skirt up to the light to see if it was wrinkled, grilling her to make sure she hadn't sat in her date's lap or she'd be pregnant.

"Fortunately, she got above that because of school," reveals Mary Ann, who helped to reeducate Natalie on the facts of life. She didn't need the information with her college beau, who merely served as an accessory for Natalie to make Jimmy jealous. Her plot was revealed before school let out for the summer, when Jimmy and a few friends were outside behind Fulton. They noticed a car circle the block, and a pair of college boys got out. A couple of Fulton students raced over to Jimmy with a message. "They said, 'This guy out here says he's Natalie's boyfriend and you've been making eyes at her, and he wants to beat you up.' " Jimmy figured out Natalie's plan. "I didn't care . . . I just walked right across that field. If he wants a piece of me, he can have it. When I was about halfway across, they drove off, and that's the last I ever heard or seen of him."

Natalie's rebellion announced itself on schedule, for she turned thirteen over the summer holiday. Not only had she declared her dating independence, she was realizing for the first time that she had a *choice* whether to act. Her father's heart condition improved enough for Nick to get a job at Warner Brothers building sets, easing some of the pressure on Natalie to work. She began to view acting from a different perspective, noticing actors whose work she admired. The turning point was that September, when she and Mary Ann went to see *A Streetcar Named Desire*, starring Vivien Leigh and Marlon Brando, directed by Elia Kazan. Natalie was transformed, in awe of Kazan and of Vivien Leigh's performance. "She wanted that part *s-o-o-o-o* bad. She wanted to be *Blanche!*" recalls Mary Ann. "Oh, God, she wanted to be Blanche du Bois. She, at a young age, knew what she could do and how *good* she could be and that she would be successful." Vivien Leigh became a role model for Natalie: a tiny, exquisite, dark-haired actress admired for her talent. Now, when Mary Ann teased her about her size, "she said, 'Well, that's all right. Because Vivien Leigh is as little as I am!' " Natalie was also struck, late that summer, by *A Place in the Sun*, enamored of actor Raymond Burr, and at how Elizabeth Taylor had made the transition from child star to ingénue.

Natalie's transition to more mature roles began that October, when she was called out of eighth grade to read for a part as Bing Crosby's daughter, Babs, in a lavish Technicolor musical for Paramount ultimately called *Just for You*. Crosby was playing a widowed Broadway song-and-dance man trying to get closer to his teenage son and daughter while courting his leading lady. Crosby chose Jane Wyman, Natalie's costar from *The Blue Veil*, to portray the actress. Mud was desperate for Natalie to play Babs, afraid that her career was over without her pigtails. She claimed later that Natalie was competing against Margaret O'Brien for the part, and that when Natalie showed up for the reading, the director "right away fell in love with her, but a producer have to approve it, too, so he gave Natalie a script, several pages, and said, 'Read this as long as you want to and then read it with me.' Ten minutes later she said, 'I'm ready, Mother. I know it by heart.' Not only her part—his, too! And he was so impressed, the producer, that they signed her up—and Margaret O'Brien lost the part."

O'Brien has no recollection being considered for Babs, but the story illustrates the pressure Natalie felt to get the part. Mud's restrictions on her hair and makeup disappeared "as soon as my mother realized that Natalie could still *work* looking older," relates Lana.

Natalie's classmates remember her as proud of playing her first role in lipstick and out of pigtails. Both she and Jane Wyman underwent radical transformations from *The Blue Veil* to *Just for You*, only six months apart. Wyman went from an aging spinster on-screen to a glamorous Broadway star. Natalie metamorphosed from a gawky girl in braids to a young woman. The movies had finally caught up with her real age. Her character, Babs Blake, was a sweet, sophisticated teen desperate to be accepted into an exclusive girls' school run by a headmistress played by the legendary Ethel Barrymore, then in her seventies.

In the picture, Crosby takes his kids to a lakeside resort, giving Natalie a chance to wear a bathing suit, showing off her budding figure. Bob Arthaud (billed as "Bob Arthur"), who played Natalie's older brother, recalls her as "a very beautiful little lady. She was 'a lady.' She was not in any way cheap or tacky or common." On location at Lake Arrowhead, where the resort scenes were shot, Natalie stuck "very close to her mother," according to Arthaud, who found her "a little aloof" with "a demeanor that was reserved." Arthaud perceived none of the awkwardness Natalie was feeling. She appeared "very controlled and poised" and was extremely feminine. Like everyone who worked with Natalie, he was impressed with her intelligence and professionalism, finding her exceptionally "focused," qualities she needed during filming, which Arthaud describes as an enjoyable but strict education.

"There was a lot at stake. It was one of Ethel Barrymore's

last films and she was quite ill. And she told the cameraman and the director that she would give everybody one chance to get her scenes right and after that it was too late. So everybody was really on their toes. She did all of her scenes in one take." Arthaud recalls a moment, off set, when he was in Barrymore's dressing room with her, listening on the radio to boxer Joe Louis's last match. "And when he lost the fight, she was propped up in bed with that mane of white hair and she said, 'Sad when a champion dies.' And I couldn't help but think that was her." Crosby had similarly high standards on the set. "What was really surprising about Bing Crosby to me was that he really was a very, very bright man. He knew everybody's lines and knew everything about the camera. He always came across as this relaxed performer, but he was far from relaxed." Wyman, whom Natalie admired, offered tips on how to look at the camera. "She said to 'look at the eye nearest the camera, don't play to both eyes, and don't dart back and forth between one eye and the other, which is what amateurs do.' And she also said that the pupil of the eye was the pinpoint of the soul and to 'look into it, when you look at other actors, you look in their eyes.' " Natalie paid attention to it all. Her performance, especially her scenes with Crosby and Wyman, was subtle and tender.

Two things about Natalie, at thirteen, stood out to Arthaud during filming. One was that she *demanded* respect. Even in the company of Barrymore, Crosby and Wyman, "she held everybody at bay." The other exceptional trait Arthaud noticed was star quality. "Noel Coward made a comment when they asked him what made a star. He said, 'A star sparkles.' And Natalie Wood sparkled."

The Hollywood trade papers agreed with Arthaud,

calling Natalie "absolutely adorable" in *Just for You* when it was released the next autumn, adding prophetically: "Her appealing performance show[s] that it is only a matter of time and growing up before she becomes a full-fledged star in her own right."

Natalie completed her scenes in *Just for You* in December and returned to junior high, making her parents $6500 richer. She was happy to be back in the realm of Jimmy Williams, whose maverick allure exerted a more powerful pull on her thirteen-year-old sensibilities than fame or money. She spent the rest of the school year trying to get him to ask her out. Jimmy was aware of Natalie's obsession ("I kept getting that word, and Mary Ann might have came to me and said, 'Jim, what are you doing?' "), but he remained irresistibly elusive. "I wasn't really into girls, if you will. I had other things in mind. We were cowboys back then . . . and of course I watched Andy Devine forever. I was impressed with *him*, but I wasn't impressed with Natalie Wood."

Natalie's nascent interest in dating made her more self-conscious about her peculiarly misshaped wrist. In *Just for You,* Natalie often kept a glove on her left wrist, one of many tricks she experimented with to disguise her deformity. That spring, she came up with the idea of covering the wrist with a huge cuff bracelet, which she wore in every scene of a movie she made that April with Ann Doran, who couldn't help but notice. Doran asked her why she always wore the bracelet. Natalie was too embarrassed to tell her what happened, saying, "Oh, I broke my arm and they didn't set it right." Wearing the bracelet was another way for Natalie to conceal the darkness in her life, which she perceived as weakness.

Hiding her disfigured wrist was a symptom of her compulsion to appear *perfect*, the flawless Hollywood beauty, relentlessly fostered by Mud. As Lana observed, "She felt that she had to appear a certain way."

Natalie was thrilled to see Ann Doran again, even though they were doing a "B" picture with such a low budget the cast had to furnish its own wardrobe. Doran and character actor Jim Backus played parents of a Rose Bowl princess pursued by the star football player in a typical fifties family film, called *The Rose Bowl Story*. Natalie was their boy-crazy younger daughter, who monopolized the phone talking to her boyfriend, or flirted with the college football players. (Backus' character finally erupts, saying, "The only way anyone could reach you in this house with that brat tying up the phone is by carrier pigeon!") It was one of the rare occasions in her child-acting career when Natalie was part of a happy family instead of a parentless child faced with a tragedy. She showed the same panache for comedy as she had in *Scudda Hoo Scudda Hay*, playing a similarly smart-mouthed kid sister, managing to be called "the cutest cutie seen in a long time" when the picture came out in October, despite her uncharacteristic baby fat.

The star of the movie, as Natalie's older sister, was a complete unknown named Vera Miles, a former Miss Texas "so doggone scared on her first picture, doing a big part, she was eager and willing to do anything," remembers Doran. "Poor little Vera Miles had a scene where she had to wear a coat and she couldn't afford to buy one. She and her husband were living on beans and rice and she was so pleased to have a job. And I loaned her my coat, since we had to furnish our own clothes, and Natalie looked at me and she said, 'You mean you're gonna let her wear your coat?' And I said, 'Of course. Because she doesn't *have* a coat.' Natalie understood immediately. She whispered, '*Oh . . . that's different.*' "

Doran and Natalie had a "wonderful time," despite the insipid plot and bizarre casting of the college football hero, played by an actor who looked old enough to own the team. "It was just the most fun, one of those close pictures. The most delightful time both of us had in a long time."

Natalie finished eighth grade after filming, capturing Jimmy long enough to sign his 1952 yearbook, hinting at her interest with this poem:

The higher the mountain
The cooler the breeze
The younger the couple
The tighter the squeeze
Lot'sa luck, "Mac"

That summer, she was invited to a Hollywood party by one of her agents at Famous Artists, where they had taken notice of her curves and decided to send her to events for publicity, hoping to create a more mature image. While she was at the party, Natalie met the actor who played Elizabeth Taylor's brother in *Father of the Bride*, Tom Irish, who was represented by the same agent. Irish was smitten by Natalie and asked her out, an idea encouraged by Famous Artists, which viewed their dating as an opportunity to publicize two clients at once. Mud still opposed Natalie dating boys from junior high, but she offered no resistance to Irish, since the dates might advance Natalie's career. Irish was twenty-one; Natalie was thirteen.

Tom Irish began calling for Natalie at the house in Northridge, picking her up for dinner dates in his car, an old hearse. Maria would greet him at the door and send her thirteen-year-old daughter off with a grown man. "She could have objected," he points out, "but she never did." Irish "never even laid eyes" on Natalie's father, "or if I did he was just in one of the other rooms, passing through." Mud's motivation was clear: to get Natalie's picture in the paper. "A lot of these things we did for publicity," Irish relates. "Publicity shots, publicity dinners and stuff . . . and then, we did a lot of things that *weren't* advertised, you might say. Non-publicity." Irish considered thirteen-year-old Natalie his girlfriend. "Somehow I never thought about the age. She looked older. She acted more mature than most people . . . she was busy doing things, and I was trying to do my little thing." Irish claims he never realized Natalie was in junior high, " 'cause we only saw each other on dates, and usually in the evening. We went to the Captain's Table restaurant, and to different restaurants on La Cienega occasionally."

Natalie was beyond her depth in the relationship, pretending to be a woman, less than a year out of pigtails. "You're not a little girl and you're not mature," as she explained to a writer four years later. "You feel so awkward. You don't know how to act or what you're supposed to be." She had no idea what to even *say* on a date. "I can remember I was so desperate for conversation that I read street signs." Natalie started reading the sports section so she had something to talk about. It was her intelligence that enabled her to straddle the age gap on her dates with Irish; inside, Natalie was still a child. She asked her parents for a canopy bed for her fourteenth birthday that July, so she could have a more "grown-up" bedroom. She was dating a twenty-one-year-old, but Natalie was still playing with her forty-seven dolls.

Fortunately, Irish in many ways was as naïve as she. He

and Natalie attended their first movie premiere together that summer, arranged by Famous Artists to get publicity shots of their young star couple arriving in formal clothes under klieg lights at the famous Grauman's Chinese Theater on Hollywood Boulevard. Irish picked up Natalie in his 1941 black Cadillac, "which either looked like I was being kept or I worked for a funeral parlor." He continues:

> We drove up to the Grauman Chinese in this car, and they opened the back door and looked around and there's nobody in there. Then they opened the front, and we looked like two peapods, because *I* was driving the car and she was sitting next to me. They drove the car away and we went in and enjoyed the movie and then we came back outside to wait for our car. And I kept hearing, "Will Lana Turner's car please . . ." "Joan Crawford's car please . . ." So-and-So's car please . . . And we stood there. We waited and we waited and we waited. And I had no idea that they didn't bring your car back to you if you don't have a *chauffeur* to drive it back to you! And there we stood, and almost everybody's gone on the street, and I said, "Well, where's my car? Why don't they bring it back?" Natalie totally was scared. 'Cause she didn't know and I didn't know. So I really did some inquiring and they said, "Oh, it's way over in such-and-such a lot." So we walked over and got it.
>
> The *next* time, I had a friend of mine drive the car, and he had a dark suit on and he put a chauffeur's cap on and his date was in the back seat with Natalie and me. And we drove up to the premiere, and they opened the back door, and of

> course we got out the way one's supposed to in that kind of car, and then my friend drove off and went around the corner. When the movie was over and they said, "Will Mr. Irish's car please . . ." my friend drove the car up, we got in the back, went around the corner, changed places, I got in the front of my car, my friend got in the back and we went on to enjoy our rest of the evening.

Mud reveled in this new aspect of Natalie's career, thrilling to the artificial reality of the Hollywood publicity machine. When a movie magazine editor suggested a pictorial of Natalie hosting a sleepover, Maria staged a slumber party for the photographer, casting students from Fulton as Natalie's girlfriends. Mary Ann telephoned them. "When the guy came to take the pictures, the girls were all sitting around in blankets and her mother was supervising the whole thing: 'I want *you* to throw a pillow, and *you* sit on the bed . . .' " Maria, the mistress of illusion, had found her natural habitat in Hollywood. "It was almost like a feeding frenzy," recalls Mary Ann of the household. "It was constant *energy* that this woman expended. It was amazing when you really think about it. All systems were going. She had the father running doing this, even little Lana was a little pitcher. Everything was clicking and in order. That's a lot of organization to put together, I give her credit for that. Things were *done*—hair appointments, everything, she had the whole thing going, it was unbelievable."

Natalie and Tom Irish faithfully performed their parts in the sideshow, dressing up for Hollywood events, attending a party "for the young up-and-coming" at Douglas Fairbanks and Mary Pickford's mansion, Pickfair, where Natalie "wouldn't even *go* in the pool." When they dated without photographers present, Irish took Natalie to dinner, or roller-skating. They occasionally visited her wealthy Russian godparents, who had moved to nearby Santa Barbara, where they owned a home that was more like a palace, with "servants with the white gloves and all that. Every time you'd turn around they'd pour this vodka—it looked like it had moss or seaweed or something in it, horrible-looking stuff—into these little glasses and they'd say something in Russian. Up and down went the vodka, and egad, you could get so sick!"

Irish found Natalie a sexual naïf, a circumstance he did not try to compromise. "Our encounters seemed to just—gosh, they went so fast. We were sitting there, mixing, at your little premiere, and you're in and you're out, and then you go off to some other spot and looking and talking to other people. There wasn't too much of being all by ourselves or up on the hill or something. We just didn't do any of that in those days." During the months they dated, Irish and Natalie did no more than pet. "It was just plain necking, there was no tongue business. Probably bored her to tears." It was pure luck that Irish, at twenty-one, was a gentleman, for Natalie, at thirteen, knew little about sex, and what she believed, via Mud, was dangerously misleading.

Late that summer, Natalie's name made its way into Hedda Hopper's column, announcing that she had been cast in Bette Davis' new picture, *The Star*. She was absolutely *thrilled* to get the chance to work with Bette Davis, Natalie said later, proof of her new maturity about acting. The script was a tour de force for Davis, then forty-something, playing a bankrupt, once-famous star unable to accept that her movie career is over. Natalie had several emotional scenes with her, as the daughter Davis was forced to abandon who idolizes her nonetheless. Tom Irish had a small part as a party guest (cut from the film), providing Natalie with company on the set. The entire production was scheduled for twenty-four days, a breakneck pace to accommodate Davis, who had to start a musical that September, according to screenwriter Dale Eunson.

The first scene scheduled for Natalie took place on a sailboat owned by actor Sterling Hayden, who was playing Davis' lover. In the scene, he takes the forgotten star (Davis) and her daughter (Natalie) sailing. Late in August, Mud and Natalie were driven to the harbor south of Los Angeles in San Pedro, where passengers catch the ferry to Santa Catalina Island, to shoot the sailboat scene. What happened during the filming of that scene remains a topic of controversy. According to Natalie, the director, Stuart Heisler, changed the script once she and Mud got to the harbor at San Pedro. "All of a sudden, it turned out that I had to jump *off* the boat and swim to a faraway raft. So there I was, faced with the threat of being *flung* into the ocean—or losing the part." During a televised tribute to Bette Davis in 1977, with Davis present, Natalie offered this anecdote of what occurred after Heisler ordered her to jump off the boat: "I went into hysterics that must have been heard all the way to Catalina. In any case, Ms. Davis certainly heard them. And she came out of her dressing room to find out what all the commotion was. This was the only time that I *ever* saw the famous Bette Davis temperament surface, and it was not on her own behalf. But she *did* tell the director that she wouldn't stand around while he threw some terrified kid into the ocean, and that if he'd wanted a swimmer he should have gotten Johnny Weissmuller."

There was more to the story, as Natalie revealed in an

interview in 1981, shortly before she drowned, eerily, from a boat moored off Catalina Island. According to this expanded account, Natalie *was* forced to jump into the ocean from Hayden's boat for the scene. "I was a complete wreck by the time I had to leap into the water," she told the reporter. "I looked over the rail and saw a huge shadow swimming by. The director told me: 'Just jump. There'll be men in rowboats to pick you up. If you get scared, just scream.' The second I hit the water, I panicked. The icy ocean took my breath away. I swam a bit, but was hysterical. They finally got me out, and used a double to shoot the scene again. The girl almost drowned in the kelp. And after all that, they cut the scene from the movie." In a separate interview, she was quoted saying she'd been "thrown into the sea and nearly drowned."

Despite the fact that Natalie, Lana and Bette Davis each at various times publicly credited Davis with coming to Natalie's rescue, Maria insisted to her last breath it was "a big lie." From what Maria said, Natalie was afraid of the director, a "tough German," and was too intimidated to tell him she couldn't jump off the boat because of her fear of the ocean and of sharks. "I've always feared sharks," Natalie acknowledged in 1981, prior to her drowning, "even before *Jaws* scared everyone else about them." In Maria's version, which Olga believes to be true, Mud advised Natalie to tell the director, Stuart Heisler, that she was willing to do the scene but her "crazy mother" wouldn't let her. "I went to him and I said, 'Mr. Heisler, Natalie don't know how to swim very good, and in dark water I won't let her.' " Heisler complained about the cost to reschedule, so Maria told him he was in breach of contract for asking Natalie to do a dangerous scene. Bette Davis, according to Maria, flew into a rage. "She said, 'Who do you think you are? You know how much money it cost to stop the movie?' I looked straight in her eyes and I stood up to her." Maria claimed that after the scene was shot, the stunt double came up to her and said, "Mrs. Gurdin, you're lucky that you wouldn't let Natalie swim. I was scared, because something was touching my legs."

Dale Eunson, who wrote the screenplay and was often on the set, knew nothing about the incident, though he confirms that his script did not require Natalie to jump off the boat, just as she said. Oddly, Sterling Hayden's wife, Betty, who was *on* the Haydens' boat during the sailing scene, never heard anything about the fracas, then or later. "I was out there while everybody else was sailing the boat—lying down with the pillow in my hand, so I wouldn't be seen on camera."

Natalie's then-beau Tom Irish, the sole survivor from *The Star* who was aware of what happened, remembers both Maria Gurdin *and* Bette Davis standing up to the director. According to Irish, Maria *did* tell Heisler that Natalie couldn't do the scene, couldn't swim and couldn't be in dark water. "Bette Davis couldn't stand the mother, with this 'Natalie can't do this' and 'Natalie can't do that' or 'Natalie's got to rest' and 'Natalie Natalie Natalie,' and she was ready to kill her. Like, 'Get this woman away and let us get on with what we're doing.' " When Heisler insisted Natalie jump off the boat or lose the part, Mud plainly sacrificed Natalie for the scene. By Irish's account, when Natalie became hysterical in the dark seawater, Bette Davis raced out to see what was wrong. "They were like two different entities. The mother did her bit, and then Bette Davis . . . came out and said, 'Now look, wait a minute, you should hire a double for this.' " Davis was able to accomplish what Maria hadn't been able to do. As the screenwriter, Eunson, notes, "With Bette Davis and a director like Stuart Heisler, *he* didn't direct, *she* directed."

For Natalie, the experience was a harrowing re-creation of the collapsing bridge on *The Green Promise*, another instance of her mother placing her in danger because of a movie. Bette Davis became a heroine. Four years later, when she told a boyfriend what happened, "she said she was crying and yelling and her mother wouldn't do anything—she was so scared—and Bette Davis came down and helped her."

Maria and Bette Davis despised each other ever after, a loathing Mud claimed began the morning they met in San Pedro, when Davis invited her for a drink and Maria, a teetotaler, ordered a 7-Up. "Oh, it's ridiculous! How ridiculous!" Davis supposedly sputtered, walking away in disgust. Sterling Hayden's wife spent most of her time during *The Star* with Davis, much of it in bars. "We were just like two women that laughed and probably drank more than we should." Betty Hayden adored Davis. "When somebody says something bad about her, I'm very defensive because I thought she was just magnificent." Natalie's friend Mary Ann, who visited the set, found Davis very businesslike. She amused Natalie and Mary Ann. "What a mouth she had! Boy, when somebody did something, oh my goodness. We, of course, would just giggle and laugh and had fun with that whole thing."

Natalie had dispensed with the cuff bracelet for her work in *The Star*, which was particularly vulnerable. She wore no makeup, playing Davis' sweetly affectionate daughter with a yearning that brought out a tenderness in Davis. "I remember for some reason a scene on the staircase in which she was particularly good," Davis said once, "and I remember telling her, you know, how much she helped me in the way she played the scene." The scene Davis was referring to was one in which a humiliated Davis tries to slip out of her ex-husband's house without being seen by her adoring daughter. As she opens the door to exit, Natalie suddenly appears at the top of the stairs in her pajamas, her sincere brown eyes seeking out Davis' with a wounded expression. "Aren't you going to come up and say goodnight, Mother?" she asks, with such longing it breaks Davis' heart. Such moments were Natalie's gift as an actress. As Ann Doran, her costar in five films, explains, "There are people that you can't stand immediately and learn to like, or there's people you can't stand and never do like, and there are people that you like immediately. That quality was in Natalie. Natalie reached out to her audience. She brought them into her world. She reached out and she got you and brought you right *into* her—you understood her." Davis would receive an Academy Award nomination for her performance as Natalie's mother, the washed-up star.

Bette Davis got her second revenge on Maria Gurdin at the end of the shoot, when Tom Irish received a telegram from Davis inviting him to bring "his fiancée Natalie" to a wrap party for the cast and crew of *The Star* at the Captain's Table. When Irish arrived at the Gurdins' to pick up Natalie, "the mother kind of looks at us both and says, 'No, I don't know, I think I'd better go with you,' and I thought, 'Oh damn!' So she puts on something and away we go." It was the only occasion Maria accompanied them on a date and it was odd, according to Irish. "She didn't say anything. She just sat in the back of the car." He continues, "So we get to the Captain's Table, the three of us, and Bette Davis is standing in the front door, with one of the dresses that she wore in *The Star*, a navy blue taffeta dress. And she was standing there with her legs sort of apart, smoking a cigarette and greeting the people that came in, like 'Oh John, how are you, darling, do come in,' 'Oh Tom, Natalie darling, do come in,' 'Tom dear, so glad you could make it.' And then she swung around and all of a sudden there's the mother. And she just stopped dead in her tracks and goes, 'Oh . . .' and takes a long drag off her cigarette, and looks at her right in the eye and just *puff*—I mean she blew smoke in her face!—and says, 'I don't remember sending *you* an invitation.' Then she just swung back into motion and said, 'But I'm so *glad* you could come anyway. Do come in.' " As Irish stood between the two women, riveted by the drama, Maria strode past Davis into the party as if nothing had occurred, "water off a duck's back."

After *The Star*, Natalie's phobia of dark seawater grew increasingly morbid. She began to believe her recurring dreams of drowning were prophetic warnings. She became simultaneously obsessed with covering the wrist she broke on *The Green Promise* as if she were hideously disfigured, when it was a minor imperfection: the bone had grown slightly below the natural position with a larger than normal bump. Natalie would not let anyone see it. "She wore big bracelets and big cuffs always, never without, *never*," declares Mary Ann. "And there was a period when she'd wear long sleeves all the time." When Irish noticed Natalie's penchant for bracelets, he bought one for her as a gift "and she never wore it." He eventually found out why. "This was a thin bracelet, and it wouldn't cover that deformed bone. I didn't realize that she even had a problem." Natalie spent hours searching for bracelets that concealed her imperfection, getting Fahd to make some for her.

—

Famous Artists' plan to transform her image from Pigtail Kid to ingénue-in-the-making overnight proceeded with a seamlessness that was disturbing. When Natalie took the much-older Tom Irish to a Lake Arrowhead hotel for the weekend to promote the Bing Crosby musical, her first film not in braids, it was accepted as a natural evolution. One movie magazine reported chirpily how Natalie had "changed her type," graduating to her "first grown-up role" and her "first premiere date," failing to disclose that her "date" was twenty-one and accompanied her for the weekend. The resort was swarming with reporters, lured by a two-day festival of stars including Tony Curtis and Janet Leigh, performing magic tricks from *Houdini*. The inappropriateness of Natalie's romance was lost in the carnival atmosphere of the weekend, which Mud attended, hobnobbing with her favorite movie gods and goddesses. A female reporter interviewed Natalie while she was at Lake Arrowhead, referring to her in the subsequent newspaper article as "that 'baby star' in pigtails," now "a growing up beauty of 14" with a boyfriend. She reported Irish's age and the fact that Natalie attended Fulton, as if there were nothing unusual about an eighth-grader "going steady" with a twenty-one-year-old. "Natalie could easily pass for 16 or 17," wrote the reporter, pointing out that Shirley Temple, Judy Garland, Elizabeth Taylor and Deanna Durbin had all "tied the knot at tender ages of 16 and 17—and untied them shortly thereafter." Natalie told the reporter *she* didn't want *any* divorces, "When I get married it will be for keeps." She was quoted as saying she wanted to be like other girls and go to school, or go on dates, "determined she won't wind up in divorce or unhappiness like the other child celebrities."

Natalie's candor, and her wisdom, contrasted with Mud,

who lied to the same reporter, telling her she chaperoned all of Natalie's dates, "tagging along" with Tom Irish. Maria wanted to create the illusion, for publicity purposes, that she was a strict parent, to camouflage the unsavory reality that she could have been in effect prostituting her junior-high daughter for a chance at more mature roles. She had no idea what Natalie and Irish were doing on their dates, and according to Mary Ann and others, Mud didn't care. "My mom would privately condone everything that was going on, and publicly denounce you," confirms Lana. "Which really, really hurts. She did it to me as well—I was like thirteen, fourteen years old when I started dating. She was a chameleon. It depended on who she was talking to, and who my mom thought they wanted her to be."

11

DESPITE HER AGENTS' AND MUD'S efforts to push her past the awkward age on-screen by sophisticating her prematurely, Natalie's career foundered when she returned to Fulton in ninth grade. She said later it was "the worst time of my life," a period of self-consciousness in which she found herself suddenly undesirable in movies, the medium that had courted her since she was four. At fourteen, she was forgotten.

She found work in television, appearing in August 1952 on the Pepsi-Cola Playhouse in *Playmates*, as a young girl who befriends a ghost. She performed live in another television drama, *Quite a Viking*, for Hollywood Playhouse, a radical experience for Natalie, who was accustomed to shooting scenes out of sequence, with multiple takes. One-Take Natalie was "cool as a cucumber," remembers Tom Irish. "I said to her, 'Aren't you nervous?'—because it was a *live show*. And she said, 'No, not at all. Why? Should I be?' I was nervous for her, thinking, 'Oh God, a live show! What happens if you goof or something?' " "I loved the feeling of beginning at the beginning and going through to the end," Natalie later told an interviewer. Her career came to a standstill that October. "There were no parts," recalls a school chum. "She was too old for some and too young for others."

Natalie embraced normalcy, leading the typical life of a girl her age for the first time since kindergarten in Santa Rosa. Jimmy Williams, the renegade who had eluded her since seventh grade, suddenly noticed Natalie that fall. The two of them "just kind of came together," by his elliptic description. "Maybe I started realizing that she was something special . . . it just come a time that I decided that I wanted to be with her. I'm talking kid stuff." "It took me two and a half years," Natalie said later of her conquest, proud of the fact that "all the girls had a terrible crush" on Jimmy. Her main rival, Jacqueline Eastes learned something about Natalie through their competition for Jimmy's affections. "When Natalie *wanted* something, it would *happen*."

She faced formidable opposition from Mud, who banned Natalie from dating Jimmy, a tenth-grader, until she was in high school, permitting her to see actor Tom Irish, who was twenty-three, anytime. Natalie's dates, under her mother's house rules, were calculated stepping-stones to stardom. "Jimmy wasn't in the *business*," as Mary Ann explains. "His folks owned a huge dairy farm that he worked on . . . very unpretentious, nice people." Natalie was frantic to see Jimmy, who was equally possessed with her. The only time they could spend together was at parties at Natalie's house, under the hawkish gaze of Maria, who was as threatened by

Jimmy's Hell's Angels persona as Natalie was exhilarated. He staged a drag race one night after cruising by the Gurdins' in his father's pickup, making a sharp right turn to avoid a police car and smashing into a telephone pole. "The kids I was drag racing with made a left turn down a street that dead-ends at the Van Nuys Airport. The police assumed they ran me off the road and started chasing them. The kids went through the fence and by that time the police had an all-points on these guys. The police had a roadblock set up, stopped them, made them get out of the car with their hands up, then one of the policeman shot this kid in the back. That was a real incident, it was all over the Van Nuys newspapers, and it cost me my driver's license until I was eighteen."

Natalie found Jimmy's hellion heroism dangerously romantic. She was drawn to dark personalities, in the opinion of a later beau, but there was more to Jimmy than a black leather jacket and jeans with the cuffs rolled up. Underneath the machismo, Jimmy was "a prince of a fellow," in the appraisal of Mary Ann. He was fiercely protective of Natalie ("She was like a child"), and had a cowboy's code of honor. "I got along with the teachers marvelously. When I did something, if they called me into the office and said, 'Did you do it?'—if it wasn't too bad, I'd say, 'Yeah, I did.' Now if it was something that was a little more *serious*, I'd deny it, even though I did it—and they'd let me go, because they knew I'd just tell the truth. So I worked that pretty hard."

Natalie was intoxicated by Jimmy. She invited friends to the house regularly just to include him, "So we started to become closer, becoming closer and closer." Natalie begged Mud to let her go to events with kids from high school so she could at least *see* him. In desperation, she dragged Maria along to a party, "because Natalie wanted to show her mother that all the kids were nice kids, and we weren't losers, and we certainly weren't smoking dope and things like that, we were just kids." Natalie's ploy worked. Mud loosened the sexual reins, permitting her to see Jimmy in a group setting.

Maria's trust was not misplaced. Van Nuys High School, in 1952, was a relatively innocent venue, even for self-proclaimed rebels such as Jimmy. "We were all good kids," as one alumna of the class of 1955 vouches. The San Fernando Valley, back then, was a flat wilderness of ranchland populated by "a few old retired movie stars, cowboy stars, and that was about it." It had been infiltrated by new subdivisions after the war, coaxing families from Los Angeles to the other side of the mountains for affordable housing. Actor Robert Redford's family was one of them. Redford, then fifteen, transferred to the class ahead of Jimmy's at Van Nuys High in 1952, just before Natalie arrived. As he recalls, "Those mountains were much more of a demarcation point as a kid in the fifties. Once you came to the Valley, it was just a wasteland, there was nothing there, and at night there were no lights out there. People spilled into the Valley, so it drew a polyglot, an eclectic mix of mostly immigrant families who could afford to live out there because it was now cheap . . . but the trade-off, for me, was horrendous: sterile, flat, boring, cookie-cutter homes in neighborhoods that had no character."

By contrast to Hollywood, Jimmy and his Van Nuys High clique were a wholesome breeze blowing through Natalie's life. "Some of us came from the 'Ronny Howard families,' the boy-next-door/girl-next-door families," remarks a classmate who went to sleepovers at Natalie's. "They were just good parents, nine-to-five parents. And then some came from celebrity families, so we were all a mixture of kids, just being kids."

Natalie fit in comfortably dating a dairy farmer's son. She had no social pretensions, according to Williams. "She was just about as down-to-earth as you could imagine." Their romance progressed sweetly, hand-holding on campus, at parties. Natalie credited Jimmy, later, as her first "genuine kiss," occurring on her living room sofa with Mud skulking nearby, swooping into the room to pull them apart, growling under her breath in heavy Russian intonations that they were "still babies." "I felt so bad that I burst into tears," recalled Natalie, confused by her mother's sexual double standard, offering her to a grown man, but pronouncing sex as something wicked with a boy her age for whom she had genuine feelings.

Natalie seldom talked about the people she met in Hollywood, or her movies, with Jimmy. "That was her job, and she wasn't overly impressed with it. She didn't carry a lot of airs with it." Becoming a movie star in the future, to Natalie, was "part of her life," reflects Williams. "I don't think it was a goal, I think it was just a given . . . she didn't know any better." Mud's fervid whispers into Natalie's ear from infancy that she was destined to become famous had implanted themselves into Natalie's subconscious and she was carrying out the prophecy as if under a hypnotist's trance.

Her overpowering attraction to a daredevil like Jimmy Williams suggested that Natalie wanted to break free. Once they started going together, he noticed, she "liked to do things that were a little risky." When they went to the amusement park at the Santa Monica Pier, Natalie pulled him onto the wildest ride, called the Pike. "They had this big drum, and you'd get in it and you'd stand and whirl, and they'd drop the bottom out of it and the centrifugal force keeps you up on the wall. And she loved it. She'd ride that thing all night long if you stayed with it." Natalie flung aside her arsenal of inhibitions in Jimmy's presence, as if his fearlessness gave her power. "She was always wanting to do a little more, go a little further, get a little more risky. I mean, she wasn't afraid."

Natalie told Jimmy she knew that she was going to drown. The premonition first came up in their conversations when Olga and her husband Lexi visited with their young sons, and invited Natalie and Jimmy to the ocean. "She'd put her toes in," he recalls, "and we'd hold hands and walk the beach and she'd let the water get on her feet, but she would not get in the water, because she was afraid of drowning. We talked about it—or I shouldn't say *we* talked. *She* talked about it and I listened. I tried to be a friend to her for this kind of thing." Natalie mentioned her recurring dreams of drowning and "believed that's the way she was going to die." She was haunted by it for as long as Jimmy knew her. "If she told me once, she told me a hundred times she loved to go to the beach, but she knew she was going to drown if she ever got in the water."

Natalie shared other confidences with Jimmy. How fond she was of her sister Olga, that Olga didn't like Fahd, because he used Natalie's money and didn't have a job. Jimmy held a similar view of Natalie's father, saying, "All the years I knew him, he never turned a hand doing anything." In his opinion, Nick was comfortable being supported by Natalie and *pushed* her to act, just like Mud, though Natalie never said a critical word to Jimmy about her father. "She felt like that's the way it was supposed to be, I think, and I guess they made a pretty good case that they were taking *care* of her, and it was because of their taking care of her that she was making this money—therefore it wasn't *hers* necessarily, but it was *family* income."

In the middle of the school year, January of 1953, Natalie skipped the last semester of ninth grade and transferred as a sophomore to Van Nuys High, though she was only fourteen. She would modestly attribute the acceleration to years of studio tutoring, but Natalie was intellectually gifted in the view of those close to her. Lana saw her report cards, nearly all A's, and described her sister, posthumously, as "quite brilliant." Mary Ann considered Natalie's intelligence her defining quality; more so than her acting, or her beauty. Jimmy was awed. "She had to have an IQ of close to 200. She was just a whiz-banger. I showed her my agriculture book one day and said, 'I've got to get a book report out of that,' and she just grabbed it out of my hand, and the next morning, I had a book report on the entire book. I didn't ask her to, I was just complaining. And I got an A+. They put it on the wall. And she didn't know anything about agriculture. She was just absolutely the smartest thing I ever met in my life."

Since Natalie was in high school, Mud reluctantly permitted her to date Jimmy under less monitored circumstances that winter. The teenagers' intense pull to each other had an urgency, suggesting something out of control. It surfaced when they spent an afternoon in the mountains around Big Bear Lake with Jimmy's brothers and Natalie's stunt double. The resort was crowded, so Jimmy's brother searched for a remote spot to ride toboggans. "He found this canyon, with good snow down and up, and I took Natalie up about thirty feet and we came down that hill. And that wasn't enough. She said, 'I want to go higher.' So we went up higher, did the same thing. And she wanted to go higher, and higher, and higher." Natalie goaded Jimmy until he took her to the top of the mountain. "I'd have *never* went to the top of that hill." Natalie was dangerously reckless; testing the boundaries of Jimmy's love, making up for a lifetime of fear and Mud's restrictions. "We started down," recalls Williams, "and she got scared, and she wanted off. And of course it was going so fast that I couldn't get her off. I tried to get her feet out, and her foot got stuck." Natalie panicked as the toboggan careened down the icy slope. Jimmy used his body to shield her, preparing to crash, "and when we hit the bottom it was going so fast, I crushed my nose—absolutely crushed it—on my knee." Natalie was hysterical. "I looked horrible," admits Williams. "I splattered my nose all over my face." When Maria saw him, dripping blood at the Gurdins' front door, "she had a hemorrhage." Jimmy's wrecked face was of no concern to Mud. She was furious that Natalie could have gotten hurt and forfeited an acting job. "I thought her mother was going to kill us," reveals Williams. She refused to let Natalie see him and "it was kind of bad for a long time."

Mud's desperation to keep Natalie working, and apart from Jimmy, led her to accept a supporting role for Natalie in a television pilot called *Pride of the Family*, a generic situation comedy starring Paul Hartman and Fay Wray (famous from 1933's *King Kong*) as a curmudgeonly ad executive and his patient wife. Natalie was playing what she later called "the idiot teenager who gave everybody trouble," and Bobby Hyatt, the child actor whom Mud had snubbed on the set of *Miracle on 34*th *Street*, was cast as "Junior," her pubescent younger brother. Maria and Natalie made it clear to Bobby and his mother that a television series was beneath their dignity because Natalie was a *movie* star, but "nobody else would hire Natalie," states Hyatt, who was thirteen to Natalie's fourteen and a half (though they were playing twelve and sixteen). "She wasn't gawky, but there weren't really a lot of roles around for teenagers in movies. TV was kind of coming into its own and there was more work for kids." Money was also an issue, according to Hyatt, who knew Natalie's father was unemployed and she was supporting the family. "I don't think they were applying for welfare, but there was no way Marie would have accepted this TV series for Natalie if they didn't really need the money."

Before they filmed the pilot, Mud signed a contract with Revue Productions for a salary of $300 for the pilot episode, which billed Natalie and Bobby as costars. When ABC bought it, accepting *Pride of the Family* as a half-hour weekly series, Maria shrewdly renegotiated Natalie's terms, refusing to let her do the show unless the producers increased her salary to $400 an episode and Natalie received top billing over Bobby Hyatt. The Hyatts got a call from their agent saying, "We've got a big problem. Mrs. Gurdin won't let Natalie sign the contract unless it says, 'starring Natalie Wood and *featuring* Bobby Hyatt.' " "Nobody could figure it out," recalls Hyatt. "I was no competition, equal status on the show, blah blah blah. It actually came down to the series being dropped if this silly conflict was not settled." Bobby and his mother capitulated. "We had to pay the rent. And I wanted to do the show because it sounded like it was fun, and plus I wanted to work with Natalie."

When they started filming the series that spring, Natalie was embarrassed that her mother had manipulated star billing over Bobby. She approached him guiltily, saying, "I want you to know I didn't have anything to do with it, and I don't feel that way. I hope you're not mad." Bobby had already forgotten about the incident, "but she hadn't." He was amazed at how nice Natalie was, and "from that point on, we became really good friends." They made jokes about the silly plotlines, and how their sitcom parents looked more like *grand*parents. "I objected to it because I don't think teenagers are dopes and idiots," Natalie remarked a few years later, "and I didn't think the show was at all funny . . . it was like being a traitor to my own class."

Natalie had to withdraw from Van Nuys High to film the series, further bonding her with Bobby in the studio classroom, where they were the only two students; whispering Maria stories, giggling at her Russian accent and squinted eyes as she dispensed career advice to Natalie. "Her favorite saying was, 'Don't be the eager beaver,' when she wanted Natalie to hold out on a contract. We would just roll on the floor laughing." Natalie eventually confessed to Bobby the reason their billing was changed. "My mother just wanted to have status over your mother at the studio," she told him. "To know that *her* daughter is the star and you're only a featured actor." Mud wouldn't let Bobby come to the house when Natalie invited him, because he wasn't a costar. "Her mother only wanted Natalie to have friends who could advance her career," a corollary to the show business commandment that had excommunicated Jimmy from Natalie's life. Bobby had a grudging admiration for "Marie," as Mud now called herself. He respected her barracuda instincts, and found her unintentionally amusing behavior endearing, despite the fact that he was near the bottom of her Hollywood caste system. "I remember Marie saying constantly, 'We can't wait to get out of this series. One movie and we're out of here.' "

Hyatt uncovered a family skeleton that spring while filming the series. One morning when Natalie and Maria stepped out of their studio limousine at Republic Studios, he caught a glimpse of Natalie's father behind the wheel. Bobby found out through Natalie that Mud had negotiated a confidential clause in Natalie's *Pride of the Family* contract providing her father a job as her chauffeur. "We were all sworn to secrecy, but that was really, at that time, his paycheck." The hidden irony was that Revue Productions had hired, for its teen star, a driver with a drinking problem. Nick's alcohol of choice, Bobby learned, was straight vodka, which he would later carry, by the pint, in his toolbox. "He wasn't drunk at first," notes Hyatt, "he was just 'nipping.' " Bobby, who occasionally rode to the studio with Natalie and Maria, had great affection for her father, whom he considered an intelligent, genial man demonized by his wife. "He's the kind of guy you wouldn't even know he was there. He'd smoke a pipe, he'd read his newspaper and drink his vodka and that's it. If you'd just leave him alone, nothing would happen. But Marie would just *naa naa naa*. What she was nagging him about, I have no idea." Occasionally Bobby would hear Nick mutter the word "bitch," "but he would always mumble it when he was drunk, never saying who he was talking about." Bobby's mother, Jean, whom Maria had befriended out of boredom at the studio, pitied Nick for his lowly position in the family hierarchy. "The mother *ruled*, Natalie came next, then the little sister, and the father comes last."

One night Maria provoked Nick, according to Hyatt, "and he just lost it when he was drunk and started throwing things around the house." Nick left in a rage and "smashed up" his car. The next morning, Mud telephoned Jean Hyatt to come over and witness the damage, threatening to divorce Nick. Bobby "couldn't figure out why he hadn't put a hammer in her head years before." Nick eventually sobered up, Mud simmered down, and Natalie's parents continued their dark dance. Natalie never talked about Fahd's drinking to Jimmy Williams, too embarrassed to disclose the family curse to the boy she adored. Nick was a cipher, to Jimmy; an anonymous figure in a back room, someone he avoided. Natalie talked more freely about Fahd to Bobby, for he had witnessed his drunken transgressions, so she couldn't pretend they didn't exist. In Bobby's view, "she loved her father, and she *liked* him as a really nice man." Natalie downplayed the psychodrama in her family even with Bobby, who saw it first-hand. Everything was an illusion in Natalie's world, he noticed, "everything except Natalie. Natalie wasn't an illusion. The people *around* her were the illusion."

The saddest member of the family, to Hyatt's mind, was Natalie's little sister, Lana, then seven, who was like the urchin Natalie played in *Driftwood* come to life. Mud tried to manipulate the series' producers into letting Lana use the studio tutor; when they refused, she simply kept her out of school and Lana wandered aimlessly about the set, carrying a starving hamster in a clear plastic purse. "Lana always looked like she just got out of bed and slipped one of those cheap cotton dresses over her and didn't take a bath," remembers Hyatt. "She was skinny, with stringy hair, and there were stains all over her teeth." Natalie took Lana along if she and Bobby had lunch at DuPar's, an industry hangout down the street. Lana brought her pet hamster, Hyatt recalls, "and she would place this poor, starving animal on the table in front of us. I insisted that she feed it and Nat joined in. Lana would pull a tiny piece of lettuce from her sandwich and place it in her plastic purse. She refused to give the poor little thing any water. I always felt Lana was showing us, through the hamster, how *she* felt." Bobby and Natalie finally refused to eat lunch with Lana unless she took care of the hamster and left it at home. Maria's solution was to keep *Lana* at home, with Nick, who became both chauffeur and babysitter. Natalie later told Bobby that when Lana got home, she put the hamster on her bed, inside the plastic purse, lay down beside it, and watched the hamster slowly die.

Mud knew that she was neglecting Lana, and that Lana "was in the shadow of Natalie, I felt it," she admitted. Not once did Maria feel guilty. Her favoritism was brazen and unapologetic. "If Natalie would tell me to," she said later in life, "I would get the moon for her! I just loved her so much." Lana's feelings for Natalie were schizophrenic. She worshipped her movie star sister, and she envied her for taking their mother from her. "I was usually home by myself because Natalie and my mom were at the studio, or Natalie and my mom were someplace else . . . and I was home." Natalie, by all accounts, treated her kid sister with affection.

The household was a model of dysfunction. The family seldom, if ever, sat down for a meal. Natalie was not required to do any chores; in exchange for her lost childhood, Mud catered to her every domestic whim. Natalie reciprocated with blind adherence to her mother's star-making schemes, staging embarrassing "sick-outs" during *Pride of the Family* whenever Maria wanted to coerce something from the producers. She loved her mother but she was god and monster to Natalie. "I wish she would just let me be a real person," Natalie would say to Bobby.

Jimmy was their battleground. Natalie crawled out windows to see him, possessed by infatuation, thrilled to defy Mud, who figured out what was going on and kept Natalie a virtual prisoner. "Marie was with her *all the time*," remembers Hyatt, who became Natalie's sole companion. "We spent a *lot* of time together, just her and I, especially in the classroom, when the teacher would leave." When they were alone, Natalie started to quiz Bobby about male genitalia, sharing information with him about the female body. "I was thirteen and she was almost fifteen and we spent day after day together, so all this stuff came out. Natalie was totally naïve about sex. She was asking *me*, and I was younger than her." After days of clumsy description, Natalie invited Bobby into her dressing room so she could see for herself. "She wasn't being dirty, she was curious. We were just kids—'I'll show you mine if you show me yours.' In fact, she was so shy that she said she would only show me her breasts." The experiment was cut short by Mud, pounding furiously on Natalie's locked dressing room door. When Maria peered in a side window, Bobby sneaked out the door. Mud apprehended him as he was leaving, calling him a pervert and advising his mother he could not be trusted with Natalie. "Marie had a radar. If Natalie was even *thinking* something, she knew it."

Maria eventually resumed friendly relations with Bobby, though she would not permit him to be alone with Natalie, and often spied on them. One day she took him aside, offering a strange bargain. "She said that if I would promise never to have any kind of physical contact with Natalie, then she would make it up to me in the future." Bobby agreed to the pact, which he considered meaningless, never imagining how Maria one day would fulfill it.

The reason for Mud's crazed vigilance revealed itself to Bobby that spring. "Marie didn't want Natalie to lose her virginity until *she* decided who was going to get it. If

Natalie was going to go to bed with somebody, she wanted it to *count*." Mud's twisted control had already created a deep-seated fear in Natalie about having a baby. Maria wanted Natalie to remain childless so she would always be available to make movies. "I *heard* her mother telling her that if she ever got pregnant, she would die. She would say, 'You're too petite. You're built too small.' " Natalie brought the subject up to Bobby in the classroom, begging him to tell her if her mother was right. "I used to say, 'Well look at *my* mother. She had *me*, and she's exactly the same size, height, and weight as *you* are.' Natalie still doubted it, it was so in her *brain* . . ."

The two teenagers continued their sex discussions on the set, while waiting for their scenes to be lit, knowing that Natalie's mother was too far away to overhear. "She could see our mouths moving," recalls Hyatt, "and she wanted to know what we were talking about." Mud furtively approached the soundman one day, asking him to turn on the overhead microphone and lower it over Natalie and Bobby. "She then listened to our private conversation with earphones. Nat was asking me what my penis looked like when it got hard and that was that. Marie stormed onto the set, grabbed Nat by the arm and marched her to her dressing room, locking the door. She refused to allow the filming to continue until the executive producers came to her dressing room for a meeting. After their meeting, one of the producers took me aside and—with a smile on his face—asked me not to talk to Natalie anymore about sex." To fool Maria, Bobby and Natalie devised code words for parts of the body, so they could continue covertly their teenage fascination with sex. Bobby's code name for penis was "Clyde." "In the morning, Nat would walk into the schoolroom and ask me, 'How's your Clyde?' "

—

By the time *Pride of the Family* debuted on ABC on Friday, October 2, 1953, Mud mysteriously lifted the boycott on Jimmy, permitting Natalie, who had turned fifteen, to go out with him at night. On their first evening date, doubling with another high school couple, Jimmy and Natalie noticed a car with a lone male driver follow them into a drive-in movie and park nearby. "If we'd get out of the car and go to the snack bar, the son-of-a-bitch would get out of the car and follow us." The same man trailed Jimmy and Natalie on subsequent dates to a pizza parlor, inside movie theaters, to drive-ins. "We knew he was there," explains Williams, who ignored the stalker, assuming he was a private detective sent by Natalie's mother. "We weren't doing anything wrong anyway. We wouldn't have done anything different if we *didn't* know he was there." By the sixth date, the Peeping Tom disappeared. Jimmy assumed it was because "there was nothing dirty to report, so her mother wouldn't pay anymore."

A short time later, Jimmy and Natalie and the couple from their double date were playing canasta in Natalie's living room, under the penetrating gaze of her mother, sitting in an adjacent chair. When Mud began to make small talk, mentioning details from the two couples' earlier date, Natalie turned to her in mock surprise. "Oh Mother," she asked innocently, "how'd you know that?" "This went on for several minutes," recalls Williams, until Maria, in the spirit of fun, confessed to having hired a detective. She gave Natalie a mischievous look. "You didn't *know* your mother had a *dick* in her, *did* you?" she grinned, unaware of the double entendre. Jimmy and his male friend forced themselves to keep straight faces. "Man, we didn't even crack a smile. I thought Natalie and her girlfriend were gonna laugh themselves right out of their chairs. I'm not even sure her mother understood what they were laughing about. If she had, there'd have been hell to pay, I can tell you."

Jimmy wondered why Natalie's mother allowed him to date Natalie at all, knowing how stridently she disapproved. According to Lana, her parents "detested" Jimmy, "but Natalie sure liked him." He was the quintessential teen rebel, by the description of Natalie's TV brother, who met Jimmy during filming. "Natalie insisted on bringing him to the studio, and he had motorcycle boots with chains, dirty jeans, leather jacket with a motorcycle club insignia on the back . . ." Jimmy was Natalie's trophy in her contest of wills with Mud, a battle she waged in mother-daughter secrecy. As Bobby noticed, "Natalie never would display any *public* displeasure with a family member. I know that behind closed doors things went on, especially when she really wanted to get mad at her mother: she would excuse everybody, or excuse herself, and take her mother in the other room and in privacy they would go at it." Natalie bleached her hair blond during her summer of love with Jimmy, a further statement of her restless youth.

The fact that Mrs. Gurdin might have a hidden agenda in permitting him to date Natalie began to enter Jimmy's mind that Thanksgiving when Natalie was invited to ride in the Santa Claus Lane Parade and her mother asked Jimmy to walk down Hollywood Boulevard, next to Natalie's float. "It was almost like a command performance. I had to be there, and I had to walk that parade, until she got off that float." Mud was aware that if anyone bothered Natalie with Jimmy around, "there wasn't much of anything I wouldn't do, honestly." When Republic began to arrange publicity dates for Natalie to promote their new television series, Maria sent Jimmy along "as a third leg."

After Natalie and her studio date would arrive at an event, "they'd take some photographs and that was the end of it, and then Natalie and I went and did our thing." One evening, the studio sent the limousine to pick up Jimmy ahead of Natalie. He got into the back of the car with Natalie's escort, a handsome young actor being promoted as the next heartthrob. On the way to Natalie's, the sex symbol to millions of girls moved in closer to Jimmy, running his fingers up Jimmy's jeans. "I did a lot of hitchhiking, and these idiots would pick me up, and the instant they put their hand on my leg I'd say, 'Stop the car.' " Jimmy kept his distance from Natalie's "date" for the rest of the night, guarding him*self* more than Natalie; observing ruefully as photographers took pictures of the young Hollywood couple out for a "romantic" evening.

Jimmy sensed, after a while, that Maria was using him. "I think she manipulated me in some of the things that she wanted me to do for Natalie's protection." What Mud hadn't counted on was the depth of their teen romance, something Mary Ann noticed at once. "This was like the storybooks . . . you know how two people look at each other and there are stars in their eyes?" Jimmy and Natalie behaved as if they were under a spell. "She was *special*," is the way he would still describe Natalie years into the future. "She was an absolute joy—humorous, spontaneous, not stuck up at all. We'd come up with some of the raunchiest jokes that you'd ever want to hear." The instant Natalie got home from filming the series, she and Jimmy were typical teenagers in love. "That was work time. When we went out, that was party time." Since Jimmy's license had been suspended, Natalie used her permit to drive them on dates, giving the wheel to Jimmy to park the car. He was a jazz fan, and took Natalie to jam sessions, introducing her to

Benny Goodman. "She loved to go to movies, and we'd go to a lot of movies, and she'd get caught up in them and get very emotional. She'd play the part as we were watching the movie." When there was a mistake, Natalie spotted it. "The tears would be coming down her eyes, and all of a sudden she'd say, 'Look at that,' and she'd see the microphone on screen, or a shadow on the wall, something that was out of whack."

There was one movie Natalie did not take Jimmy to see. Sometime after Christmas, she arranged for her mother and Jean Hyatt to take her and Bobby to a matinee of *Beneath the Twelve-Mile Reef*, starring Robert Wagner, the beautiful contract player she had passed on the Fox lot when she was eleven. In the four and a half years since Natalie had taped his eight-by-ten glossy to her bedroom wall, Wagner, now nearly twenty-four, had inched his way up the ranks of Fox bit players. His break came the year before in *With a Song in My Heart*, starring Susan Hayward as Jane Froman, a singer crippled in an airplane accident who performed for American troops. Wagner played a shell-shocked paratrooper in a wheelchair seen in the audience as Hayward performs the title song for a battalion of disabled soldiers. Although his face appeared on screen for only a few moments, something in Wagner's poignant expression as he reacted to Hayward touched a chord, "and people went out of *Song* asking, 'Who was that guy?' " The studio began to receive five thousand letters a week for Wagner from infatuated teenage girls, motivating Fox to cast him in larger parts. *Beneath the Twelve-Mile Reef* was Wagner's first romantic lead, distinguished mainly for his movie star looks and the illusion of an off-camera romance with his leading lady, starlet Terry Moore, who played along with the publicity, even though she was secretly involved with middle-aged millionaire Howard Hughes.

Natalie was ecstatic to see her fantasy husband starring in a movie, pulling Bobby aside excitedly after the matinee to find out what he thought of Robert Wagner. "I just went to the movie because Natalie and I were becoming very good friends and she was fun to be with . . . I didn't realize that she had this plan: she wanted to get my opinion about him." Bobby was brutal in the manner of fourteen-year-old boys. "I told her that Wagner was a stiff and awkward actor with a fake voice and he looked like a pretty-boy fruit ball. She punched me in the ribs and announced that she was going to marry him." "Well then, what'd you ask me for?" Bobby teased back.

By January 1954, Natalie's relationship with Jimmy had become so intense they worried about the power they held over each other. Natalie sought guidance from her sister Olga, who seemed to be preparing her for some fatalistic, bittersweet denouement, consistent with the reckless undertone of their teen love affair. "Olga didn't try to get her to break up with me, she just told her that it would come to an end, and that that wasn't bad—that we all have relationships at that age and they generally end, and the first relationship that you have like that, you never forget." Natalie took Olga's words to heart as if they were an omen. "She told me that, I can tell you, a dozen times . . . that her sister told her that it was going to end, but she'd never forget it."

Mud tried to frighten Natalie from having sex with Jimmy by instilling irrational fears, most of them related to Natalie's size, repeating the caveat that she would die if she gave birth. Maria offered horror stories of her own teen abortions in China as illustrations, lending a pseudolegitimacy to her ghoulish claims. She warned Natalie that if she had sex with a well-endowed male, she was so petite the penis would puncture her internal organs. "Whatever it took," affirms Mary Ann. "Oh, 'Mama' was very good at that. Anything she could dream of." Even at fifteen, Mary Ann understood why Natalie's mother was stigmatizing sex, and why she tried to obstruct Jimmy. She wanted Natalie under her control, at home, making movies, "because you see, 'Mommy' was living through Natalie." And Natalie was supporting her.

When Jimmy dropped out of eleventh grade in January, frustrated by an undiagnosed reading disorder, Mud's paranoia reached crisis proportions. Natalie's TV brother witnessed showdowns on the *Pride of the Family* set, when Jimmy would show up to see Natalie and she "terrorized her mother that she was going to go into her dressing room and lose her virginity." Natalie told Bobby she sometimes sneaked out to see Jimmy, until one night "her mother caught her crawling out the window. That was the end of that. That boy was forbidden." Despite Mud's dire warnings, Natalie had lost her virginity to the boy who cut off her pigtails, forfeiting the prize her mother was hoping to offer to some powerful Hollywood player. Natalie hid her phobias about sex when she was with Jimmy, though she talked to him about how worried she was about getting pregnant. "But there was no chance that she would. We made sure."

As the teen romance escalated, Mud offered to buy Natalie's best friend Mary Ann "whatever she wanted" if she could help break them apart. The relationship spun wildly, fueled by Maria's attempts to suppress it. Jimmy, who was not quite seventeen, and Natalie, still fifteen, secretly talked about marriage. She told him she wanted a family, and children, how much she wanted to get away from her mother. Jimmy was crazy in love, willing to do anything, less concerned than Natalie by Olga's warning they were "too close." He gave Natalie an engagement ring in February and she accepted it, though they didn't have specific plans when they were getting married. "At that age," he posits, "how do you think that far?" He was prepared to elope, knowing Natalie's parents would be opposed to their engagement. "I'd have married her in a heartbeat."

When Natalie wore her engagement ring home, the situation took on an electrical charge. "That's when it started. Her mother saw the way it was going, and she couldn't tolerate that." Maria's plans for "Natalie Wood," her movie star alter ego, did not include a domestic life as a dairy farmer's bride. She and Natalie had the confrontation of their lives. Afterward, Natalie drove Mud to the dairy where Jimmy worked. Mud stayed in the car while Natalie walked up to Jimmy, handing him her engagement ring. "She made her give it back to me." Jimmy looked over at Natalie's mother, who was watching from the car to make sure Natalie returned the ring. "I went out and challenged her. I told her I loved Natalie, and I was going to marry her whether she liked it or not, and she couldn't do anything about it." Maria "just sat there and listened."

As he watched Natalie and her mother drive away from the dairy farm, Jimmy had a foreboding. "I'm not sure what Natalie thought, but I think I knew that there was no chance that we'd ever marry. I didn't think her parents would ever allow it. And we were both too young, we just couldn't run off and get married, that's not practical. And I am and I was a realist, and I probably knew it was coming to an end."

Sometime in March, the high school boy who double-dated with Jimmy and Natalie approached Jimmy. "He asked me if he could take Natalie out, that she needed to go out with other people." Jimmy realized it was a setup by Natalie's mother, "and I got so mad I almost took his head off." Jimmy suspected, at that point, the future he and Natalie had planned "would never happen." A few nights later, Natalie went out with Jimmy on what was to be their last date. "She told me that night that she needed to date other people." Natalie was strangely silent; Jimmy eerily calm. "It didn't break off in a *mean* way. For whatever reason, it had come to an end, and I realized that."

According to Olga, Natalie almost eloped with Jimmy. "I said, 'Well, do you really want that kind of a life? Is that something you want to try doing? Living on a farm?' " Natalie returned the ring, relates her sister, because she didn't have enough money to elope. "All she had was an allowance." In Mary Ann's assessment, Natalie was not *strong* enough to break away from her mother, as Olga had done. "Jimmy came to the cause, and he stood up to 'Mama.' Even at that age, he had the character and the stuff to do it." Natalie was too kind to hurt her mother, her friend believed. She avoided conflict, Lana noticed; one of the consequences of seeing their mother run through the house, screaming, as their father chased after her, drunk, waving a gun.

At fifteen, Natalie had little choice but to capitulate to Mud, who restricted her from any further contact with Jimmy. Bobby Hyatt was spectator to a "huge fight" between them over Jimmy outside Natalie's dressing room, a battle in which Maria prevailed. In the final analysis, Natalie had too many fears, too deeply instilled, to overcome Maria, even for Jimmy. According to school friends, she was devastated.

Jimmy went home from their final date, found a rifle, and tried to kill himself. The blast was nearly fatal, leaving him with permanent physical damage and another scandalous headline. Mud refused to let Natalie see him. "It was a terrible thing. The whole thing was so horrible," as Mary Ann relates. Natalie blamed herself. "I mean you go through all these awful—the guilt and the this and the that. She couldn't have done anything, it was beyond her control. What could she do?" Mary Ann held Maria culpable. "Of course *I* never got along with the mother anyway. But boy, she wasn't gonna have any of that messing around. If she would have just let it alone, it probably would have burned itself out, part of growing up, first love."

Jimmy joined the service and left town, marrying a girl he met that year in Kentucky, using the ring he intended for Natalie. He stopped by Natalie's house once more, that August, to get his collection of Benny Goodman records. Maria brought them to the driveway, as Jimmy waited outside. He never saw Natalie again. "I cut it off. I had to. It wasn't any good for me, it wasn't any good for her." As years passed, they would both protect their first love. When Natalie became a movie star, realizing her mother's dream, she would tell journalists she "never dated a high school boy," guarding her relationship with Jimmy as something private. Jimmy kept his suicide attempt over Natalie a secret through forty-five years of marriage, two children and two grandchildren he "wouldn't trade for anything, even Natalie, as much as I loved her." In her yearbook inscription to Jimmy in 1953, the first time they were kept apart by her mother, Natalie foreshadowed how the relationship would end. She wrote:

Jim—

It's kind of hard to write what you want to say on the annual of someone you like very much, so I'll just wish you all the luck in the world, always, because I think that you're the best guy in Van Nuys. The best in the world. Always be as fine as you are, Jimmy, and I hope that your life will be smooth, filled with happiness, and may your every wish become true.

I'll never forget the wonderful times I've had with you.

Yours always for more fun,
All my love, Natalie

Natalie's broken love affair with Jimmy was "like a movie script," Mary Ann would later comment. It paralleled, almost eerily, the story of Deanie and Bud, the star-crossed high school sweethearts Natalie and Warren Beatty would play six years later in *Splendor in the Grass*.

12

NATALIE'S LIFE MIGHT HAVE turned out differently if she had not been forced to end her engagement to Jimmy. She was bored with the series and had little interest in being an actress. "I kept thinking that each year might be the last. I would get up every morning and go to the studio—what else did any kid do? was all I thought, if I thought about it, which I didn't." Natalie's fantasies involved Jimmy, and having a family. "Her mother disturbed all those dreams," observes Mary Ann. According to a later boyfriend, Natalie "loathed" Mud for years for "ruining her life. Her mother just said, 'You *do* this or else.' Whatever the 'or else' was, I'm not sure."

After Jimmy left town, Natalie staged a coup, telling

Mud, "*I* earn the money and *I'm* going to do what I want from now on." The two arrived at a Faustian understanding implicit in their relationship from then on: Natalie would dedicate herself to becoming a star, and Mud would permit her to come and go as she pleased, do what she pleased, with whom she pleased. Bobby Hyatt observed the shift in power, as Natalie approached her sixteenth birthday. "That's when she really started to rebel." She took up cigarettes, a classical form of teenage rebellion, though in Natalie's case, they served a dual purpose, "quieting my nerves," she said later.

Natalie's "nerves" were becoming a problem. She was developing insomnia after years of being afraid to sleep alone, talking to dolls. Her drowning nightmares continued. Jimmy had noticed she needed "to be around people," but was unaware of what Mary Ann knew, that Natalie was incapable of functioning on her own. With Jimmy gone, Natalie's daredevil behavior ended forever. She reverted to her childhood fears of airplanes, fast cars, heights, doctors, thunderstorms, earthquakes, snakes, sharks, large male sex organs, childbirth, gypsy superstitions, kidnappers—and drowning, the one phobia even Jimmy could not temporarily exorcise. Her mother, the underlying cause of her neuroses, continued to hold a power over Natalie, to Mary Ann's frustration. "You have to get to the point where you finally make a decision to stop letting people hurt you, but Natalie believed all the fictional things about motherhood and this wonderful love, and she wanted to think that of *her* mother." She and Mary Ann made an appointment for Natalie to see a psychiatrist, but went ice-skating instead, "so that was our therapy." Natalie used Mary Ann as "a sounding board, and I think it helped her a little bit."

Natalie began to wear heavy makeup, despite portraying a "typical" teenager on television. Mud's only stipulation was that she look *pretty*. Natalie was meticulous about her appearance, cognizant from her mother's constant reminders that she had an "image" to uphold. "She was almost sixteen years old, and she was getting all this fan mail from kids around the world saying, 'Oh you're beautiful,' and she was totally upset because she had no breasts," her sitcom brother recalls. Before one of their scenes together, Natalie took Bobby into her dressing room, sharing a secret: a bra that inflated by blowing through a straw. "Blow 'em up real big," Bobby coaxed. When they were called to the set, Natalie put her hot-air bosom on, under a tight sweater. "As we're walking through this dim area to get to the soundstage, all of a sudden Marie comes out of the shadows, making growling noises in a Russian accent . . . that was the end of the blow-up bra." Natalie reluctantly let the air out of her inflatable breasts and did the scene "like a little soldier." In desperation, she began to stuff napkins from the craft service table down her brassiere, acutely self-conscious of her small chest. "Finally, she and her mother made a compromise. Her mother bought her foam rubber breasts with a little nipple that she fit inside her bra," recalls Hyatt. Filming was delayed for half an hour one day when Bobby "stole one of her tits."

Natalie refused to let Bobby see her deformed left wrist, destroying publicity stills from the TV series where the bone was visible. "I told her it was all in her mind and tried to get her to go in front of the camera without a bracelet for *one day*, just to try it out. She started to, but as soon as somebody else came into the dressing room, she grabbed her bracelet and put it back on." "Don't talk to me about it anymore," she told Bobby sullenly, and left the room. He never saw Natalie's left wrist again.

Two of Natalie's other closely held secrets were nearly exposed in early April, when Fahd was in a head-on collision driving her to the studio, demolishing the Republic limousine. The accident made Louella Parsons' gossip column, where she reported that Natalie "walked away from the studio car without a scratch." Parsons did not mention the chauffeur was Natalie's father, or that he had a history of alcohol-related car accidents. Bobby shrugged it off as "one of Nick's wrecks," but Fahd's driver's license was temporarily suspended, reducing his job description to babysitter, an ignominious turn of events that plummeted Natalie's father deeper into vodka.

Later that month, Natalie dragged her pal Bobby to another Robert Wagner movie, the highly anticipated *Prince Valiant*, with Wagner in the title role, dressed in medieval tights and a Dutch Boy hairpiece. The expensive costume drama, costarring Janet Leigh, was expected to make Wagner a star. Instead, the picture received bad notices and Wagner was ridiculed for "reading his lines in a vacant monotone . . . with the skittish air of a man trying to be funny in a lady's hat," wrote a *New Yorker* critic. Bobby ribbed Natalie about her "boyfriend with the bad wig," which Wagner himself would later poke fun at, calling it his "Bette Davis look." Natalie and a million other girls swooned anyway, preserving Wagner's status as a teen heartthrob. Since she had lost her *real* love, Jimmy, Natalie fixated on her screen idol, determining that she was going to marry Robert Wagner. She came up with a plan to fire Famous Artists and hire Wagner's agent, Henry Willson, so he could introduce her to her future husband. "That was her *mission*," declares Jean Hyatt, who witnessed

Natalie in countless conversations trying to persuade her mother to sign Willson, hearing about it later from Maria, who vigorously opposed the idea.

Henry Willson, Wagner's agent, was a powerful Hollywood veteran with cultivated tastes, and a well-known homosexual. He had acquired a reputation in the industry for "discovering" Adonis-like young men and sculpting them into stars, usually changing their names, often to something absurdly rugged such as "Rock" Hudson, Tab "Hunter," or "Guy" Madison. Some of the would-be actors Willson represented were heterosexual, but a disproportionate number were homosexual, bisexual, or "cooperated" with Willson "to get gigs," in the observation of Natalie's costar Bobby Hyatt, who competed against them for parts. If a young, handsome actor had Henry Willson for an agent, "it was almost assumed he was gay, like it was written across his forehead," recalls Ann Doran, one of Willson's few female clients, who said, "Henry was a pretty boy." Maria was suspicious of homosexuals, according to Hyatt, a voyeur to Natalie's campaign to hire Willson. "Mrs. Gurdin thought that it wasn't manly—if you're going to be a man, be a man; if you're going to be a woman, be a woman. She was from that school. Her nickname for Clifton Webb, who was a big character actor at that time and a friend of Wagner's, was The King of the Faggots. She did not like Henry Willson *at all*." Since Willson showed little interest in representing Natalie, and Mud displayed less in hiring him, Natalie's scheme to meet Wagner was temporarily thwarted.

She and her mother prowled for movie roles for the summer hiatus, hoping to get Natalie off *Pride of the Family*, which she considered "dreadful." Natalie was too polite to reveal her displeasure to anyone other than Bobby, though Fay Wray, her mother on the series, sensed her "underlying restlessness," and how much "she wanted to be thought of as older." Despite the mischief she got into with Bobby, Natalie as always was the consummate professional. Wray would have "the very tenderest memories" of her from their scenes together, commenting on the same "delicate, vulnerable quality" that Orson Welles had perceived when Natalie was six, which Wray observed from "the look of her and her uncanny ability."

Natalie tested in May for a part in a Greer Garson movie for Warner Brothers called *Strange Lady in Town*. While she was on the lot, director Victor Saville and an executive named William Orr noticed her, struck by the fact that she was maturing. Both Saville and Orr thought of casting her in Saville's next picture, *The Silver Chalice*, a big-budget Greco-Roman epic. Bobby auditioned for a role around the same time, mentioning to Natalie there might be a part for her. Virginia Mayo had already been cast in a leading role as Helena, a glamorous temptress. Saville hired Natalie to play Mayo's character in her youth, as a slave girl. The fact that Mayo was a voluptuous blonde and Natalie a waif brunette did not deter Saville, or Natalie, who ambitiously dyed her hair ash blond, unconcerned that her character on *Pride of the Family* would inexplicably appear with a different hair color in the last few episodes. All that mattered to Natalie was that she was back in movies, even though it was a small role. Mud was scheming to upgrade that ranking.

The two went to Warners off and on throughout May, fitting Natalie for her Grecian costumes, screen-testing her blond hair to match Mayo's. One day while they were at the commissary, Frank Sinatra walked in, preparing for his next picture, *Young at Heart*. Sinatra either approached Natalie, or her mother sent her over to introduce herself. Maria lunged at the opportunity for Natalie to meet Sinatra, who had just won an Academy Award for *From Here to Eternity*, increasing his status in Hollywood. Sinatra was taken with Natalie, and got "a kick" out of Maria, inviting them to a party at his house. Mud eagerly accepted, whispering to Natalie afterward that she would let her go alone, urging Natalie to get close to Sinatra "because it would be good for her career." Mud had no qualms that he was separated from his wife, the tempestuous Ava Gardner, or that he was thirty-eight to Natalie's fifteen. "Her mother was a pimp," as Scott Marlowe, Natalie's later boyfriend, brutally assessed. Lana was too young to know about their mother pushing Natalie onto Sinatra, but "that wouldn't surprise me. To my mom, if you were a movie star, then you were valuable."

Natalie returned to the classroom at Republic, spilling her amazing secret to her TV brother, who recalls, "Natalie *herself* could not even believe this permission," jumping at the chance "to do something without her mother." She shared the confidence with Mary Ann, who was astonished even Maria would send Natalie alone, at fifteen, to a party at Frank Sinatra's house. "She literally threw her to the lions." The day after the party, Natalie arrived at the studio school embarrassed, telling Bobby she had something to confess. Natalie had consumed quantities of wine at Sinatra's house, and in the course of the evening, told Sinatra about "Clyde," the code name for penis Bobby had coined to fool Natalie's mother. Sinatra was so amused, he and his friends had incorporated "Clyde" into their hipster slang. Natalie felt guilty because *she* had taken credit for the word. "Here's the kind of person Natalie was. She said that my friendship was very important to her. She was going to see Sinatra that evening, and if I wanted, she would *tell* Sinatra that I invented the word." Bobby laughed it off. Some months later, he turned on the radio and heard Sinatra singing a tune called "Clyde's Song." The singer was quoted in magazines saying Clyde was his "code word" for someone he didn't trust. "Sinatra and his Rat Pack gang started using the 'Clyde' word in their Vegas act. Even JFK was saying the code word. I should have copyrighted it."

Natalie became a regular at Sinatra's that May and June, according to Hyatt, who saw her at studio school every day, keeping her secret. "I remember one Friday Natalie just couldn't wait to get out of there. She kept looking at her watch, dancing up and down, saying, 'I have to get to the hairdresser and look really beautiful tonight because—don't tell anybody—I'm going back to Frank Sinatra's house. They're having a party and I can't wait to get up there.' It was a big deal to her. Everybody was up there—Dean Martin, the Rat Pack, all the big stars, all way older than her. She was probably the only person under thirty there except for maybe some of the dancing girls from Las Vegas. I guarantee you she was the only fifteen-year-old there."

There was a mysterious, illicit quality to Natalie's relationship with Sinatra, from the point of view of Bobby, her brother-confessor. "When I asked her what was up between her and Sinatra, she said her mother told her not to say anything because if word got out that she was spending evenings at his house, it would ruin everything. I was sworn to secrecy." Bobby believed that Natalie and Sinatra were having an affair. "There was something fishy, because her mother told her not to talk to anybody about it because she was underage. I knew something was going on, because this was the first time Natalie ever told me she couldn't *tell* me something." Bobby's suspicions were confirmed in his mind when Natalie suddenly lost interest in their teenage sexual explorations. "All that stopped. No more questions about sex, no more discussions, no fooling around." Natalie "became kind of distant—not as a joking-around friend, but if I would bring up sex, she would say, 'No no no, I don't want to talk about it.' Until the Sinatra thing, Natalie was completely naïve."

Bobby's intuition about Sinatra and Natalie was probably correct, affirms her high school friend Mary Ann, who worried about Natalie. "Thank goodness, he was a nice guy . . . and you know, he was fun." Sinatra, who was devastated over his doomed, fiery marriage to Ava Gardner, found tender-hearted Natalie a soothing balm, in Mary Ann's view. "You know, he had his share of problems. Natalie always had an ear, and she could always listen. And when *she* said, 'Can I do anything to help?' she really meant it." Natalie's code words and teen giddiness were a distraction for the moody Sinatra. He said later, "She gave me the feeling that she was always glad to be alive. That she was a happy kind of a human being, and she exuded a lot of happiness when she was with you. She giggled a lot. She loved to laugh."

Natalie and Sinatra formed a fascination with each other from these early encounters that would persist for years, at times romantically, occasionally while they were in relationships with other people. Sinatra would assume the role of Natalie's "Godfather" protector the rest of his life—even after Natalie drowned, when he would intervene in classic Sinatra style.

Mary Ann and Bobby, the friends who knew of Natalie's teen liaison with Sinatra, held her mother responsible for setting her up with the married, nearly forty-year-old star. "Mrs. Gurdin was really pushing Natalie and the Sinatra thing," as Hyatt recalls. Actor Scott Marlowe, who became Natalie's boyfriend two years later, describes her then as "easily seduced," suggesting the worldly Sinatra "probably taught her a lot."

Her mother's willingness to do anything to advance Natalie's career finally pushed the volatile Mary Ann to the breaking point the summer of Sinatra, when Mrs. Gurdin took the two high school girls aside, whispering that she could arrange abortions for them. Maria told her friend Jean Hyatt she had frightened Natalie into believing she would die if she had a baby, explaining to Jean why she did it. "That was Marie's way of lying to Natalie, because . . . she wanted her to always be ready to make another picture. I don't think Marie wanted Natalie to get pregnant no matter *who* Natalie was married to. I'm not saying that she didn't love her—she did. That's all Marie thought about, is promoting Natalie."

From that point on, relates Mary Ann, "her mother and I got into it regularly." As a classmate recalls, "Mary Ann was like a grown woman in high school . . . you didn't want to get into a verbal altercation with her, because she'd just tell you off flat in one second. Natalie was a softer kind of a person." When Natalie needed to get away from home, Mary Ann was her hot line. "She would call me and whisper, 'Please come over and we'll go back to your house.' " Natalie acknowledged the debt in Mary Ann's yearbook, dedicating a page to "the most beautiful gal I know," writing, "Sometimes, when I've been sort've down in the dumps, 'funny ol' you' has always kidded me out of it." Almost wistfully, she added, "Maybe next semester I will be back at Van Nuys [High] and you and I will see lots more of each other then." It was signed "Nat."

The effect of being thrown into the adult world of Frank Sinatra, with her mother offering abortions, manifested itself in a dramatic change in Natalie's lifestyle. She smoked heavily and acquired a new adult habit, alcohol. Press releases that July from Warner Brothers, where she and Sinatra were filming their respective movies, quoted Natalie "wanting everyone to know she is ready to play sexy parts." She was frustrated playing the *younger* version of Mayo's sultry character in *The Silver Chalice*. "I had ambitions to don a frilly gown by Don Loper and a silver blue mink and embrace Cary Grant in my arms before the cameras." Paul Newman, who was making his film debut as the lead in *The Silver Chalice* after an acclaimed performance on Broadway, would remember the "marvelous sense of mystery" that Natalie projected at fifteen. She was determined to appear as sophisticated as her life had unnaturally become, identifying herself as seventeen in Warners publicity, modeling in a bathing suit at a Gem Show to cultivate a sexier image. What remained of Natalie's girlhood had vanished in a summer.

She made several new friends, one of them the delicate actress Pier Angeli, who was in *The Silver Chalice*. Another was Margaret O'Brien, the legendary child actress whose look Mud had purloined when the Gurdins arrived in Hollywood. By an irony, Natalie, driven by Mud's ambition, was now working more steadily than O'Brien, whose amazing popularity had dimmed in adolescence. Although Margaret was seventeen to Natalie's fifteen, she had lived a sheltered life in the confines of her studio, MGM, and was kept further sequestered by her rigidly conservative mother. "Margaret was sweet and kind and very naïve about life and people," as a girlfriend of Natalie's recalls. An actor who spent time with them both then states, "Natalie had pizzazz. Margaret was more withdrawn. Very ladylike. If you were to say 'pooey,' it would be a bad word. Natalie was a little more loose and Margaret was—let's say strung a little tighter."

What they had in common was a childhood lost to Hollywood, with their mothers controlling them every hour of the day—although they never discussed their child star pasts, according to O'Brien, who had enjoyed that period in her life and believed Natalie did too. Natalie had fully embraced her mother's dream by the time she met Margaret, and was consumed with becoming a famous movie star. "She was very ambitious with her career and Hollywood, and I guess I had at that time experienced a little bit more stardom, so I wasn't as gung-ho on it as she was. She was very driven. Even if we were out, or having a good time, if a call came to go on an interview, she'd drop everything and go." Natalie never mentioned her TV series to Margaret, which was being considered for renewal that summer. "It was like it didn't exist. She wanted to be a film actress." Both of the dark-haired former child stars idolized Vivien Leigh. "She's the only person I ever wanted to meet and get an autograph from," states O'Brien. "We tried to copy her." Natalie wore one of Leigh's dresses from *A Streetcar Named Desire* to a masquerade party, arriving as Blanche du Bois, the role she desperately wanted to play. "I remember she went to the studio and got it," said a chum, "and she was the exact same measurements as Vivien Leigh."

On July 13, a week before Natalie turned sixteen, Irving Pichel died under circumstances as murky as his purported attempt to adopt her. There were whispers within his family that the sixty-three-year-old director's jealous wife,

Violette, had procrastinated in getting his heart medication to him. After his death, his widow destroyed all of Pichel's papers related to his films. Natalie did not attend her mentor's funeral, which was private, though many years later when she met Pichel's son Marlowe, "she made it clear she was very devoted to my dad and very grateful for what he'd done for her." Maria took immediate advantage of Pichel's demise by further embellishing the myth she had created of how Natalie became a child star. She told a periodical associated with *Parents* magazine that Irving Pichel had simply appeared at their door in Santa Rosa while he was directing *Happy Land*, offering Maria a small part and giving Natasha the nickname "Cinderella," sending her a telegram two years later begging her to be in *Tomorrow Is Forever*. Natalie implicitly endorsed her mother's tall tale about her and Pichel, posing for pictures with Lana in the same magazine, further blurring the hazy line between fantasy and reality in her increasingly make-believe life.

The sense of illusion carried over to her sixteenth birthday, when Natalie was reported to be eighteen in Louella Parsons' column, which now mentioned the names of whoever she was dating as gossip items. Natalie's sweet-sixteen present from Mud and Fahd, paid for with her earnings, was a pink Thunderbird convertible. "She couldn't wait to show that T-Bird to me," recalls Jackie Eastes, a former student at Van Nuys High who was getting close to Natalie. "She picked me up at my house and we cruised Van Nuys Boulevard, ending up at Bob's Big Boy, the Valley hangout. We used to go to Bob's and she had bacon-tomato-avocado-and-lettuce sandwiches." It was rare for Natalie to make a new friend from high school, where "most of the girls were thrilled when she left school to do another film," intimidated by her fame. Jackie, a star-struck strawberry blonde, clung to her celebrity classmate like a trail of perfume, "living through her life vicariously."

To Jackie, Natalie was a goddess inhabiting a glittering world. When she spent a Friday night with Natalie, they would get up late and go out to lunch in Natalie's T-Bird convertible. After lunch, Natalie would shop. "That was a major production. She'd go to the House of Seven and Nine and she'd spend eight hundred to nine hundred dollars in one afternoon buying clothes. That was a lot of money, when you consider I worked all week as an usher at a movie theater for fourteen dollars a week." The instant Natalie got her unrestricted license, she became a fixture at every popular restaurant in Hollywood and the Valley, stopping first in her pink Thunderbird to pick up Jackie. "She would take me out, because she knew I couldn't afford it. We had breakfast, lunch and dinners out." Unlike Mary Ann, who had a healthy disdain for Hollywood, Jackie at times felt that it was "tough being with someone like Natalie, who was beautiful, famous—and thin, too. Who could eat anything she wanted and never put on a pound. I wore a size twelve, if I was lucky. She was perfectly proportioned, and very tiny—ninety-five pounds."

Jackie found it impossible to resent Natalie, even though she believed Natalie had it all. "You couldn't know Natalie and not adore her. She was extremely warm and open. She was friendly, she was funny, she was witty. I'll never forget her infectious laugh. It was probably the best time in my life, knowing her." Natalie's consuming obsession with her career fostered her new friendship with Jackie, who idolized movie stars and tacitly supported Natalie's goal: "Achieving stardom was all she lived for."

—

The week Natalie turned sixteen, her family moved from Northridge to a cozy house set diagonally on a winding curve at the top of Valley Vista, "which at the time was the best address to have in the Valley." The Gurdins' new home was south of Ventura in suburban Sherman Oaks, closer to Van Nuys High, and to Hollywood. Natalie chose wallpaper with tiny pink roses for her bedroom, to match her T-Bird, choosing fabrics in shades of pink chintz. "She was going through her pink phase. The room was decorated in pink, the car was pink, everything was pink."

She appeared in public steeped in the sort of glamour she and Mud associated with movie stars, driving around town in her convertible T-Bird, secretly smoking Kool menthol cigarettes with Dunhill's crystal filters, reeking of Jungle Gardenia by Tuvaché, her new signature scent, cultivating the image of a Hollywood star. If there was a chance anyone might see her, "she always had to present herself in a certain fashion," recalls Lana, who watched, fascinated, as her big sister transformed herself into the star, "Natalie Wood": putting on her makeup, coiffing her hair, covering her imperfect wrist with a bracelet, dripping in borrowed mink and Jungle Gardenia. "I'm sure a great deal of it was perpetuated by my mom," attests Lana, "who felt you had to look a certain way or you were unacceptable."

Maria's fantasies of becoming a movie star had successfully transferred to Natalie. "She loved everything to do with stardom," relates Margaret O'Brien. "She just loved the life. The glamour and the going to premieres and all that." Jerry Eastes, Jackie's handsome older brother, escorted Natalie to a movie premiere that summer. "She wore long white leather gloves and a white mink stole, and her hair was done up in a French roll," recalls Jackie, who watched out the window, wishing that she could be

Natalie, stepping into a limousine sent by Warner Brothers. "She was beautiful in a full-length, strapless ice-blue satin sheath with a peplum that formed a train to the floor."

Natalie drew Margaret O'Brien out of her shell, coaxing the reserved actress, who had seldom been anywhere without her mother or a chaperone, to go dancing at trendy nightspots like Peter Potter's, taking Margaret to jazz clubs to hear Al Hirt. "She kind of got me going out," credits O'Brien, who remembers Natalie being "all excited to see a movie star." Natalie had taken on other characteristics of her star-worshipping mother. When she went to a movie with Margaret, "she would go up and say, 'We're in the movies and I'm Natalie Wood,' and she got us in all the movies free." Her celebrity status provided Natalie an entrée in restaurants to smoke and to drink alcohol, infractions that would have gotten her expelled from Van Nuys High School.

O'Brien's lasting image of Natalie at sixteen is in a nightclub, a mink stole thrown over her shoulder, smoking from a long cigarette holder, balancing a cocktail in a gloved hand, laughing gaily, the center of attention of every male in the room.

Natalie reminded her school friend Jackie of Scarlett O'Hara in *Gone With the Wind*—"Boys followed her around like puppy dogs." Natalie's boyfriends ranged from high school football players like Jackie's brother Jerry, to fun-loving "All-American young men" such as Sonny Belcher, a sound technician at Fox, or Bob Allen, a college student preparing to go into the Army.

One beau, Rad Fulton, a darkly handsome aspiring actor of nineteen, gave Natalie the nickname "Squirt." She exuded effervescence and the promise of a good time, like bubbles in a glass of champagne. "All she wanted to do is laugh," he recalls. "We never talked about careers, we just had fun with each other."

Natalie generously passed her old boyfriends to Margaret, encouraging her demure friend to break away from her dominating mother. "Mrs. Gurdin didn't have much control over Natalie. When she wanted to go out, she went out, if she wanted to meet a boyfriend, she met one. Natalie could never understand my mother. She'd say, 'We could be better friends if your mother wasn't so strict.' " O'Brien eventually became serious about one of Natalie's hand-me-down beaus, Bob Allen, marrying him in 1959. She acknowledges, "Natalie kind of helped me grow up."

As teens, Margaret marveled that Natalie had negotiated her freedom. Bob Allen, the boyfriend they shared, was witness to a "scene" between Natalie and her mother over a curfew, during which their arrangement post-Jimmy was revealed. "Natalie said something about, 'I make the money in this family so you be quiet.' "

Her girlfriend Jackie, who spent a lot of time at the Gurdins', thought Natalie's relationship with her mother was strange. "I never, ever saw them fight in the house. It was like there was no emotion whatsoever. If they did have screaming, hollering fights it wasn't in front of me. The whole family revolved around Natalie, because she was the breadwinner. That was a very strange position for a young person to be in."

Despite Natalie's personal liberation, Mud retained some control, for Natalie occasionally asked Jackie to act as a "beard" while she went on dates. "Her mother would think that she was out with me, and she wasn't of course. I would leave with her and do my thing, and then come back and pick her up." Mud continued to keep Natalie under her surveillance. "I tried to stay out of Mrs. Gurdin's way,"

Jackie asserts, "because she was always nosing into everything. And she always had to know where Natalie was and what she was doing. She was like a police person."

Rad Fulton, Natalie's actor boyfriend, found Mrs. Gurdin "so tough she was like nails" when he picked up Natalie. "I never spent more than two minutes around her mother. She was very, very difficult. Very protective."

Mud's true stronghold over Natalie was psychological. Even when Natalie was out of the house, Jackie noticed, "she'd check with her mother ten times a day." Maria had woven herself into her daughter's persona so intricately, neither could exist without the other, a codependency even Natalie's teen anarchy could not extinguish.

Late in August, Natalie spent the night at Margaret O'Brien's house, an experience she found unsettling. As she later told former child actor Dickie Moore, "I was in a very rebellious phase, feeling that my parents were too strict. And then I saw Margaret's home life and I was absolutely astonished . . . Margaret had this extreme overprotection, which I had been rebelling against for a couple of years."

Though Margaret's mother liked Natalie, she viewed her as a potentially disruptive influence. When the then sixteen- and seventeen-year-old girlfriends decided to see a matinee in Hollywood, Mrs. O'Brien insisted on dropping them off in front of the theater and made arrangements to meet them in the lobby after the movie.

While they were buying their tickets, Natalie and Margaret found out that actor Jimmy Dean and a few of his pals had driven up on motorcycles to Googie's, an industry hangout down the street. Natalie was instantly intrigued, having heard a buzz about the talented, eccentric actor that summer at Warner Brothers, where Dean was making *East of Eden*, his first film. Margaret was curious more than interested, but she was up for an adventure. "We snuck out and walked over to Googie's, and Jimmy Dean was there with his roughy-toughy, offbeat young fellows that would hang around there with their motorcycles."

As Natalie and Margaret approached Dean's table, Mrs. O'Brien happened to drive by, spotting them through the window. "She got really mad and yanked us out of there, in front of Jimmy Dean and everything," recalls O'Brien. Natalie was mortified. "My mother drove Natalie to my house and called her mother and there was this big argument and everything." As Natalie told the story later, "Margaret seemed to accept it, but I was absolutely horrified . . . I couldn't wait to get home and tell my parents that they weren't so bad after all. I was driving way too fast in my desire to get home, and I got into a terrible car crash."

According to the papers, Natalie was almost killed. She took a curve too fast on a mountain road on her way back to the Valley, spinning out of control and flipping over her T-bird, knocking down forty feet of guardrail. Louella Parsons reported a second time in less than a year when Natalie walked away from a demolished car:

> Natalie Wood, former child actress and currently a teenage favorite on TV, narrowly escaped death yesterday . . . her car careened, went over an embankment and hit a tree, which saved her from falling into a ravine.

Natalie's chief concern as her car flipped over the embankment was how she would look at an audition the next day. "She had presence of mind enough to put her hands over her face," wrote Parsons, adding that Natalie went into shock, emerging with only bruises.

Mrs. O'Brien's disapproval of Natalie stemmed from a deep fear—that Margaret, her star-child, would fall in love and leave home. "My mother wasn't worried about drinking. She was worried that we would get in trouble with boys, and that Natalie was leading me to do it. She was having a hard time, like Natalie's mother, of letting go. And I think she thought, 'Well, Natalie's the one that's taking her away.' "

The two stage mothers maintained a vulture's vigilance over their daughters' boyfriends. Jackie Eastes was at the Gurdins' house for a double-date with Natalie when Bob Allen arrived, surprising Natalie with a sheath dress lined in mink, "and her parents were really upset that this guy had bought her this, because it was obviously a very expensive gift, and their first reaction was, 'What does he want for this gift?' " Maria even resented Jackie. "Looking back, I don't think she liked *anyone* that took up Natalie's time."

Natalie empathized that year when Margaret O'Brien fell in love and her mother tried to block the romance, just as Mud had with Jimmy. "This was my first love, and Natalie would help me sneak out to see him. We'd pretend we were going someplace, and then I'd go over and see him, and *she'd* go over and see somebody *she* wanted to see. Bob Allen would be a go-between, poor Sonny was a go-between. I'd pretend I was out with Sonny, and then I'd go see this other fellow."

One night when Natalie was covering for Margaret, Mrs. O'Brien called the chief of police. Natalie was brought to the police station, along with Margaret and her boyfriend, all minors. "It was just a mess for Natalie at the time," relates O'Brien, who was pressured to stop seeing the boy she loved. "My mother ruined that romance."

There was a dangerous momentum building around Natalie. From the outside, she appeared to be living every teenage girl's fantasy, bubbling with happiness like her nickname, Squirt. The boyfriend who gave the name to her, Rad Fulton, "never heard Natalie complain about anything—she had it made." No matter what the circumstances, Jackie noticed, Natalie was "on." "I don't remember her ever being depressed or unhappy about anything." In time, Jackie recognized Natalie's perpetual cheerfulness as a *performance*, part of the image Natalie believed a star should project. "She always remained the actor—always on stage and in control."

Lana could see their mother exerting tremendous pressure on Natalie to create movie star glamour, pressure that Natalie, the perfectionist, internalized. "My sister was very concerned about how the public would perceive her at all times—the makeup, the clothing, behaving a certain way, saying the right things, being liked." As a result, Lana noticed, Natalie became "very controlling of her feelings and emotions," suppressing her real self to enact the part of a star. "She would never walk out of the house without her face made up to look perfect," observed Jackie. Mud instructed her never to gossip. "To Natalie, everyone was wonderful. She said her mother used to tell her, 'If you can't say something nice about someone, say nothing at all.' "

Natalie's identity was further lost to her. She had already confused Natasha—her true self—with the movie characters she played. Now her mother was creating a glamorous persona for "Natalie Wood," Movie Star, that was an amalgam of Natalie and Mud. "She never really allowed Natalie to just be herself," declares Lana. "To see if people would accept her or not, which is really, really, really sad. That's just devastatingly sad to me."

The strain on Natalie was already evident. Actress Steffi Skolsky Sidney, then a college student, remembers being shocked to see Natalie in a tight dress, drinking Zombies at the bar at a fraternity party in the Hollywood hills. Steffi, who was the daughter of a well-known Hollywood gossip columnist, Sidney Skolsky, thought, "Uh-oh, this is not good," aware that Natalie was only sixteen. "The next thing I knew, I went downstairs to use the ladies room and Natalie was passed out on the bed." Steffi searched the house in alarm for Natalie's date, demanding he take Natalie home. "I didn't know her at all, but suddenly, all the motherly instinct in me came out and I felt very protective." Steffi kept the incident a secret from her columnist father, protecting Natalie from possible scandal, remaining mum when she and Natalie became acquainted the next year on *Rebel Without a Cause*. "I didn't say anything. It was none of my business."

Natalie was in trouble if she consumed more than a few drinks. "She was only ninety-five pounds," Jackie points out. "She couldn't drink a lot of liquor without getting smashed." Margaret O'Brien noticed Natalie had a difficult time holding alcohol when they were at clubs together, or if their dates used false I.D.s. "It wasn't terrible, it wasn't like she was falling down or things like that. She'd just get a little tipsy." Margaret, who was permitted wine at home, seldom drank. "But Natalie I don't think was allowed to drink in her family, so this was like a rebellion." "Not a lot of teenagers were drinking at that time," recalls Jackie. "It was a different era. Drinking was chic, it was 'in,' it was the thing to do."

A part of Natalie regretted her already spent youth. Years later she said, "I wanted to do all the things the other kids were doing. The life of the average teenager was something I read or heard about, rather than experienced. While they were at the senior prom, I was sipping drinks at Ciro's with older men. This made me look like a flaming rebel, even though it wasn't unusual for movie kids to act this way." The irony, Margaret O'Brien points out, is that "although movie children are worldly-wise, it takes them longer to *emotionally* mature." Natalie's teen costar from *The Green Promise*, Ted Donaldson, estimates that child actors tend to be four to five years *behind* their peers emotionally, creating a warped imbalance between their adult lifestyles and their childlike emotions. Natalie, in O'Brien's view, fit that pattern when they went out together. "She'd be real mature one minute, and then she'd be real childish." Natalie's sophistication, like so much in her life, was illusory—"a feint, a look, an attitude . . . the cigarette holder, dragging the fur."

Natasha, the real Natalie, was submerged inside the star persona of "Natalie Wood" as if she were an alter ego, a personality created by Maria to present if anyone was with her. Behind the façade of forced gaiety and glamour, Natalie was a mass of insecurities and neuroses. Being alone made her increasingly anxious. As Jackie recalls, "She always had to have tons of people around her. There were *never* enough people." Natalie started to take sleeping pills as a nightly routine, unable to fall asleep on her own, haunted by fears of kidnappers or nightmares of drowning, despite her contingent of storybook dolls. Eight-year-old Lana watched her sister's drill: "It's time to go to bed: you wash your face and you brush your teeth, you put on your pajamas and you take a sleeping pill."

The tortured Fahd's drinking worsened. One night, Lana remembers, "I saw him broadside Natalie with a record player." Mud's midnight flights from the house, taking Natalie and Lana to the safety of a motel room, or to a neighbor's they barely knew, were becoming almost as regular as Natalie's pills to put her to sleep.

She was desperate to break away from this harrowing existence, yet unprepared psychologically or emotionally to live by herself. She saw boys, or men, as her salvation—and her means of escape. The line of suitors at Natalie's house, one beau wryly observed, went around the block. "She wouldn't stick with one boy," Natalie's friend Margaret witnessed. "She'd want to go see one here, then she'd want to go see one there, and one at the other place—four or five in one day." The handsome young actor James Darren, who was selling shoes then, was an infatuation. "I remember," O'Brien laughs, "we walked over to the store in the Beverly Wilshire Hotel where he was working, and we tried on a lot of shoes!"

It was easy for Natalie to develop a crush on someone, and she would have more than one crush at the same time. "She loved flirting, and was young," explains O'Brien. "I don't think there was anything terrible about that or anything." Margaret did not consider Natalie promiscuous. "Not from what I could see. But she did like to flirt, and I think she liked the attention. She liked attention, and a lot of it was that."

Actor Rad Fulton saw a great deal of Natalie at that time. They frequently went to parties, or restaurants, sometimes to the beach, occasionally to Rad's bachelor apartment in Silver Lake, near downtown. He and Natalie were secretly photographed making out on the sofa at a friend's party; the picture suggests a furtive, reckless sexuality, as Natalie puts her head back submissively and Rad leans into her with a forceful kiss. "I will say she was a hot little girl, but she was a *nice* little girl . . . adorable and sweet and lovely."

Natalie's desperation to leave home was tragically apparent. She suggested marriage to Rad, a struggling actor of nineteen to her sixteen. "I said no. It wouldn't have happened with her mother, and she was only a kid—I knew all that. I was too young myself. I told her, 'There's a whole life out there. Don't miss it.' I said, 'Wait until you're twenty-one.' " Rad found Natalie "naïve in a lot of ways." She didn't smoke with him, and drank very little—sharing a beer. His feeling was that Natalie asked to marry him because she "wanted to get into a dream world."

ABC chose not to renew *Pride of the Family* for the 1954–55 TV season, freeing Natalie that fall to return to Van Nuys High, where she had missed over a year. She was still determined to maintain the normalcy of public school, and had registered the previous spring on a break from screen-testing as a blonde for *The Silver Chalice*. During registration, she crossed paths with graduating senior Robert Redford—an athlete regarded as friendly, though not one of the "cool kids," evincing "no sense of what he was to become." Redford, who would have embraced that description, was eager to get out of Van Nuys High and Los Angeles, displaying his maverick streak in his brush with Natalie Wood at registration. As he recalls:

> Bunch of the ballplayers were spared the ordeal of having to go through registration day in the auditorium if they would man the doors. Kind of a

"duh" job, which was fine with us, because we didn't want to have to sit through this stiff indoctrination ceremony where people make speeches you've heard before in a very unspectacular way. I was a total goofball in school, just a worthless student, always looking for a way out of going to class or a way to have more fun than I was having, or to *escape*—to hooky out. That was my chief modus operandi.

There were about four or five doors going all the way around the oval-shaped auditorium, and each door had an alphabetical sequence over it—A through F, G through L. There were two guys at each door, and of course, we were kind of competing with each other to see who would get people into the auditorium fastest because as soon as you got them in there and shut the door, you were free to split, and we were headed to the beach or the pool hall.

So we were rushing to get through it, and we were all ready to shut the doors and this little girl comes running down—tiny little thing—and wants to come in the door. And I just was a complete jerk. I said, "Hold on. What's your name?" I didn't have a clue who she was. First of all, she had her hair very blond because she was doing a movie—though I'm not sure I would have recognized her [anyway]. I said, "Hold it," and then it becomes sort of this machismo bullshit: "Where are *you* going?"—giving her a hard time. She says, "Please let me in. Please." And I said, "What's your name?" She said, "Please. Let me in the door. I'm embarrassed." And then she says, "Wood," and I said, "That's W's. That's all the way around the other side." And she said, "Please. I don't want to cause a scene going in there." I said,

"Well . . . you don't wanna cause a *scene*, huh?" And the guy with me started to hyperventilate. He's trying to send me signals that it's Natalie Wood.

Anyway, I just continued to just be a jerk, and give her a hard time. I said, "Sorry! Name is Wood? All the way around." I said, "Does this give you permission to change your name? Go around to the other side." And then she just let me *have* it. Got madder 'n hell and says, "You son-of-a-bitch" and sped off. And the guy with me goes, "Ho ho! I guess she told *you!* That was Natalie Wood." I said, "Are you kiddin' me?" And then I was glad I had pushed her around to the side . . . because I had a dim view of movie people.

Robert Redford would not see Natalie for another ten years, when ironically, she would help launch his career as a movie star.

Natalie blended in gracefully when she returned to high school that fall, accelerating to become a senior, like Mary Ann. Phoebe Kassebaum, who was in a choral group Natalie joined, was amazed at how friendly she was. "I never got the feeling that she was braggadocious, or wanting to impress me. It was rather *me* being impressed by *her*. She had this very exciting life outside of high school, and to us that was a very unbelievable, glamorous thing. I earned twenty-five cents an hour babysitting, and here's this beautiful girl who has everything—the look, the voice, the figure—and she's in movies. I didn't know anything about the Hollywood scene, I just knew that this girl was famous, and that she was a very nice girl."

Natalie was proud of her decision to go to Fulton, and then to Van Nuys High, telling Margaret O'Brien she "would have been really unhappy if she hadn't gone to regular school." As ferociously as she pursued her inherited fantasy of becoming a movie star, Natalie paradoxically longed for a real life.

She and Mud reacted to the cancellation of the TV series with relief, escalating their dogged search for a part that would make Natalie a famous movie star, the quest that had occupied Maria daily since Natasha was five.

Natalie interviewed for what would be the Leslie Caron role in *Daddy Long Legs* in October, but had to content herself with guest appearances on Studio 57 (*The Plot Against Mrs. Pomeroy*) and NBC Ford Theater, where she starred as a teenager who finds a dream date for the prom in a comedy with the ironic title *Too Old for Dolls*. Teen actor Robert Kendall, who played her date, a young Arab prince, found Natalie fresh and natural, without the pseudo-sophistication she donned to appear glamorous. He wrote later how "her heart shone through her big brown eyes, electric with excitement." Natalie's hair had grown back to its natural shade, light brown, and on television she looked like a typical teenage girl, though as her friend Jackie would observe, Natalie was no longer a teenager "in the true sense of the word."

She returned to campus in late October, sharing her experiences with the shy Phoebe, who couldn't believe that Natalie Wood was talking to *her*. Natalie would listen with compassion as Phoebe talked about her recently deceased father. "She had those really warm brown eyes, and that sweet little set of lips—she was just a sweet person, and she carried that presence about her no matter where she was, I think. Certainly when she was with me, in that class, she couldn't have been any nicer."

Natalie was more consumed than ever with her scheme to hire Henry Willson, so she could meet and marry Robert Wagner, her dream husband. She asked Rad Fulton, who was represented by Willson, to help convince the agent to sign her. As Robert Hyatt recalls, "Natalie went on a strike with her mother that if Henry Willson wasn't her agent so she didn't at some point meet R.J. [Wagner], that she wouldn't work." Natalie signed with Henry Willson on November 10, 1954.

Maria had grave reservations. She was concerned about Natalie associating with the homosexual Willson. Fulton had met Willson as a teenager while he was working as a model under his real name, Jim Westmoreland. Willson changed Westmoreland's name to Rad Fulton while getting him started in movies. Fulton worshipped the powerful Willson as "a guide, [who] made sure you met the right people at parties, met the right girls."

Natalie's objective upon signing Willson was to arrange a date with Wagner, certain it would lead to marrying him. Mud held a dim a view of this. Natalie campaigned Willson relentlessly. He finally agreed he would set up the date with Wagner, then twenty-four, once Natalie turned eighteen in a few years.

The month she signed with Willson, Natalie was cast in a CBS live half-hour drama for General Electric Theater called *I Am a Fool*, based on a Sherwood Anderson story about a drifter who falls in love with a small-town beauty and lets her slip away. Eddie Albert narrated the story, told in flashback, with Natalie cast as the ingénue. "That was my first love scene, and I remember my agent saying to me, 'It'll either be with actor John Smith or else they might use this new young kid, some guy from New York . . . some kid named Jimmy Dean.' " Natalie later told actor Dick Moore that the producers were disappointed when they found out they were "stuck" with James Dean, who was rumored to be avant-garde.

Natalie, who had chased Dean into Googie's three months earlier, was excited and nervous to work with the unconventional rising star. He arrived late for the first rehearsal, roaring in on his motorcycle dressed in jeans, a dirty T-shirt, and a large safety pin holding his fly together. "He was exactly what I expected. A junior version of Marlon Brando. He mumbled so you could hardly hear what he was saying, and he seemed very exotic and eccentric and attractive." The producer worried that Natalie, at sixteen, "didn't quite know how to deal with" Dean, who "could be alternately jolly, charming, and funny, then twenty minutes later off by himself 'sulking.' But he only appeared to be sulking—he was actually inside of himself."

Dean barely spoke to Natalie that morning, but trailed her out the door during the lunch break, inviting her on his motorcycle. "I was thrilled. We went speeding off to some greasy spoon." When Dean turned on a portable radio, Natalie expected to hear bongo drums. Instead, "he played beautiful classical music." Dean chatted with Natalie about the script at lunch, relaxing her. Suddenly, he put down his sandwich. "I know you," he said challengingly. "You're a child actor." Natalie, who sensed he was testing her, responded, "That's true. But it's better than acting like a child." Dean "didn't get it for a moment," she later recalled. "Then he started to laugh. Then I started to laugh, and that's how our wonderful friendship began."

Natalie was encountering James Dean on the precipice of fame, in the final few months before the release of *East of Eden*. The public had never seen Jimmy Dean in a movie, but he was acquiring a mystical status in Hollywood, where word was circulating that his sensitive performance in *Eden* was certain to make him a star. The Dean with whom Natalie had lunch was a broken man, reeling from a break-up with Pier Angeli, whose mother had objected to Dean not being Italian, or Catholic.

Dean's shattered emotions brought out Natalie's gift for empathy. As they left the café, strolling past a newsstand, his eye drifted toward the covers of a few movie magazines, reporting Angeli's new romance with Italian-Catholic singer Vic Damone. Natalie would recall Dean picking up a few of them and reading them:

> Since Pier was a big star, her picture was on all the magazines, with articles about how her mother had broken up the romance between Pier and some eccentric kid from New York. Jimmy . . . was very upset, because he was obviously in love with her. He was fascinated by her stardom, and he was fascinated by the fact that he was becoming a celebrity—yet not wanting it, not wanting fame.

According to Mary Ann, when Angeli unexpectedly married Damone the next week, a few days after *I Am a Fool* aired on CBS, Natalie spent the evening consoling Dean. "He almost OD'd that night—oh God, that was terrible—and Natalie babysat with him and stayed with him. It was awful, poor guy."

Natalie was struck as if by lightning performing live with Dean, whose intensity as an artist ignited her. Up to that point, she said later, acting was something she had taken for granted, "like being a girl." Dean inspired Natalie to be a serious actress, in addition to a movie star. If there was more to the attraction, it had not surfaced yet.

Within days of Natalie's creative awakening, Henry Willson sent her to audition for the part of a twelve-year-old in a far-fetched Universal-International costume drama called *Tacey*, later changed to *One Desire*. Louella Parsons, the Hollywood scribe, reported the following Monday:

> Natalie Wood returns to Universal-International after an absence of 10 years. She was a little girl of 7 when she was called one of the most promising child stars in Hollywood.
>
> Natalie gets an important role in *Tacey* with Anne Baxter, Rock Hudson and Julia [sic] Adams . . . she got the job by putting her hair in pigtails and proving to producer Ross Hunter that she could look that young.

Natalie was humiliated. A year later she wrote, "I've been the Pigtail Kid in Hollywood for so many years nobody thought I would ever grow up—least of all me."

13

FOR NATALIE, THE HIGHLIGHT OF *One Desire* was hearing Rock Hudson wolf-whistle at her as she walked on set in a wasp-waisted hoopskirt, hair upswept, for a scene as a late teenager. Throughout the rest of filming, Thanksgiving to Christmas 1954, she suffered the ignominy of pretending to be twelve, another movie waif-child in braids.

Natalie was impatient to grow up, bursting to express the artistic impulses stirred by playing James Dean's lost love.

She got a mink stole for Christmas, the essence of Hollywood in Mud's *Modern Screen* mentality; for Natalie, wearing a mink symbolized sex and sophistication; the antidote, she believed, to her child star stigma.

In her eagerness to appear older than sixteen, and to project the image she and Mud considered starlike, Natalie tended to wear too much of everything. "There were some times she didn't have the best taste in what she'd put together. She'd wear prints and plaids all at the same time." A dancer who knew her recalls, "Natalie loved clothes, but she didn't have real fashion sense at all." When Max Factor hired her to do print ads, Natalie took home boxes of makeup, overpainting her face with a little girl's idea of glamour. She appeared blond in ads for Lustre Crème, promoting *The Silver Chalice*, which came out at Christmas. She still presented herself in the guise of the movie star alter ego Mud had created for them both, but Natalie aspired to something more. "I didn't know what I wanted," she said later, "except to be a great actress."

Around the time she started her last semester at Van Nuys High, January 1955, Natalie got a call from Bobby Hyatt that seemed an eerily answered prayer. Bobby had just met with the director of a modestly budgeted film in development at Warner Brothers about teenage alienation. He was reading for the role of a high school boy named Plato, and noticed there was a teenage character named Judy. Bobby suggested Natalie get a copy of the script from Henry Willson. The movie was called *Rebel Without a Cause*. The creative elements were a confluence of everything Natalie was hungry for as an actress: the director of the film, Nicholas Ray, was a protégé of her idol, Elia Kazan; James Dean, her muse from *I Am a Fool*, had just been cast as the lead; and the story was dark and provocative.

When Natalie read the script, she wept. As a friend recalls, "She said there was actually a little voice buzzing in her head saying, 'You *are* Judy!' " The story mirrored themes from Natalie's rebellious teen years. The screenplay opened with Judy and several friends under interrogation at a police station, as Natalie and Margaret O'Brien had been the year before. The title character, who becomes Judy's boyfriend—a sensitive youth in rebellion against authority—was a prototype of Natalie's fugitive love Jimmy Williams, down to the rolled-up jeans. His name was even Jim, as was the actor who would play him, Jimmy Dean. The Judy character came from a cold home with a remote father and yearned to create a utopian family with Jim.

"I felt exactly the way the girl did in the picture toward her parents," Natalie said later. "It was about a high school girl rebelling, and it was very close to home. It was really about my own life."

The story was the brainchild of avant-garde director Nick Ray, who was intrigued by the idea of a film about juvenile delinquency in Eisenhower-conservative America. He had hoped to collaborate with his mentor, playwright Clifford Odets, but Warners assigned the commercially successful Leon Uris to write the screenplay, and suggested that Ray adapt the story from a published case study written by psychiatrist Dr. Robert M. Lindner called *Rebel Without a Cause: The Story of a Criminal Psychopath*. Ray rejected the case study in favor of his own plotline but kept the main title, eventually replacing Uris with screenwriter Irving Shulman, who was superseded by Stewart Stern. Stern had come into the project via composer Leonard Rosenman, an East Coast friend of James Dean whom Ray hired to create the score.

The quasi-intellectual, sociological background of the

film enthralled Natalie, who desired an entrée into this rarefied circle. Her reaction to the script and the concept of *Rebel Without a Cause* was visceral. She said later, "I felt an instant communication with the role, an absolute necessity for playing it. I just had to have that part, in order to express something inside of me that I had never felt before . . . because I had been playing ingénue roles up to then and here was a sensational part that had to be played by an ingénue but wasn't one of those sweet-young-thing roles—it was a real, gutty character part. I loved it." In future years, she would describe her response as the moment when *she* made the decision to be an actress, as opposed to following a path chosen for her by her mother. It would also establish a precedent of Natalie gravitating to film characters with whom she could identify.

She phoned Hyatt to thank him, sharing a giggle at the similarity between herself and Judy; then she called Mary Ann, telling her she *had* to have the part. "Oh, she wanted that *s-o-o-o-o-o-o* bad."

Natalie's first obstacle was Mud, who was suspicious of the gritty Nicholas Ray school of filmmaking; Maria's idea of Hollywood was klieg lights, studio limousines and red-carpeted premieres with stars in sable coats. She was nervous that a movie about teenagers fighting with their parents would tarnish Natalie's image and jeopardize her destiny as a movie star.

"She did not want Natalie to take that part," recalls Natalie's friend Jackie, who heard the details of an incendiary argument between Natalie and her mother over the role. Fahd disapproved as well, though his approach was to reason with Natalie. As Mary Ann explains, "It was rather an iffy film at the time . . . it was really very controversial. There were a lot of people who said, 'Don't get involved with this.' "

Margaret O'Brien's mother had dissuaded her for that reason. O'Brien, ironically, was the first actress Nick Ray had in mind to play Judy. Unknown to Natalie, Ray had approached Margaret and her mother at Romanoff's that autumn, before James Dean had been cast. "He said, 'I have the perfect movie for you.' " Mrs. O'Brien vetoed it after a first meeting with the unconventional Ray. "My mother loved this film called *Glory*, which I hated, about a horse, so that's what she was steering me toward." Ray himself had misgivings after the meeting, worried that O'Brien was too respectful to play Judy. She also lacked Natalie's adoration of James Dean. "I thought he was weird, to be perfectly frank."

Natalie, according to Mary Ann, had the vision to see *Rebel's* potential. "She recognized it when she read the script. She was the one that really had the foresight. Everybody saw her as a young girl, but she had years of so much experience . . . she was perfect for it and she knew it."

Natalie stood up to Mud for a second time, threatening to "run away from home and become an actual juvenile delinquent unless I was given the chance to test for the part," implicitly modifying their tacit pact so that *she* had control over her career. "For the first time, I got serious about my work and vowed to derive some satisfaction for myself. I was no longer going to do what I was told if it conflicted with my instincts." Fahd was a silent observer. As Lana would note, "My father . . . just sort of threw his hands up and said, 'I don't like it. Nothing I can do about it,' and my dad, unfortunately, began to drink even more heavily."

Natalie would consider her stand on *Rebel* one of the most critical decisions of her life. "I'd allowed studios and my parents to guide my life and career . . . I was rebelling against being overprotected."

It was a development that would create a permanent schism in Natalie. For the rest of her acting career, she would struggle to reconcile her own inclination toward serious filmmakers she respected versus the powerful influence of Mud and the studio system, pulling her toward mainstream Hollywood material and stardom for stardom's sake. She launched her campaign to be cast in *Rebel* with an altered perspective. "I don't know if I wanted to be a star," she said later. "I just wanted to be great."

Mud acquiesced, partly because she realized that a lead role in a Warner Brothers picture, even a controversial one, was the vehicle she and Natalie had been on a quest to find since the TV series. Maria wanted her back in movies—so they could both fulfill her destiny—with the same life or death intensity that Natalie coveted the part of Judy. "I would have done *anything* to get the lead in *Rebel Without a Cause*," Natalie told starlet Joan Collins a few years later.

According to actor Nick Adams, who would play a gang member in *Rebel*, Natalie showed up at the Warners casting office clutching a script and begging to read for Nick Ray—dressed in opera pumps, a tight black sheath, and a black-veiled hat. She would tell columnist Sidney Skolsky that people in the industry still thought of her as a girl in pigtails then, "and I wasn't about to become an ingénue." Under Maria's *über*-Hollywood influence, she believed that her "Natalie Wood" persona would convince Ray that she was a star, and dramatically illustrate she was not in pigtails.

Natalie later would tell her stand-in that by the time she and her agent met with Ray, she was so nervous to be in his presence, her knees shook and her voice gave out.

Panicking, "she jumped up and started pounding on his desk, 'I *am* Judy! . . . you can't give the part to anyone else . . . you must let me do a test!' " Ray later wrote, "I wasn't going to cast Natalie Wood in the picture because she's a child actress, and the only child actress who ever made it as far as I'm concerned was Helen Hayes." Then he became intrigued. "After Nat's interview, she left, and outside waiting for her was this kid with a fresh scar on his face, so I said, 'Let's talk again.' She seemed to be on that kind of a trip." Ray's idea—unknown to Natalie—was to test her for a part as a friend of Judy's.

Adams, who became a pal after meeting her in the casting office, noticed that Natalie was worried she would not hear back from Ray. According to the star-struck Jackie, who became her lady-in-waiting throughout *Rebel*, she and Natalie "ate, slept, and drank" Judy. When the trades reported that Terry Moore and Lori Nelson were being considered for the part, Natalie took action in Mud's aggressive style. "We kept going to the commissary at Warners, so she could run into Nick Ray."

Both sixteen-year-olds were in awe of the iconoclastic forty-three-year-old director. Natalie flaunted her star image during these seemingly casual encounters, desperate to appear older after Ray's disparaging comment about child actors. Jackie remembers, "I wore white bucks and pencil skirts and sweaters—I mean, I looked like a kid—and she would dress up, with the high heels, and she'd be all decked out like a movie star." British pinup Joan Collins, who met Natalie in this period, observed, "She always dressed and behaved like the ultimate star. Spending money with abandon on clothes, furs and jewelry . . . she was incredibly insecure as a person and about her physical attributes. She always wore high-heeled shoes to maximize her height, and she always wore a thick gold bracelet to cover a slightly protruding bone in her wrist."

She got Ray's attention. One day as Natalie and Jackie strolled into the commissary, Ray was on his way out. He told the maitre d' to put the girls on his tab, and invited Natalie to have lunch with him the next day. As soon as he was gone, Natalie asked Jackie to go with her. "She had the life I dreamed of, and always included me when she could—and I think she was a little afraid to be alone with him. I know I was terrified." Ray inspired strong reactions. He was physically imposing—tall and lanky, like Abe Lincoln, with a long face and drooping features that gave him a slightly doleful expression. He dressed like an elegant bohemian, occasionally directing in his bare feet. Hollywood's Old Guard considered the East Coast director odd.

Lunch with Nick Ray was a mystical experience for the two teenagers. "There was something about Nick," Jackie tried to explain later. "First of all, he was probably the most intelligent human being I ever met. Very well read. He had a way of making you feel that you were the most important person in the world to him. He concentrated on your every word." Natalie was flattered that Ray wanted *her* thoughts about the script, and the way teenagers behaved. Throughout lunch, Jackie noticed he kept staring at Natalie's face. When he asked Natalie why she was wearing makeup, "she looked at him quizzically." Jackie, who sensed that Ray disapproved, came up with the excuse that Natalie had just come from a Max Factor layout.

By the time the check arrived, Natalie had fallen under Ray's spell. "I was madly in love with him, too," states Jackie. "It wasn't that he was a particularly handsome man, but he had such charisma. Nick Ray was probably the most exciting, sexiest man."

Natalie shared her Nick Ray experience with Mary Ann, who remembers her as "very, very adoring of him—because of his position, because of his experience, because of him being who he was . . . he was extremely different and charming and really knew his business, which *she* respected very highly in a man."

For several days afterward, Natalie haunted the Warners commissary hoping to see Ray, "all made up like a sophisticate." Finally, Jackie pointed out to her, "If you want the part of Judy, you've got to go in there looking like a teenager." Natalie returned to the commissary in flats, a skirt and a sweater, wearing very little makeup, her hair in a ponytail. Ray did a double take, telling her she looked beautiful and suggesting she stop by his office, where he invited her to dinner to discuss the part. Natalie "drove directly to the House of Seven and Nine and bought a new four-hundred-dollar wardrobe."

Jackie stopped by her house that night to assist in Natalie's ruse that Ray had invited them to meet him at the Chateau Marmont, a hotel resembling a castle on the Sunset Strip where Ray had rented a bungalow and conducted script sessions. Natalie dropped Jackie off at home and went to the Chateau alone; Ray took her to dinner at a restaurant called the Luau. She went to dinner alone with Ray several times after that, according to Jackie, who continued to tell the Gurdins she was with Natalie.

Natalie brought her *Rebel* script along when she met Ray, with her notes written in the margins. She was bursting with observations, ecstatic that Ray was interested in her comments, delirious at the possibility of playing Judy. "He was helping her, because she'd practice and read [with him]," recalls Mary Ann, who went to Ray's bungalow with Natalie a few times. "And he spent a *lot* of time with her."

atalie's mother, Maria Zudilova, with her family in Siberia, 1919. Maria claimed they were)manovs. Seated from left: Maria's father, Stepan Zudilov, 42; aria, 11; her "aristocrat" mother, also named Maria, 36; sister Zoia, 12; brothers Gleb, 4, d Boris, 6. Back row from left: half-sister Kallisfenia (Kalia), 13; lf-brother Mikhael, 20; half-sister Apollinaria (Lilia), 17; half-brother Semen, 18.

usia as Queen of the Russian Invalids ll in San Francisco in 1936, assuming ose like the Russian royalty she imed to be.

Courtesy of Phyllis Quinn

Musia with her trophies as Queen of the White Russian Veterans Balls in San Francisco, a glory she would relive while channeling her dreams through Natasha.

Courtesy of Ed Canevari

Natasha's first publicity photo, a few weeks after producers changed her name to "Natalie Wood." She mailed it to her only friend, Edwin, on May 2, 1945, signing her real name, Natasha, in parenthesis, signifying the beginning of the split in her persona.

Natasha at the christening of baby sister Svetlana in 1946, when "Natalie Wood" first appeared on-screen in *Tomorrow Is Forever.*

Courtesy of Lana Wo

Courtesy of Constantine Liuzunie

The three sisters – Natasha, Olga, and Svetlana – with their mother, the formidable Maria/Musia/Mud.

Natalie in 1948 with the cast of *The Green Promise*, the movie where she injured her left wrist and nearly drowned. The wrist healed improperly and she wore a bracelet over it for the rest of her life. From left: Marguerite Chapman, Natalie, Walter Brennan, Connie Marshall, unidentified man, Ted Donaldson.

Michael Panieff's ballet class reads Christmas cards. At left is Natalie; at right "Taffy" Paul; second from right is Jill Oppenheimer. Natalie would marry actor Robert Wagner twice; Taffy would change her name to Stefanie Powers and play Wagner's wife on TV; Jill would become Jill St. John, Wagner's third wife.

Robert Banas Collection, courtesy of Robert Banas

opposite top:
An enigmatic Natalie at 16, before *Rebel Without a Cause*. She gave this picture to her beau Rad Fulton, signed "Squirt," his nickname for her.

Natalie, 11, before she began to wear a bracelet over her disfigured left wrist.

Natalie and her first love, Jimmy Williams. Their tragic romance would be mirrored by her role as Deanie opposite Beatty in *Splendor in the Grass*. Williams would become her personal prototype for Jimmy Dean in *Rebel Without a Cause*.

Jimmy Williams' favorite photo of Natalie, smiling for him at Fulton Jr. High.

Photos above and at right courtesy of Jim Williams

Jim Westmoreland collection, courtesy of Jim Westmoreland

From the collection of Steffi Sidney, courtesy of Steffi Sidney

The historic first read-through of *Rebel Without a Cause* in Nick Ray's bungalow at the Chateau Marmont, March 1955. Clockwise from lower left corner: Ray, Jim Backus, Natalie, Nick Adams, Mitzi McCall, Leonard Rosenman (on sofa at right), Bev Long (in ponytail).

Sixteen-year-old Natalie and her 43-year-old lover Nick Ray with Clifford Odets and actress Steffi Skolsky in Ray's bungalow.

From the collection of Steffi Sidney, courtesy of Steffi Sidney

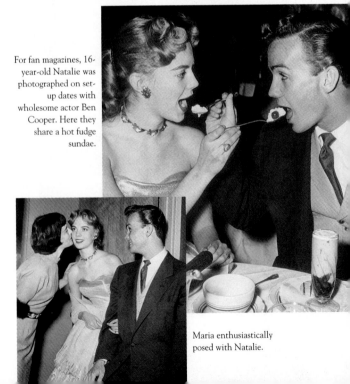

For fan magazines, 16-year-old Natalie was photographed on set-up dates with wholesome actor Ben Cooper. Here they share a hot fudge sundae.

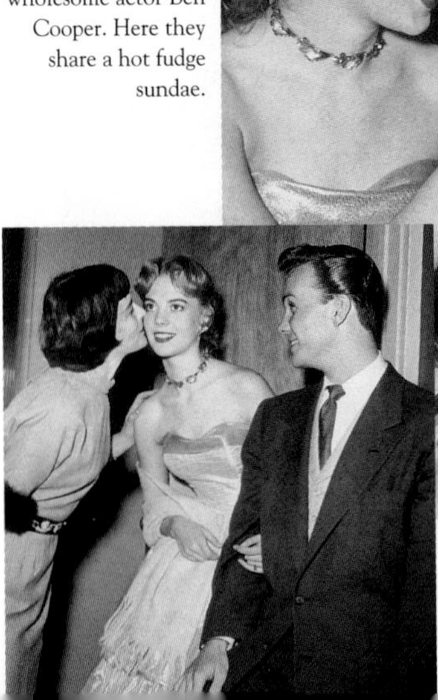

Maria enthusiastically posed with Natalie.

Perry Lopez Collection, courtesy of Perry Lopez

Natalie, Jimmy Dean, and actor Perry Lopez in a Warner Brothers ressing room during *Rebel ithout a Cause*. Lopez still thinks of Natalie every day.

atalie at the height teen stardom in fall 56, arriving with star Tab Hunter for e New York premiere of *e Burning Hills*.

Behind the scenes at Natalie's first wedding to Robert Wagner, December 28, 1957. Faye Nuell congratulates them as Lana, barely visible, stands beside Nuell and Maria lurks behind Natalie, her ever-present shadow.

Natalie and R.J. go over photos with Steffi Skolsky for their profile in *Datebook*. This photograph was taken in R.J.'s dressing room at Fox circa November 1958.

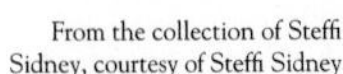

From the collection of Steffi Sidney, courtesy of Steffi Sidney

According to Mary Ann, Ray and Natalie were on similar intellectual planes. "Natalie's head was always clicking with ideas, and all of a sudden here's somebody who thinks the same way." Natalie said later Ray was the first director "who wanted my ideas."

The relationship turned romantic quickly. In Mary Ann's view, "the affection and everything started because of the mutual respect for each other." Natalie was clearly enthralled by Ray, who stimulated her intellectually, introducing her to the works of Hemingway, Poe, Fitzgerald, Wolfe, as well as *The Little Prince* by Antoine de Saint-Exupéry, a magical French fable about the innocence of childhood that would remain Natalie's favorite book the rest of her life.

She was close-mouthed about her sexual relationship with the forty-three-year-old director, even with close friends, though she and Jackie sighed like the high school girls they were at the romantic way he seduced her. Natalie told Jackie that Ray had taken her to a tiny, candlelit restaurant with pink tablecloths—Natalie's favorite color—where they drank champagne. After dinner, they went back to Ray's bungalow, where he told her, "I want to make love with you." Natalie found Ray's prelude to sex eloquent. "She said, 'All the other guys just want to screw me. He wants to make love *with* me.' It had a different connotation and it touched her. She said that when she had her first experience with him, she felt like a virgin for the first time." Natalie was nervous about undressing with the much older, revered Nicholas Ray. "She felt like she had never done anything before. It was just a very special thing."

Ray gave Natalie the key to his bungalow, and told her he wanted her to read for the part of Judy. Natalie, hoping the role was hers already, seemed upset. Ray continued to test other actresses through January and February—Moore, Nelson, Patricia Crowley, Kathryn Grant, Gloria Castillo—keeping his relationship with sixteen-year-old Natalie secret. "Nick Ray did not want anyone to know they were having an affair, and he wasn't about to disclose this. Nor was Natalie. She was jailbait."

Mud knew that Natalie was sexually involved with Ray, but she had lost the power struggle preceding *Rebel*—the dynamics between mother and daughter had changed and Natalie was in semi-control. "She was a little crazy about it at first," concedes Lana. When Natalie left the house at night to meet Ray at the Chateau Marmont, Mud would sneak out, taking eight-year-old Lana with her to spy on her older sister. "Mrs. Gurdin was a shrewd woman," as Jackie would observe. "She was out to protect her meal ticket."

Maria parked on a side street with a view to the pool area adjacent to the Chateau, and would fix her piercing gaze on Nick Ray's bungalow, waiting for Natalie to emerge. "She used to drag me out at night and we'd sit in the dark car, on the street, and watch the time—see when Natalie went in, when Natalie came out," Lana recalls. "I used to fall asleep in the back seat, praying that we could just go home and I could go to bed." At the first sign of Natalie leaving Ray's bungalow, Mud would rouse Lana from her slumber so they could scrutinize Natalie's appearance for evidence of sexual activity. " 'What condition? Was her lipstick messed up?' I felt like a detective on a stakeout."

Her mother accepted the affair with Ray, observes Lana, "because it was helpful to Natalie's career." "Believe me," observes Robert Hyatt, "if Marie did not want Natalie in there, she'd have gone in there, grabbed her by the hair and yanked her out. This was a break of a lifetime for Natalie and they knew it. The professional movie mother of all movie mothers said, '*This is it, you're a star, go get this picture—do anything with anybody.*' " Interestingly, the normally garrulous Mud kept this aspect of her management of Natalie to herself, though close friends such as the Hyatts knew about it. "Marie didn't want to talk about promoting Natalie to date older men for her career purposes." Jean Hyatt, her good friend, was aware Maria supported Natalie trying out for *Rebel*, though Mud kept to herself Natalie's trysts with Nick Ray in Bungalow #2.

Fahd played out his tragic role as a tormented Russian soul, turning a blind eye to his teen daughter's love affair with a twice-married director the same age as he. "He knew, but you *see* what you want to see," as Mary Ann would describe Nick's response, "and he had had a heart condition." "I remember my dad being *really* angry," Lana said later. The sad truth was that Fahd was a shadow figure in his own household. As Hyatt would observe, "Nick never had a thing to say about any of it."

Natalie and her teen friends romanticized her affair with Nicholas Ray, even the straightlaced Margaret O'Brien. None, including O'Brien, believed that Natalie was sleeping with Ray so he would cast her as Judy. "She did fall in love with Nick Ray, there was no question about it," declares Jackie, who lived the experience vicariously. The worldly-wise Mary Ann felt Natalie "knew going in" the involvement was not permanent. "We all experience those love affairs where 'who *cares* about next week, *today* is wonderful,' which is part of growing up. And he was a very *kind* man, and he taught her a lot more than just the film." Years later, Natalie would describe Ray's impact on her life by saying, "He opened the door to a whole new world for me. It was just glorious."

Natalie took inspiration from the great literary heroines in her borrowed novels from Ray, especially those of F. Scott Fitzgerald. She identified with Fitzgerald's brilliant but tragic wife, Zelda, enamored of Zelda's brazen sexuality and daring behavior, comparing it to her affair with Ray. "She became aware of these sort of historical female figures in romantic novels and so on—the independent woman."

Natalie costarred with Gigi Perreau, her child actress rival, in a CBS Four-Star Playhouse called *The Wild Bunch* in February, where they played sisters, as they had in *Never a Dull Moment*. Gigi, who at fourteen still considered herself a child, was astonished at the change in Natalie in four years. "She was very beautiful, and seemed very exciting and very glamorous. I thought, 'Oh my goodness, I will not ever be that old.' " The constant, for Perreau, was Natalie's drive. "She announced many, many times, 'I will do anything to be a star.' Usually you have other things in your life that you want—it's not such a burning, such a *single* goal." Jackie reveals: "She wanted to win the Oscar—oh God—more than life itself."

She clung to Ray during preproduction for *Rebel Without a Cause*. When he was busy, Natalie took her acolyte, Jackie, to sunbathe by the Chateau Marmont pool using Ray's key, dressed in a leopard bikini and ogling his reclusive neighbor, Marlon Brando. Once, when they were poolside while Brando swam, Natalie "dismissed" Jackie to talk to a cast member. "She realized later she was 'playing the star,' and then she realized it wasn't a kind thing to do. She said, 'I'm very sorry, and it will never happen again,' and it never did." Typically, Natalie was kind to a fault. When Nick Ray telephoned one morning to invite her to Romanoff's and Jackie had spent the night, Natalie included Jackie in the lovers' lunch, buying her a new dress to wear. She waved her hand and laughed, "You can pay me back when you're rich and famous!"

The luncheon was a young girl's fantasy. Ray kissed the sixteen-year-olds' hands as they walked into show-bizzy Romanoff's, ordering them screwdrivers. During lunch, he studied Jackie as if she were "under a microscope," asking for suggestions to make the teen characters in *Rebel* more realistic. The big news was that Ray had made arrangements for Natalie to screen-test. Because James Dean was in New York, he wanted her to do the test with Dennis Hopper, an eighteen-year-old he had just cast as a gang member. Ray raved about Hopper's talent, and asked Natalie if she and Jackie would "show him around town," handing Natalie five hundred dollars.

Natalie arrived for the test in full Natalie Wood makeup, facing "an assembly line" of Warner Brothers actresses, all reading with Hopper. According to Hopper, Natalie called him the next night. "She had to identify herself to me over the telephone for me to know which one she was, because I tested with about ten women that day."

As Hopper relates the story, Natalie propositioned him almost before he said hello. "She was really funny. She told me she thought I was great looking and she really liked me and she wanted to have sex with me—which never happened before or since. Helluva line." Hopper was instantly fascinated. "In the fifties, to be aggressive like that as a woman was really amazing—it was an amazing *turn*-on to me, for one thing. But it was certainly contrary to any kind of movement, or idea, at the time." Natalie told him later she was emulating Zelda Fitzgerald.

Hopper relates that he picked her up at the Chateau and they spent the evening in the car necking, talking passionately "about acting, and wanting to be the best, and our place in history." It was the beginning of an intense friendship between Natalie and Hopper, tainted by Natalie's disclosure—which Hopper states came as they prepared to make love—that she had just left Ray's bed. "I thought it was *weird*, okay? At the time. I was eighteen years old! I thought it was strange, I thought it was weird of her to be *doing* it . . . he was having an affair with a minor. It was illegal for me, too, but at least I was only a couple years older." Hopper asserts they made love that night.

Natalie's friend Jackie, who knew nothing about Natalie's tryst with Hopper, expected, from Ray's description, to meet someone Rock Hudson– handsome, with electric presence. Jackie found Hopper sweet and shy, with "interesting" looks, Kansas-naïve, with "this wonderful little boy quality that melted your heart." Jackie remembers him hanging on Natalie's stories about Hollywood, asking to see the movie star handprints in front of Grauman's Chinese Theater; Natalie compared her hand size to Elizabeth Taylor's, announcing, "One day I'm gonna be here." They showed Hopper the Hollywood hangouts—Googie's, the Villa Capri, the Luau—accompanied by Natalie's pal, Nick Adams. After a few days, they were all fast friends.

Hopper asserts that he and Natalie were "boy/girlfriend" from the time they met through the end of filming. "She was seeing Ray, but she was *with me*." Natalie's close friend Mary Ann believed that Natalie was interested in Hopper "as a friend, as a coworker," the same impression Jackie and the cast of *Rebel* would have. Their perception was that "Dennis was just madly in love with Natalie," and she considered him a pal. Hopper responds, "I wasn't in *love* with Natalie. I loved her. She was my best friend. But I wasn't *possessing* her, as an object, which I do know about. We didn't have that kind of relationship. It was really much more complicated, and much more interesting, and much more *involved* kind of relationship for two young people."

Adams, an impish blond, who worshipped Hollywood stars and was desperate to be famous, shared Hopper's fascination for Natalie, recognizing that she viewed him as a buddy. "He chose the friendship over the romance because he just wanted to be around her. She was that kind of a person." Natalie and Adams gave each other the nickname "Chort," Ukrainian for "little devil," enjoying a teasing, flirtatious friendship. Once, when Natalie was lying on the bed in her room, Adams dove on top of her and they rolled around, laughing until tears ran down Natalie's cheeks. "Boy, we could never be lovers," she giggled. "We could never stop laughing!" Adams had even charmed Mud, whose sense of mischief could be as vivid as her sense of drama, under the right circumstances. "I remember him coming into the house, grabbing Natalie's mother and throwing her around, then planting a big kiss on her cheek."

Nick Ray had concerns, after seeing Natalie's filmed test, extending beyond her makeup. The director thought she appeared too thin on screen, and her voice was childishly high-pitched. Although Natalie took an attitude from the beginning, especially with Mary Ann, that "she knew she was going to get the part *period*," privately she was insecure, with good reason. Jackie, who was at Natalie's side throughout, points out, "Nick was trying to bring the best out of her, but he was real critical, like 'I don't like the way you walk.' She didn't swing her hips enough, or she just wasn't sexy enough . . . he wasn't sure in his own mind whether she could handle it or not." In memos to Warner Brothers in January, Ray was leaning to actress Carroll Baker to play Judy, after rejecting Lee Remick, an earlier choice, as lacking the "right quality" for the part.

Natalie was confronting complex realities concerning Nick Ray. Throughout their clandestine involvement, Ray was simultaneously dating actress Shelley Winters. According to Natalie's eventual stand-in, and to composer Leonard Rosenman, the director was also seeing Jayne Mansfield, another candidate for the part of Judy. Ray would claim later that Mansfield was "an hallucination" of the casting department, and that he "didn't even put any film in the camera for her screen test," an assertion Rosenman, working on the score with Ray, disputes. "He tested her. I think that Jack Warner just said no." Hopper, who read with Mansfield, considered it a "serious test."

However serious Ray was about Mansfield, personally or professionally, the emotional and career stakes were staggeringly high for a sixteen-year-old. Even though Mary Ann thought Natalie could handle it, she conceded that her friend was starry-eyed teenaged "in love" with Ray, whose feelings for Natalie were those of a "loving" sexually sophisticated forty-three-year-old man. As she distinguishes, " 'Loving' someone and being 'in love' are two different things."

Natalie had agonizing doubts whether she would get *Rebel*. She told Hedda Hopper a few months later, "I wanted this picture more than anything. I was in Nick Ray's office daily for a month waiting to see what would happen after my screen test. Practically everyone had tested for the role—Debbie Reynolds, Pat Crowley, Lori Nelson, and Jayne Mansfield."

In this vulnerable period, Natalie suffered one of the great traumas of her life at the hands of one of her childhood idols, a powerful, married movie star more than twenty years older than her. She went to Jackie the morning after it happened, in hysterics; that afternoon, she showed up, berserk, at Dennis Hopper's apartment. The following year, Natalie would confide the secret to actor Scott Marlowe, her then-boyfriend. At least several other people knew about it from Natalie, including Mary Ann, and Faye Nuell, a friend from *Rebel*. She revealed the star's identity to each of them.

Natalie's account to Jackie, the morning after, was that the famous actor asked her to his hotel suite to read for a part. When she arrived at the suite, "he offered her a drink, they started to talk, and she asked about the part. He told her, 'I've always wanted to fuck you.' The script was just a ruse. He said he liked young girls, and he said he always wanted to fuck a teenager. She probably wasn't the only one. It was really nasty and verbally abusive."

Natalie told Jackie she reached for her purse and started to leave, but the star dragged her across the room and threw her on the bed. "She begged him to stop. She tried to fight him, but he told her if she fought, it would be painful. She didn't have a chance. He just absolutely tore her clothes off." According to Jackie, Natalie said the star was so violent that she bled. "He knew he'd raped her. Natalie started to cover herself with her coat, and he said, 'If you tell anyone, it'll be the last thing you do.' "

Jackie heard this account around eight in the morning, when Natalie located her at a girlfriend's house. "She tracked me down and came to pick me up, and she was hysterical. She looked like hell—her eyes were swollen and red. She had no makeup on. She was shaking. She fumbled for her sunglasses and told me, 'I was raped last night.' "

They drove to a restaurant, then to Natalie's house. "She was afraid to tell her mother. She threw herself on her bed and sobbed, 'It was awful. I was so scared.' " Natalie was terrified she might be pregnant, thinking she would die. She cleaned herself up compulsively, saying, "What am I going to do?"

Hopper recalls Natalie appearing at his door, raving, the afternoon after she was raped. "I remember I was painting. She came in, rushed into the apartment, grabbed my bullwhip and said, 'Lay down, let me whip you' . . . and she was really angry. I'd never seen her so angry. She told me what had happened." Hopper recollects Natalie telling him the rape occurred in a car. "She told me that she had woke up from being unconscious—she thought he'd given her a pill or something—and that she was laying half-in and half-out of the car. And her clothes had been taken off—at least the bottom parts were off, and he was whipping her, very hard, on her thigh. And she woke up screaming, and then he raped her. She didn't say anything about why she was with him or any of that. I never knew." Natalie told Hopper the star "had hurt her really bad."

Natalie's account to Scott Marlowe the next year was similar to what she told Jackie. She explained to Marlowe that the movie star had lured her to a hotel room (Marlowe thought it was on a Warners' tour), "made up some elaborate little scheme, and then raped her, according to Natalie . . . he just threw her in his room and *fucked* her. I mean she'd been around, but she hadn't seen anything like *that*. That kind of *rage*." Natalie told Marlowe she eventually had to confide in her mother because she needed to treat the pain at a hospital and stop the bleeding.

Mud offered no maternal tenderness or emotional support to Natalie. According to Mary Ann, Maria "thought it was great" that Natalie spent an evening with "Mr. Show Biz," Mary Ann's sarcastic description of the famous actor. Jackie and Hopper, who each suggested that Natalie call the police, both remember she was worried that if she reported that the popular, powerful movie star had raped her it would ruin her career. ("It would have," asserts Hopper. "At that time, the studio system controlled us, really.") Lana, who was never told, is certain her mother would have hushed the star's assault on Natalie because of his status in Hollywood. "That would be my mom's concern, it really would."

Though her five close friends' memories of some details or timing differ after forty-five years, the essence of what each recalls Natalie confiding to them is the same: that the same married film star lured or tricked Natalie, raped her so brutally she was physically injured, and she was too frightened or intimidated to report it to the police.

Natalie "hated" her former screen idol afterward, "shuddering" if she heard his name. She would keep the horrible secret, and behave as if nothing happened whenever their paths intersected, too schooled by Mud in the politics of Hollywood to cross a powerful movie star.

Mary Ann, who never feared confrontation, found it heartbreaking. "If you knew Natalie, you know what a dear soul she was, and so when things like that would happen, it'd just kill you because she wouldn't fight back and she wouldn't say a word because of that stupid mother of hers." Jackie wonders still "how this man can live with himself. Today that would have been front-page news and the bastard would have gone to jail for rape and sexual harassment."

Though Natalie "snapped back," the brutality of the star's sexual assault on her had an effect on her relationships with men. Mud used it to validate her perverse propaganda that it was dangerous for Natalie to have sex with well-endowed males, intensifying Natalie's sexual phobias and fears of pregnancy. "Her mother told Natalie she mustn't go to bed with anybody. She said, 'Some men are too big, and you shouldn't do that with *big guys*.' She put all that stuff in her mind." Faye Nuell, who would become Natalie's stand-in on *Rebel Without a Cause*, noticed that after Natalie told her that she had been raped, Natalie was "vulnerable" to men who would be "loving." Natalie also became more reckless in her behavior. "It's no wonder that I broke out in a big way," she would say in future years.

Natalie was a bundle of nerves by mid-February. Ray was preparing to start *Rebel* in March, and the role of Judy was not cast. Although part of Natalie was convinced "she *was* it," her insecure side—or, in this case, realistic—worried. "Nick really left her out to dry as to whether she had the part or she didn't have the part."

Hopper, whose role was set, suggested that Natalie and Jackie meet him at Googie's for lunch during this interlude. Natalie was uncharacteristically quiet, distressed that she hadn't heard from Ray. As they were leaving Googie's, she proposed they go to the Villa Capri for a glass of wine to calm her nerves, and then continued to order wine until the restaurant served dinner. The three teenagers left in Hopper's car and drank from midafternoon until the Villa Capri closed at eleven, as Natalie obsessed over Ray and the movie. According to Jackie, "No one ever questioned whether we drank," the dubious privilege of a juvenile celebrity.

The trio, heavily intoxicated, stumbled into Hopper's car before midnight. Natalie was upset, recalls Jackie, "because

Nick was supposed to call her." Hopper stopped to buy a bottle of whiskey at a liquor store and they drove up twisting Laurel Canyon Boulevard into the hills. As a classmate of Natalie's from Van Nuys High recalls, "Laurel Canyon was the big deal then—it was a big deal, if you could drive it."

Hopper parked on Mulholland, a scenic drive off Laurel Canyon with spectacular views, and they sat drunkenly "looking at the stars." Jackie, who was in the back seat, remembers observing Hopper drink half the bottle of whiskey before she fell asleep from too much wine. She woke up to see Natalie outside the car, vomiting, with Hopper nervously muttering, "It's all my fault, I shouldn't have bought that bottle." When it began to rain, they decided to drive back to Googie's to get Natalie's car.

Hopper, who was deeply drunk, started down the slippery, snakelike turns of Laurel Canyon, driving "almost too slow," he recalls, because of the rain. As he was coming out of a curve, "a guy came way across the line, didn't know where he was going and we had a head-on."

Hopper's car flipped, remembers Jackie: "Natalie was thrown into the middle of the street, and I was thrown on top of her, and she was knocked cold. I thought she was dead." Hopper, who landed atop Jackie, was miraculously unhurt. "I don't even remember having cuts. But I gotta tell ya, I was so concerned about Natalie that I could have had my *head* in my hands and not known it."

Jackie, who also escaped injury, screamed, "*Wake up!*" over Natalie's lifeless body, as Hopper got up and frantically paced, repeating, "Oh man, this is all my fault," like a mantra of guilt. Natalie drifted in and out of consciousness, wondering why her face was wet and complaining that her head hurt, as neighbors appeared with blankets, an ambulance pulled up with its siren blaring, and Jackie pitched into the brush Hopper's open whiskey bottle, tangible evidence of their criminal activities.

When they got to the emergency room, doctors examined Natalie while Hopper and Jackie, scared sober, conferred over whom they should notify. "We needed a spokesperson, because we obviously had been drinking and it didn't look good." Jackie told Hopper to call Nick Ray, "because he communicated on our level."

Natalie had the same thought, for different reasons. "I was sort of semiconscious," she said in a later documentary about Ray. "And the police were called and they were asking me my parents' phone number, and I kept saying, 'Nick Ray. Call Nick Ray. And the number is so forth and so forth. I'm at the Chateau Marmont.' And I just kept repeating that."

Ray called his physician to meet him at the hospital, then he phoned Natalie's parents. When the director arrived at the E.R. shortly after the Gurdins, he stormed over to Hopper, "grabs me and throws me against a wall. I was trying to explain to him, and I guess he was a little hysterical, and he slapped me very, very hard, pushed me against the wall, and said, 'Shut up, and straighten up.' "

Once the doctors reported that Natalie had a concussion but would be all right, "she didn't want to see her parents first," Ray would recall, "she wanted to see me." When the director approached her bed, Natalie pulled him next to her face and whispered, "Nick! They called me a goddamn juvenile delinquent! *Now* do I get the part?"

Jackie and Hopper, who were skulking nearby, remember hearing Ray say to the doctor, as he left Natalie's room, "Take good care of this young lady, she's the star of my next movie."

14 NATALIE "LUCKED OUT" TO GET the part in *Rebel Without a Cause*, in the opinion of her next beau, Scott Marlowe, whom she talked to about how Ray had "dangled" her until the strangely fortuitous car accident.

Whether anyone called Natalie a juvenile delinquent that night, or if she was being theatrical to manipulate Ray—in the tradition of Maria—is her secret, for no one else heard the comment, and Natalie would later ascribe it to different people. "Why would they have called her a juvenile delinquent when she was fucking unconscious?" queries Hopper. "She may have *said* that. Because I'm sure that the reason—I thought so at the time and still do—the reason she kept 'wanting to see Nick Ray, see Nick Ray, call Nick, call Nick,' is because she hadn't gotten the part in the fucking movie! And she wanted him to see her—not like a Hollywood type, but really in trouble."

One adult who came close to calling one of the teenagers a delinquent was Mud, who glared in the E.R. at Jackie, Natalie's companion in crime, as if she was hell's angel, smelling her breath and demanding to know if she had been drinking. Jackie lied to cover for Natalie, whose vices were an open secret with the morally flexible Mud.

On February 23, *Variety* ran a blind item about the teenagers' drunken escapade, calling them "overenthusiastic wannabe juvenile delinquents" who "got overenthusiastic for director Ray, and lotsa nicked noses resulted." The accident made Natalie more fearful of fast cars. "She told me they actually almost went over the edge of Laurel Canyon," relates a classmate. "It was very, very, very frightening to her." According to Marlowe, Natalie was "terrified" of Laurel Canyon afterward.

Almost perversely, she still had not clinched the role. Her forty-three-year-old lover, Nick Ray, was committed to Natalie, while ironically, the studio perceived her as a child, because she was playing twelve in *One Desire*. Warner Brothers also wanted a major star for the part of Judy, pushing Ray to cast Debbie Reynolds. Reynolds, who was at MGM, had no idea Warners was promoting her, and "wasn't interested" in *Rebel*. "I was in musical comedy, and I at the time didn't really want to do drama . . . I just wanted to be lighthearted and do lighthearted roles." For Natalie, the stakes were "live or die."

To appease the studio, Ray tested an army of actresses the last week of February. One of the eventual gang members, actress Beverly Long, remembers standing in the hall outside Ray's office with Natalie during the tests. "She was very, very into it. She was not a star or anything then, I mean she was just a person. She was so nervous." "I think there were fifty of us to begin with," Natalie later recalled, "and it sort of narrowed down, and the second day it was down to ten, and the third day I think it was down to five or six. But the big problem was that I'd really up to that point only played children . . . and so I was finding it difficult to convince—and Nick was also finding it difficult to convince—the studio that I was out of pigtails."

On March 1, Ray sent a memo to Warners taking an aggressive stance. "We've just spent three days testing thirty-two kids," he wrote. "There is only one girl that has shown the capacity to play Judy and that is Natalie Wood. Although there has been talk of Debbie Reynolds, I think the studio might develop a star of its own with Natalie Wood. I'd be happy to close with her." He acknowledged Natalie's shortcomings, adding, "I could start work on [her] voice, wardrobe and hair."

Long, who weighed a mere 107 pounds and was exactly Natalie's height—five foot one and a half—"felt like a big moose around her. She was about ninety to ninety-five pounds and much thinner-boned than I, very fragile. She had no butt, no hips, no breasts. She looked like a twelve-year-old boy when she was naked." Natalie said later she "had to make a lot of screen tests" to convince the producers she was the right age.

Nick Ray finally prevailed over Warner Brothers the middle of March. When Henry Willson pressured the studio for a "big price" to sign Natalie, "I spoiled it all by blurting out to Jack Warner, 'Are you kidding? I'd do this part for nothing.' " Natalie told her friend Nuell "she would've sat on Jack Warner's lap." She behaved in what would become the contractual equivalent, agreeing to a seven-year option contract with Warner Brothers beginning at $400 a week. "Well, I would have signed almost anything to play that part, so I signed."

For Natalie, winning the part in *Rebel* set up a complex of emotions, some of which were destructive. It led her to believe she could get anything she wanted, and it sent the message that Mud had been right to push her onto Pichel's lap. Robert Blake, her occasional confidant, recognized how vulnerable Natalie was underneath the mink and the makeup. Blake believed that being cast in *Rebel* gave Natalie "the only confidence and security that she ever had—knowing that as a young, frightened teenager, she went in and she got it." The fact that she successfully used her "aura of sexuality" to achieve it at the tender age of sixteen was a commentary on the legacy her mother began for her at four.

Once Natalie got the part, her insecurities came out like evils from Pandora's mythic box. "She was scared to death, because she felt that James Dean could act circles around her, and this was either make it or break it from being a kid actress to an ingénue." The fact that Natalie had to grow up too fast was obvious by the disguises Ray and the wardrobe department devised to make her appear more sexually mature: cushioning to create the illusion of hips, a "butt pad," and a special bra to enhance her childlike bust, which still caused Natalie great anxiety. "That was the era of Jayne Mansfield and Marilyn Monroe. If you didn't have big boobs, you were nothing."

Nick Ray masterminded every detail. "He was always looking for ways to make Natalie more seductive, kind of the Pygmalion thing." Ray told Natalie he had created his ex-wife Gloria Grahame's sexy on-screen pout by stuffing cotton under her top lip. He hired a voice coach to work with Natalie to lower her girlish timbre, and found someone to teach her to walk more provocatively. At the same time, he toned down her makeup, and darkened her hair, advising her to cut it below her ears in soft waves.

Natalie's makeover was essentially complete by the time Ray gathered the cast in his bungalow the last week of February to begin night rehearsals. He spent his days polishing the script and looking for an actor to play Plato, the troubled boy who shares Judy's idolatry of Dean's character. Ray would later assert that he spotted swarthy, sensual Sal Mineo in a lineup of actors trying out for the gang. Jackie, Natalie's school friend, recounts that it was she who suggested Mineo to Ray, after noticing the teen actor in *Six Bridges to Cross* that month with her parents. According to Jackie, Ray was so grateful, he took her to lunch at Romanoff's with Natalie, "and he put two hundred dollars down on the table and he said, 'I want you to buy yourself something.' "

The nighttime rehearsals at Nick Ray's bungalow had a loose, "family atmosphere," with Ray a sort of bohemian patriarch to his largely youthful cast, including Jimmy Dean, who had arrived from New York. "Jimmy trusted Nick a great deal," Natalie observed, "and I think Nick was very fatherly towards Jimmy. I mean he was to Sal and to myself as well." For Natalie, who had been rigidly disciplined from age five to memorize everyone's parts, show up on time, and hit her marks, rehearsing with Ray—who encouraged actors to improvise—was a journey to an alternate creative universe.

"No director that I'd ever worked with had ever improvised. And Nick's bungalow at the Chateau Marmont, where he lived—the set was built *from* that, so that when we rehearsed, we really rehearsed as though in a set. And we improvised most of the scenes." Natalie wanted desperately to be brilliant, to earn the respect of Ray and Dean, but she felt naked without a script. "Natalie liked *structure*," according to Lana. Ray, recalls actor Corey Allen (who played Buzz), "just said, 'Read, and see what you want to do.' He didn't lay anything special on us. He just said, 'Take it easy and explore.' "

When they were working together, Natalie and Ray were "all business," though bubbly ingénue Mitzi McCall, who was cast as a carhop in a scene that was cut before filming, knew during rehearsals that the director and his teen star were romantically involved, as did composer Leonard Rosenman. McCall, who was in the midst of a brief romance with James Dean, considered the much-older Ray "sexy." Rosenman, who was a more mature thirty, took a dim view of Ray's conduct. "He was having several affairs, with different people . . . I liked Nick, but I *didn't* like him, too. He was a weird guy."

A few years earlier, Ray had been part of a love triangle that scandalized Hollywood. He told Natalie he found out that actress Gloria Grahame, his second wife, was having a secret affair with his teenaged son Tony, her stepson (whom Grahame would marry in 1961). "It was a strange situation, because Tony was *around* us at the Chateau . . . it was bizarre."

Mary Ann felt that Natalie could cope with the complexities of her involvement with Ray, and that he would not hurt her. "It's part of the business, and you go with it or you get out. And if you're going to roll with it, you've got to be grown-up."

Natalie left the first rehearsal in the thrall of Jimmy Dean, her actor-god. She revered the way he worked as a new thespian gospel, saying later, "He was serious about his acting. He felt a deep responsibility about his role in *Rebel*." When Dean told her they had to "*live* their roles," Natalie found his words to be an aphrodisiac.

The next day, she and Jackie went to see Dean in *East of Eden*, which had opened at the Egyptian Theater in Hollywood. "She walked out and said, 'I'm gonna marry him.' " Natalie later admitted she had "a big crush" on Dean. "I remember going with my school girlfriends to see *East of Eden* like fifteen times, sitting there sobbing when he tried to give the money to his father. We knew every scene by heart."

Natalie was infatuated with what Dean *represented*—a higher form of cinematic art, the same attraction Nicholas Ray held for her. She was also confusing her own identity with Judy, her character, who falls in love with Dean's character, Jim Stark. "I didn't have a strong sense of my own self," she later analyzed, recognizing that she often took on the emotional characteristics of her characters. The parallels between herself and Judy further blurred the line between fantasy and reality for Natalie, powerfully so in what Dean embodied. Not only did he play her character's boyfriend Jim, Jimmy Dean was an icon for Jimmy Williams, Natalie's own rebel love.

A few nights before filming began, Ray called the entire cast to his bungalow to do a read-through, an event memorialized in photographs. The actors can be seen sitting on folding chairs in a circle around Ray, looking down at their scripts in fierce concentration. Natalie is a tiny figure in a too-sexy dress, her face rapt in thought. The feeling from the photograph is one of collective intensity; it was a "weird night," describes one participant. Marsha Hunt, a veteran stage actress cast as Dean's mother, found the reading fascinating. "The cast sat around and mumbled. Nobody was audible but me!"

Natalie entered what she later would call the "golden world" of Nick Ray on March 30, 1955, the first day of shooting. She developed a ritual: at 5:30 A.M., she would pick up Jackie and they would go to breakfast, where Natalie ordered egg yolks; then she drove to Warner Brothers, going straight to the makeup department. Her ritualistic breakfasts at 5:30 "were the only time Natalie was ever without makeup."

On set, she gave the appearance of being self-assured, but the actors playing gang members, who were older, could tell that Natalie was nervous about working in Ray's loose style, in her first mature part. "It was palpable, and it came out in the role," Corey Allen, who played her boyfriend in the early scenes of the film, recalls. "She didn't seem to me to be familiar, or particularly comfortable, with exploring the things which are awkward for any adolescent . . . and not only sexually." Natalie, in Allen's opinion, had a hard time exposing herself emotionally. "Nick had a wonderfully nurturing effect on Natalie, which enabled her to go much deeper than she otherwise would have gone. I don't mean that she didn't *have* it. I mean that she hadn't attained it yet." Natalie seemed hungry for Ray's input, "[like] a novice, who was really willing to work, and who was responsive to Nick's direction."

Ray's influence can be seen to startling effect by comparing Natalie's textured, emotional performance as Judy to her more facile portrayal of a teenager in *The Wild Bunch* a month earlier. His Pygmalion-like suggestions to darken and cut her hair brought out Natalie's sensitive brown eyes, and the more subdued makeup revealed her natural beauty. "The camera loved her," observed Debbie Reynolds, the studio's choice for the role. "She had features for the camera like Elizabeth Taylor and Marilyn Monroe. They were so beautiful, and the camera loved their faces! It was a love affair with the camera, and Natalie had that, with those big brown eyes, little nose, little mouth."

While Natalie hero-worshipped Ray, she was in awe of Dean. A few months later she said reverently, "Great directors Elia Kazan and George Stevens said that Jimmy was the finest of young actors, and I knew how right they were when I had only worked in one or two sequences with him." Sal Mineo observed, "He was all she could talk about. Every night for weeks in a row, she went to see *East of Eden*—she must have seen it over fifty times. She even taught me to play the theme song from the picture on the piano." According to Natalie's tutor, "She would hang around him as much as possible . . . she was very flirtatious with him."

By nearly everyone's accounts, Dean at times treated the adoring Natalie perversely. "He would *do* things to her off-camera. He would taunt her . . . Natalie would be in a close-up, and he'd get on a ladder behind Nick Ray and the camera, and Jimmy would say, '*Woo-woo-woo-woo*' and imitate a train." Dean's disciples considered it a form of "Method" acting: that Dean was staying in the character of Jim Stark, the alienated outsider, between scenes. "Natalie was schooled that when the scene is over, you drop it and you go away and become 'Natalie Wood' again. But Jimmy was Jim Stark all the time. It was a different kind of atmosphere for her."

She said later, "I kept hearing about the Method, and just about everybody on the set was carrying a copy of Chekhov's book, *To an Actor*, and using phrases like sense memory, and emotion memory." They were techniques invented by Stanislavsky, taught at the Actors Studio in New York. Natalie idealized Studio devotees—Kazan, Brando—as gods of drama, embarrassed by her child star past. "Natalie and I took acting as a job," observes Margaret O'Brien. "We went in to do our best, we had responsibilities. When I left the job, I didn't think about it anymore, and neither did Natalie." O'Brien considered the Method "a lot of hooey," and believed it destroyed actors' lives by instructing them to become their characters. Natalie was "fascinated" by the Actors Studio methodology, concedes O'Brien. "She loved the Brandos and the Deans. These were people that were like from another planet, you know?"

Dean, a costar observed, would "toy" with Natalie in the guise of Method acting, occasionally crossing the line to cruelty. She would defend his behavior passionately, saying that it was part of Jimmy's "brilliance," though later,

Natalie privately expressed disappointment about a few of Dean's taunts. She yearned to measure up to his standards, to emulate the mysteries of his genius. "I think she was a little scared of him, too," assesses Bev Long. "Or more like, 'wow.' He was extraordinary as an actor, but he was very weird as a person. He was very moody and all that stuff." Long's heart went out to Natalie during her scenes with Dean. "She was so vulnerable. She was really 'right there,' all the time—really working, and really trying to do something. Working with Jimmy was quite a feat, because he would behave so badly sometimes . . . and it was hard, I think, with her, to get close to him."

Natalie's access to a deeper part of herself in her scenes with Dean was evident. Reynolds, who might have played Judy, noticed "a lot of depth and soul" when she saw Natalie's performance. "She was not just a little cute thing . . . she had a lot of courage, and she fully fulfilled the role and brought to it color and unexpected moments, which is what makes a star." Natalie's feelings of inadequacy were unfounded, assesses Robert Blake. "She didn't need the Method—she was instinctual." Hopper, who was there, concurs. "She did it without a lot of baggage, without having to go through a lot of great metamorphosis to become Judy."

Natalie lacked that confidence or insight. She felt inferior to anyone with Studio training and embarrassed by her ignorance of Stanislavsky. Her insecurity manifested itself in a jealous fixation on actress Susan Strasberg, the seventeen-year-old daughter of Lee Strasberg, founder of the Actors Studio, who represented everything Natalie felt *she* was not. On set, Ray would whisper encouragement to Natalie before a scene, or pull her aside to suggest how to do it differently. He used his sexuality to bring out the young actors. "He would come up to Jimmy or Sal or Natalie, and he put his arm around their shoulders and walked them away from the crowd, and then he would say, 'Well, what I want to see . . .' and be very vague and strange and moody and mysterious . . . very sensual. That's how he made the connection."

However, it was Dean—not Nick Ray—who was the dominant presence. According to Corey Allen, "Nick told me that he made an agreement with Jim not to rush Jim. And so sometimes we would wait thirty or forty minutes for Jim to come out of his trailer." Dean wanted to "prepare" until he felt ready to shoot a scene.

Marsha Hunt, the actress signed to play Dean's mother, left the picture the day Ray was to shoot the opening sequence at the police station ("I was already committed to a play . . . and I finally had to make a choice"). The no-nonsense character actress Ann Doran got a call at five in the morning from her agent, telling her to drive to Warners to replace Hunt in a Nick Ray picture. "I thought 'Nick Ray? Who the hell was Nick Ray?' I didn't even know what I was going to be doing." Ray had cast comedian Jim Backus against type as Dean's tortured father, which meant that Doran and Backus would be portraying husband and wife, as they had three years earlier in *The Rose Bowl Story*.

Backus stuck his head inside Doran's dressing room door. "I hadn't seen Nick Ray yet. I hadn't even been on the *set* yet. And Jim [Backus] came in and said, 'Good to see you,' and all that kind of stuff. And then he said, 'Natalie's on the picture, too.' I said, 'But I haven't met this boy who's playing my son,' and Jim said, 'Whoo! Wait'll you meet him!' "

The old-school actors decided to get a closer look at James Dean. "So we crept up to the set, and sat way, way behind the camera to watch him in a scene." Once the camera was in place, Doran and Backus waited for Ray to call for action. "All of a sudden everything got quiet and [Dean] got down in this fetal position. We waited and waited. *Finally* he stood up, and they said, 'Action!' Jim [Backus] and I practically fell on the floor laughing. We had never seen such a bunch of crap in our lives. We snuck out, because we broke up the scene by our laughing."

Doran considered Ray "a wimp" as a director for giving his star such license. By the end of filming, Doran's opinion of the youth-oriented Ray had not changed. "He said, 'Turn 'em over,' 'Action,' and 'Cut,' and that's about all he did. Jimmy [Dean] just took over the picture," an opinion seconded by Hopper, Rosenman and Steffi Skolsky, who was cast as a gang member. Doran came to admire Dean, once she figured out what he was doing. "Jimmy and I kind of squared off. He was not too sure of me. The first scene we did together was at the police station, where he was rattled—rattled as a person, rattled as a character. So he was fighting back at anybody . . . that's just the way he worked. And I tried to play it to him, to give it to him, to be a little too sweet . . . it gave *him* something to bump off of. And as I watched him work, and worked with him, it was wonderful, because there was this wonderful giving *to* you, and giving it back."

Doran could tell Natalie was in distress the first day. "When we worked before, she had been fourteen, and now she was gonna play a grown-up, and it scared her to work with Jim, this weird thing! Very difficult for her to get *into* that mood." Doran, who had been in five pictures with Natalie by then and admired her acting "tremendously," recognized that Natalie had a completely different approach to acting than Dean. She observed of Natalie, as Orson Welles had when she was six, "Whatever she did, she did it from the heart. From the heart first, and from the mind second."

Natalie had a panic attack just before the emotional scene when Judy bursts into tears at the police station. Long found her in the bathroom. "She was saying, 'I can't do it, I can't do it, I can't, I just can't . . . I can't *cry*," and then she started crying. I said, 'Natalie, yes you can. Look—you're crying now. Just stay in that moment, that feeling, whatever it is.' "

"It" was Natalie's past: the pressure, at six, to cry on cue; envisioning her dog killed; seeing Mud tear apart a live butterfly.

"I told her, 'Let's go back to the set, quick, while you're crying.' "

Natalie felt she couldn't do it. When Long left the bathroom, she was alone with her secret. "She had a little ring made, with a cup on it, and she put Vicks in there. And when she had to do a crying scene, she'd rub the Vicks into her eye. That's how she cried in the scene in *Rebel*."

Doran noticed Natalie was fixated on Dean, who could be "rude, nasty." (Doran once slapped him for taking *her* on a wild motorcycle ride.) "If he would have said, 'Get down and crawl over there,' she would have gotten right down and crawled."

Natalie's friend Jackie, who cut class to be on set, believed Natalie was serious about wanting to marry Dean, whom Jackie felt was contemptuous of Natalie for being too "Hollywood"—the Maria component of the "Natalie Wood" composite personality. "Jimmy liked the innocence of Pier. He had this image of Natalie that she wanted to be with him just because of his fame, which was not true." According to Jackie, Natalie tried to hide her affair with Ray so Dean wouldn't think less of her.

She was embarrassed that she still had to have a welfare worker on set, irritated that she had to study with a tutor, and indignant that the studio was required to use a double for her when shooting after midnight. Ray tried to hire Jackie to be Natalie's welfare worker, until Warner Brothers realized that Jackie was in the eleventh grade. Ray finessed it so that Tom Hennessy, a tutor for the studio, served as both Natalie's teacher *and* welfare worker, and got a "special dispensation" from Maria authorizing Hennessy to stand in for her as Natalie's guardian on the set.

Hennessy, a handsome former football player who sometimes worked as a stunt man, was as straight an arrow as Ray was "a free spirit," in Hennessy's words. He recalls Natalie "could be moody. She resented the fact that the other 'kids' were out there doing their thing . . . when she had to be restricted to the schoolroom or trailer, but basically she was cooperative." Natalie later told *Look* that she and Mineo, Hennessy's other charge, "would tell him that we had arranged interviews for [him for] an acting job . . . we made up the interviews to get rid of him." Skolsky remembers, "She just wanted to grow up. She wanted to be eighteen so she could be out of her mother's reach. And she was always trying to sneak a smoke."

Hennessy took it as his responsibility to shield Natalie from the *Rebel* gang. "He had a big meeting and he told the producers and Nick Ray that we were smoking and swearing around Natalie, and that we were a bad influence. We just howled, because she smoked more than we did—and swore!"

There was an absurd, Fellini quality to the illusion of Natalie being under the protection of a studio welfare worker, when she was sexually involved off-set with the forty-three-year-old director. Faye Nuell, a pretty dancer with a passing resemblance to Natalie, whom Ray hired as her double, became Natalie's friend and used to go to Ray's bungalow with her at all hours. Nuell was aware that Natalie was involved with Ray, but "she didn't really talk about that stuff very much. I mean she adored him—that was very clear . . . I think it was hero-worship on her part." Nuell considered Ray's involvement with Natalie "ego" driven: "She was an adorable, sexy young girl. *We*, of course, thought he was an old man—a sexy old man."

According to Nuell, Ray's affair with Natalie was taboo on the set. "If it was thought about, it was whispered and nobody wanted to talk about it. She was underage. To my knowledge, people didn't really know at the time. It was years later that Natalie was a little more open about it." Others described it as a quiet buzz. "We all knew," Doran said in 1999. "Jim [Backus] and I talked about it." Backus told Doran, "Well, I hope she doesn't get pregnant."

Hopper, who had been persecuted by Ray since filming began, came to the conclusion Ray was using him as a smokescreen for his illegal affair with Natalie. "The day of the chickie run scene, Natalie's parents had arrived on the set, and Nick suddenly started yelling at me and sent me to my trailer, in front of her parents. Which is when I realized that the reason I was getting into this kind of a problem with Nick was because of Nick Ray's relationship with Natalie and *my* relationship with Natalie." Hopper figured that the studio or her parents had complained that Natalie was having an affair, and Ray told them it was with *Hopper*. "I realized that I could be expendable in Nick Ray's world. And he could blame *me* and get off. And I wasn't gonna let it happen."

That night, before the chicken run scene, Hopper took Ray aside. "I said, 'Nick, I *know* that you've been fucking

Natalie. You're now using that against *me*. I know that you've now told the studio that I'm having an affair with her. This has gotta *stop* . . . [or] I'm gonna beat the shit out of you right now.' And I took some sort of boxing pose." Hopper would never forget Ray's response. "He said, 'See, that's your problem. You have to use your fists. You can't use your brain. Someday you're gonna have to start using your brains.' And he turned and walked away."

Whether the studio *did* know about Ray's affair with Natalie is unclear. Hennessy, who was working for Warners as Natalie's chaperon/tutor and on-set guardian, "was suspicious" because of her frequent night and weekend rehearsals at the director's bungalow, "but she gave me the impression that there wasn't much that I could do about it." Since Hennessy wasn't legally required to be at Ray's bungalow, he felt "it was up to her mother and her parents to be in charge." Natalie's increasing control over her mother was apparent by the fact that Maria delegated her guardianship of Natalie on the set to Hennessy, who recalls, "Her mother wasn't around all that much."

The tutor was on "friendly relations" with Maria, who considered it in her best interests to be polite to anyone affiliated with the studio. To the *Rebel* gang who had minor roles, she was "such a bitch. She used to throw us out of the dressing room if she wanted to take a nap. I remember being very intimidated by her." In her middle age, Maria had cut her bush of hair into a severe Dutch bob she dyed until it was the color of indigo ink; the contrast against her Russian-pale skin, and the intensity she projected, gave her the appearance of a prison matron in a film noir. "She seemed very stern, with the black hair, and the way she looked."

Maria's lack of outward affection was a mirror of what

Natalie was experiencing playing Judy, whose father slaps her when she tries to kiss him on the cheek. One of the gang recalls, "I never saw Natalie hug her mother and chat with her mother, and her mother certainly never associated with any of us."

Natalie had powerfully deep and conflicting emotions about Mud. As Faye Nuell would observe, "She kept trying to keep a distance, she very much wanted to be her own person," but "there was an incredible bond there." Nuell, who was privy to Natalie's feelings about Maria, perceived their mother-daughter symbiosis as a uniquely Russian, "strange, mystical connection." Natalie told Nuell many times about the gypsy's warning, "Beware of dark water," as if *she* and the prophecy were somehow entwined, even though it was said to her mother. She revealed to Nuell the secret she and Mud shared: that it was Natalie's destiny, as Maria's second-born child, to be known throughout the world as a great beauty. Nuell found it all mystic and fascinating, "but Maria wasn't *my* mother."

Fahd, who got a job as a carpenter on miniature sets at Warners through Natalie's connections and Mud's finagling, "somehow seemed to know that he wasn't important" by comparison to the gothic drama of Maria and Natalie. Nuell could tell that Natalie loved her Fahd "and he loved Natalie tremendously . . . but I don't think she respected him then."

Natalie embraced Nuell as part of the magic circle of Nick Ray, as she did Hopper, Adams and actor Perry Lopez, who were disciples of Dean and whom Natalie viewed as extensions of Dean. She told biographer Albert Goldman years later, "They were the gods. I just wanted to be exactly like them." They frequented foreign films, Hopper recalls, "trying to find another way of, like, working . . . we were very ambitious to change things." The Dean acolytes adopted angst as an artistic affectation, and Natalie cheerfully suffered with them: "What we used to talk about was how unhappy we were. Whoever was the unhappiest, whoever came closest to suicide the night before, he was the winner."

She hinted at their other exploits, saying that Nick Ray had taught her about books, while Hopper and Adams offered a fast course in cigarettes, drinking and cussing—their imitation of "wild, crazed Hollywood icons," reveals Hopper.

"All three of them—Natalie, Dennis, and Nick Adams—had a leaning to the wild side," remembers Natalie's tutor. Adams later told a magazine, "Natalie thought that being grown up meant being free of the rules . . . for a few months, she spent most of her time rebelling against everything and everybody." Nuell believed that Natalie's fast life with Adams and Hopper was an attempt to exorcise the superstitions and gypsy magic Mud had brainwashed her into believing.

As its only female member, Natalie became the golden goddess of the cult to Dean. Adams loved her as if under a spell. Hopper said later of his friendship with Natalie, "It's one of the best relationships I've ever had in my life." What Hopper admired most about Natalie was her honesty, audacity, "and her *balls*. I mean she really had balls." Lopez remembered Natalie as "up for anything." She filled a room with her tinkling laugh, sparkling with creative energy.

Natalie also gave her complete attention when she listened, fixing her expressive velvet eyes on whoever was talking, mirroring that person's emotions. "Hopper and Perry Lopez . . . these guys were all running in the fast lanes, and getting themselves messed up. And bless her heart, for *hours and hours and hours* she would sit and just be consoling. She always had time for them." In his old age, Lopez, a handsome bit player in *Rebel*, would cry at the mention of Natalie's name, saying, "Meeting her was the best day of my life. I still think of her twice a day."

Some questioned whether the ambitious Adams and Hopper had additional reasons for getting close to Natalie. "I remember being in Dennis' dressing room with Nick [Adams] and Natalie," states actor Jack Grinnage, one of the gang members in *Rebel*. "I don't know which one of them said this—it was Nick or Dennis—but he said, 'We're gonna hang on to her bra straps.' Meaning up the career ladder." Natalie's tutor, who knew Hopper and Adams off set, said, "Both of those two guys were all over her . . . because they could see that this movie was going to be a big thing for Natalie . . . they were game for anything in order to be noticed and to get ahead in the business."

Opinions were passionate, and divided, about the two actors. Ann Doran considered Hopper "an opportunist" but liked Adams ("he was a nice kid, very straightforward that he wanted to be an actor"). Skolsky and Long championed Hopper, calling Adams "an asshole" whose "motives were never pure." Natalie openheartedly adopted them both; the comical Adams became a best friend. "Natalie was very naïve in many ways," observes Steffi (Skolsky) Sidney, "and she didn't realize he was such an operator."

As part of their desire to make their marks in the history of cinema, the triumvirate of Hopper, Natalie, and Adams fancied becoming their era's romantic icons, patterning themselves after notorious screen legends from the past. "We were always envious of the generations *before* us," reveals Hopper. "People think that *we* were wild, but man, we had a lot to come up to, in our opinion, from the generation that had just, like, disappeared—the John Garfields and the Lana Turners, Ava Gardners. In a strange way, we were trying to emulate some sort of past glory."

One night, possibly after *Rebel*, they decided to have an "orgy," because they read that Garfield had them. Natalie's Hollywood-glamour idea of an orgy was to bathe in champagne. As Hopper recalls, "I think she had heard that Jean Harlow or somebody had had a champagne bath." Hopper and Adams eagerly rushed out to buy several cases of champagne, pouring the contents of the bottles into a hot bath at Adams' cabin in La Cañada. Natalie put a dainty foot into the tub and smiled, imagining herself as Harlow. When she sat down in the champagne bath, she let out a scream and jumped out, her vagina burned from the alcohol. "That stopped *everything*," Hopper would remark.

Natalie laughed about the "orgy" afterward with Nuell. "Natalie was adventurous about sex and life. She was going to explore it all. She thought it sounded so glamorous—they bathe in champagne—and her whole vagina was burned by the alcohol!"

Nuell considered Natalie's sexual adventurism a form of rebellion. "I saw the fights with her mother in the house a lot. It was, 'You have to be home by such and such time.' 'No, you can't wear this.' 'You are wearing too much makeup.' If Maria could have kept her a baby forever, she would have been very happy." The mixed message to Natalie from her mother—that it was acceptable to have sex with middle-aged, married men with power in Hollywood, but not with boys her age—created moral confusion in Natalie.

Nuell observed, "I think there was an *amorality* with Natalie. There was a big thing about breaking the rules: she wanted to break the rules. She followed whatever her feelings were and it wasn't about making judgments. That's not always the healthiest thing to do, or the smartest. That was her modus operandi. That was her appetite, too. She would become fascinated with somebody and the sexual part of it was just the natural part of wanting to get to know them."

Hopper felt that Natalie was living out "the goddess syndrome, and the outrageous behavior of the female stars during the forties and so on." She had been trained for this idolatry since she was two, pasting pictures of Hedy Lamarr, Veronica Lake and other forties' glamour girls into the family scrapbook of stars.

In the case of her behavior with Hopper and Adams, Natalie was also fueled by the desire to belong to the kingdom of James Dean. "She went along with things, thinking she was being the 'in' person—naïvely, with these guys, who were on the make for *everything*. She was very enamored of that whole—the legitimacy that title gave: you know, 'method acting.' " Hopper contends, "It was almost that we were naïve to the point, 'If people did drugs and alcohol and were nymphomaniacs, then that must be the way to creativity, and creativity's where we wanna be. We wanna be the *best*.' She always wanted to be the best."

There was a schizophrenic quality to Natalie's life. In reality, she was having an illicit affair with a director her father's age, participating in wild escapades with Hopper and Adams; for fan magazines, her publicist would send a young, wholesome actor to her house, accompanied by a photographer, and the trio would travel to a restaurant, where Natalie and her arranged escort would be photographed on a "typical date."

Actor Ben Cooper, who got the assignment more than once, kept photos from one choreographed evening. In the first photograph, Cooper, a boyish twenty-two, stands in front of the Gurdins' open front door, as a smiling Maria—in a mink-trimmed dress—kisses a ponytailed Natalie goodbye. In the second photo, Natalie, wearing an evening gown, and Cooper, in a three-piece suit, feed each other cherries off the top of a hot fudge sundae. *That* was the image of Natalie Wood press agents created for the public.

Not surprisingly, "Marie was an expert at the set-up date," observes Robert Hyatt, who witnessed her in action when he and Natalie were at Republic. Mud, who took credit for inventing Natasha's star persona, considered *herself* to be "Natalie Wood," as much as her daughter. If Natalie got dressed to go to a premiere, Mud put on a formal gown as if *she* were going. Mary Ann recalls, "Natalie and I used to laugh about it all the time. Natalie would say, 'Well I think I'll wear this . . . unless *Mom's* gonna wear it!' "

Cooper, Natalie's staged date that spring, became friendly with her, howling over the fan magazine's "screamingly funny" demand they share an ice cream sundae. Once the photographer was gone, "we went out and had a bite to eat, and talked." Cooper, who had starred on Broadway as a child and worked with Nick Ray the year before in *Johnny Guitar*, had a similar enough background that he and Natalie related, though Cooper was a conservative, "kind of mature for my age."

Cooper found Natalie to be "just a terrifically nice, sweet person" who was being consumed by insecurity and drive, "to do *more*, to be the *best*," which she equated with Dean and the Method. Cooper got the impression Dean and his followers had her under a Svengali-like spell, "that they were manipulating and controlling her, and that she would do just about anything, at anytime," which distressed him. "Here she was, a fabulous actress—just incredibly good, from the time she was a child, devastatingly good, and well-known—and it seemed that she needed *more*, and was allowing herself to be used by this group of guys, as if that was her acceptance. I felt that she felt she *had* to go along with whatever they wanted."

Cooper drove Natalie home, "trying to see if I could get her to kind of pull away from Jimmy Dean and that group. Not for *me*, I just felt she was caught in a quagmire, and I really liked her very much."

The second time Cooper was set up with Natalie, he spent a few minutes with her mother, giving him a glimpse into the reason behind Natalie's secretly sybaritic lifestyle. "Her mother was firm, Russian: 'You *vill* do this, you *vill* do that.' " Cooper found it revealing that Natalie "didn't tell me *anything* unhappy about being a child actor. She shied away from talking about her mother. It was almost as if, 'No, I'd rather not.' " Cooper analyzed that Natalie participated in Dean's cult as the only way available to rebel, "because in film, the work is so structured you can't be too rebellious *there*, or they're not going to use you. So where else *could* she?"

Natalie's sometime beau, Rad Fulton, was dismayed by the change. "It was like looking at a pretty little girl on one page, turn it over, you see an adult. She became a nasty little girl, as far as morals. Sometimes she spoke like a truck driver. Kind of hard to fathom, that happening that fast." Actress Debbie Reynolds, who was twenty-two then, remembers seeing sixteen-year-old Natalie at parties, often with Nick Adams. Reynolds thought of her as "a woman with a young girl's face."

Jackie, who was with Natalie almost daily, began to worry that her behavior "sometimes felt destructive." She noticed that Natalie needed to be the center of attention, in the midst of clamor, at all times. "If she was at home and the phone wasn't ringing, she was unhappy—but it was always ringing—and if we were out someplace, she'd call her mother a hundred times to see if anybody had called. Like she wanted to fill her life with people so she didn't have to think about anything."

There was something vaguely melancholy about Natalie to Bev Long. "She always seemed a little tentative, a little frightened. She was sweet and lovely, and I never heard her say a bad word about anybody, but she was not a boisterously happy person. She was kind of delicate. I always felt she was vulnerable, and sensitive—which she was." Long, who was only slightly older than Natalie, "felt terrible" when she found out Natalie was intimate with Ray. "So many times I wanted to say something, like, 'God, Natalie . . .' I used to think, 'God, she doesn't need to do that, why is she doing that?' " Long observed that Natalie always had to be with somebody, "particularly men."

She flirted at the commissary with her tutor, the handsome but stalwart Hennessy, or when he took her to dinner during a night shoot. "She'd kind of play games like that, but I told her to knock it off—I didn't want any kind of suspicion of anything like that."

"Natalie wanted an affair with *me*," asserts Leonard Rosenman, the film's composer. Rosenman, while flattered ("I thought to myself, 'Oh boy, I wish I was 150 years younger!"), chose to be Natalie's friend, and to counsel her. He was impressed by her intellect, suggesting she go to college after she finished *Rebel*. Natalie seemed interested, but told Rosenman it was impossible. "She said that her mother just constantly wanted her to work." ("She could have been *anything*," avers Mary Ann, "she was so smart.") The composer urged Natalie to get therapy, concerned about her home life and the fact that, at sixteen, she was involved with a forty-three-year-old man.

The perception among the young female cast was that Natalie was promiscuous. "I never understood it," said Long. "Why did she need to do that? She was such a wonderful girl on her own." Natalie's close friend Nuell felt that Natalie was "pressing the limits" in defiance of her mother. "Somewhere, probably, she wanted someone to say, 'Stop it. Don't do that.' "

Throughout filming, Natalie was obsessed with a smoky, melancholy song recorded by Peggy Lee, called "When the World Was Young," a bittersweet lament to lost youth that she sang constantly. "The song reminded her of *her*," Jackie observed:

They call me coquette and mademoiselle,
And I must admit, I like it quite well.
It's something to be the darling of all,
La grande femme fatale, the belle of the ball.

There's nothing as gay as life in Paree,
There's no other person I'd rather be.
I like what I do, I like what I see.
But where is the schoolgirl that used to be me?

You'll see me at Cap d'Antibes or in Spain.
I follow the sun by boat or by plane.
It's any old millionaire in a storm,
For I've got my mink to keep my heart warm.

And sometimes I drink too much with a crowd,
And sometimes I laugh a little too loud.
My head may be aching, but it's unbowed,
And sometimes I see it all through a cloud.

Ah . . . the apple trees,
And the hive of bees, where we once got stung.
Summers at Bordeaux, rowing the bateau,
Where the willow hung, just a dream ago
When the world was young.

"It was sad . . . 'where's the little girl that used to be me?' " reflects Jackie. "And I think that was the way she perceived a lot of her life, especially in those years. Because she was being kind of used, and even though she felt in love with Nick Ray, I'm sure there was a point where she's saying, 'Why am I sixteen, having sex with somebody that's that old?' "

Jackie believed that Natalie "was such a sensitive person," she fell in love with every man with whom she was intimate. Scott Marlowe, Natalie's subsequent boyfriend, got the impression Natalie wanted to marry Nicholas Ray, suggesting that the relationship was not casual on her part.

Natalie and her great friend Mary Ann had soul-searching conversations about their relationships with men. Underneath her sexually rebellious behavior, Natalie was influenced by old-fashioned mores. "We got into heavy discussions about how men and women go in and out of heavy love affairs, and how *men* seem to function without a problem—hello/goodbye—and *women* are just devastated. And why? Is it the nesting syndrome?" Natalie felt incapable of fleeting sexual relationships without an emotional attachment, and was frustrated by the 1950s double standard dictating that "it 'wasn't nice' " for women to enjoy their sexuality. According to Mary Ann, in Natalie's heart, she wanted to find one true love, marry him, and live happily ever after. "She was—quote unquote—'seeking bliss.' "

She was also desperate to escape Fahd's alcoholic rages and the gypsy-mystic regime of her obsessively ambitious mother, flinging herself into relationships in the hope she would find the security and love that was missing in her life.

Natalie said later her favorite scene from *Rebel* was one between herself and Dean that was cut from the film. The choice reveals much about what Natalie was feeling at the time:

> It was in the car. I was waiting for him and he comes up and we talk to each other. There was a section of the scene where I imply that I've sort of been around, that I'm not really pure.
>
> I say to him, "Do you think that's bad?" And he says, "No, I just think it's lonely. It's the loneliest time."
>
> I thought it was a wonderful line—right on the cutting room floor.

Sometime during filming, Natalie's affair with Nick Ray came to a bittersweet end. She told Mary Ann that Ray had cut it off, "but she had been in the business long enough to realize that these things happen . . . it was a little bumpy for her, but it was best." Natalie offered a more poetic version to Jackie, saying she had gone to Ray's bungalow one day when he was out, leaving behind her key, and the books he had loaned her, as a romantic gesture their affair was over.

Jackie thought that Natalie broke off the relationship

with Ray in the hope that Dean would see her in a romantic way. "She and Jimmy were having a big fight when they shot their love scene, and it was really upsetting to her. She complained because she'd come on the set and he wouldn't speak to her." In Jackie's view, Dean's disinterest intensified Natalie's desire. "She always wanted what she couldn't have."

Ann Doran would recall that Natalie finally "meshed" with Dean creatively. "Sal Mineo told me afterwards that he used to talk to her. Sal was a kind soul. He'd say, 'Honey, it's *his* way of doing things. Just get *with* him.' And Natalie finally *got* with it."

By the end of filming, she and Dean became close friends, with Natalie resuming her role as "Nurse Nancy," comforting Dean through his distress over the news that Pier Angeli—still married to Vic Damone under pressure from her mother—was pregnant. "Pier was Jimmy's whole life, I mean eat, live, sleep, breathe—it was so sad, that whole thing," asserts Mary Ann, who often was present when Dean "poured his heart out" to Natalie. "She felt close to him, because the same type of situation had happened to her with Jimmy [Williams]. It was a few years before, but those wounds take a long time to get over." In Mary Ann's view, Dean brought out Natalie's "huge maternal instincts. She was always going to make everybody better."

Jackie saw Natalie's friendship with Dean as a consolation prize after she was unable to turn the relationship into something romantic, an analog to Nick Adams' friendship with *her*. "She wanted Jimmy, and she tried every way she could think of to get him to go out with her. If she couldn't seduce him, she would take the friendship."

Though Natalie told reporters, later, that she briefly "dated" Dean, all her friends understood the relationship to be platonic. (Hopper believes that Dean would not have become involved with a minor at such a critical stage in his career, and that he wanted to keep his personal life separate from the work.) Lana remembers him coming to the house to see Natalie, as would Maria, who described James Dean, later, as a "very nice boy" who surprised her by singing a song, in Russian, for her.

Lana confirms her sister was "obsessed" with Dean; Natalie's later comments about him suggest that she idealized Dean even before his fatal car accident.

Once, when she was at Dean's house with Jackie, Natalie found a scrapbook he put together. She sneaked it out for a few days so she could look at it, and as Jackie recalls, "It was the most pensive, sweetest . . . he had pictures of babies, and he had his favorite poem, Edgar Allan Poe's 'Annabel Lee.' The sensitivity of this human being! In the back of the book, there was a little thing cut out of a newspaper, and it said, 'Ways for a Boy to Get a Dog,' and if that didn't tear me apart!"

Natalie would later compare Jimmy Dean to the Little Prince, the magical character in the allegorical fable she adored, who believed "It is only with the heart that one can see rightly." She explained the dichotomy between the tender, poetic Jimmy Dean she idolized and the intermittently provocative costar who taunted her, by saying, "It was like two separate people: there was the Jimmy I was working with, and there was this other person on the screen."

That June, while *Rebel* was in postproduction, Natalie drove onto the Warner Brothers lot with Faye Nuell, planning to have lunch at the commissary and loop some lines from the film. When she pulled onto the studio lot, the parking places were taken. As Nuell recalls, "There was a security guard standing there and he said, *'Oh! Miss Wood!'* And he moved one of the sawhorses and made a parking place for her.

"She looked at me, and she said, 'You saw that?' "

Natalie knew, in that instant, that *Rebel Without a Cause* had made her a star at Warner Brothers, four months before its release.

15

NICK RAY GAVE NATALIE A TOY tiger after they completed *Rebel*, a gift suggesting her sexual paradox as a child-woman. She started to collect stuffed tigers with frenzy, acquiring so many she briefly would become known as "Tiger."

Natalie had not set foot in Van Nuys High for months, but she considered it an accomplishment to graduate with the class of 1955, a symbol of her striving for a *real* life. She was deprived of even that opportunity to be herself when photographers showed up on June sixteenth to take shots of Natalie Wood, the star, as she left her house to attend the commencement ceremony. Natalie posed for them with Mud in countless contrived scenes at the front door, smiling effervescently in her cap and gown. Once she was alone, she burst in tears at losing a moment Natalie considered hers, not Hollywood's. She and Margaret O'Brien celebrated their joint graduations that night at Peter Potter's Supper Club, where Natalie resumed the Natalie Wood persona, "flouncing in with her fur," making sure she got to the stage to give a live interview.

She spoke wistfully to a fan magazine of going to college one day to study art and literature, testing in the top ten percentile. Natalie was on a movie set within hours of graduating, canceling a vacation in Hawaii to start *The Searchers*, director John Ford's now-legendary western about a loner with a deep hatred for Indians, played by John Wayne, who embarks on a five-year quest to recover his niece from Comanches, who kidnapped her in a vicious raid.

Although Natalie, who would be playing Debbie, the niece, thought "it was a big deal to do a picture with John Wayne" and considered her small part to be pivotal, the true reason she accepted *The Searchers* was that John Ford had agreed to Mud's idea to cast eight-year-old Lana as young Debbie in the scenes through the kidnapping. (Ford had only one stipulation, according to Lana. "I was brought into the office to meet John Wayne, and John Ford said, 'Can you pick her up?' So he lifted me off the ground, held me up, said 'Okay,' and that was it.")

Fan magazines would trill how Natalie's little sister Svetlana Gurdin had chosen the stage name of "Lana Lisa Wood," and that she was excitedly following in Natalie's footsteps as a child actress, but it was all Mud's doing. "She pushed me massively," reveals Lana, who was filling the void in their mother's life that Natalie's growing independence created. Mud's approach with "Lana Lisa" bore no resemblance to her consuming attention to Natalie, her golden girl. "She said, 'This is what you're doing, you're going to work on this film. Get up, get showered, I'm taking you to a set, these are your lines, learn them.' "

Natalie would recall the imperious Ford as "tough, but kind to me" during the shoot, which took place on a Navajo reservation in the blistering summer heat of

Monument Valley, Utah. The authenticity of the setting ("just dust and heat") led to Natalie "frying" her skin from sunbathing, and spooked Lana, "because every night you could hear the Indians chanting and singing, and then there was a dust storm and we got trapped in the commissary." The cast semi-roughed it, staying at the Goulding Trading Post, where Ford took his evening meals, expecting John Wayne and the rest of his stars to join him, "as he sat holding court at this long table . . . and we were all there to do his bidding." That was the recollection of Wayne's handsome son Patrick, who had a small role in the picture.

As the only teenagers on the remote location, Pat Wayne and Natalie drifted together, enjoying a mutual crush that was a sweet contrast to her adult experiences on *Rebel.* Patrick Wayne recalls, "We didn't have to fake being in the frontier, we were living in it, so you were really looking anywhere for any kind of amusement. There were no movies, there was no radio, there was no television, there was nothing!" Outside the influence of her provocateurs, Hopper and Adams, Natalie turned to more innocent pleasures, playing cards or board games with Pat. "We spent a lot of time talking together on the set, and just related as two young teenagers about the same age. And I had a great deal of fondness for her, even puppy love."

Pat Wayne, barely sixteen, was slightly awed by Natalie's "world of experience, and the stories that she would tell me about things that she had done." He was shocked that someone as dazzling as Natalie could be "neurotic" about a tiny bump on her wrist, which she showed him in secrecy one day, "but I guess she just had no sense of the fact that her charisma or her presence would overcome anything." Natalie's ambition to be a star nearly overwhelmed the relaxed Pat. "It wasn't unattractive, but . . . she seemed like a person that had figured out that she was going to do what it took to be a success."

She impressed Ford, who came back to the Trading Post after directing the climactic scene where John Wayne finds Natalie living among the Comanches, saying, "That girl was brilliant today."

"Duke Wayne was a great guy for eyes," costar Harry Carey, Jr., said later. "And every confrontation that was very dramatic that he had with Natalie—because he really wanted to kill her [character] because she'd been living with the Comanches for so long—he said she had such great eye contact, that she gave so much . . . he couldn't stand actors or actresses that didn't really look at him when they talked to him, and this with Natalie impressed him very much."

John Wayne's only personal comment about Natalie was to his son Pat. "He noticed that we were spending a lot of time together, and he said, 'Just be careful where you're going.' I guess he was concerned that I was gonna become too involved with her and get upset or whatever. He was being fatherly."

Natalie celebrated her seventeenth birthday on location for *The Searchers*, coming back to L.A. a year closer to the magic age of eighteen she believed would set her free. She splurged on a new Thunderbird convertible, gambling that Warners would exercise her option and she would have the security of a salary again.

She finished the summer in a social whirl—at a beach party in Malibu with actor Hugh O'Brian; spotted by gossip columnists having dinner with Pat Wayne; mugging with Nick Adams in a Hollywood costume shop; on the arm of

Perry Lopez for the opening of the Greek Theater, then on to Ciro's. Most of the "dates" were set up by publicists for the purpose of generating pictures for fan magazines of up-and-coming young stars at play, and Natalie threw herself into them with the élan she gave everything. In the photographs, she is always animated, makeup Max Factor perfect, a different bracelet over her left wrist at every event, her beau gazing at her magnetized.

Natalie was like a whirligig, spinning between boyfriends and phone calls and photo shoots and parties, making sure there were no empty moments. She said tellingly, "Actors are basically lonely people," admitting to one writer that she was frequently lonely and depressed. Her bedroom had become a zoo of toy tigers—including a stuffed tiger's head mounted on the wall, given to her by Mud. Dennis Hopper "thought it was cute and eccentric," recalling "stuffed animals *everywhere*." Natalie's tigers were a replacement for the collection of storybook dolls that had been her nighttime companions up to then, hinting in interviews at her fear of being alone. "That's why I have toy tigers around me—to keep me from getting lonely and depressed."

Some of the young actors from her publicity dates buzzed around Natalie on their own time—so many that Mud and Fahd called her Scarlett, a role Natalie had a "burning ambition" to play. The beaus—Hopper, Adams, Lopez, actor Martin Milner—seemed to be more *friends* than boyfriends. Hopper fell into this curiously ambiguous category after they completed *Rebel*, "when we got into a relationship where we were going out to parties together and we would score for each other. She'd say, 'I'd really like to have a date with *him*,' and I'd say, 'I'd really like to have a date with *her*,' and we had great fun procuring for each other . . . we weren't blind to the fact that we could see other people, but we were having sex all through our relationship."

Natalie set up Hopper with Margaret O'Brien on a blind date, a mismatch that signaled the two child stars' drifts in different directions. O'Brien recalls, "He was not my cup of tea, and I wasn't his cup of tea . . . he was trying to be Jimmy Dean and I didn't understand that scene at all, so I think he thought I was boring and I thought he was strange."

Maria used a portion of Natalie's Warner Brothers earnings to construct a swimming pool in the backyard, "so she could *monitor* the *Rebel* boys—Hopper and Adams," according to Robert Hyatt, who heard her grouse about Natalie's boyfriends, paranoid that Natalie would get pregnant, or fall in love, and leave home. Since Natalie had stripped her of her earlier power, Mud had to resort to subterfuge to try to retain control over her alter ego. She came up with the idea of building a pool to entice Natalie's swarm of beaus to the house, so she could keep an eye on them—a plan that was not only manipulative but oddly perverse, since she and Natalie were terrified of drowning, and there was barely space for a wading pool. Lana recalls, "Natalie would get in, get wet and get out."

Maria "tolerated" Hopper and Adams, in the Hyatts' opinion. Hopper remembers Natalie's mother having "talks" with him. "She never went into any details, it was just a lot of attitude. A *lot* of attitude. Didn't like me, didn't trust me. And it wasn't dumb of her. Natalie did what she wanted to do." Hopper, who inspired Natalie's sexually liberated Zelda Fitzgerald personality, believed she was enjoying her sexual freedom "and didn't have moral hang-ups in those areas," unaware that Natalie would agonize over moral issues with her friend Mary Ann, who asserts "she wasn't a 'player.' "

Ed Canevari, who stayed with the Gurdins that September to visit his childhood best friend, found her to be the "same old Natalie" she was at four, when they baked cookies in her play-oven in Santa Rosa. The only difference was the mink stole Natalie threw over her sundress as they posed for pictures with her parents and Lana.

On September 29, Warner Brothers exercised the option on the first year of Natalie's seven-year contract, but she was still clawing for recognition as an actress. From what she later told Scott Marlowe, she was upset at the way Warners had placed her credits at the beginning of *Rebel Without a Cause*, which she saw at an early screening. "Her billing was just lousy—she was just thrown in with everybody . . . so she went to Henry Willson and said, 'Please, Henry, do something to change that billing, because I think this movie is going to help me a lot.' And he was terrified of Jack Warner. So she went in on her own and *begged* him to change the billing."

Natalie felt Warners was dismissing her as "just an ex–child star, and ex–child stars *never* did well historically." She had a continuing inferiority complex vis-à-vis the Actors Studio, which she tried to disguise by demeaning it in interviews, saying, "I don't like technique in acting . . . I believe if you have a feeling for acting it comes to you naturally, that you don't need any training." In truth, Marlowe reveals, "she wanted to model herself, in a strange way, after Jimmy [Dean]," demonstrated by a "beatnik phase" Natalie went through that fall, strolling barefoot with Nick Adams, mimicking strangers.

She was ecstatic to be cast as Clara in *Heidi*, a television special to be broadcast from New York starring Jo Van Fleet, Dean's costar from *East of Eden*, another Kazan protégé whom Natalie regarded in "tongue-tied" awe. Warner Brothers made arrangements to send Adams and Sal Mineo to Manhattan with her to start promoting *Rebel*, scheduled for release in early October.

Natalie had to reconfront her fear of airplanes, a carryover from her trip to New York at the age of six, when pregnant Mud was unable to fly with her. She came up with a bizarre ritual of carrying her stuffed tigers with her, believing they were talismans, a superstition similar to Mud's gypsy magic. "I won't fly without them," she said the next year. "I also have people write notes to me when I fly—silly little notes. That, plus the tigers, constitutes my good luck charms."

While she was in New York, Natalie saw her first play on Broadway, "crying her eyes out" through two performances of *Anastasia*, a haunting mystery about the young grand duchess rumored to have survived the execution of the Romanovs, whose family portraits Natalie saw from her crib as a child. It was the role she would be preparing to play as her stage debut twenty-six years later, before she drowned.

The night before Natalie filmed *Heidi*, a Friday, September thirtieth, actor Dick Davalos, who played Dean's brother in *East of Eden*, invited her and Adams and Mineo, Dean's costars in *Rebel*, to dinner in Chinatown. "We were all together—all Jimmy's friends," Natalie would recall. "We were talking about what a great future he had, and how in a few years he'd be the greatest thing that ever hit Hollywood. Then Nick said he was sure Jimmy wouldn't live past thirty, with all his rodeo riding and his racing." Natalie told the group, "Jimmy's going to outlive every one of us at this table." The next morning, "We read the terrible, unbelievable news of Jimmy's death in an auto accident. And we realized that he had been killed almost as we were talking about him the night before."

Dean's fatal accident in a speeding Porsche along Route 466 on his way to the races in Salinas, California, would have similarly eerie reverberations throughout the country, and on *Rebel Without a Cause*, which came out at the time of his funeral. "The way the world reacted to Jimmy's death was what I had heard, but was not old enough to remember, about Valentino's death," observed one of the *Rebel* gang. Actor Corey Allen, whose character drives off a cliff while racing against Dean's character (seen through much of the movie in a red jacket), remembers, after the movie opened, "young men running around in red windbreakers, and talking with their lips barely moving, and thinking that they would somehow become Jimmy."

Theaters showing *Rebel Without a Cause* offered grieving fans a temple to worship Jimmy Dean as an actor, to mourn his passing, and to wonder what might have been, turning Nick Ray's personal statement into "an epic," and Natalie Wood into a star. "It's a gruesome thought that she owes her stardom to James Dean's bad driving, but it's certainly true that his death helped establish him as an icon and that her association with him benefited her," film critic Stanley Kauffman observed years later. "What might have happened otherwise, who knows?"

Natalie called it "a lucky picture" for her, "because that part had such dimension to it—more than the normal ingénue role for a fifteen-year-old girl, so I think that helped me get into more mature roles."

While it was a lurid coincidence that car accidents contributed to Natalie's fame from *Rebel Without a Cause* in three ways—Hopper's head-on collision on Laurel Canyon helped her get the part, a tragic crash was the climax of the "chickie run" scene, and Dean's fatal smash-up in his Porsche ignited the movie's cult success—her poignant performance was memorable on its own. *The Hollywood Reporter* called Natalie "splendid," with Ray proclaiming her "the greatest young actress since Helen Hayes." She had the same vulnerability on-screen as an ingénue as she had playing an Austrian waif-child at six, clinging to Orson Welles. "She had an endearing quality," as her actor pal Ben Cooper observed, "and I don't think people can *fake* that."

Natalie found out about Dean's death during the taping of *Heidi*, reacting hysterically. She broke down in tears at the press premiere of *Rebel*, and kept a miniature bust of Dean as a shrine, recalls Lana. For days, reporters would call Natalie for stories about him, designating her the keeper of Dean's flame. "I was embarrassed," she told Hollywood correspondent Vernon Scott months later, "because it made me look as if I were capitalizing on his fame." At the same time, she loyally defended her friend Nick Adams to Steffi Skolsky when she heard that Skolsky was "badmouthing" Adams for selling Dean trivia, a rumor Nuell and others confirm was true, though Natalie was too faithful a friend to believe it.

Her role as James Dean's girlfriend in *Rebel Without a Cause* not only established Natalie as a mature actress, she suddenly became her generation's idealized teenage girl. Her brown eyes sparkled from the cover of every movie magazine, featuring articles with headlines such as: "Natalie Wood Speaks Out," "Teenage Siren," "Natalie's Teenage World," "Going Steady with Stardom," "The Dance She Couldn't Miss," "It's a Wonderful Whirl," "Togs for A Teen," "It's a Date!"

Natalie's personality buried itself further as "Natalie Wood" became more famous. She felt pressure, in public, to become the air-brushed fantasy figure smiling from the pages of fan magazines, to *please* everyone, to be *perfect*, the way Mud trained her, to look beautiful at all times, to be a *star*. "She was very concerned about how her fans felt about her," her sister Lana observed. "It was sometimes a burden for her, because she felt so indebted to everyone, felt that she had to appear a certain way, had to *be* a certain way."

"I have to be '*Natalie Wood*,' " she would tell her friend Robert Hyatt.

Hopper recalls, "People would come to the table—we'd be sitting eating, in the commissary, or a restaurant or whatever—and Natalie would turn on this *smile*. This smile, you know? And the *second* the person left, the smile would drop and she would just go right back. She'd turn it on, and turn it off—it was incredible. I used to say, 'I don't know how you can do that, Natalie. How do you do that?' She said, 'Practice.' "

Every moment in Natalie's day was dedicated to the pursuit of stardom. Even the court hearing for approval of her new contract at Warner Brothers—required by law because she was a minor—became a photo opportunity for Natalie Wood, her star alter ego—and her mother's. She and Mud went to court together, with Natalie dressed to the nines, carrying her toy white poodle, Fifi. As they left the judge's chambers, Natalie held up Fifi for UPI photographers, mugging adorably with her poodle, a picture that made newspapers across the country the next day, with captions such as "Pats of Joy," reporting Natalie Wood's new seven-year movie contract.

She opened her first checking account, depositing part of

her Warners salary at the discretion of Maria, who controlled the rest as family income. Natalie had no concept how to function outside the artificial world Mud had created for her. "My first official act was to overdraw $400," she said to a Hollywood editor. "I'm not very bright about money. I'm not domestic either. If I don't learn how to cook, maybe I won't have to."

She cooperated fully with Maria's star-driven regime, even though her own dream was to be a serious actress like Jo Van Fleet and other protégés of Kazan, creating an internal conflict that contributed to Natalie's confusion about her identity. Her struggle to reconcile these two competing goals is evident from this interview she gave then:

> Stardom is only a by-product of acting . . . I don't think being a movie star is a good enough reason for existing. I want to contribute something of myself. I feel that it's possible to be a star, yet be a good actor—like Brando, Clift, Eva Marie Saint and people like that. On the other hand, there are certain stars who are not actors. I don't want to be that type. I know there are certain rewards for stardom. I can't help being touched when fans want my autograph, but I like to think it's because they like my work, because they like what I've done—not because I wear long earrings or drive a Thunderbird.
>
> . . . It would be foolish of me to say I don't want to be a star. But if I didn't believe in what I'm doing, I'd rather go to work in a dime store.

That fall, Natalie heard about a picture in development at Alan and Sue Ladd's production company on the Warners lot. The script was by novelist David Dortort, an

Emmy nominee for adapting *The Oxbow Incident*, featuring character actor Raymond Burr. Dortort recommended the dark, heavy-set Burr, then thirty-eight, as the villain in the small-budgeted noir drama he was writing for the Ladds' company, called *A Cry in the Night*. Burr was playing a sexual stalker who kidnaps a beautiful girl after he spies her necking in a car with her boyfriend. The stalker knocks out the boyfriend and drags the girl to a secret lair, where he intends to rape and possibly kill her before her boyfriend and her father, a police captain, can discover where he's taken her.

Natalie "staged a campaign" to play the intended rape victim, which not only challenged her as an actress, but had obvious parallels to her violent encounter with the star she said held her sexual hostage. "It was so absolutely unbelievable," recalls Dortort, who was unaware of Natalie's experience. "She would come up, and practically break down the door, and say, 'I want to play that girl!' . . . she *really* had some deep *feelings*, and an emotional response, to the character for some reason."

Dortort had conversations with Natalie about the character, which he had written with a plot twist. "At first she's terrified, but . . . she slowly but surely begins to *dominate* the man that kidnaps her and was going to rape and kill her." Dortort asked Natalie to read a few scenes. "Watching her—and watching the animated face, and the eyes, she had wonderful eyes—she convinced me that she not only *could* do this part, but she almost *needed* to do this part." For days, Natalie lobbied the producers. "She'd meet the Ladds on one of the studio streets and implore them, beg them, 'I can do it. I was born to do this part.' " As with Judy, in *Rebel*, Natalie *related* to the character, and felt a passion to *become* her on-screen.

Natalie got what she wanted, again—approaching *A Cry in the Night* as if it were Chekhov, not a B movie, and she was Helen Hayes. "She always did the best job she could," observed Hopper. "If she was doing something that was not important at all, she gave it the same energy as something that was going to be great. She really loved her work. That was her *life*."

Her first day of shooting, early November, Natalie invited Richard Anderson, a reserved, contemplative actor loaned by MGM to play her boyfriend, to meet in her dressing room so they could go over their scenes, a rare gesture in a low-budget contract movie. Anderson, who was a mature twenty-nine to Natalie's seventeen, remembers her as "very watchful," "always fighting for better stuff," a "fully engrossed actress" who was "really *there*."

Lana, who had to be forced into doing *The Searchers*, was awestruck by her older sister's absolute dedication to acting. "Every day of her life, she never thought about doing something else. She thought of what she could do to be better. She would analyze her script and write notes in the margins, and she was very, very careful, very meticulous with *all* of her roles. She would get an idea of who that individual was long before she would start the film."

Natalie merged with her victim character in *A Cry in the Night*, forming a bond with Raymond Burr, her movie stalker. Their costar, Richard Anderson, noticed they "caught on immediately professionally," and "had great sympathy for one another's work, and what they were both trying to do." Burr, a closeted homosexual or bisexual who seemed "overwhelmingly lonely," according to screenwriter David Dortort, brought sympathy to the sexual psychopath, playing him as a persecuted mama's boy with a kind heart beneath his brutish exterior. Burr's gestures during script readings with Dortort—"bringing his hands around, fluttering a little bit"—suggested the rapist was secretly homosexual, like Burr, "and I put that into the character: that he wanted someone to *talk* to, someone who would appreciate him for what he was, and not criticize him."

Natalie, whose character responds sensitively to her captor, found herself similarly drawn to the gentle giant Burr, who had infatuated her ever since she saw his deep-set bedroom eyes in *A Place in the Sun* with Mary Ann. Burr, a gourmand, invited her to dinner one night, ordering escargots at an elegant restaurant. Natalie had no idea they would be eating snails, setting the tone for Burr's "Orson Welles makeover" of her that fall. "Burr was a very classy guy, and he saw her talent, and the potential in her, and he really wanted to cultivate her, the way Orson Welles did with Rita Hayworth," suggests Mary Ann, "and it was done very lovingly."

Natalie went out with Burr throughout filming, and afterward. "Natalie was so crazy about Raymond Burr," Jackie recalls. "That was when she was kind of branching out, and learning more about literature. She said that when she would go over to his house, he could recite poetry. He was a real sensitive human being, and she had a wonderful time with him—fine wines, wonderful cook, extremely intelligent—but at the end of the day, he'd kiss her on the cheek and say, 'Goodnight, Natalie.' "

According to Jackie, "It was the most devastating thing when she found that Raymond Burr was gay and there was no way they were going to have an affair, because she tried her darndest. She thought with her charm she could make the difference." Burr's preference for men stimulated Natalie's tendency to "want what she couldn't have." She continued their relationship, in the hope she could "change" or seduce him, "like Elizabeth Taylor and Monty Clift."

After Natalie's confession she had been raped sadistically by a powerful star, the males in her life were either *pseudo*-boyfriends—Hopper, Adams, Perry Lopez, Martin Milner—or men of sensitivity, such as Nick Ray and Jimmy Dean, who possessed her Fahd's tender, artistic nature. Her attraction to the gentle, homosexual or bisexual Burr followed this trend, providing Natalie with what Debbie Reynolds referred to as a "safety net." Hopper, who performed in an ABC King's Row Theater production of *The Wedding Gift* with Natalie that December, knew that she was seeing Burr and that Natalie considered it "dating," not a friendship, speculating "She may have gone into a period where she was interested in gay men."

Her next serious boyfriend, Marlowe, believed that Natalie also viewed Burr as representative of a fantasy. "He was a protector of sorts. He would tell her things, worldly things—*he* thought were worldly and *she* thought were worldly. She *wanted* somewhere . . . she wanted a world, outside the world that was created for her: the child actress, the Warner Brothers contract; that mother, the dragon. She was living a frightening fairy tale."

Natalie, moreover, may have found the relationship with Burr a catharsis from her confessed rape, since Burr played her attacker on screen, and her character formed a sympathetic attachment to him, managing to escape sexual assault.

Most of Natalie's friends assumed that Burr was using the relationship partially as a "beard" to "cover his gayness," as Hopper put it, a common practice in the repressed fifties. Burr claimed to have been married multiple times, to wives who died or disappeared under untraceable circumstances.

"In those days, they were all in the closet," asserts Dortort, who felt sorry for Burr. "To admit it was suicide. Absolute death." Others presumed Burr dated Natalie to get his name in the gossip columns. Burr later told Robert Benevides, his longtime male companion, he was in love with Natalie.

Toward the end of filming, Warner Brothers got word their seventeen-year-old starlet was dating the corpulent, thirty-eight-year-old villain of their stalker movie. "Everything gets upstairs," Anderson would say. "Whatever happens on the set—they have their watchers." The studio pressured Natalie to stop dating Burr, considering the relationship destructive to her image and their film.

Natalie ended the year 1955 as she began it, embroiled in a complicated, scandalous, futile relationship with a middle-aged man.

16

IN HER NEW YEAR'S DAY COLUMN, Hedda Hopper predicted Natalie Wood as one of her "top picks for stardom" in 1956, a harbinger of what would be the most glamorous, clamorous year of Natalie's life.

Warner Brothers launched a dizzying campaign to get Natalie nominated for an Academy Award for her performance in *Rebel Without a Cause*, capitalizing on her emerging popularity as a teen idol. They scheduled five separate magazine layouts in the Gurdins' backyard at intervals, with an ecstatic-looking Natalie dressed in a variety of bikinis and bold bracelets to cover her left wrist, pretending to dive into the tiny kidney-shaped pool she avoided, in real life, like a death trap.

"We'd all get her in the pool and she'd do a little dog paddle," one of the Hopper clique recalls. "I'd say, 'Come on, you gotta learn to swim, I can teach you and we'll take it slow,' but the water was terrifying to her. We'd make fun of her when she would paddle around like a little dog, and we'd laugh, and call her all sorts of dumb names."

Natalie demonstrated an obsessive dedication to Warners' publicity department, helping to create an artificial version of her life for fan magazines to foster the studio's image of Natalie Wood. She was still the people-pleasing Natasha she was at four—curtsying for grown-ups, singing songs with hand gestures, desperate that people like her.

The publicity was effective; a few months into 1956, Natalie was receiving more fan mail than any other star on the Warners lot. But the line separating Natalie from "Natalie Wood" blurred with each publicity layout she did. "They were very strange," she said later. "It was like reading about somebody else. I didn't feel synthetic, but lots of the stories were simply made up . . . there was so much invention." Years later, in 1980, she would compare her experience to Brooke Shields' teen fame:

> The constant attention is what is so difficult. People say, "Come here, do this, do that, let me take your picture, get up early, go on this tour, go out with that person, don't go there, do that, wear that dress." That's where all the confusion sets in.
>
> If there were no publicity and acting was your only job, I don't think anybody would get into very much emotional trouble.
>
> That's why I feel sorry for Brooke Shields . . . the stress of a relentless career where she's being photographed every day, playing the sex symbol, doing commercials, posing for the cover of *Vogue*—being so visible, such a *star!* That's difficult.

As she posed for fan layouts, Natalie was simultaneously completing the grueling abduction scenes in *A Cry in the Night*, performing with such intensity she dropped to ninety-one pounds and gashed her thigh on a rusty nail, prompting the studio physician to recommend time off, a warning Natalie ignored.

She continued her forbidden romance with Burr, which she told one close friend had become physical. Natalie was so engrossed with her career and with Burr—who sent her flowers every other day—her head was barely turned at a Thalians party at Ciro's in January, when she chanced to encounter Robert Wagner, the Fox heartthrob she had been maneuvering to marry since she was eleven. They shared a dance and flirted enough to be mentioned in a gossip column the next day as "in a spin . . . and loving the spin they were in," but nothing more came of it.

That winter, Warner Brothers capitalized on Natalie's popularity, putting her in the first of two low-budget movies with Tab Hunter, the blond teen idol, who was also under contract to Warners. To promote them as romantic costars, the publicity department created the impression that Natalie and Hunter were dating *off*screen, sending them to glamorous events photographed as a couple, planting suggestive items in columns ("Natalie Wood was seen coming out of Noel's candy store with a red heart, on Tab Hunter's arm"). "They were pushing us, so they really built us up," recalls Hunter.

Natalie's true personal life—puffing from dramatic cigarette holders, sipping champagne at supper clubs with her beau, thirty-eight-year-old screen heavy Ray Burr—was causing problems between her and Warner Brothers. She and Burr were pictured together at the Coconut Grove over cocktails, listening to Peggy Lee: Burr is in a tuxedo;

seventeen-year-old Natalie wears an ultrasophisticated one-shouldered gown, her mink beside her to keep her heart warm, as Lee performs "When the World Was Young," Natalie's poignant trademark song. That month, Natalie's Revlon-red smile radiated from the cover of *People and Places*, quoting her wanting to play a "femme fatale."

Warners waged war over Natalie's romance with Burr, and her glamorous nightlife, forbidding both. The end of January, Hollywood writer Joan Curtis ran into her at a party for forty "up-and-coming" young actors:

> Natalie sat in a corner sulking . . . over the fact that the older man she was then tingling over had been declared off-limits by her studio, and as she was still under 18, she had been requested *not* to pose for any pictures with a drink in her hand. In fact, a studio man was present to see the edict was carried out. Her poured-on slinky black dress (which she borrowed from wardrobe) and heavy makeup seemed out of place for one so young . . .

The party—at a restaurant called the Oyster House—ironically was hosted by Robert Wagner. "My husband and I wondered why Natalie and Bob hadn't discovered each other romantically," Curtis commented for a magazine after the party. "Bob's blond handsomeness seemed to compliment [sic] Natalie's dark beauty to perfection." Natalie, according to Curtis, thought only of her taboo boyfriend, Ray Burr. "Nick Adams confided to me that he was particularly distressed over the deep depression she was in."

The same week, Jack Warner—the head of Warner

Brothers—"chaperoned" Tab Hunter and Natalie to an industry banquet, sending an emphatic message about the image the studio wanted to promote. Hunter recalls: "Natalie and I used to kid, we used to say, 'Oh my God, don't tell me they're gonna try to make us into William Powell and Myrna Loy!' Then we'd laugh like crazy about this."

On February 10, the new Warner Brothers duo started filming *The Burning Hills*, a Louis L'Amour western in which Natalie wore a cascade of black hair and deep tan makeup to play a Mexican spitfire tending to Hunter's cowboy wounds, a picture so camp, "she used to make jokes about it . . . and do all those terrible Spanish lines." (Hunter, who later became a rancher, would remark, "The best thing in it was my horse.") After living her part in *Rebel*, and as Burr's near-rape victim, Natalie's only comment to friends about *The Burning Hills* was, 'Oh, hell, I've got to be up at five . . .' She was more worried about wardrobe—to make sure that she had a bosom lift."

Natalie's pique at Warners for pressuring her to stop seeing Burr, and forcing her into a "Carmen Miranda accent" in a picture she found absurd, revealed itself when she began staging sick-outs on the set, behavior she had learned from Mud. Stuart Heisler—the same director who had forced her to dive from Sterling Hayden's boat during *The Star*—telephoned a Warner Brothers executive one evening to complain, saying:

> Something happened to Natalie Wood today and I just found out about it, and the more I think about it the madder I get . . . she went over to the lunch wagon, ordered a huge hamburger, ate it and then ordered a ham and egg sandwich on top of that.

> Then when it's time for her to work (even though she was a little late in getting fixed up) she suddenly gets sick . . .
>
> Unless Jack Warner or Steve Trilling tells me otherwise, I'm really going to let this girl have it. From what I get from the crew tonight, this seems to have been a pre-arranged sickness—and if she goes to a premiere tonight (which I have heard she may do) then I'll really bawl the hell out of her . . . we will never finish the picture the way we want to and will do if this girl is going to start acting up . . .

Natalie was frustrated, telling a writer her goal was to be the "greatest actress" she could be, to play "character parts with realistic emotions," using the model of Jo Van Fleet or Vivien Leigh, hoping she would "still be creaking on the stage at eighty." During the first days of shooting the embarrassing *Burning Hills*, she received an Academy Award nomination as Best Supporting Actress for her performance in *Rebel Without a Cause*, an exceptional accomplishment at seventeen. Natalie got a standing ovation on the set—validating her consuming passion to play Judy.

While she was struggling through *The Burning Hills*, Natalie found out that Warner Brothers had acquired the film rights to Herman Wouk's popular novel *Marjorie Morningstar*, forming a similar obsession with its title character, a sheltered Jewish ingénue inspired to be a great actress, whose heart is broken by a middle-aged composer-director. "She read the book and she just threw the book down and she said, 'This is my next movie. I'm gonna do this. I love this character—it's just me!' " *Variety* announced in March that Warners had Elizabeth Taylor and Marlon Brando in mind, but Natalie was possessed to play Marjorie, another character with whom she identified, telling *Seventeen* magazine later, "Almost every girl falls in love with the wrong man, I suppose it's part of growing up," a reference to her affairs with Nick Ray and Raymond Burr.

Her verboten relationship with Burr took a more serious turn in early spring. He took Natalie to the Philharmonic, continuing his real-life role as Henry Higgins to her eager Eliza Doolittle. They went out several times a week, arranging to costar as Anne Boleyn and Henry VIII in a production of *Anne of 1000 Days* at the Pasadena Playhouse, where Burr regularly appeared onstage. The two made plans to go to Korea on a USO tour Burr was organizing that spring.

"He was just so good to her and for her," thought Tab Hunter, whom the studio *wanted* Natalie to date. "She was like a colt, finding its legs—experimenting with things, learning about herself, trying to find herself as an actress. Raymond Burr was like a father figure, in many ways."

Natalie told columnist Sheilah Graham that she and Burr had "an understanding for the future," with Graham reporting, "It's beginning to look like a marriage for young Natalie Wood and Raymond Burr." When Louella Parsons put an item in her March 15 column denying any romance between Natalie Wood and Tab Hunter, stating, "Her real heart is Ray Burr, who'll escort her to the Oscars," Warners took drastic action. Within a week, *Variety* reported that *Hunter* would be Natalie's date to the Academy Awards on March 21, with Natalie retracting her comments about Burr to Graham, saying, "He just helps me with my acting."

Burr, who was cast within months as *Perry Mason*, said later, "I was very attracted to her and she was to me. Maybe I was too old for her, but there was so much pressure upon us from the outside and the studio, it got awkward for us to go around together." According to Robert Benevides, Burr's companion in the last thirty years of his life, "He was a little bitter about it. He was really in love with her, I guess."

Natalie, trained by Maria to defer her own needs to the studio's—whether it meant being terrified by water in a scene, keeping secret a broken wrist from a faulty stunt, or in this instance, losing someone she loved—accepted Burr's immediate exile in exchange for Warner Brothers' star-making buildup of Natalie Wood.

She attended the Academy Awards on the arm of Tab Hunter, chopping off her hair as her sole expression of rebellion. (Hunter had popped into her dressing room that afternoon as the studio hairdresser was styling it, and teased Natalie to "just cut it all off." When he returned a few minutes later in his dinner jacket, Natalie said, "Surprise!" and twirled around, revealing a pixie cut she later called "plumas locas." "She started a whole new trend that went all over—she made publicity all over the world with that.")

Going to her first Oscars ceremony without Burr was not the only disappointment Natalie faced that night. She failed to win an Academy Award for *Rebel Without a Cause*, though the consolation was that she lost to Jo Van Fleet for her performance in *East of Eden*, which Natalie knew by heart. As ever, Natalie had her fur to keep her heart warm: a silver stole, identified in Warners' publicity as a gift from her parents—paid for, by Mud, with Natalie's money.

Within a few days, Warner Brothers announced its second picture to pair Natalie Wood and Tab Hunter, beginning in May. *The Girl He Left Behind* (or *The Girl with the Left Behind*, as Natalie later would deride it) was another "schlocky" production, so low-budget the studio would decide to shoot the picture in black and white. "Warner Brothers made me do [it]," she later conceded, a condition of the studio's pact to make Natalie into a movie star in the old Hollywood tradition.

She returned to her submissive, dutiful self, "dating" up a storm with Tab Hunter, photographed in movie magazines dancing with him at a UCLA fraternity party where she served as Queen of the Dublin Ball, the model of a wholesome fifties teenager. While she was at UCLA, she ran into a few of her classmates from Van Nuys High, including one of Jimmy Williams' former teammates, who found Natalie "totally unaffected and totally sweet," despite her burst of fame, though it was clear, to all of them, she could no longer even pretend to fit into their world. "She honored us with her presence," as the student chairman of the Dublin Ball would put it.

Natalie's absorption in her career, and her mother's drive to make her a star at all costs, affected her close camaraderie with Mary Ann, who had always been leery of Hollywood, and of Maria. "I was approached for auditions and stuff and I just backed off. It's not my thing. I wouldn't like that whole thing. And of course as I got older and I saw what was happening, I *really* backed off. Natalie kinda went one way, and I went one." Though their paths diverged, the friendship remained sacred. A Van Nuys graduate who talked to Natalie at the UCLA ball remembers, "The first words out of her mouth were 'Do you ever see Mary Ann?' "

Mud was on cloud nine over Warners' publicity campaign to launch Natalie Wood as its newest star, and by the studio's invented romance between Natalie and Tab Hunter, whom she considered "safe." Maria had always been impressed by "gentlemen," and was flattered that the well-mannered, respectful Hunter unfailingly addressed her as "Mrs. Gurdin," presenting himself as the anti-Hopper. "I think it's all in how the parent perceives who their daughter is going out with," suggests Hunter. "For example, if I toot the horn and expect Natalie to come running out, or I'm a real slob about the whole thing. But I would *never* go over there without a jacket or tie on—unless it were a casual date—and I'd take Natalie to a nice place. And Mrs. Gurdin liked that."

Warner Brothers promised Natalie a spring break in Hawaii between her back-to-back pictures with Hunter, purportedly as a bonus for breaking off her relationship with Burr. A few weeks before she left for her Hawaiian holiday, she spotted an actor of eighteen named Scott Marlowe, a dark, handsome, curly-haired intellectual with a Byronic intensity. Natalie was instantly captivated. "I was at the airport picking somebody up, and she just went—*something*," Marlowe remembers. "She got a real vibration from me. We were very attracted to each other. And her mother was with her, and her kid sister, and maybe the father, I'm not sure—it was very early in the morning."

Natalie boldly approached Marlowe, as she apparently had Hopper, offering her best imitation of a fearless flapper as romanticized by Fitzgerald. "She said, 'Oh, I'd really love to see you and meet you again.' She was just *taken* with me, I could hear it." Marlowe, who had been living in New York taking classes at the Actors Studio, was "a little cocky" about dating a seventeen-year-old product of Hollywood. "I thought, 'Well you know, this kid . . .' " When Natalie asked for his home phone number and then called him, "I was shocked." She invited Marlowe to a movie premiere, accompanied by Nick Adams, Natalie's constant companion.

Natalie was smitten with Marlowe, who represented, for

her, the magic of both the Actors Studio and James Dean, once a friend of Marlowe's, whose anti-Hollywood sentiments he shared. "She was so responsive to me. She'd see my work, or she'd come on the set to visit me, and I would tell her stuff that I had learned at the Actors Studio, at Lee Strasberg's, all those people that I had studied with—and Kazan. She adored Kazan, and he discovered me in New York, and I used to tell her stories about him, and she just loved it."

Natalie went to see *A Streetcar Named Desire* over and over again, seeming to "meld together" her awe for Kazan, for the movie, for Warner Brothers, and for Vivien Leigh, who was suffering from bouts of manic-depression. "She felt a great identification with her," Marlowe noticed. "Wanted to *be* like her. And the lady was *so* sick."

In Scott Marlowe, Natalie found someone to love who combined the artistic integrity she admired in Jimmy Dean with the intelligence that drew her to Raymond Burr and Nick Ray. Like Ray, Marlowe provided Natalie with books to stimulate her hungry intellect. "I was into philosophers, and I'd given her Spinoza and Schopenhauer, and a lot of kid stuff—Nietzsche and stuff like that—because I was going through a phase of learning, and wanting to know *everything*. I gave her a lot of plays—a book of 'twenty best plays'—she had *never* read stuff like that. All she'd ever read was movie scripts, and bad movie scripts, usually."

Natalie talked to Marlowe about her obsession to play Herman Wouk's character, Marjorie Morningstar. "She was desperate to get anything that would further her. She had an incredible drive . . . I don't know if she picked it up from her mother or it was forced on her, but she had an incredible sense of destiny and where she should be."

Natalie took singing lessons that spring with a voice

coach named Eddie Sammuels, who wrote a song for her called "Eilatan," "Natalie" spelled backwards. Warner Brothers announced that Natalie would be going on a nightclub tour with a forty-minute song-and-dance routine prepared by Sammuels, plans that never materialized, though as Marlowe recalls, "She wanted to sing well, badly."

On the surface, Natalie's life seemed like a Sandra Dee movie fantasy of a teenage star: she had breakfast in her canopy bed every morning, brought to her by her mother, served on a tray in her cotton-candy-pink bedroom filled with toy tigers—gifts from famous male admirers, who called on her constantly ringing, pink rhinestone phone.

Warner Brothers flew her to Honolulu that April on an all-expense-paid "holiday," with sightseeing activities scheduled by the studio, in the company of reporters and photographers from *Movie Parade* and *Photoplay*, recording her activities as a "diary" for Natalie's fans. Maria went along, ostensibly as her chaperone, though she was really in Hawaii as the "shadow" Natalie Wood.

Natalie spent her private time reading Nietzsche's *Thus Spake Zarathustra*, and *Band of Angels* by Robert Penn Warren, books from Scott Marlowe she carted onto the plane, along with her "lucky" toy tigers to protect her; *Natalie Wood*, the actress, was photographed for fan magazines on a catamaran in the ocean off Waikiki, arranged by Warner Brothers. The ride on the catamaran, a combination sailboat/outrigger canoe, was Natalie's first time on a boat. According to her *Movie Parade* diary, she leaned too far over the side and fell into the ocean. "We were pretty far out when it happened," Natalie was quoted as saying. "Maybe I could have swam back—and maybe I couldn't. Two native boys jumped in after me and helped me back in the boat. Whew! I get cold just thinking about it."

After two weeks, Natalie was restless to get home "and to work." She and Mud took an ocean liner, the SS *Lurline*, from Hawaii to San Francisco, re-tracing the last leg of the days-long journey young Marusia made with her first daughter, baby Olga, a quarter of a century before aboard the battleship *Asama Maru*, when she arrived to a mistress and a home that was one room of a hovel crammed with Russian sailors. *This* time, when Maria disembarked at San Francisco's Port of Angels, paparazzi swarmed the dock, snapping pictures of her and her daughter as they clamored for a shot of Natalie Wood, the movie star composite of Maria and Natasha.

They spent a day or two with Olga, who had divorced herself from her mother's and sisters' Hollywood lives, living a quiet existence in San Francisco with her husband, Lexi, an insurance agent, and their two sons, five-year-old Lexi and three-year-old Dmitri. Natalie posed with her nephews for the San Francisco paper, with the headline "S.F. Actress Visits Here." Olga, who once dreamed of a career in voice, contented herself with singing in the choir at the Russian Orthodox Church where her mother and Nick were married when she was ten.

"Sometimes when I visit my sister and see her two children, I wonder if she missed a lot by getting married," Natalie told a movie magazine when she got home. "But when I look at her, she *seems* happy, and I guess that's the difference between her and me. Right now, nothing could be further from my mind than getting married."

Scott Marlowe, who picked up Natalie when she flew in from San Francisco and was with her every day in the weeks afterward, sensed deep disturbance beneath her outwardly glowing "actress" personality, which he traced directly to Maria.

"I was onto that mother from the very first date. Very first date. She looked me over with such a jaundiced eye and thought, 'Uh-oh, there's a problem here, I can see it.' I think she spotted it at the airport, the very first day."

Mud correctly assessed Marlowe as a threat to her possession of Natalie, in the same way Jimmy Williams was. Like Williams, Marlowe possessed a rebel strength capable of standing up to Mud. "I was a maverick," Marlowe explains, "and Natalie liked that." Natalie was also "madly in love with Scott," observed her sister Lana, increasing the possibility she might leave home, abandoning Mud and the glamorous career they shared. Tab Hunter, who was filming his second movie with Natalie, recalls, "Natalie loved the fact that Scott was part of the Studio and that very kind of crazed crowd like Jimmy [Dean] . . . he was opposed to the 'Hollywood' image."

Marlowe felt that Natalie's mother had prostituted her to make her a star from the age of four, when she met Pichel, revealing itself as he and Natalie became intimate. "She was very, very experienced for a very young girl. She *knew* too much, more than a kid that age should know. She *knew* about all the men's body parts, and about what to do, how to please, or how to get herself loved. She knew all those little things, and it was very sad. I was aware of it from the beginning."

Natalie "had a very wistful kind of quality" that touched Marlowe, "a very sort of sad orphan's quality. She was just incredibly appealing."

He recognized Natalie's terror of being injured during intercourse or of becoming pregnant as phobias instilled by her mother to keep her at home, making movies. "Her mother knew what she was doing. Her mother knew that she was with me, and she just made her fearful. Just scared her, all the time."

When he found out that Natalie was afraid to be alone, a fear her mother encouraged, Marlowe refused to go out with Natalie at certain times, pushing her to spend time by herself so she could become independent.

"There was an edition of Freud that came in six paperbacks, that went through all his phases in analysis and therapy in women," recalls Marlowe, who loaned his set to Natalie. "She devoured them." When Natalie expressed suicidal feelings "in a very general way, in a sort of dramatic way," Marlowe took her to see his therapist, concluding she wasn't "seriously" suicidal. "She just wanted away from that scene: that mother, that father." He perceived Natalie's occasional drinking and heavy smoking as a way "to drown out all that stuff."

Natalie's "twisted and broken" wrist became a metaphor for *her*, the child abused at the hands of her mother and the studios. "That would have been so easy to fix," Marlowe observed. "It was such a minor thing. But she wore it like a cross, a medal. Her mother also put it in her head that it would have laid her up too long in a cast."

According to Lana, Natalie was *afraid* to have a doctor operate on her wrist, "for the same reason that she used to talk about plastic surgery and say, 'I'm just going to have to grow old, because I'm too terrified to have anything done.' " Maria had attached herself to Natalie so symbiotically, Natalie assumed her mother's phobia of doctors, just as she had her fears of drowning and dark water. For that reason among others, Lana would one day interpret her mother's neglect as her own saving grace. "That's what my analyst told me. I was saying, 'Poor me, the forgotten, horrible, nobody cared . . .' and my analyst told me, 'No, you're very lucky. Your mother didn't *influence* you.' "

The bracelets that Natalie used to cover her left wrist in public were symbolic of the split, in her mind, between herself and "Natalie Wood"; when she put on the bracelet, she became the flawless movie star who was always glamorous and beautiful, the only standard Maria would accept.

Marlowe's influence in getting Natalie to start therapy made him even more of a danger to Maria. "She did not like any kind of analysis at any time," witnessed Lana. "She would get very angry: 'What do you talk about when you go to the doctor? You probably talk about *me* with that doctor . . .' " In analysis, "Natalie realized how she'd been manipulated and used," her later confidant Mart Crowley would comment. "She felt angry about it. With good reason." According to Lana, "She just really didn't like our mom. She liked our dad a lot, but she didn't like the kind of person our mom was."

Marlowe would recall attending an actors' soiree at the Chateau Marmont with Natalie, where a hypnotist put her in a trance as a party trick. "He hypnotized Natalie in a room with thirty people . . . and just created the most nightmarish thing that came out of Natalie about the death of a dog. And she *sobbed* and *sobbed*." Natalie was still disturbed when she came out of the trance. As they left the party, she told Marlowe how her mother had forced her to re-live her dog being crushed, to get her to cry for Pichel. "That mother was *ruthless*." The incident was so unnerving to Marlowe, he avoided hypnosis afterward. "I remember taking Natalie home, at like six o'clock in the morning, and the mother was out of her mind with worry. I had a very old junky car. But it had nothing to do with our doing anything wrong—it was just that Natalie had to go on location for *The Girl He Left Behind*. *She* never cared where she was."

Marlowe had deep feelings for Natalie, saying later, "She was the most meaningful woman in my life, Natalie Wood, the most wonderful woman." According to Marlowe, she possessed the same fragile, vulnerable quality with him as she projected on camera. "That was *real*. That was *all* real."

Natalie's admiration for Marlowe was apparent while she was filming her second "B" picture with Hunter, playing the girlfriend of a reluctant Army trainee. "Scott was very serious and very dramatic and so 'Method,' " Hunter recalls. "I remember one time Nat and I were doing a scene and we'd had a little bit of an argument and I said to her in the scene, 'Well, what do you want?' And she was really mad at me when we did the take, and she said, 'I want to see some signs of you growing up!'—and she yelled this at me, she was so involved. So when we cut, I said, 'Thank you, Rod Steiger.' " (*The Hollywood Reporter* would notice her efforts in its review, calling Natalie "one of those rare beautiful young women who gives you the feeling there is thought going on behind her lovely brow.")

Through Marlowe, Natalie met an Actors Studio graduate that summer named Norma Crane, a blond actress nearly ten years older, who would become her closest friend around 1959 and until Crane's premature death in 1973 from cancer, when Natalie quietly would pay all her medical bills and arrange for her funeral.

About the same time as she met Crane, Natalie acquired another new girlfriend, named Barbara Gould, a Fox bit player near her age, with whom she was close for the next year or two.

By June, Natalie was living part-time with Scott

Marlowe, alarming Mud into the surveillance activities she had used on Jimmy Williams, Natalie's first love. "Her mother would open my mail! Just dumb things, like a phone bill, anything, a personal letter." She induced Nick Adams to follow Marlowe when he was with Natalie. "The mother had him actually spying on us and reporting back. I don't know if he was being paid or not." Mud *did* pay a struggling actor named Nicky Blair, who had a tiny role in Natalie's new film, "and he had nothing to say, really, except that I used bad language. I had a vile, filthy mouth. I used to say 'fuck' a lot when I was a kid—I was just trying to be older—and he went to the mother and said that I had this filthy mouth."

A few weeks prior to her eighteenth birthday, after an argument with Mud, Natalie proposed to Marlowe, in a manner reminiscent of Jimmy. "We were walking on the beach. She said, 'Let's get married.' And I said, 'Really?' and she said, "Yeah, I want to get away from her. I want to get away from orders. And I feel that you're my harbor and my shelter.' " Marlowe demonstrated Jimmy's strength of character. "I said, 'Well, I don't know if I can do *that*, but *you* certainly can get away from these *people*.'

"She wanted to marry me. I didn't particularly want to get married. But I knew that, probably, was the only way we would ever stay together, is if we got married, so I agreed. It was mostly her . . . she wanted to get away from that whole family and background stuff, away from that awful childhood."

Though Natalie told movie magazines she felt sorry for her sister Olga because Olga missed a glamorous career to start a family, Natalie, in her heart, still desired what she sought with Jimmy at fifteen. "She wanted to have a normal life, and have a husband and kids," she revealed to

Marlowe. "Kids were very, very important to her." How much of that was fantasy, or seeking "time lost" from her own childhood, Marlowe could not be sure.

Louella Parsons announced Natalie's engagement to Scott Marlowe in a banner headline on July 2, quoting Natalie saying, "I've never loved any other man." When Parsons suggested they might marry on Natalie's eighteenth birthday—July 20—because she would no longer need her parents' consent, Mud reacted like a Fury, setting out to sabotage Marlowe. "Her mother got frantic—frantic—and she gave out this story that I would never go to premieres."

Mud warned publicists at Warner Brothers that Marlowe could ruin Natalie's image because he disliked publicity and drove a "junk heap." When he took Natalie to the opening of *Moby Dick* in his 1940 Cadillac on a rainy night, accidentally stepping on a woman's train, "I was just taken to task in the press, saying that I was not good for her." Maria escalated the anti-Marlowe campaign, enlisting Nick Adams, who gave interviews to fan magazines accusing Marlowe of using Natalie to further his career.

Warners took seriously Maria's propaganda to break up the relationship with Marlowe, who had never played by studio rules. "When I came to this town, I was so inaccessible to those gossip people that they were out to destroy me. I'm not overreacting, either: they were out to destroy me. I was a threat to Warner Brothers and to Natalie. They just wanted to end it. And get on with *her*."

Natalie was caught in a tug-of-war between her respect for Marlowe's disdain of cheap publicity, versus her mother's powerful influence and her now ingrained obsession with image and the pursuit of stardom. As she admitted a decade later, "I [even] used to worry about the *fan* mags!"

Mud's scheme to discredit Marlowe extended to Warners' publicity department, which issued "erroneous" press releases in mid-July stating that Natalie was demanding they cast Marlowe in her next picture or sign him to a contract. "It was a nightmare for me. Warner Brothers just tried to keep her *away* from me."

The day she turned eighteen, July 20, Natalie had her first date with Robert Wagner, to attend a press screening of his new Paramount picture, *The Mountain*, followed by a dessert party with forty-eight other film stars and the press.

Over time, the Natalie Wood legend has been that Wagner telephoned Natalie to invite her to the premiere after photographers posed them together at an industry event, a publicity story that began to circulate after they married. Natalie and Wagner gave conflicting versions of the industry event—Wagner said it was a charity luncheon at the Beverly Wilshire, Natalie wrote that it was a nighttime "Hollywood party–fashion show." They also offered differing accounts of *when* he phoned her for the date: Wagner said he was "captivated" and called right away, Natalie wrote that it was "a few weeks later." Suspiciously, there is no record in the press of an event matching either description.

According to Bobby Hyatt, whose mother and he were still in close contact with the Gurdins, Wagner took Natalie to the July 20 press screening of *The Mountain* as an *arranged* date to fulfill agent Henry Willson's earlier promise to Natalie that she could go out with Wagner when she turned eighteen.

Maria and others would also recall it as a studio "set-up" date, as would Marlowe, who was still engaged to Natalie and begged off going to the *Mountain* premiere, preferring to spend the evening at a friend's place at the Chateau

Marmont, where Natalie began the evening. "I remember she got dressed at the Chateau, and went on the date."

Natalie chose a sea-blue chiffon dress and a tiny diamond tiara for her night with her childhood Prince Charming, though it was not the romantic fantasy she had envisioned at eleven. Robert John Wagner ("R.J." to friends), who was twenty-six to Natalie's eighteen, worshipped the older, conservative bastions of Hollywood, copying the style and mannerisms of Cary Grant and Fred Astaire, to whom he had ingratiated himself as a teenager while caddying at the Bel Air Country Club, next door to his wealthy parents' home. His perfect manners, polished prep school charm, and penchant for fifties slang like "the gonest" and "the coolest," were the antithesis of the intellectual-poet-rebels who fascinated Natalie.

"She was sort of all into that whole Actors Group, and I was sort of a Happy Jack Squirrel kid, you know, with nothing on my mind, much, but my hair," was the amusing, self-deprecating way Wagner would remember it in the late seventies, when he and Natalie were married to each other a second time. He admitted, "I really *liked* Natalie a lot, and I really wanted to strike up a little conversation . . . and she sort of resisted me a bit, actually, at the beginning, because I was so different than all the rest of them."

Ironically, it was Wagner, not Natalie, who was starstruck in their first extended encounter after Natalie's schoolgirl crush on the Fox lot in braces and braids. ("She was so beautiful—those eyes!") Wagner, a high school graduate more interested in mimicking Hollywood stars than in his studies, found Natalie "a great intellect—she read like crazy." Wagner's career, from Fox bit player to *Prince Valiant*, had primarily been as a pin-up boy for teenage girls. He was awestruck by Natalie's "wonderful talent . . . that driving ambition to be somebody." His recognition of his limitations, and Natalie's superior gifts, was honest almost to the point of poignancy. "She was much more accomplished an actor than I will ever be," he said in midlife.

Their first evening together underlined the differences. Natalie would recall Wagner doing "perfect imitations of movie stars," while *he* remembered, "She was so honest. She was real and very vulnerable."

Maria, who had been worried about Natalie's girlish infatuation with Wagner because of his representation by the homosexual Willson, dismissed him completely that night. "He came in and I thought, 'Well, at least the studio sent one with good manners.' That was my first impression of R.J."

In her studio publicity, after she married Wagner, Natalie would help create the illusion she waited by the phone for Wagner to call from the time he brought her home from the premiere. Marlowe recalls, "She came back and we met at the Chateau later that night . . . and she said, 'I had the *most* boring evening. He's very sweet—and so boring. *So* boring. *Please* don't let me do that again.' And I said, 'I can't go to them. I can't. I can't sit through those Warner Brothers things.'"

The next day, Wagner, the perfect gentleman, sent Natalie flowers to thank her for the date. She put them in a vase and went to the backyard to burn an effigy of her studio welfare worker, in ritualistic celebration of the fact that she was eighteen, and the law no longer required a guardian for her on the set.

Years later, Wagner seemed defensive about the impression he made on Natalie. "I was a different type than she was used to . . . she was running around with Jimmy

Dean and those guys—you know, part of the rebel movement. Me, I was around the elite of Hollywood. Power, Webb, Stanwyck . . . Bogie, Betty, Coop—these were the people I was going around with, and it was a whole new world to her." After sending the flowers, Wagner made no attempt to contact Natalie. It was just another date, he told columnist Sidney Skolsky the next year.

Natalie spent the next few days making plans for an imminent wedding to Marlowe, "And she made the mistake of telling her mother," he recalls. "I think Barbara was gonna be the maid of honor, Barbara Gould. Natalie wanted Nick [Adams], and I just said, 'No.' " Their plans were to have a simple ceremony, with just a few guests.

That week, Marlowe was called to New York to do a play, putting the wedding in limbo. Natalie aligned herself with her anti-establishment fiancé. He recalls, "She told Warners she wouldn't go to any premieres again, or do publicity, and they got *really* insane. They got really crazy."

Natalie's second bold move was to fire Henry Willson, who had served his original purpose: setting her up on a date with Wagner. Willson was "screwing her career," in Marlowe's opinion, because he was too attentive to "his boys, the Rock Hudsons and so forth." Natalie's chief complaint was that Willson had not been aggressive enough.

Jackie Eastes was at Natalie's house when Willson phoned for the last time. "She wanted *Marjorie Morningstar*, and he wouldn't go to bat for her. He said, 'You're not right for the part.' And she said, 'If you don't get me this part, you're fired.' I'd never seen her so forceful." Years later, Natalie would ridicule Willson to the *London Times*, saying, "There was a Hollywood agent who made up names for his actors—Race Gentry, Rock Hudson, Tab Hunter. He knew what he's doing, I guess, but Tab's the name of a soft drink. Low calorie."

A desperate Maria implored Nick Adams to persuade Natalie to delay marrying Marlowe. Adams further assisted by "planting" a story in Army Archerd's August fifteenth column in *Daily Variety*, stating that *he* and Natalie "might elope," to Las Vegas, a "set-up" about which Natalie later bitterly complained.

She succumbed to mounting pressure from Warner Brothers and Mud, demonstrating the part of her personality that craved stardom, by participating in a month-long publicity tour to New York, Chicago and St. Louis with Tab Hunter to promote the release of *The Burning Hills* and *The Girl He Left Behind*, arriving at the Los Angeles airport on August 21 in a plunging neckline, carrying her good-luck toy tigers to make it through the flight.

Natalie and Hunter were mobbed at the New York premiere of *The Burning Hills*, with fans swarming them like bees at each city Warners arranged for them to visit. "The tours we went on were phenomenal," as Hunter recalls. "That kind of exposure when the studio gets behind you, it's incredible . . . they wanted to make stars out of the both of us. We were the last of that sort of era."

While Natalie was in New York, she had lunch at the society restaurant Twenty-One, with author Herman Wouk, hoping to convince him to cast her as the title character of his novel, the demure Marjorie Morningstar. She dressed for the luncheon with the same display of allure she had when she met Nick Ray to campaign to play Judy—mistakenly believing that glamour, rather than authenticity, would sell her, an influence of Maria's that would stay with Natalie her life long. Wouk would write:

> It was obvious to me, almost from the moment I saw her, that she was wrong for the part. This was not my "Marjorie" . . . she had a precocious, worldly look and an assured, fetching manner, which made her entirely different from my poor Central Park West dreamer. She wore a seductively cut red dress, a little too chic, I thought, for her age. Her hair was arranged in smart black bangs. Her make-up was stunningly smooth.
>
> In answers to my questions about her background and her career she gave a fine performance of girlish demureness; too good a performance.
>
> My Marjorie would have been stammering and feeble talking to a novelist 20 years older than herself. She would have said the wrong things. She would have spilled coffee, or dropped a fork. Natalie Wood carried off the interview with unshaken aplomb. She took charge . . .
>
> An hour or so later, talking to the producer of the picture on the telephone, I advised him that I had met Natalie Wood, that she was probably a very good actress but, in my opinion, was out of the question for the role of Marjorie Morningstar.

Natalie's seriously artistic side revealed itself in New York, as she sat in on classes at the Actors Studio, which Marlowe had arranged for her. Later, she would compare Stanislavsky's teachings to "the way I'd been working all along. 'Emotion memory' is recalling something sad when you have a sad scene to do, and very early on I used to get myself in the right mood by thinking of a pet dog that died."

Natalie returned from her star-making Warners tour the first few days of September, joining Marlowe for a "hideaway at the beach, to get away from her mother." They rented a cottage in a Malibu hotel for a few days, resuming their discussions about getting married, a possibility that created panic in Maria and alarm in Warner Brothers executives, who were desperate to sever the maverick Marlowe from Natalie's life.

While they were in Malibu, Nick Adams "*appeared* at our hotel," Marlowe would recall, bringing his newest famous friend, Elvis Presley, to meet Natalie. Adams had encountered Presley, then twenty-one, a little over a week before on the set of Presley's first movie, *Love Me Tender*. Presley, who deeply admired James Dean's acting, knew every line in *Rebel Without a Cause*, and wanted to meet Natalie Wood because she had worked with Dean.

Presley, Natalie and Adams instantly became "almost a threesome—having a lot of fun together," Natalie said then. They were spotted that week at a cinema in Hollywood called the Iris, seeing *Hot Rod Girls* and *Girls in Prison*, the day before Presley flew to New York for his historic first appearance on *The Ed Sullivan Show*, turning him into a cultural phenomenon.

With the world's most famous singer expressing an interest in Natalie, Maria exerted the full measure of her power over her daughter to end her romance with Scott Marlowe, abetted by equally potent pressure from Warner Brothers. Natalie Wood, the movie star, relented. "I don't know if you can imagine those days," Marlowe later would reflect. "Everything was geared to publicity. Studios got together and made people's lives, and had clauses in their contracts: what time they could go out, what time they had to be home, what they had to wear, what their hair was, what their photographs were like. They dictated how they lived or *not* lived. They said, 'You do this and you'll be okay; you *don't* do this and things will be bad for you.' And they meant it."

The effect of Natalie's enforced breakup with Marlowe was as devastating, in its way, as her broken engagement to Jimmy Williams, her earlier opportunity for a "real" life. "The mother just fucked it—just screwed it all up," remarks Marlowe. "I was kind of a fort for Natalie. I just was there for her all the time."

After the breakup with Marlowe, Natalie took her first trip to New York without her mother or a chaperone, to appear on *The Perry Como Show*. The experience was so disconcerting, she decided not to move out of her parents' home until she got married. A friend she made that fall, actress Judi Meredith, noticed that Natalie needed to have "someone around her all the time." "And when they are not," Meredith said at the time, "she keeps in touch by phone. That's why she calls her mother practically every hour, why she calls me at three and four in the morning, why she constantly talks to her agent, to the studio, a dozen different people. Even at home she can't be alone for a moment."

Natalie wanted to escape from Mud and her dysfunctional family, but the very neuroses Mud had instilled—primarily the fear of being alone—bound Natalie to her mother, as if Maria were a snake coiled around her neck.

With Marlowe exorcised from her life, Natalie spent more time with Elvis Presley and his companions from

Tennessee, who had taken over part of the Beverly Wilshire Hotel as their stomping grounds. Lamar Fike, a Presley pal with a rollicking Southern sense of humor, adored "the raving ingénue," as he later described Natalie. "We used to call her the Mad Nat. Elvis and I thought it up. Natalie used to get so dramatic! I came in one day to his room at the Beverly Wilshire and she got up on the windowsill and opened the window up. And I said, 'Elvis, Jesus Christ, she's going to jump!' And he said, 'No, no,' and then he said, 'Nat, come and sit down and quit being so dramatic.' And he was right. So we called her the Mad Nat."

Her mother "pushed" the relationship with Presley, according to Hyatt. Maria visited Presley on his movie set with Natalie and struck up conversations with his mother, Gladys. Even Fahd liked Presley, according to Maria, who would remember her husband buying Elvis Presley records that fall. "Natalie was crazy about Elvis," she claimed in later years. Natalie bought matching velvet shirts for herself and Presley, sneaking into movies with him throughout the late fall, finding him "complex and lonely," not unlike herself. "Natalie was attracted to dark personalities," Marlowe observed.

Her school friend Jackie, who was still friendly with Natalie, remembers Natalie telling her "what a polite, wonderful human being" Presley was, but "he was not what she wanted romantically." Later in life, Natalie gave an interview to Presley biographer Albert Goldman, discussing her relationship with the singer:

> He was the first person of my age group I had ever met who said to me: "How come you're wearing makeup? Why do you want to go to New York? Why

> do you want to be on your own? Why don't you want to stay home and be a sweet little girl? It's nice to stay home." We'd go to P.C. Brown's and have a hot fudge sundae. We'd go to Hamburger Hamlet and have a burger and a Coke. He didn't drink. He didn't swear. He didn't even smoke! . . . I thought it was really wild!

At the height of her friendship with Presley, in October, Natalie was sent to New York to appear in a live television drama called *Carnival* on NBC's Kaiser Aluminum Hour, costarring Dennis Hopper, directed by George Roy Hill. Natalie played the daughter of a drunken carny worker who takes a job as a "cooch dancer" in a desperate bid to save her father's job, then lies to cover for him. She would later refer to it as her best work as an actress, perhaps because she related to her character, who was supporting her alcoholic father.

Ironically, Scott Marlowe was NBC's first choice to play Hopper's role as the carnival barker in a tender romance with Natalie's character. "I was doing a television show, and I couldn't do it. My heart was wrenched." Marlowe, who was still in contact with Natalie through "secret" phone calls she made to him through friends, watched her perform that night. "She was brilliant. The camera came in close and she had this big, big scene, she had to burst into tears—and she did it and she was brilliant. She burst right into tears. God, she was magnificent." *Daily Variety* agreed with Marlowe, calling Natalie "touching and effective."

She returned to Hollywood from her television triumph to begin dating an intense young actor she met before she left town, when she saw him perform onstage in *End as a*

Man. Her companion that night was Ben Cooper, who recalls their reaction to actor Robert Vaughn, when they met him after the play at a small party: "Bob played a real rat, just a despicable bastard. And I told him, 'If you don't mind, I'd like to talk to you later; right now I still hate you.' And he laughed and he said, 'Thank you very much.' He was just magnetic. You would hardly remember any of the other actors who were in the play. So when he and Natalie met, there was a lot of electricity." Vaughn would say, "Being a reasonably sensitive fellow, it was apparent from the git-go that the girl and yours truly would see each other again—she had that look."

By the time Natalie returned from New York, Vaughn had been signed to a two-picture-a-year deal with Hecht-Hill-Lancaster, and moved from a one-room apartment shared with his mother "into a magnificent three-story, ten-room penthouse on Orchid Avenue overlooking the lights of my newly discovered Hollywood." Natalie introduced him to Hollywood's haunts, as she earlier had Hopper. "My first Hollywood premiere was with Nat, who as a result of *Rebel*, was now the toast of *Photoplay* and *Modern Screen*, etcetera." Vaughn simultaneously went out with Natalie's friend Judi Meredith, "[and] since neither Judi or Natalie seemed to be concerned about the other's role in my life—that life was good."

Natalie was juggling Vaughn with Elvis Presley, who invited her to Graceland, his Memphis home, over Halloween. According to Marlowe, "She did a weekend, to make me *jealous*, with Elvis. That's *all* it was about. She wanted to get back with me and so she took off with him."

Natalie left town abruptly, without telling the studio or her new agency, William Morris, missing a publicity event and flying under an assumed name. Her "secret" visit to

Graceland was captured by photographers moments after Nick Adams picked her up at the airport in Memphis, where she and Presley were stalked by fans everywhere they went: riding on his motorcycle, tooling around town in his Lincoln Continental, stopping at the Fairgrounds or for ice cream. Presley's later friend Jerry Schilling remembers, "I was fourteen years old, playing touch football, and who should drive up but Elvis on a motorcycle, and who's sitting behind him but Natalie Wood! All I could do was just stand there and stare."

Presley allowed his fans to do almost anything, even look through his windows. He explained why to a bewildered Natalie, who recalled, "I hadn't been around anyone who was religious. He felt he had been given this gift, this talent, by God. He didn't take it for granted. He thought it was something that he had to protect. He had to be nice to people, otherwise, God would take it all away."

Both Lana and Maria would later say that Natalie phoned home toward the end of her visit, asking Mud "in code" to call her back on the ruse that Warner Brothers needed her in Los Angeles. Presley's friend Fike, who was in Memphis, claims that was "a lie," that "Natalie really cared for Elvis," though he acknowledges "it just didn't work out" between them. "She just didn't like the whole set-up, didn't like the guys around, which most girls didn't." Faye Nuell, Natalie's friend from *Rebel*, still a confidante, felt Natalie, who preferred "worldly" men, had always considered Presley more a friend than a boyfriend.

Natalie flew back to Hollywood from Memphis in tight toreador pants, clutching her stuffed tigers, greeted at the airport by Robert Vaughn and by photographers, eager to snap Elvis' "new girlfriend." Pictures of Natalie Wood, smiling ebulliently, waving to her fans, appeared in newspapers across the world the next day. Michael Zimring, her new William Morris agent, saw Natalie privately, "and when she came back she looked like a rat that died. I don't think she'd been to sleep for a week." Zimring took Natalie to task for leaving town without informing him or the studio, though he felt sorry for her. "I tell you, she had a tough family thing. She was a good kid. She was a little wild, but basically she really was a good kid. I really was fond of her. She took care of her family: I mean let's face it, she supported them. Her father was a mess."

Marlowe recalls, "She appeared at my door the following weekend," still hoping to marry him. "She wanted to be married badly—to *somebody*—I know. I think she just wanted out—of that mother, and that relationship. And out of feeling suicidal so much." Natalie and Marlowe gave it a last go, but it was "not meant to be," they would both say. "Barbara Gould tried to get us back together, but we split up."

In the end, Scott Marlowe, like Jimmy Williams, Natalie's true loves, represented a too extreme break from her codependent relationship with Maria, and their shared Hollywood fantasy, movie star "Natalie Wood."

Robert Vaughn briefly filled the void in Natalie's life through November. He remembers her then as "a full blooming late teenager, with all the passion, humor, vulnerability and craziness that time suggests. She could also drink a Volga boatman under the table. She introduced me to the 'way of the world' in Hollywood's last glamorous days, and I shall treasure our fleeting time upon that 'wicked stage' all of my days." At the same time, Vaughn had a strange premonition about Natalie, a disturbing feeling that something was wrong. "Even then, I had some concern, based on her zest for life, that she might not realize her full 'Biblical' four score and ten, and said so to my friends."

When Vaughn escorted Natalie to a party given by Elvis Presley that December at the Santa Monica Pier, which Presley had "bought out" for his friends for the evening, "Natalie, with profound sadness, stared at the black waters, and told me how deeply afraid she was of drowning."

ACT THREE

Movie Star

1957–1966

"I thought back then I'd have such a happy life ahead of me.
Where is it?"

Anton Chekhov
Three Sisters

17

NATALIE FINISHED THE HEADY, tumultuous, high-pressure year of 1956 in a burst of fame, winning a Golden Globe as Outstanding Newcomer (shared with Carroll Baker and Jayne Mansfield), after being named "Most Popular New Star of 1956" by *Modern Screen* in a ceremony hosted by Louella Parsons on Sunday, December 3, broadcast live from CBS in Hollywood to *The Ed Sullivan Show*.

At one event, the movie star whom Natalie told her close friends had raped her sat near her during a ceremony, flashing his charismatic grin as if nothing had ever happened. Natalie Wood, the always-beautiful, always-happy star, beamed radiantly throughout the event, pretending to adore the famous actor beside her whom she despised.

Dennis Hopper would later observe that Natalie did her best acting "playing" Natalie Wood. Natalie worried about the fact that *she* was lost inside her screen persona, telling her sister Lana she felt that "very few people liked her just for *her*. They liked her because she was 'Natalie Wood.' Including guys. That was always foremost on her mind."

At a party after the *Modern Screen* ceremony, Natalie bumped into Robert Wagner, whom she hadn't seen since their unexciting publicity date five months earlier. He was worried about how much weight she had lost—"neuroses" kept her thin, Natalie told a magazine—and invited her to meet him at his studio commissary for lunch the next day. Natalie's indifference, and Wagner's easy-going nature, are suggested by the fact that she arrived three hours late, to a patiently waiting Wagner, still in good humor.

Natalie found Wagner's mellow manner a soothing balm for her increasingly frazzled nerves, accepting a date on his new sailboat, *My Lady*, moored at Newport, south of L.A. *My Lady* was Wagner's first of many boats, paid for with his "movie money," and he was intoxicated with her, and with the ocean. Natalie discovered that sailing off to sea, where she could not be reached, was a relaxing panacea from the stresses of the studio and the demands on her. "At night, when the sky is full of stars and the sea is still you get the wonderful sensation that you are floating in space," she said. "You don't even *think* words, yet you get the glorious feeling that you are tuned in on the universe." She spent that night—December 6—aboard *My Lady*, which she and Wagner would celebrate in future years as their most sentimental anniversary, commemorating their first date and the first time they were intimate.

Natalie's fear of dark water—seawater—was still with her, but she somehow separated it from being on a boat. "I don't think it occurred to her that she would go in the water, or go off the boat," her then close friend, Judi Meredith, noticed. "R.J. always had a boat, and it started out with a smaller one, and then it just grew. And she was going with R.J., and I don't think it would have occurred to her to say, 'No, this is not for me.' 'Cause Nat was gung-ho for life."

Wagner said later he "fell head over heels in love" with Natalie "the way they write about in songs," describing their relationship as "intense," but in fact they saw each other only sporadically the next few months. Natalie was seeing several other suitors, including hotel heir Nicky Hilton, Elizabeth Taylor's first husband, whom she met a few weeks later as part of a "star junket" to promote the opening of a new Hilton hotel in Mexico City. Natalie "liked the idea" of dating the dark and dashing Hilton, according to her friend Meredith, and was eager to emulate Elizabeth Taylor, in the opinions of Robert Blake and Marlowe. She juggled three boyfriends on her trip to Mexico City: Bob Neal, a wealthy businessman in Hollywood circles, took her to the airport, Hilton was with her in Mexico City, and Wagner picked her up by limousine when she flew home.

Respected character actor Karl Malden, who was playing Natalie's father in a Warners potboiler they shot that winter eventually called *Bombers B-52*, remembers beaus "swarming" around Natalie on the set, "There must have been five or six boys around all the time—and you know, it was funny, they'd come together. Two or three of them'd come in, and hang around . . . She was always a serious actress, that was her profession, she really cherished it, she worked on it, so she was always conscientious there, but as a person—boy, she had a good time at eighteen." Malden glimpsed the loneliness underneath Natalie's surface gaiety when he discovered she had never been on a family picnic, and arranged to take her on one. She told him, afterward, that it was one of the happiest days of her life, which Malden found desperately sad.

Natalie paid for the Gurdins' new house that December—perversely, on Laurel Canyon, the street she feared—fashioning her bedroom into a separate "wing" so that she could pretend she was in her own apartment, something she was still too terrified to do. She surrendered her schoolgirl pink canopy bed for modern bedroom furniture, all in black, and acquired a private phone line so she could "talk all night" with Nick Adams or Barbara Gould or Judi Meredith, the friends who kept her company through the long nights that frightened her, "sometimes falling asleep on the phone."

The "ambition of her life" was to play the part intended for Elizabeth Taylor in *Marjorie Morningstar*, a role she was certain would catapult her to true movie stardom, which consumed her thoughts more than any of the boyfriends who phoned with "love talk" night and day, according to the neighbor who shared her party line. "For fun, I work," Natalie told *Cosmopolitan* in 1957, which described her "demonic ambition." She tested for the part of Marjorie in January with a drove of actresses amid great publicity over who would play the coveted role. Natalie anguished into spring, as the tests continued.

"Warner Brothers tortured her over *Marjorie*," recalls Marlowe, who still had occasional taboo contact with Natalie by phone. Her agent at the time, Mike Zimring, was aware of what the studio was doing. "I *knew* Natalie was going to play the part, but I had to play this game. The studio wanted to test all these other girls for publicity—because it was a big deal, who would be Marjorie Morningstar. I always felt so damn guilty about that." Natalie even adopted a Brooklyn accent with her friends, pretending to be Jewish, desperate to play Marjorie not only as her ticket to stardom, but a chance to prove herself again as a serious actress, disgusted by the pictures she was being forced to make for Warner Brothers.

She exhibited some of her old "rebel" behavior, engaging in swearing contests for sport with her friend Meredith and their "core monster group" of Hopper and Adams and occasionally actor Robert Conrad. "We were so full of B.S., running around and terrorizing theaters and things, putting our feet in the back of people's seats so they'd move, and dressing in black leather. Oh God, we were like Peck's bad boys, but it was just to make ourselves laugh. We didn't care what anybody else thought."

Natalie added a new swain to her assortment of men that spring, the young and wealthy Lance Reventlow, who took her to the Academy Awards. In April, she was seen with Frank Sinatra, her mentor in the ways of Hollywood at fifteen. Sinatra was courting her for his next movie, *Kings Go Forth*, as well as personally, according to Natalie's chum Nuell, who recalls how Sinatra "adored" her. Natalie told a movie magazine it was not uncommon for her to have three dates on the same night—Hilton, Wagner, Reventlow, Robert Vaughn, Bob Neal, Nick Adams, Dennis Hopper, and the list went on.

By late spring, Natalie was pilloried in the press. Hedda Hopper warned her, in print, she was going to "burn out"; columnist Sheilah Graham wrote, "Tomorrow won't come for Natalie Wood if she doesn't slow down"; *Look* published a profile of Natalie, querying, "Is she riding for a fall?" *Movieland* criticized her for dating Sinatra, calling him "her most incongruous escort," writing that he was "old enough to be her dad." Even *Variety* took a shot, tittering, "Natalie Wood's either got a great press agent or she's boy crazy."

Judi Meredith, Natalie's close friend, considered the attacks unjustified. Meredith, who had her own apartment, acted as a "beard" for Natalie when she spent the night with Hilton, because Natalie's father disapproved of him, an arrangement Maria—impressed by Hilton's name—encouraged. "Her mom told her dad that she was staying overnight with me, but she wasn't. Natalie got pretty much whatever she wanted." Meredith largely discounted the negative gossip about Natalie's male harem, saying they were "*purely* platonic" for the most part. "Nick [Adams] was just sort of the kid next door. So was Dennis [Hopper]. Dennis the Menace, for God's sake. [I think] he was just inventive."

Natalie's school friend Jackie, who was still around her quite a bit, felt "Natalie couldn't be faithful to one boy then." Several years later, Natalie admitted that she fell in love much too easily, observing poignantly, "It's not really love, though; I guess you call it fascination." "She could have had anyone," observed Jackie. "She was looking for happiness." Natalie told a magazine she was looking for a man who was "intense about *something*." With Scott Marlowe evicted from her life, she seemed to spiral downward. A female friend who remained unnamed described Natalie during this period to *Coronet* magazine, later, as reminding her "of an F. Scott Fitzgerald heroine. She was burning herself up. I was frightened and I waited for something to happen."

There was evidence. Amanda Duff, who met Natalie years earlier during *The Ghost and Mrs. Muir*, written by Duff's husband Philip Dunne, recalls seeing Natalie at a party, smoking heavily, noticing that "her hands were shaking." At another party in this period, Natalie encountered actress Anna Lee, who had a small part in *The Ghost and Mrs. Muir* as George Sanders' screen wife. Natalie, who was only eight when she made the movie, was curious about her screen mother, the beautiful Gene Tierney, who had suffered a nervous breakdown in the interim. "She wanted to know what my scenes with Gene Tierney were like."

Natalie's childhood hypochondria returned with a vengeance. She missed several days shooting *Bombers B-52* because she thought she had a "nervous heart," driven by car from the set by Hilton. "Every time she reads a book about a disease or hears a person discuss a sickness," her friend Meredith wrote at the time, "she's promptly convinced that she has it, too. During the past six months, she was convinced she had hardening of the arteries, TB, rheumatism, sclerosis of the liver, leukemia, and half a dozen other diseases I never even heard about . . . luckily, just as quickly as she identifies these 'symptoms,' she gets over them."

Photoplay, then the most influential movie magazine, published a two-part cover series on Natalie, describing her as "controversial," frighteningly ambitious, "flashy," criticizing her for having so many boyfriends, reporting there was "talk she won't make it in her personal life." *Movie TV*, another popular magazine, wrote that Warner Brothers had been warned there would be no more fan magazine covers for Natalie if she "doesn't slow down on men," prompting the studio to exert pressure on Natalie to rehabilitate her image. Natalie would complain, later, that the fan magazines "tried to make me look like a femme fatale."

She narrowed the field of suitors to Hilton and Wagner by May, just after Warners announced she would play Marjorie Morningstar, the same week Wagner left for Japan to shoot a movie with Joan Collins. Troy Donahue, who was seeing Judi Meredith and double-dated with Natalie, recalls her "trying to make up her mind—I remember—between R.J. and Nicky." According to Olga, Hilton invited Natalie and their mother to the family mansion to meet his father, Conrad Hilton, to discuss terms for a marriage, with Conrad Hilton attempting to "bribe" Maria, who thought at the time that Natalie would choose Hilton over Wagner. "That was very serious," recalls Lana of the

Natalie–Nicky Hilton romance. "He was like part of the family or something."

Wagner inundated Natalie with phone calls from Tokyo, sometimes every three minutes; by the time he returned to Hollywood on July 2, she was cooling the romance with the violent-tempered Hilton in favor of R.J., telling friends how gentlemanly and attentive R.J. was, traits she valued after her confessed rape. "She was crazy in love with Nicky," recalls Troy Donahue, "but knew it wouldn't be the best thing." Friends noticed that Natalie was also drawn to men who were handsome, like her father. Wagner took her out on his boat for her nineteenth birthday on July 20, surprising Natalie with a Black Mist mink stole, the perfect symbol of the glamorous life they would have together.

The studio was ecstatic with Natalie's romance with Wagner, who worshipped at the altar of Hollywood and posed endlessly with Natalie for fan magazines, flashing his dazzling movie-star smile as they quickly became the era's favorite new celebrity couple, joining the ranks of Debbie Reynolds and Eddie Fisher, Tony Curtis and Janet Leigh. Natalie acquired a "personal" couturier, Howard Shoup, the costume designer from *Bombers B-52*, who "taught her how to dress" and created special costumes for her with "boob uplifts" to create the illusion of the larger breasts she had coveted since *Pride of the Family*.

Wagner's and Warner Brothers' joint influences on Natalie were startlingly obvious when she arrived in New York that summer to test with supporting actors for *Marjorie Morningstar*. Natalie was pictured in the *Tribune* in a glamorous off-the-shoulder white gown, quoted as criticizing the New York "method" actors she earlier had worshipped, saying, "They don't like movies so, I say, why don't they leave Hollywood and go back to the stage. Or better still they shouldn't go to Hollywood in the first place. I for one am tired of hearing them complain about Hollywood. I resent kids who say movies are terrible, noncreative and all that. That's just talk."

The star-driven, "Maria" aspect of Natalie's personality had assumed center stage via her budding romance with Robert Wagner, to the delight of her studio. By early August, rumors that Natalie would marry Wagner—who called her "Bug"—began to pop up in the trades. When Natalie, increasingly afraid to fly, took the train to the East Coast in mid-August to start filming *Marjorie Morningstar*, Wagner tagged along, staying at the same Adirondacks resort hotel on Schroon Lake as Natalie, Maria and Lana. The fan magazines, and Warner Brothers, embraced the couple, putting them on covers in dreamy, romantic poses—Wagner tenderly kissing Natalie on the forehead, or the two of them gazing into each other's eyes—with headlines such as, "Natalie Wood and Bob Wagner: It's the Romance of the Year!" or "Natalie's Love Search Has Ended!" Louella Parsons bubbled that they would marry, writing that Wagner had become accustomed to being called "Mr. Wood."

By the end of summer, Natalie's disenchantment with *Marjorie Morningstar* was summed up by her private comments about the director, Irving Rapper, to a friend: "I'd rather spend my life in a crapper than do another picture with Irving Rapper!" Actress Ruta Lee, who had a small part in the film as a rival of Marjorie Morningstar's, remembers Natalie being "not too crazy" about their "old guard, somewhat dogmatic" director, and vocalizing it.

The Lithuanian, outgoing Ruta Lee bonded with Natalie over their ethnic backgrounds and shared rituals. "She was very real, very down-to-earth . . . and she had a wonderful, dirty giggle. Loved a bawdy story. Was very earthy and very wonderful . . . and yet there was something about her that, even though I was very, very young, wanted me to reach out and kind of make a haven for her, and *protect* her in some sort of way."

Wagner celebrated his and Natalie's joint return to Hollywood in September by buying a new forty-two-foot powerboat, which he planned to name *The Natalie*, but changed to *My Other Lady*. The two spent increasing amounts of time on Wagner's boat, out at sea, one of the few places where Natalie found it possible both to drop the "Natalie Wood" mask and to relax, something she found difficult with her driven, intense nature. She confessed to *Seventeen* magazine she hadn't had a day off in two and a half years, since *Rebel*.

Natalie kept up the pace, beginning in November the film for which Sinatra had pursued her, *Kings Go Forth*. It was a war drama set in the Mediterranean, with Natalie playing a French-speaking mulatta driven to a suicide attempt by a playboy soldier (Tony Curtis), rescued by Sinatra's character. She spent her time between scenes listening to Sinatra records ("He's from greatsville!" she told a reporter from *Bride* magazine, sounding like Wagner), or knitting an afghan, to use on the boat, as a surprise for R.J.

On December 6, the anniversary of their first date aboard *My Lady*, Wagner arrived at the Gurdins' to take Natalie to Romanoff's, carrying a bottle of Dom Perignon and two crystal glasses. When he filled Natalie's glass with champagne, she discovered a pearl-and-diamond ring on the bottom, engraved with the words "Marry me?" At Romanoff's, Wagner discreetly dropped a pair of diamond earrings in Natalie's glass, the way Cary Grant, his role model, might have done on screen.

Their first call was to Hollywood reporter Louella Parsons, who wrote breathlessly about R.J. and Natalie's movie-scripted engagement in her column the next day. In keeping with the Hollywood theme, Natalie hired her movie costume designer, Howard Shoup, to create a wedding gown for her, with Shoup sketching a beautiful short white lace dress and romantic lace coverlet for her head.

When Wagner showed up on the set of *Kings Go Forth* to see Natalie, Sinatra, who had a special relationship with Natalie that Faye Nuell, Janet Leigh and others perceived as romantic then, pulled him aside, giving Wagner "the Hoboken guide of, 'Don't you do anything to hurt her,' " recalls Nuell, who happened to be visiting Natalie. "He said, 'If you ever hurt her, you'll have to answer to me.' "

That week, Natalie had lunch with her oldest and dearest friend, Mary Ann, rhapsodizing about R.J. and their engagement, telling Mary Ann how "perfect" he was, how "perfect" their marriage would be, reminding Mary Ann how she once had seen Wagner on the Fox lot and fantasized marrying him, how this was her fairy tale come true.

Mary Ann expressed her concern. "R.J. presented such a grandiose thing. She was in love with love. And he was extremely handsome, surfacely [sic] extremely charming, and she was being pushed by all sides—studio, Mama, *everybody*. And it seemed almost . . . you know how when things seem to be *too* perfect? I told her, 'Nothing's *that perfect*.' "

Mary Ann's caveat about Robert Wagner caused a rift between the two friends. "She believed everything he said. But sometimes you've got to *listen*. She was hearing what she wanted to hear. And the studios were pushing, and

Mom. She was into this, both hands, both feet, everything—all systems go."

Natalie had a similar experience with her friend Jackie. "I hadn't seen her in a long time, because she was making all these movies. And she called me one day and she said, 'What are you doing? I want to take you to Romanoff's for lunch, I have something to tell you.' " Jackie expected to see Natalie in her T-Bird, "but she had a black Cadillac, and the whole persona of Natalie had suddenly changed to this very sophisticated—she had a black turban on, and a black jersey sheath, and a cigarette holder, and the leather gloves. So we march into Romanoff's, and we're talking, and she pulled off the glove, and there is the diamond on her finger. She said, 'I'm marrying Robert Wagner.' " Like Mary Ann, Jackie had concerns.

Within three weeks of finding a pearl-and-diamond ring in the bottom of her champagne glass, Natalie was on a train to Arizona with Robert Wagner to get married—on such short notice, even her sister Olga was unable to attend. Olga believed that Natalie married so young "to get away, maybe . . . although I think she was in love with R.J. They were fun to watch together. I remember they came to San Francisco and we went out to dinner. And they always would make a production—if she was going to the bathroom, they'd have all these farewells! They had this little act together."

Her mother, remembers Olga, was "not always" happy about Natalie's decision to marry Wagner, partly because, "for Mother, it was a big blow when Natalie decided to be on her own, and Mother wasn't to interfere. That was a blow."

Jean Hyatt was a witness to her close friend Maria's

devastation at losing her star-child, the outcome that Mud had schemed to prevent since Natalie was a little girl, frightening her with grotesque lies about sex and pregnancy. Maria's motivation to keep Natalie at home was to some degree financial, as "a lot of her meal ticket would go away when Natalie married somebody." But the more primal reason for Mud's hysteria over losing her daughter was survival, for as Maria's friend Jean points out, "She lived and breathed through Natalie."

Maria had a foreboding about Natalie marrying Robert Wagner. She told Natalie, "No good will come of this."

Though her older sister had insufficient notice to attend Natalie's wedding to Wagner, a fan magazine reporter and photographer were present every second, even on the train to Scottsdale, where R.J.'s parents had a home. Barbara Gould was Natalie's maid of honor, just as she would have been if Natalie had married Scott Marlowe the year before. The only other guests at the Wood-Wagner wedding were Mary Anita Loos and Richard Sale (whom Natalie had met on *Driftwood*), Nick Adams, Faye Nuell, the Gurdins, the Wagners, and a few other family or friends.

But the photographs, and all the details, were available to anyone who bought the March 1958 issues of *Photoplay*, *Modern Screen*, or *Motion Picture*.

18

IRONICALLY, BOATS—AND BOAT mishaps—would be a recurring theme in the joined lives of Natalie and Robert Wagner.

Their first honeymoon began with a misadventure at sea. Because Natalie was afraid to fly, the Wagners and their sixteen pieces of luggage took the *Silver Streak* to Miami, where they had booked passage on a chartered boat for a month-long cruise, an opportunity for Natalie to relax—with no telephones—after the grueling schedule of filming *Marjorie Morningstar* and *Kings Go Forth* almost back-to-back.

"So what happens?" Wagner queried Louella Parsons after the honeymoon. "The worst storm to hit the Florida coast in fifteen years blows up! They called it a storm—ha! It was really a typhoon." Natalie and R.J.'s honeymoon cruise became a nightmare, as their boat lurched its way back to port. "It was pitching like a wild horse. Dishes and glasses were crashing . . . all the furniture that wasn't nailed down was sliding from wall to wall. It was all but impossible for our skipper to see one wave ahead of us. I was so worried about Nat. It was an awful ordeal for her."

The newlyweds shifted their honeymoon to New York, where they checked into the Waldorf Towers, accompanied, rather bizarrely, by Nick Adams, Natalie's perpetual sidekick. (Actor Robert Conrad, Adams' best friend then, did not consider the arrangement strange. "Nick was a very entertaining guy, and they were pals. He was with them all the time, always hanging out. He was referred to by his friends as 'Emperor Adams'—he was charming, he was funny, he was outrageous, and you had a sense that he really cared about you.")

The next few weeks were a public spectacle, with photographers chronicling the Wagners' comings and goings to Manhattan restaurants and Broadway plays, including *West Side Story*, Natalie's eventual film classic. They left New York mid-January, buying a new Corvette to drive home, another way for Natalie to avoid airplanes. Natalie and R.J.'s motor trip back to California was a surreal exercise in movie star fame: each time they drove to a different city, a local radio station announced their arrival and fans would mob the car.

When they returned to Hollywood from their honeymoon, the Wagners had barely spent a waking hour alone. They holed up aboard *My Other Lady*, moored off Catalina Island, the glamorous little hideaway two hours by sea from the port south of Los Angeles. "The best part was the last week," Natalie would say a year later, of her honeymoon. "We spent it on R.J.'s boat, off the coast of Catalina, in a dense fog for four days." The experience would forever hold a glow for both Natalie and R.J., who romanticized Catalina, and their boat, as the perfect expression of their love.

Natalie spent her first days as Mrs. Robert Wagner writing one thousand personal thank-you letters on pastel blue note cards monogrammed "NWW," acknowledging wedding gifts she and R.J. had received, with thoughtful greetings to every person she addressed. It was typically Natalie, her sister Lana would observe. "The same as she took acting very seriously, she took being a wife very seriously. And gave it her all . . . she did everything meticulously, and very thoroughly and completely."

Outwardly, the newly wed Wagners appeared to have achieved romantic nirvana; however, the movie star façade that was "Natalie Wood" concealed the person inside, gasping for breath. "It was a mystery to me. I loved my husband, we were healthy, we were desirable according to the press, but all I felt was torment. I was unable to make a decision of any kind. People had told me what to do all my life, and now I was expected to function as an adult woman."

After nineteen years of possessing a human shadow,

Natalie was experiencing the same separation anxiety from her mother as Maria—her alter ego—was from her. She included Mud in all her movie contracts for the rest of her life, paid by the studio to autograph fan photos, with Maria signing as "Natalie Wood," their shared identity.

Natalie and R.J. kept up the illusion of movie magazine bliss, with Natalie ensconcing herself in her husband's cozy bachelor quarters, a two-bedroom duplex apartment on Durant, in Beverly Hills, with barely enough space for their star wardrobes.

Mud's protective antennae went up the first time she visited Wagner's tiny apartment, when the door was opened by a much older man with an English accent, identifying himself as R.J.'s butler. Mud made it her mission to rid Wagner of his live-in houseman before he married Natalie. "Her mother disapproved of the butler," relates Maria's friend Jean Hyatt, "and being that type of a person, she didn't want Natalie to have anything to do with Wagner."

According to Bobby Hyatt, Natalie was also "questioning why Wagner had that guy. She was trying to get him to get rid of him. And the joke became that after they got married, not only did R.J. *not* get rid of the guy, but *moved* the guy into their apartment." A fan magazine even reported on the oddity after the Wagners divorced:

> Natalie and her former husband, Robert John Wagner, were living then in this nice but very dinky garden apartment duplex in Beverly Hills. There wasn't room to swing a cat by the tail, in case that was your idea of fun, but there was a butler. He was a *bona fide* butler all right, with all sorts of movie star credentials and references. But in that apartment it was like keeping a polar bear in

a broom closet . . . Natalie and R.J. would weave in and out around the butler . . .

Jean Hyatt recalls, "I used to go over there with Marie Gurdin and the butler, of whom Mud disapproved, would answer the door. From then on, Maria complained to Jean Hyatt incessantly. "She mainly said, 'I don't know why Natalie would marry R.J. in the first place.' And she just went on and on about the butler. And she'd say it right in front of Natalie—she said she didn't care whether he heard her or not. She was very outspoken, Marie was. Not to hurt you, but that was just the way she was."

Natalie wanted desperately to live the fairy tale she imagined for herself as a child, with the handsome prince she fantasized about at eleven. When her costar of so many movies, Ann Doran, ran into her in the Fox commissary, she was "ecstatic over her new husband. This was 'it!' "

Natalie made a romantic pact with R.J. never to be separated, and they vowed not to exploit their relationship by appearing in a film together. As a symbol of her love, Natalie balked at making a six-city tour to promote *Marjorie Morningstar*, since R.J. would be filming a movie called *The Hunters* and they would be apart.

When the studio prevailed, bowing to her preference to travel by train, Natalie got a viral infection at the station before she even left Los Angeles, and was sick throughout the tour. Her insistence that her husband be with her at all times was probably as much a symptom of her emotional dependency and fear of solitude as a romantic gesture.

Natalie was in a tug-of-war with Warner Brothers from the time she returned from her honeymoon in January through summer, refusing to accept the pictures they were offering—*The Miracle* and *A Summer Place*—as a bargaining tool to renegotiate her contract. Natalie had no idea what to do with herself, or her time, away from a movie set, admitting sadly she was "more at home on a soundstage than in my own home." She joined R.J. on *his* set, appearing so often she was given a canvas chair with the title "Associate Producer" while he filmed *In Love and War* that June. Natalie followed the cast to the Monterey Peninsula, near the Stanford campus, where yet another movie magazine, *Screen Album*, took pictures of her and R.J., posing like lovebirds in the picturesque setting.

By July, studio executives were losing patience with Natalie. The star whom the *Los Angeles Examiner* described as the "queen of the Warner Brothers lot" hadn't worked for six months. That summer, she was offered a huge salary as the female lead in a prestige film. Natalie turned it down, saying she couldn't be separated from R.J., resulting in publicity that made her appear either capricious or unreasonably demanding. The underlying reason, which Natalie did not disclose, was that one of the figures associated with the project was the famous, powerful actor she said had raped her.

The tension with Warner Brothers reached a climax on July 14, when Natalie failed to show up for a meeting to discuss *The Philadelphian*, a courtroom drama costarring Paul Newman (later changed to *The Young Philadelphians*). She made the cover of *Variety* the next day for the wrong reasons: to report that Warner Brothers had placed Natalie Wood on unpaid suspension for refusing to appear in *The Philadelphian*.

Natalie offered several principled explanations for her suspension in later years: that she refused to do "silly press," she wanted the right to make pictures for other studios, and she wanted a voice in the roles offered to her by Warner

Brothers. She was also unhappy with her salary, which was less than she was making as a child, at Fox.

Natalie turned twenty a few days after she was suspended, celebrating her birthday by picking up the $27,050 in bonds that had accrued in her name since she became a child actress, money the Wagners needed without her salary. That same month, Natalie's parents moved into a new house in Van Nuys, a few blocks from the Hyatts, offering the Laurel Canyon home to R.J. and Natalie.

She spent the rest of the year out of work, a circumstance utterly alien to Natalie, who had acted for so much of her childhood she "didn't know how to play." She idled away some of her restlessness on the boat, with R.J. Occasionally they would sail to Catalina with their business manager, Andrew Maree III, and his wife, Prudence, who were in their wedding party. Prudence Maree recalls she and Natalie "kind of *learned* to like it, because the boat was a great love of R.J.'s." Natalie also considered it "a place to get away from everything—ringing phones and fans and all the rest of it." According to both the Marees, they would moor at Catalina and stay on the boat all weekend, playing cards and cooking on a hibachi. "Natalie was an excellent gin player," recalls Andrew Maree. Neither wife set foot in the water.

Natalie and R.J. discussed their boat with columnist Hedda Hopper then, in what would become an eerie interview in light of Natalie's eventual drowning from their last boat, the *Splendour*. Wagner told Hopper, "I had my first boat before we were married, and Nat didn't know anything about it. So she started reading books to learn how to run it, so if I fell overboard, she could come back and pick me up." Natalie confessed to Hopper, in the same interview, that she would never set foot in the ocean. "It looks so dark down there, and I'm scared of fish. I sort of thought when the boat went along, the fish would swim away from it."

Faye Nuell, still a close friend, always found it odd that Natalie and R.J. had a boat, since Natalie was so terrified of dark seawater. Natalie addressed that question in a joint interview with R.J. for a magazine, after he teased her that he felt ignored when she took naps on the boat. Her comments are haunting, in view of how she died: "Don't you realize that here I am, out in the middle of the ocean?" she asked him. "The boat could sink, a storm could come up, anything might happen. But am I afraid? No. So I lie in the sun and fall asleep—a little. Why? Because with you I feel safe, secure, but most of all happy. That's a compliment."

R.J. taught Natalie to play gin rummy and poker, a game she enjoyed with wicked delight, beating her husband, Frank Sinatra, and Dean Martin on regular poker nights. The Wagners became fringe members of Sinatra's "Clan," taking the train to Vegas to play blackjack with Dino, Frank, or Peter Lawford, and to catch a show by Eddie Fisher.

Steffi (Skolsky) Sidney, Natalie's *Rebel* costar, was writing for a fan magazine called *Datebook* that November, and interviewed Natalie and R.J. for an "at home" profile on America's sweethearts. While Sidney sat in their living room, R.J. rehearsed a dance number for his next movie, *Say One for Me*, as Natalie appeared, wearing a leopard-skin robe and slippers, accompanied by her poodles, Chi Chi and Chou Chou. She sat on the sofa beside Sidney, surrounded by her stuffed tigers, talking about how stars *are* different, how she wanted to bring glamour into peoples' lives.

Sidney found them both charming and adorable, but she left the Wagners' home with a disturbing feeling that the marriage was doomed. She thought Natalie was too young, "and there was something about it that wasn't real." When Sidney tried to include her opinions in the article, the Wagners' publicist struck her lines.

By the end of the year, around the time of her first wedding anniversary, Natalie's problems with the studio began to lift, triggered by Jack Warner's return to work after a serious car accident, and Natalie's discovery of *Splendor in the Grass*, which Elia Kazan, her movie god, had begun to develop at Warner Brothers.

Both Kazan and Warners had Natalie in mind for the picture in its earliest stages. Her name appears in Kazan's first handwritten casting notes (along with Jane Fonda and a crossed-out Lee Remick), and in his original letter of intent to Warner Brothers in January 1959 (with no other actress mentioned). He told his friend Richard Sylbert, and the *Saturday Evening Post*, that when he saw Natalie in *Rebel*, she stayed in his head.

Warner Brothers was already intimating they would cast Natalie in *Splendor* while she was on suspension: the December 12, 1958, *Hollywood Reporter* reported that the studio had just "bought Inge's *Splendor* for Natalie Wood."

As further confirmation, Natalie *herself* said later that Warner Brothers had promised her the lead in *Splendor in the Grass* if she would come back to the studio and first appear in *Cash McCall*, which is how it happened. She agreed to a new contract on February 24, 1959, after a seven-month suspension. By her new terms, she was permitted to make one non–Warner Brothers picture a year, and her salary increased to $1000 a week. In early

April, she was gritting her teeth through *Cash McCall*, a vehicle to exploit James Garner's television popularity as *Maverick*.

The Wagners burst into the second year of their marriage spending money with reckless abandon. They bought each other matching Jaguars, and purchased a snow white showcase house at 714 North Beverly in the heart of Beverly Hills, announcing they wanted to "live like stars." They hired the art director from *Cash McCall* and a decorator named Dewey Spriegel to turn their mansion into a Greek Revival masterpiece with white marble floors, gold rococo in the master bedroom, a saltwater pool, sunken tub, lanai, "His" and "Hers" Greek statuary, and a sixteen-foot wardrobe for Natalie's clothes. R.J.'s butler followed them to the house on Beverly, where the surroundings were more suited to a manservant.

"It was the very end of glamour with a capital G, movie star with a capital MS," Natalie's friend Judi Meredith remembers.

The mistress of the mansion wandered the halls like a stranger. "I had never thought about furniture or things like that," Natalie later told the author of a book on child stars. "All I'd thought about is acting, and whether I got the part or not. When the decorator said, 'What about the coffee table?' I realized I'd never even noticed what goes on a coffee table. I'd never looked. I didn't have any opinion about the kind of furniture I wanted. I'd always been so worried about being shy, or what people were going to think of me, or what I was going to say, that I'd never notice *anything* when I entered a room."

Natalie started to see a psychoanalyst, to learn how to "just *be*," struggling to reclaim the identity that was lost to her at six, when she became the actress Natalie Wood. "I didn't know who the hell I was. I was whoever *they* wanted me to be, *they* being agents, producers, directors, or whoever else I was trying to please at the time." Natalie, in her sister Lana's later observation, needed analysis as a place where she could "be naked and real." R.J. was against it. He was threatened by the idea of his wife in analysis, just as Mud had been when Natalie briefly went to Marlowe's therapist, perceiving it as a reflection on him. "I was afraid of it," Wagner said later.

Robert Hyatt came back into Natalie's life in 1959, after a stint in the Army, and saw her fairly often, since he and his mother lived near the Gurdins. He and Natalie talked about her therapist, an elderly doctor on Rodeo Drive in Beverly Hills. Natalie told Hyatt she needed therapy because she wanted to have a baby, and she was terrified to get pregnant because of Mud's horror stories. Scott Marlowe experienced Natalie's pregnancy fears when they were dating. "Oh my *God*, she was just frightened to death. We had to be very careful. We were very, very careful. Again, it was the mother."

When Maria tried to force thirteen-year-old "Lana Lisa" into show business—pushing her to interview for a *National Velvet* television series and other acting jobs—Lana called Natalie in desperation. Natalie moved her little sister into her house on Beverly temporarily, even permitting Lana to sleep in the same bed with her and R.J. "Natalie protected her like she was Lana's mother," recalls Natalie's agent, Zimring. Mud harrumphed to a movie magazine that Natalie "spoiled" Lana, whom she called "lazy." "Which is why I became so attached to Natalie," explains Lana. "Because she grew up and away and was married and I could go and stay with her. It was like actually being with somebody who cared about you."

Natalie's tenderness toward Lana, shielding her sister from their mother's ambition, spoke volumes about the way Natalie perceived her own tragic childhood. She developed a fascination, that year, with a popular San Francisco–based artist named Margaret Keane, identifying with Keane's paintings, which usually depicted a wispy waif-child with enormous, sad eyes. "She was obsessed with them," recalls Dennis Hopper. "She thought they looked like *her*."

Natalie commissioned Keane to paint her the way she had looked as a child, and sat for a portrait of herself at nearly twenty-one. Keane would remember Natalie posing for her, hours upon hours, without complaining or moving a muscle; still the little girl who would do anything to please. Keane's adult portrait of Natalie, childlike in a simple black dress, gazing soulfully with dark, tragic eyes, was on display wherever Natalie lived for years afterward, representing her image of herself as a fragile figure of immense sadness. It was reminiscent of the refrain of her long-ago favorite song: "*Where is the schoolgirl who used to be me?*"

Her glamorous life with R.J. showed signs of strain. When Hyatt visited Natalie at the house on Beverly, he noticed enormous bottles of prescription pills in the medicine cabinet, with thousands of Seconals, Dexedrines, Nembutal, and Dexatrim. "Natalie would get up in the morning and take a Dexie, then she would have a bowl of chicken noodle soup and a glass of white wine for breakfast." Hyatt considered her anorexic, before the term came into vogue. "She was worried about her weight, because she noticed her mother had gotten fatter as she got older, and she was afraid it would happen to her."

Lana, who stayed for several weeks with her sister and R.J. after "running away," was aware that her sister still took sleeping pills. A publicist who played poker at the Wagners' recalls Natalie and R.J. using her colored prescription pills as "chips" in the poker game. Natalie's diet and sleeping pills were commonplace in their crowd, asserts Faye Nuell. "It was like something people did then. It wasn't thought of as drugs in those days. That was the day of the Dr. Feel-Goods—there were all these drugs. I knew Cary Grant when he was doing LSD with his psychiatrist. That was all before the sixties drug culture. Nobody thought about it."

Natalie's rebel years of drinking ended with her teens. Once she got married, she would have an occasional glass of champagne or wine (her favorite was Pouilly Fuissé). Hyatt noticed that when he visited the Wagners' house, R.J. often had a bourbon-and-water in his hand.

Natalie and R.J. blended his Old Guard cronies with her younger contemporaries in their social life. According to actor Robert Conrad, part of a group called "the pack" then, "R.J. and Natalie had 'pocket friends.' One night or two nights it would be the young, contract, we're-all-trying-to-make-it group, and then it would be the Fred Astaire, high-powered, Abe Lastfogel, president and head of William Morris. It was like that. And they entertained every night."

The strange fascination between Frank Sinatra and Natalie continued after her marriage to R.J. One of the few people who knew about Natalie's teenage friendship with Sinatra, Bobby Hyatt, recalls that Sinatra was a frequent guest at the Wagners' when he was there. Natalie would be upstairs giggling with Sinatra, while R.J. played poker downstairs in the den, the only room not under construction.

In July, Sinatra cohosted with R.J. an extravagant surprise twenty-first birthday party for Natalie at Romanoff's, serenading her in song with Dean Martin.

Natalie's friend Judi Meredith, who met Sinatra at the party and began a months-long romance with him, observed, that night, that Natalie was "smitten" with Sinatra, who "did treat Natalie with deference." When Meredith started to date Sinatra, "Natalie would talk about Frank a lot, about how he treated her so beautifully." In August, Sinatra invited the Wagners to New York with him and Meredith. They traveled together by train, spending several days on the East Coast, going to nightclubs like the Blue Angel and Monsignor's.

Sometime the next year, when they were all four at a dinner party at Romanoff's, Meredith was startled to have "a rift" with Natalie in the powder room over Sinatra. "I'm not confrontational at all, neither was Nat, but a couple of comments were made by each of us." Natalie made it clear, in the encounter, she had a crush on Sinatra, "and I didn't know it . . . and I think my being the center of attention with him—and at one point, very serious—that threw her, she didn't expect it."

The jealous confrontation over Sinatra ended the friendship between Natalie and Meredith, who thought Natalie's infatuation was "a crush on a megastar. Sinatra was a magic person, an icon I guess. I don't know if it was like something you think about—everybody fantasizes on what would have been, what could have been, what should have been but doesn't. There's a huge line between fantasy and acting out. We all make reality out of dreams."

Natalie and R.J.'s profligate spending and fast life with such as Sinatra, Elizabeth Taylor and Eddie Fisher, Tony Curtis and Janet Leigh, began to catch up with them by the end of 1959. "It was like we were playing house with play money," Natalie said later, "and when it ran out—that was it." To recoup their financial losses, they agreed to break their marital agreement to not make a picture together after MGM offered Natalie $150,000 to cast her with R.J. in a Southern Gothic soap opera ultimately called *All the Fine Young Cannibals*.

Natalie approached it with her usual dedication, moving a dialect coach into the house to teach her and R.J. the proper Texas accents, but the picture would come to be known as the fiasco of her career. Hyatt visited her on the set, where Natalie was worried whether her husband could handle a dramatic role.

Although Natalie joined R.J. earlier that year ridiculing "nose-picking fringe Method actors" in the *New York Times*, she was embarrassed by the bad Hollywood films she had made since accepting her star-making Faustian pact with Warner Brothers, beginning with the Tab Hunter pictures. It rankled her to be forced into *Cash McCall* by the studio, which had caused her to forfeit an opportunity to costar with Laurence Olivier in *The Entertainer*, which she wanted "desperately."

All of her hopes and dreams for her career seemed to reside with *Splendor in the Grass*, the picture Warners had dangled to get her to return to the studio. She saw *Splendor*, and its director, Kazan, as her last best hope to restore her integrity as an actress. As with *Rebel*, *A Cry in the Night*, and *Marjorie Morningstar*, her three earlier passion projects, Natalie deeply identified with the character in *Splendor* because of parallels to her own life. Wilma Dean, "Deanie," the sweet high school girl in *Splendor*, was almost *too* close to Natalie for comfort.

In the script, by William Inge, Deanie has a weak but tender father and an overbearing mother who demonizes sex and tries to keep her from the high school boy she loves, with tragic results, leading Deanie into a mental institution for psychoanalysis. Natalie recognized herself, and Jimmy Williams, in the thwarted teen lovers Deanie and Bud, though in the movie it is Deanie—not Bud—who tries to commit suicide. The role excited her because of the storyline with the controlling mother, Natalie told her friend Bobby. At the same time, "I always had a bit of inner resistance to doing that part," she said later, "because I felt I would have to open doors and relive a lot of feelings that I had put the lid on. I had a hunch that emotionally it wasn't going to be good for me . . . [that it would] open up a lot of wounds."

The script also called for the character of Deanie to sob in several scenes, to walk on a high ledge, to submerge her head under water in a bathtub, and try to drown herself—some of Natalie's most deep-seated fears. Natalie ultimately decided she had to play Deanie, despite the emotional risks, because of a greater fear: she told Kazan, when they met, she was afraid her *career* was in danger.

Natalie's first encounter with the director she idolized since seeing *A Streetcar Named Desire* at thirteen was a dramatic illustration of the Natalie/Maria schism in actress "Natalie Wood." Her by now best friend Norma Crane, a graduate of the Actors Studio, was with Natalie as she was dressing at the Waldorf in New York to see Kazan about playing Deanie. As Crane would recall, "The girl in *Splendor* is the purest, most virginal girl in the world, and Natalie was putting on mascara, high heels up to here, false eyelashes, bracelets, rings. I said: 'You're going to meet Kazan. The part!' She said: 'I'm Natalie Wood and that's how I go out at 7 at night.' "

Kazan's encounter with Natalie was illuminating for the director. Although she was his original choice to play

Deanie, he said later that he had second thoughts while he was developing the project at Warner Brothers, worried about hiring a "has-been child star." According to Leonard Hirshan, one of Natalie's agents at Morris, Kazan also "-didn't feel that she looked as virginal as he wanted . . . he was looking for a quality that he didn't see in her then."

Upon meeting Natalie, the shrewd Kazan, who was famous for psychoanalyzing his actors, correctly perceived Natalie as half-child, half-woman, "like a doll dressed up by adults." He saw a "desperate twinkle" underneath the makeup and recognized an "unsatisfied hunger" in Natalie to excel. He looked past her mink, and believed Natalie when she told him she was "disgusted with the image" she had acquired.

He recalled, two years later, "I put paint remover on her, took off her glamorous clothes, and put her up there, naked and gasping. She wanted a new career, and I guess I gave her a new career. She had tremendous willpower to be good. So many actors, you feel they have a private life, a husband and kids, and acting has a place. But with her, acting is her whole life."

Natalie told Kazan she would do anything for him in the picture, with one exception: she confessed her terror of "feeling helpless in dark water," saying that she would require a double for the scene where Deanie tries to drown herself. What else she confided only they knew.

Before Natalie arrived on the East Coast to begin *Splendor*, assistant director Don Kranze recalls, "I remember Kazan saying to us—because Natalie was sort of a lightweight from the Kazan standpoint, okay?—he said, 'You're going to see a Natalie Wood that you've never seen before.' So he had something in mind."

Natalie and R.J. left Hollywood like movie stars on April 8, 1960, for Natalie to begin *Splendor in the Grass*, taking the luxurious *Super Chief*, accompanied by Eddie Fisher and Elizabeth Taylor, who was on her way back to New York to complete *Butterfield 8*. The Wagners rented an apartment on Sutton Place overlooking the East River, where R.J. practiced the piano for a picture that never materialized, *Solo*, despondent over his career, which he said later was "going downhill."

Natalie started *Splendor* with the mingled fear and pleasure she had *Rebel*, describing her work with Kazan as a return to the "golden world" of Nick Ray. She would recall Kazan encouraging her, "Don't be afraid to make a fool of yourself," to be bold, be free, to "shock herself," helping Natalie to realize that her perfectionism was inhibiting her. She was stimulated by the cramped, makeshift New York stages where they were shooting, so unlike the artificiality of Hollywood. "She worked as if her life depended upon it," as Kazan famously would later say.

Kazan's makeup person, Bob Jiras ("B.J."), had been preparing for Natalie's arrival with the same idea of transforming her. "I knew that Kazan didn't like makeup that much, and I went to see a couple of Natalie's films, and she was always very heavily made-up. And I knew that Kazan wouldn't want that." Jiras used "a very simple make-up" on Natalie in a filmed test as the sweet Deanie—less, even, than in *Rebel Without a Cause*—leaving it to Kazan to convince her that she would still look beautiful without her Natalie Wood mask.

Kazan watched the test with Natalie and Jiras, as Natalie gasped at her nearly naked face, "and Kazan turned to Natalie and said, 'B.J. is really talented, don't you think?' And that's how he got her. He could feel her negativism, so we had to present it as that's the look *she* wanted, instead of her saying, 'Don't you think I need more lipstick?' It ended right there." Natalie was enamored of the way she looked in *Splendor* because *Kazan* was. She became instant close friends with the affable, talented Jiras and requested him on nearly every subsequent picture.

Natalie's costar in *Splendor in the Grass* was Warren Beatty, a gorgeous, intense young actor making his film debut as Deanie's teen love, Bud, on the recommendation of William Inge, who had earlier cast Beatty in an unprofitable production of his play *A Loss of Roses*, Beatty's only other credit. "Warren, hell, hadn't done anything," as Pat Hingle, the Kazan protégé who played Beatty's/Bud's tyrannical father recalls. "Warren had been in a Bill Inge play that didn't succeed . . . he could hardly have been more of a neophyte."

The popular mythology in Hollywood, in future years, would be that Natalie and Beatty began a love affair while making *Splendor*, under the noses of Robert Wagner and Beatty's fiancée, Joan Collins, who left for London early in the production to star in *Esther and the King*. The rumor about Natalie and Beatty became so pervasive by 1988, that Kazan included it as fact in his memoir published that year.

In truth, Natalie and Beatty disliked each other throughout the filming of *Splendor in the Grass*. Natalie talked about it in later years, in interviews with the *New York Times*, *Interview*, and *Cosmopolitan*, describing Beatty as "difficult to work with." Bob Jiras, who was doing her makeup, confirms Natalie found him problematic.

"Warren was a pain in the ass," affirms Kranze, the assistant director. "He was very young, anyway, but his emotional maturity was about thirteen . . . we all sort of felt about Warren that he's an immature boy playing a man's game." Richard Sylbert, the Oscar-winning production designer who worked on *Splendor*, one of Beatty's best friends, admits, "He was a real pain in the ass. The crew called him 'donkey dick.' He was the Warren Beatty he was gonna become, meaning—and I say this, this is all good—he was gonna do what he wanted to do. He didn't care what anybody thought."

Natalie became so annoyed with Beatty she asked Kazan's right-hand man, Charlie Maguire, his associate producer, to keep Beatty out of her dressing room. As Kranze explains, "In New York it wasn't so fancy shmancy. We didn't have a separate room for her and a separate room for him, so they shared the makeup area. Charlie said she didn't want him in there. 'She can't stand him, she wants him out of there.' That was his remark to me." Natalie would later tell several Hollywood writers, for publication, that she and Beatty had so much friction, she worried whether they would be convincing in their love scenes.

Natalie repeated this to Robert Redford, when they became friends later. "She told me she didn't like him. That's not when they got together." The production designer, Sylbert, one of Beatty's best friends and a friend of Natalie's, confirms, "There was nothing going on during the film. And not only that, they didn't like each other. Nothing happened, I guarantee it. And he's told me that, and she told me that." Natalie's confidant, Jiras, states flatly, "There was no love affair. There was nothing."

Joan Collins, who flew to New York on weekends to see her fiancé, further denies there was an affair between Natalie and Beatty. "She wouldn't let him out of her sight," Jiras says of Collins. As filming progressed, Natalie began to respect Beatty's talent, and found him attractive, Jiras noticed, but she still considered him a pain. Natalie gave

Beatty the secret nickname "Mental Anguish." "Here comes 'Mental Anguish,' " she would whisper to Jiras. "Then it was shortened to 'M.A.' "

During an in-depth interview between her two marriages to Wagner, Natalie addressed the rumor she had an affair with Beatty, calling it "complete, utter nonsense."

As free-spirited as Natalie was in her rebellious teen years, when boyfriends lined around the block, once she married, she respected her marriage vows, as those close to her knew. The image of gaiety that became associated with Natalie from her zany movie magazine covers as America's Teen was "Natalie Wood," not Natalie. Lana comments, "Natalie was—I don't want to say that she was more serious than she was fun, but if you had to draw lines, she was. Even her type of 'fun' was more serious than anyone else's."

Natalie viewed her marriage to R.J. as her one-and-only, her fantasy fulfilled, and she committed herself in the only way she knew how to do things, all or nothing. "She really wanted these things to work," observes her friend Sylbert. "Not that people don't have affairs in Hollywood, but it's not something, I don't think, that she would have done—by nature. She wasn't gonna be married and have an affair at the same time."

Natalie's love affair on *Splendor* was with Deanie, the movie, and working with Kazan, who brought her to the greatest emotional heights of her career. The experience was exhilarating but wrenching for Natalie, who faced her demons on *Splendor*.

She was panicky about shooting the bathtub scene, where Deanie has a volatile confrontation with her mother about sex and purity, ending by Deanie dunking her head in the bath water, then standing up, naked and hysterical, shouting, "I'm a *good* little girl, Mom!" Natalie dreaded the scene, confessing to Kazan ("Gadge," as friends called him) that she had an emotional block about crying on cue. According to Lana:

> Elia Kazan—Gadge—said to her, "Do you not understand the scene? Do you not understand how you're feeling?" She said, "Yes, I do, I do. I just don't think I can shed tears. I won't be able to cry."
>
> And he said, "Aha." And he said, "Okay," and he asked [actress] Barbara Loden to come over, and he said, "Could you cry for Natalie?" And Barbara said, "Sure," put her head down for a moment, lifted her head up and tears were streaming down her face. Kazan said, "Thanks."
>
> Barbara left, and he said to Natalie, "Well, how did that make you feel?" And Natalie said, "Well, it makes me feel terrible. I can't do it!" And he said, "No, no, you're missing the point. How did it make you *feel?* What were you feeling when you were watching her cry?" And Natalie said, "Well, I was in awe that she could do it."
>
> And he said, "Yes, but did you feel empathy? Were you moved?" And she said, "Well, no." And he said, "Exactly. There's a big difference between just being able to turn on tears and actually feeling something and have that come true in your scene, in your acting. As long as you know what it is that you are feeling, and it's true for the character, it doesn't matter if you shed a tear or not. It's still going to be moving."
>
> And then she felt better about that.

According to Kranze, the assistant director, Kazan put off the bathtub scene for several weeks, knowing Natalie was frantic about crying, and about putting her head under water. She would also be performing wearing only pasties. As he was preparing to shoot the scene, Kazan cleverly baited Natalie by telling her he could shoot the scene without showing her face if she didn't think she could be emotional enough.

Then he whispered into the ear of Audrey Christie, the actress who was playing Natalie's mother, to stand offstage and taunt Natalie before the cameras started to roll. "He had Audrey say a line which he knew would set me off. It wasn't the line in the script. But it was a line which, when I was little, used to drive me crazy. You know that mother's tone, so sweet: 'Darling, is there something bothering you? Is there something I can do to help?' Audrey just said that line in that sweet tone, and I went off the way I always used to [with my mother] and they shot it and that was it."

Kazan may also have come up with the idea to have Natalie remove her "magic" bracelet, knowing that the feeling of insecurity that caused would heighten her performance, for she is not wearing a bracelet in the bathtub scene in *Splendor*, one of the few times when Natalie's misshaped left wrist was exposed to the camera.

The combination of Kazan's wizardry, Natalie's emotional connection to the mother/daughter conflict in the scene, the panic of dousing her head under the bath water, and the vulnerability she felt at being seen "naked"—without her bracelet—produced a hysteria in Natalie that may be her most powerful moment as an actress.

"She broke wide open that day," recalls Kazan's assistant director, Don Kranze. "That was her first day where she really—she hit the scene. And it was clear that she was just terrific. I know Kazan felt good that day. He felt that he had really hit something. And we all did. Anyone who really was thinking about the movie other than their paycheck, saw something pretty good happening."

According to Kranze, "From then on, it was easy" with Natalie. "She broke open. She became a full-fledged—she was gonna hit that role out of the park after that day." Kranze noticed that when Natalie finished the mother/daughter confrontation scene in the bathtub, "she was emotionally moved . . . she felt lousy afterwards."

According to Natalie, Kazan employed other "tricks" to provoke her into an emotional state, related to her fear of heights and of water. She told the *London Times* that Gadge lied to her about the scene where she had to walk on a high ledge, telling her that his assistant would be holding her hand off-camera. As soon as Kazan called action, the assistant released Natalie's hand, terrifying her—the reaction he wanted for the scene.

Kazan was more diabolical toward the end of filming, when the cast and crew traveled to a reservoir at High Falls in upstate New York to film the sequence where Deanie tries to commit suicide by jumping off a ledge into a waterfall, the scene Gadge promised Natalie he would hire a double to perform. Several versions exist as to what happened. Natalie said later:

> Elia Kazan assured me a double would do the scene where I was required to swim under an eight-foot waterfall. But then it turned out the double couldn't swim at all, and I had to do it. I told Kazan: "I'll do it only if you take me out to the waterfall and throw me in. I know I can't swim that far, and I'm scared besides." And that's what they did. They threw me in, and had to get me out fast before I drowned.

Kazan denied it, after Natalie died. "How could you use a damn double? You had to go ten miles away," he protested, claiming that he "gentled her into it," and used his assistant, Charlie Maguire, to stay near her under the water for reassurance, admitting she was "not entirely reassured."

There *was* a double. Natalie gave an interview to the *New York Mirror* that June, shortly after filming the waterfall scene, complaining about her bruised legs, scraped hand and swollen right wrist, offering the same account of how Kazan had hired a double who couldn't swim well. Less than two months later, a bit player named Martha Linda Martin threatened to sue Warner Brothers over Natalie's comments in the press, alleging that *she* was Natalie's double for the scene, and that she *could* swim—suggesting that Kazan *had* employed a double, but misled Natalie that the double couldn't swim to deceive her into doing the scene.

Kazan's assistant director, Don Kranze, "won't say it's not true, because when we talk about Kazan tricking actors into doing things, that's Kazan. He's a great, great director, but a more ruthless man you will not find when it comes to getting what he wants. As all directors must be. Directors must be ruthless—and psychiatrists and psychologists and liars and manipulators and actors and whatever. They play a host of parts. I can't deny that he tricked Natalie into something because that's Kazan's method." Maguire, Kazan's assistant, recalls holding Natalie's hand during the waterfall scene, but is vague about the rest. Her hairdresser, Willis Hanchett, remembers the double, and learning that the double couldn't swim, "so Natalie, being the trouper that she was, said, 'I will do it,' and she did."

Natalie was "tremendously proud of having done it

herself, she was ecstatic—though she was also furious that she had been hoodwinked into this," although Natalie had known, since *Rebel*, that Kazan was famous for manipulating his actors, something she and Dennis Hopper had talked about frequently in their "bull" sessions about acting.

According to Kranze, who helped to set up both the waterfall and the ledge scenes for Kazan, "I can tell you, when Natalie had to get into that water, in that river, she was deadly afraid of the water. I mean deadly. And where we were, she had a good reason to be, although I didn't know it at the time. We were in a stupid place. We were on the edge of a waterfall, a slow-moving waterfall. What I didn't realize at the time, or what the production manager should have realized, is that we should have kept checking upstream to see if there were any dams on that river that they might let it loose. I don't think we even thought of the possibility of a heavy rainstorm fifty miles away. And it could have been dangerous. We should have done a lot more checking before working there."

Natalie earned the respect and affection of everyone concerned with *Splendor*, creating such an indelible portrait of the Kansas innocent Wilma Dean, "it was so easy for me to forget that she was Natalie, and believe that she was just this high school kid called Deanie," praises Pat Hingle, an Actors Studio great. "In my mind right now, when I think of her, the picture comes to me is of this teenage girl in bobby socks and that sort of thing. I am from that neck of the woods, so I know well the Midwest, and I don't think that she could possibly have had any kind of a background like that, but she was very believable as a small-town girl. And to my mind, that's acting."

Actor Gary Lockwood, who played the cad who tries to

seduce Deanie before her suicide attempt, felt "Kazan and Natalie were a terrific marriage, because you had this beautiful girl, and you had somebody that could get things out of her." Lockwood characterized R.J., who was often on the *Splendor* set to see Natalie and would later work with Lockwood's first wife, Stefanie Powers, as a "professional" movie star. "Natalie was a bona fide movie star. I don't give a shit that she didn't do Broadway or whatever, but I mean, the camera looked at her, and she turned her head to the right, and she was vulnerable, and beautiful, and you can't buy that."

Kazan's favorite scene in *Splendor* was the last one, when a worldly, mature Deanie (Natalie—looking radiant and beautiful in a white dress and a white, wide-brimmed hat) goes back to see her lost first love, Bud (Beatty—in overalls), finding he has married a simple girl and is living on a farm. "It's terribly touching to me. I still like it when I see it." Kazan's bittersweet ending illustrates poignantly paths not taken, as Natalie's voiceover, as Deanie, is heard to quote from Wordsworth's "Ode on Intimations of Immortality," saying:

> *Though nothing can bring back the hour*
> *Of splendour in the grass, glory in the flower;*
> *We will grieve not, rather find*
> *Strength in what remains behind.*

The lines in Wordsworth's poem, and Deanie's emotions, had special pathos for Natalie, reminding her of herself with Jimmy, the "old wounds" she had anticipated opening when she hesitated whether to take the role. Kazan was unaware of Natalie's heartbreaking first love, though he recognized, as he was shooting the scene, that it struck a personal chord with Natalie, saying later, "[The scene] is wonderful because of *her*—because of her own pain about it. Whatever that came from, I don't know. But you didn't have to direct that. She had it right off. She understood it."

While she was in the middle of shooting *Splendor in the Grass*, Natalie got an urgent call from her agent, saying that the Mirisch Company wanted her for the part of Maria in the film version of *West Side Story*, which director Robert Wise was preparing to start shooting with no leading lady in sight. The way it came about was "an odd situation," Natalie would say later.

She had been approached about *West Side Story* a year earlier, around her twenty-first birthday, when the Mirisch Company was developing it with its creator and choreographer Jerome Robbins, and with Wise. Wise, and Walter Mirisch, wanted to cast the original Maria on Broadway, stage actress Carol Lawrence, but decided she "was not young enough anymore to play it in the film." At an early production meeting, someone mentioned they needed "a fawn in the forest" to play the innocent, vulnerable Puerto Rican girl Maria, prompting casting director Lynn Stalmaster to suggest Natalie Wood. The suggestion was taken seriously enough to make the trades that July, and Natalie told Hedda Hopper in the beginning of 1960 she had been offered the part.

In the six months that followed, the Mirisches and the film's codirectors, Wise and Robbins, "wanted to find an unknown who could sing," but who "also had the acting chops" to play Maria, resulting in what assistant director Robert Relyea called "the largest testing, searching program probably ever in Hollywood's history." When the quest proved futile, Wise and Robbins tested actresses Anna

Maria Alberghetti, Suzanne Pleshette, Diane Baker, Pier Angeli, Angie Dickinson, Jane Fonda, Hope Lange, and Susan Kohner. By late June 1960, with only a few weeks before filming, "panic set in," and Natalie reemerged as a top contender, even though she was not a professional singer or dancer, nor was she Puerto Rican.

According to Wise, the Mirisches decided they needed a "name" actress around the time they all saw a screen test of Warren Beatty from *Splendor*, whom they briefly contemplated to play Tony, Maria's boyfriend. When Natalie appeared on camera as the innocent Deanie, "we said, 'That's our Maria.' " Jerome Robbins said later he was impressed by Natalie's "depth."

Natalie was not eager to play another ingénue and was unsure she was right for the part, dangling the Mirisches into July, while she was filming *Splendor*. She celebrated her twenty-second birthday on the twentieth with a small on-set party, surprised by a lavish birthday dinner that night at Pierre's, arranged by R.J., who flew in Mud from California to blow out the candles on Natalie's birthday cake. ("All was a secret," Maria said after Natalie's death, still thrilled at the memory. "She was shooting that day, and she came to the hotel room and R.J. had me in the closet. She didn't know that I was there. And R.J. said, 'Well, you're tired, we're not gonna have a party or anything, just you and me will go to this restaurant.' He said, 'Go in the closet and get something pretty and we'll celebrate, just you and me, very romantic.' She open the door and there I was standing there!") Sinatra, who was rehearsing at the 500 Club in Atlantic City, sent twenty-two bouquets of flowers to the restaurant every half hour, hiring musicians to sing to Natalie "Nothing Like a Dame."

That weekend, as Natalie and R.J. left for New Jersey to

attend Sinatra's opening night, Natalie's agent, Leonard Hirshan, got an emergency call, as Wise and Robbins began to film the New York exterior scenes in *West Side Story*:

> Bobby Wise finally, at the eleventh hour, made the decision that he would like to go with Natalie Wood, but he wanted to meet with her that weekend . . . and I said, "She's going to Asbury Park to see Frank Sinatra, who's performing at a club." So I told Bobby Wise and Jerome Robbins that if they wanted to meet her this weekend, they're going to have to go to Asbury Park, and they said, "Okay, how about 9 A.M. Sunday morning?"
>
> Saturday night, Natalie was seeing Frank Sinatra. I flew to Philadelphia, drove down to Asbury Park and joined Natalie and R.J. seeing Frank Sinatra perform two shows, eating dinner with him in the kitchen—Natalie, R.J., and the boys—and then going back to Sinatra's suite until about 4:00 in the morning.
>
> At 9 A.M., we had the meeting with the two gentlemen. It was very brief, very nice, and Bobby said, "We would love to have you do the picture," and she said, "I'd love to do it."

Hirshan, an associate of Joe Schoenfeld, Natalie's primary agent at William Morris, boasted, before he left for the East Coast, that he could get Natalie $250,000 for the part, an astronomical sum in 1960. After the meeting with Wise and Robbins, Harold Mirisch agreed to the figure. When Hirshan flew back to L.A., "Harold Mirisch says, 'Look, I know I said $250,000, but would you take into consideration *$200,000* plus 5% of the profits?' " Joe Schoenfeld demanded the straight $250,000 salary. "Some people like to get whatever you can up front. Me, I'm a believer in royalty," asserts Hirshan. "I, in later years, found out that 5% of the profits was worth one million dollars! Therefore, by taking 250 instead of 200, that extra 50,000 caused Natalie to give up a million dollars." Two years later, Natalie said sheepishly, "Don't think I'm smart; I was offered a percentage on *West Side Story* and didn't take it."

Natalie signed to play Maria during her emotionally trying last three weeks as Deanie, saying later she was "so busy concentrating," she hardly thought of the musical aspects of the role, requiring her to perform complex dance numbers and a light operatic score. At the same time, it was the opportunity to sing that intrigued Natalie to *star* in *West Side Story*.

The agreement that was reached about the use of her singing voice is somewhat unclear. Producer Walter Mirisch recalls her agent, Schoenfeld, telling him that Natalie "thought she could do it and wanted the chance." According to Mirisch, she accepted the part on the condition they would let her *try*, with only an "outside chance" they would use her singing voice. Director Robert Wise has a similar "we'll try it and see" recollection, though Saul Chaplin, the associate producer in charge of music, claimed later he knew from the beginning they would have to dub Natalie.

Natalie's perception, clearly, was different. She arranged for voice lessons to begin as soon as she returned to L.A., excited at working with an orchestra. Marni Nixon, who eventually dubbed her voice, felt Natalie "really did believe" her voice would be used. "Natalie wanted to sing more than she wanted to breathe," asserts her friend Robert Blake, who would play the guitar for her while Natalie sang. "She loved being a singer."

—

Natalie attended a wrap party in New York for *Splendor* the middle of August, bidding farewell to her incompatible costar, Beatty, whose gag gift from Kazan at the party was a hand mirror that said, "Good God, Warren." According to Kazan's assistant director, Kranze, the mirror was a symbol for Beatty's vanity during filming. "I recall distinctly getting on the set early in the morning and he's in there before his makeup call . . . he's in front of a mirror, a set stage, where the mirror's right on the stage—and he's got a straight pin, right? He's putting that pin into each eyelash, and separating and moving them forward. He's separating every goddamn eyelash! He's going one by one by one. Oh my God, this is six feet of pure ego!"

In later years, Natalie would describe Beatty's behavior filming *Splendor* more charitably, saying that he was "insecure." The impression *she* left on the cast and crew at the end of the picture was as "a very nice, professional young girl," in Kranze's view. "Pert, likeable, lively, with it, can take a joke, friendly, vivacious." Kranze perceived "that was not her personality, but that's what I saw. I guess she was darker than I'm suggesting." Production designer Dick Sylbert knew and liked Nick Gurdin from his carpentry work at the studios. "I always called her 'Natasha,' " he said of Natalie. "That was my sort of name for her. She was terrific. Natalie was not a snob. She really liked the people who make movies."

One of them, a young "gofer" named Mart Crowley, who would eventually write the groundbreaking play *The Boys in the Band*, "fell in love with Natalie so much," recalled Maria, "even if he is a homosexual. When she finish the movie, he start to cry and say, 'Oh, I'm not gonna see you.' So she said, 'Okay, you gonna be my secretary,' and so she took him to L.A." Crowley became, as Mud would put it,

Natalie's "best girlfriend." He also became her "caretaker," Nuell said later, someone to hold Natalie's hand during long, insomniac nights.

Beatty and his fiancée, Joan Collins, who was back from London, went their romantic way, as Natalie and R.J. departed for Hollywood by train on August 19 for Natalie to start rehearsals on *West Side Story*. They arrived to find their white Scott-and-Zelda mansion in a state of lavish disrepair, with the floor sagging under Natalie's sunken six-foot-square tub, and the extravagant staircases wobbling. She and R.J. fired the contractor and escaped to the haven of their boat for a week so Natalie could shake off the intense emotions from *Splendor*, before the taxing *West Side Story* shoot. R.J. was having problems with his studio, Fox, over changes they made to *Solo*, and his "phone wasn't ringing" with offers.

The Wagners' new house on Beverly, which Natalie would later complain was unfairly maligned as "Miss Havisham's mansion," was beautiful, recalls Faye Nuell. Natalie and R.J. had purchased extraordinary pieces from Hearst's castle at San Simeon, including antique balustrades, wrought iron gates, and an ornate fifteenth-century eight-foot bed with a massive oak headboard in the upstairs master bedroom.

R.J.'s live-in butler, and an occasional daytime maid, completed the picture of the "mad young millionaires," as Louella Parsons wrote of the Wagners. Bobby Hyatt recalls R.J.'s valet as "creepy. He was an elderly, thin guy with gray hair, and he had a tendency to wear a white dress shirt with the sleeves rolled up, and he pulled his slacks up as high as he could and cinched the belt so that his testicles would be on display. When he'd [go] by to his back room, Nat would whisper to me, 'I hate him!' " Hyatt suggested that Natalie fire the butler, "and she said she couldn't, that he belonged to R.J. That was a continuing argument—about the only thing they ever argued about."

Leonard Hirshan, the agent who guided Natalie through *West Side Story* daily, and socialized with the Wagners, remembers them as "terrific, a very nice, compatible, easygoing couple. They were fun to be with."

Natalie plunged into her new musical on a punishing schedule of twelve-hour rehearsals each day, trying to catch up to the cast of professional singer/dancers, many of whom were in the Broadway show, and who resented and envied Natalie as a "movie star." Rita Moreno, a Tony-winning Broadway singer-dancer-actress who would win an Oscar playing the fiery Anita in *West Side Story*, recalls "a few groans from a few people" when Natalie arrived on set.

The perfectionist Natalie, still emotionally drained from *Splendor*, felt insecure about her singing voice, her dancing, and her attempt to play a Puerto Rican, throwing herself into one rehearsal with such intensity she fell to the floor and Wise thought she was injured. According to Moreno, "She couldn't get it right" during the mambo scene in the gymnasium, forcing everyone to repeat the dance many times without apologizing. "I remember at the time being rather dismayed that there seemed to be no acknowledgment of the work the other people were doing in this. Not getting it right was not really her fault, but she didn't address it." The other dancers—including Moreno—interpreted Natalie's insecurity as "indifference . . . I don't know that there was resentment, but there were sarcastic remarks."

"Natalie was miserable," recalls Lana. "She loved Jerry Robbins and she liked that entire process, but she just didn't get along too well other than that. She just was unhappy on it . . . it was very demanding, she was very concerned about the makeup, about the look, about people accepting her as a Puerto Rican—about everything."

Natalie asked Moreno to help her with her accent during one of the early rehearsals, "and I went into her room and started to tape record her dialogue, and somewhere along the middle she sort of lost interest. I made a tape for thirty minutes, and that was that." Natalie's Puerto Rican accent was "terrible," in Moreno's opinion. "Awful. It could have been really so much better." At the time, Moreno thought Natalie was lazy, "but maybe when you feel you're not up to the job, you sort of give up on it, you go through the motions, and it's very possible that's what she was doing."

Lana recalls Natalie as on the verge of a nervous collapse, missing work by calling in sick, spending lunch hours in her trailer, on the telephone with her analyst. When Jerome Robbins was fired as codirector in October, "Natalie was left without her guru," as assistant director Relyea relates. Saul Chaplin recalls, "She was adamant and she threatened not to show up. But of course she not only showed up, she was terrific."

Natalie's saving grace was Tony Mordente, one of the "Jets" dancers, whom Robert Wise and Natalie requested to work with her on the remaining musical numbers. Mordente "was hesitant about it," perceiving Natalie the same way some of the other dancers had. "There were kids in the company who thought that Natalie was kind of a snob—same kind of feeling I got. I thought, 'Oh, wow, she's really a snobbish, standoffish, Miss Star, Miss Hollywood.' But she was quite the opposite, very much the opposite."

Mordente spent every night, and weekends, going over dance routines with Natalie at her house on Beverly:

> And as it turned out, I found her absolutely—she was like a human Alka Seltzer, she was just the most bubbling, effervescent person, and she was so easy to work with. I mean she certainly had her likes and her dislikes, and she certainly knew what she wanted to do. What she needed *me* to do was to help get her to what she wanted to do. And she worked really hard, I think the first day we worked twelve hours. But the work was what she wanted to do, and what she wanted to do was get it right.
>
> And she really did a wonderful job, for somebody who was basically a non-dancer . . . and she was a lady who had rhythm, who could move.

As Mordente spent more time with Natalie, he discovered how insecure she was in the part, and how much she wanted people to like her—just as she had at Fulton Junior High, with Mary Ann. "She was very genuinely worried about what the entire cast thought about her. She would always ask me, 'What do you think? What do you think they're thinking?' In a sense, she was shy around the company. I said, 'What are you worried about? They're not even in the scene with you, forget about 'em.' She was worried about other people's perception of her as a person, and what they thought of her as a performer. She was so concerned that people like her, and she wanted them to think she was good."

Natalie talked to Mordente, for hours, about her Puerto Rican accent. "I know she worked on it all day long. She used to talk to *me* like that. We'd be out to dinner, and suddenly she'd be breaking into it. She was always concerned about it. She was always concerned that things were going to be exactly the way she wanted them. She wanted them to be perfect all the time."

If Natalie had a flaw, in Mordente's opinion, "it would be that she wanted people to like her, and she wanted to be a great actress . . . she strived to be the perfect actress. There was no question. She wanted to be the best actress in Hollywood, even the world, there was no question about that. The Academy Award was very big to her."

Mordente saw Natalie virtually every day from the time Robbins was fired in October, until the end of filming *West Side Story* in February. "I became friendly with Natalie, and R.J., and we spent a lot of time together, going to dinner and so forth. R.J. became a very good friend of mine. And he was going through a very tough period at the time, because he had been suspended by Fox . . . and I think R.J. had his ego, and his ego was being a little bit tossed around because Natalie was peaking, and he was sliding, at that time, in no man's land, not knowing what he was going to do next."

Mordente considered the marriage "good," though he allowed, "They had their problems. And I think their problems stemmed from Natalie really driving to stardom, and the possibility of winning an Academy Award, and R.J. saying, 'Where's my career going next?' Natalie was a very ambitious lady, I make no bones about that."

While filming *West Side Story*, Natalie said positive things to Mordente about Warren Beatty as an actor, never mentioning him otherwise. Nor did Mordente see Beatty around Natalie from October 1960 to February 1961. Natalie's intimate, Bob Jiras, who did her makeup on *West Side Story*, confirms Beatty was never there. In Mordente's view, "there couldn't have been" any personal contact between Natalie and Beatty during filming. "Because, I'm not going to exaggerate, Natalie and I spent five nights a week together. Going to dinner, or talking, or laughing, or playing games, or shopping, or going to the movies—and it was always with R.J., and Natalie, and/or Mart. Mart was always there." Beatty, in fact, had been living with fiancée Joan Collins since shooting *Splendor in the Grass*, and left for Europe in December to shoot a movie, *The Roman Spring of Mrs. Stone*, accompanied by Collins.

Sometime during filming, Natalie was told that singer Marni Nixon was going to dub the high notes in Natalie's song tracks as Maria. Nixon recalled, "They were telling her she was wonderful, and we on the sidelines were going, 'Oh my God! How could they let that go on?' They would turn to me and they would wink." Natalie was deceived about her voice being used until the end of the film, when Wise and the producers informed her that Nixon would be dubbing all of her songs as Maria. "She wanted so much to do her own singing, but in the final analysis, her voice just wasn't good enough," reveals Wise. "She was more than upset," relates Mordente. "She was pissed. She was steamed." Mostly, Natalie was heartbroken.

They had gotten their fawn in the forest, nearly destroying her, like Bambi. While millions of moviegoers, for decades to come, would be dazzled by the dancing and singing in *West Side Story*, it is Natalie who would move them, with her heartbreakingly vulnerable performance as Maria.

After she finished *West Side Story*, Natalie was admitted to St. John's Hospital for a tonsillectomy, which she had delayed for weeks. Mordente recalls her with a "throat problem" toward the end of filming, "and R.J. was saying, 'Maybe we should get a doctor.' " According to Mordente, Natalie's mother did not want her to see a doctor, an attitude Mordente felt bordered on "witchcraft."

During her April 7 tonsillectomy, Natalie developed complications and nearly died, hemorrhaging for four hours, according to reports published at the time. R.J. took an adjoining room at the hospital for two nights, holding Natalie's hand while she recovered. She was released from the hospital in mid-April, missing an appearance as a presenter at the Academy Awards.

Before she was hospitalized, Natalie turned down a picture that Warner Brothers was pressuring her to make called *The Inspector* (or *Lisa*). She spent the next few weeks of spring contemplating other movie offers and resting, as R.J. rehearsed for his first movie under a new nonexclusive contract with Columbia Studios. The picture, *Sail a Crooked Ship*, starring Ernie Kovacs, began filming in Los Angeles on May 1, 1961.

Natalie visited the set of *Sail a Crooked Ship* occasionally in May and June, as she and R.J. coordinated their work schedules to go to Italy together in July, Natalie's first time abroad. R.J. had arranged to meet with Darryl Zanuck in Rome to discuss appearing in the war drama *The Longest Day*, while Natalie filmed the Warner Brothers romantic drama *Lovers Must Learn* (later changed to *Rome Adventure*), costarring Troy Donahue, which she accepted the end of May.

The Wagners kept up their glittering social schedule in June, as R.J. completed his film with Ernie Kovacs, sparkling together at a party the first week of the month, given by their friends Elizabeth Taylor and Eddie Fisher at Au Petit Jean, radiantly hand-in-hand mid-June at a Warner Brothers Jubilee dinner of stars, where they were a foursome with Warren Beatty and Joan Collins, who had just returned from Europe.

A day or so later, R.J. completed *Sail a Crooked Ship*, with Natalie romantically anticipating their coming trip to Europe. After they went to bed that night, Natalie went to a neighbor's house in her nightgown and banged on the door, using their phone to call her mother.

Lana, who was in junior high, remembers her sister arriving at the house in Van Nuys that night, frantic, her hand bleeding from cut glass, sobbing that her marriage was over. "She was really, really upset."

Natalie would not tell her sister at the time what occurred that night. "My mom told me a couple of things that Natalie said," reveals Lana.

Natalie shut herself in one of the bedrooms at her parents' home that night, swallowing sleeping pills, "and I guess she had taken too many, because Mrs. Gurdin called my house immediately," relates Jean Hyatt. "But I was asleep and Bobby answered the phone." Robert Hyatt remembers, "It was late at night, and Marie started telling me everything.

Mud and Fahd, according to Jean Hyatt, "took Natalie to the hospital and had her stomach pumped, they weren't taking any chances. The poor little thing, I think that she was in such shock, that she took the pills to go to sleep, not to commit suicide. Of course in that state, she could have overdosed without even realizing it."

Natalie told Bobby Hyatt, sometime afterward, she "wasn't trying to kill herself."

19

NATALIE STAYED IN HIDING FOR a week, dropping ten pounds from stress. One of her first calls was to summon her old friend Mary Ann, whom she hadn't seen since their difference of opinion over Natalie marrying R.J.

"Oh God, it was awful. I said, 'Honey, you have to accept it now . . . you've got to face what we're talking about here.'

In Mary Ann's view, the end of her fairy tale marriage to R.J. was the end of a fantasy that had sustained Natalie since childhood. "It was the *whole picture*, it wasn't just him as an individual." Natalie discovered "there is no golden rainbow. And it was tough to say it's all going to be better. And her demons were just going wild, because she was bright and she was smart . . . 'but it can't be, but it *is*.' Ah, Jeez, it was awful."

Natalie "just lost it," in the observation of Mary Ann. "Years later, I could see pictures of her and I could see her heartbreak—she *never* got over it."

Natalie's lifeline was her analyst, whom she began to see every day from the night she left R.J., struggling to separate from the merged personality Maria had created between them, to overcome the fear of being by herself that her mother had fostered to keep Natalie at home. She would be in daily therapy for the next eight years. "My parents wanted me to come back to live with them, but I felt strongly that I didn't need my parents," she told author/actor Dick Moore in 1981. "I needed, in today's words, to get my head together. I needed psychiatry. I knew I needed to be independent, but I was still terrified of being alone, and I went to stay with friends. I had always been dependent on someone—first on my parents, then on R.J. This feeling that it was somehow dangerous to be alone was deeply instilled."

Natalie subsequently kept secret what she said had happened the night she left R.J. "The iron curtain went down," as Robert Hyatt put it. "It was a big deal to keep quiet. We were not supposed to talk to anybody about it, and I never would. Natalie told her mother that if she talked about it, she would never speak to her again and would cut her off her salary, which Natalie provided. That kept Marie quiet."

Natalie "never got over R.J.," Lana observed. Family friend Jean Hyatt, who saw Natalie during her hideout, felt "she was still in love with Bob Wagner, . . . she always carried him in her heart." Or as Mary Ann analyzed, Natalie cherished the *illusion* of what R.J. represented. "Natalie didn't want to get a divorce," Wagner said in 1986, "but people said, 'Go your separate ways and see how it feels.' "

The Wagners' then close friend Prudence Maree remembers, "R.J. was destroyed by that first separation. He'd just sit and look in the distance, which is not like R.J. at all, he has great charm, great charisma, and he was stunned. And never talked about it, but just sat in our home and I'd take care of him as best I could." Years later, Wagner said, "I should have hung in there, and things probably would have been different. We never wanted to break up, and we thought we would get back together, but there were lots of interventions—our careers, other people . . . but that *feeling* between us was there. The love was there."

Their ambivalence and affection was evident in a two-paragraph statement issued by the Wagners' publicist four days after Natalie went underground, announcing a trial separation with "no immediate plans for divorce. Both are hopeful the problems that exist between them can be worked out satisfactorily."

The news of Natalie and R.J.'s separation hit Hollywood like a bomb, a foreign correspondent would observe. *Variety* commented the Wagners had "fooled everyone"; the *Los*

Angeles Mirror reported show business circles as "baffled"; their friend Elizabeth Taylor was reputed to be under sedation, holding Natalie and R.J. as her role models for a happy marriage. No one in Hollywood had any idea why its golden couple had split up. "Natalie, come out of hiding," implored *The Hollywood Reporter*.

Warner Brothers executives were frantic to find their missing star, needed for wardrobe tests for the ironically titled *Lovers Must Learn*, set to shoot in Rome in a few weeks. Natalie finally checked in with the studio on June 23, asking that her whereabouts be kept secret. She called Louella Parsons a few days later, telling Parsons she hadn't spoken to anyone because she "had the flu" and had lost weight. Natalie told the columnist that what had occurred between her and R.J. was "too personal to discuss," admitting she was "not up" to meeting with anyone at Warners about her new movie.

"Louella Parsons and they were all looking for her," remembers Jean Hyatt, "and she *was* sick. What she *saw* made her sick—and taking those pills." She was also afraid to be seen looking anything less than the glamorous "Natalie Wood," Robert Hyatt remembers.

On June 30, Warren Beatty, who had been in New York for several weeks to promote *Splendor*, returned to Hollywood, just as Natalie "really felt I might crack up." She temporarily moved back into the Beverly house, and as she later told the story, "R.J. came back home one night to pick up some things and we both had our guard up. We said some hurtful things and he left. I started to shake. I went into the bathroom and looked at myself in the mirror and I was ready to let go. In another minute they would have had to carry me out. But I said to myself, 'Don't do it. Don't let it happen.' And I got through the night."

From then on, Natalie would need someone to keep her company through the night, and on airplanes, no longer comforted by her toy tigers or storybook dolls. She began to turn to secretary/companions who stayed with her, the first being Mart Crowley, who eventually wrote *The Boys in the Band* in Natalie's guesthouse. "He, in a significant way, was taking care of Natalie after the breakup," asserts Bob Jiras, her friend, makeup man, and occasional fill-in for Crowley.

Natalie was emotionally unable to star in *Lovers Must Learn*, or any other picture. On July 3, Warner Brothers sent her a legal letter accepting Natalie's request for a leave of absence without pay for an undetermined period for "reasons personal to her," eventually casting Suzanne Pleshette in *Lovers Must Learn*, renamed *Rome Adventure*. (Troy Donahue would be grateful for costarring with Pleshette, whom he married.) Natalie admitted, later, she was almost "over the edge." She moved out of the white dream home on Beverly ("too many memories"), into a small, hidden house along a curve on Chalon Road in Bel Air Estates behind an imposing brick wall, a metaphor for her private torment.

Mid-July, Natalie and Warren Beatty began bumping into each other at parties. By a coincidence, Beatty's romance with Joan Collins was coming to an end, an outcome hastened by Natalie's sudden availability. Collins observes, "It amused me actually, because knowing Warren was the most ambitious person I'd ever met, a sizzling romance with the hottest film star helped him *enormously*. Don't forget he dumped Jane Fonda for me and I introduced him to everyone I knew in Hollywood."

For Natalie, the suddenly unattached, talented, devastatingly handsome Beatty was a godsend for her shattered sense of self-worth. After the marriage ended, "she went through, 'It's my fault. What's wrong with me?' Fortunately Beatty came along," comments Mary Ann. "The timing was good and he was what the doctor ordered. And he was a nice guy, and he had a brain in his head."

On July 27, Beatty took Natalie to an early screening of *West Side Story*, their first public date. Within a few days, her elderly analyst died. Though she would quickly replace him, "it hit me at a crucial point in our marriage, like the death of a father," Natalie said later, "and shortly after that, the marriage sank like a ship going down for the last time." Natalie signed a friendly property settlement with R.J. on August 15, evenly dividing their assets, and she and Beatty were together constantly from then on, though Natalie still had not filed for divorce, an indication of her emotional ambivalence about severing the relationship with R.J.

R.J. fled to the comparative anonymity of Europe, undergoing psychoanalysis, taking small roles in pictures by respected Italian filmmaker Vittorio De Sica, hoping to transform himself and his career, saying, "My life went into a tailspin." Wagner would later credit therapy, which he had feared during his first marriage to Natalie, for "curing" him. "Lots of years of analysis," he told the *Los Angeles Times* in 1977. "I had to learn a great deal . . . first I had to learn to like and respect myself, to find security within me, and in that way to achieve a kind of emotional strength I hadn't known before." R.J. rented a flat in London, and then took a penthouse apartment off Rome's Via Po.

By happenstance, Joan Collins was in London shooting *The Road to Hong Kong*—a movie that Natalie, with whom she was friendly, helped her get—when R.J. arrived in the U.K. to begin filming *The Longest Day*. Much was made in gossip columns of the fact that R.J. and Collins were seen in London having dinner while their exes, Natalie and Beatty, were romantically involved in Hollywood. The "dates" between Collins and R.J. were nothing more than old friends and costars spending time together, for Collins was in ardent courtship with Anthony Newley, soon to be her husband. She scoffs at the gossip that was published then, painting her as a woman scorned. "I never resented Natalie dating Warren . . . I was madly in love with Anthony Newley, so I couldn't have cared less!"

The fact that Natalie—still technically a married woman—was conducting a public romance with rising star Beatty, vacationing with him while he was on location in Key West for *All Fall Down*, created a furor of gossip. According to Mary Ann, Natalie was suicidal at the time, "destroyed" by the dissolution of her dream. "She didn't even think about the outside world, how it looked or anything. She was just trying to survive. I didn't think she was ever going to pull out of it. And Beatty just happened to fall in, which was good, it helped her."

With only whispers about what *really* ended the Wagner marriage, Louella Parsons and other columnists at first offered ridiculous theories, mostly centering on "the horrors" of Natalie and R.J.'s "white elephant" mansion, "literally falling down around them." When Natalie began dating Beatty, the gossips seized upon a new explanation, speculating the two costars must have begun a "secret" affair during *Splendor*, tarring Beatty as the playboy predator who broke up the Wagners' idyllic marriage, and casting Natalie as the scarlet woman.

Natalie selflessly accepted a rumor that she had an extramarital fling. The Natalie-R.J.-Warren triangle would become part of the Natalie Wood Myth, with Natalie's explanation for the breakup of their marriage known only to an intimate few. Mart Crowley, who was glued to Natalie from *Splendor* on, conceded in 1999, "Their marriage did not end because Warren Beatty came along," hinting, "There were problems between the two of them that they needed help in working them out . . . sometimes love is just not enough."

The illogic of the gossip that Natalie left R.J. because she fell madly in love with Beatty is apparent in all of the articles about Natalie at the time, characterizing her as wounded, sad, and distrustful of marriage, already recognizing with poignancy that the free-spirited Beatty would not be a permanent part of her life. Asked by one reporter if she had found happiness, Natalie looked wistful. "Doesn't everyone search for happiness? I think most people search for what makes them happy . . . but I guess I haven't found it yet." Natalie equated happiness, at the time, with finding someone to love. "Love is the most important thing there is. I don't see how people can exist without love, let alone work without it."

Despite the fact that she was the fragile victim, Natalie's image, suddenly, was as a "callous," heartless glamour girl who discarded her husband, stole Joan Collins' fiancé, and would stop at nothing for stardom.

When *Splendor in the Grass* and *West Side Story* had gala New York openings nearly simultaneously in mid-October, Natalie and Beatty became the most-photographed celebrity couple in the world. They appeared, arm-in-arm, at the glittering premieres: Russian-dark Natalie, lush in white mink and white satin, her bust pushed to the skies by Hollywood magic, holding on to a sultry, sensual, formally attired Beatty as if he were her life preserver, which he was. They were the breathtaking gods of the movies, almost too beautiful to be real.

On December 5, Natalie placed her handprints in the cement at Grauman's Chinese Theater, as she had vowed at sixteen, when she and Jackie Eastes took Dennis Hopper to gape at the movie star signatures. She laughed gaily for the television cameras filming the ceremony, holding her hands up to show the wet cement, cocking her head to the side, flashing a Natalie Wood smile, but Natalie's animation seemed like a wind-up doll, and her dark, dancing eyes appeared troubled.

Her career kept soaring. By Christmas, *Splendor* and *West Side* were playing across the street from each other on Hollywood Boulevard. *West Side Story* would play continuously in the same Paris cinema for seven years.

Natalie began the year 1962 with an Oscar nomination for *Splendor in the Grass* and a role she had been coveting for eighteen months, Gypsy Rose Lee. Natalie was driven by demons to play the stripper with the stage mother of all stage mothers, Mama Rose—played in the film by Rosalind Russell—viewing *Gypsy* as the catharsis for all her years as a child star under the tyranny of Mud. Lana recalls, "She used to kid that Rosalind Russell was actually portraying our mom." Maria raved against the movie—even *The Hollywood Reporter* ran an item about it—recognizing, though she would never admit it, that *she* was Mama Rose.

Three major magazines dispatched reporters to Hollywood to interview Natalie for cover stories during the filming of *Gypsy* that winter—*Newsweek*, *Saturday Evening Post*, and *Show*—with all three journalists delivering unflattering profiles of her as neurotic and driven, mocking her perfectionism with asides about "rehearsing for *Gypsy* as if it were *Otello*." Her friend Henry Silva, a well-known screen villain, remembers Natalie as "crushed" by what was written about her in *Newsweek*. She complained, later, that the *Saturday Evening Post* writer only spent nine minutes with her.

Morgan Brittany, the then nine-year-old actress who played Dainty June, spent hours on the set observing Natalie, whom she idolized, noticing every nuance of her dress, behavior, and mien at the peak of her career. "I didn't know charisma at the time, but when she walked in the room, everything stopped. I remember her coming in with high, high heels, like four inches, Capri pants, and an angora sweater, white, with white pearls. She always wore a bracelet—sometimes it made a lot of noise, rattling. She loved to sit and watch us rehearse . . . she smoked, constantly smoked. I never saw her without a cigarette, ever." Brittany never noticed Natalie *not* look like a star. "It was the furs, the cigarette, the sunglasses, jewelry, pearls, the bracelet."

Brittany recalls Natalie as fragile, insecure that her voice would be dubbed after what happened to her on *West Side Story*, constantly being reassured by director Mervyn LeRoy that her character "wasn't supposed to be a good singer." She was nervous that her breasts would not look voluptuous enough, intimidated by playing a big-boned stripper nearly six feet tall. "She had a tough time doing the numbers, worrying that she wasn't doing a good job. I remember she had a problem with the last strip tease number; she wanted only one brief shot when she got down to next to nothing on."

Orry-Kelly, the famous dress designer, employed the same artifices as Nick Ray had with Natalie on *Rebel*, padding her hips and the base of her brassieres to give her curves, using a French cut on the costumes to optically lengthen her legs.

Harry Stradling, a respected director of photography

known for the flattering way he photographed female stars, made sure tiny, delicate Natalie was alone on stage when she did her strip tease so she would not appear dwarfed by the other statuesque dancers, and photographed her from low angles, shooting up.

Still, "there was a lot of tension," acknowledges Brittany, who remembers everybody, including Rosalind Russell, "walking on eggshells" around Natalie. "She'd get into moods and smoke and smoke. She was Queen of the Warner Brothers lot, so she had a lot of power then, and she'd get angry about something, and go off to a corner, stomping her feet." When Warren Beatty came to the set, "she'd sit on his lap and she'd whisper in his ear and he would reassure her," observed Brittany, who wondered what her idol saw in Beatty, who wore thick "Coke bottle" glasses. "She just had this *power* over him. He adored her."

Preteen Ann Jillian, who played Baby June, had a similar experience:

> I always used to look at Natalie and, "Oh my Lord, she's so gorgeous, and she's so petite and beautiful, and everything is so feminine." And I would watch her when we started filming, and how she would put on her makeup, her eye makeup particularly, with one little pinkie up.
>
> And I was standing there one time watching her, and I felt the presence of a man come in, and I turned to the side, and I didn't know who he was, and he was watching the same thing I was. And I looked at him and I said, "She's so beautiful." And he said, "Yes, she is." And I later realized that was Warren Beatty.

Costar Karl Malden, who had worked with Natalie when she was a boy-crazy teen on *Bombers B-52*, observed, as many in the industry would, how "as Natalie grew up, she became more beautiful, and more beautiful."

Malden knew that Natalie struggled with the musical numbers. "It was challenging for *both* of us. I'm not a singer and a dancer, she wasn't a singer and a dancer, and we both went at it. She wanted to do it badly, and so did I. It was something we never would have gotten a test for if we hadn't been under contract with Warners, so we said, 'Let's do it.' In a crazy way, but we did it. The one place where she was really scared stiff was when she did the strip number. She was scared stiff that Gypsy Rose Lee was there and was gonna tell her things, *and* that she was having to strip. And I thought she was magnificent." Malden recalls only one piece of advice the famed stripper offered Natalie: "Gypsy would say, 'When you take the sleeve off, don't do it fast, take time, take all the time in the world.' "

Child actress Ann Jillian, whose mother grew up in Russia and was Lithuanian, felt a kinship with Natalie, sensing an ineffable sadness, a "brooding," that touched her. "Children can have a sense in that way. On the top there was this wonderful giggle she had that was so endearing and delightful, but her eyes said something else."

As it had been since she was a child, Natalie's star shone in the quiet, poignant moments, such as when, as the young Louise, she tenderly sang "Little Lamb." Jillian recalls Natalie being terribly nervous beforehand, "and Mervyn had to tell her, 'Everything's gonna be fine.' He comforted her in telling her that exactly what she was feeling was exactly what was needed for that scene."

Natalie brought all the pathos of her lost childhood to the song, touching Jillian. "Because it was such a plaintive little song. You know: 'I wonder how old I am, do you think I'll get my wish, little lamb, little lamb, I wonder how old I am.' And then the little breath that she took at the end—'little lamb . . .'—on a sustained note, and the way her voice kind of trailed off and slightly, almost very delicately, broke off."

Jillian could sense "there was so much more behind that. You could feel the depths from where she was bringing it. She was very childlike, and I could tell she was calling up certain things, like what comes earlier:

Little cat, little cat, and why do you look so blue
When somebody pets you? Or is it your birthday, too?"

"I think she had to come to grips that she was a used child star who missed out on a childhood," Lana said later of Natalie's experience on *Gypsy*. "The resentment toward my mom for all the pushing and the long hours and the this and the that."

Watching from the wings, as she had since Natalie was six, on *Tomorrow Is Forever*, stood Mud, fixing her compelling gaze on her star, unfazed by the tear in her daughter's voice singing "Little Lamb," or the anguish behind her eyes.

Jillian's lasting image of Natalie, from *Gypsy*, "is from a series of Russian fairy tale story plates that I have, one of which is the Snow Queen. And I see these enormous, beautiful chocolate eyes, with this beautiful raven hair and vanilla white skin, dressed regally in the jewel tone colors of her region . . . Natalie was the Russian princess, who came here and had the American dream."

—

The Academy Awards took place on April 9, at the end of *Gypsy*. The editors of *Life* magazine were so certain Natalie would win as Best Actress for *Splendor in the Grass*, they assigned a photographer to follow her throughout the day. He sat in the row behind Natalie and Beatty in the auditorium, with Natalie under instruction to turn around so that he could photograph her reaction to winning an Academy Award. When Sophia Loren's name was announced, Natalie not only faced the disappointment of losing, but the ignominy of watching the photographer from *Life* fold up his camera equipment and prepare to leave. She would laugh about it, fifteen years later, but in April 1962, it stung.

West Side Story, for which she was *not* nominated, received ten Academy Awards that night, making Natalie's loss for *Splendor* all the more bittersweet.

Later that week, she appeared in court to file for divorce from R.J., dressed in black from her turban to her silk stockings, a clue to Natalie's emotions. She and Beatty left shortly afterward for a two-month trip to Europe, where the Wagners, ironically, had planned to go before their separation.

Natalie's romance with the unabashedly ambitious, marriage-phobic, sexually driven Beatty was more impressive in photographs than in reality. She would describe it, later, as "changes of heart, flying jars of cold cream, protestations of renewed love, and clashing of egos." He and Natalie had moved into a glass house at the top of San Ysidro in Benedict Canyon leased by Natalie, where they both obsessed about their careers more than each other.

"Natalie's entire relationship with Warren was a very passionate, tumultuous one," remembers Lana, who briefly lived with Natalie and Beatty later that year after secretly marrying at sixteen in a ceremony in Tijuana that was quickly annulled. The elopement was the first in a series of abrupt, failed marriages for Lana, who had unexpectedly developed into a buxom ingénue, half-heartedly pursuing the family business of acting, with help from Natalie, who also gave her little sister a gold Jaguar and a mink coat for her sixteenth birthday. Lana recalls the dynamics of Natalie's love affair with Beatty as, " '*Warren didn't show up on time to go to the party,*' '*Warren didn't get home for dinner,*' '*Where was Warren?*' Not a match made in heaven."

The Natalie-and-Warren trip to Europe the summer of 1962 was glamorously recorded in photographs by almost as many magazines as Natalie and R.J.'s 1957 wedding. *Life* made Natalie its June 15 cover girl when she and Beatty attended the Cannes Film Festival, and she was photographed in Paris, discovering haute couture, the beginning of a chic new image for Natalie. While at Cannes, Natalie charmed the Russian delegation by folk dancing, speaking to the Russians in their native tongue. It would later be falsely reported that she and Beatty traveled to Russia together, stimulating him to develop his future film *Reds*. Beatty may have gotten the idea from time spent with Natalie and the Russian delegates in Cannes, but Natalie would not visit her parents' homeland for the first time until much later.

The couple did stop in Rome, so Natalie could discuss potential projects with Françoise Sagan and director Federico Fellini, and to greet Elizabeth Taylor, who was filming *Cleopatra*. By a coincidence so bizarre it would inspire a play by Mart Crowley called *Remote Asylum*, she and Beatty had drinks one night at the Hostario Del Orso, a Rome nightclub, where they ran into R.J. with former actress Marion Marshall, whom he had met when both were bit players in *Halls of Montezuma* in 1949, when Natalie spotted Wagner on the Fox lot. Marshall lived in Rome with her two young sons by ex-husband Stanley Donen, and had offered friendship and support to the emotionally destroyed Wagner since he relocated to Europe.

From what Natalie later told her friend, writer Thomas Thompson, R.J. invited her and Beatty to come to his table for a drink, "almost perversely" ordering her favorite wine, Pouilly Fuissé. She recalled the encounter as bittersweet, with R.J. sitting next to Marion and Natalie beside Beatty, while she and R.J. exchanged meaningful looks across the table. She described the feeling as a "bond of sadness." Later that night, R.J. tried to telephone Natalie at her Rome hotel for hours, unable to get through because Beatty was tied up on the line with career-related calls. "I never knew he tried to call me until years later," Natalie told Thompson. "I was in my hotel room for a week, crying my eyes out. If that call had come through, I think I would have dropped everything and gone running back to him." R.J. later would refer to it, poignantly, as "that night in Rome."

"Things might have been different," he said.

Instead, Natalie fulfilled her sad destiny, returning to the house on San Ysidro to celebrate her twenty-fourth birthday with Beatty, who told the *Saturday Evening Post*, that July, he was "confused" about marriage, a signal of the state of their love affair.

She and Beatty went to a party in early August, possibly at Peter Lawford's in Malibu, attended by Marilyn Monroe, who was thirty-six. Natalie would recall Monroe mumbling to herself, all night, "*Thirty-six, thirty-six, thirty-six—it's all over.*" The experience haunted Natalie, who said later she was thinking, "I don't want to join that long gray line of faded movie stars who are left with yellowed scrapbooks and memories." When Monroe was found dead from an overdose a few days later, Natalie phoned Mud in the middle of the night, desperately worried she would "end up like Marilyn," dead and alone, taking too many pills.

Thomas Thompson, who became a close friend of Natalie's the year before while writing for *Life*, would compare Natalie to Monroe in this period, using the metaphor of the front end of a roller-coaster going down. "I remember evenings when Natalie would disappear into her bathroom and take her Seconals and then beseech me to sit beside her until they took effect, until her eyes were falling and her words were blurring and she was finally able to achieve a few hours of drugged blackness until an unwelcome dawn. Had the headline writers found the same tragic verbs for her as they had for Marilyn Monroe, it would have saddened but not surprised most of her close friends."

The only rainbow over the horizon for Natalie was a script called *Love with the Proper Stranger*, for which she rejected *Charade*, typically forming a bond with the character, in this case an endearingly plucky Macy's salesgirl from a close Italian-American family who falls in love backward, by first getting pregnant and then being courted. The storyline, which featured a near-abortion, was controversial for 1963, but Natalie recognized the intelligence of the script and the dimensions of Angie, the brave, scrappy salesgirl from Little Italy struggling to break away from her overprotective family, unwilling to settle for anything less than romance that was real.

"She loved it," recalls Lana. "She loved the character,

she liked everything about it. Natalie felt that it was one of the chances she got to show people that she could act. That she wasn't just a little cookie, that she was an actress."

It appealed to Natalie that Angie was an ordinary girl, that she was "real," saying later that she drew on "the healthier parts" of herself to play her, meeting with the screenwriter, Arnold Schulman, so that he could use aspects of *her* in Angie, proud of the fact that Angie was her "least neurotic role." The film was even shot in naturalistic black-and-white, part of the French New Wave, then in vogue.

Natalie and Beatty had already broken up several times before she arrived in New York in March of 1963 to start *Love with the Proper Stranger*. Their romance was in its last gasp during filming, as Beatty flew back and forth between New York, Hollywood and London, preparing to star in *Lilith*. Natalie's costars in the new picture were Edie Adams, stage actor Tom Bosley (later the father on *Happy Days*), and a sexy Steve McQueen, playing Angie's hipster musician boyfriend who is averse to marriage.

"She was able to use, obviously, her relationship with Beatty in some of the scenes with McQueen, there's no question about it," recalls Bosley, who was aware of the tenuousness of Natalie's romance with Beatty, as was Edie Adams. "She was vulnerable to anything at that point," in Adams' view. "She was more fragile than people thought. We all took care to take care."

Natalie would remember *Love with the Proper Stranger* as "the most rewarding experience I had in films, all the way around . . . my personal life was quite meager then, and the picture was 'it.' We were like a family." In fact, Natalie met two of the people she would request on future pictures:

costume designer Edith Head, and a hairdresser named Maryce Bates (known also as "Sugar", "Ginger", and currently as Ginger Blymyer).

McQueen's petite brunette wife, Neile Adams, who was on set constantly, felt Natalie was "a little crazed" and "was making a play" for Steve. She mentioned it to her husband. "During the movie, she'd do things like—you know, she'd always bump into him, or she'd see him on the street and she'd say, 'Hi, Steven,' and position herself for that. She was there—much like Steve used to do when he and I were going together in New York, where I would look around and he would be there."

Bill Claxton, a photographer who took movie stills of the actors and became close to Natalie and especially McQueen, believed Natalie "fell in love with Steve," a suggestion Lana, who was at the location in New York with Maria, questions. Natalie said later she thought she and McQueen "were good together," referring to their on-screen dynamics.

Neile Adams did not consider Natalie's flirting a "big, serious thing," and found her "darling," "warm," and "kind." Adams was confident "nothing ever happened" between Natalie and her husband during filming, an opinion Lana shares. "Natalie didn't do that. She really didn't do things like that." Lana, who was seventeen with a divorce in her past by then, was surprised at her older sister's "very old-fashioned moral code." Natalie told Lana that when she went to bed with a man, it was "a commitment."

Natalie's chemistry with McQueen, her affinity for Angie, and her camaraderie with her costars contributed to one of her best, most natural performances, leading to a third Academy Award nomination the following winter.

Edie Adams, who was a friend of Marilyn Monroe's,

noticed a similar quality in Natalie as an actress to Monroe. "She had this way of communicating her innermost thoughts and feelings as if it was just for *you*, and the camera was the person watching. Everybody in the movie theater thought, 'My God, she's doing that just for me.' " Adams also noticed that Natalie, like Monroe, "didn't really realize how good she was. She would take you through every thought she had, without saying words, as Marilyn did."

Natalie and the rest of the cast completed their New York location work on *Love with the Proper Stranger* the middle of April. Director Robert Mulligan shot the last five days at a studio in Hollywood filming interior scenes, many of them with a slightly nervous Tom Bosley, who joined the cast late and was starring in his first picture.

Natalie returned to the house atop San Ysidro, and the gypsy Beatty flew to L.A. to join her for a few days prior to beginning *Lilith* on the East Coast. Lana later recalled things "coming to a head" one night when Beatty was late for a dinner party, resulting in an explosive argument with Beatty slamming the door. "He was a beast, you know," Sugar Bates, Natalie's hairdresser, recalls, only half in jest. "She'd have something for them to do, and he'd never tell her where he was. He always kept her on the edge. I always felt he was really good for a girl to go out with, because boy, she'd appreciate the next person she went with!"

On April 26, Tom Bosley's last day of filming, Natalie left the set early. Bosley was disappointed he had not gotten to express his appreciation to Natalie "for being so nice during the filming," since he was leaving for New York that night. While he was in his hotel room packing, he got a call from a woman working for Natalie, "who said, 'Mr. Bosley, Miss Wood apologizes for not getting to say goodbye to you. She would like you and your wife to join her for dinner at Chasen's tonight.' " When Bosley explained that he had airline tickets for that night, "she said, 'That's already been taken care of. You're flying back tomorrow.' "

Natalie hadn't arrived when Bosley and his wife, Jean, walked into Chasen's at eight, but producer Alan Pakula was waiting for them, with actress Hope Lange, Pakula's girlfriend and a friend of Natalie's. Lange ordered a Hobo steak, "and it takes a couple of hours to cook the damn thing, so we talked and no Natalie," recalls Bosley. "So the evening went on—nine, nine-thirty, and no Natalie. And my wife kept saying, 'Where's Miss Wood?' and I said, 'Honey, it's *Natalie*, I've worked with her, you can call her Natalie.' And I could tell from the look in Alan's face that he kind of knew where she was. And she finally showed up, had to be between ten and ten-thirty."

When Natalie got to the table, "she was obviously shaken," remembers Bosley. She apologized for being late, explaining to Pakula, Hope Lange and the Bosleys, "she was at the airport breaking off with Beatty. It was the final kiss-off." Natalie was charming to Bosley and his wife, but Bosley noticed she kept giving Pakula and Lange "that look, 'Shit, look what I just went through.' " According to Bosley, Natalie "was strong about it, because I understand *she* did the breaking off, not he. He wanted her to come and say goodbye to him at the airport and she decided to say goodbye to *him*."

The story would eventually circulate—another of the Natalie Wood myths and legends—that Natalie's romance with Beatty ended at Chasen's when he excused himself to go to the men's room and left with a blond hatcheck girl for a week, returning to Natalie's house to find all his clothes burned to ashes.

Natalie did set fire to Beatty's clothes when he flew to

New York to make *Lilith*, from what she told Joan Collins, but she remained on friendly terms with Beatty after the breakup, contrary to Natalie Wood lore. "Because Natalie was very—she knew what Warren was like," Lana explains. "I mean, you cannot ever dislike Warren, because he's completely open and honest and adorable."

Natalie was at sea without a man in her life, or her movie family, to keep her company. "I remember the last day in *Love with the Proper Stranger*," she told the *New York Times* two years later. "I was supposed to cry in my last scene, but I could not cry for the camera. Then, during the wrap party, I could not stop crying." Mud's closest friend heard about Natalie's constant calls to her mother. "There was nobody in her life and she would get very depressed."

Natalie removed the photograph of Beatty from an eight-by-ten frame next to her bed, "and on the cardboard that was in the frame, she drew a big question mark, like, 'Who's gonna be next?' " She found a new rental house below Mulholland, a terra-cotta cottage on Coldwater Canyon, and set out to find the man whose picture could replace Beatty's in her frame.

She encountered him at a party in May. Natalie's new boyfriend was an old friend named Arthur Loew, Jr., the lanky, middle-aged heir to the Loews' Theater fortune, who specialized in rescuing high-profile Hollywood beauties in the aftermath of painful breakups, setting them free when a more exciting man came along. His damsels in distress had included Janet Leigh, Joan Collins, Debbie Reynolds, Tyrone Power's widow, Debbie, and now Natalie. "He was a friend to all of us," Reynolds explains, "and he loved women and he loved to be your boyfriend without taking you to bed. He really wanted to hold your hand and be the gentleman, take you out and teach you about all the good things in life. Arthur, who was a very, very rich man, was the sweetest."

Natalie needed a soothing man after the emotional tempests with Beatty, someone to chase away her hobgoblins. "With Arthur Loew, Jr., she used to laugh a lot," recalls Edd Byrnes, who was married to actress Asa Maynor, one of Natalie's closest friends. The angular-looking Loew, who bore a slight resemblance to playwright Arthur Miller, was not the Greek god Beatty was, but "Arthur was the funniest man I've ever known," acknowledges Natalie's makeup man and companion, Jiras. "Nicest, kindest, generous . . . but what is important is that Arthur was all laughs."

When R.J. moved back to Hollywood and married Marion Marshall, two days after Natalie's twenty-fifth birthday, Natalie began to suggest, in the gossip columns, that she might marry Loew, who gave her a $10,000 sable coat that fall.

She tried to fill the emotional void in her life with fame, and by starting a new picture, *Sex and the Single Girl*, the title of a pop bestseller by Helen Gurley Brown, the editor of *Cosmopolitan*. Warner Brothers bought the film rights for $200,000, essentially buying the title, since the book did not have a plot. The original screenwriter created a romantic comedy with Natalie as Helen Brown, a famous author-psychologist, wooed by a sexy but sleazy journalist, played by Tony Curtis. Director Richard Quine hired Joseph Heller, the author of *Catch-22*, to do a rewrite. Heller recalled, "Natalie Wood owed a picture to Warner Brothers and she wanted to get it out of the way, and Richard Quine needed money to buy a house."

Natalie's contractual list of demands to appear in the

movie was almost as long as the script, beginning with a salary of $160,000. In the pantheon of female stars, she had achieved a degree of power second only to Elizabeth Taylor, whom she still looked to as a role model. Natalie's Warner Brothers contract set forth, in minutiae, requirements for a luxurious portable dressing room (down to the color of the phone). She requested white cigarette holders from a shop in London, a special oil of gardenia available in Cairo, and stipulated days off during her menstrual period, when "she would get twisted, really terrible," recalls assistant director Phil Ball. "The lower part of the skin under her eyes would practically get black, and we just couldn't photograph her."

Natalie insisted on Bob Jiras or Eddie Butterworth to do her makeup, Sugar Bates or Sydney Guilaroff to style her hair, Edith Head to design her costumes, and Roselle Gordon as her stand-in. She included the standard clause employing her mother to answer her fan mail, with Maria signing publicity stills "Natalie Wood." Mart Crowley continued as Natalie's "best girlfriend," and she hired a dancer she met on *West Side Story*, Howard Jeffrey, as a fill-in personal secretary/companion. Jeffrey and Crowley "were an item."

Natalie's movie star entourage, as it would be viewed, was really an emotional support system; a family, of sorts, to keep her from being alone. She admitted, in a televised documentary, that she would "panic" without them on set. Tony Curtis, her three-time costar, noticed, "Natalie *always* needed *somebody*. Always needed somebody running her life. She always had two or three guys, or somebody."

She bought an extra ticket every time she had to fly, making sure someone from her trusted circle was beside her on the plane. "She didn't like to fly, but to fly alone, it was hell for her," states Jiras. Once in 1964, when Jiras missed a flight, Natalie refused to speak to him for days, even though her business secretary, Mona Clark, was on the plane next to her. "I was *alone*," she later told Jiras.

The two invisible members of Natalie's entourage were her psychoanalyst, Dr. John Lindon; and Maria. She phoned them both, every day, in ritualistic fashion: her mother in the morning, and Dr. Lindon at noon.

Maria continued to live as the shadow "Natalie Wood," signing autographs as Natalie, lurking on the set, attending Natalie's premieres, managing her career moves, using the phone as an umbilical cord when Natalie was not with her. Her frequent companion was Shirley Moore, a neighbor who adored "Marie." "She just was the most fun person to be around. She would tell you story after story after story. I remember once a neighbor came over to her house and said, 'Oh, Marie! Look at the ring on your little finger. I just love your little finger ring.' She took it off and gave it to her."

Moore saw Natalie and Maria together often, describing them as "very close," characterizing Natalie as "a *wonderful* daughter." Every Christmas Eve, "Natalie would put a $5000 check under her mother's plate—and then we'd go car-hunting!" Moore witnessed the unusual relationship between Maria and Nick, whom she found to be a "sweetheart," even though his vodka rages had become so frequent, and so violent, Moore provided Maria with a key to her house so she could spend the night on the occasions Nick chased after her with a gun.

Mud retreated into further fantasy, still spinning dreams about marrying her Russian captain, with whom she kept in touch. "She did *nothing* but talk about him," remembers Mann, who felt, nonetheless, "Marie loved Nick, he was such a handsome man."

Nick was a heartbreaking character to Robert Hyatt, who

used to see him at the bus stop "after he had too many drunk drivings and smashed into the back of some parked car, so they took away his license." Hyatt would pick up Fahd and drive him to his carpentry job at the studio, taking him home at night. "We would always go to this little bar and he would blast down the vodka, then go next door to the liquor store, buy a pint of vodka, stick it in his tool box, go home, go in his room, read his newspaper and drink the vodka until he passed out. He'd just given up." Natalie was disgusted by his drinking, but anguished over her beloved Fahd, worried the next phone call would be from a hospital, to inform her he was dead.

Natalie pretended she was in love with Loew, flashing a fourteen-karat diamond engagement ring to Mud and her friend Shirley Mann on the set of *Sex and the Single Girl*, refusing to take it off before her scenes, "so they turned the ring around and put tape on it, because they didn't want the ring showing in the movie."

Loew was an also-ran to Natalie's real passion, stardom. By the end of filming, she was named "Star of the Year" by the United Theater Owners, and had been nominated for her third Oscar. David Wolper produced a documentary about Natalie that winter called *Hollywood's Child*, Warner Brothers prepared a Natalie Wood movie trailer, "Born in a Trunk," and *Life* published a lengthy profile, "Born to Be a Star," in December 1963, featuring a famous picture of Natalie at the head of a long conference table in a chic black suit and hat, holding court over her retinue of attorneys, agents, publicists, and business manager. Wolper filmed her for the documentary sitting up in bed, dressed in a peignoir, taking occasional puffs on a long cigarette holder, purring instructions to her agent over the phone as a maid walked in, carrying a tray with juice and coffee.

Her costar, Tony Curtis, perceived Natalie in desperate pursuit of "the sweet smell of success. She was ready to sacrifice anything and everything for it." Curtis, who had known Natalie since her late teens, attributed it to Maria. "Natalie was brought up in that profession and she wasn't going to let anything stand in her way. She was searching for that *ultimate hit*. I personally don't feel anything was as important to her."

Sex and the Single Girl, despite its confused and eccentric history, was a hilarious romp of confused identities and a slapstick chase scene, "mirth that was mine," Heller would say. Natalie had a natural flair for comedy, something she dismissed, recalls her teen friend Jackie, "because she wanted to be a *dramatic* actress." Jiras felt that Natalie possessed Carole Lombard's combination of beauty and screwball comedy. "She adored the original, outrageous things Mel Brooks did with Carl Reiner, so that ought to give you a clue how funny she was. She used to quote his things."

Later in life, Tony Curtis would say he had better chemistry with Natalie than any other costar, citing his psychotherapy scenes with her in *Sex* as "about the funniest things I've ever seen. It was a wonderful dance. You can't get it better. We never stepped on each other. She always gave me my moments and vice-versa." He reveals, "Natalie and I had to be careful, because we found each other quite attractive, but I just didn't want to degenerate the relationship and neither did she." At the same time, Curtis "never felt *aroused*," admitting, "Natalie's boom-booms weren't big enough. To each his own."

Curtis was aware, from his years around Natalie, that "Natalie Wood," the movie star, was an invented personality. "Natalie never allowed herself the privilege to be who she wanted to be. Everything about her was very organized: the way she presented herself, the way she worked, her social life. I never felt much of a spontaneity, I always felt that it was somewhat under control." Curtis also knew that her mother was the one who had created, and enforced, the star persona. "And Natalie didn't want that, but there was absolutely *nothing* she could do about it. She knew that if she blew the whistle on her mother, a lot of people in town would take that as a bad gesture, and since she was so professionally oriented, she didn't want *anything* to interfere with her career, so therefore she put up with her mother's machinations."

The tragedy for Natalie, in Curtis' opinion, was that "her sense of who she was, her needs, were completely different from what she got from her profession. She would have been much happier as a nun or a hooker." He noticed, when he was with her, "she had these depressions. I could see a cloud—some shadow in her sweet face, and I knew that she was suffering."

Curtis also witnessed Natalie's water phobia, in a scene where her character jumps off a Malibu pier to "rescue" Curtis' character. A stunt double made the jump, but Natalie was needed for close-ups in the seawater, as she struggles to save Curtis' character from drowning. Richard Quine, the director, shot the close-ups using a huge tank on the Warners lot. By what has become an unsettling coincidence, David Wolper shot footage of Natalie in the water scene for his documentary, *Hollywood's Child*, providing a haunting record of Natalie, gingerly stepping down a ladder into the dark water, clinging to trained divers. Wolper's documentary footage shows her once the scene is completed, standing in the water tank with a cigarette holder, glamorous and seemingly amused. What Wolper did not include was Natalie, at the end of the scene, with her head submerged in the dark tank. As she popped out of the water, "she flipped out," recalls the on-set photographer, Bill Claxton.

After finishing *Sex and the Single Girl*, Natalie faced a painful disappointment, failing to win an Academy Award for *Love with the Proper Stranger*, her third Oscar loss and her last nomination. The evening was doubly poignant, for one of her competitors that night was French actress Leslie Caron, on Warren Beatty's arm.

Natalie broke off her ambiguous engagement to Arthur Loew, Jr., a week later, returning to their former status as friends, leaving her alone, except for her paid companions.

Five days after the papers announced she had dissolved her wedding plans, Natalie spent a quiet evening with Lana at the booth she and R.J. used to share at La Scala, a celebrity haunt in Beverly Hills. By a cruel coincidence, R.J. happened to walk in that night, rushing to announce to friends that he was the father of a baby girl named Katharine. R.J. darted from booth to booth passing out cigars, while Natalie summoned all of her gifts as an actress to congratulate him. She broke down in the car, with Lana, weeping inconsolably "for myself and what might have been."

R.J.'s news punctuated Natalie's loneliness, and resurrected her loss over the dream life she thought she would have with R.J. When he married the older, mature Marion Marshall, Natalie had not been as traumatized. Their daughter, Katie Wagner, as an adult, would say, "They're really *friends*."

R.J. becoming a father was a different emotional anguish

for Natalie, who had longed for a baby when they were married, blocked by her fear of childbirth and R.J.'s resistance, "and now, here he was, telling me about the birth of his daughter by another woman." After seeing him at La Scala, passing out cigars, Natalie plunged into a dark abyss, muttering to Lana, "I've got to have a baby, I've got to have a baby."

"She wanted desperately to have a child," states Lana. "She used to say that if she couldn't find anybody to marry, and father this child that she so desperately wanted, she really wanted Gregory Peck to father the child!" That month, Natalie was a guest at then-producer Dominick Dunne and his wife Lenny's tenth anniversary Black and White anniversary party, attended by the gods and goddesses of the cinema. In later years, writing about the party, Dunne would pronounce Natalie Wood the most beautiful of them all, a strange irony for a woman unable to find someone to love her.

The Great Race, Natalie's next picture, came at the worst possible time emotionally. Warners had forced her into it by promising to cast her in *Inside Daisy Clover*, an Alan Pakula/Robert Mulligan project Natalie found out about while she was making *Sex and the Single Girl*, pursuing Mulligan "relentlessly" to play Daisy, a teenage star created and then nearly destroyed by the studio system.

Tony Curtis, who went from *Sex and the Single Girl* into *The Great Race* with Natalie, knew "she wasn't happy with the way her career was going," and that she believed Daisy Clover was the role that would bring her recognition. "She never felt that she achieved the height of what she wanted, and she wanted that so bad she could taste it. I know that for a fact. So she put up with an awful lot of movies and relationships in order to try to achieve that. The only way she could make herself available for *Clover* was to do *The Great Race*, because Jack Warner wanted it that way. And she wasn't really interested."

Natalie and Curtis became estranged between the end of *Sex and the Single Girl* and the start of *The Great Race*, according to Curtis' first wife, Janet Leigh, and by the observations of Martin Jurow, who produced *The Great Race*, and Jurow's wife, Erin. Erin Jurow recalls, "We knew about the angst . . . because Tony was very vocal about it. He just didn't really want to work with her." Curtis refers, now, to a conversation he had with Jack Warner before shooting. "He asked me if I would give her some of my percentage so that she would do the movie." Curtis balked. "I couldn't give her anything to make her *want* to do the movie."

The Great Race, which began filming June 15, 1964, was a big-budget farce about a turn-of-the-century car race in which Natalie played a fiery suffragette in fabulous Edith Head costumes, "torn between two macho men, an evil one and a noble one," played by Jack Lemmon and Curtis, as "Professor Fate" and "The Great Leslie." Director Blake Edwards, a comic genius who "worshipped that kind of slapstick comedy where the girl got the pie in the face," created what Natalie called a "party atmosphere" that she disliked. "I prefer a closed set, with no visitors . . . *The Great Race* went on forever, and then came the day when we had about five hundred extras, and the director turned loose a man dressed as a gorilla. Just for a joke, you understand."

Edwards ignored Natalie, assigning her to his producing partner, Martin Jurow, so he could concentrate on Curtis, Lemmon, and actor Peter Falk, who played Lemmon's moronic sidekick. "Blake was more interested in the humor that he was getting out of Jack and Peter," Jurow recalls, "and he was a person who didn't worry too much about rehearsing. Natalie was not as important [to him]."

According to Jurow, Curtis "bothered" Natalie throughout filming, "like little boys in the playground pick on certain little girls, very juvenile," as Jurow's wife describes. He set up a "lunch club" with himself as maitre d', excluding Natalie. At one point, they stopped speaking to each other. "She established, very early, an equality with Jack and Tony, and she wasn't going to be put down on a lower level, and Tony was trying to do that," relates Jurow. "She went to Blake, and she fought for her position. We loved her for it."

The elaborate production, which required location shooting in Salzburg, Vienna, Paris and throughout California, was "not a thrill" for Natalie, concurs Lana, who was on set quite a bit. Curtis acknowledges, "She wanted [to play] that part a certain way, and she wasn't getting it. She worked at it very hard, because she wasn't allowed or given any indication in the playing of the scenes . . . and I think that was probably the dilemma, and her difficulty, I believe. She needed help on the set, like we all do."

When Natalie celebrated her twenty-sixth birthday on location in July, the Jurows were concerned about her, noticing that "her eyes were glazed, and she was not herself," Erin Jurow recalls. "I think she was abusing herself with pills, and alcohol. Definitely alcohol, because she was drinking too much at the table. And she was miserable." Later in life, Natalie provided a hint of what she was feeling: "At my birthday parties, the guests were always my lawyer, my agent, my publicist, my accountant, and my mother." Curtis also attributed Natalie's emotional state to her unhappiness with the film. "Tony told me, 'She's under pressure, she's had it now,' " Erin Jurow remembers.

The Great Race was *still* in production four months later, requiring a shaky Natalie to get on airplanes repeatedly, including crossings to and from Europe. "She wanted to get out from it," recalls Curtis, "but the problem was, she didn't realize how long it would take. She thought she could do it and get out, but it went on and on and on. They went so far over budget that everybody gave up on it."

Few, including her stand-in, saw Natalie's torment, under the Natalie Wood mask. The assistant directors on *The Great Race* remember her as "a lot of laughs, a lot of fun," a consummate professional. At twenty-six, she was still the little girl programmed to please. As Curtis observed, "I know that on the set she wanted no static from anybody, that she just wanted to be well-liked, and she was *always* well-prepared."

Natalie's unhappiness was nowhere visible as the spunky, glamorous suffragette Maggie DuBois, the prettiest Natalie ever looked, in Lana's opinion, though Lana was aware, by the end of the shoot, "it was physically taxing" for Natalie. "And she wasn't overly fond of the antics . . . the practical jokes were troublesome to her. It just wasn't the way she was accustomed to working, so it was kind of tough on her."

On a Friday at the end of filming, November 27, Natalie spent the day at Warner Brothers, dubbing her lines from *The Great Race*. She left the studio and drove home to the "bachelorette" French Tudor mansion she recently had purchased in Brentwood, an indication she had resigned herself to being single.

She had plans to spend the weekend in Las Vegas with English actor Tom Courtenay, whom she met at a party the week before, following a location romance with Hope Lange's brother David, an assistant on *The Great Race*, one of Natalie's "interim men," Jiras would say. She had also been on a few dates with an agent named Sandy Whitelaw, and reconnected with Frank Sinatra, her recurring fascination, cochairing an October benefit for *My Fair Lady* with him, sharing intimate dinners in show biz restaurants. Earlier in the week, Hedda Hopper had written a cautionary column mentioning that she "wished Natalie could find stability in her personal life," observing it was the first time in years Natalie was not married, engaged, or dating someone steadily.

Sometime that Friday night, like her haunting vision of Marilyn Monroe, Natalie swallowed a bottle of prescription pills, saying later she didn't want to live. She groggily telephoned Mart Crowley immediately afterward, suggesting it was really a cry for help. "All I can say about it is it was very serious, she almost did die," he said later. Crowley crawled through a doggy door, remembers Olga, rushing Natalie to Cedars of Lebanon, where she admitted herself, ironically, as Natasha Gurdin, her lost self.

Mike Connolly, a veteran journalist who knew Natalie well, published a cryptic item in his column in *The Hollywood Reporter* on November 30, mentioning that Natalie had been hospitalized at Cedars over the weekend for "mal-de-motorcycle," his code phrase for an overdose. Several movie magazines would speculate Natalie was upset about losing the lead in *Hawaii*, which Walter Mirisch had just offered to Julie Andrews. Mirisch would have no such recollection.

Her sister Lana never knew about this suicide attempt; nor, possibly, did Mud, whose "deep and complicated" relationship with Natalie was one of the underlying reasons for it. "I felt bitter about life and resentful of my parents," she told a journalist years later, alluding to "inner conflicts" she needed to resolve, referring to her struggle to figure out who Natasha was, submerged so long within Natalie Wood.

Just as compellingly, Natalie felt "alone and empty," triggered by seeing R.J. at La Scala, so ecstatic over the birth of his baby girl. She was afraid she would never have the happy life she envisioned when she married R.J.

Her analyst talked her into living, she told Thomas Thompson. "If it weren't for . . . analysis, I'd probably be dead today," she said in 1975. "There didn't seem much even worth losing," she said of her life at the end of 1964.

Tony Curtis, who was sliding into a serious drug problem, commented later on the irony of his and Natalie's lives: "We both looked like we had everything—we just had *everything*, we were the *envy* of so many people—when in fact, we both were just reaching out. That's why she needed that analysis; that's why I needed it too."

20

1965 AND 1966 WOULD PROVE TO be the best of times, and the worst of times, for Natalie.

Inside Daisy Clover and *This Property Is Condemned*—two dream projects—were in place at the beginning of 1965, films she wholeheartedly believed would move her away from frothy romantic comedies back to the "golden world" of Kazan and Ray.

She began 1965 in an emotional freefall, leaving the country within a few weeks of her suicide attempt, against her analyst's advice, to spend New Year's Eve in Gstaad with actor David Niven's twenty-three-year-old son, David Jr., a Rome-based talent agent for William Morris. "She was ready to let it rip and that's what we did."

Niven, Jr., and Natalie met when the Morris Agency assigned him to watch over her while she was in Europe filming *The Great Race*. "She and Elizabeth Taylor were the two highest-paid actresses in the world, so I was told that I had to make sure that nothing went wrong." The charming, fun-loving young Niven had a week's fling with Natalie in Vienna, the basis for her impulsive Swiss holiday. "Which created a big stir," recalls Niven, "because it's a major no-no at the William Morris Agency. You're never supposed to fuck your clients."

Natalie wanted to get as far away from reality as her fears would permit after the suicide attempt. "I remember one of her remarks was, 'Is that real snow?' when we drove from the Geneva airport up to the house. She was just sort of wide-eyed about everything that was going on. Everything was different, everything was exciting." Though she was "up for anything," as Niven remembers, Natalie was "constantly" in touch with her analyst, who had misgivings about her being "so far away" after a pill overdose. "The shrink wasn't too sure about me, anyway . . . it was touch and go."

Natalie, who was afraid to ski, spent her time party hopping with the very social Niven, who noticed she was eager for "anything that was non-Hollywood, with people who didn't even know about it or wouldn't talk about it." She was in that milieu on New Year's Eve at the ballroom of the Palace Hotel in Gstaad, where the guests, most of them rich Europeans, were invited to dress as children or infants for a "Back to Babyland" costume party.

Natalie went as Shirley Temple, briefly meeting a "crazed Yugoslavian" from Caracas in the shoe business named Ladislao Blatnik, or "Ladi," who was wearing a diaper. "He would come to Europe twice a year and spend, spend, spend, spend, all the money he had made. Now he did, however, have one trick, which would get anyone's attention. Which was, if you had a glass of champagne, he had a glass of champagne. And then he would drink his champagne after the toast, and then he would eat the entire glass." After the party, Blatnik took Niven aside, inquiring about his movie star date.

A few weeks later, Niven and Natalie took a train to his apartment in Rome, where *West Side Story* was still playing and Natalie was "a mega megastar. There were paparazzi all over the place." They enjoyed a "fairly serious, fun" romance that was "more than a fling but less than an engagement."

When Natalie returned to Hollywood to play Daisy Clover, Ladi Blatnik turned up at the Beverly Hills Hotel. By March, Blatnik was calling Niven in Rome to let him know he was dating Natalie, "saying, 'Listen, I've got to tell you something. This is what is going on.' So you do the gracious thing. I said, 'Terrific, good for you, well done, keep her in the club,' or some stupid, inane remark."

Niven hung up, thinking, "This is doomed, totally doomed." He had known Blatnik since he was seventeen, and considered him "a major con artist . . . a total whirlpool who would just suck up everything around him." Not long afterward, Niven got a call from Natalie, telling him it was getting serious between her and Blatnik. "I said, 'Listen, congratulations.' And she said, 'Well, what do you think about it?' I said, 'I think congratulations will do.' What are you going to say? It's a no-win situation. So you say congratulations and just drop it."

People close to Natalie were horrified, by and large, by her romance with Ladi Blatnik, with descriptions of him ranging from "a sweet buffoon" (Lana), to "big fat slob, phony baloney" (Shirley Moore), to "he was a nightclub act" (Tom Mankiewicz). "It was totally not Natalie," pronounces Bob Jiras.

Ladi Blatnik provided Natalie comic relief, and a radical change from Hollywood, the two things she had sought when she went to Switzerland after her overdose. "He'd fly in mysteriously," recalls her friend Edd Byrnes. "We would be sitting in her living room, and all of a sudden I'd see somebody run by, outside by the pool. Open the door, and it'd be Ladi, who had flown in from Caracas. He would do all these crazy things. Crunch wine glasses up in his teeth. He faked a suicide in Palm Springs. He was this kind of adventurous Robin Hood. Natalie liked him a lot." Blatnik was a fixture on the set of *Inside Daisy Clover* that spring, when he and Natalie announced their engagement.

Creatively, she was back in her element with *Inside Daisy Clover*, a dark fable produced by the prestigious team of Pakula/Mulligan. "I have only had this kind of a reaction on one other thing, really, and that was *Rebel Without a Cause*," Natalie said at the time. "Where I *instantly* realized that no matter what, I *have* to [play this part]."

Natalie said later, "I felt close to Daisy." In the script, the teen character of Daisy Clover lives in poverty on the Santa Monica pier with her eccentric, superstitious mother; she becomes a musical star under the complete control of the studio, and falls in love with their most handsome leading man, who marries Daisy, concealing his homosexuality. Gavin Lambert, who wrote both the book and the screenplay, said, "She identified with the character . . . I never discussed the part with her. It was hardly necessary, because she seemed to understand it, know about it, and know how she was going to do it."

Natalie had sky-high hopes for the picture, putting her heart and soul into Daisy, a performance praised as "eloquent" and "moving," which she hoped would redeem her career; instead, the film was intrinsically flawed, a tremendous setback for Natalie.

What she did derive from *Daisy* were two important friendships, with actors whose careers she instrumentally assisted. One was Ruth Gordon, whom Natalie approved to play Daisy's borderline-crazy mother, reinventing Gordon as a film actress. The other was Robert Redford, Natalie's former classmate, whom she did not remember from Van Nuys High, but had admired late in 1961 when she and Beatty saw him in the play *Sunday in New York*, stopping backstage to meet him. "I vaguely remember her coming, and being very dressed up, like a movie star." Redford was now starring on Broadway in *Barefoot in the Park*, but had inconsequential film credits. Pakula and Mulligan jump-started his movie career by offering him the role of Daisy's secretly homosexual movie star husband, a breakthrough that Redford credits to Natalie. "I *know* that she played a role in my being brought in for that part . . . the word that filtered back was that she wanted me to play the part."

Redford accepted the role in accord with Pakula and Mulligan that he would play Wade Lewis, Daisy's husband, not as a homosexual but as a bisexual narcissist "just *completely* on the take . . . men, women, children. That, to me, was a more interesting character to play, and also one that I thought I could play more believably . . . so that's who I played. A character who was sort of just mysterious: you didn't know where he was, and you didn't know what he was, but he was charming and very seductive, and that mystery surrounding his character was what drove Daisy a little crazy."

Natalie loved how the New York–trained, maverick Redford "really created a character," especially after her misery on *The Great Race*, inspiring her the way that Dean, Marlowe, McQueen, Kazan, Ray, and to some extent Beatty had. "I wouldn't have expected a Hollywood movie person to be that dedicated to want to go for the craft, and she did," Redford recalls. "She really worked hard, she got herself completely into the role."

Working with Redford, identifying with Daisy Clover, her character, brought out the intrinsic part of Natalie that wanted to do serious work, as opposed to being a movie star, the Maria-dominated side of her personality. Redford noticed it, too: "There's always that veneer of a Hollywood 'star' performance, giving the audience what you've learned works well. But there wasn't a whole lot of that . . . particularly if you could break through that sometime shield that would come over her—'I'm giving you my Natalie Wood performance.' When you could break *through* that, which we did, you got in touch with what was really the best of her, which was this totally *alive* quality."

Natalie was exhilarated, saying later, "What I really enjoy is acting itself; not the premieres, not the setting-up, but the moment you can really get down to it on a set where everyone knows his job, and gets on with it." She had one of her most fulfilling screen partnerships with Redford, developing "a wonderful working relationship that turned into a friendship, that carried on through the years after that. I enjoyed her immensely, on that film. We had a *great* time. She *surprised* me, because there was not a star—she made fun of that. She was very self-effacing about her 'star' category."

Redford assessed Natalie in this way: "I think that Natalie, underneath everything, was a very sweet, genuinely down-to-earth person who was slightly colored by the warped life of being a star at such an early age. But she herself, as a human being, shone through that. She was a real person. And I responded to that."

Natalie confided in Redford, revealing how her mother had tortured a butterfly to get her to cry on cue; how lonely she was, her longing to be married, to have a child. The happily married Redford wasn't sure whether Natalie realized what a caricature her fiancé, Blatnik, was. "*I* sure did. That was depressing." He noticed Natalie "couldn't be alone, she couldn't be," finding her vulnerable. "I think that vulnerability was part of her attractiveness as a performer. She had a girl-woman quality: she was a little girl, but a woman at the same time. And the child was vulnerable, and that vulnerability came through, and was very appealing."

Redford became aware of Natalie's terror of water during a scene, ironically, on a boat. By a further coincidence, in the scene, Natalie and Redford, as Daisy Clover and her screen idol husband, have escaped to his boat to get away from the pressures of Hollywood. Redford remembers:

> We were off the coast of Ventura, shooting this scene where we're shacked up on a yacht and someone comes and tries to find us or something . . . we got out there, and it was rough. The boat was going back and forth. And it got *detached,* [like] a runaway boat.
>
> And I was out there alone with Natalie. And I held on to her. She hid it beautifully—she made jokes and so forth, she was great—but she was *not* a happy camper. But I had a hold of her—in other words, I assured her it was gonna be okay. But it got a *little* weird there for a while, and then they somehow got us.

Both Natalie and Redford were disappointed by *Inside Daisy Clover*, which Redford felt "had a *stiffness* to it." Natalie later told her friend Peggy Griffin, and guests at a film festival, that she was upset her ironic voiceover narration had been partially eliminated. "There was also a scene where they left just half a song in and I found that very painful," she told an English reporter in 1969. Natalie was reminded of her hurtful experience being dubbed on *West Side Story*, saying, "I'd like to do a musical again, but I want an absolute guarantee that the songs, sung by me, stay in the picture."

Redford felt similarly deceived on *Daisy Clover*. "I had problems with it—I had a couple problems, but one was egregious at the time." Redford found out that the film had been altered after it was completed, changing his character from a bisexual. "I was told that they previewed the film . . . and the filmmakers decided they needed to do something to shock the audience, to keep their attention. So they decided to turn the character back into a homosexual—by looping a line with another character who's in a conversation with Daisy, Natalie's character. They looped the character to say, 'Don't you know he prefers young *boys?*' which was never in the scene. That was supposed to get a shocking reaction. I didn't know this. They never told me. I then confronted Pakula and Mulligan . . . I just said, 'Hey, it wasn't too cool. You could have told me, and done me the courtesy, so I was at least prepared for the fact that you turned my character into something I didn't play.' But because I liked them, and I was pretty young, I chose not to make a big deal out of it, just went on with my life."

Natalie asked Redford, while they were filming *Inside Daisy Clover*, if he would costar with her that fall in *This Property*

Is Condemned, a compliment to Redford, for Natalie saw her role as Alva, which originated in a one-act play by Tennessee Williams, as "probably the closest I'll ever get to playing Blanche DuBois," her dream part. For a time, Vivien Leigh, her idol, had even been attached to the project as Alva's mother, and John Huston was going to direct. Prior to Natalie's involvement, Elizabeth Taylor and Montgomery Clift were the leads. By the time Redford read the script, it had become "a mish-mosh," he recalls. "It had everybody's fingerprints on it."

Natalie secured Redford as her leading man and flew to Caracas that June to meet Blatnik's parents and consider moving to Venezuela, an experience that cooled her romance with him and caused her to delay their wedding until Christmas.

When she returned from Caracas, Natalie addressed the problem of who would direct her Tennessee Williams movie, which was scheduled to begin in October. As Redford reconstructs, "They were running down through the director's lists and they were down to the bottom, and I started to panic. Because I wanted to do the film, and I wanted to work with *her* again, but it was a mess, it needed somebody to straighten it out, and the top directors were turning it down."

Natalie, who had contractual rights to approve her director, costars, and virtually everything else, discussed it with Redford, who suggested a "completely unknown" Sydney Pollack, an actor he had worked with in a 1962 film called *War Hunt*. Since they acted together, Pollack had directed a few television shows and *The Slender Thread*. Redford recommended Pollack to Natalie "as self-preservation, as much as anything, because I liked him. We were the same sensibility, young guys roughly the same age. I just liked his sensibility. He had been trained in New York, and I just thought we'd have a better shot with this."

Redford did a desperate selling job on Natalie. "She said, 'Who is Sydney Pollack?' I said, 'Oh! Hey listen! This guy is so hot! If you can get this guy—if you're *lucky* enough to get him—he's the hot new guy.' Which he wasn't, right? He was just my friend." A few days later, Redford heard from an astonished Sydney Pollack, "saying, 'Bob, what are you doin'? I got a call from Natalie Wood!' He says, 'What am I gonna do? My palms are sweating.' I said, 'Well, don't shake hands when you go in to meet her. Keep your hands in your pocket!' "

Pollack, who had had a crush on Natalie since *West Side Story*, was sent to her house on Bentley, arranged by Joe Schoenfeld, their mutual agent. "I was very nervous. I didn't know how a director was supposed to 'audition.' I remember she lived in a house that was built on a slope, and you went downstairs to the living room, and it was sort of off-beige and very luxurious, and I remember thinking, 'God, this is all very impressive, very movie-starrish.' The lady that worked for her asked if I wanted a drink . . . and Natalie came down looking absolutely incredible, and she was very, very sweet. She made it easy. She was very anxious to find out what I thought about the script, how I thought it might be improved."

Pollack was added to the list of people who would credit Natalie for giving them their first break. He checked into a motel in San Jose with eleven versions of the screenplay, "cutting and pasting," emerging two days later with a mock-up final script.

The filming of *This Property Is Condemned*, beginning that October in the Deep South, was intense for Natalie, who had Blatnik with her in Mississippi. "We all knew it was a challenge for her creatively," reveals Pollack. "It was a Tennessee Williams heroine, and it had a certain kind of creative level that's required." Redford found Natalie as committed to Alva as she had been to Daisy, doing careful work to create a Southern character and an accent with nuances. "She was gonna go for it. She allowed Sydney to really *work* with her . . . she was very willing to take chances."

In a difficult sequence where Alva gets drunk and seduces her mother's boyfriend, Pollack suggested Natalie have some wine before she shot the scene. "I don't necessarily believe in tricks like that, but in this case, I thought it worked very well. She had two glasses of wine and it just took the edge off." Natalie later considered *This Property Is Condemned* some of her best work.

Emotionally, Natalie was dancing on the edge of a cliff, trying to keep herself from falling off. She abruptly canceled her Christmas wedding to Ladislao Blatnik over Thanksgiving, when the movie company returned to Hollywood to film. Maria's friend Shirley Moore recalls someone (probably Mud) hiring "a lot of spies to check up on him, and when they found out when or what he really was, Natalie got rid of him quick." Edd Byrnes heard, at the time, that Blatnik was receiving money from friends in South America "to keep on romancing Natalie and play the game, sponsoring him to marry this movie star." Marion Picciotto, who married the playboy "Ladi" in 1972, had no idea why Natalie and Blatnik, an eventual suicide, called off their wedding. "Better a long engagement than a short marriage," Natalie gamely told columnists.

Privately in deep despair, Natalie went through daily psychoanalysis with Dr. Lindon. Pollack remembers "seeing her blue Mercedes dart away at lunchtime, and come back afterwards, and the back of her dress would be all wrinkled from lying down on the couch." He knew "she worried about being an actress and being single and getting to be thirty years old and not having a child . . . she wanted children badly."

At Christmas, Natalie suffered a blow when early reviews of *Inside Daisy Clover* came out prior to its February release. Critics praised the performances but demeaned the picture as a "failure," a "not-bad idea gone wrong," diminishing Natalie's hopes that her poignant portrayal of Daisy would lead to the Oscar she needed to validate her artistic talent, and wanted as the ultimate symbol of stardom.

Pollack soothed his leading lady through the remaining weeks of *This Property Is Condemned*. Thirty-three years later, with the wisdom of experience, he would say:

> It's very rare to meet an actor or an actress who doesn't have a very neurotic side, and sometimes that neurosis is a big part of what gets transformed in their work. I had a teacher once who said that talent was a kind of liquefied trouble.
>
> Natalie wasn't neurotic in the sense that she made trouble on the set, but she was a very emotional young lady. She was really Russian to the core, and had that sort of Russian sense of tragedy. Sobbing, and the sort of conventional attitude you get from Dostoesvky.
>
> There was a fragility in her, and the emotions were very close to the surface: scratch her and get to an emotional color right away. There's something breathless about her, and you feel it, you can feel a kind of quivering just below the surface, a very

> appealing and vulnerable part of her. She had it in person. I've only seen that color twice in actresses. In her, and years ago, I sat at a dinner table with Elizabeth Taylor, and she had the same thing. There was a kind of breathless vulnerability. You want to say, "It's going to be okay."
>
> And Natalie had that quality, along with this volatile emotionalism.

During the Christmas season, Natalie lost her long-time secretary, Mona Clark, who got married. She replaced her with an affable Englishman named Tony Costello, the son of her live-in housekeeper of several years, Frances Helen McKeating, whom she called "Mac." Costello joined his mother at Natalie's mansion, coincidentally ushering a "British" phase into her life. That December, she was introduced to Michael Caine, who took her on a few casual dates, a diversion from her increasing depression.

Natalie's deepest emotional connection was with the solidly married Sydney Pollack, who plainly "adored" her, recalls her secretary-in-residence, Costello. When filming on *This Property Is Condemned* came to an end toward late January, Natalie no longer had the character of Alva to inhabit, or Pollack and her movie family to provide emotional support, leaving her alone with her demons.

"I was aware that something very bad happened, just right before I was to do the dubbing, where you come in and do the looping of the voice for the picture," remembers Pollack. "Because there was a period of time when I was not able to reach her to try to schedule this. I knew that something had happened, I knew she'd been hospitalized. And there was a rumor around that she'd taken some pills . . . I heard from her girlfriend, who was Norma Crane, that she had been very upset. I didn't ever know if it was a real serious attempt, or if it was one of those dramatic attempts."

Costello reveals it was his mother, Mac, Natalie's live-in housekeeper, who called Norma Crane after finding Natalie overdosed, characterizing it as "a bid for attention. She was on Valium and Librium and God knows what else. She kept a good supply on hand." Mac was also present for Natalie's suicide attempt at the end of *The Great Race*, when she began to put a single gardenia, Natalie's favorite flower, in a shallow bowl beside her bed. "Most of the occasions were quietly hushed up. My mother would never discuss any details, even to me. My mother did say to me that all of the attempts were for attention and not in earnest, except for one occasion when Natalie cut herself, which was probably deep depression."

Costello, who considered Natalie "delightful," did not believe she wanted to die, "She loved life too much. She was a *brave* woman." He and his mother Mac kept the overdose in early 1966 under wraps. "Her family had no idea. It was call a friend, come on over, discreetly head to the doctor. When in doubt, call Norma."

Norma Crane, who had a brief, long-distance marriage to New Yorker Herb Sargent, lived across the freeway from Natalie and was frequently around, recalls Costello, who saw her skinny-dip with Natalie, possibly the only time Natalie went in her kidney-shaped pool. Scott Marlowe, who had introduced Crane to Natalie, felt, "Natalie, in a sense, used Norma as a mother—the mother she never really had. That's how the relationship evolved—neither one really saying that was the reason, but it was. Norma was a very loving person and it fulfilled them, each for each other."

Natalie's overdose catalyzed her into drastic changes that winter, orchestrated by her analyst, whom she hoped could help her resurrect Natasha, the self she had lost at six to "Natalie Wood."

"It was mainly a matter of getting to the point where I could say, 'Hey, I'm not such a bad person to hang out with.' I had a lot of monkeys to get off my back."

At Dr. Lindon's direction, Natalie banned Mud from her house on Bentley. Maria's only contact with her daughter that winter was a package of publicity photos for fans that Mud received from Costello each week, to autograph as Natalie Wood.

Fahd's visits to the house were restricted, and when he came, Natalie locked the bar. "She just didn't like to see her father when he was drinking," Costello declares. "When her father called, she would say, 'Have you been drinking?' " Costello never saw Natalie drink more than an occasional glass of wine, and she became almost militant about alcohol. "She did not approve of *my* drinking."

Natalie and her analyst came up with the idea she audit night classes at UCLA, taking subjects she was interested in as a child. By an odd irony, one of her first assignments in her English Literature class was Wordsworth's "Ode on Intimations of Immortality." Natalie would recall, "That carried me right back to the classroom scene in *Splendor in the Grass*, where the teacher was reading the same poem."

Typically, she went to extremes, listening to classical music by Sibelius "until I liked it," quoting Prufrock, reading Thoreau, Kafka and Erich Fromm, studying art, collecting paintings by Bonnard, Courbet and Matisse, donating artifacts to UCLA. Hollywood columnists satirized Natalie, designating early 1966 as her "culture-vulture period," missing the point that she was trying to learn, not impress; as her friend Robert Blake observed, "For Natalie it was life or death."

"I really didn't know how to *be*, other than acting," she reflected. "I didn't really know what pleased me. I sort of had to figure all that out." Her secretary's 1966 memory of Natalie, at home, is curled up, lost in a book, or listening to music. The articles about her in movie magazines then featured Natalie posing in her house, showing off rooms she decorated herself. She developed an obsession to star in *I Never Promised You a Rose Garden*, about a girl who had lived in an imaginary world struggling to achieve reality with the help of a psychiatrist, another character that mirrored her life. It was the first of several projects related to mental illness that would captivate Natalie, another being actress Frances Farmer's memoir, *Will There Really Be a Morning?*

Natalie's epiphany, in analysis, was that "Natalie Wood" may have craved stardom, but *she* always desired a family, the dream denied her when Mud banished Jimmy, forging their pact to make Natalie Wood a star. Her constant refrain was, "It took me ten years of analysis to help me find what I wanted." When she talked to Olga now, Natalie would tell her married sister, who had three boys and an insurance broker husband who adored her, "*You're* the lucky one."

That March, Natalie re-met an analytical young actor who aspired to write plays, named Henry Jaglom, with whom she became intrigued in November, after an introduction at a summer party in Malibu. Jaglom, who studied with Strasberg and viewed Hollywood warily, fascinated Natalie as the sort of artistic maverick she had admired since Dean and Marlowe; while Natalie Wood, the movie star, resisted.

Jaglom witnessed the schism in Natalie's personality early in their affair. When they were at her home, "she was this sweet, lovely girl—open and vulnerable and probing and curious." If they went out in public, he noticed, she would put on her bracelet, and "she *became* somebody *else*. Sort of fake and formal, and had this *smile*."

As "this unemployed actor kid" with strong political opinions, Jaglom was alternately excited and repelled by the "glittering, glowing, jeweled unreality" of the Old Hollywood parties Natalie was invited to attend, with guests like Rosalind Russell, Garson Kanin, Ruth Gordon, Cary Grant, Van Johnson. He encouraged Natalie, who was only twenty-seven, to seek a younger crowd, visit The Actors Studio West, smoke pot. "Which, at that time, shocked Natalie. I actually introduced her to pot. Her reaction was the same as my mother: 'It didn't *do* anything.' I didn't smoke a *lot* of dope, it's just that I was so anti-drinking at that point. I remember parties at Dean Martin's house, dinner parties, and they all got totally loaded, and it was boring and stupid. And it was compounded by the fact that nobody paid attention to the fact that there was a war. They were talking about *tennis* games, and cutlery."

The two had an intense, "push-pull" romance, with Jaglom imploring Natalie to reject *Penelope*, a glossy romantic comedy that he warned her would be "another *Sex and the Single Girl*." Natalie's decision to accept the role—for $750,000, the use of a white Rolls-Royce, and thirty-five lavish Edith Head costumes—was a signal that the Maria aspect of Natalie's personality would be dominant, and of the futility of her relationship with the avant-garde Jaglom.

One night, Jaglom confronted Natalie about the way she

behaved in public, discovering an astonishing thing. "She said there was *her*, and there was '*The Badge*.' " The Badge was "Natalie Wood," her star persona. "She would say, 'I'm putting on The Badge,' which was her movie star role. She talked about it as if it wasn't her. We went to a movie theater once and I got in line, and she said, 'Well, we don't have to get in line. Watch. I'll just use 'The Badge.' Walked to the front, walked in line—I felt really weird! I was still in my sixties sensibility then."

Natalie eventually became embarrassed by Jaglom's rebel attitude at Hollywood events. "She'd say, 'Why'd you have to say this to so-and-so?' " Not only was part of Natalie drawn to that world of old Hollywood stars, noticed Jaglom, she also could not handle confrontation. "Natalie *hated* that, *hated* it, because I would inevitably get into some sort of tension. Her hatred of tension, any kind of tension—it was unbelievable."

Lana traced this to their experience as children, having to escape to neighbors' houses when a drunken Fahd chased Mud with a gun. In 1966, Jaglom wrote this about Natalie in his journal, observations that would take on greater meaning after her drowning: "*She turns off cold if there is any unpleasant vibration within her sensory reach. If it comes to a head between two other people, she cries. If it happens between her and somebody else, she stabs.*" Jaglom further noticed, that summer, how Natalie had an inability to relax, carrying her tension between her eyes. "There was a frown there, and I used to rub it and say, 'Okay, let's try to relax . . .' And she thought it was funny, and then got annoyed, of course."

Jaglom's ill-mannered behavior at Natalie's A-list events made him "the bad boy" to her Hollywood friends. "They thought I was obnoxious, and bad for her."

That spring, Natalie and Jaglom spent a long weekend in Palm Springs, where he noticed "a white car following us, driven by a goon." When they got back to Natalie's house on Bentley, they discovered it was someone sent by Sinatra. "The phone rang, and Roz Russell was on the phone. And Natalie did what she always did, which was whisper, 'Come here!' and motioned for me to get on. And then I hear Roz Russell warning her that Frank is very concerned about me, and she's checking to make sure that Natalie is okay. And she got all the wrong information—that I was some street kid who did drugs."

Jaglom decided not to go out with Natalie in public anymore, frustrated by her Hollywood lifestyle and by her alter ego, The Badge. "I finally just said to Natalie, 'Look, I don't want to go to these huge things where everybody talks about nothing.' " He moved into her house for a few weeks to write, where he had a strange encounter with Sinatra, whom Mud, by phone, was encouraging Natalie to marry. "I remember going downstairs and saying to Sinatra, 'Natalie'll just be five minutes.' Then he'd look at me, thinking, 'Is he a homosexual or something?' He couldn't quite figure it out." When Jaglom offered Sinatra a drink, "he said, 'I know where the bar is!' Very adolescent, like a kid who had a thing for her."

According to Costello, Natalie was rejecting Sinatra, because he was then involved with her friend Mia Farrow. His continuing surveillance and protection of Natalie even extended to Lana, who remembers a Sinatra employee following her through Europe. Composer Leslie Bricusse, who cowrote the title song for *Penelope* and was a friend to Natalie and Sinatra, knew there was "a little ring-a-ding" between them, analyzing Sinatra's behavior toward Natalie as vintage Frank. "He was like a huge father figure, he was a great taker-carer of people . . . and I think probably, the other part of Frank, is that he was probably keeping his options warm with Natalie."

Sinatra, Jaglom, and Michael Caine were only three of Natalie's "boys of 1966," as Costello called them. She also reportedly received a car as a gift from millionaire Del Coleman, spent a week in New York with actor Stuart Whitman during location shooting for *Penelope*, received ardent calls from author William Peter Blatty, and dated a handsome young lawyer named David Gorton, whom she met at UCLA as part of a Career Day panel. "Anyone who came in contact with her fell in love with her," recalls Costello, including himself, by the way "she made you want to protect her."

Gorton, who had never been around a movie star, was surprised to find Natalie a little nervous. "In a way, it was charming, because rather than being arrogant, she seemed more just like a normal person." They spent a weekend on a yacht off Catalina, talking, ironically, about their "shared fear of drowning." It was Natalie who suggested the excursion. "On a boat like that, we felt pretty safe. I don't think either of us would have gone out on a dinghy." Gorton didn't expect their relationship to go further, sensing Natalie "needed somebody a little more sensitive and with more presence."

None of the men in Natalie's life, nor anyone in connection with *Penelope*, were aware of an overdose she had that summer, though director Arthur Hiller recalls, "There was an insecurity. And you had to be daddy, pat her on the back, sometimes slap her wrist. I was almost like father-and-child with her. It makes sense looking back and looking forward . . . I had to be daddy."

"The attempt in the summer of '66 was discovered by my

mother," recalls Costello. "And she made a phone call, I don't know who to, but I would say Dr. Lindon, Paul Ziffren, Mart, or Norma. I was out for the night and knew nothing until the following day."

Lana heard about the suicide attempt from a catatonic Maria, who asked her to take clothes to the hospital for Natalie. Mud was barred. When Lana arrived, she could hear Natalie and Dr. Lindon shouting. Natalie told her, "I didn't want to live."

In the years after her drowning, the Natalie Wood lore would unfairly assign the blame to Warren Beatty for her suicide attempt during *Penelope*, based on a conversation between Lana and Mart Crowley. Lana recalls Crowley, who was not fond of Beatty, telling her that he heard the "raised voices" of Natalie and Beatty before she overdosed, implying that something Beatty said might have provoked Natalie to try to kill herself.

Tony Costello, whose mother found Natalie after her overdose and who lived at Bentley, remembers her blaming Dr. Lindon. "She was ranting and raving at the hospital, shouting and cursing at her therapist." Costello never heard a word about Beatty. "This was a very tough summer for Natalie. *Property* was a stinker and she knew *Penelope* would flop, so her self-esteem was at a low point."

Beatty was around Natalie that summer, hoping to coax her into playing Bonnie in *Bonnie and Clyde*, his pet film project, which she resisted. Natalie was so friendly with Beatty that she and Jaglom double-dated with him and a Bolshoi ballerina named Maya Plisetskaya in June, with Natalie acting as a translator for Beatty and his Russian girlfriend. Jaglom, whose 1966 journal recorded his contact with Natalie, recalls her as "joking and comfortable" with Beatty throughout the summer.

In 1968, Beatty spoke fondly of Natalie in an interview, mentioning his last conversation with her about costarring as Bonnie to his Clyde, revealing nothing to suggest an argument. "We met at her house, and she kept on taking phone calls while I tried to tell her about the picture. I guess I wasn't too persuasive; at that point I wasn't getting a lot of offers and Natalie was riding the crest of her career. Well, it didn't take long to see she wasn't interested in doing a picture with me. Besides, she figured the idea didn't have a chance."

In later years, Natalie would say that she turned down *Bonnie and Clyde* because it was filming in Texas and she couldn't be apart from her analyst, a decision she would regret. "I loved the script and I loved the part," she said in 1969, "but I had personal reasons. I didn't want to go to Texas on location and well, Warren and I are friends, but working with him had been difficult before."

Ironically, it was a role that might have brought Natalie the artistic validation she was seeking. Her rejection of the gritty, realistic *Bonnie and Clyde* was a further indication she was hesitant to veer too far outside the Hollywood mainstream and the studio system that weaned her, Mud's concept of what movie acting was all about. Natalie was being called "the last great Studio star," a symbol of an era that was fading, superseded by independent filmmakers, and actors and actresses who eschewed glamour. At the same time, *she* still wanted to do serious work, as she had since meeting James Dean, breaking out in hives from playing the flighty Penelope.

Earlier that spring, prior to *Penelope*, the Harvard Lampoon organization named Natalie the "worst actress of last year, this year and next," two months after she received a Golden Globe Award as World Film Favorite, illustrating that her stardom had eclipsed the perception of Natalie as a serious actress. She seemed amused by the Lampoon's "Natalie Wood Award," which impressed Jaglom. "She got it for the joke it was." Natalie, tutored by the shrewd Maria in the art of publicity, came up with an inspired idea. "I decided to accept it in person, and delivered an Academy Award acceptance sort of speech, telling them I was moved to tears." Her clever joke turned an embarrassment into a triumph. She appeared on *What's My Line?* while she was on the East Coast, where panelist Bennett Cerf, a Harvard man, pronounced Natalie "the best sport in Hollywood." The Lampoon Award would become a Harvard/Hollywood tradition, a tongue-in-cheek honor.

After her overdose, Natalie continued to be friends with Warren Beatty, making it even less likely he had anything to do with her suicide attempt. In fact, she would invite him to her next wedding.

Natalie was so adept at playing "Natalie Wood," the glamorous, effervescent star, her attempted suicide that summer stunned even Lana. "She never seemed suicidal to me," states her sister. "Ever. But Natalie was also very controlling of her feelings. That was why she needed analysis. She needed one avenue where she didn't worry about her makeup. She spent an awful lot of time not being able to be exactly as she was." Natalie's "puffy, scared" face in the hospital, stripped of cosmetics, "didn't seem real" to her sister, accustomed to seeing the mask of Natalie Wood.

So effective was Natalie at putting on The Badge, Sinatra, who dated her throughout her three suicide attempts and had known her from the time she was fifteen, would remember her as "laughing all the time," saying, after her death, "I have never known her to be depressed. What used to amaze me about her was a wonderful warmth and sweetness all the time, I don't care what conditions prevailed."

Only an inner circle saw the real Natalie. Costello, who lived in her house, comments, "She put on a great front as being independent and a savvy lady, which she was, but she had a lot of demons . . . she did need constant support." Costello was startled to find out, during *Penelope*, how uncertain Natalie was about her talent as an actress. "Lila Kedrova had a small part, and honest to God, Natalie was afraid that she was going to be upstaged, she was so in awe of Kedrova. Natalie knew she was a star, but she was unsure about being an actress. When you're unsure in your own profession, and yet you're a goddess, it's *really* got to be tough."

In the days after her overdose, Natalie talked to Jaglom about her desire to be "real," the dream she had nurtured since childhood, when she longed for friends at a birthday party, enrolling in junior high to blend in. Jaglom remembers her, that summer, as "searching." She appeared to be "yearning for more, very insecure and very committed to figuring it all out, and figuring out how to be happy." Natalie occasionally invited her parents to dinner, against her psychiatrist's advice. Jaglom, who was present, saw how "it would always be very complicated and hard for her to have them around, and yet she somehow wanted to be the good *daughter*. It would be civil, but there would be a chill. It was clearly very fraught." Maria, he observed, was deferential to Natalie to the point of obsequiousness. "Her mother's whole identity was wrapped up with—not *Natalie* actually, but with 'Natalie Wood,' the movie star."

Jaglom became a quasi-therapist for Natalie, who

revealed some of her emotional scars from being a child actress, which always seemed to come back to the trauma of being forced to cry on cue. "Natalie always said, 'How do you expect me to be normal when I learned that the most attention I could get was the harder I cried? And the harder I cried, the more, technically, I felt *sad*—and the happier everybody *around* me was, and how they all *loved* me.' So it was very clear that her sadness and her success and pleasure were all mixed up."

On July 20, toward the end of the *Penelope* shoot, Norma Crane and Tony Costello gave a surprise twenty-eighth birthday party for Natalie around the blue pool at Bentley, inviting faces from her Hollywood past. "Norma put up the money. It was a stupendous party, out in her garden. When Natalie came home from the studio, B.J. drove her home. As he turned into the big horseshoe drive, we put all the outside lights on." Once everyone yelled, "*Surprise*," Costello sent Natalie upstairs to change into "a beautiful dress that Edith had made for her."

There is a snapshot taken in the garden of Natalie, obviously moved, standing beside her birthday cake in her Edith Head dress with her eyes closed, smiling with the exuberant joy of a little girl.

One of the guests at the party that night was William Goetz, the producer of *Tomorrow Is Forever*, the picture that turned Natasha Gurdin into the child star, Natalie Wood. As she would later tell the story, "I remember him standing up and proposing a toast, 'Here's to Natalie! I've known her since she was five and I named her!' " Natalie would poignantly recall an angry voice from the back of the garden, coming from the normally shy Fahd, who disdained Hollywood gatherings. "My father immediately jumped to his feet and said, 'I knew her before Mr. Goetz, and I named her first.' "

Natalie broke her contract with Warner Brothers that summer, after eleven years as Queen of the Warners lot, agreeing to pay the studio $175,000 to set herself free. That August, after she finished *Penelope*, she fired her agents, publicists, accountant, business manager and lawyers, drawing a black "x" through each of their faces on the famous *Life* magazine photo of her at the head of a conference table.

She forced herself to spend an entire night alone in her house, the first time Natalie had not had somebody to hold her hand, or talk her through the post-midnight hours that had frightened her since childhood, when she used to lie awake, afraid she would be kidnapped. The next day, she drove to Dr. Lindon's office to announce, "I did it! I spent the night with nobody in the house!"

A few days later, Natalie asked Jaglom to drive her to the airport, where she boarded a plane, by herself, to fly to New York. When she arrived at her favorite hotel, the Sherry Netherland, Natalie received a telegram from her inner circle, congratulating her. "It must sound silly except to anyone else who never did anything for herself," she told Thomas Thompson, "but to me, it was a step-by-step progression to normalcy." At twenty-eight, she had made an astonishing forty films, and appeared in roughly thirty television productions, over the course of a career spanning a quarter of a century.

She returned to Los Angeles after a few days of shopping in New York, ready to begin a life outside the movies, as the *person* behind The Badge, Natalie Wood.

As *Natasha*.

ACT FOUR

Motherhood

1966–1979

"I feel like I'm sailing. There's this enormous pale, pale sky and I'm gliding around in circles with these great white birds . . ."

ANTON CHEKHOV
Three Sisters

21

NATALIE HIRED CREATIVE management Associates, or CMA, to replace the William Morris Agency in August 1966, but her real focus was on finding a husband.

She was then at the height of her infatuation with Englishmen, which had begun with Tom Courtenay the end of 1964, carrying through to Michael Caine. In fall 1966, she tried to launch projects with British actors Alan Bates and Albert Finney, a "crush"; and she began a romance with English actor Richard Johnson, known as a ladies' man.

That September, she was introduced to another British "Richard," Richard Gregson, a suave London agent born in 1930, the same year as R.J., with similarly handsome features that, probably not coincidentally, resembled Fahd's. Gregson had recently established a Hollywood branch of his U.K. agency, partially to distract himself from a complicated divorce in London. One of his clients and a "very close pal," English composer Leslie Bricusse, a recent friend of Natalie's, played Cupid.

Bricusse recalls, "Natalie used to come to our house for parties, and she was always alone, and I got the impression she was lonely. And Richard was in the middle of his divorce and he had a bunch of kids in London, and had moved his life to L.A. . . . so he was wandering around." The introduction took place at a party at Leslie and Evie

Bricusse's, attended by Natalie's occasional publicist, Rupert Allan, who would mistakenly be credited with the matchup.

Bricusse had noticed, before setting her up with Gregson, Natalie's tendency to seek refuge in Mart Crowley and Howard Jeffrey, "to have some gay friends to fall back on, so she had good company, she didn't have to go out on a 'date' per se, she could be with people and yet feel protected."

Gregson, as Natalie's secretary Tony Costello observed, "was in the right place at the right time" for Natalie, arriving on the scene during her Anglophile period, when, as Lana put it, "she desperately wanted to have a child."

Although Natalie later would be quoted as saying she and Gregson looked at each other and "that was it," Lana remembers helping her sister draw up a list comparing the two Richards—Gregson and Johnson—so Natalie could choose which man to make her husband. "I remember going over all their different qualities, and Natalie said there was only one problem. She said, 'I've slept with Richard Gregson.' I said, 'Then you've made your decision, haven't you?' Because that, to Natalie, meant something." Gregson himself would refer to Natalie having a "high moral code."

Bricusse, who knew all parties well, felt that Natalie made a wise choice in the "more stable" Gregson, whom she settled on after a final date with David Gorton at a party on Bentley to which she invited the Bricusses, accompanied by Gregson. "Richard's very low-key and quiet," observes Bricusse. "Nice sense of humor, immensely bright, and I think Natalie absolutely adored him, she felt very safe with him. And he was, I think, good for her, because she had been kind of looking around, and I felt from the very beginning that she was a little girl lost, because she looked that part—you know, that face—she looked very much that role, so the relationship firmed up very quickly once they got to know each other." Sugar Bates, Natalie's longtime hairdresser, says simply, "She just wanted someone to love her."

By October, Natalie was at Gregson's side for the London premiere of *This Property Is Condemned,* taking up part-time residence at his townhouse in Pimlico, telling reporters she was ready to give up her career to marry Richard and have children.

Neither of Natalie's sisters considered Gregson to be a great passion, though Costello describes her as "gushing" when they began dating. Olga recalls, "She said at the time that she wanted to have children, and that she wanted to step down. This was her choice. She was ready to be a mother and to live a good life. There must have *been* love there, to get married, but I don't think that was a great love of her life."

Natalie's comments about Gregson, then, suggest that he was a father figure, someone who took care of business so she could have a private life. "I don't have to make endless decisions anymore," she said in one interview. "Richard is a strong man with integrity and good judgment. He assumes most of the burdens that were once mine. I don't need work as a security blanket anymore. And the thought of going back to six nights of dates every week is quite sad. I don't think I could go through it again."

Her new romance with Gregson eased the pain of the reviews for *Penelope* ("a waste of comedy talent," "flimsy and ludicrous"), which Natalie read during a trip back to New York from London that November, arriving at JFK in a leopard coat and hat like the movie star she was trained to be.

She spent the next two years patiently waiting for Gregson's divorce to go through, dreaming of a honeymoon in Russia and of her longed-for child. Between October 1966 and October 1968, Natalie flew back and forth with Gregson from London to Los Angeles to New York, attending plays, dining out, doting on his school-age children, Charlotte, Sarah and Hugo. "I certainly overcame my fear of flying during those two years," she later told a magazine. "I flew to London about once a month and Richard came here even more often, sometimes just to spend a weekend." Natalie's routine was to board the plane, set her watch ahead, and take a sleeping pill, waking up just before landing.

She took French lessons and tennis lessons, studied interior decorating, and enrolled in cooking classes at Le Cordon Bleu, approaching domesticity with the same perfectionism as she had acting, rejecting roles in *Diary of a Mad Housewife* and *Goodbye Columbus*. The only acting project for which Natalie displayed her former passion was to play the schizophrenic teenager in *I Never Promised You a Rose Garden*, which she tried, in vain, to produce with Sydney Pollack, who also tried to set her up in a film with Oskar Werner that never materialized, called *Very Special People*. "I have been working steadily since I was *five*," she said later. "I had to have two years of just—just *living*. Catching up. And I was thrilled to discover that I didn't have the *need* to work. There was a time when if I wasn't working, I felt at a loss."

Though she no longer had her coterie of attendants, Natalie still presented herself as an old-fashioned movie star, dressing up for her flights to and from London in high glamour, wearing Jackie Onassis oversized sunglasses, a variety of fur coats, and ensembles ranging from chic Yves

St. Laurent and Chanel sixties mini-dresses to chocolate brown suede pantsuits, accessorized with bracelets, rings, necklaces and often dangly hoop earrings. She had let her dark hair grow long to please Gregson, and adopted mod sixties makeup, wearing several pairs of false eyelashes and eyeliner, painting individual black lashes below her eyes. On anyone else, the excess would have been garish; somehow, it suited Natalie's dark Russian beauty and still-girlish face.

One of her teenaged fans in this period, a New Yorker named Diane Wells, used to meet all of Natalie's flights into JFK or Newark, wait for her to emerge from the Sherry-Netherland, and follow her and Gregson to Broadway shows with a camera. Natalie signed countless autographs and posed endlessly for Wells, even letting the teenager up to her hotel suite to take pictures. "She was an angel," comments Wells. In the suite, Natalie did whatever the thirteen-year-old asked, pretending to answer the phone, crossing her legs, putting on her sunglasses, taking off her coat while Wells snapped photos—behaving with the same doll-like, eager-to-please wistfulness she had at four, when she sat on Pichel's lap and entertained him with her song.

Gregson, who was not a celebrity, occasionally became irritated by Natalie's patience with her fans, tapping his feet while she posed for yet another picture. "My first wife wasn't a professional," he said later, "so Natalie was the first big challenge for me. I got very upset at her temper tantrums, I couldn't cope with her ego. It took me three years to learn." Natalie once hinted at the same thing, saying, "We both have tempers. We have some stormy fights. There are periods almost as stormy as with Warren. But for now, the void is filled."

Not everyone in Natalie's circle approved of Gregson.

David Niven, Jr., who remained close to Natalie after their fling in 1965, as did his father, "didn't see the warmth" in Gregson though he acknowledged that "He was a very shrewd, tough agent." Natalie's secretary, Tony Costello, left her employ when she became engaged, as did his mother, Mac. "A lot of us didn't like Gregson and we all quit."

Natalie loyally supported her fiancé, hiring him as her agent and recommending him in 1967 to her friend Redford, who recalls, "It was really Natalie who came to me and said, 'You oughta *go* with this guy.' She suggested it, because I wasn't happy with my agency situation. And she said, 'Look. Why don't you go with this guy? He's a hotshot guy from England. He's taken the place by storm. He's really cool. He's very da-da-da-da . . .' I met him, I thought he was suave, I said yes, he became my agent."

Redford and his wife, Lola, developed what he calls "a good, really good friendship" with Natalie while she was involved with Gregson, spending time together as couples at the Redfords' Utah ranch. Natalie and Redford talked about appearing in a play together, while he and Gregson discussed producing a movie.

In May of 1968, Gregson closed the L.A. branch of his agency, London International Artists. According to his friend Bricusse, "Richard made a lot of money very quickly. He sold his agency to a bigger agency, and the bigger agency was taken over immediately afterward, so he made a double killing. And I think he then decided to move on and do other things." One of those things was to form a company with Redford, who wanted to produce and star in a film he admired called *Downhill Racer*, about a professional skier. "He was a pretty ambitious guy," Redford states of Gregson. "And we formed a company called

Wildwood. And since he was going with Natalie, that put us all in a triumvirate of sorts."

Gregson and Natalie summered at David Niven, Sr.'s villa on the Riviera, where they met up with Leslie Bricusse and his wife, Evie, with whom they spent a disturbing afternoon on the Mediterranean. Bricusse remembers, "We took Richard and Natalie out on our Riva speedboat. We were going to St. Tropez, and it was a very, very hot day, and halfway we stopped to have a swim, quite a long way out to sea. It was a beautiful day and the sea was perfectly calm. And we all splashed around, and suddenly Natalie panicked, really panicked, screaming and everything. When you're out in deep water, it's dark, the water itself, and I think she was just afraid of the water, and maybe what's down there, that feeling. Richard and I got her back on the boat, and she was lying on her back, breathing very heavily. When Natalie could talk, she said, 'I have this dream where I'm going to die in dark water.' "

Bricusse found the experience chilling. "I never, ever forgot that."

Natalie had made dramatic progress since her last overdose the summer of 1966, but she was still a fragile soul. "She was afraid to be alone *at all*," noticed Bricusse. "She was very immature in those kind of ways." Joseph Lewis, a writer who had spent considerable time with Natalie since the mid-sixties, once working with her on her life story, reinterviewed her in the backyard at Bentley just prior to her summer in the Mediterranean. Lewis described her as "faintly tragic," referring to "fleeting moments of unyielding sadness" that flickered across her face, comparing Natalie to romantic, doomed heroines such as Madame Bovary, Anna Karenina, and, ironically, Blanche DuBois. "When the demons are upon Natasha," he wrote, "she locks herself in her bedroom . . . [to] read poems (Andrey Voznesensky is one of her favorite poets), play records or write in her journal."

Natalie spoke to Lewis of making progress, through analysis, in her relations with her parents, saying that she was able to see them for the first time "as people, real human beings with all their love and imperfections." She was trying to disengage from therapy, recognizing "not even analysis, by itself, can transform you . . . you must still do the changing yourself." In a poignant admission, Natalie acknowledged she was better, as an actress, in "sad things," telling Lewis her goal now was "to play a happy lady—and do it convincingly."

That August, she accepted the part of Carol, the hip, loving wife on a quest for sexual honesty in the social satire *Bob and Carol and Ted and Alice*, a script she considered "witty, original and rare." The project was the brainchild of neophyte director Paul Mazursky, who said later he had doubts whether Natalie could do satire. They were dispelled "in ten seconds" when he met her for lunch at Claridge's in London, when for the first time, Natalie dressed simply to meet a director, impressing Mazursky with her down-to-earth friendliness. In truth, she was nervous about the comedy, and "I didn't know how I would feel, coming back to work after having not worked for two years . . . my God, I thought, what if I don't like it anymore? What if I forgot how to do it?"

Agreeing to star in the unknown Mazursky's controversial parody about wife-swapping and the swinging mores of the late '60s was a brave move by Natalie, who was the only major star in the ensemble cast. Elliott Gould, who played

Ted, initially "shied away" from the picture, finding it "exploitative, and I was not confident and really quite scared about it." Natalie made it clear she would not perform a nude scene, displaying further shrewdness by accepting a percentage of the profits as compensation for a reduced salary of $250,000. She had become astute with money since the financial fiasco of her early marriage to Wagner. Costello, who wrote Natalie's checks when he was her secretary, remembers, "No matter what, she went over the bills with me regularly and marked them to be paid or explained . . . she was very particular. In one instance, she received a bill and she had me go to the restaurant and check the price of the wine. She was a very tough cookie when it came to a dollar."

The filming of *Bob and Carol and Ted and Alice*, shot in Los Angeles and Las Vegas roughly from Halloween to Christmas of 1968, was a halcyon interlude for Natalie. Sugar Bates, who styled her hair as she had since 1963, recalls, "Paul Mazursky, the director, was wonderful, and when they started working, she had a great time." Natalie appeared to be over the moon about Gregson, whose divorce was finally falling into place. "She was so happy. Richard would call her all the time, and it was so romantic and she was just thrilled, and that was the first time I ever saw her feel that way." Natalie, Bates observed, deeply wanted her marriage to Gregson to work.

Natalie's focus on her personal life, and the anti-glamour that defined the "new Hollywood," influenced by political unrest and the breakup of the studio system, reflected itself in her shrinking attendants on *Bob and Carol and Ted and Alice*. Natalie even did her own makeup. "There was no silly star crap," as Mazursky put it.

In a *New York Times* interview on location, taking place

in a Las Vegas casino, Natalie mocked her former self, the studio queen with clauses specifying the color of phone cords. "When you start out . . . you have great fun making them put all that in your contract: 'I want so-and-so or I'm not playing!' . . . There's a time for that. I've had mine." She even alluded to her "Natalie Wood" alter ego, The Badge, during her interview, referring to it as "The Image" or "The Face." She mused to the *Times* reporter, "The whole 'star' business seems so far away," saying she was after "the really reals, they're what I believe in." While saying it, Natalie was wearing a silver lamé Chloe mini-dress and a fur coat. When a fan strolled past in the casino to admire her mink, she murmured, "Sable, darling," displaying the still-extant split between Natalie and "Natalie Wood."

She endeared herself forever to the awed, slightly nervous Elliott Gould, who pronounced Natalie "perfect, she was perfect." Gould was especially anxious about the famous last scene in the film, where Bob, Carol, Ted and Alice (Robert Culp, Natalie, Gould and Dyan Cannon) are in bed together to swap spouses. Gould, who was to remove his underwear while beneath the covers and fling them to the floor, wore an extra pair of "rugby jockey shorts" because he "just couldn't be naked" next to Natalie Wood. "We were all embarrassed as hell," Natalie later told Tom Snyder. "And Dyan and I really were making sure that we were all covered up, and that we weren't nude. It seemed so *shocking!*"

Mazursky shot the scene as improvisation, with the option for the actors to go as far as they wanted in terms of nudity and swapping. "I recall there was some degree of manipulation going on for the four of us to physically interact . . . but I couldn't do it," states Gould. "Bob would have liked to have, and I think that Dyan was hysterical enough to perhaps go on and use her hysteria, but the anchor there was Natalie." Gould was devoted to Natalie for her integrity and dignity. "Natalie was not just there as a star, she was there as a fellow human being, like a sister."

After finishing *Bob and Carol*, Natalie tagged along to Austria the first three months of 1969 to watch Gregson and Redford film *Downhill Racer*, rolling up her sleeves to become a "functioning groupie," Redford would joke. "She was just a *great gal*. She helped out, and loved doing it. She went around and carried things. It was just fun. She was just a lot of fun."

While in Austria, Natalie pushed herself to learn to snow ski, which terrified her, for she was still under Mud's spell that she was too fragile for sports. "She was very gutty," Redford recalls of her skiing. "She'd *charge* into things, and try them." True to Maria's forewarning, Natalie broke her leg in early April, flying back with a cast to be a presenter at the Academy Awards.

The first of May, when Gregson's divorce entered its final phase, Natalie sent invitations to her May 30 wedding, flaunting Mud's warning, "May weddings bring tears," one of Maria's litany of ancient Siberian superstitions.

Natalie tried to convince herself she didn't believe her mother's Russian-gypsy lore, while at the same time, she incorporated it into her wedding, an elaborate "crowning" ceremony similar to Olga's, taking place at Maria's Russian-Orthodox cathedral, the Church of the Holy Virgin Mary. Significantly, Natalie wore shafts of wheat in her loose, long hair, a symbol of fertility in Mud's Old World shamanism. Edith Head had designed a wedding gown inspired by eighteenth-century Russian Court dresses, with Natalie looking like the Russian czarina Fahd made her at birth in her carriage fit for a Romanov. Gregson chose

Robert Redford to be his best man, and Norma Crane was Natalie's maid of honor. Among the guests was Warren Beatty, with his then-girlfriend, Julie Christie. Pictures of the wedding were like stills from *Dr. Zhivago*, with beautiful people in extravagant costumes in a moment of romantic ecstasy that was doomed.

Natalie spent the rest of the year "radiating happiness," as newspaper accounts describe her, barely fazed by the surprise success of *Bob and Carol and Ted and Alice* that September, making Natalie three million dollars and "shooting her back . . . as a *movie star*," Mazursky would boast. She would later tell Rex Reed this "was not the movie I would want to be remembered by." More to the point, Natalie's obsession was no longer movies, but motherhood.

She learned she was going to have a baby the beginning of 1970, when she was thirty-one, a moment of supreme happiness for Natalie, who finally had overcome her mother's gothic warnings about childbirth. "There's nothing like finding out for the very first time that you're going to be pregnant, and to go through that first pregnancy," she said later, "because no matter how fantastic the next one is, there's just nothing quite as miraculous as that."

Natalie announced she was semiretiring to devote herself to her baby, telling an L.A. newspaper she was having a "delayed childhood," realizing she had "never had time to play" when she was growing up, for she had lost herself to child actress "Natalie Wood," who was too busy pretending to be Maureen O'Hara's daughter or Orson Welles' ward to let Natasha be herself.

In the months before she gave birth, Natalie supervised

the construction of a nursery, knitting baby clothes while Gregson flew back and forth to London on business. That June, when she was six months pregnant and Gregson was in the U.K., she accepted an invitation on a rainy night to what she would later call a "fateful" dinner party at the home of producer John Foreman and his wife, Linda, friends of hers and R.J.'s. Oddly, the Foremans had invited R.J., who was quietly separated from his wife, seating him next to Natalie, who would claim she never knew he was estranged from Marshall.

"We spent the whole evening together and reminisced about our love for our boat and the sea . . . we recalled all the good things," Natalie said later. "We just sat there and talked. It wasn't flirty or anything like that." When the party ended, R.J. walked her to her car. "It was raining, and he was worried about my driving home to Bel Air by myself." R.J. followed Natalie to her house, then stood on her front porch to say goodnight. "It was awkward, and I finally said, 'Well, are you happy, R.J.?' " Neither R.J. nor Natalie would address the question, focusing on her happiness at being pregnant. Wagner said later he drove around the corner afterward, stopped his car, and cried.

Natalie later would call this the "important night" in their eventual reunion, and he would refer to it as "the greatest unexpected meeting of my life." Whether there was more to the encounter than they shared publicly, or with friends, is unknown, though R.J. would later hint that Natalie was "experiencing unhappiness" in her marriage. "I think we realized there was still something between us," Natalie later told a magazine.

The next day, R.J. sent Natalie roses, as he had after their first arranged date, "with a little note," she would remember. "It totally dissolved me. I sat and cried for a while, and thought that was that."

Lana would later reflect, "There was just something that Natalie could never get out of her mind about R.J. He was never gone out of her heart."

To Natalie, R.J. represented a dream, the happily-ever-after she had imagined as a child, the idol whose picture she taped on her wall at eleven and fantasized marrying. Those powerful images were the reason she had been so traumatized when their marriage fell apart, and they were what pulled her toward him afterward, in the hope of restoring a cherished ideal that she had lost. "I always cherished that early marriage of ours," she said of her reaction to seeing R.J. again. "Sort of a bittersweet reaction of what had happened to us. My memories of it were beautiful, and sad . . . I was tremendously moved at John's party."

After her poignant encounter with R.J., Natalie devoted herself to two other long-held dreams: the impending birth of her child, and a future trip to Russia, set up as a television special by Gregson, with himself as executive producer. Gregson also made arrangements to produce a film, starring Natalie, called *Thank You, Dr. Reinmuth*.

At the end of the summer, *Downhill Racer*, Gregson's debut film with Redford, was given a sneak preview. The pregnant Natalie, her husband, and Redford all attended, with great expectations. It was a "disaster," Redford recalls:

> We're sitting in a theater in Santa Barbara for the preview of the film. And I'd never been through it before in my life. It was my first film producing, and we made it for no money, and I put my heart and soul into it.

> So we were sitting there, in this screening, where the studio did some incredibly stupid thing: they ran it in a double bill with *Midnight Cowboy*, with no intermission. It's so depressing, that film, and then they went right into *our* movie. And I could hear the audience, people saying, "*Skiing?*" All these octogenarians were getting up and leaving. And I was sitting in there, just sliding down, further and further in my seat.
>
> All the while this is going on—people are getting up in droves, leaving—Natalie whispered, "That's okay. This happens all the time in Hollywood." And she's giving me a lot of encouragement, saying, "They'll come back. They have to go to the bathroom because they weren't able to go to the bathroom." Except they weren't coming back!
>
> Finally *whole rows* were getting up and leaving! By the end of the movie, there were about eight people left in the audience. And she leans over and whispers—because she could see me now, practically on the floor—and she says, "Don't worry about it." I said, "Don't *worry* about it?" And she said, "It's okay. In *my* film *All the Fine Young Cannibals*, they threw stuff at the screen!" It was very sweet. I can remember being totally charmed by that. I remember that moment.

Redford and Natalie veered in different directions afterward. "She was married and decided to try motherhood, to go down that road, and was committing to that." Gregson stepped away from Wildwood Productions around the same time. "Our partnership broke up, because he moved on to other, greener fields," explains Redford.

"He had a bigger fish to fry. I think he had a more ambitious program than mine, with just our company, because he moved on to other things."

On September 29, Natalie's fondest dream was realized when she went through natural childbirth at Cedars in Beverly Hills, giving birth to a daughter who was a virtual re-creation of herself as a baby, with flashing brown eyes and an elfin face. "I can definitely say that was the happiest moment of my life," she later reflected.

Natalie chose to name her baby Natasha, the identity that had been taken from her; "giving herself another chance to start a childhood," perceived Lana, who listened to Natalie talk about how she was going to rear her children, which would not include stardom. "She just wanted them to have a *childhood* . . . a real childhood, and not have any kind of concerns about anything other than being a child, getting along at school, having friends." When Natalie noticed Mud begin to circle around baby Natasha, whispering to her that she was a "lucky" baby, "Natalie got upset," recalls Lana, and kept Natasha away from her, eerily reminded of how Mud used to throw coins on the sidewalk and tell her that she was a magical child. Fahd simply was entranced with Natasha, as he had been with his first Natasha, calling his granddaughter "Natashinka."

When Natalie talked about having become a mother, it was clear she saw Natasha as a resurrection of her lost self, and that the void in her life had been filled:

> I never knew motherhood could be so truly gratifying until I had Natasha. As a person, one thinks about one's self. And as an actress, you tend to think about

> yourself to an even greater degree—how you look, what you wear, how you move and talk. Then you have a child, and suddenly you're faced with a helpless little being who is utterly dependent upon you. She loves you like no one else has before, because she is an extension of you. You want to give her everything you have—to protect her, to teach her, to explain to her. And in turn, she brings you out of yourself. You open up, not only to her, but to the entire world. A child changes your perspective on the world, because you are also seeing it through that child's eyes.

Natalie exhibited a glow that winter and into the next summer that had not been in evidence since before her trauma with R.J., posing proudly with Natasha in magazines with headlines such as "How I Was Saved." The new Natalie, as she was being called, described her lifestyle as a homebody, telling *Pageant* in the July 1971 issue, "For the first time I feel an inner emotional security. There is reality and dependability. My life revolves around Richard and the baby . . . independence is fine, but not for me."

While the magazine was still on newsstands, Natalie abruptly ended her marriage to Gregson. She took extreme measures, demanding that Gregson leave the house immediately. Natalie gathered all his clothes, wrapped them in a sheet, and threw them on the driveway, calling her attorney that night to instruct him to file for divorce. She refused to take Gregson's calls and got a restraining order to keep him away from her and Natasha. "Natalie was really angry," remembers Lana. "She had people posted outside the house. Seriously, he could not drive onto the driveway."

Gregson was beside himself. "He called *me* to see if I could help patch them up," recalls Olga. "And I can't change Natalie's mind when she decides that she's not gonna go back to him. And he never spoke to me after that! It was like pffft!"

22

NATALIE'S SUDDEN DIVORCE WAS the talk of Hollywood. Rumors whispered across town the first week in August, even showing up in gossip columns, where Natalie tersely responded, "No comment."

She isolated herself in the house on Bentley, bereft over the failure of her marriage and the fact that Natasha would grow up as a child of divorce. Natalie took tranquilizers to calm her nerves, unable to eat, humiliated and angry and miserable, questioning whether she ever wanted to be married again. She decided to disappear from Hollywood for a while, asking Olga to go with her on a cruise around Sardinia, accompanied by Natasha and by Mart Crowley, her buffer from being alone.

While Natalie was at this low point, she received an unexpected call from R.J., who was living in London for the summer to film an ABC movie called *Madame Sin*, costarring Bette Davis. By a turn of fate, his marriage had ended since his emotional encounter with Natalie the summer before, and he was now engaged to Frank Sinatra's twenty-three-year-old actress daughter, Tina, who reportedly had a crush on R.J. as a child.

R.J. had flown into L.A. for a few days early in August for a deposition in a thorny lawsuit with Universal over residuals and his right to star in outside projects, when he happened to read about Natalie's divorce.

"He called and said he was sorry and that he understood what an unhappy time it was for me," she later recounted. "He asked if there was anything he could do." Wagner said later, "I just called to see if she needed anything or if I could be of help." He left a few days later to return to London. "R.J. never knew how touched I was by that telephone call," Natalie would remember. "I was actually crying when we talked that day, but he never knew it."

Natalie departed for her sad cruise around Sardinia in September, with Olga to hold her hand, and help her with Natasha, who was only a year old. Olga recalls, "It was important to *me*, because Natalie had never asked me to do anything for her before . . . so I told my boss I needed to take a month or so off to go with my sister."

Olga was heartbroken when she saw Natalie. "She was very depressed. She had lost so much weight, she looked like Audrey Hepburn—anorexic. Her bones stuck out. She had been in the business for God knows how long, since four years old. She had really decided to get married, to have children, and she was a good mother. She *really* wanted Natasha, and she nursed her, she took care of her, she worried about her. She was ready to have a *life*. It was a real letdown for her."

Natalie spent the cruise fantasizing about a reunion with R.J., hoping to make things in her life right again. "She was *thinking* about R.J., even in Sardinia," recalls Olga. During the holiday, Natalie kept analyzing whether his call to her was consoling, or something more. As she said later, "He's very thoughtful and it was the kind of thing he would do, without romantic motives." Olga recalls her sister as worried about R.J.'s engagement to Tina Sinatra, which he implied was "cooling." Natalie mused whether it could ever work out for her and R.J. a second time. "She was asking me, 'How can I . . . ?' or 'What do *you* think?' She was sort of thinking about it."

Natalie went through a period of "desperate" unhappiness after she and Natasha came home from Sardinia in early October, when R.J.'s divorce came through and Hank Grant of the *Hollywood Reporter* wrote, "The question is not when he'll marry Tina Sinatra, but where." R.J. and Tina Sinatra were in the south of France, staying with her father, Frank, at David Niven's villa, where Natalie holidayed with Gregson in summers before.

Actor Steve McQueen, who was recently separated from his wife, Neile Adams, invited Natalie to dinner the middle of October, giving the former costars an opportunity to act on their attraction from *Love with the Proper Stranger*. Natalie "thought the world of Steve," calling him "one of the smartest cookies you'll ever come up against." They went to a few high-profile restaurants together and bought $800 solid-gold sunglasses, but "it was not a serious thing," observed Adams, who was still friendly with her estranged husband. "I think they went together for about ten days, something like that. It was no big deal. Natalie was a child of Hollywood, and she really represented everything that Steve didn't even like about Hollywood. When he first began, everything was new—the premieres, the parties and all that—but by the time he and I divorced, that was old. But Natalie still loved doing that. She always loved doing that."

In November, Natalie had a few highly publicized dates with California governor Jerry Brown, but she was not a content woman. "I'd been thinking of R.J. almost constantly since my divorce," she said later. When he returned from Europe, R.J. spoke to Natalie on the phone a few times, but he was still seeing Tina Sinatra.

When she met Richard Smedley, Lana's third husband, over Thanksgiving, Smedley noticed that Natalie was under a strain. Even Natasha, who was less than two, sensed her mother was vulnerable, saying later, "Subconsciously I have a lot of memories of sort of being with her all the time and wanting to sort of protect her, take care of her and stuff." Natalie considered Natasha her "perfect love." She was at her happiest singing nursery rhymes with her, tape-recording their songs as forget-me-nots.

She did a favor for an old friend in December, during the depths of her depression, flying to Oakland to appear in a cameo as herself in Redford's second foray as a producer, *The Candidate*. According to Redford, Natalie accepted "without a thought, without a question . . . she just came and did it. There was no calling the agent, no deals. She said, 'I'm just gonna do it.' That kind of stuff I'm a pretty old-fashioned guy about, that kind of loyalty and commitment. That meant a lot. And we had great fun, doing it."

Natalie arrived on set in jeans and a mink coat, a perfect metaphor for the dichotomy between Natalie the person and The Badge, charming the crew with reminiscences about *Splendor in the Grass*, making the poignant remark that she had been playing the last scene too often in her real life. She would not see Redford again, though he would consider Natalie a fond friend evermore.

Actress Edie Adams, who had a large circle of friends, remembers a plaintive call she got from Natalie in this period. "It was very late at night, and she sounded like she was crying and very sad, and she said, 'Edie, I'm so out of things, are you giving any parties, what's happening?' She just sounded awful, and *so sad*. And I tried to include her in things, or say, 'Why don't you go ask Natalie out?' "

Natalie spent a forlorn Christmas at a party at the house of Dean Martin's ex-wife Jeanne, while R.J. announced plans to take Tina Sinatra to producer Irwin Allen's house for New Year's Eve. Somewhere in between, he stopped by Natalie's house with Christmas gifts for her and Natasha, "And when he left," Natalie recalled, "there was kind of a feeling we would see more of one another."

A few weeks later, on January 19, 1972, *The Hollywood Reporter* broke the news that Natalie and R.J. were "dating again," ending his engagement to Tina Sinatra. ("They were going separate directions," observed his assistant.)

R.J. would later say that he was feeling sentimental that Christmas, and took out a box with some old newspaper and magazine clippings. "I was suddenly overwhelmed by the number of stories about Nat and me that had been published over the years," he said, inspiring him to telephone her for a date. The fact that Natalie looked upon R.J. as the symbol of a dream she hoped to recapture was obvious by her reaction to his call. "I thought my heart would stop . . . it was like I was eleven years old again." The same age she was when she first saw Robert Wagner on the Fox lot.

R.J. invited Natalie to his home in Palm Springs the weekend of January 26, a date they would celebrate in the coming years with the same nostalgia as December 6, their first time together on R.J.'s original boat, *My Lady*, in 1956. As soon as Natalie got off the plane, R.J. said then, "It was instant reaction." From that point on, he and Natalie had an understanding they would remarry. "We started going out again . . . mostly out in Palm Springs, before anybody knew it. We fell in love all over again."

This time, there was a better balance in Natalie and R.J.'s

professional lives. During their first marriage, he accepted self-effacingly the role of "Mr. Wood," the handsome face married to a full-blown movie star. Since then, R.J. had capitalized on his enormous personal charm, and the style he copied from Cary Grant, to transform himself into a popular television idol by playing a character—Alexander Mundy in *It Takes a Thief—patterned* after Grant in *To Catch a Thief*.

Natalie was still a "movie star" with all the prestige that connoted when she and R.J. remet in early 1972, but she had acted in only one picture, *Bob and Carol and Ted and Alice*, in six years, and her three previous films (*Inside Daisy Clover*, *This Property Is Condemned*, and *Penelope*) were disappointments. Financially, she had amassed a fortune, which she shared with the cash-poor R.J. "Frankly, she bailed me out. I was a financial disaster at the time, what with the divorce and back taxes and committing money to an unproduced movie. But off we started again. It was the most highly emotional and most marvelous time of my life."

Lana, who knew how devastated Natalie was when her marriage ended in 1961, had concerns that winter when they arrived at a dinner party at Natalie's house, and she surprised them with R.J., implying they would remarry.

Natalie later told Lana, "The devil you know is better than the devil you don't know." Lana explains, "Here was a person whose problems she *knew*, and could cope with, rather than having to deal with the unknown . . . she knew there were problems with R.J., but she'd say, 'These things will not hurt me; I can deal with these.' She was very good at preserving an image, at holding things in, at living up to the public perception of her." According to Hyatt, Natalie believed things with R.J. would be different at least because he had been through analysis in Europe.

Natalie entered her new relationship with R.J. with eyes wide open, desperately in need of what he offered her: adoration, stability, and the illusion, at least, of the fairy tale she sought. "I think she got precisely what she wanted," declared Lana. "She told me she never stopped loving R.J., that she would always love him." While she was adrift in her single years, Natalie often mused to Sugar Bates, "R.J. was so nice, if I couldn't get along with him, who could I get along with?"

Mud was still opposed to Natalie's involvement with R.J., grumbling about it to the Hyatts, but at nearly thirty-three, with a lonely life as her possible alternative, Natalie chose to ignore her dominating mother, placing Maria further on the sidelines, although the Gurdins moved into a townhouse in Palm Springs within footsteps of Natalie, who happily left her Bentley house when R.J. swept back into her life.

As Natasha, who was a toddler then, would touchingly say of R.J., "He was like this *Romeo* that came and just *saved* us, and took us away, and was so fabulous."

To Natalie and to Natasha, he was Prince Valiant.

On April 10, Natalie and R.J. were invited to be joint presenters at the Academy Awards, as they had been fourteen years earlier, in March of 1958, shortly after their honeymoon off Catalina. The Oscar ceremony in 1972 was R.J. and Natalie's first public event together since reuniting, and they arrived on the red carpet radiating an old-fashioned glamour that was electric, looking as movie star gorgeous at forty-two and thirty-three as they had at twenty-eight and nineteen. The public was so captivated by their storybook renewed romance, they needed bodyguards to walk through the crowd. A friend of the Wagners used the word "*Zeitensprung*," a German musical term for an intermission between dances, to describe Natalie and R.J.'s interrupted romance, a poetic concept they, and the public, romantically embraced.

The Hollywood-worshipping qualities in R.J. that had given Natalie pause on their arranged first date in 1956 united them in 1972, when Natalie had accepted the dominance of the star-driven, *Maria* side of the "Natalie Wood" persona. By choosing to remarry R.J., Natalie was choosing Old Hollywood, sublimating the part of her that was drawn to the "golden world" of Ray and Kazan.

After the Oscars, Natalie and R.J. set sail on a luxury crossing aboard the *Queen Mary II*, bound for London, to publicize *Madame Sin* and to enjoy a "pre-honeymoon." Oddly, R.J. had seldom been on the water *between* his two marriages to Natalie. "When we got back together," he said later, "we wanted to get back to sea." In the freak manner of their original honeymoon cruise out of Florida, they encountered what R.J. described as "one of the worst storms at sea recorded in more than 100 years," making headlines in newspapers and putting them in England two days late.

In their gilded tradition as a celebrity couple, they invited photographer Michael Childers on their pre-honeymoon. "We went off to Venice together, the three of us, it was great fun," recalled Childers, who described Natalie as "the most glamorous star of that era. When she walked into a room, the room lit up! First of all, it smelled like Jungle Gardenia, a thousand gardenias. You never forgot an entrance. She was like the old school of actors: they knew that the camera was what brought them alive. They made love to the camera."

Natalie and R.J. chose July 16, 1972, four days before her thirty-fourth birthday, as a wedding day, guided by astrologer Carroll Righter. Neither was conventionally religious, and both had an interest in New Age spirituality. Natalie still resisted Maria's occult ways, but she "was fascinated by universal New Age teachings," according to her friend Faye Nuell. "She read a lot about it, she was always seeking."

In a sentimental nod to their romantic few days off Catalina at the end of their first honeymoon, R.J. and Natalie decided to have their ceremony on a boat, at sunset, borrowing a friend's yacht, called *The Ramblin' Rose*, moored at Malibu in Paradise Cove. The only guests were family and a few friends, with Natalie and Natasha wearing matching gingham dresses, with a picnic for a reception. "It was marvelous in spite of the sea," was Maria's ironic comment to a magazine a few years later:

> We all thought it would be grand; however, in reality it was not such a good idea. I remember everyone kept asking when the boat was going to stop. Some of the guests were seasick before we were halfway there, and the others were well on the way to being sick . . . it was all everyone could do to stand for the ceremony.
>
> There was a boat of photographers that followed us, and they kept circling the boat and causing it to rock, which only added to everyone's misery. I think I was crying and gagging at the same time.

When they came back from their honeymoon cruise, R.J. and Natalie began "hunting all over the world for *our* boat," as R.J. later put it, a quest that would take several years and lead to *The Splendour*, where Natalie would spend her last tragic night.

The Wagners spent the honeymoon months of their second marriage as gypsies, traveling back and forth from Palm Springs to Bentley to Natalie's place in Tahoe to a townhouse in the Mayfair district of London, where R.J. was filming a BBC miniseries called *Colditz* to circumvent a restriction that blocked him from appearing on TV in the U.S., part of his legal dispute with Universal.

Maria sometimes went along as a nanny for Natasha, under Natalie's close scrutiny. R.J.'s assistant, Peggy Griffin, who became close to Natalie early in the second marriage to R.J., remembers her relationship with her mother as "on and off" then. "Natalie had 'issues,' " as Griffin describes it, "but she was also very family-oriented."

Natalie's purest relationship in her family was with Olga, whom she respected, admired, and had come to realize, with irony, was the happiest one in their Russian-Chekhov family of three sisters—the one who chose a simple life, leaving Hollywood, and their star-crazed mother, behind. "She thought the world of Olga. She always wished that they had lived in proximity to each other."

Lana, like Natalie, was struggling to overcome a childhood warped by their mother's mad genius. The effect on Lana of having felt invisible, worshipping and envying her famous sister, created complex issues between them, erupting when Lana's husband sold pictures of Natalie and R.J.'s second wedding. R.J. bore a grudge. Natalie eventually forgave Lana, but their relationship was strained. As Lana perceives:

> It was tough for Natalie, because she was constantly trying to bridge the gap between who I was to her: was I her baby sister, was I her friend? She was constantly walking that tightrope, so there were a lot

> of things that she chose not to tell me . . . we were moving closer to being friends, but it was really tough for her to know how open she could be with me. She was protective of me. It was a lot easier for me, which I didn't realize at the time. I could go and say 'I need you,' and she would help me, and everything would be fine. But for Natalie, it was really strange, because she didn't know how to *be* with me at all times. I was a burden.

After years pining over what might have been, Natalie put her marriage to R.J. ahead of the complex and burdensome ties to her parents and younger sister, directing her perfectionism into being a wife. "She was very, very nice to R.J., she went out of her way to be nice to him," observed Sugar Bates. "She would make life as good as possible for him—she sort of ran the house, but also she was the wifey kind of person, too."

The vibrancy Natalie displayed as a teenager bubbled back after she remarried R.J. "She was always up to something," recalls girlfriend Peggy Griffin, who palled with Natalie when R.J. was working. "She was a total 'girl' girl, always shopping and talking clothes and makeup and gossip and diets. She was such fun."

R.J.'s influence on Natalie's career was evident their first spring together. She retreated from an opportunity to be considered to play Daisy in *The Great Gatsby*, instead embracing a television movie-of-the-week produced by Aaron Spelling and Leonard Goldberg, costarring R.J., called *Love Song*, the first time since becoming a movie star that Natalie had considered television. There was a soupçon of reluctance in an interview Natalie gave early that summer, when she admitted that TV had less "prestige," suggesting gamely that if George C. Scott could do it, so could she.

Two things attracted Natalie to the role, according to Gilbert Cates, the director she and R.J. requested: she would be playing a woman crippled by polio, "which would have been unique for her," and the character, a lonely songwriter, had a scene in which she performs a song. "R.J. loved the idea, obviously, of the two of them doing the movie together." There was a curious scene—either a strange coincidence or an intended parallel to their real lives—where Natalie's character crushes a glass in her hands when R.J.'s character breaks her heart.

That June, Natalie wrote a letter to her friend, actress Ruth Gordon, Natasha's godmother, expressing her new domestic bliss, including hers and R.J.'s plans for a third honeymoon in Mart Crowley's guest house, followed by a few weeks by the beach, or house sitting for the vacationing Gregory and Veronique Peck. She was excited about the *Love Song* script, but even more thrilled by the short shooting schedule for television movies. Natalie seemed unenthused about returning to London for R.J. to film *Colditz* ("Jan—Feb.—cold—ugh!!"), prattling to Gordon about remodeling R.J.'s house in Palm Springs. "We're wildly happy," she wrote Gordon, teasing that three-year-old Natasha was "running the whole house—I'm now not sure whether she's going to be an actress or a director." She signed it "xxxooo Natalie."

Natalie cut off her long, sixties straight hair before starting *Love Song* (later called *The Affair*) that summer. "I remember when it came to learning how to walk like her character did, she wanted it to be authentic," states Cates. "She had great respect not only for authenticity, but for other people's feelings, two qualities that were not associated with conventional stars during that period. And I remember we got a nurse, and we brought someone in with the disease, and she watched how the person walked, and it was quite impressive." Ironically, Natalie again faced opposition to using her singing voice. Cates recalls, "She and I absolutely wanted it to be her voice; Aaron Spelling wasn't quite so sure." Natalie prevailed. "She had a very sweet voice, and she had great commitment . . . 90% of it's commitment," assesses Cates.

A few weeks before shooting began in Santa Barbara, Natalie found out she was pregnant, placing the TV movie in jeopardy. Cates had three concerns. "Firstly, healthwise for her, whether she could do the rigors of the movie. Secondly, whether we could do it in time before she'd show. Thirdly, she had horseback riding scenes." Cates hired a double for the riding scenes, and Natalie and R.J. ensconced themselves in a glass house by the sea in Malibu to shoot *The Affair*, choosing the name Courtney, the character Natalie was playing, for their unborn child.

Natalie spent her thirty-fifth birthday, July 20, 1973, pregnant with R.J.'s child, shooting their second film together as husband and wife. The years of holding back tears through birthdays spent with business managers, and Mud, were in the past. That autumn, Natalie happily knitted a baby blanket, cheerfully disregarding the extra weight she was gaining, decorating a nursery in Palm Springs for what she was calling "the most wanted baby in the world."

After years hidden behind The Badge, Natalie was rediscovering who she was. "She just was meant to be a mother," her friend Griffin observed. "She just loved it. She read all the books about child rearing, and if she'd meet anybody with children, the topic would immediately go there. And it wasn't just her kids, she just really liked kids." Natalie became intrigued with the idea of doing a picture about what would have happened to her if her parents had stayed in Russia, part of her inner journey to understand "Natasha Gurdin."

The only cloud over Natalie's seemingly charmed life that fall was the cancer death of her nurturing friend Norma Crane, at forty-two. Natalie paid for all her medical bills and arranged Crane's burial at Westwood Cemetery, near the remains of Marilyn Monroe. She ran into her old love, Scott Marlowe, at the funeral. "She started to cry when she saw me. R.J. grabbed my hand, and just was very warm. Natalie was devastated. She gave the closing speech. She handled the first part of it okay, then she totally folded. It was the saddest thing I've ever seen. She was down on her knees, by the open grave." Eight years later, at forty-three, Natalie would be buried beside Crane, in the shadow of Marilyn Monroe.

All of Maria's dark, disturbing warnings to Natalie that she was too small to have a baby came back to haunt her on March 9, when she was admitted to the emergency room at Cedars to give birth to her daughter with R.J. "I was in labor but the baby wasn't falling. I was so scared. And physically, I was a wreck . . . I didn't really know just what was going on. I thought something was wrong with the baby and they weren't telling me." Natalie started "fantasizing about terrible things," she said later. After nine "hellish hours," she delivered by emergency caesarean, a result of the umbilical cord being wrapped around the baby's neck. It was a "disaster," Natalie told writer Rex Reed.

Courtney Brook Wagner would be Natalie's last child,

though she often spoke of wanting more, especially a little boy.

While Natalie was nursing Courtney, she was offered a quarter of a million dollars to play what became the Faye Dunaway role in *The Towering Inferno*, a picture R.J. would be making at Fox that spring. She turned it down as "boring, insipid and worthless," though she was restless after two years of quiet bliss in Palm Springs. "Palm Springs was wonderful," Natalie said later. "But it got to be a bit *much*, you know? House guests every weekend. And then, during the week, nobody." Her friend Tommy Thompson compared her to Napoleon in exile.

Natalie felt disconnected from "Natalie Wood," from Hollywood, the only world she had known from the age of six. She convinced R.J. to look for a house in Los Angeles, and accepted a role that intrigued her as an erotically glamorous heiress in a Raymond Chandler–style caper ultimately called *Peeper*, costarring her brief flame Michael Caine. Natalie later told Tom Snyder she grew up believing it wasn't possible to be a mother and an actress at the same time—Mud's way of keeping her focus on work. Natalie decided to exorcise that demon.

She chose *Peeper* in part because it was filmed at Fox, where R.J. was working on *The Towering Inferno*, and where she could bring Natasha and Courtney to the set. Since Natalie was dabbling in movies again, she and R.J. made an agreement that one or the other of them would be with the girls at all times, a pact both took seriously.

Natalie went on a rigid 800-calorie diet to lose the fifty pounds she gained with Courtney. By June, when she started filming *Peeper*, she had a twenty-two inch waist and looked ravishing, according to the director of photography,

Courtesy of Janet Leigh

Natalie and R.J. congratulate publicist Warren Cowan and actress Barbara Rush at their wedding in Janet Leigh and Tony Curtis's home.

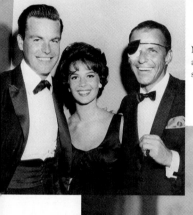

Natalie at her twenty-first birthday party at Romanoff's, cohosted by R.J. and her secret crush, Frank Sinatra.

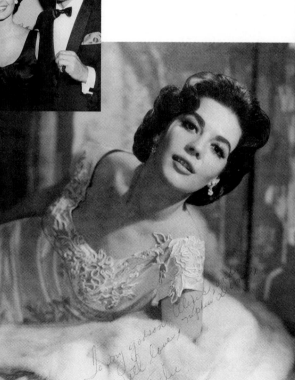

A glamour shot of "Natalie Wood," Natalie's movie star persona, from the early 1960s. She signed this one for her sister Olga's son Alexis.

Olga Viripaeff Collection, courtesy of Olga Viripaeff

Dancer Tony Mordente goes over Natalie's steps for a number in *West Side Story*. The other dancers thought she was aloof; she was actually deeply insecure about her singing and dancing.

Bettman/CORBIS

Natalie with Warren Beatty at the Academy Awards in 1962. Contrary to gossip, he was not the reason she left Robert Wagner.

By permission of Delmar Watson

Natalie, 23, fulfills the vow she made at 16: to put her handprints in the cement at Grauman's. Behind her smile, she was devastated by her recent breakup with R.J.

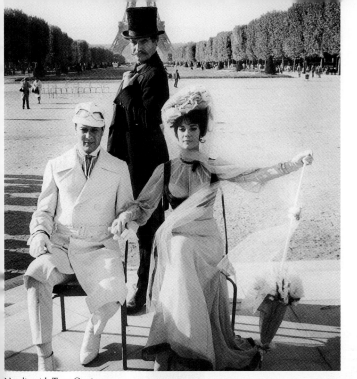

Natalie with Tony Curtis and Jack Lemmon in Paris during *The Great Race*, her least favorite shoot. She made a suicide attempt at the end of filming, November 1964.

Natalie with beau Henry Jaglom, spring 1966. Later that year, Frank Sinatra would hire someone to follow them.

Henry Jaglom Collection, courtesy of Henry Jaglom

Courtesy of David Gorton

Natalie boating off Catalina with her date, lawyer David Gorton, one of her "boys of '66." The couple to their left are Edd Byrnes and Asa Maynor, Natalie's good friends.

Natalie attends the fall '66 London premiere of *This Property Is Condemned* with director Sydney Pollack, who credits her with his big break.

Courtesy of Wayne Case

Natalie, touched by her ovation during a tribute at the San Francisco Film Festival in October 1976. She thought no one would remember her.

Natalie and fiancé Gregson on the set of *Downhill Racer* with director Michael Ritchie (far left) and Gregson's producing partner and Natalie's close friend Robert Redford (far right). Taken in Idaho Springs, Colorado, April 1969.

Three generations: Maria, Natalie, and Natasha, whose birth gave Natalie another chance at childhood.

Courtesy of Peggy Griffin

Natalie holds daughter Courtney at a backyard birthday party with best friend Peggy Griffin circa 1975. Nanny and cook Willie Mae Northen is in the background at left.

Courtesy of Peggy Griffin

Probably the only photo taken of Natalie cooking: aboard the *Splendour* in 1977, making her famous huevos rancheros. She was at the peak of her happiness.

Natalie's last visit to San Francisco, June 1981, the summer before she drowned. At left is her daughter Courtney; on the other side, daughter Natasha.

Courtesy of Betty Battausa

One of Olga's favorite pictures: Natalie talks to Frank Sinatra's pianist while Olga and her son Michael look on.

Fahd's last days. Taken in the backyard at Canon with Mud, R.J., and Natalie, who held his hand at the end.

Photo courtesy of Betty Battansa

The *Valiant*, the Wagners' dinghy, in the cove at Blue Cavern Point where it was found tangled in kelp at 5:30 A.M. on Sunday, November 29, 1981.

The Spendour– "the boat that took her away," Mud described it.

Natalie's final glamour shot and one of her last autographs as "Natalie Wood," signed with her usual warmth to two-time screen daughter Tonya Crowe.

Tonya Crowe Collection, courtesy of Tonya Crowe

Earl Rath, Jr. "She was getting a little older then, so I used a little softer lens, just to enhance the quality of her face. Every shot, I'd glamorize. I'd make her look beautiful, which was not hard to do."

Natalie was excited to be working again. She gave a party for the cast and crew the first day, and seemed "very up" throughout the highly technical production, which included night shooting and complicated interior shots on the *Queen Mary*. "She was right on top of it, knew her lines, and got it done," recalls Rath, who found Natalie to be a "very nice, happy, bouncy kind of woman. She'd come in with a limo in the evening, we'd work all night long, and R.J. would drive down and pick her up."

Natalie's sole concern about *Peeper* was a shot in silhouette, when her character steps from the shadows in a transparent peignoir to meet Michael Caine. "She was nervous," remembers Rath. "It was a morality thing. She didn't want to be seen in the nude, so I lit her from the back so you couldn't see her and we used a body suit. It just silhouetted her so you see the beautiful legs as she opened up her robe with a flourish to tease Michael Caine. It was a pretty interesting shot—beautiful."

Reviewers admired Natalie's beauty and spunk, but little else, with one observing that her legendary vulnerability worked against her, writing, "She's like an appealing waif who smears her face with mascara and rouge, climbs into mama's slinky dress and says: 'Aren't I naughty?' " Natalie was stung by the negative reviews for *Peeper*, saying publicly that she and Caine "gave it their all." Privately, she admitted, "It just didn't work."

However, by the time the picture came out at the end of 1975, sixteen months after she finished it, Natalie had retreated into motherhood and domesticity again. She was inspired into "semi-retirement" by Natasha's enrollment in nursery school, and by the family's move into singer Patti Page's former house in Beverly Hills: a cozy Colonial on Canon Drive that seemed to coax out every one of Natalie's nesting instincts.

Faye Nuell described the house on Canon as a less showy version of Natalie and R.J.'s dream house from their first marriage, potent symbolism for Natalie, whose nature was to "make things right in the end." She created a happy haven for Natasha and Courtney, making needlepoint pillows, taping up their crayon drawings, cluttering the yard with cats, dogs, chickens, rabbits, trees to climb, even a white picket fence.

She made up for her sad, lonely birthdays as a child by making her daughters' holidays magical, to be sure they experienced what she missed: a normal family life. "She just loved, *loved* Christmas!" recalls Peggy Griffin. "I always used to say to her, 'You turn into Currier and Ives.' She just couldn't do enough, with the decorations, and having Santa Claus there, planning children's parties—with a gift for every child at the party, and knowing their names and seeing these little kids' faces just light up."

Natasha said later, "I think Mommy had a real zest for life. Everything mattered to her, you know? The holidays mattered to her. Birthdays mattered. We were *it* for her, I think. I really think that."

"I am personally enjoying their childhood more than I did mine," Natalie admitted once to *L'Officiel*. "Whereas, as a child, I always had the feeling of my nose pressed against the window looking in, my daughters have none of that. They are growing up more traditionally. I love being involved in their schools, their friends, their lives."

Natalie made it clear to Lana and to Faye Nuell that "she

wanted to be the mom *she* didn't have," indulging her daughters to the point that Natasha would admit later she was "spoiled rotten." Natalie even sought guidance from a female analyst to make sure she did not inflict on Natasha or Courtney any of the phobias Mud instilled in her, especially about childbirth and sex. She told Natasha the facts of life at four, as she would Courtney. Natasha would remember, "We talked about sex and it was never a dirty thing. It was always a beautiful, empowering thing." Natalie's comment was: "I wouldn't want them to be especially proper, I would like them to be unafraid . . . and feel free enough to express themselves." Peggy Griffin recalls Natalie aggressively shielding Courtney and Natasha from Mud's superstitions.

She was adamant that *her* daughters *not* become child actors, Natalie's most eloquent expression of the pain she experienced as a child of Hollywood. "It was absolutely not an option to even consider acting," Natasha would recall. "My mom never had a childhood, and it was one of her great sadnesses. One of her most important wishes was that my sister and I have a normal childhood."

New Yorker Rex Reed would remember going with Natalie to every Christmas tree lot in Beverly Hills one December, sniffing the branches to find the perfect tree "because she wanted her house to smell like Christmas." She and R.J. invited celebrity friends and civilians like Peggy Griffin or realtor Delphine Mann, Natalie's other close chum, to an open house each December 25, serving eggnog, turkey and ham in shifts from eleven in the morning until midnight, with generous supplies of wine and other alcohol, an essential part of their style of entertaining. Natalie was still on her guard about liquor, though she drank her favorite wine, Pouilly Fuissé, and alcohol was part of R.J.'s lifestyle, from highballs to fine wines.

They regularly opened their guest cottage to David Niven, Fred Astaire, Elia Kazan, Laurence Olivier—with Natalie hand-painting personalized signs above the door, such as "Gadge's Gulch," to make each of them feel welcome. "Natalie just had her house filled with friends at all times," observed Peggy Griffin. "She really just crammed so much living into every given day."

By the third year of their remarriage, the entertainment industry had embraced Natalie and R.J. as its romantic icons, beloved ambassadors of the celebrity community, a mantle that Natalie, the child of Hollywood, taught to worship stardom, and R.J., its biggest booster, felt comfortable assuming. The mayor chose R.J. and Natalie, accompanied by their daughters, to lead the televised Santa Claus Lane Parade along Hollywood Boulevard the following Thanksgiving. Whereas Richard Gregson had little tolerance for the pomp and circumstance of stardom, "Natalie and Robert Wagner made a wonderful Hollywood couple," Karl Malden observes, "and they performed properly for the profession, at all sorts of affairs."

One of R.J.'s most thoughtful traits as a husband was what seemed to be his egoless deference to Natalie's status as a movie star of legendary proportions, his attentiveness to her, graciously putting Natalie on center stage when they were in public, or interviewed together, providing her with the adulation that "Natalie Wood," her star persona, both needed and desired, particularly as her career was waning.

By 1975, R.J. resolved his dispute with Universal and was cast in the CBS series *Switch*, providing structure to his and Natalie's idyllic family life. While R.J. was at Universal filming the series, Natalie drove Natasha to nursery school, read aloud to Courtney from her long-ago favorite book, *The Little Prince*, helped friends decorate their houses, attended PTA meetings—observing, "Normal things have a mystique for me because I've never had them." Courtney, their "love child," was a tow-headed toddler with the pastel beauty of her father and the wistfulness of Natalie. When R.J.'s pretty blond daughter Katie came to spend weekends, Natalie had three daughters, just like Mud; Natasha, ironically, was the middle of three sisters, just like her mother.

Natalie invited her former stepchildren for summers in the guest cottage, healing wounds from the failure of her marriage to Richard Gregson, who had disappeared to a farm in the U.K. and remarried. "His life changed so dramatically," recalls Bricusse. "He suddenly went to live in Wales and write." Though Natasha saw her real father from time to time, she called R.J. "Daddy."

In the fall, R.J. came upon "*the*" boat he had been searching for since remarrying Natalie, a white sixty-foot powerboat with an outer deck and spacious cabin with room to sleep eight, a shower, a galley, and handsome dark wood trim with polished brass fittings. He showed it off to a reporter like a proud father, saying, "We looked in the South of France and England. Finally we found her . . . I know every boatman thinks his is *the* boat, but come on down and take a look . . ."

Natalie and R.J. sentimentally named their boat *Splendour*, after *Splendor in the Grass*, the movie that had such deep significance to Natalie; as a wink, they called the small, attached dinghy *Valiant*, after R.J.'s spectacular disaster, *Prince Valiant*. Natalie helped paint the engine and decorated the cabin herself, choosing Early American furniture, hand-crocheting pillows, knitting blankets, hanging family photographs, creating a homey ambience without a trace of movie star glamour.

Though Maria would later tearfully lament, "*Oh, why did they buy their boat?*" the *Splendour* brought R.J., and Natalie, interludes of great joy. Mart Crowley would later call to mind a memory of Natalie at the end of 1975, sitting on the deck with Courtney in her arms, "And she saw me staring at her. And she looked me in the eye and said, 'There's no movie in the world that's worth *this* little thing!' "

The Wagners leased a mooring from Doug Bombard at Emerald Bay, off Catalina Island, where they spent most weekends when they were aboard the *Splendour*, often inviting friends. Bombard remembers the girls, and R.J., as "waterdogs," while Natalie "liked the social part of it, but she used to kind of sun on the bow cap of the *Splendour*, sitting there reading, with a big floppy hat. I would never see her in a wet suit, or swimming." She was famous among friends for her Spanish eggs on Sunday mornings, cooking in the little galley on the *Splendour*, the only time Natalie went near a stove. She lavished love on every room inside the Canon house with Martha Stewart detail, but "the kitchen was not her place," chuckled her pal Griffin.

That year, when Natalie was thirty-seven and R.J. forty-five, they achieved the happiness in their married life that fans fantasized existed the first time, when their movie star faces graced the covers of every magazine in tender poses suggesting eternal bliss. Except for an "occasional fix-up," Natalie quit therapy after nineteen years, ten of them in analysis every day. "I'm fixed!" she laughed to Peggy Griffin.

With her newfound contentment, Natalie became more understanding of Mud, reaching a point where she was grateful for the *positive* things her child stardom brought her, since it led her to this happy stage. The fact that she would never have become a movie star without Mud, or that her mother had made it all happen "wasn't lost on Natalie," observes Griffin, "because Natalie loved her life, and she knew she couldn't have it both ways." Although she loved her mother, a part of Natalie still resented Mud for her lost childhood, the identity she forsook to create "Natalie Wood." "We're all human," as Griffin points out, "and sometimes we're contradictions within ourselves."

Friends who had known her in her fragile twenties marveled at Natalie's transformation. Leslie Bricusse thought of her as an iron butterfly. "She had tremendous courage, and you could tell that she wasn't as strong as she sometimes appeared to be." Yet Natalie was stronger than her vulnerability would suggest. That was the paradox.

She described *herself*, with pride, as "a survivor." It was Natasha, Natalie admitted, who brought her back from the dark side. "She said to me, 'A lot changed when I had Natasha,' " remembers her friend Griffin. "She suddenly realized she had to provide for her child and she had to account for herself."

The practical change was in Natalie's finances, which she placed in the management of a shrewd lawyer named Paul Ziffren during the great purge of 1966. More miraculous was the emotional strength she summoned once she became a mother. When Natasha would later watch *Rebel Without a Cause*, she hardly recognized the "hysterical and volatile and electric" actress she saw on the screen. "That's not how I remember her at all. I remember Mommy as this solid, grounded, direct, funny woman. Obviously there were times when she wasn't like that, but by the time she chose to have children she was very clear, strong and protective. She wasn't like the characters she played, these fragile girls. I felt safe around her."

The place inside Natalie where her monsters still resided troubled her, even at the height of her fulfillment. "Don't make it sound too terrific!" she superstitiously warned her writer friend Thomas Thompson that summer, as he prepared a magazine profile about her life with R.J. "Because, God knows, I don't have all the answers . . . I'm so happy now it's scary. I'm afraid to even talk about it for fear it will crumble or something."

23

MOTHERHOOD HELPED NATALIE rediscover her lost self, but it was still hard for her to be seen in public without The Badge, The Image, The Face, or any of the other names she devised for "Natalie Wood," the star personality she and Maria had created.

She made fun of being "a star" when she was with close friends like Peggy Griffin, as she had with Redford, yet Griffin noticed Natalie could never go out without her bracelet and "it was important to her to always look great, not just because she was a star . . . she spent a lot of time 'doing' herself." Griffin traced this insecurity to Mud, "who raised Natalie to never walk out of the house without the war paint glamour going, because you never know what producer's going to see you."

"She got herself done up *every single day*," stresses Lana, who had watched her sister since childhood in front of a makeup mirror, transforming herself into "Natalie Wood." Once, around 1976, when Lana picked up Natalie to take her to a dermatologist's office so they could both have face peels, "she had on full makeup." Lana was startled. "I said, 'What are you doing? They're gonna make you take it all off!' " "Well what if somebody sees me?" Natalie responded uncertainly.

She envied Lana for her ability to relax and be herself. "Natalie told me that when she would go on talk shows, she would pretend to be me. Because she was accustomed to having things scripted, and she was so afraid that she wouldn't be able to think of something to say, or that she would say something that wasn't quite right."

Natalie still possessed a compulsion to please, to entertain, to be perfect, even with a close chum like Peggy Griffin, who observed, "Natalie was always so happy. There was nothing sad about Natalie. She was happy and giggly and funny and just full of the devil. She wasn't sad at all." Other longer-term friends, such as Leslie Bricusse, who had witnessed her panic attack in the Mediterranean, believed that Natalie's vibrancy concealed a still fragile soul. "She was a very emotional girl, and I think instability was never far away, if she didn't have a support system around her."

Natalie's complex, at times conflicting, needs included expressing herself as an actress, even though motherhood fulfilled her.

She had not buried her dream to play Blanche DuBois, reacting with excitement to an unexpected offer the end of 1975 from Sir Laurence Olivier asking her to play the sensual Maggie the Cat to his Big Daddy, with R.J. as the alcoholic, homosexual Brick, in a televised production of Tennessee Williams' *Cat on a Hot Tin Roof*.

The invitation was "like a gift that fell out of the sky," Natalie said, giving her an opportunity to act with Olivier, the idol of *her* idol, Vivien Leigh, in a play by the creator of Blanche DuBois. As an added attraction, Olivier arranged to film the production in Manchester, England, set up like a play, with five weeks of rehearsal, shot in sequence.

Natalie spent two hours with Tennessee Williams in Cannes beforehand to make notes about her characterization of Maggie, and listened to friends from Mississippi to create an accent, turning hoarse from the screaming required to play the feisty Maggie, whom she would name with Alva, her other Tennessee Williams character, as the most challenging roles of her career. She compared acting with Olivier to starring with James Dean, describing them both as "fluid."

Olivier was "insane about Natalie," according to their costar Maureen Stapleton. Olivier, ironically, was in awe of Natalie's beauty, the very thing Vivien Leigh, her idol and his ex-wife, worried overshadowed *her* reputation as a serious actress. It was Natalie's insecurity about her movie star persona—The Badge—that encouraged Olivier to focus on her looks; in particular, a habit she had, at dinner, of checking her face in the blade of a knife. "She would just hold the knife horizontally across the front of her eyes," Bricusse recalls, "and move her face up and down so she could see everything on the blade. I thought that was rather cute." Olivier teased Natalie about it, Stapleton recalls. "He would hand her a knife and she would look in, like it was a mirror . . . and she was teasing *herself*."

That October, before NBC aired *Cat on a Hot Tin Roof*, the San Francisco Film Festival chose to honor Natalie for her contribution to films. The other honoree was actor Jack Nicholson, who had won the Oscar that year for *One Flew Over the Cuckoo's Nest*.

The public was invited to attend the afternoon event, which was to begin with a tribute to Nicholson, followed by an intermission. Afterward, the organizers of the festival planned to show film clips from Natalie's movies and then bring her onstage for a question-and-answer session. For Natalie, the tribute was especially poignant, since she was born in San Francisco, and it was the thirtieth anniversary of her 1946 film debut as "Natalie Wood" in *Tomorrow Is Forever*.

Mud, naturally, planned to attend, for it was *her* creation—actress "Natalie Wood"—that was being celebrated. The surprise was the reticent Fahd, who never went to any of Natalie's premieres and shyly avoided the limelight. For moral support, Natalie asked Peggy Griffin, Mart Crowley, and Howard Jeffrey to accompany her and R.J.

"She was very nervous at the last minute," recalls Griffin, who had coffee with Natalie in her hotel room the morning of the tribute. Griffin finally asked Natalie what was wrong. "And she hemmed and hawed, and she finally said, 'I just hope I'm not embarrassed out there. I'm gonna follow Jack Nicholson. Who comes to these things? All young kids. They hardly remember who I am. I'm going to walk out there after the montage of my films that they probably haven't even seen. What if nobody has a single question?' " Natalie was nervous, she told Griffin, "because she'd been out of the public eye for a long time, she'd been doing the 'mom thing.' "

When Natalie's part of the program finally came, Griffin recalls, "They showed this endless montage of her work—such a brilliant body of work—and all of us, even those of us who knew her, were just sitting there saying, 'Oh my God, she really did all this!' After it was over, the applause was deafening."

Natalie stood onstage beaming, clasping her hands together and holding them to her chest, touched that people remembered her. She told the audience it was odd to view her entire life on a movie screen, to see herself again as Margaret, the Austrian waif in *Tomorrow Is Forever*. "I was such a tiny little thing," she remarked wistfully, telling the audience that Natasha, her six-year-old daughter, looked exactly like *she* did in *Tomorrow Is Forever*.

"And when they started the Q&A," Griffin recalls, "it had to be almost an hour and a half later, when only forty-five minutes was allotted—that the moderator just said, 'I really have to limit this, folks.' They couldn't stop. They just went mad for her."

Maureen Stapleton, who had just appeared with Natalie in *Cat on a Hot Tin Roof*, later offered what may be the best description of Natalie's enduring appeal: "She had a quality that made you want things to turn out well for her in the end."

Natalie's most memorable moment occurred after she left the stage. As Griffin remembers, "She and I were standing there talking, and her dad, Nick, came up to her at the end, which wasn't like him. I remember he had tears in his eyes, and he couldn't get the words out of his mouth. He had this sweet little Russian accent, and he said, 'Natasha, I just realized how much work you've done.' She was on a high for the rest of the night."

The next spring, Natalie was nominated for an Emmy for *Cat on a Hot Tin Roof*, though she did not win. Worse, the production received wildly mixed reviews when it aired on NBC December 6, 1976, the twentieth anniversary of the date celebrated by Natalie and R.J. as their first night together. *TV Guide* had praised Natalie's Maggie as glowing with passion, "the performance of her career," while the *New York Times* reviewer excoriated her as "offering a campy imitation of Bette Davis," wearing "an inordinate amount of makeup for the sweltering Deep South," savaging R.J. for a performance "so low keyed that it is an effort to remember he is there at all."

Natalie's glamorous, sexy Maggie suffered by association with weaknesses in the production, as had her Alva in *This Property Is Condemned*. *Cat on a Hot Tin Roof* had been a rewarding experience creatively and personally for the Wagners, but it was not the triumph Natalie envisioned.

Though she doted on her daughters, by 1977 she was losing interest in decorating other people's houses, which had become a boutique business for Natalie, who half-jested that she and R.J. had become "middle-aged squares." They entertained their wide circle of adoring friends, many of them Hollywood royalty like Natalie, as she channeled her creativity into parties, hiring magicians and pianists to perform at the house, even hosting a Russian-themed dinner written about in *Bon Appetit*, with recipes courtesy of Mud.

Most of Natalie's interviews centered on her family life, with frequent references to time spent on the *Splendour*, which she had reproduced in miniature as a fifth anniversary gift for R.J. Natalie spoke of how she liked to be "on the water, and near the water, but not *in* the water." Peggy Griffin, who went out on the boat with the Wagners on occasional weekends, stayed on the deck with Natalie, sunbathing, while everyone else Jet-Skied or swam. "Our idea of athletics was putting suntan lotion on."

In early fall 1977, a few months after her thirty-ninth birthday, Natalie accepted a part in the big-budget special effects film *Meteor*, out of restlessness or boredom. There was only one thing about *Meteor* that interested Natalie, both she and director Ronald Neame would later confess:

the opportunity to play a Russian. Leslie Bricusse had recommended her to Neame for the role of a Russian translator assisting Sean Connery, whose character was trying to avert a meteor from colliding with Earth.

Natalie approached the part of the translator with the meticulous preparation she had Maggie, or Alva, listening to tapes of Mud speaking Russian to study the inflections. Griffin recalls, "She went to Berlitz and learned Russian, which she really didn't know. People don't give her enough credit for that. They thought she knew it; she understood words here and there, but her parents never taught her Russian. She crash-coursed it, which is very hard to do, with a different alphabet."

Natalie fine-tuned her Russian dialect to perfection to lose her parents' Ukrainian accent, hoping to create a "characterization," Kazan style, out of a stock character in a disaster movie, a frustrating experience for her. She was also approaching forty. "Aging in general was really tough for her," recalls Lana. "It's tough for any woman who is making her living by her appearance. Your face is six feet large on a gigantic screen, with people going, 'Wow, do you believe what she looks like now?' And Natalie was always worried that the film she was working on would be her last."

"One of the things that intrigued me to work with Natalie was her age," reveals Neame. "I was curious to see if she could make the transition from leading lady to character actress. Some women make that change perfectly—Kate Hepburn is one, Bette Davis. There are others that can't." Unfortunately for Neame, and for Natalie, her part was too one-dimensional for him to make the appraisal.

Natalie's hairdresser, Sugar Bates, recalls Neame as piqued with Natalie for wearing too much makeup to portray a translator from Russia, a habit that was ingrained in Natalie by Mud, part of Mud's concept of "Natalie Wood," the movie star. At thirty-nine, Natalie was more insecure about upholding that image. "The makeup man always tried to discourage her from wearing that heavy eye makeup, but she didn't care what period it was or anything, that was *her*."

To add to her distress on *Meteor*, Natalie knew she was being lit unflatteringly. Neame admits, "The cameraman was more concerned with the overall special effects in the film than making people look good." When Natalie viewed the rushes, "she didn't like what she saw . . . she looked a little hard," recalls an assistant director. "It really depicted what the film was, as opposed to her looking soft and gorgeous." Natalie asked Bates to bring her a mirror before every scene, "so she could look at herself and see how she was lit. She was smart." For the rest of the film, there was a struggle between Natalie and the cameraman, with Neame in the middle. "Natalie liked to look good," Neame discloses, "and I don't blame her." Neame's assistant, Ginger Mason, recalls, "It was not a great, happy, fun set."

Mason sensed that Natalie was going through a rough patch in her life because of her age, commenting, "Natalie, at that time, didn't seem very happy." Mason, who was an attractive and younger thirty-six, considered Natalie to be "really rude" to her, behavior that was uncharacteristic of Natalie, "who went out of her way to be kind to people," observed Sugar Bates, who had worked with Natalie for over fifteen years.

Natalie discussed with Bates, during filming, her concerns about how she was aging on screen, revealing that she would not have more than one glass of wine at night because it would show up the next day on camera. "She used to chew bubble gum to exercise her chin, because she was worried she had a double chin, and I said, 'Come on! You're so perfect!' She would laugh about stuff like that."

Bates ascribed Natalie's concern to "professional vanity," her legitimate worry that she would get fewer offers if she looked older. "Which was really smart, because she was selling herself as a product, and she wanted to look good." Natalie toyed with the idea of plastic surgery around her eyes, but in the end her phobia of doctors prevailed. Her friend Griffin observes, "Natalie was one of those people who would only think of surgery if it was life or death." Ironically, Mud, the source of her paranoia, had her eyes done then.

Ginger Mason noticed that when R.J. visited the set, Natalie was "insecure and possessive," which Mason interpreted as part of Natalie's concern about turning forty. "It was just my instinct . . . from whatever she was going through at the time, that period of life or something. He would always say hello or try to talk to me, and then he would back off. She was always very somber."

According to Lana, Natalie had an abiding fear that she would lose R.J. because of what had happened in their first marriage, and watched him closely.

Production designer Richard Sylbert, Natalie's friend since *Splendor in the Grass*, sat next to her and R.J. at a tribute to John Houseman during *Meteor*, accompanied by his wife, Sharmagne. Both were struck by how melancholy Natalie was, "one of those curious details" that lingered in their minds. Sharmagne Sylbert watched Natalie follow R.J. with her eyes all night, acting "horribly insecure." Natalie became distressed by a comment that she might be too old to play the schizophrenic teenager in *I Never Promised You a Rose Garden*, the passion project she had been trying to get made for years. "She looked really depressed," Richard Sylbert appraised that night, noticing a similar malaise in R.J. "She was not happy. I could feel it coming out of her pores. She really wanted this marriage to work."

Natalie's longtime friend and hairdresser, Bates, saw strains in the marriage during *Meteor* that were not present when she worked with Natalie on *The Affair*. Natalie suggested the cause was R.J.'s drinking. "That was how the industry was. After work, he'd have a few drinks, and it takes its toll." Natalie enjoyed her Pouilly Fuissé, but she was not by nature or by choice a heavy drinker, because of what she had witnessed with Fahd. "It was a way to relax after a hard day of shooting," as her stand-in and friend of twenty years, Roselle Gordon, describes.

No one questioned whether Natalie and R.J. were devoted to each other, or to their girls. "They *just adored* each other," extols Gordon, who watched them together over many years. "It was wonderful to see. What a caring, loving relationship, both of them. Sometimes you'd ask her something and she'd say, 'Well, let me ask R.J.,' and she would consult him. They were just courteous and kind and gentle with each other and loved each other. And I think it was better the second time than the first time, because they were both older, and lived longer and were able to find each other again and appreciate the marriage."

Natalie had another of her freakish water-related incidents while filming *Meteor*, when she and the rest of the cast were nearly buried in special effects water-based mud ("evil-looking stuff—thin and runny") on the MGM lot. "I remember tremendous courage from her," states Neame, who knew that Natalie was afraid to shoot those sequences.

"I said, 'Natalie, how can I help you?' and she insisted on doing it."

Even her ultramasculine costars, Sean Connery and Karl Malden, had trepidations. Malden recalls, "Those were difficult scenes for everybody, because it was very real. It was very real. The whole set was filled with tanks which would throw the mud down. There were a couple of times when I was *under*—when that mud was above me—and it was heavy mud, it wasn't just water. It was heavy, and you had a hard time raising yourself, and if you were under, you had a hard time to get up. And so you had to be careful and protect yourself as much as you could. But Natalie never said anything." According to Neame's on-set assistant, Connery "protected" Natalie during shooting the same way his character did, "and it wasn't theatrics."

During a break in filming the mud scene, Natalie had what is now a haunting interview with a reporter, foreshadowing her death. "My major concern isn't remembering the Russian, or getting my accent straight, it's not *drowning* in the mud. It's unpredictable. There's no question that there's a certain amount of pain. People can break an elbow or a leg or whatever by slipping and falling in their bathrooms or kitchens from a little water on the floor. But when you're involved with slippery mud and you don't know what kind of objects are in it—they can control it only to a certain point—there is always the possibility of something going awry. So everybody, including the stunt people, is a little nervous about this sequence."

In the same conversation, Natalie talked about her recurring near-accidents in water scenes, starting with *The Green Promise*. She brought up another one, from *The Great Race*, that the actors with her in the scene—Jack Lemmon, Peter Falk and Tony Curtis—strangely would not recall.

Natalie's account was eerily prescient of the way she would drown, off Catalina, a few years hence. "I remember there was an iceberg, and we got swept under it! I was wearing all of these furs and heavy things and because there was machinery underneath—the wave-makers that made everything move—if you got swept underneath there, I hate to think about what could have happened."

Meteor was not only a difficult shoot for Natalie physically and emotionally, "the special effects were so disastrous," Neame forthrightly admits, "the picture also was a disaster." Natalie would promote it with her usual enthusiasm when it came out late in 1979, over a year behind schedule, though for the first time since the early sixties, she requested to travel by train.

Though she concealed it, Natalie was still a prisoner of her fears and phobias, which made her continuing confrontation of them all the more brave.

Around the time she turned forty, July 1978, Natalie began acting more, unable to completely exorcise "Natalie Wood," the actress personality that dominated her life from the age of six to twenty-eight. "I think that's what I *do:* I'm an actress," as she struggled to explain the next year. "That's my work. That's what I know how to do, and that's what I get pleasure out of doing. That's my *expression*."

She admitted in interviews that she needed a "balance" between family and career, something Mud had taught her to believe was impossible. Natalie's solution was to take Natasha and Courtney, who were seven and four, to the set with her. "She loved the acting," acknowledges Peggy Griffin. "And quite frankly, to make a good living."

R.J. and Natalie reconfirmed their agreement that if one

of them was on location, the other would stay at home with their daughters. When Courtney was born, they had been fortunate to find a live-in cook/nanny named Willie Mae, who had become a trusted member of the family.

Although Natalie, with Elizabeth Taylor, was considered the last of the great movie stars, she was not a box office attraction, or a leading lady, anymore. *Bob and Carol and Ted and Alice* was her last commercial success, a sixties film that seemed frozen in another era. Natalie was clear-eyed about her declining stature, following R.J.'s lead by accepting a miniseries, where her illustrious name assured her a star role and star treatment, if not prestige. "She didn't hesitate to do television," Griffin recalls.

Natalie's choice in projects was the Deborah Kerr role in a CBS remake of *From Here to Eternity*, which she shot in Hawaii that summer. R.J., whose TV series had been abruptly canceled that spring, filmed the ABC miniseries *Pearl* in Hawaii prior to Natalie's television movie, providing the Wagners with a tropical summer vacation with Natasha and Courtney. Natalie had fun making *From Here to Eternity* for CBS, receiving a Golden Globe for her work, but it was not *Splendor in the Grass*, nor was it *Rebel Without a Cause*, or *Gypsy*.

R.J. was acutely aware that he was a television star, married to a legend. That June, while he was in Hawaii, director Tom Mankiewicz flew to the island to offer him what would be his next television series, the romantic comedy- drama *Hart to Hart*, which Mankiewicz was hoping he could convince R.J. and Natalie to star in together for ABC. Mankiewicz would later recall R.J.'s poignant response. "I sell soap," he told Mankiewicz. "My wife sells tickets."

Natalie did appear in the pilot episode of *Hart to Hart* in a cameo that fall, dressed as Scarlett O'Hara, the Vivien Leigh role she had always longed to play, listed in the credits as "Natasha Gurdin." *Hart to Hart*, which was produced by the Wagners' company, would make them wealthier than they already were, and enshrine R.J.'s television persona as the David Nivenish sophisticate he had been mimicking since he was a teenaged caddy. It would also foster a friendship between R.J. and his costar, Stefanie Powers, including Natalie, according to her friend Faye Nuell, who described R.J. and Powers as "brother and sister."

By November 1978, Natalie and R.J. seemed to have regained their emotional footing since the rocky period surrounding *Meteor*. R.J. was content starring in *Hart to Hart*, a surprise hit, and Natalie was in heaven portraying a vulnerable, wisecracking wife and mother admitted to a psychiatric ward for alcoholism, a role that finally gave expression to her passion for a project about emotional illness. The story also touched on subjects Natalie knew intimately: therapy, and drinking problems. The movie for television was based on a true story based on the life of producer Joyce Burditt, from Burditt's autobiographical book, *The Cracker Factory*.

"She had read the book," recalls Burditt, "and she loved it. She thought it was a real story about a real person, and it resonated with her. What the heroine in the book goes through requires some courage, and I think she identified with that. She loved the character, and I began to feel in the course of making this movie with her that I understood why it resonated with her: I think *she* was a very brave person with a good heart."

After the debacle of *Meteor*, Natalie leapt to appear in the very sort of movie that appealed to her: an intense drama with a character she related to, shot in a structured, controlled setting. "I've decided to go on instinct a lot," she told reporter Brian Linehan, "in terms of how I respond to material, rather than following a lot of advice. The times that I have done something that I didn't respond to emotionally right away, it's generally not worked out too well."

When Burditt found out that Natalie Wood was interested in playing her in the TV movie, "my first reaction was, 'My God, she's a movie star!' I was amazed." Burditt worked closely with Natalie, who originally wanted to produce the movie, but ABC had already optioned the book.

According to Burditt, Natalie took charge, quasi producing and directing the ABC movie, which was shot in Cleveland, and at the Veterans Administration Hospital in west L.A. "She had sort of an extreme focus on what she was doing, and what was going on around her in the production. She was a better producer than the producer. She was like the antithesis of the prima donna. It was not only 'Let's get it done,' but 'Let's get it done *right*.' She was a particular person. She was particular about the lighting, her makeup had to be right, the atmosphere on the set had to be right, it had to be totally professional. She didn't like a lax set, which I admired. She would have just been a great producer. It was her film."

Natalie said later, "I was just in *love* with *Cracker Factory*. They don't come along every minute. I think it's very fortunate to get a project like that once in a while, that your whole heart and soul is in."

She was the Natalie of old during *The Cracker Factory*, impassioned with every aspect of the movie, impressing each person by her kindness. John Martinelli, then a young assistant director, was charmed by Natalie's refusal to let him run any errands for her. "She did everything herself and demanded nothing from anybody. She was a delight. It was a role that called for no makeup in some scenes and she took it off and had no complaints. Just a beautiful lady." Richard Shapiro, the writer-producer, recalls, "It was sincere, she really wanted people to love her."

Natalie told Shapiro there were three things that were important to her. "The first thing was family—and her house, whatever project she was working on at the house. The second thing was work, which was very important to her. And she talked about a third, friendship. The first and most important was the family, then friends. People *adored* Natalie."

The production manager, Ed Ledding, would later make the comment that it sold Natalie short to call her a consummate professional. "She was gifted, and knowledgeable. A lot of people are professional that aren't necessarily gifted. *And* she was very nice. A lot of people that are professional are not particularly nice. She was very nice, she was very talented, and she was *very* knowledgeable."

Lola McNally, a sweet-natured veteran Hollywood hairdresser who was Natalie's choice to do her hair, saw the hidden, fragile side of Natalie during six weeks filming in Cleveland in the dead of winter. McNally recalls, "She took a liking to me right away and followed me around like a little puppy. When we'd be on the set, she'd come up every time before she did a scene and give me a hug, like, 'Let me get my breath.' "

One of the first nights the movie company was in Cleveland, McNally heard a knock on her hotel room door. When she opened it, Natalie was standing outside in her nightclothes. "She just said, 'Do you mind if I just come in and sleep with you?' I said, 'Fine. I'm from a big family. It doesn't matter to me.' And almost every night after that she'd come and crawl in bed with me because she didn't want to be alone. She was a little girl, even though she was grown up."

Natalie drew close to Lola McNally as if McNally were her mother all through filming, eating dinner with her every night, sleeping in McNally's bed with her, showing McNally the bump on her wrist, explaining how she was afraid to get it fixed. She talked about her fear of dark water and of drowning off a boat, which had happened to McNally's husband. McNally washed Natalie's hair for her the way Mud did when Natalie was a little girl, because she was afraid to put her head in the water: "We used to *bend* her over the bathtub and wash it." Natalie had McNally play child's games with her in the snow between takes. "We had a little contest sliding our shoes on the ice—little kid's stuff—sliding down the hallways to see who could go the fastest. She'd say that she won and I'd say, 'No, you didn't win, *I* won today.' And we'd go looking around the gardens, trying to figure out what flower was coming up, because they were covered with snow and ice."

Natalie, who had spent her childhood with Mud at her side every second of every day, even in the bathroom, felt lost without her alter ego, needing a mother figure to replace Maria, the missing half of "Natalie Wood."

Even when R.J. came to Cleveland for an extended visit, Natalie knocked on McNally's door, wistfully, asking to spend the night in her bed. "I think Natalie was a little girl. That's the only way I can put it. Like there's some little girls that are outgoing, and then there's those who sit back and suck their thumbs."

After Natalie's drowning, R.J. would allude to the ghosts from Natalie's childhood, saying, "She worked on herself for a very long time. And she wanted to be content. She wanted to be pleased about herself. Obviously, she was being pursued, inside, somehow. Some demons were in there pursuing her. Who knows?"

Natalie's private fragility, the lost little girl she revealed to McNally, gave special pathos to her identification with the character in *The Cracker Factory*, whose essence was Natalie. As Burditt describes, "The character is very, very vulnerable, and always trying to do her best . . . that constant striving, and that vulnerability, and looking for reasons to go on. And then going on *without* reasons—even if you don't have a reason you can understand, you go on anyway."

Burditt noticed, while Natalie was playing the part, "It's almost like different personalities would come up. When it required an intensity, you would see that in the determination, the intelligence; and then when it was appropriate for her to be vulnerable, you just wanted to take care of her. It was all in Natalie's personality. It was very real."

Natalie's divided personality as a child-woman was evident in the impressions she left on Burditt, who found her "very verbal, very persuasive. She was very generous, very openhearted, an amazingly complex woman in a good way. A lot of women with her drive, and determination to be perfect, don't have the empathy that she did. She had all of it, and she used all of it as an actress, too. I just thought the world of her. I thought she was brave and funny and very true to herself. She was a star, in the best sense, and didn't seem to do a lot of stuff that stars do."

—

That same winter, Natalie bought a condominium on Goshen in west Los Angeles for her aging parents. Fahd was a frail sixty-six, recently in intensive care for an irregular heartbeat. Mud, at seventy, still dwelled in the fanciful world of her imagination, decorating the new condominium with Natalie Wood glamour shots and the sad-eyed Keane portrait of her daughter hanging in the living room, "living Natalie's life," as Sugar Bates put it. Mud spent her time in Natalie's movie trailer, often with Natasha and Courtney. "Natalie was always doing things for her," recalls her stand-in. "She just *did* things for people." That summer, Lana prepared to marry for a fifth time. At forty, Natalie was still caretaker of the lost souls in her family, as she had been at six.

She accepted a part in a feature film the first few months of 1979, called *The Last Married Couple in America*, directed by her friend Gil Cates, who brought the script to Natalie. The movie was a lighthearted look at a couple with problems in their marriage who, in the end, choose the sanctity of the family—a theme that reflected Natalie's life, and drew her to the role. "She thought it was really a good part for her, so she and I became partners in crime. We figured out, Okay, who would be the best actor for this? At that time, it was George Segal."

The stresses in the Wagner marriage were revealed to Lola McNally, who had observed Natalie arguing in Cleveland with R.J. over the nights he spent out, drinking. "She wanted to be with him *alone*, and he wanted to be with the crew." John Martinelli, the A.D. on *Cracker Factory*, thought Natalie and R.J. were a great couple, "all class—class, class, class," though he noticed, as others did, "she and R.J. were checking each other out all the time, like they were making sure they weren't running off with somebody else."

There was also great tenderness. Joyce Burditt, who accompanied Natalie when she promoted *The Cracker Factory* that March, was backstage while Natalie did *The Merv Griffin Show*. "R.J. was watching the feed in the green room, and he was just sitting there, and I thought, 'Oh my God, he's so proud of her.' You could just see it in his face. He had been chatting, he was a very charming guy, with a wonderful sense of humor, and the minute she started to talk, he just looked at the monitor at the feed and was really into it, and I thought, 'How nice. How nice for her, how nice for him.' It gave me a really good feeling."

Burditt's perception was that "it seemed to be a good time in Natalie's life. R.J. was there, they were very sweet with each other, he was so supportive of her. She was a nice person who liked her life, liked her kids, liked her husband, and that showed, too."

That spring, as she was finishing *The Last Married Couple in America*, Natalie gave a spate of interviews comparing her marriage with R.J. to the couple she and George Segal were playing in the picture, a husband and wife who go through a rocky time and come through in the end, the way Natalie liked things to turn out. The *Saturday Evening Post* profile of her and R.J. that March was even called "Happily Ever After." Just like the fairy tale that Natalie had longed for as a child.

When she finished filming *The Last Married Couple* in April, Natalie finally fulfilled her lifelong dream to travel to Russia, part of her journey to rediscover Natasha Gurdin. The trip was to film an NBC documentary called *Treasures of the Hermitage*, an on-camera tour of the museum, hosted by Natalie and Peter Ustinov.

Natalie envisioned the trip as a romantic odyssey to her

homeland, the Russia she knew from sitting on Fahd's lap, looking at the drawings in his fairy storybooks. Or the Russia she heard about from Mud, who spoke in whispers about jeweled aristocrats in ballgowns carrying mink muffs on wintry nights. She imagined herself Anna Karenina, riding the *Trans-Siberian Express* eating caviar by candlelight, listening to the balalaika.

Natalie had planned that she and R.J. would take Natasha and Courtney to Russia, with Mud and Fahd as guides. Fahd refused to go. "Her father still had great anger at what happened after they left Russia," recalls Peggy Griffin. "Their family members were all killed. Actually, he got very stressful when Natalie agreed to do that show." Maria wanted no part of Russia, still traumatized over seeing her brother hanged, paranoid that she would be killed, insistent that Natalie take a bodyguard.

Natalie and R.J. decided to fly to Moscow without their daughters, accompanied by Natalie's friend, writer Thomas Thompson. She made arrangements to telephone Natasha and Courtney twice daily, worried about the two-week separation.

Natalie landed in Moscow wrapped in sable, her image of Russia. The Russia she encountered in person—drab, stifling, unemotional—was nothing like the magical place in her mind. "I went through so many different emotions: seeing the place where my parents were born, viewing all the things I'd read about . . . I found it a very moving experience, and yet, it made me feel more deeply American than ever."

When she and R.J. went through customs in New York, Thompson said later, Natalie burst into "The Star-Spangled Banner."

—

As the Wagners returned home to Beverly Hills, their faces were on the cover of *Look* magazine, with the headline "Hollywood's Most Exciting Couple."

Inside was a stunning full-page shot of Natalie, at forty, wearing only her magic bracelet, with the caption "NATALIE WOOD: HOLLYWOOD'S NUMBER ONE SURVIVOR." The article, written by her friend Thomas Thompson, began:

> The bottom-line fascination we hold for Hollywood is not the gold, not even the magic, but the suspense of tragedy—the waiting for those absurdly beautiful people to fall off the tightrope and wreck their lives. James Dean was handsome and strange, but he wrapped his body in a fatal gesture that was somehow appropriate. Marilyn Monroe died with the dark roots of her blonde hair showing, her toe nails in need of clipping, her stomach full of barbiturates . . .
>
> This melancholy and melodramatic throat-clearing is by way of making a few comments about a woman who refuses to fall. If winning is surviving, then Natalie Wood is the number one seed. For almost 20 years she and I have been friends, but not until the last years have I stopped holding my breath . . .

Natalie, Thompson concluded, had fought her demons and won.

ACT FIVE

Dark Water

(1980–1981)

"You'll be lost at sea, no question, absolutely vanish, but not quite without a trace: because, don't think that someone like you won't have an influence."

Anton Chekhov

[*Three Sisters*]

24

AROUND THE TIME SHE RETURNED from Russia, Natalie began to gather her thoughts for an autobiography, scribbling notes on a yellow legal pad late at night, when R.J. was frequently out for the evening and her two daughters, six cats and several dogs were asleep, leaving the house on Canon quiet and still.

Olga remembers Natalie asking their mother to record her memories of Siberia, and of Harbin, into a tape player, so that Natalie could include in her memoir her Russian heritage, which defined Natalie to herself, even though Maria's doubtlessly fantastical version of her childhood in Russia would be more properly written as fiction. Natalie hid her early musings, a few lines from a chapter or two, in a fur closet, possibly wrapped inside the sable coat she wore in Leningrad during her quest to unearth "Natasha."

She once joked to Mart Crowley that if she ever wrote the story of her life, she was going to call it *I Got What I Wanted.* In Natalie's star-crossed existence, the title is an ironic reminder of the passage from a play by Oscar Wilde: "In this world, there are only two tragedies. One is not getting what one wants, and the other is getting it."

One thing Natalie did reveal about the book she intended to write was a theme that would relate to her deep fear of dark water, she told a writer for the *New York Daily News* in 1979. "I've been terrified of the water . . . and yet it seems I'm forced to go into it on every movie that I make."

She would have that experience one last time later that year, in a television movie called *The Memory of Eva Ryker*, which she accepted as a disappointing alternative to the part she really desired, the repressed mother in *Ordinary People*, the psychological drama Robert Redford had chosen as his first film to direct. At the time, neither *Meteor* nor *The Last Married Couple in America* had been released. Natalie's only other feature in a decade was the unremarkable *Peeper*.

Redford knew Natalie's movie career was on the wane. "She started declining in her work—not that the work wasn't good, she just did less. She had decided to try motherhood, and that took her away from the career. And you don't come back easy." When Redford heard that Natalie was interested in the part of the mother in *Ordinary People*, he felt wrenched. "She had been out of work for a while, and her name came up, and I would have loved to have made it work, but I couldn't. I really had Mary Tyler Moore in mind, and I was convicted on that. And Natalie had requested just a conversation about it, and that was kind of painful. I would love to have done it, but I just didn't see her for that particular role."

Natalie's request would be their last contact before she drowned, to the chagrin of Redford, who not only had deep feelings for Natalie, but also felt an emotional debt to her for choosing him as her costar in *Inside Daisy Clover*.

That same summer, Natalie, a prolific reader, bought William Styron's powerful bestseller, *Sophie's Choice*, about the tragic Polish émigré forced to choose which child to sacrifice to Nazis. She developed an instant passion for the book, and its central character, reacting as she had years before to Marjorie Morningstar. "We were on the boat," recalls Peggy Griffin, "and she was telling me about this incredible character. Of course she was relating to everything—to the actress, to the mother-child story—and she was almost *acting* it, she got so excited. I remember she did a little scene from it, with an accent."

Natalie kept a close eye on the film rights, "drooling" to play Sophie, the kind of challenging role that would revitalize her feature career. When *Meteor* was finally released that November, the reviews were as dismal as filming it had been for Natalie, criticisms she admitted were hurtful. *The Cracker Factory*, the TV movie she had put her heart and soul into, was a modest success that spring, though Natalie would not be nominated for an Emmy, an oversight Joyce Burditt found "unfathomable."

Fahd was in declining health, suffering a series of small heart attacks that Peggy Griffin associated with his stress over Natalie's trip to Russia. "Who knows what stirred it up? It didn't happen right there on the spot, but it wasn't long after." Natalie spent increasing amounts of time at her parents' condominium, hoping to get closer to her father. When Griffin mentioned to Natalie how *she* had taken *her* father out for his seventieth birthday, just the two of them, Natalie's face lit up. "And a couple of days later, she called me and said, 'I just called Fahd and asked him to have dinner with me alone.' " At the last minute, Fahd canceled. "Natalie said she always knew that was Mud, not wanting it to happen—finding some health reason or something."

In the weeks before Christmas, Natalie filmed *The Memory of Eva Ryker*, a movie for CBS in which she played an heiress with a repressed childhood memory of seeing her mother drown aboard the *Queen Anne* luxury liner in 1939. In flashback, Natalie also portrayed the heiress's mother, submerged in water as the *Queen Anne* sinks into the sea.

"Oh, she hated that movie," recalls Griffin. "She just thought everything, including herself, was terrible in it." Even the art director, Duane Alt, was surprised to work with Natalie Wood. "She was certainly, what should I say, much more talented than to really have done this little movie of the week thing, and she obviously was used to doing big number pictures . . . but she was 100% into this thing. There was something very, very personal that she felt about this."

Natalie arranged to be hypnotized for the regression scene, studying how different parts of the body physically react in the moments before death. In a macabre foreshadowing, she "practiced" drowning to prepare for the flashback scene on the boat, which was going to be shot on the *Queen Mary*, in Long Beach, where a luxurious dressing room had been prepared for Natalie. "At dinner at our house one night," she told a reporter, "everyone did his version of how the death scene should be played. If anyone looked in the window that night, he would have thought we were all crazy." Once filming began, it was like a series of Chinese water tortures for Natalie.

According to Walter Grauman, the director, Natalie could tolerate the scene where she floated through the ship's waterlogged cabin, "because of the controlled circumstances," though Grauman "knew she was scared."

What panicked Natalie, he found out, was a sequence in the Pacific Ocean with actor Bradford Dillman, to be filmed at Paradise Cove, where Natalie and R.J. were married on the *Ramblin' Rose*. "I was explaining to her a scene where Brad chases her down the beach, on the sand, and then she plunges down into the water, and he pursues her into the water and there's this desperate struggle between them." Natalie responded, "Walter, I'll do anything you ask, but there's one thing I'm deathly afraid of, and that's dark water—deep, dark water." Grauman recalls, "She had had premonitions and dreams about dark water." Natalie had similar conversations during filming with her costume designer, Grady Hunt, telling Hunt about a recurring premonition she was going to die in dark water.

Grauman's solution was to show Natalie running on the sand and then insert a cutaway of her in a close-up shot in a water tank, "and then I had a stunt double go in the *real* ocean. Natalie was panic-stricken over dark water, deep dark water."

She was even terrified to get into the water tank at the studio. "I remember *I* went in the tank," recalls Bradford Dillman. "I was the guy to be the guinea pig to specify exactly where she could stand to show her that her head would still be above water. She was really kind of pathologically frightened . . . ultimately she did go in, and I remember that she was holding on to the edge rather fearfully. Eventually she had to let go of the edge and she had to tread water, or pretend to be treading water, and she *did* it, and we all gave her a round of applause."

Actor Robert Foxworth, who was also in the tank sequence with Natalie, remembers holding her in his arms, with Natalie "just shaking like a leaf." Duane Alt, who set up the scene, comments: "I think everybody really remembers that day very specifically because she was petrified . . . I really was shocked how frightened she was."

With the exception of her demons, Natalie was in command on *Eva Ryker*, as she had been on *The Cracker Factory*. "You thought this was *her* film," a crewman recalls. "It seemed that important. She was so focused, and watching the details." Dillman, an Actors Studio graduate, found Natalie "driven to be the best she possibly could be."

He was fascinated by her technique, which he considered to be the opposite of Method acting, "in the sense that she acted from the outside in. Hers was a very different kind of a technique. It was *technical*, meaning knowing where her marks were, where the lights were, where the key lights were . . . that she would show to advantage. There are certain actresses who could care less about how they look. They're there to be admired as *actresses*. That was not Natalie's game. She wanted everything to be perfect for her."

Exactly the way Mud had trained her, from the age of six.

Sugar Bates returned to do Natalie's hair during *Eva Ryker*, noticing that Natalie was under a great deal of stress in her personal life, exacerbated by R.J.'s drinking, which Bates said Natalie had told her had worsened since *Meteor*. "*She* just seemed really in good shape and she loved the kids, but Wagner was drinking quite a lot," Bates sympathized with Natalie. "My husband was, too, so we had a lot of talks about that."

Natalie had been on a health kick since the mid-sixties, and successfully quit smoking that year. Although she still took a sleeping pill every night, an occasional diet pill, and prescription mood regulators as needed, she was uncomfortable with social drugs, which were popular in Hollywood. "We had a talk about it," states Bates. "She just wasn't into drugs. She said, 'I'm not going to those parties where they put out the line of cocaine and stuff.' " The Wagners' older Hollywood crowd "didn't take drugs and things," observed Bates. "They just drank."

Alcohol was one of the demons in Natalie's life, beginning when she was a little girl, cowering in a corner during Fahd's drunken rages. She knew the dangers of drinking, part of what had drawn her to *The Cracker Factory*. She told Sugar Bates she had learned in analysis to be firm with alcoholics, the reason she locked the liquor cabinet if Fahd was around, and once paid for Mart Crowley to get therapy. "When Mart was drinking a lot, she finally banned him from her house. She was such a loyal friend, and she had always been so giving, but finally she learned that it wasn't helpful. She was learning not to be an enabler."

Natalie's own drinking was sporadic. After her "Volga boatman" period as a rebel teen, she scaled back to a glass or two of Pouilly Fuissé, a martini, or a drink called a Scorpion on social occasions. By the time she made *Eva Ryker*, she was drinking more than in previous years, partly as a result of the Wagners' lifestyle. "Natalie may have enjoyed drinking wine, but she never got sloppy or falling down. She never pushed it," observed Lana. "I never saw her out of control. Wine is also a very European thing—you have wine with dinner; in sophisticated circles, you drink wine with dinner."

Walter Grauman, Natalie's director on *Eva Ryker*, went out with the Wagners one night. "All I know is that we put away a number of bottles of wine when we were out to dinner. We had a marvelous time, but I had a hangover the next morning, and I assume that they did, too."

Duane Alt, one of the production crew, was a drinking buddy of R.J.'s from previous TV projects. "We'd just kill the afternoon, shooting the bull in the back part of the stage and *he* liked to drink, I know that. He'd say, 'Hey, why don't we take off and go get a beer or something? Let's go get something.' " Alt, a Hollywood veteran, understood that alcohol relieved the pressures of stardom. "I think that's something the public doesn't understand.

When you live at such an intense level, and you have to be seen as the best you can be, it's a tough, tough thing. You've got to find some relaxation out of it to survive."

That December 6, after a long day's filming, Bates styled Natalie's hair in her dressing room on the *Queen Mary*, while Natalie put on something spectacular to meet R.J. for their special anniversary. "She was really tired, but he loved to celebrate, he loved to do these lovely parties and things. But she wasn't looking forward to it, because she knew what was going to happen."

Bates recalls commiserating while Natalie talked about R.J.'s drinking. "I was thinking, 'Where will she go from here?' Because he loved the kids, too. My gut feeling at that point was that the family was the most important, and she would have done anything she could have done to make it work. She'd gotten old enough that she knew you don't just run off and expect to find somebody else. If you don't solve what you're doing, it's not going to get any better. She had done enough work on herself that she knew that. I didn't get the feeling that she'd walk away unless something worse happened."

The Wagners began the new year of 1980 in Hollywood style. Mud accompanied them to the premiere of *The Last Married Couple in America* early in February, enjoying what would be her last blush in the public spotlight of Natalie Wood.

Natalie did a round of interviews to promote her film about the sanctity of marriage, saying publicly what Bates privately intuited in her dressing room. "A lot of people just walk away from a relationship rather than trying to make it work," Natalie told an interviewer. "Really, that's not very healthy."

Natalie surprised R.J. a few days later with a lavish party at a starry, stylish Beverly Hills restaurant called the Bistro, celebrating his fiftieth birthday on February 10. Natalie invited their close friends as well as the extraordinary personages of Hollywood within their magic circle—David Niven, Christopher Plummer, Gene Kelly, Henry Fonda, Robert Mitchum—part of the glue that held them together as a couple.

The Wagners, like F. Scott Fitzgerald's observation about the very rich, were different, even among their peers. "They were *stars*," Bradford Dillman muses. "R.J. was married to Hollywood and the idea of stardom. And there are people, of course, who just luxuriate in that." Roderick Mann, a Hollywood correspondent who had known Natalie and R.J. since the 1950s, described their partnership as a kind of prestige. "To pull in people like that for a friendly party—full of directors and movie stars, everybody was there. They were just terrific, and they were generous friends."

Peggy Griffin characterized them as "a team," for they were joint partners in a Hollywood fairy tale. Sue Russell, a British journalist based in Los Angeles, observed the Wagners sitting for a magazine cover in this period. She was spellbound watching them carry on a conversation with each other at the same time as the photographer was taking their pictures—holding their smiles as they discussed their plans for the day behind clenched teeth, like ventriloquists.

Natalie received enthusiastic reviews for her comedy turn, and her beauty, in *The Last Married Couple in America*, but the film was dismissed as a second-rate *Bob and Carol and Ted and Alice*, as *New York Times* critic Vincent Canby suggested. During filming, Natalie bemoaned to George Segal, "It's one typed role after another, and pretty soon you forget everything. You forget why you're here, why you're doing it."

She would spend the whole of 1980 away from the camera, enjoying a family holiday with R.J. and the girls in Europe during R.J.'s spring hiatus from *Hart to Hart*. The British Film Institute honored Natalie in April with a retrospective, and then the Wagners visited David Niven in France, a spring tradition.

Niven, like all of Hollywood, adored Natalie. "David always said she gave off an aura of sex like musk," relates Roderick Mann, who regularly saw the Wagners on their trips to Europe.

Mann sensed from his encounters with Natalie that she was a lonely woman, "even when she was married to Bob. It was like two separate people in some way. Sometimes two people meld together and are really one. They were sort of separate, I always felt." In Mann's view, R.J.'s charm masked a serious, sometimes dull nature. He compared Natalie to a joyous child. "Very hard to resist Natalie. She was never boring." Mann observed that Natalie was the dominant spouse, as did Lana, who felt that R.J., at times, resented being "Mr. Wood," which came out in "little verbal barbs here and there." Mann observed, "Natalie was her own person. Very much so, and she was stronger than Bob. Maybe that's a Russian thing, but there was strength there, beneath that childish exterior." Mann witnessed a few rows between R.J. and Natalie, including one "that went on a bit," when R.J. told Mann that Natalie "took an ugly pill. And they'd be at each other for whatever the reason."

They returned from their trip abroad in May to an unspectacular reaction to *The Memory of Eva Ryker* on CBS. Natalie signed a contract to renew an earlier agreement with ICM as her talent agency, where Michael Black and the powerful Guy McElwaine represented her. She still longed to play Sophie in *Sophie's Choice*, which her friend Alan Pakula had optioned as a feature film; looking for ways to revitalize her career.

She spent all of the summer, and the fall, tending to motherly duties or at Fahd's bedside, for he was weakening from a bad heart, exacerbated by years of alcohol abuse. "She was constantly at the hospital with Nick," states Peggy Griffin. "Months and months and months. There was one point at which Nick was in the hospital in Long Beach and R.J. pulled his back out and he was in traction at Cedars, and Natalie was back and forth between the two of them, plus picking the kids up at school. And she just did it all. She wasn't one to say, 'Oh, why me?' or call in an army of maids to do this and that. They needed *her*, not somebody she'd send."

In October, when Fahd had his final heart attack, Natalie kept a promise to let him die at home, arranging for a hospital bed in his den and a round-the-clock nurse. Natalie, Lana believed, had made peace with their father's alcoholic rage. Shirley Moore, Maria's close friend, recalls Natalie at the Gurdins' condominium, sitting with a bowl of her mother's Russian eggplant, next to Fahd's frail body, staring into his still-handsome face. "She was there every day. She was holding his hand, and reading to him, and just so sweet to him. That's where he died. It was kind of sad."

Natalie made arrangements for a memorial service at Westwood Chapel, though Fahd's final resting place would be a Serbian cemetery south of San Francisco. The night before the wake, Natalie scheduled a viewing of the body, a Russian Orthodox tradition. "People got confused, and nobody, not one person, came to the viewing," recalls Griffin. "Natalie was there alone." She told Griffin afterward, "I had such a peaceful sense of being alone with him for the first time."

Fahd's death was a powerfully emotional experience for Natalie, who was struggling, still, to vanquish the ghosts of her childhood, conflicted with feelings of love and loss and unresolved resentment. "She was just so filled with grief for her father, I can't even describe it," remembers Griffin. Natalie gave the eulogy at the Westwood Chapel on November 7, 1980, a tender tribute to the papa who spent all his money in 1938 to buy his Natasha the finest carriage in San Francisco, fit for Anastasia:

> I used to call him Papa. Lana called him Pop. To R.J. he was Fahd. Then, when he had his grandchildren, Natasha, Courtney, and Evie, they called him Deda. So did Katie . . . he was always surrounded by his family of little women . . .
>
> I am his firstborn daughter and I will always have so many memories of my Papa, my Deda, my Fahd . . . his wife who loved him and shared his life for over forty years, he called Musia. My mother, Musia, was so devoted to him during his long and difficult illness—she cooked his special dishes and went without sleep herself . . . shall no doubt miss him most of all. But it must be a comfort for her to know that she was the love of his life . . .
>
> When we used to tell Natasha and Courtney stories about the three bears—when Goldilocks breaks the littlest bear's chair—we always added "But never mind, Deda will fix it" because he always seemed to be able to fix anything for us . . .
>
> I think many of us here have had the supreme pleasure of watching and listening to him play his

> balalaika . . . Fahd loved music, singing, dancing and he was never embarrassed to let his feelings show. He was far too much a man to ever worry about having anyone see his tears. He sometimes cried in sorrow, but often in joy . . .
>
> Aren't we lucky to have witnessed some of his rich, wonderful Russian explosions. He was passionate and could be wild—but his underside was soft and gentle . . .
>
> My daughter, Natasha, wrote a beautiful letter to her Deda . . . "Deda, I didn't believe you would die and I never will because you're alive with me . . . Natasha."
>
> My youngest daughter, Courtney . . . wrote "Dear Deda—I hope you have a nice time in heaven, Love Courtney."
>
> And now I must say my farewell. I would like to say to my father a last goodnight—"*Spakoynee Noch*" . . . *Spakoynee noch, Papachka.*

Six weeks after Fahd's death, Natalie asked her friend Peggy Griffin to go with her and Natasha and Courtney to a final memorial service, a Russian tradition. Griffin would never forget Natalie's face as she said her last farewell to her Fahd. "I think she had a lot of unfinished business, and she really loved him. She just loved him."

Natalie's deep and complicated feelings for Fahd were not unlike her love for R.J. Both R.J. and Nick were tender, handsome, artistic men with a tendency to be weak, and to have a drink to escape a private anguish.

That New Year's Eve, Natalie and R.J. gave a glittering black-tie dinner at their house on Canon, one of the legendary soirees they would be remembered by. "To be at a party at the Wagners' was really extraordinary," Gil Cates would say. "I went to several New Year's Eve parties there where everyone from David Niven to—I remember one New Year's Eve party, about 1:30 in the morning—Cary Grant dropped by, just to say hello." The magnet was Natalie. "Natalie attracted people in an amazing way. People loved being around her, and not because she was a star, because I know a lot of stars that people don't love to be around. She was fun, she had this tinkly laugh, it was just so adorable—I can hear it, it was just light and merry—just this merry, merry laugh."

At the stroke of midnight on December 31, 1980, R.J., in his tuxedo, picked up his glass of Dom Perignon and held it up to a sparklingly glamorous Natalie, as their crush of celebrated guests fell silent. "I love you, my darling Natalie," he said, in a toast reminiscent of the Cary Grant–romantic way he had dropped an engagement ring into her champagne glass on a December night, twenty-three years before. "In fact," he added, "you take my breath away."

It would be Natalie's last New Year's Eve.

25

NATALIE AND MARIA, THE TWO personalities intertwined in the actress persona of "Natalie Wood," each began 1981 in upheaval.

For all her fantasizing about her sea captain, and the stress of living with Fahd's brooding, brawling Russian despair, Mud was bereft without the matinee-handsome husband who gave her what she considered her greatest gift: Natasha.

She reacted to Nick's passing with her usual high drama, going into "the fits," drawing Olga to Los Angeles so the three sisters could figure out what to do with Musia. Mud went back and forth from her condominium to Lana's apartment to the place she felt she belonged, with Natalie, an arrangement that strained Natalie and R.J.'s increasingly delicate balance.

Something was stirring in Natalie that began during Fahd's long illness. She was going through a creative reawakening, harkening to her youthful passion for projects that stimulated the artist side of her rather than the "movie star" personality that reflected Maria and was reinforced by her Hollywood marriage to R.J.

As Fahd lay dying, Natalie read a version of *Anastasia*, the play that had moved her as a teenager, serendipitously presented to her late in 1980 by her friend Robert Fryer, the artistic director at the Ahmanson Theater, who hoped to interest Natalie in playing the lead role on the stage. During this interval of heightened family drama, less than a year after her trip to Russia, the mystery story of the putative Romanov duchess sparked something in Natalie, who in the sixties had dreamt of costarring on stage with Robert Redford. "The play was even more wonderful than I remembered," she said that year. "I had a strong emotional reaction to it and, perhaps because of my Russian heritage, I identified with the characters. All my life I have had my best experiences when I have responded to material with my heart before my mind."

Mud gathered together with great excitement her treasured photographs of the Romanovs, still in their frames, ecstatic at her beloved Natasha playing a member of the Russian royal family that she had always claimed as her own. Natalie immersed herself in her mother's buried treasures to prepare for the role, asking Mud if she could use the family portrait of the Zudilovs taken in Siberia in 1919 as a prop when she played Anastasia. "She told me, 'Mud, can I borrow it? I can put it on the stage.' She said, 'Can I have the Romanov family, too, so it will be very authentic on the stage, too?' "

Natalie's true inspiration for *Anastasia* was Fahd. She told her friend Roderick Mann how her father had slept with a picture of the Romanovs in his bedroom, where she had seen it from her crib. "To him they were saints," she explained. "He was always talking about the tragedy of the massacre."

Natalie approached the February 1982 stage production with the same mingled terror and elation she had *Rebel* and *Splendor in the Grass*, part of what attracted her to it. She even quoted Kazan's long-ago advice to her—"Don't be afraid to make a fool of yourself"—as a catalyst.

Lana noticed unease in Natalie that winter. "There was contentment, definitely—she had her kids and she had a lovely home and she had R.J., who she just absolutely was madly in love with—but she was concerned about her work, and she was concerned about *life*."

At forty-two, with lackluster films and television movies becoming her stock in trade, Natalie made other sweeping changes. Early in 1981, she formed a production company with Bill Storke, a television executive friend of R.J.'s, acquiring rights to a few books to adapt into films, explaining, "The business side of acting—movies anyway—is changing to the point where I don't think it's practical to sit around and wait for scripts to come in. I find I enjoy buying books and working with writers. And that's an area I didn't think I'd ever find myself in." Her friend Griffin observes, "Natalie was so smart and realistic. She knew, at forty-two, she wasn't going to be the leading lady anymore. And she was a survivor."

She clearly wanted to resurrect her gloried Kazan/Ray past, telling a writer, "I've always thought it was good to be ambitious in terms of growing and realizing your potential . . . I want to take some risks and work." Natalie watched in despair from the sidelines as other actresses vied for *Sophie's Choice*, where once *she* would have been the frontrunner. She was "not overly thrilled" with her own recent films.

Natalie saw an opportunity to be involved in something substantive by playing Zelda Fitzgerald, the schizophrenic flapper she had emulated at sixteen with Hopper and Adams. She made overtures to Nancy Milford, the New York–based biographer of the respected *Zelda*, arranging for Milford to fly to Beverly Hills to convince her that she was Zelda, as she had done with Nick Ray when she wanted to play Judy, or Kazan for the part of Deanie, or Herman Wouk, to play Marjorie Morningstar. Natalie wanted the rights to *Zelda* desperately, Milford could tell, "to do a serious piece of work."

The schism between Natalie the star, and Natalie the artist, was evident in her encounters with the New York author. Milford recalls Natalie in a "ridiculous" cowboy hat, taking her to a party at John Schlesinger's house, introducing her to Richard Gere, trying to impress her. She noticed the Wagners had matching Mercedes "with little shag rugs inside, which had intertwined initials. Which seemed to me almost outrageous—which, of course, may be just a Hollywood gesture."

Milford at first questioned whether Natalie was capable of portraying the intricate Zelda. "So as I would pull back a little, she would be more aggressively, 'Well, what kind of person do you want me to *be?*' or 'Do you want me to be *crazier?*' There was this dance going on. On the one hand, she was trying to charm me or trying to sell me or trying to give me the feeling that she could *be* this complex woman, and on the other hand, looking right *at* you, smoldering dark eyes, and yet very wary." Natalie let Milford know "she knew whereof she spoke" concerning neurotic behavior. "She *was* intense, and quite lovely, and sort of *screwy*, I thought."

While Milford was in town, Natalie took her to Cedars to visit R.J., who was in the hospital for a herniated disc. Mart Crowley, who was now working for R.J., went along, carrying a plastic cup appearing to be a malted milk, "and in fact it was loaded with vodka or booze of some sort." Like naughty children, Crowley and Natalie sneaked the glass to R.J..

Milford perceived, as had Lana, that Natalie "was not in great shape" emotionally. "She was at that—sort of feeling like her career was washed up. She was a woman who seemed to be profoundly unsure of herself, while behaving as if, or acting as if, everything's fine: great marriage to a great guy, great kids, great house . . . 'but I'm a *complicated* woman.' " When Milford left L.A., she verbally agreed to let Natalie option her book, "more favorably impressed by her than I thought I would be." She caught glimpses of Natalie's vulnerability, finding her fragile in some way. "I thought she *could* have been a remarkable Zelda. I know it seems unlikely, but I did."

Natalie spent most of that winter and early spring under the same roof with the husbandless Mud, who had swept into the Wagners' house, where she passed her days devising elaborate ways to provoke arguments between Natalie and R.J. "She just was a busybody," as Bates oversimplified it, "and always on Natalie's case. The mother just drove her crazy, with her ways. Natalie would have liked to have been away from her, not worry about her—'Just let me live my life'—but her mother would always come in and cause upsets and things. And I can't tell you exactly what it was, because I don't know."

In public, Maria hero-worshipped the suave, charming R.J., reveling in the Wagners' prestige as Hollywood's favorite couple. Away from the spotlight, Mud muttered darkly and superstitiously about "no good coming of this," creating further tension over his drinking. "Natalie was mad at her mother," relates Robert Hyatt, who heard all about it from his mother Jean, and from Mud. "Marie was in the guest house, taking care of the kids, like a built-in babysitter. She was next to Natalie—that was her gig. But she was constantly trying to get Natalie to leave Wagner, constantly, and I think she had crossed the line, had told some stories to the kids, I don't know what about. Whatever it was, Natalie got pissed."

The straw, for Natalie, was Mud's fixation on ten-year-old Natasha, her namesake, look-alike daughter. When Natalie saw her mother fawn over Natasha, ignoring seven-year-old Courtney, it brought back all the ghosts of Natalie's star-child past with Lana, the invisible sister. To protect her daughters and preserve her marriage, Natalie evicted Mud. "Wagner threw Marie out," states Hyatt. Mud sought refuge, ironically, with Lana, who was newly divorced, living with *her* daughter, Evan.

The rift between Natalie and Maria did not sever their unholy bond; Natalie continued to phone her alter ego every morning, and Mud still worshipped the ground on which Natalie walked. Peggy Griffin, Natalie's close friend, did not characterize Natalie's feelings for Mud as "love-hate," even at this extreme stage. "I don't think the word 'hate' would ever come into it, maybe some resentment. But if there was a problem, Natalie was there. She was very family-oriented."

After learning that *Hart to Hart* had been renewed, the Wagners escaped to the south of France for their spring pilgrimage, stopping in Paris. While she and R.J. were at Maxim's having dinner, Natalie took a call from John Foreman, the producer friend who reunited them at his "fateful" 1970 dinner party.

Foreman tracked Natalie down in Paris to tell her about a part he was developing for her in an unusual MGM feature about an experimental machine with sensory devices allowing one person to experience the emotions of another, even during death. The screenwriter's idea was "to take the audience through a death experience, and explore that mystery." The script was called *Brainstorm*. Because the premise was science fiction, Foreman had chosen a gifted young expert in special effects named Douglas Trumbull, famous for his electronic wizardry in *2001: A Space Odyssey*, as director.

Natalie was intrigued. When she and R.J. flew back to Hollywood a few weeks later, she told Roderick Mann why. "In the film I'm estranged from my husband . . . but through his being able to experience my feelings and see things through my eyes, and vice versa, we get back together again."

En route from Paris to Los Angeles, the Wagners stopped in New York for Natalie to pose for a Blackglama fur advertisement, part of the company's successful "What Becomes a Legend Most?" campaign featuring icons in glamorous furs. Natalie got to keep her sumptuous black mink to add to her fur closet, near the notes she was making for her eventual memoirs.

She and R.J. stayed at the elegant Pierre Hotel, where they invited a longtime fan of Natalie's, Bill Goulding, up to their suite. By contrast to Richard Gregson, who would appear to hurry Natalie along in irritation, R.J. chatted with Natalie's fan, assuming his role as the perfect consort, posing in seeming self-effacement next to Natalie. The casual photos of the Wagners from that summer day, with R.J. dressed in designer blue jeans, their arms around each other's waists, and Natalie smiling as R.J. looks at her adoringly, reveal no evidence of stress. They both looked a few pounds heavier than their Hollywood ideal, with evidence they were fifty-one and forty-two, but they were still the golden couple.

When they got back to L.A. in mid-June, Natalie's new agents at William Morris, back in her good graces after the mass firings of 1966, announced her casting in *Brainstorm*.

26

ALTHOUGH SHE NO LONGER HAD costar approval as she had in her glory days at Warners, Natalie had input in the casting of her scientist husband in *Brainstorm*, the film's central character. Foreman's choice was the edgy thirty-eight-year-old Christopher Walken, who had received the Academy Award a few years earlier for his mesmerizing performance as a psychotic Vietnam veteran in *The Deer Hunter*.

Screenwriter Bob Stitzel, who was revising his *Brainstorm* script to enhance Natalie's fairly minor part, was with her when she attended a private screening of *The Dogs of War*, Walken's most recent film, to assess whether she was amenable to Walken as her leading man. "The only thing I remember her saying is that she liked his physical look. And she also felt that he was a very good actor—but I think she was mostly reacting to *Deer Hunter*."

According to Stitzel, MGM had high expectations for *Brainstorm* that summer as a breakthrough special effects film, because of Trumbull's technical genius, Walken's combustible talent, and Natalie's name. Natalie, he observed, seemed "very much into this movie." Actress Louise Fletcher, who was playing Walken's research partner, knew from her conversations with Natalie that she considered the film important to her career. "I think it was sort of like—God, I don't want to say making a comeback, 'cause it wasn't that—but it was the first picture she'd made in a while, and I think it meant a lot to her to look good, to be good."

Natalie told Stitzel she was worried about the love scenes between her and Walken because he was thirty-eight and she was turning forty-three. "You know, 'Would that work?' Would people laugh at her?" He also found her "extremely sensitive" about her weight, "It was written on her face, written in how she behaved. She was looking a little rounded."

During their script discussions that summer, Stitzel was privy to the division between Natalie and her other self, "Natalie Wood," or The Badge. On the one hand, "she never went anywhere, believe me, without the clothes, the jewelry, the makeup—'I'm Natalie Wood, I look great'—period." But Stitzel saw that was not Natalie. "She seemed like a real homebody, the kind that would be baking cookies for the grandchildren . . . she seemed very much a mother type. She would talk a lot about family things, and what they were doing as a family."

Natalie's insecurities about her career, and the way she looked, came from her efforts to perpetuate the movie star alter ego Mud had created for them both. "She was carrying a heavy burden around of being 'Natalie Wood,' " Stitzel observed. "There was a concern like, What's 'Natalie Wood' going to be when she's fifty? What's 'Natalie Wood' going to be when she's forty-five? What's 'Natalie Wood' going to be now?"

The month of July was trying for Natalie. She started on a rigid diet to lose weight before *Brainstorm*, exercising on a Pilates machine, eating so little that Louise Fletcher's sister worried. In the latter half of the month, she turned forty-three the day after it was announced Meryl Streep was cast in *Sophie's Choice*. Peggy Griffin, Natalie's good friend, recalls, "I never saw her so wishful about getting a part that somebody else got."

Lana had a discomfiting feeling about her sister. "She was going through a bad time, she was just going through something in her own head. In terms of herself, where she was going, what she was going to be doing."

One day, when Lana was at the house watching Natalie put on her makeup, the way Lana had when she was seven and Natalie was fifteen, Natalie turned to her, suddenly pensive, and said, "Do you know what I want? I want yesterday."

Before her birthday, Natalie telephoned her older sister, Olga, in San Francisco for a long chat. "She asked me, 'What do you miss most about my being a movie star?' I say, 'Well, what I miss most is we don't see enough of each other as a family.' "

Natalie called her sister back a while later to say that she and R.J. and the girls were coming to San Francisco and

Santa Rosa—where Natalie spent what little childhood she had—in a thirty-five-foot R.V. "So they piled into this—just before she died—they piled into this thing. And R.J. was driving, because his driver was on strike, so he had to get used to driving this van, because it's so long. And they came with Courtney and with Natasha, who came with a little girlfriend, and R.J. parked the van right in front of my house. And the neighbors all around came and were asking for autographs."

Photographs from the Wagners' summer vacation in northern California with Olga and her family show Natalie as the "real person" she always longed to be: standing with her daughters on a street in Chinatown, smiling while her husband snapped their picture; enjoying lunch at the touristy Spinnaker Restaurant overlooking the Bay, with both sisters' families sprawled at one long table and Natasha in Natalie's lap, playing with Natalie's necklace.

At the same time, Olga noticed, something seemed to be bothering Natalie, for she stayed in the R.V. by herself on occasion, seemingly withdrawn.

When the Wagners returned from their holiday, director Doug Trumbull made arrangements for Natalie, John Foreman, screenwriter Bob Stitzel, Louise Fletcher, actor Cliff Robertson (who had been cast in *Brainstorm*) and himself to spend a few days under the supervision of Dr. Stanislav Grof at the experimental Esalen Institute near Big Sur. Trumbull's esoteric idea was to research the life-after-death concept in *Brainstorm* by having everyone take a hallucinogenic drug that simulated death. "The only person that didn't come up was Walken, who was doing something else," recalls Stitzel. Once they arrived, "it turned out there was a little legal problem with this drug."

In its place, the Esalen Institute included Trumbull's *Brainstorm* group in a rebirthing seminar, with everyone lying on the floor listening to a tape, using slow, rhythmic deep breathing until their muscles contracted and they went through emotional states from hysterical laughter to sobbing, simulating life after death. "The only person that didn't do it was Natalie," recalls Stitzel. "Because stars don't lie down on floors and weep and pound. She might look vulnerable. She stayed in her room, mostly, the whole time."

Fletcher considered the exercise "insane. I couldn't wait to get out of it. We had one guy stand up and rip his clothes off and he was being reborn and he was a warrior. Doug [Trumbull] was into it, because he had some idea about death. I mean, *please*. I'm too pragmatic and I just went along with it because I had to."

Natalie took her costume designer, Donfeld, with her to Esalen, taking walks, calling her daughters, and appointing Donfeld her "diet watchdog." "The rest of us were getting into nude hot tubbing," states Stitzel. "Natalie wouldn't get naked," laughs Fletcher. "She was smart. I was forced into it, or felt forced into it, but Natalie said, 'I'm going to take a nap.' She just wasn't about to do that." Stitzel found Natalie "very proper and very prim, almost prudish."

Natalie had struggled with her inhibitions while she was making *Rebel Without a Cause* and *Splendor in the Grass*, part of her perfectionism, her obsession with presenting herself as "Natalie Wood," the glamorous alter ego her mother invented—The Badge—symbolized by the bracelet she always wore in public to cover her flawed wrist. "She couldn't let her hair down," reveals Stitzel. "She had to look real together all the time. She was a movie child, raised on sets. That was her life: looking good. Doing her very best acting bit playing the role of a star." Dennis Hopper had noticed the same thing, twenty-five years earlier, commenting that Natalie's best performance was as "Natalie Wood."

Early in September, Trumbull initiated another bold idea by conventional Hollywood standards, gathering Stitzel and the *Brainstorm* cast—Natalie, Walken, Louise Fletcher and Cliff Robertson—at a table on a soundstage at MGM to go through the script together, a process that lasted almost two weeks. In Stitzel's view, it turned into "utter chaos," with the intense, Actors Studio–trained Walken making changes in the scenes and rewriting dialogue, eventually "wrestling power" from the cerebral Trumbull.

For Natalie, the script sessions were a flashback to the emotionally charged script readings for *Rebel Without a Cause* led by the intellectual Nick Ray at the Chateau Marmont, the "golden world" she had romanticized in her mind, with the New York–based, avant-garde Walken assuming the role Jimmy Dean had when she was sixteen.

At one point in the *Brainstorm* script read-through, Walken pulled Natalie aside and said, "Let's put the script away, Natalie, and let's improvise," just as Dean had done with her in 1955. Natalie's initial reaction to Walken was similar to her original, intimidated response to Dean. "You could look at the terror in her face," recalls Stitzel. "She was like, 'Okay,' with her earrings all dangling. And she was trying to improvise with him." Walken, per Stitzel, "had that East Coast, 'I'm an actor' kind of thing: 'I'm an artist, what am I doing in this stupid special effects movie?' " The neophyte Trumbull, Stitzel observed, was "way, way over his head, particularly with this cast. They had him by the end of the rehearsal that day."

Natalie's relationship with Walken was "cordial" during the fortnight of rehearsals in L.A. that early September, but it was clear she had been stimulated creatively. Walken sparked the same excitement in Natalie that Dean, Kazan, Ray, and Scott Marlowe had, bringing out the artist side of Natalie's actress personality that had been suppressed since her movie star–style second marriage to R.J., at a time when Natalie was hungering to do serious work, to recapture "yesterday."

Lana recalls, "She was enjoying working with Walken. She had a great deal of respect for him. She felt that he was another one of those really serious New York actors, which meant a lot to her. She was very respectful of that whole acting process, that she did feel was very different than it is out here in Hollywood."

Natalie's career spirits lifted as she prepared to go on location for six weeks in Raleigh, North Carolina, to begin filming *Brainstorm*, energized at the thought of working with Walken, anxious to be in a big-budget feature film again. She finalized her option for the film rights to *Zelda*, and made plans to portray the suicidal poet Anne Sexton, another of the dark, complex, fragile women who drew her. The jewel in her crown was *Anastasia*, her homage to Fahd, to Mud, to Natasha Gurdin.

"She was getting rejuvenated about her career," relates Peggy Griffin, then Natalie's closest friend. "The kids were getting older, Natasha was eleven. Natalie had a sense that—you know how eleven-year-old girls are—they want to be with their friends, they don't want to be with Mommy. Courtney was heading in that direction, and Natalie had a sense of 'This is something I might want to do again.' " Since R.J. was filming *Hart to Hart* at the studio, there would be a parent at home with Natasha and

Courtney while Natalie was making *Brainstorm*, part of the Wagners' marital pact.

When the time came for Natalie to leave for Raleigh in late September, it was wrenching. Natasha had a morbid fixation that her mother was going to die, because a playmate's stepfather had recently had a sudden heart attack. "Tasha developed this little kind of drama that every time Natalie went out the door, Natasha started this, 'I don't want you to go, Mommy. What if you die? What if you die in the car?' " recalls Griffin. "She was developing this out of control fear of death, and Natalie didn't want her to have a fear." Griffin suggested Natalie just *tell* Natasha that Mommy wasn't going to die. Natalie's response was eerily prescient. "She said, 'How could I say that? What if something ever really happened to me? Who would she ever trust to believe again?' "

Courtney was so distraught that her mother would be away for six weeks that Natalie took a later flight from the rest of the cast so she could drive both her daughters to school, arranging for costumer Donfeld to fly to Raleigh in the seat beside her. "Natalie was terrified of plane travel," he said later. "At the start of our trip that day, I pointed out some of the things about her past and personality that might be responsible for her fear. She hung on every word, and I thought I helped her."

Natalie checked into the Pinehurst Hotel in North Carolina to start *Brainstorm* ridden with guilt, desperately missing her little girls. "I remember her telling me that this was the first thing she'd worked on in a long time away from her family and she was feeling a bit weird about it," relates costar Louise Fletcher, who was at the hotel in Pinehurst when Natalie arrived. "But she was *excited* about doing this movie, and it was sort of striking out on her own in a way."

Natalie made herculean efforts to be the perfect mother while still fulfilling her creative needs. Within a few days of arriving in North Carolina, she flew back across the country for Natasha's September 29 birthday party, despite her fear of airplanes. "I got there for dinner," recalls Griffin, "and there was like a mob of people, kids and all that stuff. Natalie was on a flight out almost at dawn because she had to be back in North Carolina. It was a hard trip for her because it was a turnaround. We hugged and she said, 'I'll see you at Thanksgiving.' "

When she returned to Raleigh, Fletcher noticed, Natalie had a difficult time without a support system around her, separated from her daughters. "She was always talking about her kids. Missing them, what they were like. She mentioned them all the time, and called them, having conversations at night." Creatively, Fletcher thought Natalie "was having a very good time. When we worked together in scenes, she was in a very good mood and very, very funny. She would be talking under her breath, trying to make me laugh—and she succeeded."

The production itself seemed doomed. The word filtering back to Stitzel in Los Angeles was that "it was chaotic because of Trumbull's complete lack of control over what was going on, and Walken was pretty much directing his own scenes and doing his own thing." Fletcher says diplomatically, "The producers and the director didn't have a creative meeting of the minds."

By the middle of October, *Brainstorm* was so far behind schedule that executive producer Jack Grossberg "cleaned out the entire production department" and made an emergency call to a first assistant director named David McGiffert. "He said, 'You owe me a favor,' and he was kind of laughing. He said, 'They've got a problem on *Brainstorm*, this movie being shot by Doug Trumbull. We've got to take over this show. They're in North Carolina, and we've gotta go in and get it right.' "

McGiffert's perception, when he arrived on location, was similar to Stitzel's during rehearsal. "It seemed as though a lot of the production was in chaos . . . for some reason, it was difficult for Doug [Trumbull] to impart his brilliance, to communicate it to actors." Stitzel heard from his contacts on location that Natalie "really fell under Walken's spell and followed his direction more than Trumbull's."

Louise Fletcher, who was there and had numerous scenes with Walken, observes, "Chris is just too *crazy* to take over. Natalie, believe me, was grounded in her craft, and I don't believe that Chris was going to take her over in any way. He may have given her suggestions or an extra glass of wine, I don't know. He's a marvelous actor. He made me laugh a lot . . . right before the scene would start, he would do something completely different just to get the energy going, like he'd drop his pants or something. He's not over in his own space. He's kind of intrusive, but everybody's got their own way of working."

Walken's off-the-wall style and Method approach were similar to the way Natalie's movie-god Jimmy Dean behaved with her during *Rebel*, striking an emotional chord in her. "She would look at Chris and he'd do some funny thing that nobody would see on the set, and she'd just fall over laughing," observed McGiffert. "Chris was trying to get her to loosen up in her role, because I think Natalie really wanted to do well, and that actually impaired her relaxing to do the part. Chris gets with his parts, and he lives in that guy, and he wanted Natalie to sense this woman."

Walken, according to McGiffert, who was responsible for

keeping track of the cast, assuaged Natalie's "huge" insecurities about her age and weight—the pressure to be "Natalie Wood"—that Stitzel noticed prior to filming. She was especially insecure about a wedding flashback scene depicting her and Walken in their early twenties.

"She was really, really afraid of how she was going to look," states the A.D. "Lots of time in makeup." The morning of the scene, "Natalie didn't want to do it. You could tell she was stressed, and Chris had this goofy little kind of thing he did . . . to get her on the point where she needed to be, without upsetting her emotionally."

Natalie's concern that she needed to look like "Natalie Wood" was touching to McGiffert. When the scene was over, he went up to her and said sympathetically, "Look, you look good. And you can't go back. You know, you can't be that girl again."

Natalie spent most of her down time in Raleigh on the telephone with her daughters, or in the trailer with Walken, who occasionally went to dinner with her. With Walken, she violated her longstanding rule to drink no more than one glass of wine during filming. "Wardrobe was going crazy because she was putting on weight from all the wine," recalls Faye Nuell, who was then a production executive at MGM. "Suddenly she had these matronly arms and they were having to let out the clothes."

"I think that she was in over her head, that's what I think, in every which way," submits Fletcher. "If Natalie had *one* glass of wine, she could be—she just couldn't handle any kind of alcohol, and I think unfortunately a couple of times she had more than one glass. And I'm not saying she was alcoholic or anything like that. It's just that I think she was kind of in *limbo* out there in North Carolina and didn't really feel that she had her community right here, and I think that a couple of times it may have looked like she and Chris were drunk."

In the awful aftermath of her drowning, a month or so later, Walken would acknowledge that Natalie "wasn't much of a drinker."

R.J. would later tell a family employee he was irritated about Natalie's location shooting in North Carolina because he had to film an episode of *Hart to Hart* in Hawaii that October while she was in Raleigh, leaving Natasha and Courtney without one parent at home for a few days, a violation of the Wagners' marital understanding. R.J. felt Natalie was the one who should be home with the girls, not him.

McGiffert, who interacted with Natalie and Walken many times a day on and off the set, liked them both and had a "light relationship" with them. McGiffert construed Natalie's occasional wine consumption with Walken as a way for her to relax. "They weren't drunk, but they were buzzed. Not to the point where it was impairing their work, but they were a little giddier than usual . . . she just looked to me like a woman who was opening up a little more."

People who knew Natalie well, such as her hairdresser and friend of eighteen years, Sugar Bates, or her sister Lana, find it unimaginable that Natalie would ever have had an affair with Walken. "I think she was probably having a flirtation, which is different than having an affair," contends Lana. "I really don't think that she would do that. There may have been those kind of boy-girl little attention games going on. A genuine affair, I don't believe it for an instant. I would just never believe it of her. I really don't believe she would do that. Ever ever ever ever. She would not have risked her marriage."

If she had, it would have been Natalie's first known

extramarital affair, something she did not condone.

What Natalie unmistakably experienced was an emotional connection with Walken that filled a void in her life, stimulating her in a way that was powerfully evocative of Jimmy Dean's effect on her during *Rebel Without a Cause*. McGiffert, who was around them throughout filming, sensed that Natalie was "transformed" by the relationship with Walken. "It was a dramatic, uplifting thing for her, you could tell that she was fulfilled, that she was refocused. And it was nice to see . . . I think she was blown away. This weird guy from New York, he said these goofy things, and put her in these goofy positions, and he'd show her up and play jokes on her."

Natalie was in conflict in *herself* that fall, or selves. The serious actress part of her that was drawn to Kazan and Dean was excited by Walken and the chance to express herself artistically, while the star-driven "Natalie Wood" side of her was comfortable in the celebrity world she and R.J. symbolized. "They were the king and queen of the Hollywood parade," as Fletcher observed, "and when you spend that much time in Hollywood—and I'm using that word 'Hollywood' on purpose—if you start out that young, you kind of *believe* what you read in the paper, that you *are* royal in some way: you know, 'Hollywood royalty.' And she *was*. She was a member of that old school . . . she and R.J. kind of are the way they were. Together they felt *special*."

The true Natalie, Natalie the mother, was isolated and lost without Natasha and Courtney. "She called all the time," recalls Peggy Griffin. "I'd go over there and have a bite to eat with R.J. and she was always on the phone. Constantly. With the kids."

McGiffert, their on-set liaison during those charged last weeks on *Brainstorm*, had fond feelings for Natalie, and liked Walken. "She was the kind of person I would like to have for a friend. She had long periods of being lonely and had spent a lot of time figuring out what was important to her. And the things that were important to her were unexpected from someone of her magnitude: simple truths, affection and honesty. And she was in a business where all three of those things are in short supply."

While Natalie and Walken filmed the last scene in the script, Fletcher, who was not on set heard that Natalie had "had a tough time that night . . . in *her* case, it would probably have been like two glasses of wine. She was so little, and she couldn't handle it."

By the first week in November, the star-crossed *Brainstorm* company returned to L.A. to finish the last month of shooting on the soundstage at MGM.

Walken checked into a hotel and Natalie reunited with her family in the house on Canon, showing up at MGM as needed for her scenes, carrying out the mundane errands of motherhood she found so fulfilling, taking lessons to strengthen her voice for *Anastasia*, which would start rehearsals after Thanksgiving and open at the Ahmanson Theater in February. "To be live on stage absolutely terrified her," recalls Stitzel, one of the many to whom Natalie mentioned her fear.

"We were all talking about what we might do to help her," actor David Dukes, who was cast as Rasputin, would recall. "We felt we'd probably go with body mikes because she certainly wouldn't have the voice for a theater like that."

Her conversations with Lana then, and an interview she gave when she got back from North Carolina, suggest that Natalie was disenchanted with *Brainstorm*. She told Lana it was a "so-so" movie, and said to a reporter, "Today's films are so technological that an actor becomes starved for roles that deal with human relationships. My friends seem more excited about my doing *Anastasia* than about *Brainstorm* . . . and to tell you the truth, I feel the same way."

Child actress Tonya Crowe, who played Natalie's daughter both in *Cracker Factory* and *Eva Ryker*, stopped to see her mid-November on the *Brainstorm* set. Crowe remembers Natalie as bubbling over about *Anastasia*, autographing, with typical warmth, what would be her last "Natalie Wood" glamour shot, "to my favorite screen daughter." To Crowe, Natalie was not only the epitome of a star, she was the epitome of a mother. "All I know is that she took me under her wing in such a motherly way. I worked with Donna Mills as my mother on *Knots Landing* and Donna Mills loved having a child on the set, but it wasn't anything like Natalie. Natalie adored being a mother. She had total respect for children—not just love, but respect."

She posed for a portrait that month as the mystery woman claiming to be Anastasia, used in advertisements announcing the forthcoming play, a haunting preview of what might have been. It was a stunning photograph of Natalie as the putative Romanov duchess, in a plunging gown, wearing an ornate jeweled necklace, her hair upswept and her dark Russian eyes smoldering; the closest she would get to fulfilling her fantasy to honor Mud and Fahd's reverence for the Russian royal family and her own buried identity as Natasha Gurdin.

Brainstorm continued on its troubled, anarchic course through November. David McGiffert, who carried on as first assistant director in L.A., noticed that "things were a little more contentious" between Trumbull and the united force of Natalie and Walken once filming began on the MGM lot. "They were now aligned to what they were doing with the script, and obviously their relationship was playing into the relationship on the screen: the relationship on the screen was of a couple that was having trouble, and the *offscreen* friendship was of two people who were having a great time."

The charged friendship between Walken and Natalie was still evident after she was back home with R.J. "The dynamics that went into that were funny, they were hazy, they would change a lot," appraised McGiffert. "Lots of mood swings about what was going on." McGiffert noticed Natalie seemed to open up around Walken in a way that was similar to what Redford described during the times *they* acted together when she dropped the "Natalie Wood" movie star persona. As McGiffert remembers, "She was really alive. She had a beautiful laugh, and a beautiful way of just letting go, and she'd just get all goofy and fall over things. It was fun to watch, because she was usually pretty controlled, and she'd just get giddy and it was infectious. And it would make Chris want to do more to make her laugh, and he was good at that."

What is clear, and becomes significant, is that there was a *perception*, however mistaken, that her friendship with Walken had become deeper, at least among the people involved with *Brainstorm*, to the point that McGiffert, the first assistant director, was certain R.J. was aware of it by Thanksgiving.

Natalie alluded to colleagues on the set that R.J.'s drinking was bothering her, just as she had to Sugar Bates during the trying *Eva Ryker* shoot exactly two years before, when Natalie was preoccupied with premonitions she would drown in dark water. Outwardly, Natalie and R.J. appeared "just, oh, madly in love" to their mutual close friend Griffin that pre-Thanksgiving, who described them as "a happy couple; very playful, very respectful, very supportive. A team at all times, on every level."

Faye Nuell, who was working on the lot, stopped by Natalie's *Brainstorm* set the fortnight before Thanksgiving for what would be their last conversation. Nuell and Natalie stood in a doorway in one of the buildings on the MGM lot, both suddenly experiencing a "total flashback" to when they met in 1955 on *Rebel Without a Cause*. They were struck by how many of their friends from the movie had died early—Jimmy Dean, Sal Mineo, Nick Adams. "It was like, 'Oh my God, we're still here!' "

That same week, in what would be a cruel irony, actor William Holden, the longtime companion of Stefanie Powers, R.J.'s costar on *Hart to Hart*, was found dead in his bedroom after tripping and gashing his head while under the influence of alcohol. R.J. comforted Powers over the needless loss of her great love, as she would do for him less than two weeks later, under circumstances that were also engendered by the effects of excessive alcohol, the true demon surrounding Natalie from earliest childhood in a household haunted by Fahd's vodka-inflamed rage.

On Thanksgiving morning, Natalie and her friend Griffin had a long phone conversation about their weekend plans. *Brainstorm* was winding down, and Natalie was excited about starting rehearsals on Monday for *Anastasia*. "Everything about this whole sad time to me was so ironic," observes Griffin. "For years, my tradition was that I had Thanksgiving with my parents, and then in the early evening, about 6:00, I'd go over to Natalie and R.J.'s and have dessert and coffee. And this particular year I had a friend in the hospital, and my whole Thanksgiving Day got kind of turned around."

Griffin told Natalie she couldn't make it for dessert that night, and they discussed Natalie and R.J.'s plans to spend Friday through Sunday off Catalina, on the *Splendour*. The Wagners planned to take Natalie's close friend, realtor Delphine Mann. Griffin was invited, but declined. "I never went on the boat in the winter. It's very confining. You don't have the freedom of doing all those things you do in the summer."

She and Natalie said their goodbyes, and set a date to see a movie together that Sunday night after Natalie got back from Catalina. "I still remember the movie we were going to see," Griffin recalls sadly. "*Absence of Malice*, with Paul Newman. And to this day, I've never seen the movie. I just couldn't see it."

That night, a few close friends and family dropped in and out of the Wagners' house for their traditional Thanksgiving buffet. Mud was there, Lana and her daughter, Mart Crowley, Delphine Mann, R.J.'s mother, and for a time Walken, whose wife was on the East Coast. Natalie had invited Walken on the boat for the weekend. It was not untypical of the socially gregarious Wagners to bring costars on the *Splendour* as their guests.

More typically, the boat was a family affair, with Natasha or Courtney inviting chums along to swim and Jet-Ski with R.J., while Natalie sat in the galley or in the wheelhouse reading scripts or the latest bestseller. She never swam, never Jet-Skied, and would not participate in anything water-related. If the *Splendour* was moored, Natalie might take the girls or a guest to shore in the *Valiant*, the

Wagners' motorized dinghy, but she would never get in the dinghy alone at night.

Later that Thanksgiving evening, she asked Crowley if he wanted to join her and R.J. on the *Splendour* with Walken and Delphine Mann. Crowley had a conflict, and at the last minute, Delphine Mann canceled. "She had some things coming up that weekend," explains Griffin, "and so she changed her plans." Mann would later agonize over her eleventh-hour decision not to go to Catalina with Natalie and R.J. and Walken. As Griffin would observe wistfully, "You think, 'Well maybe, if someone else was there, it might change just *anything* . . .'"

Lana, who was banned from the *Splendour*, along with Mud, felt Natalie "seemed odd" that Thanksgiving night, the last time she saw her sister alive. "Like something was bothering her. Nothing specific, just lots of little bitty things."

What would forever haunt Lana was Natasha's hysterical reaction to her mother's plans to leave for Catalina in the morning. Natasha begged Natalie to stay home, not to go on the boat that weekend.

Normally, Natalie would indulge her daughters anything. But in this case, she said no to Natasha. She didn't want Natasha to grow up with the kind of deep-seated fears Mud had instilled in her.

27

THE TRAGIC, ANOMALOUS EVENTS of Natalie's sad, last, lost weekend off Catalina Island, leading to her greatest fear realized—drowning in deep, dark water—have been speculated about and exploited throughout the twenty years since she died, threatening to eclipse the memory of her poignant performances, and the grace with which she lived her life, which is how she should be remembered.

Because the circumstances surrounding Natalie's drowning have been the subject of such speculation, this examination of her last hours is offered to help clarify, at least, what is known and what has been offered in explanation by the participants, some of it for the first time, though the full details of that night may be lost in an alcoholic haze and remain a mystery.

Of the four people on the *Splendour* that weekend—Natalie, R.J., Christopher Walken, and the Wagners' private captain, Dennis Davern—only Davern has talked publicly at length about what he claimed happened, and his stories have trickled out through the years in tabloids, for remuneration; in a British documentary and in *Vanity Fair*. His public accounts have stopped short of the climactic last moments when Natalie went off the boat, which he says he knows, hoping at some point to disclose for profit in a book, or as his coauthor put it, "his day to reveal the truth." Natalie cannot give witness, and R.J. and Walken have each maintained silence other than through two statements given by each to authorities, a brief interview by Walken, and in R.J.'s case, a four-paragraph public statement.

Consequently, Natalie's last weekend can only be patched together from statements given by the principals to L.A. Sheriff's investigators, supplemented by the recorded statements and twenty-year-old memories of witnesses, or from Davern's subsequent accounts in the media.

By any interpretation, using all of the versions available, the last thirty-six hours of Natalie's too-short life consisted of an almost surreal, alcoholically charged chain of circumstances and behavior unlike hers or R.J.'s, building, like grand opera, to a tragic climax, the details of which may remain as murky as the dark seawater she had a premonition would take her life.

Natalie, R.J., Walken, and Davern, the skipper R.J. brought to California to keep in his employ when he bought the *Splendour* in 1975, set sail for Catalina Island from Marina Del Rey before noon the Friday after Thanksgiving, the beginning of a cold, gray November weekend so unpleasant Davern suggested they go a different time. Natalie "was out for a wonderful weekend, to entertain her guest," Davern would recall to a friend, and Catalina was the Wagners' sentimental favorite, because of their romantic first honeymoon in 1958, tucked aboard *My Other Lady*.

Davern, a slight, bearded, lanky New Jersey native of thirty-three, "worshipped" Natalie and R.J., friends recalled, thrilled to be included in his celebrity bosses' family activities during weekend getaways on the *Splendour*, "helping to raise" Courtney and Natasha. As his childhood friend and coauthor Margaret Rulli would rhapsodize, "It was just like an unheard of Hollywood lifestyle. They really *had* the marriage. Robert Wagner loved Natalie Wood, his love for her took his breath away."

The rough crossing to Catalina that Friday afternoon harbingered strange tempests of emotion gathering momentum on the *Splendour*. Davern could sense it in the air. "As soon as Christopher and Natalie and R.J. entered the boat is when there was a feeling of *negativity* going on between R.J. and Christopher," he told a British documentary group. "And it just kept on getting more like that as the time would go on."

Alcohol was the leitmotiv. The East Coast–based Walken, who was an inexperienced sailor, started the voyage with two Bloody Marys, according to his later statement, becoming so seasick he had to lie down for the rest of the cruise. By the time he roused, around five in the afternoon, the *Splendour* was moored a quarter of a mile from the historic domed casino at Avalon, the tourist-populated side of Catalina Island, a picturesque seaside village of boutiques and restaurants associated with carefree gaiety.

Shortly after Walken got up, he and Natalie and R.J. took the *Valiant*, the Wagners' motorized dinghy, to shore, leaving Davern behind to prepare dinner. As revealed in Walken and R.J.'s statements to police, they and Natalie spent a cold, drizzly afternoon into evening drinking beer and margaritas, beginning at a Mexican restaurant and ending at El Galleon, a popular waterfront bar with an outdoor veranda where Natalie and R.J. once celebrated one of their special private anniversaries.

Between barhopping, the trio shopped a bit in a nearby arcade, where Walken wandered into a gallery, purchasing a painting, and the Wagners browsed at David Stein Jeweler's. Natalie bought an early Christmas gift to surprise the skipper, and R.J. indulged Natalie with a $5000 one-carat diamond necklace set in a barnacle she admired in one of the display cases.

The manager of the bar at the El Galleon, the actors' last stop, remembered them as leaving for the dock around ten P.M., which meant they had been consuming alcohol on and off for five hours from the time they arrived onshore, in addition to Walken's earlier two Bloody Marys and whatever Natalie and R.J. may have been drinking aboard the *Splendour* from noon to five. The emotional dynamics during those five hours from five to ten P.M. when Walken was drinking with Natalie and R.J. in

Avalon is unknown, though Davern later said in the same British documentary that R.J. was even more "irritated" by the attention Natalie paid to Walken once they returned from shore.

According to both R.J. and Walken's later statements, when they got to the dock, Natalie did not want to get into the motorized rubber dinghy to go back to sea where the *Splendour* was moored, even with R.J. and Walken beside her, "because it was dark, it was cold, and she was afraid she would get wet." Natalie told R.J. she wanted to ride back to the *Splendour* in a larger shoreboat. He eventually "talked her into" getting in the *Valiant* with him and Walken, R.J.'s statement reveals, and all three returned to the *Splendour* together, where Davern was preparing a barbecue.

Walken recalled "more drinking" on the boat, until he felt ill and went to his stateroom, leaving Natalie, R.J., and Davern to dine without him.

What happened next set the tone for the disturbing, mysterious rest of the weekend. During R.J.'s final police interview on December 4, he would tell authorities the sea had high swells that Friday night and everyone on the boat discussed crossing the channel to return to the mainland—although, in their statements, neither Walken nor Davern would mention any group discussion of a night crossing cutting their trip short. Duane Rasure, the lead investigator, noted R.J. telling him that Natalie "didn't want to go back at night in the dark."

In R.J.'s December 4 statement, he said he and Natalie had a "strong disagreement" about whether to move the boat closer to shore Friday night to get out of the rough waves. R.J. told authorities Natalie objected to repositioning the boat, so he told her to spend the night in a hotel in Avalon and take Davern with her.

Davern's second statement on December 10, with lawyers R.J. hired for Davern present on his behalf, he concurred with R.J.'s follow-up statement, saying the sea was "grumpy" that night, and that the Wagners disagreed about whether to move the boat, though Davern stated it was *Natalie's* idea for her to stay in a hotel in Avalon that night.

When Walken was interviewed the second time, he told sheriff's investigators he heard "some sort of hubbub" between Natalie and R.J. after he had been in bed, seasick, for twenty minutes; then he heard what sounded like an anchor chain, and Natalie knocked on his door to say, "He wants to cross during the night." By Walken's account, Natalie left the room and Davern appeared, asking Walken to come to the main salon to mediate. Walken told Davern, "Never get involved in an argument between a man and a wife." When Davern left his room, Walken went back to sleep, evidently until morning, though he felt the boat move and noticed through the porthole that they were closer to shore.

Davern says that he then knocked on Walken's door, seeking his intervention. When Walken refused, Davern "thought the best thing for me to do was to go ashore with her," he told a British television documentary.

Davern drove Natalie to shore in the *Valiant,* by his and R.J.'s accounts, leaving R.J. on the boat, agitated, and Natalie's guest, Walken, in his cabin, seasick and asleep.

Natalie walked the few short blocks from the dock at Avalon to her and R.J.'s sentimental favorite spot, El Galleon, distressed, deeply intoxicated, with only a duffel bag, and Davern, from the statements of witnesses. Paul Reynolds, the manager of El Galleon who saw Natalie leave with R.J. and Walken that night at ten, reencountered her in the bar at eleven, accompanied by a "man with a beard" he identified as Davern. Natalie wanted to know when the next public boat was leaving for the mainland, which was not until morning.

Then she asked Reynolds to help her find two available hotel rooms. While the bartender called to make reservations at a modest motel a few doors down called the Pavilion Lodge, Natalie and Davern, according to Reynolds, had "a couple of drinks," ogled by other patrons "looking at [Natalie Wood] get tipsy."

This awful drama carried over to the Pavilion Lodge, where Natalie walked in with Davern close to 11:15 P.M., both so intoxicated they had trouble getting in the door, as later told to police by the night clerk, Ann Laughton, who would remember Natalie wearing a red quilted jacket, the same thing she would have on approximately twenty-four hours later during her desperate struggle to keep from drowning.

Natalie prepaid by American Express for rooms 126 and 219, asking Laughton for some ice. Laughton showed Natalie and Davern how to use the ice machine and escorted them, together, to room 126, one of the Pavilion's standard motel-style rooms, with a king-sized bed. When Laughton asked Natalie if she wanted to see room 219, Natalie responded, "Not at this time, we'll see it later." The maids' records would reveal that room 219 was undisturbed the next day.

In Davern's second statement, with attorneys he disclosed that he spent Friday night at the Pavilion Lodge with Natalie, acting "as her bodyguard" at R.J.'s request. R.J. confirmed Natalie's Friday night in Avalon when he was questioned for the second time.

While they were in room 126 at the Pavilion Lodge with

midnight approaching, Natalie asked Davern to stay with her through the night; afraid, as she always was, to be alone at night. They drank more wine, he would remember, and talked.

Natalie got up before eight A.M. and wanted to go home, hoping to telephone Lana, Davern would recall to friend and coauthor Rulli. "Natalie tried to call Lana that morning to leave the island. She wasn't going to go back to the boat." Davern did not want to return either, he told Rulli. "Why put trouble on top of trouble?"

Natalie left Davern in room 126 at 8:00 and went to the front desk with the key to room 219, telling the day clerk, "Excuse me, I can't find my room." The clerk, Linda Winkler, astonished to see Natalie Wood at the Pavilion Lodge, directed her to room 219, noticing Natalie was "disoriented," as Winkler told investigators.

Natalie left Winkler for about twenty minutes, returning to pay her bill, surprised to find out she had paid it by credit card the night before. Natalie asked the clerk where she could catch a boat back to the mainland. Winkler was "amazed that a movie star like Miss Wood would be taking public transportation back to the mainland." Natalie told the clerk she was on her way to the boat dock, and to send "the captain" there.

When Davern joined Natalie at the dock fifteen minutes later, she had changed her mind about taking a public cruise line home, after looking them over. Instead, they got into the *Valiant* together and Davern steered the rubber dinghy back to the *Splendour* that Saturday morning, November 28, another chilly, overcast day. Sometime that morning, Walken would tell authorities, Natalie woke him up in his cabin on the *Splendour* to tell him that she was taking a seaplane back to Los Angeles and she wanted to know if he was staying on the boat. "I'm not in this," was Walken's all-too-wise reply.

The mood on the boat, especially Natalie's, shifted again, drastically, by the time Walken got up and went to the main salon, where he saw Natalie busy cooking her famous huevos rancheros. Suddenly, "everybody seemed happy," Walken later told police. Natalie dropped her plans to go home, telling Walken they were taking the *Splendour* over to the Isthmus at Two Harbors, the remote side of Catalina Island. Davern was as puzzled as Walken by the sea change in the Wagners' behavior. "Everyone acted like nothing happened," Davern told *Vanity Fair*, "and everything was beautiful again."

R.J. suggested to Walken they do some fishing once they got to Two Harbors, though after what R.J. described to police as a "nice ride" across the ocean from Avalon, where they were recorded by the harbor patrolman as leaving at 11:30 that morning, he and Walken decided to take a nap. Natalie read screenplays in the main salon and Davern went for a short ride on the dinghy.

The harbormaster at the Isthmus assigned the Wagners Mooring #N1, about a hundred yards from shore, where the *Splendour* was one of an assemblage of fifty to seventy pleasure boats moored in front of Two Harbors that blustery Thanksgiving weekend. For some reason, R.J. chose not to use the Wagners' permanent mooring at Emerald Bay, possibly because the Isthmus was closer to Doug's Harbor Reef Restaurant in Two Harbors, where the group planned to have dinner on what would be Natalie's last night.

By early afternoon, as the weather turned drizzly and threatening, Davern returned from his dinghy ride and settled in to take a nap. As he and R.J. snoozed, Walken awakened around 2:00 and he and Natalie decided to take the *Valiant* to Two Harbors, leaving a note for R.J. that they had gone ashore, as R.J. would later tell police. Natalie put on her red quilted jacket over a pair of designer blue jeans, a yellow turtleneck sweater, and high-heeled suede shoes, carrying a red-white-and-blue bag.

The two co-stars sat on stools in the wood-paneled inside bar at Doug's Harbor Reef, a "funky" quasi-nautical, tropical-themed restaurant that was literally the only place to go in desolate, rustic Two Harbors. When the weather was warm, the outdoor bar at Doug's was like a Jimmy Buffett tune, flowing with margaritas and weekend revelers in from their boats for a good time. This gloomy, wet November afternoon, any action at Doug's was removed to the indoor bar, where Walken and Natalie continued the weekend bacchanal. Inside the bar, they resumed their playfulness from the *Brainstorm* set, discussing their last few weeks of filming, in which Natalie had two or three scenes.

When R.J. woke up from his nap to find Natalie ashore with Walken, sometime before 4:00 in the afternoon, R.J. took a shoreboat to Two Harbors with Davern, in search of Natalie and Walken, who had the dinghy tied at the dock at Two Harbors.

When he found them, drinking at the bar, "Natalie and Chris were having such a good time that I think it started to really upset R.J.," Davern disclosed to the British documentary team in 1999. He told *Vanity Fair* that Walken and Natalie "were out of it—giggling and laughing," an observation that comports with the memory of waitress Michelle Mileski, who passed Natalie in the bar off and on from four P.M., and later served her dinner. "She was buzzed, she was screwed up in the afternoon, if you want to know the truth." (Mileski, who came on duty at four, thought Davern and R.J. had preceded Natalie and Walken into the bar.)

Natalie's internal conflict between her "Natalie Wood" movie star personality, created by Mud, and the serious actress who longed for the Kazan/Ray/Dean "golden world" collided that afternoon and evening, in the charged company of R.J. and Walken, who represented the competing sides of her complex dual identity. This struggle would come out in her mercurial behavior that night at Doug's Harbor Reef.

R.J. made a 7:00 reservation in the dining room, and then he and Davern joined Walken and Natalie at the bar, where they would spend the next three hours, as a storm gusted outside. Davern would later tell his coauthor he noticed R.J. simmering while he was watching Natalie and Walken share private jokes from their movie, leaving R.J. the odd man out.

Sometime before dinner, Natalie and R.J. expressed displeasure with the wine list, asking Davern to go back to the *Splendour* and choose something from the wine cellar. Davern told *Vanity Fair* he and Walken rode the dinghy back, smoking a joint on the *Splendour* before selecting three bottles of wine, one of which they left in the *Valiant*. When he and Walken got back to Doug's Harbor Reef, Davern was "right in tune with Christopher and Natalie—high as a kite."

By the time Natalie, R.J., Walken and Davern sat down for dinner in the adjoining dining room at seven, they were all "inebriated," in the description of Doug's host/manager, Don Whiting. Whiting seated them in the corner at a round table big enough for eight people, with R.J. taking the "King's chair," Natalie to his right, Walken to *her* right, and Davern to the left of R.J. Whiting told police, later, "he was of the impression that Robert Wagner was a little bit irritated with his wife."

Christina Quinn, their original waitress, noticed that Natalie's mood shifted quickly, "from light to dark, not in the brightest of spirits." She fussed about the lighting, the size of the table, the freshness of her fish, eventually sending her meal back, saying she would "just drink her dinner."

Michelle Mileski, a waitress with more experience at Doug's, recalls that Quinn eventually found the Wagner group "such pain in the butts that I took 'em over for her." Mileski felt a "strange" vibration from R.J. directed toward Natalie and Walken. "There definitely was something going on, the table just felt weird, that's why Christina was just not into it that much. So then we both kind of waited on them."

The "eerie" feeling at the Wagners' table, as Mileski described it, was made more incendiary by massive quantities of alcohol. During dinner, from seven to ten P.M.—as recalled by both waitresses, who also gave statements to the police—the already inebriated Wagner party consumed two bottles of wine from the *Splendour*, two bottles of champagne and cocktails sent by star-struck fellow diners, daiquiris ordered by Walken, and cognac for R.J. and Davern. That was in addition to the drinks they all had earlier at the bar.

Mileski observed that R.J. seemed detached from the group somehow, less visibly intoxicated at the table, an outsider to Natalie and Walken's conversations. "I remember thinking along the line like, 'He's not even partying with them.' "

John Ryan, a fifteen-year-old at the table next to the Wagners, talked back and forth with them throughout the evening after Ryan's "Uncle Warren" Archer, who owned a boat called the *Vantage*, sent a bottle of champagne to

Natalie and R.J., who reciprocated. Ryan found Natalie spectacularly beautiful that night, "a babe," her hair and makeup done up as "Natalie Wood," even on a casual boating weekend. She flirted sweetly with Ryan, flattering his teenage ego, impressing him as "more together" than Walken and R.J., whom Ryan, his mother, and Archer observed as "whacked out, particularly Robert Wagner," whose behavior seemed, to them, bizarre. "He and Walken were not with all their faculties."

Laurel Page and Dennis Bowen, a young engaged couple staying on a boat moored near the *Splendour*, dined at Doug's that night and formed the same impressions as Ryan during their encounters with the Wagner group. "She was very nice, very personable," recalls Bowen. "But Wagner was pretty whacked." Page had a chance to express to Natalie how much she appreciated her work, "and she thanked me very much and was nice and friendly to me . . . she was just approachable and was just—God, she really was something." As the evening progressed, Page noticed, "Robert Wagner was really out of it, swaying, just so drunk . . . could have, in his condition, fallen on the floor. Really drunk."

Natalie expressed several times to people in the bar or restaurant that night that she was missing her daughters. When R.J. sent their first waitress, Christina Quinn, to the small bathroom to check on Natalie because she had been away from the table for a long time, Quinn walked in on a "very tender moment" between Natalie and a young girl of nine or so, almost the age of Natasha. They were sitting in front of a big, lighted mirror. "Natalie was behind the young girl and looking into the mirror, stroking the girl's hair, telling her what a pretty young girl she was, and how lucky she was to be a young girl. Honoring the little girl and her childhood, telling her how important childhood was, how valuable that time was. It was a really nice thing in my mind and heart."

Laurel Page wandered into the ladies' room before or after Quinn, noticing Natalie with the same little girl and another child, finding herself touched in the same way Quinn was. "Natalie was just sitting there combing their hair, the way a mother would comb—the right hand has the comb and your left hand goes over the hair—smiling, looking in their faces. I watched her comb their hair for a while. Because it was in the bathroom, so private, I was able to have a moment with her. It was a really maternal, tender moment. I'm glad I got to see that. She was reflecting on her daughters." Or, possibly, her own lost childhood.

Mileski would recall Natalie inviting the young girl to her table afterward, braiding her hair—the way Mud used to do for Natalie, when she was the Pigtail Kid. Dawn Powers, the little girl, felt a sense of 'peace' from Natalie, a serenity and kindness.

When an accordion player stopped by the Wagners' table to play a song on his accordion for Natalie—the haunting "Lara's Theme" from *Dr. Zhivago*—it seemed, another diner would recall for police, "to make her happy," perhaps reminding Natalie of her Fahd and his balalaika. Such poignancy was fleeting. A while later, Mileski would say, "she was fooling around, it seemed like, with Christopher more." As both Mileski and Quinn would tell police, Natalie suddenly got up and threw a wine glass at the wall next to the Wagners' table, "and I figured there was a spat going on," states Mileski. Mileski also felt it was a bid for attention. "Everybody kind of stopped and looked, is what I thought she wanted." Quinn considered it a "human" reaction of emotion.

Walken would later tell police it was "my fault. I recall that we were making a toast while drinking. At the conclusion of this toast I threw my glass to the floor as I always do, and I remember Natalie, and I think everybody else, did the same." Walken told police Natalie made the remark that she was Russian, and Russians did this.

Quinn and Mileski stand by their statements that Natalie was the only one to smash a wine glass that night.

Susan Bernard, an Orange County resident who was having dinner with a girlfriend at Doug's, told investigators she saw Natalie break the glass, and a second glass, which she observed, from a distance, as "a touch of drama."

The restaurant manager, Don Whiting, now deceased, corroborated to police the waitresses' version of Natalie smashing the glass, mentioning that another glass was broken by accident. "He thought at the time there was a possible problem between Robert Wagner and his wife," as Duane Rasure, the lead investigator, wrote in Whiting's statement. "He remembers a glass was broken, possibly thrown." Dawn Powers, whose hair Natalie had braided earlier, noticed "a fuss going on" or "a commotion" at the Wagner table before the glass was broken. "There was a lot of commotion at their table that night." Rasure's partner, Roy Hamilton, noted in his report that Whiting told them Wagner was "irate" with Natalie.

The escalating tension seemed to build to a crescendo around ten o'clock, when R.J. got up to leave the restaurant. Natalie was reluctant to go back to the *Splendour*, Davern would say in a later interview. She had trouble zipping up her jacket, Quinn told the police, and had a hard time walking, Mileski observed. Whiting, the host/manager, noticed R.J. and Natalie in a private tête-à-tête as R.J. put his pea coat around Natalie, shrouding her, Mileski felt, from the stares of other diners. "It was sprinkling out, and he put his coat over her head and they walked out, and she smacked into this wood tiki pole at the front door."

Both Mileski and Whiting were so concerned about the Wagner party's level of intoxication, and the slick weather, they made separate calls to Kurt Craig, who was at the dinghy dock in the Harbor Patrol office. Mileski recalls, "I said, 'They're coming out, they're screwed up, just keep an eye on them.' "

Craig, who went off-duty at 10:30, recalled for police a call from Whiting at 10:00 saying the four were "very drunk," with Whiting advising him to be sure they got aboard the *Splendour* safely. Craig watched them at the dock as they all stepped into the Wagners' dinghy, when he heard Natalie scream. "He thought she may have been drunk and was unhappy with something that happened at the restaurant." A shoreboat driver named William Peterson, who was near the dock, heard Natalie yell and saw her stumble as she tried to get into the dinghy, with Davern assisting her. Davern would later say in a British documentary, "We got back to the boat and Natalie's in a giggling state by now, talking with Christopher and being pretty chummy. And it was beginning to upset R.J. to the point where he had to explode."

Walken's and R.J.'s statements to the police indicate all four went to the main salon as soon as they returned to the *Splendour*, where, Davern would say in later media interviews, Natalie lit candles, he and R.J. drank scotch, and they opened another bottle of wine. What occurred next would set in motion the tragic denouement of the lost weekend.

In his first interview with authorities, Walken volunteered that he and R.J. got into a "small beef" soon after they got to the salon that night, and that Natalie seemed "disturbed" afterward.

Walken elaborated on the "beef" between himself and R.J. during his second interview with police. Duane Rasure, the lead investigator, recorded Walken's expanded account as: "They had all been drinking, and they had one of those conversations going where you kind of put your cards on the table. R.J. was making statements and complaining that [Natalie] was away from home too much, that she was away from the kids, and it was hurting their home life. Walken stated he also got involved in this discussion, supporting [Natalie's] view: that she was an actress, she was an important person; this was her life. He suddenly realized he was violating his own view about getting involved in an argument between man and wife."

The investigator's record of Walken's account continued, "[Walken] stepped outside for some air, and when he returned everybody was apologizing, particularly he and Robert Wagner, and everything seemed fine. He further recalled that about this time, when Natalie left the salon and went down to her bedroom, he thought she was tired of listening to them." Rasure's partner, Roy Hamilton, wrote in his notes: "Walken said he thought Natalie went to bed, and that she thought he and R.J. were a bunch of assholes."

When Davern was interviewed a second time by police, in the presence of attorneys he alluded to the argument: "[Davern] recalled that R.J. and Natalie got into a discussion about her being gone, and how R.J. missed her. During this discussion between them, Chris Walken entered into it and supported Natalie's view. Davern felt R.J. was being upset over this, and he recalled Chris getting up and going outside for a while. At about this time, Natalie went to the master stateroom to go to bed."

In R.J.'s second interview with police, he acknowledged,

"There was a discussion about [Natalie] being away from home and the kids so much." Sheriff's investigators noted R.J.'s explanation as, "Natalie went down to bed. And at this point in time, [Wagner] recalled Chris Walken stepping outside on the deck for a while. When Chris returned inside the salon, they continued talking."

R.J.'s told police that Natalie went to bed, he went to her bedroom, then they noticed that she and the dinghy were missing. In his second statement, R.J. said that after his "discussion" with Walken, Natalie went to her bedroom and Walken stood outside on the deck for "a while." He and Walken then talked and then he went to Natalie's bedroom to check on her and she and the dinghy were gone.

Walken's first statement was that he was on the deck for "a few minutes" after his "beef" with R.J., when Natalie went to bed. He "next remembered the captain making a remark that the dinghy was gone; at about the same time, they noticed that Natalie was gone." Walken thought it might be sometime just after midnight. In Walken's second statement, he repeated that Natalie went to bed as soon as R.J. got upset, "[and] the next thing [Walken] recalled was that within a short time the captain made mention that the dinghy was missing. At about the same time, Robert Wagner checked the bedroom and observed that Natalie was missing."

Davern told police in his first interview that Natalie went to bed, "and it was after this he noticed the Zodiac [dinghy] was gone." Davern's follow-up statement related that Natalie went to bed, and "after some time passed, R.J. went to see where Natalie was. When they noticed she was gone, at about the same time they noticed the Zodiac was gone."

According to Sheriff's records, Warren Archer, the diner

from the *Vantage* who shared a bottle of champagne with the Wagners that night, told investigators he radioed R.J. on the *Splendour* when he got back to his boat from dinner (sometime around eleven) to invite the Wagner party to the *Vantage* for drinks. Archer told investigators R.J. said no, and he heard noise in the background giving him the impression that there might have been an argument going on. Archer told a shoreboat operator later that night that he had noticed the Wagners' dinghy tied to the rear of the *Splendour*, which was moored near from Archer's boat.

R.J.'s first known call to report that Natalie was missing was picked up at 1:30 A.M. Sunday, when he used the hailing and frequency channel 16 on the ship's radio, saying, "This is the *Splendour*, we need help. Somebody's missing from the boat."

Don Whiting, the host/manager at Doug's Harbor Reef who had seated the intoxicated Wagner party and called the dock operator to be sure they got back to the *Splendour*, happened to be awake on his sailboat at 1:30, listening to the VHF marine radio. He recognized Robert Wagner's voice, "sounding drunk," he later told police. Whiting responded to the radio call from R.J.

R.J. told Whiting via the ship's radio that Natalie was not on the *Splendour*, and he thought she might be at the bar at Doug's. R.J. asked Whiting if he would check the bar for Natalie, and see if the dinghy was at the Two Harbors dock.

Why R.J. seems to have waited until 1:30 A.M. to ask for help to find Natalie, or to report her as missing from the boat, is one of the lingering questions from that fraught, alcohol-fueled night, since all three men appear to have noticed she was overboard or missing between 10:45 and midnight, according to their police statements.

By happenstance, Paul Wintler, an employee who lived on the campgrounds in Two Harbors, had been awakened by loud music just before 1:30 and turned on his radio monitor to pick up the emergency airwaves. Wintler overheard R.J.'s radio distress call to Whiting and immediately got in touch with Whiting to offer his help.

The search for Natalie Wood, who was missing in the Pacific Ocean off Catalina Island, proceeded at the direction of a restaurant host at Doug's Harbor Reef instructing a campgrounds maintenance man.

Wintler looked around shore for Natalie, and then checked the pier for the *Valiant*. When he didn't see Natalie or the dinghy, the campgrounds employee borrowed Harbor Patrol Boat #10 to go out to the *Splendour* to talk to R.J., around two in the morning. Wintler described R.J. to police as "drunk and a little panicky." He asked Wintler to drop him off at shore so he could look for her.

Wintler used the Harbor Patrol boat to drop R.J. off at the pier at Two Harbors and began to search the dark waters off Catalina for Natalie or the dinghy sometime after two A.M. "I kind of figured out which way is the wind blowing," he recalls, "and I kind of went along the shore . . . and I didn't find anything." After fifteen minutes or so, R.J. flagged down Wintler from the pier to take him back to the *Splendour*, "agitated" that Wintler couldn't find Natalie. "He was saying, 'Where is she?' and I can't answer, and after a while you get tired of that."

R.J. repeated to Wintler he believed Natalie was in the dinghy. Wintler brought R.J. back to the *Splendour* around 2:30 A.M., "thinking, 'I got to call somebody [for help].' " By that time, Don Whiting and his boat mate, Bill Coleman, the cook at Doug's Harbor Reef, had arrived at the Two Harbors pier, where they coordinated with Wintler to expand their makeshift search for Natalie, sending a few local residents in harbor boats to patrol the water.

Shortly after 2:30 A.M., by Whiting's statement, he and Wintler realized they needed guidance in their search for a movie star lost at sea. They decided to awaken the local harbormaster, Doug Oudin. Oudin quickly got dressed and took a skiff out to the *Splendour*, where he encountered R.J. and Davern, Walken, at that time, was in his cabin. Oudin tried to get details from R.J. and the captain to assist him in the search for Natalie and the *Valiant:* "What kind of dinghy is it, how much fuel did you have . . . did she know how to run the boat, how was she dressed?

Both R.J. and Davern told the harbormaster they thought Natalie was wearing a nightgown at the time she disappeared from the boat. Davern and R.J. told Oudin that Natalie had gone to bed, "and she just didn't want to sit around with the boys while they were drinking and partying."

R.J. told Oudin it was "completely out of character" for Natalie to take the dinghy out at night alone. "He said she wouldn't have." R.J. also told Oudin that Natalie was afraid of the water.

The harbormaster left R.J. and Davern sometime around 2:45 A.M. to arrange for an expanded search, thinking he was going to find Natalie with the dinghy. Both men, he observed as he got in his skiff, "were scared-looking."

Oudin arranged for five little harbor outboards to search the beach, sending one boat to Emerald Bay and another toward Blue Caverns, searching the coastline. He sent Wintler on a "land patrol" up to the campground. After forty-five minutes, Oudin took his skiff back to the

Splendour, informing R.J. he was "not having any luck" and needed to call the Coast Guard. Whiting, who was with Oudin, recalled R.J. and Davern as "a little dazed." Whiting told police, "The skipper said to R.J., 'Boss, do you think she could have gone to the mainland?' and Wagner said, 'Yes, that's a possibility.' "

Oudin called the Coast Guard at 3:30 A.M.

Meanwhile, a few small Isthmus harbor boats, manned by volunteers, continued to sweep the shark-infested waters off Catalina for signs of Natalie or the *Valiant*.

The first call to a Baywatch lifeguard to begin a search for Natalie in the 85- to 100-foot, 54-degree waters around the *Splendour*, and in the Isthmus harbor, was not until 5:15 on Sunday morning, six hours after she disappeared from the boat. The Coast Guard initiated the call to a pair of experienced divers named Roger Smith and Jean-Claude Stonier, who in turn called Bill Kroll at the Sheriff's Department in Avalon.

While Smith and Stonier dove under the *Splendour* between 5:30 and 6:00 A.M., searching for Natalie, Deputy Kroll questioned Robert Wagner.

R.J. told Kroll that he, Natalie, Walken, and Davern had been drinking in the main cabin of the boat "when we realized Natalie wasn't around. We searched the boat and found the Zodiac dinghy was missing. We then thought that Natalie had gone ashore to the bar. This all took place around 12 midnight. When she didn't return by 1:30 A.M., I got on the radio and called the Isthmus to see if she was there. I got a hold of some guys who worked at the Isthmus and asked if they could check the Isthmus for Natalie . . . they contacted the Coast Guard."

At the same time R.J. was giving his statement to Kroll and divers were searching in the choppy waters around the

Splendour, the night manager and the cook from Doug's Harbor Reef spotted the *Valiant* tangled in kelp inside a small cave at Blue Cavern Point, where it had drifted about one and a quarter miles northeast of the Isthmus pier.

According to the police statements of Whiting and Coleman (both now deceased), the key was turned off, in neutral, with the oars still in place, suggesting that Natalie had never been in the dinghy. The two boat mates also noted there was a wine bottle inside the *Valiant*; presumably the third bottle that Davern and Walken had retrieved from the *Splendour* for dinner the night before.

However, Roger Smith, one of the Baywatch lifeguards, asserts that he and his diving partner found the dinghy. "We swam it out of the cove . . . and when we swam it out, all the oars were in disarray. Everything was in disarray, as if somebody had been trying to climb back into it." Smith also noticed "scratch marks" on the *Valiant*.

Whiting later told police that once the *Valiant* was taken out of Blue Cavern Point, he and Coleman used it to continue the search for Natalie. As a result, the dinghy's evidentiary value was compromised, which lifeguard Smith found typical of the search for Natalie Wood. "Several errors were made. The one thing was not calling us out to begin with, to search for her, soon after she was missing . . . they had *shore boat operators* out there looking for her!"

The discovery of the dinghy at 5:30 A.M., with no Natalie, was an almost certain indication that her worst fear came true, and she had been helpless in deep, dark seawater.

The grim drama reached its nightmarish final act at first light, when Doug Bombard, the owner of Doug's Harbor Reef, who had the flu the night before, joined the search team at the Isthmus, using a small Harbor 4 patrol boat. "I was hoping that we'd find her clinging to the rocks or sitting up on the hill. I kept running the boat right up next to the beach, thinking that if she had drowned, that she'd probably be inside the kelp line, because the current comes down the island and swings in."

While Bombard was trolling about a hundred to a hundred fifty yards off Blue Cavern Point, close to 7:45 A.M., "I saw something red, and that was her down jacket. It ballooned up, and had enough air so it acted as a kind of life preserver." Bombard used his boat radio to alert Baywatch he thought he had spotted Natalie. Lifeguard Roger Smith immediately radioed back to the Isthmus Harbor Patrol to alert Bombard to locate her but not touch her "because we might be talking about a homicide. I wanted to recover her onto the Baywatch. And so I saw them speeding over there really fast, and Doug pulled her out of the water just as we got there." Smith was too late.

Bombard steered the boat closer to the jacket, discovering what he hoped he would not find. "Natalie was hanging underneath the jacket, which buoyed her. A lot of times when a person drowns, if they don't have a lot of fat, they go to the bottom. There was only one thing that kept her up, and that was that coat. She wasn't floating, she was hanging, actually, almost in a standing position, with her face down and her eyes open."

Underneath the red jacket, Natalie had on a floral print flannel nightgown, no undergarments, and blue slipper/socks, not the way Natalie Wood would dress to go to a bar. Coroner's records would note she was wearing four rings, an I.D. bracelet on her right wrist (a gift from R.J. she kept on always), and a gold chain around her waist. There was no cuff bracelet on her left wrist—suggesting that

Natalie did not intend to go anywhere, for she would not have been seen in public without The Badge. She had died as Natasha, not as "Natalie Wood."

Smith, the lifeguard who assisted Bombard in lifting her out of the water that morning, was struck by how beautiful Natalie was.

"All I remember is her eyes."

28 THE LOS ANGELES COUNTY Sheriff's Department rotation elected Detective Duane Rasure, a good-natured, self-described cowboy in his forties whose wife, ironically, idolized Natalie Wood, as the investigator sent to Catalina early that Sunday morning to find out how she came to disappear from the *Splendour* the night before, wearing only a flannel nightgown and a quilted jacket.

On his way, Rasure stopped at the heliport in Long Beach to question R.J. and Walken, who were flown back to the mainland as a courtesy by a Sheriff's Department helicopter, two hours after Bombard found Natalie off Blue Cavern Point. R.J. had asked the skipper to stay in Two Harbors to identify Natalie's body.

By the time sheriff's investigators took statements from R.J. and Walken the end of that long Thanksgiving weekend, news that Natalie Wood had been found floating near a cove off Catalina Island was on radio and television, sending shock waves around the world, inciting international gossip. Los Angeles coroner Dr. Thomas Noguchi, who had been notified of the drowning around 8:00 A.M. had already sent his investigator, Pamela Eaker, to examine Natalie's body.

Rasure met with R.J. at 9:54 A.M. Sunday to interview him about the events leading to Natalie's drowning. This, in paraphrase, is the sheriff's complete report of R.J.'s statement for police of what happened that night:

> He stated that Natalie went to her bedroom and shortly thereafter they noticed that she and the dinghy were missing. He first called to see if she went back to the restaurant, and the next thing he recalled they were unable to find her and people were searching.

Rasure noted in his report: "Mr. Wagner was in an emotional state at this time, at this interview, so it was terminated."

The detective was satisfied with R.J.'s explanation. "Really, I had the basics of what I needed," he states, acknowledging that he was already forming the opinion that "it was an accident." According to Rasure, the Sheriff's Department viewed Natalie's death that morning as "nothing more than a big-time celebrity drowning, in our minds. I've got nothing so far to make me think that anything's wrong. We had an accidental drowning."

Moments after he spoke to R.J., Rasure met with Walken in an office at the heliport. Rasure and his partner, Detective Roy Hamilton, spent a few more minutes with Walken than they had R.J. Rasure found Walken forthcoming, and he provided more details than R.J. had. After discussing "the beef" between himself and R.J., Walken told Rasure that Natalie went to her room. Walken thought she had gone to bed:

> He next remembers the captain making a remark that the dinghy was gone. At about the same time, they

> noticed that Natalie was gone. They noticed that she was missing from her bedroom. He stated he thought this was sometime just after midnight. He added he did not hear a motor or a small boat. He next remembered a shore boat coming alongside, and Mr. Wagner went ashore to look for her. He recalled Mr. Wagner saying that neither she nor the dinghy had been found.

After taking R.J.'s and Walken's statements on the fly, Rasure and Hamilton departed for Catalina to interview people on the Island who had seen Natalie that weekend, and to take a statement from Davern. The skipper, who had just completed the gruesome task of identifying Natalie's body, was questioned at greater length by the two detectives than either R.J. or Walken, providing an equally hazy account of how Natalie got off the boat and of his, R.J.'s and Walken's activities before and after. Davern told police:

> They all went back aboard the *Splendour* and sometime later he observed that the Zodiac, which was usually tied to the stern, was gone. He recalls that he next called for the harbor patrol.

Mud had spent Saturday night at Lana's house when a friend of Lana's woke them up by phone Sunday morning to tell them she heard on television Natalie had drowned off Catalina. R.J. had not phoned to break the news to Natalie's mother or to her younger sister, though he made several calls from Bombard's office in Two Harbors before flying back to the mainland, including one to Mart Crowley, and another to make arrangements for a child psychologist to counsel Natasha and Courtney.

Lana wept incessantly. Maria let out a primal scream and fell to the floor, shaking convulsively, just as she first had in childhood when she saw her brother hanging in front of the family's house in Siberia. When she opened her eyes, she was in a hospital; too drugged, at first, to recall the awful news. "Suddenly I remember and I started to scream again. I said, 'No! I wanna go, and find Natalie is alive. She is *alive!* It couldn't happen to her.' "

The twisted genius who had created "Natalie Wood," the intertwined movie star alter ego of mother and daughter, did not want to go on without her other half. "I don't wanna live. I didn't eat. I didn't sleep," she described to a friend later. "I was losing three, four pounds a day. Imagine. I didn't care. I wanna die, I wanna be with Natalie. I just didn't want to live without Natalie, couldn't live without her. She was my whole life. She was so much part of me."

Olga immediately flew to Los Angeles on Sunday to see her mother through the only crisis that ever threatened Maria's indomitable Russian spirit. Maria's kindly, most contented daughter, who was going through her own grief accepting that Natalie had drowned, reflected back on her shared childhood with Natasha, remembering how afraid she used to be to even wash her hair, terrified she was going to drown because of the gypsy's dark prophecy to their mother. Olga said to Mud, when she arrived in L.A., "I guess the gypsy was wrong, and that it was *Natalie* who was going to die that way, not you—so you can relax now." Her mother, she would recall, "just looked at me."

Lana, who had lived in the shadow of her famous older sister for all of her life, felt that the gypsy was right, saying later, "My mother basically *did* die when Natalie drowned."

Mud spoke in theatrical whispers, under her breath,

about the *Splendour*, "the boat that took her away," sobbing, when she regained consciousness, at the thought of Natalie. A Russian Orthodox priest finally told her, "Don't cry about Natalie. You're drowning her with tears. You're hurting her." "That did it," Maria would say later, explaining how she was able to go on.

Mud stopped weeping, but her spirit seemed to have departed with Natalie. "Every morning, ten o'clock," she said later, "it doesn't matter what Natalie was doing, even if she was in a studio, she would call me: 'Mud? Are you okay? Everything is fine?' *Every* day. She called me. So every ten o'clock, I feel sad."

Monday, November 30, the day after Natalie's body was found in the sea off Blue Cavern Point, as the public outpouring of grief, shock, and gossip over her death began to intensify, R.J. issued a statement through his lawyer, Paul Ziffren, as an explanation of what happened:

> Mr. and Mrs. Wagner had dinner last night in a restaurant on the Isthmus, after which they returned to their boat.
>
> While Mr. Wagner was in the cabin, Mrs. Wagner apparently went to their stateroom. When Mr. Wagner went to join her, he found that she was not there and that the dinghy (a small inflatable boat) was also gone.
>
> Since Mrs. Wagner often took the dinghy out alone, Mr. Wagner was not immediately concerned.
>
> However, when she did not return in 10 or 15 minutes, Mr. Wagner took his small cruiser and went to look for her. When this proved unsuccessful, he immediately contacted the Coast Guard, who then continued the search and made the discovery early this morning.

That same day, Dr. Thomas Noguchi held a press conference to disclose his initial findings on the cause, manner, and circumstances of Natalie's drowning; compelled, he would say later, to respond to what he described as "extraordinary interest among the news media."

Dr. Noguchi informed reporters that Natalie fell from the *Splendour*, speculating that she was trying to get into the dinghy from the swim step at the stern, to "separate herself from the group." The coroner's initial opinion was that Natalie hit her head on either the boat or the dinghy, which was tied to the stern, and she plunged into the sea. Noguchi based his theory that Natalie may have hit her head on a scratch, or "abrasion," he found on her left cheek. "There is no evidence of foul play," he said.

The coroner stated that Natalie was "slightly intoxicated," revealing that she had .14% alcohol in her system at the time of her autopsy, what Noguchi described as the equivalent of "seven or eight glasses of wine." Natalie's level of intoxication, he suggested, "was one of the factors involved in her not being able to respond in case of emergency after she was in the water."

In his question-and-answer session with reporters afterward, Noguchi was asked why Natalie would want to "separate herself" from the men on the boat. One journalist asked if there had been a dispute between Walken and Wagner. According to Noguchi, he conferred for a moment with his assistant coroner, Richard Wilson, who had been briefed on the sheriff's investigation by Rasure's partner, Roy Hamilton. Noguchi asserts that Wilson whispered to him that Hamilton informed him there was an argument between Walken and Wagner. Noguchi further claims that reporters overheard the comment in the microphone, setting off a bombshell at the press conference, with journalists demanding to know what kind of an argument occurred between Wagner and Walken. Wilson, who had met with Detective Hamilton, told reporters it was "nonviolent."

R.J., who had been in seclusion since he got home from Catalina, semi-sequestered himself in his bedroom in total darkness, barely getting out of bed, seeing only his doctor, his psychiatrist, and those closest to him, clearly haunted by what happened to Natalie. As Katie, his daughter by Marion Marshall, then seventeen, would say later, "There's his wife's children, looking him in the eyes, and wondering where their Mommy is and how they're gonna get through *life*. And he's wondering the same damn thing: how's *he* gonna get through life? 'Where's the love of my life?' "

Mud, who was under heavy sedation, finally told Lana, "I want to go and see R.J." She would recall Olga and Lana taking her to the house on Canon that first day or so, so that she could look in the eyes of possibly the last person to see Natalie alive. "And I ask him, I said, 'I know you won't be able to tell me any details, because you know I'll get too upset, but tell me please: 'Did she suffer when she died?' He said, 'No, no,' so that make me feel better."

Olga remembers R.J. as "totally broken. He was lying on his big king-size bed and his two stepsons, Josh and Peter, were guarding the door. So I finally went upstairs and just walked through to the bed, where R.J. was."

Lana wanted to know details of what happened to her sister. R.J. told Lana that it was an accident; that Natalie had gone to bed while he and Walken were talking and that she must have fallen overboard. Lana asked her brother-in-law why he hadn't heard a splash, or Natalie's screams for help. R.J. told Lana that he didn't hear anything, begging her to believe that it was an accident.

Monday, November 30, the same day Noguchi held his press conference, Duane Rasure, the lead detective investigating Natalie's drowning, told reporters for the *London Daily News* he was "putting together" Natalie's last moments, based on the Sheriff's Department's detective work. "What we think is that Natalie Wood needed a breath of fresh air . . . and went out on the deck. Maybe she wanted to go out for a little float around. Maybe she decided to go for a swim."

Army Archerd, a columnist at *Daily Variety* who had known Natalie and R.J. since the 1950s, spent part of that same Monday afternoon with anguished Hollywood friends of Natalie's, such as Elizabeth Taylor, Roddy McDowall, and agent Guy McElwaine, gathered in the living room and den of the Wagners' home on Canon, where the mesmerizing poster of Natalie, as Anastasia, was propped against a wall, a haunting reminder of the play she would have been rehearsing were she alive. Walken came by for a while, Archerd reported, sitting near the bar, where he "stared out in space."

R.J. wandered in, Archerd would write in his column, "his eyes wet with old and new tears," mingling with Natalie's stricken friends. According to Archerd, a few of them asked R.J. why he thought Natalie might have got in the dinghy by herself that night, as he said in his press release issued the day before.

The next day, Tuesday December 1, Detective Rasure talked to Paul Connew of the *London Daily News*, suggesting, "Natalie may have fallen overboard from the yacht and knocked the rubber dinghy, which was moored alongside, adrift as she fell. Or she could have decided to take the dinghy out for a cruise."

Natalie's funeral on Wednesday, December 2, touched and stunned the Hollywood community in a way perhaps no celebrity's had before. Natalie was not only beloved by the actors, directors, producers, and crews who worked with her and knew her, she was a *child* of Hollywood, taken tragically, while young and still beautiful; leaving behind two small, grieving daughters and a husband barely able to get through the services.

The honorary pallbearers were the legends with whom Natalie had grown up, literally, in the movies—Rock Hudson, Frank Sinatra, Sir Laurence Olivier, Elia Kazan, Gregory Peck, David Niven, Fred Astaire—Hollywood royalty, like she was. In the background were the strains of a balalaika playing the Russian melodies she loved. The casket was laden with gardenias—a thousand gardenias—the fragrance that announced Natalie was in a room. "It was so tragic, and so sad," recalls producer Martin Manulis, one of the guests.

Natasha, the daughter Natalie named for the identity and childhood she lost to become "Natalie Wood," was "hysterical" when she found out her mother drowned, recalls Peggy Griffin. By the day of the funeral, Natasha—who had begged Natalie not to go on the boat—was almost supernaturally calm, perhaps because Natalie prepared her by telling her the truth she would die some day. Natasha wrote a private farewell note to her mother, which she had put in Natalie's coffin, the way Natalie had placed Natasha's and Courtney's letters to Fahd, only a year before.

Eight-year-old Courtney, the "most wanted baby in the world" as Natalie once called her, was still in denial at the funeral, remembers Griffin. She would have a hard time, as years passed, accepting her mother's death. "A lot of times in my dreams, for instance, she'll come back, and I'll just think, 'Oh God! You're here! Where have you *been?*' And she hasn't been dead, she's been somewhere else."

At Natalie's star-studded funeral, R.J. picked up three gardenias and tenderly handing one to each of Natalie's daughters, the three sisters, Katie, Natasha, and Courtney; bending over to kiss the casket in a final farewell to Natalie, photographed and published in newspapers across the world, as had almost every gesture exchanged between R.J. and Natalie since their first publicity-arranged date in 1956.

"Weren't we all lucky to have known Natalie?" a dazed Mud, heavily tranquilized, said to each person who came over to console her. "Weren't we all blessed?"

The destroyed, displaced, delusional Maria met a fan outside the funeral who bore an uncanny resemblance to Natalie, and who said that her name was Natasha. Maria attached herself to "Natasha" for months afterward, introducing her to people as her secret, illegitimate daughter by her Russian sea captain, bizarrely fulfilling her long-ago pact with Natalie's TV costar Robert Hyatt by offering him "Natasha" as a substitute for Natalie, since Hyatt had kept his word not to "experiment" sexually with Natalie anymore. Mud carried on conversations, after Natalie drowned, "as if she were expecting her," handing out studio glossies she continued to sign for fans as "Natalie Wood." "She had to keep Natalie alive as much as possible," recalls her nephew, Constantine Liuzunie. "She couldn't let Natalie die, otherwise *she* would."

Natalie was buried under a camphor tree near her late friend Norma Crane. Her final resting place was at Westwood Cemetery, where Marilyn Monroe, whose sad, solitary overdose at thirty-six had alarmed her, was in a crypt, amid a galaxy of other Hollywood stars still worshipped by fans leaving flowers on their graves. Ironically, Natalie's fans would leave her pennies, like the coins Mud used to surreptitiously toss in front of her on the sidewalk, leading Natasha to believe she would have a charmed life.

R.J.'s last interview with investigators was December 4 from his bed, in his bedroom, where he was still in isolation, wearing pajamas.

Ziffren, who issued the press release setting forth what R.J. said happened the night Natalie drowned, was in the bedroom to advise R.J. during Rasure's questioning.

In this final interview with police, R.J. offered a few more details about the events on the Friday and Saturday before Natalie died. R.J. told Rasure he went to Natalie's bedroom and noticed she was gone, and they observed that the dinghy was missing. Their first thought, R.J. said, was that Natalie had taken the dinghy to shore.

According to Rasure, "The only conclusion [R.J.] could come to" was that Natalie had gotten in the dinghy alone to go back to the restaurant.

Walken's second and last statement repeated the theory that Natalie had gone ashore in the dinghy to return to the restaurant. He told Rasure he went to his cabin, and when he woke up the next morning, R.J. told him that Natalie might have drowned.

Davern offered nothing specific in his final statement about Natalie's disappearance, merely confirming R.J. and Walken's contentions they thought Natalie took the dinghy to shore.

On December 11, less than two weeks after Natalie drowned, the Sheriff's Department pronounced the case closed.

"As the thing progressed," Rasure explains, "my mind was getting made up and made up and made up, and I'm thinking this is verifying what I was thinking. I think I was totally satisfied within five days that this was an accidental drowning."

Frank Salerno, who was Rasure's supervisor in the Sheriff's Department overseeing the Natalie Wood case, states, "The investigation is completed. As far as the department is concerned, there is no mystery." How Natalie happened to get into the ocean that night "is getting into theory," asserts Salerno, "because you never know."

In Salerno's view, "It was just a tragic accident, that's all. It's no more, no less. It just involved a very famous person. In most death investigations, you never have all the answers. It's not like you can go from A to Z and in each slot there's an answer to that question. Because we weren't there. They may never figure out exactly what happened."

With questions still lingering about how and why Natalie ended up in the dark seawater she found terrifying, the media looked to Dr. Thomas Noguchi, since it was the coroner's responsibility to certify the cause, manner, and circumstances of death.

The cause and manner of Natalie's death were clarified within a day by Noguchi's deputy examiner, Dr. Joseph Choi, who performed the autopsy under Noguchi's supervision, determining that she died by drowning and hypothermia. Based on a "substantial amount of ocean water" in her lungs, Choi determined Natalie was still alive when she fell in the ocean. How long she remained alive in the 54-degree water was less clear. Choi felt "she may have struggled. I didn't think she died right away." In Choi's medical opinion, Natalie likely succumbed to hypothermia within "maybe an hour . . . but I don't think it was *hours*."

The other details of Natalie's autopsy included her blood-alcohol level, which Noguchi accurately reported in his press conference as .14, though Choi observed that Natalie had a higher reading when she went overboard. Choi found two drugs in Natalie's bloodstream: a seasickness pill called Cyclivine, and the painkiller Darvon, which Choi believed caused a "much more drunken state" with the alcohol.

No sleeping pill was detected, indicating that Natalie had not made her final preparations to go to sleep, since she had taken a sleeping pill as part of her bedtime routine for twenty-eight years.

Choi observed a "mostly fresh group of bruises," including the abrasion on Natalie's left cheek, a scratch on the left knee, and bruises along the right and left foreleg, as well as both feet. Noguchi later described a "recent widespread bruise" on Natalie's right arm above the wrist and a slight bruise on her left wrist. Both Choi and Noguchi detected "no evidence of foul play" from the autopsy.

Choi "thought it was likely" that Natalie died around midnight, designating that as her official time of death, saying it was "difficult to pinpoint."

Normally, Noguchi observes, medical examiners "don't generally get involved in circumstances, motives, and so forth. We just interpret medical and autopsy findings and express opinions."

In the case of Natalie's drowning, Noguchi asserts, he decided to hold a press conference to offer his preliminary opinion of how she died because of the rumors, media uproar, "and it's my belief in telling it like it is to the public, straight, when somebody dies under mysterious circumstances."

Noguchi's decision to go public with the circumstances surrounding Natalie's death, particularly the 'beef' between Walken and R.J., eventually cost him his position as chief coroner. His attorney, Godfrey Isaacs, states, "That argument was the trigger of the removal of Tom [Noguchi], or Tom leaving the Coroner's office." Noguchi was also criticized for revealing that Natalie was legally intoxicated, which he had been chastised for disclosing to the public a few weeks earlier in the death of William Holden, who stumbled while inebriated and struck his head.

Noguchi comments, "[It is the] duty of medical examiners to look into it straightforward, and reveal to the public what happened. Of course, people are not entitled to know every minor detail, but [they are entitled to know] what happened and why death occurred. We can't help Natalie Wood anymore, but hope that the public will realize that there are certain things that the preventive aspect can be developed . . . to make sure that a similar death will not occur."

Noguchi continued his investigation into Natalie's drowning, conferring with his consultant on ocean-related accidents, Paul Miller, who examined the *Splendour* and the *Valiant*, and was preparing a report for the coroner as an advisory opinion.

On December 5, a coroner's office spokesman pronounced the Natalie Wood case closed, ruling that it was an accidental drowning.

On December 27, after the sheriff's and coroner's offices closed their investigations, R.J. was quoted in the media, through a friend, with what would be his second and last public comment about the night Natalie drowned.

The information R.J. released in late December was that he and Walken had a "friendly political debate" at the restaurant, "and continued the discussion" on the *Splendour* until Natalie went to bed. R.J. offered his second theory of how Natalie might have fallen into the water, suggesting that she could have been bothered by the sound of the rubber dinghy banging against the side of the boat and went on deck to secure it, slipping into the ocean.

Over the years, this would become the standard theory offered for Natalie's drowning and would be accepted as perfectly plausible by Noguchi when he published his memoirs two years later, utilizing the advisory report he commissioned from Paul Miller, his expert in ocean-related accidents.

After reading Miller's findings, Noguchi revised his early opinion that Natalie was trying to board the dinghy. He thought it was possible, as R.J. proposed, that she went on the deck to adjust the line of the dinghy, lost her balance, and fell into the water, holding on to the *Valiant*. If that were the case, Noguchi theorized, the widespread bruise on Natalie's lower right arm could have been from "hooking her arm" over the side of the dinghy to stay afloat.

Based on Miller's report that there were scratch marks on the side of the dinghy—as lifeguard Smith observed—Noguchi presumed Natalie held on to it and was swept to sea by strong currents and the wind.

Noguchi's conjecture was that Natalie tried to hoist herself over the large, cylindrical sides of the dinghy, possibly by the motor, which he felt could account for the bruises on her lower legs. Noguchi believed that Natalie's red quilted down jacket—which kept her afloat after she drowned—prevented her from getting into the dinghy because it was heavy from being waterlogged. The vertical scratch he noticed on her left cheek "fit well" with Natalie "hanging on in tight contact with the dinghy frame." The coroner surmised that Natalie clung to the sides of the dinghy, trying to kick it toward shore, until hypothermia set in.

Noguchi's 1983 analysis that Natalie held on to the dinghy, kicking it toward shore as it swept out to sea, was based on his consultant Miller's mistaken belief that Natalie's body was found *with* the dinghy; Miller was unaware the *Valiant* had washed up in a cove 100 yards away from where Natalie was. "That's a surprise to me," admits Miller. "I was told that they were found together. If they were found together, I speculated that she had probably been alive for quite a while. But if they were not found together, well then I would be surprised that she could stay alive that long."

Miller still thinks that Natalie "was with the dinghy for a while because of the scratches, and I think she was probably hanging on to that bar line and she and the dinghy were floating around out there." Even this is conjecture, since the dinghy was *used* in the search, and had been washed up in the cove, banging against the rocks.

Natalie's closest friend, Peggy Griffin, is certain that Natalie was kept awake by the dinghy and was trying to re-tie it when she fell overboard.

According to Griffin, she and Natalie would become annoyed when they were sunbathing on the sun deck of the *Splendour*, next to the stern, because the rope tying the dinghy to the stern would get slack. "The dinghy would start bumping against the back because the waves were not regular and it would drive you crazy, and you had to go unhook the little gate that was in front of the swim-step, and step down on it, and untie the dinghy—pull it really tight and tie the knot again. And then it was good maybe for an hour before it would start knocking again."

If there was no one else on the boat, Griffin and Natalie reluctantly took turns retying the knot:

> Both of us would be half-asleep in the sun, and you'd hear the thing starting, and I'd be thinking, "Oh, I hope she does it," "Oh, I hope she doesn't ask me to do it," because you hated doing it. And then finally one of us would do it.
>
> But it was a foolish thing to do yourself. It wasn't easy to do it. It's strong, to keep your balance and pull a thing back like that and tie it up. You had to be really careful, because seaweed would wash up on that little step.
>
> Now it's one thing in the broad daylight, when you know what you're doing and you're balanced . . . it must be a whole other deal when it's nighttime, you've got those mukluks, stupid slippers that are leather on the bottom, and a big parka because it's freezing. I can see how in a second, you could lose your balance.

One question casting doubt on the bumping dinghy theory was why Natalie, who was afraid to be alone at night, terrified of dark water, would have gone to the slippery swim-step in her nightgown to retie the dinghy close to eleven o'clock on a cold, drizzly night with choppy waves, when there were three men to do it for her, including a skipper. Bob Jiras, her makeup man and confidant of twenty years, suggests that Natalie would have called out to R.J., "using these words, 'R.J., would you tie up that fucking dinghy, it's keeping me awake.' "

If she did try to move the dinghy, Griffin concedes, it violated Natalie's own rules about stepping onto the swim-step, even in the daytime. "She was very strict about safety, and always had to wear tennis shoes. I remember once she made me take my sandals off as too dangerous." Griffin feels "she broke all her own rules that night. Which people do. How often do you run a red light, when you know you shouldn't do it? Just for that one second."

There was another, more critical, flaw in the bumping-dinghy theory, according to boating specialist Paul Miller, who examined the Wagners' dinghy and analyzed the soundproofing inside the *Splendour* for Noguchi. Miller claims that even if the inflatable dinghy bumped against the *Splendour* that night, it "wouldn't make any noise at all" inside Natalie's cabin. "It's *rubber* . . . and they tied it off behind the stern step. It was a *very large* power boat."

Based on his analysis for Noguchi, Paul Miller believes that Natalie "fell over the side" in an accident. How it happened, he acknowledges, would be "completely a guess."

Noguchi, twenty years later, observes there are "some unanswered questions" about Natalie's drowning, adding, "I personally don't have personal information to add any more, and I, we, our profession generally try to stick with the scientific facts. I have nothing more to offer."

Since that devastating night in 1981, R.J.'s only public comments about the events of that weekend have been the

November 30 press release issued by Ziffren, and his quotes, through a friend, that late December.

Walken has rarely discussed Natalie's death in the media in the twenty years since her drowning, "out of respect for the family." He told reporter Barbara Howar, in 1983, "[Natalie] drowned and nobody knows how she drowned or what happened, except her. Nobody will ever know."

One person who claims to know is the skipper, Dennis Davern, the wild card in the deck from that disturbing lost weekend in Catalina, who has talked publicly and has offered glimpses into the events of that night, but his tale is clouded by his secretive behaviour, tainted by his profit motive and riddled with his own inconsistencies and piecemeal revelations.

What really happened on that awful, aberrant night may never be known. In the end, one is left with a sense of overwhelming loss, of tragedy, and of mystery; a feeling that Natalie should not have drowned during that strange, alcoholic, incoherent night on the *Splendour*, made even more heartbreaking and harrowing by her recurring dream she would die in water that was dark, her deepest fear.

The second tragedy is that Natalie, who lived to please, who always wanted things to turn out well in the end—a "good soul," as her friend Redford said in simple eloquence—has been shadowed by the irresolution of the events from a night that was so unlike her.

As Christopher Walken would say of the movie they had not quite completed together, "Things that are left hanging are difficult." Natalie's older sister, Olga, would view her disappearance from the *Splendour* as a mystery, which it remains. "Who knows what happened?"

What is important, finally, is to remember Natalie's *life*, and the characters she created on-screen—the poignant Austrian waif in *Tomorrow Is Forever* . . . precocious Susan in *Miracle on 34th Street* . . . tender, luminous Maria in *West Side Story* . . . Judy, the sensitive teenager in *Rebel Without a Cause* . . . brave, plucky Angie in *Love with the Proper Stranger* . . . vulnerable Deanie in *Splendor in the Grass*—the gifts Natalie gave her fans at the expense of her own identity.

"Natalie Wood," her actress alter ego, lives on in the movies. What has been lost is Natasha.

"Ootra Vechereem Moodreunaya," as Natalie said at the end of her eulogy for her Fahd. "Now we feel so sad about losing you, as one sometimes feels sad at nightfall. But we will have our morning when our spirits will lift, our sadness will lighten and we will realize we haven't really lost you, because your uniqueness to us all will always live in our hearts."

Spakoynee noch, Natasha.

Filmography

1944

Happy Land (Twentieth Century Fox). Director: Irving Pichel; Producer: Kenneth MacGowan; Screenwriters: Julian Josephson & Kathryn Scola; Novel: MacKinlay Kantor

1946

Tomorrow Is Forever (RKO). Director: Irving Pichel; Producer: David Lewis; Screenwriters: Gwen Bristow & Lenore J. Coffee

The Bride Wore Boots (Paramount). Director: Irving Pichel; Producer: Seton I. Miller; Screenwriter: Dwight Mitchell Wiley

1947

Miracle on 34th Street (Twentieth Century Fox). Director: George Seaton; Producer: William Perlberg; Screenwriter: George Seaton

The Ghost and Mrs. Muir (Twentieth Century Fox). Director: Joseph L. Mankiewicz; Producer: Fred Kohlmar; Screenwriter: Philip Dunne

Driftwood (Republic). Director: Allan Dwan; Producer: Allan Dwan; Screenwriters: Mary Loos & Richard Sale

1948

Scudda Hoo Scudda Hay (Twentieth Century Fox). Director: F. Hugh Herbert; Producer: Walter Morosco; Screenwriter: F. Hugh Herbert

1949

Chicken Every Sunday (Twentieth Century Fox). Director: George Seaton;
Producer: William Perlberg; Screenwriters: George Seaton & Valentine Davies

The Green Promise (RKO). Director: William D. Russell; Producers: Glenn McCarthy, Robert Paige; Screenwriter: Monty Collins

Father Was a Fullback (Twentieth Century Fox). Director: John M. Stahl;
Producer: Fred Kohlmar; Screenwriters: Aleen Leslie, Casey Robinson,
Mary Loos, Richard Sale

1950

No Sad Songs for Me (Columbia). Director: Rudolph Mate; Producer: Buddy Adler; Screenwriter: Howard Koch

Our Very Own (Goldwyn). Director: David Miller; Producer: Sam Goldwyn; Screenwriter: F. Hugh Herbert

Jackpot (Twentieth Century Fox). Director: Walter Lang; Producer: Samuel G. Engel; Screenwriters: Phoebe & Henry Ephron

1951

Never a Dull Moment (RKO). Director: George Marshall; Producer: Harriet Parsons; Screenwriters: Lou Breslow & Doris Anderson; Novel: Kay Swift

Dear Brat (Paramount). Director: William Seiter; Producer: Mel Epstein;
Screenwriter: Devery Freeman

The Blue Veil (RKO). Director: Curtis Bernhardt; Producers: Jerry Wald & Norman Krasna; Screenwriter: Norman Corwin

1952

Just for You (Paramount). Director: Elliott Nugent; Producer: Pat Duggan;
Screenwriter: Robert Carson

The Rose Bowl Story (Monogram/Republic). Director: William

Beaudine; Producers: Richard Heermance & Walter Mirisch; Screenwriter: Charles R. Marion

The Star (Twentieth Century Fox). Director: Stuart Heisler; Producer: Bert E. Friedlob; Screenwriters: Katherine Albert & Dale Eunson

1954

The Silver Chalice (Warner Brothers). Director/Producer: Victor Saville;
Screenwriter: Lesser Samuels; Novel: Thomas Costain

1955

One Desire (Universal/International). Director: Jerry Hopper; Producer: Ross Hunter; Screenwriters: Lawrence Roman & Robert Blees; Novel: Conrad Richter

Rebel Without a Cause (Warner Brothers). Director: Nicholas Ray;
Producer: David Weisbart; Screenwriter: Stewart Stern, Adapted by Irving Schulman, Story by Nicholas Ray

1956

The Searchers (Warner Brothers). Director: John Ford; Executive Producer: Merian C. Cooper; Associate Producer: Patrick Ford; Screenwriter: Frank S. Nugent;
Novel: Alan LeMay

A Cry in the Night (Warner Brothers). Director: Frank Tuttle; Producer: Alan Ladd; Screenwriter: David Dortort

The Burning Hills (Warner Brothers). Director: Stuart Heisler; Producer: Richard Whorf; Screenplay: Irving Wallace

The Girl He Left Behind (Warner Brothers). Director: David Butler; Producer:
Frank Rosenberg; Screenwriter: Guy Trosper

1957

Bombers B-52 (Warner Brothers). Director: Gordon Douglas; Producer: Richard Whorf; Screenwriter: Irving Wallace; Story: Sam Rolfe

1958

Marjorie Morningstar (Warner Brothers). Director: Irving Rapper; Producer: Milton Sperling; Screenwriter: Everett Freeman; Novel: Herman Wouk

Kings Go Forth (United Artists). Director: Delmer Daves; Producer: Frank Ross; Screenwriter: Merle Miller

1960

Cash McCall (Warner Brothers). Director: Joseph Pevney; Producer: Henry Blanke; Screenwriters: Lenore Coffee & Marion Hargrove

All the Fine Young Cannibals (MGM). Director: Michael Anderson; Producer: Pandro S. Berman; Screenwriter: Robert Thom; Story: Rosamond Marshall

1961

Splendor in the Grass (Warner Brothers). Director: Elia Kazan; Producer: Elia Kazan; Screenwriter: William Inge

West Side Story (United Artists). Codirectors: Robert Wise & Jerome Robbins;
Producer: Robert Wise; Associate Producer: Saul Chaplin; Screenwriter: Ernest Lehman; Book: Arthur Laurents

1962

Gypsy (Warner Brothers). Director: Mervyn LeRoy; Producer: Mervyn LeRoy; Screenwriter: Leonard Spigelgass

1963

Love with the Proper Stranger (Paramount). Director: Robert Mulligan;
Producer: Alan J. Pakula; Screenwriter: Arnold Schulman

1964

Sex and the Single Girl (Warner Brothers). Director: Richard Quine; Producer: William T. Orr; Screenwriters: Joseph Heller & David R. Schwartz; Story: Joseph Hoffman; Book: Helen Gurley Brown

1965

The Great Race (Warner Brothers). Director: Blake Edwards; Producer: Martin Jurow; Screenwriter: Arthur Ross

1966

Inside Daisy Clover (Warner Brothers). Director: Robert Mulligan;
Producer: Alan J. Pakula; Screenwriter: Gavin Lambert

This Property Is Condemned (Paramount). Director: Sydney Pollack;
Producers: Ray Stark, John Houseman; Screenwriters: Francis Ford Coppola,
Fred Coe & Edith Sommer; Play: Tennessee Williams

Penelope (MGM). Director: Arthur Hiller; Producer: Arthur Loew, Jr.;
Screenwriter: George Wells; Novel: E. V. Cunningham

1969

Bob and Carol and Ted and Alice (Columbia). Director: Paul Mazursky;
Executive Producer: Michael J. Frankovich; Producer: Larry Tucker;
Screenwriters: Paul Mazursky & Larry Tucker

1972

The Candidate (Warner Brothers)—cameo as Natalie Wood. Director: Michael Ritchie; Producer: Walter Coblenz; Screenwriter: Jeremy Larner

1975

Peeper (Twentieth Century Fox). Director: Peter Hyams; Producers: Robert Chartoff & Irwin Winkler; Screenwriter: W. D. Richter; Novel: Keith Laumer

1979

Meteor (Universal/International). Director: Ronald Neame; Producers: Arnold Orgolini & Theodore Parvin; Screenwriters: Stanley Mann & Edmund H. North; Story: Edmund H. North

1980

The Last Married Couple in America (Universal). Director: Gilbert Cates; Producers: Edward S. Feldman & John Herman Shaner; Screenwriter: John Herman Shaner

1982

Brainstorm (MGM). Director/Producer: Douglas Trumbull; Executive Producer: Joel L. Freeman; Producer: John Foreman;
Screenwriters: Robert Stitzel & Philip Frank Messina

Television Appearances

1952
Playmates, NBC, Schaefer Century Theater
Quite a Viking, NN, Hollywood Playhouse

1953
Pride of the Family, ABC series

1954
Pride of the Family, ABC series
Return of the Dead, CBS, *Public Defender*
The Plot Against Mrs. Pomeroy, NN, Studio '57
I Am a Fool, CBS, General Electric Theater
Alice in Wonderland
Opening Night
Somebody I Know
Life with Luigi

1955
The Wild Bunch, CBS, Four Star Playhouse
Too Old for Dolls, NBC, Ford Theater
The Old Triangle, NN, Mayor of the Town
Heidi, NBC
Feathertop, CBS, General Electric Theater
Miracle at Potter's Farm, CBS, Studio One
The Wedding Gift, ABC, King's Row Theater

1956
The Deadly Riddle, ABC, Warner Brothers
Perry Como Show, guest appearance
Carnival, NBC, Kaiser Aluminum Hour

House Party with Art Linkletter
Ed Sullivan, CBS, Modern Screen Awards

1957
Girl on a Subway, ABC, Conflict
The Bob Hope Show (Special), NBC, guest appearance

1958
The Bob Hope Show (Special), NBC, guest appearance
Sinatra Show, ABC, guest appearance

1959
The Bob Hope Show (Special), NBC, guest appearance

1960
Jack Benny Show, CBS, guest appearance with Robert Wagner

1973
The Affair (telefilm), ABC

1975
The Cruise Ship Murders, CBS, *Switch*, guest appearance

1976
Cat on a Hot Tin Roof (special telefilm), NBC

1977
A Salute to Bette Davis, CBS

1978
Stars Salute Israel at 80, ABC

1979
From Here to Eternity (miniseries), NBC
The Cracker Factory (telefilm), ABC
Hart to Hart (pilot), ABC (cameo as Natasha Gurdin)
Treasures of the Hermitage (special), NBC

1980
The Memory of Eva Ryker (telefilm), CBS

Notes

[SF=Suzanne Finstad]

ACT ONE

CHAPTER 1

3 NATALIE'S REAL NAME: Birth certificate #4866, County of San Francisco

3 MARIA WAS COLORFUL: Lois Tenney to SF, 6/13/99; Constantine Liuzunie et al. to SF, 7/10/99; Shirley Moore Mann to SF, 2/2/00; Phyllis Quinn to SF, 4/28/99; Randal Malone to SF, 1/25/00

3 DEVIOUS: Scott Marlowe to SF, 6/8/99; Maryann Marinkovich Brooks to SF, 11/4/99

3 PATHOLOGICAL LIAR: Lana Wood to SF, 8/19/99 & 8/24/99

4 OBSESSED W/NATALIE: Phyllis Quinn to SF; Lana Wood to SF; Shirley Mann to SF; etc.

4 NOT SURE WHERE BORN: Olga Viripaeff to SF, 7/11/99; Phyllis Quinn to SF

4 BORN BARNAUL: Olga Viripaeff to SF, 5/7/99; Kalia's birth certificate; ship's log

4 BORN TOMSK: Maria Gurdin to Sue Russell, 1/10/87, for *Star Mothers*, Georgia Holt and Phyllis Quinn with Sue Russell, Simon and Schuster, 1988; *Natalie:* A

Memoir By Her Sister, Lana Wood and Jake Enterprises Ltd., G.P. Putnam's Sons, 1984

4 PALATIAL ESTATE: Shirley Mann to SF; Olga Viripaeff to SF; Randal Malone to SF, 1/25/00

4 YOUNG ACTOR: Randal Malone to SF

4, 5 MARIA'S GENEALOGY: Constantine Liuzunie to SF; Maria Gurdin to Phyllis Quinn; etc.

5 "CLOSE RELATIONS" TO: Maria Gurdin to Sue Russell, 1/10/87, for *Star Mothers*

5 BORN MARIA KULEVA: Constantine Liuzunie to SF; Marriage and death certificates of Maria Gurdin

5 SOMEONE A COUNTESS: Constantine Liuzunie to SF

5 RUSSIAN SCHOLAR: Professor Stefan Frank, UCLA Russian History Department, to SF, 2/8/00

5 PARENTS TOOK HER TO CHINA: Robert Hyatt to SF, 5/10/99

6 KNEW HOW TO SPEAK FRENCH: Olga Viripaeff to SF, 5/7/99

6 KALIA COULDN'T: Constantine Liuzunie to SF

6 NAT TRIBUTE: *A Tribute to a Very Special Lady*, KCOP-TV, written and directed by Gary Davis, produced by Peter Schlesinger and Harry Kooperstein

6 FOUND ON HILLSIDE: Lana Wood to SF, 8/19/99

6 MARIA LAUGHED: Shirley Mann to SF

6 HOGWASH: Constantine Liuzunie to SF

6 LANA DIDN'T BELIEVE: Lana Wood to SF, 8/19/99

6 BORN IN DACHA: Olga Viripaeff to SF, 5/7/99

7 FAMILY PHOTO: Olga Viripaeff to SF, 5/7/99; Phyllis Quinn to SF; Constantine Liuzunie to SF

7 TWINS: Maria Gurdin to Sue Russell for *Star Mothers*

8 SHE BELIEVED IT: Randal Malone to SF

8 WEIGHED 2 POUNDS: Phyllis Quinn to SF; Maria Gurdin to Sue Russell, 1/10/87

8 EYES LIKE FATHER'S: Maria Gurdin to Sue Russell, 1/10/87

8 GRAY-BLUE: Olga Viripaeff to SF, 5/7/99
8 BLACK AND BEADY: Sue Russell to SF, 4/30/99
8, 9 SWORE/JEWELRY: Olga Viripaeff to SF, 5/7/99
9 KEPT BOOKS, WORSHIPPED: Maria Gurdin to Phyllis Quinn, 11/85
9 KALIA SUPPORTED: Constantine and George Liuzunie et al. to SF
9 FOOTNOTE: RUSSIAN SCHOLAR: Professor Stefan Frank to SF
9 TOWN NAMED: Maria Gurdin to Sue Russell, 1/10/87
9 ARRANGED MARRIAGE: Olga Viripaeff to SF, 5/7/99
9 DIDN'T COOK: Constantine Liuzunie to SF
10 FAMILY HISTORY: Olga Viripaeff to SF, 5/7/99; Constantine Liuzunie to SF; Maria Gurdin to Phyllis Quinn
11 SCHOLAR: Professor Frank to SF
11 PROMISE: Olga Viripaeff to SF, 5/7/99
11 DEMENTED: Nina Arrabit to SF, 1/27/00
11, 12 QIQIHAR ANGELS: Olga Viripaeff to SF, 5/7/99; Maria Gurdin to Phyllis Quinn; Shirley Mann to SF
12 HARBIN LIKE RUSSIA, "NICE" STREET: Professor Olga Yokoyama to SF
12 YOUNG BOYS, GREAT DANCER: Randal Malone to SF
12 CHURCH TO EYE BOYS: Maria Gurdin to Phyllis Quinn
12 BALLET: Olga Viripaeff to SF, 5/7/99; Maria Gurdin to Phyllis Quinn
13 LOOKING IN MIRROR: Olga Viripaeff to SF, 5/7/99
13 GYPSY SAID SHE'D DROWN: Faye Nuell Mayo to SF, 2/24/99; Olga Viripaeff to SF, 5/7/99; Lana Wood to SF, 8/19/99; Maria Gurdin to Phyllis Quinn
13 GYPSY SAID 2ND CHILD A BEAUTY: Faye Nuell Mayo to SF, 2/24/99
13 TATULIAN, STRICT, GIRLFRIENDS DESIRED HIM: Maria Gurdin to Phyllis Quinn
13 ELOPED, LED REGIMENT, LADIES' MAN: Olga

Viripaeff to SF, 5/7/99; Maria Gurdin to Phyllis Quinn

13 HAD ABORTIONS: Randal Malone to SF

13,14 CHILDBIRTH EXPERIENCE: Olga Viripaeff to SF, 5/7/99; Maria Gurdin to Sue Russell

14 OVSANNA BAPTISM: Olga Viripaeff to SF, 5/7/99

14 MOVE TO AMERICA: Olga Viripaeff to SF, 5/7/99; Maria Gurdin to Phyllis Quinn

14 ALEXEI'S VOYAGE: U.S. customs records/ship's logs

14 UNDERWEIGHT: Olga Viripaeff to SF, 5/7/99; Maria Gurdin to Phyllis Quinn

14 BEER AND MILK: Olga Viripaeff to SF, 5/7/99

14, 15 BOOKKEEPING, BREAST-FED: Maria Gurdin to Phyllis Quinn

14, 15 MARIA'S VOYAGE: U.S. customs records/ship's logs

CHAPTER 2

15 MISTRESS: Maria Gurdin to Phyllis Quinn; Olga Viripaeff to SF; Shirley Mann to SF

15 ADDRESS, LIVING ARRANGEMENTS: OlgaViripaeff to SF; ship's records; Maria Gurdin to Phyllis Quinn

15 HALLUCINOGENIC: Nina Arrabit to SF

15 MOVIE CRAZY: Olga Viripaeff to SF, 5/7/99

15 DEALT IN ILLUSION; BELIEVE IN THE BEST: Randal Malone to SF

16 LEFT IN PARK, BALLET: Olga Viripaeff to SF, 6/12/99

16 SOCIAL CLIMBER, "TOOK" A DRESS, "NOT TWO PENNIES": Nina Arrabit to SF

16 PAID DRESSMAKER, FELL ASLEEP: Olga Viripaeff to SF, 6/12/99

16 WANTED TO BE ACTRESS: Josephine Paulson via Lois Tenney to SF, 6/13/99

16 READ PALMS/TAROT: Lois Tenney & Olga Viripaeff to SF

16 ALWAYS INTO: Lois Tenney to SF, 6/13/99
17 NEAR-DEATH EXPERIENCE: Lois Tenney to SF, Olga Viripaeff to SF, Shirley Mann to SF, Maria Gurdin to Phyllis Quinn, Josephine Paulson to Lois Tenney to SF
17 CAPTAIN HER PASSION: Olga Viripaeff to SF, 5/7/99; Shirley Mann to SF
17 NICK HANDSOME/WANTED HIM: Maria Gurdin to Phyllis Quinn
17 MUSIA PET NAME: Natalie Wood's eulogy for Nick Gurdin, 11/7/80, Westwood Village Chapel
17 WON PRIZES: Dmitri Zakharenko to SF, 6/27/99
18 NICK VIOLENT: Maria Gurdin to Phyllis Quinn; Olga Viripaeff to SF, 6/12/99, Shirley Mann to SF, Dmitri Zakharenko to SF
18 ZAKHARENKO HISTORY: Dmitri Zakharenko to SF
19 LIVED WITH NICK: San Francisco city directories, 1936–1937; Olga Viripaeff to SF
19 TATULOV DIVORCE: *Marie/Maria Tatuloff v. Alexander Tatuloff*, Case No. 264481, Superior Court of California, San Francisco County
19 INFATUATED WITH GEORGE: Olga Viripaeff to SF, 5/7/99; Shirley Mann to SF
19 NICK BELIEVED STERILE: Maria Gurdin to Phyllis Quinn; *Star Mothers*
19, 20 WHY MARIA CHOSE NICK: Olga Viripaeff to SF, 5/7/99
20 GAVE HER NATALIE: Randal Malone to SF

CHAPTER 3

20 CHOSE LOYS FOR MONEY: Lana Wood to SF, 9/13/99
20 STAGE-MANAGED: Maryann Marinkovich Brooks to SF
20 CHINA DOLL: Nina Arrabit to SF

21 NAMED FOR NATALIA, LOPATINS: Natalia Shabalina Bazigin to SF, 1/27/00

21 NO MONEY, BROUGHT THEM LUCK: Maria Gurdin to Phyllis Quinn

21 WAGNER SAID: Robert Wagner, Lifetime's "Intimate Portrait of Natalie Wood"

21 RAISED HER TO BE STAR: "Their Mother Neglected Lana," Harriman Jamis, *Photoplay*, 8/67

21 BREAST-FED HER AT MOVIES: Olga Viripaeff to SF, 5/7/99

21 WORE MASKS: Maria Gurdin to Phyllis Quinn; Olga Viripaeff to SF, 5/7/99

21, 22 GOOFY, BOUGHT CARRIAGE: Nina Arrabit to SF

21 SO BRAVE: Natalie Wood's eulogy for Nick Gurdin

22 RUSSIAN EYES: George Segal in "The Last American Girl," The Movies, 310 Madison Ave., NY, *The Movies*, 10/83, vol. 1, #4

22, 23 PAPA, MEELAYA, LOVED TO READ: Natalie's eulogy for Nick Gurdin

22 CHRISTENING GOWN: Natalia Shabalina Bazigin to SF

22 IGNORED NICK AND OLGA: Olga Viripaeff to SF, Nina Arrabit to SF, Liuzunies to SF, 8/67 *Photoplay*

22 COULD TAKE CARE OF SELF: 8/67 *Photoplay*

22 BABYSAT: Olga Viripaeff to SF, 5/24/99

23 READ FAIRY STORIES: "Natasha & Natalie," Barbara Giasone, *Biarritz*, July 1980

23 SMART LITTLE THING: Josephine Paulson to Lois Tenney to SF

23 NATASHA WAS BRILLIANT: Maria Gurdin to Phyllis Quinn

23 SPOKE "AMERICAN": "6-Year-Old Siren," Connee Curtis, *Motion Picture*, (circa July) 1945

23, 24 NO BABY TALK, CHANGED NAME, CURTSY, FOUL LANGUAGE, UNAFFECTIONATE, MARIA SET HIM OFF: Olga Viripaeff to SF, 5/7/99

24 STRICT EUROPEAN: *Twinkle Twinkle Little Star*, Dick Moore, Harper & Row, NY, 1984

24 CHILDREN IN CORNER: "Natalie Wood's Secrets for Blending a Busy Career and a Bustling Family," Marcia Borie, *Motion Picture*, 12/77

24 MARIA UNDEMONSTRATIVE: Olga Viripaeff to SF, 8/13/99

24 NICK LOVED LIFE, ADVENTURES, COMPLICATED: Natalie's eulogy for Nick Gurdin

24 BROKE BALALAIKA: Olga Viripaeff to SF, 5/24/99

24 OLGA BELIEVED: Olga Viripaeff to SF, 5/24/99 [Dmitri Zakharenko, Nick's brother, recalls their grandfather dying of natural causes during the revolution]

24 HATED CONFRONTATION: Lana Wood to SF, 8/19/99

24 "PRETEND" HER FAVORITE WORD: 7/45 *Motion Picture*

24 PLAYLETS: Lois Tenney to SF; Olga Viripaeff to SF, 5/24/99, Constantine Liuzunie to SF

25 PUT ON SKITS: Olga Viripaeff to SF, Lois Tenney to SF

25 SCRAPBOOK, TAUGHT HAND MOVEMENTS: Olga Viripaeff to SF, 5/24/99

25 WHEN WE WALKED: "What Ever Happened To Baby Natalie?" Joseph Lewis, *Cosmopolitan*, November 1968

25 BRAINWASHED NATASHA: Faye Nuell Mayo to SF, 2/24/99

25 POSED FOR CAMERA: "The Taming Of The Shrewd," Aljean Meltsir, *Coronet*, February 1960; "Natalie Wood: Star Into Actress," Richard Lemmons, *Newsweek*, 2/26/62

25 REMEMBERED FROM TWO: "Don't Sell Natalie Short," Richard Gehman, *Photoplay*, September 1957

26 EASY WITH HER, GOT PIANO: 8/67 *Photoplay*

26 SHE WAS DIFFERENT: Lana Wood to SF, 8/19/99

26 MARIA KEPT SECRET: Lana Wood to SF, Faye Nuell Mayo to SF

26 MOTHER THOUGHT SHE'D DROWN: Olga Viripaeff to SF, 8/13/99

26 MARIA SAID SHE WAS AFRAID OF DARK WATERS: Maria Gurdin to Phyllis Quinn

26 NATASHA WAS AFRAID TO WASH HER HAIR: Maria Gurdin to Randal Malone

26 MOTHER CREATED AN IMPRESSION, CONTRIBUTED TO THE FEAR: Olga Viripaeff to SF, 5/7/99

27 CREATED PARANOIA IN HER: Natasha Gregson Wagner on "Intimate Portrait: Natalie Wood," Lifetime

27 NICK WOULD NOT LET HER IN CROWDS: Shirley Mann to SF

CHAPTER 4

27 THOUGHT JAPANESE WOULD BOMB S.F., MOVED TO SUNNYVALE: Nina Arrabit to SF

27 LIVED IN PROJECTS: Lois Tenney to SF

27 NICK WORKED AT SHIPYARD: Olga Viripaeff to SF, 5/24/9; Maria Gurdin to Phyllis Quinn

28 MARIA'S HOUSE PURCHASE: Olga Viripaeff to SF, 5/7/99 and 5/24/99; Maria Gurdin to Phyllis Quinn

29 MARIA FOLLOWED THE CREW, NATASHA WENT ALONG, GOT SOCIAL SECURITY CARD, MARIA WAS FUN: Olga Viripaeff to SF, 5/7/99, 5/24/99

29 NATASHA ALWAYS ACTING: Maria Gurdin to Phyllis Quinn

29, 30 EDNA MAY DAY: "10-Year-Old S.R. Girl Gets Chance at Role in Movies!" *Santa Rosa Press Democrat:* 7/28/42; "City Plans Welcome to 'Cinderella Girl' " 10/18/42; " 'Edna May Day' Will Be Observed Here,"

10/24/42; "City Welcomes Child Actress with Rally," 10/25/42

30 "STANDING ON CORNER," "TOUCH MY DAD": Edna May Wonacott Green to SF, 2/4/00

30, 31 STAGE MOTHER, PLAYED HUSBAND, WATCHED HER, WATER FEAR, CALLED BUTCH, PLOT TO POISON: Ed Canevari to SF, 5/28/99 and 11/24/99

30 NEVER PHYSICAL, TAUGHT HER EMBROIDERY: Maria Gurdin to Phyllis Quinn

31 PICKED CHERRIES: Olga Viripaeff to SF, 5/7/99 and 8/13/99

31 GOT DRUNK, BETTER HE BE SOMEPLACE ELSE: Maria Gurdin to Phyllis Quinn

31 DYSFUNCTIONAL FAMILY: Outtakes of Robert Blake interview, "E True Hollywood Story: Natalie Wood"

32 KIDS LOVED HER: Ethel Polhemus to SF, 2/2/00

32 PITIED FISH: 2/26/62 *Newsweek*

32 PUPPY KILLED: Olga Viripaeff to SF, 6/12/99

32 GIRLS STOOD ON CORNERS: Edna May Wonacott Green to SF

33 POWDERED HER HAIR: "Natalie Wood: A Bride Again," Mike Connolly, *Screen Stories*, April 1964

33 GOT INTO THE MOOD: "Hello, Natalie Wood!" Allen Rivkin and Laura Kerr, *Vogue*, June 1962

33 NEWSPAPER ARTICLE: "Movie Stars to Arrive in S.R. Today," *Santa Rosa Press Democrat*, 6/13/43

33 PICHEL SAW "SHADOW": *Natalie Wood: A Biography in Pictures*, Christopher Nickens, Dolphin, 1986

33 BASED ON NOVEL: " 'Happy Land,' Second Movie Made Here," *Santa Rosa Press Democrat*, 1/22/44

33 KNOWN FOR ANTI-NAZI: 10/54 *Films in Review*

34 DESTINED TO BE MAGICAL, DUTIFUL: "Natalie Wood: Rebel at 20," Mark Alan, *Screen Parade*, June 1969; 11/68 *Cosmopolitan*

34, 35 PICHEL NOTICED CHILD, TRAGIC EXAMPLE, ENCOUNTER WITH NATASHA: "Modern Pied Piper," Faith Service, *Silver Screen*, February 1947

34. 35 MAKE IMPRESSION, MARIA ASKED HOW IT WORKED, NATALIE DESCRIBED IT, GO SING: *Twinkle Twinkle Little Star*

35 SANG "IN MY ARMS": *Twinkle Twinkle Little Star*

35 KNEW RUSSIAN, FELL IN LOVE, OLGA TAUGHT HAND MOVEMENT: Olga Viripaeff to SF, 1/6/99, 5/7/99, 7/11/99

35 THOSE EYES . . .: 2/60 *Coronet*

35 IF NICE TO MEN: June 1969 *Screen Parade*

35 PICHEL SPOTTED HER IN CROWD: Phyllis Quinn to SF

36 NATASHA JUMPED IN LAP: Shirley Mann to SF; 9/57 *Photoplay*; "Seventeen, Seventeen," Jane Wilkie, *Modern Screen*, January 1956; "We Solved the Natalie Wood Mystery," Claire Sills, *Movie Show*, November 1957

36 NICK DIDN'T OBJECT: Olga Viripaeff to SF, 5/24/99

36 MARIA MADE DECISIONS: 8/67 *Photoplay*

36 DIDN'T SEEM EXCITED: Olga Viripaeff to SF, 5/24/99; Ed Canevari to SF, 5/28/99

36 SEE IT IN HER FACE: Ed Canevari to SF, 5/28/99

36 WASN'T SHY: *Twinkle Twinkle Little Star*

36, 37 EDWIN RAN OFF, LIKE A SHADOW: Ed Canevari to SF, 5/28/99

37 WITH TEARS: Maria Gurdin to Phyllis Quinn

37 DRESSED IN TRAILER, PAIRED HER: Olga Viripaeff to SF, 5/24/99

37, 38 ANN PICKED HER UP, MARIA KEPT HER UNDERFOOT: *Twinkle Twinkle Little Star*

38 PICHEL FELL IN LOVE: 2/47 *Silver Screen*

38 "HE SAID TO MY MOTHER . . .": *Twinkle Twinkle Little Star*

38 OLGA'S MEMORY OF PICHEL: Olga Viripaeff to SF, 5/7/99

38 WANTED TO BUY NATASHA: Maria Gurdin to Sue Russell for *Star Mothers*, November 1985
39 PICHEL'S CHILDREN: Estate of Irving Pichel, Los Angeles County, 7/19/54
39 PICHEL'S SONS' ACCOUNTS: SF interviews with Pichel W. Pichel 3/29/99, Dr. Julian Pichel 4/2/99, Marlowe Pichel 3/29/99
39 MRS. PICHEL RESENTED MOVIE INDUSTRY: Aaron Pichel to SF, 4/2/99 & 10/18/99, Dr. Julian Pichel to SF, 4/2/99
39 PICHEL IN MAGAZINE: 2/47 *Silver Screen*
39 FABRICATION: Lana Wood to SF, 8/19/99
39 PROMISED HER PART: September 1957 *Photoplay*
39 WARNED MARIA: Olga Viripaeff to SF, 5/7/99; 2/47 *Silver Screen*
40 BIG DAY: *Twinkle Twinkle Little Star*
40 NEVER MENTIONED MOVIES, PLAYED IN YARD: Ed Canevari to SF, 5/28/99
40 MOTHER EXCITED, OLGA CARED LESS: Olga Viripaeff to SF, 5/7/99
40 VOLUMINOUS, GIFTS: 2/47 *Silver Screen*
40, 41 TOLD NEIGHBORS, MARIE EMBARRASSED: Shirley Mann to SF
41 CUT SCENE: Olga Viripaeff to SF, 5/24/99
41 SHE WAS GOING TO OFFER: Lana Wood, "Intimate Portrait: Natalie Wood," Lifetime
41 NO EVIDENCE: Olga Viripaeff to SF, 5/24/99; Ed Canevari to SF, 5/28/99
41, 42 WALKED TO JOB, TOOK GIRLS, WENT TO CHURCH: Olga Viripaeff to SF
42 STUDIOS WERE GOLD: "Natalie At Ease," Roy Loynd, *Los Angeles Herald-Examiner*, 7/23/67; 2/26/62 *Newsweek*
42 IDENTIFIED STARS, INVENTED A GAME: September 1957 *Photoplay*; 1/56 *Modern Screen*

42 MAYBE KNEW PICHEL, GYPSY MAGIC, GOT HIM TO SELL: Olga Viripaeff to SF, 5/24/99

43 HOUSE GONNA SELL, GOT THREE TIMES: Maria Gurdin to Phyllis Quinn

43 SOLD HOUSE LIKE WONACOTTS, ALL WENT TOGETHER: Olga Viripaeff to SF, 5/7/99, 5/24/99, 7/11/99; (Gurdins moved year to LA year before *Tomorrow Is Forever*): 1/56 *Modern Screen*

43 DEED TO HUMBOLDT: Volume 611 of Official Records, Page 70, Sonoma County

43, 44 ARTICLE: Santa Rosa newspaper clipping from scrapbook of the Canevari family

CHAPTER 5

44 FELT BURDEN: Lana Wood to SF; numerous published Natalie Wood interviews

44 KILLED ME: Ed Canevari to SF, 5/28/99

45 SORRY MOVED, HER DESTINY: Olga Viripaeff to SF, 8/13/99

45 DESTINED FOR THIS LIFE: Scott Marlowe to SF, 6/8/99

45 DROVE ALL NIGHT, HITCHHIKER: Olga Viripaeff to SF, 7/11/99

45 SOB ACT: Scott Marlowe to SF, 6/8/99

45 PICHEL DISMAYED: 2/47 *Silver Screen*

46 HARD MOVE: Lois Tenney to SF

46 EXPECTED VELVET: 7/23/67 *Los Angeles Herald-Examiner*

46, 47 PHOTOS: Letter with photos from Natasha Gurdin to Edwin Canevari dated 9/30/44

47 READ TRADES, TRIED FOR DIFFERENT THINGS: Olga Viripaeff to SF, 8/13/99, 5/24/99

47 REJECTION: "I'm Going to Live My Life," John Hallowell, *New York Times*, 3/9/69

47 PRAYED: "Bride-to-Be Natalie Wood Tells All," Jon Lawton, *Motion Picture*, March 1964

47 CARPENTER THROUGH PICHEL, NICK MADE SWING: Olga Viripaeff to SF, 5/24/99

47 NICK GOT CONSTRUCTION JOB IN STUDIO: January 1956 *Modern Screen*

48 MOTHER GOT EXCITED: Olga Viripaeff to SF, 5/7/99

48 PICHEL WAS DEPRESSED: 2/47 *Silver Screen*

48 BE ACTRESS, WAITING FOR BREAK: "How Eight Famous Stars Got Their First Acting Job," *Movie Life*, October 1970

49 TOLD LANA: *Natalie: A Memoir by Her Sister*

49 SCHEMED HOW TO STAND OUT: Olga Viripaeff to SF, 5/24/99

49 DRESSED THE WAY SHE PLAYS: Maria Gurdin to Phyllis Quinn

49 PICHEL ADVISED HER: Maria Gurdin to Phyllis Quinn, Shirley Mann to SF

49 IMITATED O'BRIEN: Margaret O'Brien to SF, 1/26/00; Randal Malone to SF, 1/25/00

50 FLAWLESS: studio biographies of Natalie Wood, Maria Gurdin to Phyllis Quinn et al.

50 NOT VERY GOOD, PICHEL RELIEVED: 2/47 *Silver Screen*

50, 51 PROUD SHE HADN'T CRIED, A COMMOTION, COUNTED CRYING SCENES: *Twinkle Twinkle Little Star*

50, 51 MARIA WAS UPSET, GOT NATASHA TO CRY, SEEMED TO GET THROUGH IT: Olga Viripaeff to SF, 5/24/99

50 MARIA HAD NATASHA CALL: *Twinkle Twinkle Little Star*; 2/47 *Silver Screen*

51 TOOK OUT OF SCHOOL, TOLD HER ABOUT DOG: Olga Viripaeff to SF, 5/24/99

51 BUTTERFLY: Robert Redford to SF, 2/16/00

51 TEARS FROM DEPTH, BROKE HIS HEART, SHE WAS IN THE MOVIES: 2/47 *Silver Screen*

52 NEVER BE THE SAME/CRYING: Scott Marlowe to SF, 6/8/99; "Natalie Wood Hits Promo Trail," Mary Blume,

Los Angeles Times, 8/2/70; "Don't Sell Natalie Short—Part II," Richard Gehman, *Photoplay*, September 1957; Lana Wood to SF

52 MOTHER LIVED THROUGH HER: "Natalie, More Than the Hollywood Stereotype," Anthony Korba, *Orange Coast*, October 1979; Natalie Wood interview excerpt on "Intimate Portrait: Natalie Wood"

52 MARIE'S DREAM: Randal Malone to SF

52, 53 MOVIE CONTRACT/SCREEN NAME: Case #503232, *In the Matter of the Contract between International Pictures Inc. and Natasha Gurdin*, Superior Court, Los Angeles County, Los Angeles, California, filed 6/22/45

52 READ SMALL PRINT: Maria Gurdin to Phyllis Quinn

53 NAME CHANGE: Natalie Wood excerpt on "Intimate Portrait: Natalie Wood"; 10/79 *Orange Coast*; 7/80 *Biarritz*

53 WOOD WALKED BY: "Hollywood Throwback," Bill Davidson, *Saturday Evening Post*, 4/7/62

53 HATED IT, "DON'T FRET": "A Star Is Born Again," Bob Lardine, *New York Daily News Sunday News Magazine*, 2/11/79

53 MUD ADMONISHED HER: Maria Gurdin to Phyllis Quinn; 6/69 *Screen Parade*

54 BE NICE TO DIRECTOR: 6/69 *Screen Parade*

54 WIND-UP DOLL: Pauline Kael, as quoted in "Natalie Wood," Kevin Lewis, *Films in Review*, 1986

54 I HAD TO DO IT: Natalie Wood as excerpted on AMC *Hollywood Real to Reel*, "Hollywood Legends: Starring Natalie Wood"

54 NO VOICE COACH: Olga Viripaeff to SF, 5/24/99

54 IQ 150: Robert Blake outtakes

54 MEMORIZED EVERYONE'S PARTS: Maria Gurdin to Phyllis Quinn

54, 55 MEMORIZED QUICKLY, EXPLAINED IN LANGUAGE SHE UNDERSTOOD: "Boy Meets Girl," Richard Baxter, *Seventeen*, January 1964

54 MOTHER DID SOMETHING: Scott Marlowe to SF, 6/8/99

55 PLAYING HOUSE: "A Last Visit with Natalie Wood," Dick Moore, *McCall's*, October 1984

55 FEELINGS SUBMERGED: "Natalie Wood & Robert Wagner," Marshall Berges, *Los Angeles Times Home Magazine*, October 9, 1977

55 YOU CAN'T MAKE HIM: 2/47 *Silver Screen*

55, 56 ACCOUNTS OF *TOMORROW* FILMING: USC Special Collections, *Tomorrow Is Forever* file, esp. Daily Production Report

55 EXPECTED TINSEL AND GLITTER: 2/26/62 *Newsweek*; "Care and Feeding of Child Stars," Charles Champlin, *Los Angeles Times*, 5/26/65

55, 56, 57 FIRST LEADING MAN, IN LOVE, BLEW HIS TAKES, EYES REFLECTED TRAGEDY: Orson Welles, "Tribute to a Very Special Lady"

55 HELPFUL TO HER: Natalie Wood interview excerpt on AMC's *Hollywood Real to Reel*

56 TERRIFYING: "New Movie Moppet," *Life*, 11/26/45

56 WELLES HAD A LOT OF EXPERIENCE: 2/26/62 *Newsweek*

55, 58 BOOMING VOICE, TAUGHT MAGIC: October 1984 *McCall's*

56, 58, 59 KNOW LINES, TERRIFIED TO CRY, GOT HER WORKED UP, SHORTY, COLBERT, WELLES CHANGED LIGHTING, MUD GOT HER WORKED UP: *Twinkle Twinkle Little Star*

56 PERFECTIONISM: Olga Viripaeff to SF

57 BEST AT SAD CHARACTERS: 6/69 *Screen Parade*

57, 59 ACTS FROM HEART; COLBERT SAID SMART: "Natalie Wood: Teenager with a Past," *Movie Life*, July 1956

57 THE WAY IT WORKS: Robert Hyatt to SF, 5/10/99

58 I HAD TO TAKE: Natalie Wood on *Tomorrow* with Tom Snyder, 2/14/80

58 HORRENDOUS STORIES: Mart Crowley, "Intimate Portrait: Natalie Wood"

58 TAUGHT MAGIC TRICKS: *San Francisco Chronicle*, 3/22/46; "Natalie Wood Makes It As Actress," Bruce Bahrenburg, *Newark Sunday News*, 6/15/69; Erskine Johnson column, *Los Angeles Mirror-News*, 7/7/56

59 LOVED GROWN-UPS: 3/64 *Motion Picture*

59 WATCHING TO BE BETTER: November 1957 *Movie Show*

59 COLBERT KIND, MATERNAL: *Claudette Colbert* unsourced biography, Academy Colbert collection

60 LETTER TO EDWIN: Letter and photo from Natasha Gurdin to Edwin Canevari received 5/22/45

61 I INVENTED HER: Maria Gurdin to Randal Malone

CHAPTER 6

61 FAN MAGAZINE: (circa July) 1945 *Motion Picture*

61 FRIGHTENED TO BE ALONE, MUD NEVER LET HER: "Natalie Wood's Own Story," Patricia Reynolds, *Pageant*, July 1971; *Natalie: A Memoir by Her Sister*

61 KIDNAPPED: 6/69 *Screen Parade*; 11/68 *Cosmopolitan*

61 DANGEROUS: 10/84 *McCall's*

61, 62 DREADED BEDTIME, STORYBOOK DOLLS, CALLED "FATHER," LIVED IN IMAGINATION, BEST FRIEND PICHEL: 6/45 *Motion Picture*

61 DOLLS KEPT HER COMPANY: Maryann Marinkovich Brooks to SF

61 TALKED TO HER DOLLS: 11/68 *Cosmopolitan*

62 SOLE COMPANION: Olga Viripaeff to SF, 7/11/99; 6/45 *Motion Picture*

62 FANTASIZED RUSSIA: 7/80 *Biarritz*; "Natalie Wood's Russian Roots," Roderick Mann, *Los Angeles Times*, 2/15/79

62 BIRTHDAY PARTY: "Am I Too Young to Be a Good Mother?" Frank Collins, *Motion Picture*, July 1958
63 ENAMORED OF: Mrs. Gregory (Lily) Muradian to SF, 2/9/99
63 PERFUME: 7/7/56 *Los Angeles Mirror-News*
63 11/26/45 *Life*
64 TO BACK UP THE LIE: Maria Gurdin to Shirley Mann to SF; Maria Gurdin to Sue Russell, 11/85; Maria Gurdin to Randal Malone
64 STORY LANA WAS TOLD: Lana Wood to Dennis Bartok at the American Cinematheque Tribute to Natalie Wood, Hollywood, California, 9/2/99
64 GENIUS, FOOT IN THE DOOR: Randal Malone to SF
65 PUT A LOT INTO HER: Robert Wagner, "Intimate Portrait: Natalie Wood"
65 DECIDED TO WORK; NOT EXCITED ABOUT MOVIES: Olga Viripaeff to SF, 5/24/99
65 NO MATTER WHAT: "Just for Variety," Army Archerd, *Daily Variety*, 11/8/78
65, 67 DEFINED ACTING; BULGING CALVES: 6/45 *Motion Picture*
65, 66 MARIA'S STORY: Maria Gurdin to Sue Russell and Phyllis Quinn for *Star Mothers*, 11/85
66 GAIL REMEMBERED HER: Gail Lumet Buckley letter to SF
66 TREAT TO GO TO MOVIE, BIT HER CHEEK, WET HER PANTS: Olga Viripaeff to SF, 5/24/99
66 NATALIE SAW HER PARENTS AS GODS: 11/68 *Cosmopolitan*; 6/69 *Screen Parade*
66 94 STARS: 2/60 *Coronet*
66 PLAYED MAKING MOVIES: 11/57 *Movie Show*
66 NICK WAS PROUD: Dmitri Zakharenko to SF
67 GOSSIP IN SAN FRANCISCO: Nina Arrabit to SF
67 NICK WAS UNHAPPY: Lana Wood to SF, 8/19/99
67 RUBBED OIL, SAID NO: 8/67 *Photoplay*

67 TOLD HER SHE WAS FRAIL, SHE IMAGINED ILLNESSES: 3/62 *Photoplay*

67 WOULDN'T LET HER RUN: Robert Wagner, "Intimate Portrait: Natalie Wood"

67 SO OVERPROTECTED: "Natalie's Happy To Be Back In Films," Kevin Thomas, *Los Angeles Times*, 10/30/69

67, 68 MISPLACED FEAR, CHILD ABUSE: Robert Blake outtakes

67, 68 NICK HELD A KNIFE, MARIA IN CONTACT WITH CAPTAIN, MARIA WAS AFRAID: Olga Viripaeff to SF, 5/24/99

68 GOSSIP ABOUT HOLLYWOOD PRODUCER: Nina Arrabit to SF

68 MEAN DRUNK: Lana Wood to SF, 8/24/99

69 AIRPLANE FEAR: Robert B. Jiras to SF, 9/16/99; Faye Nuell Mayo to SF; various Natalie Wood published interviews

69 PULLED PIGTAILS, AFRAID: *Twinkle Twinkle Little Star*; 8/2/70 *Los Angeles Times*

69 GABRIELLA, THRILLED BY SNOW: 7/56 *Movie Life*; *Hollywood Top 10 Scandals* 1963

69 SELDOM NEGATIVE, WOULDN'T WANT HER OWN CHILD: "Natalie Wood: A Young Wife's Tragic Story", *Modern Screen*, December 1961; 4/64 *Screen Stories*

70 RELINQUISHED LANA TO OLGA: Lana Wood to SF; Olga Viripaeff to SF; Constantine Liuzunie to SF; Randal Malone to SF; 8/67 *Photoplay*

70 RUMORS SVETLANA WAS OLGA'S BABY: Olga Viripaeff to SF, *Natalie: A Memoir by Her Sister*

70 IT WAS THE LAW; "THEIR MOTHER NEGLECTED LANA . . .": 8/67 *Photoplay*

70 NON-PERSON, THINKS SHE LIVED THERE, NO GODPARENT OR CURTSYING: Lana Wood to SF, 8/19/99

70 PRESENTED NATALIE WOOD: 3/22/46 *San Francisco Chronicle*

70 MAGAZINE PRAISED NATALIE: *Tomorrow Is Forever*, *Look*, 3/19/46

70, 71 OLGA WORRIED ABOUT GRADES, FIRED NANNY: Olga Viripaeff to SF, Maria Gurdin to Phyllis Quinn, Lana Wood to SF

71, 72 DAYS CONSISTED OF DRINKING; MARIA WAS UNHAPPY, SHE'LL SING: Lana Wood to SF, 8/24/99, 8/19/99

71 NATASHA FELT GUILTY: 3/79 *Saturday Evening Post*; 10/79 *Orange Coast*

71 MARIA'S COMPANION POSITS: Randal Malone to SF

72 EAT YOUR HEART: Louella Parsons column, *Los Angeles Herald-Examiner*, 4/5/46

CHAPTER 7

72 BRENT TOOK HER TO FAMOUS ARTISTS: 9/57 *Photoplay*; 8/67 *Photoplay*

72 CONTRACT WITH FAMOUS ARTISTS: Case #503232, Los Angeles Superior Court

73 SHE'D STILL READ THE TRADES; OLGA STAYED BEHIND: Olga Viripaeff to SF, 5/24/99

73 MARIA NEGOTIATED: Robert Hyatt to SF, 5/10/99

73 MOTHER MANAGED MY CAREER: 6/67 *Pageant*

74 DIDN'T LIKE SCHOOL: 9/57 *Photoplay*

74 DIDN'T KNOW NEIGHBORS; BITTY HOUSE: Lana Wood to SF, 8/19/99

74 NATALIE FELT AWFUL: "Natalie Wood Gets Back In the Ring," Patrick Pacheco, *After Dark*, 10/79

74–77 TITLES; SUGGESTED WHILE VACATIONING; NATALIE FLEW ON 11/17: "Vital Statistics on *Miracle on 34th Street*," Harry Brand, Director of Publicity,

Twentieth Century Fox, circa 1947 [from the Fox archives, Los Angeles]

75 FILMED AS B MOVIE: Robert Hyatt to SF, 5/10/99

75 ZANUCK SENT A NOTE, ASSIGNED O'HARA AND PAYNE: Fox Archives, Los Angeles

75 I WAS ONLY EIGHT: "Exclusive Interview: Natalie Wood," Flanzy Lewis, *Preview*, 1978, USC Archives, Natalie Wood Collection

75 MARGARET WAS THE TOP: Randal Malone to SF

75, 76 THERE WERE A MILLION; COACHED HER TO "BE MARGARET"; PEOPLE THINK IT'S ME: Margaret O'Brien to SF

76 ZANUCK'S NOTES ON *GHOST*; MOOD STORY: "Vital Statistics on 'The Ghost & Mrs. Muir,'" Harry Brand, Director of Publicity, Twentieth Century Fox circa 1947 [Fox collection, Los Angeles]

76 TRACY DROPPED OUT: Amanda Duff Dunne to SF, 6/22/99

77 MANKIEWICZ'S COMMENTS: Mankiewicz Q&A at the Director's Guild of America, Los Angeles, 1986, as quoted in *Films In Review 1986*

77 MAUREEN HADN'T READ IT; ORDERED BACK; NOT SO MAD: Maureen O'Hara to SF, 6/16/99

77 MAGIC: Maureen O'Hara to SF, 6/16/99; "Charming Christmas Story Brings O'Hara Back," Mark Dawidziak, *Calgary Herald*, 12/17/95

77 BELIEVED HE WAS SANTA: Maureen O'Hara to SF, 6/16/99; "Maureen O'Hara Hopes She Has Made Her Second Christmas Classic," Walt Belcher, *The Tampa Tribune*, 12/17/95

77 FELL MADLY IN LOVE: "Tennessee Williams Took His Name Off It," Rex Reed, *New York Times*, 1/16/66

78 ONE-TAKE NATALIE: Nina Arrabit to SF

78 SEATON WAS AMAZED; INSTINCTIVE SENSE OF TIMING: 2/60 *Coronet*

78 MARIE NEVER INTERFERED: Robert Hyatt to SF, 5/10/99

78 MOST VIVID MEMORY: 7/7/56 *Los Angeles Mirror-News*

78 NATALIE'S TECHNIQUE: *Twinkle Twinkle Little Star*; 1/64 *Seventeen*

79 SPELLED MANKIEWICZ, KNEW SHE'D BE AN ACTRESS: Mankiewicz Q&A as quoted in *Films in Review 1986*

80 WHAT A WONDERFUL TIME: "Recalling the Happy Times with Natalie Wood," Donfeld, *Los Angeles Times*, 9/30/83

80 HAD TO BE PAMPERED: Amanda Duff Dunne to SF, 6/22/99

80 LEE RECOLLECTIONS: Anna Lee Nathan to SF, 6/3/99

81 O'HARA RECOLLECTIONS: Maureen O'Hara to SF, 6/16/99

81 GOOD LITTLE GIRL: Natalie Wood interview, *Peeper* press release from Gordon Armstrong, Publicity Director, Twentieth Century Fox, 1975

81 MAYBE SHE WAS BEATEN: Scott Marlowe to SF, 6/8/99

81, 82 THREATENED WITH PIANO: Twentieth Century Fox press release

82 BOBBY HYATT RECOLLECTIONS: Robert Hyatt to SF, 5/10/99, Robert Hyatt letter to SF, 5/99

82 JEAN HYATT RECOLLECTIONS: Jean Hyatt to SF, 5/6/99

84 *SCUDDA HOO* BACKGROUND: "Vital Statistics on 'Scudda Hoo Scudda Hay,'" Harry Brand, Director of Publicity, Twentieth Century Fox [Fox collection]

86 IN ONE I WAS: "Falling Stars," David Castell, *Sunday Telegraph*, 12/6/81

86 I WAS PLAYING: 3/9/69 *New York Times*

86 I TOOK ON THE CHARACTERISTICS: 7/71 *Pageant*

86 DIFFICULT TO SEPARATE THE REALITY: *Twinkle Twinkle Little Star*

86 STILL VAGUELY BELIEVED IN SANTA: Natalie Wood on AMC *Hollywood Real to Reel*
86 NATALIE WAS PARALYZED: 2/60 *Coronet*
87 ALWAYS BEEN FRAIL: 3/62 *Photoplay*
87 IT WAS TERRIBLE: Scott Marlowe to SF, 6/8/99
87 PLAYED CANASTA: Robert Hyatt to SF, 5/10/99

CHAPTER 8

88 LOUELLA GUSHED: Louella Parsons columns, *Los Angeles Herald-Examiner*, 5/3/47, 6/14/47
88 MARIA'S DIRTY TRICK: Maria Gurdin to Phyllis Quinn; Maria Gurdin to Sue Russell for *Star Mothers*, 1/10/87
89 NICK WAS TOO DRUNK: Olga Viripaeff to SF, 5/24/99
89 LANA'S STORMY RECOLLECTIONS: Lana Wood to SF, 8/19/99
89 SHOW BUSINESS HER SOLUTION: Robert Blake, "E True Hollywood Story: Natalie Wood"
89 BELIEVED SHE WAS SEXUALLY ABUSED: Robert Blake outtakes
90 THE SIGNS WERE THERE: Scott Marlowe to SF, 6/8/99
90 KEEP HANDS OUT OF BEDCOVERS: Lana Wood to SF, 8/19/99, Olga Viripaeff to SF, 5/24/99
90 TOLD NATALIE SHE WOULD DIE: Robert Hyatt to SF, 5/10/99
90 FAHD WAS IN THE BACKGROUND: Margaret O'Brien to SF
90, 91, 92 NICK PRETENDED, FLIPPED OUT, SENSITIVE TOPIC, NATALIE KNEW RUSSIAN, KIMONOS: Robert Hyatt to SF, 5/10/99
91 LANA HATES SHOUTING, NATALIE HATED CONFRONTATION: Lana Wood to SF, 8/19/99
91 OLGA AND LEXI, SHE WAS MORE RUSSIAN: Olga Viripaeff to SF, 8/13/99

92 RUSSIAN FOODS: "Natalie Wood and Robert Wagner," Barbara Wilkins, *Bon Appetit* October 1977

92 DACHAS HIDDEN IN FORESTS: 2/15/79 *Los Angeles Times*

92 GOAL TO BE BEST BALLERINA: 9/57 *Photoplay*

93 WHAT INTRIGUED DWAN: *Who the Devil Made It*, Peter Bogdanovich, 1997, Knopf

93 IT WAS A SLEEPER: Robert Hyatt to SF, 5/10/99

93 *The New Yorker*, 6/14/17, "Santa Out of Season"

94 *Hollywood Reporter* 5/2/47, " 'Miracle on 34th Street' Delightful Surprise Hit"

94 A NOVELTY; LOST TO VIEW: " 'Ghost and Mrs. Muir' Scores as Novelty," Edwin Schallert, *Los Angeles Times* 7/4/47

94 FOX CONTRACT: Los Angeles Superior Court Case #531936, *In the Matter of the Contract Between Twentieth Century Fox Film Corporation and Natalie Gurdin*, filed 7/10/47

94 NO CONCEPTION OF MONEY: *Twinkle Twinkle Little Star*

95 HEDDA USED TO: "The Natalie Wood Story—Child Star To Glamor Girl," Hedda Hopper, 6/26/55, *Chicago Tribune Magazine*

95 INFUHR MEMORIES: Dr. Ted Infuhr to SF, 6/2/99

96 NATALIE'S FAVORITE SCENE/GLAMOUR GIRL: 7/7/56 *Los Angeles Mirror-News*

96 NATALIE WAS DELIGHTFUL, ADORED LANA: Mrs. Frank Arrigo to SF, 6/26/99

96 CALLED HER LANA, LANA CRIED: Lana Wood to SF, 8/19/99

96 LANA A NERVOUS CHILD: 8/67 *Photoplay*

96 LANA WAS JEALOUS: Maria Gurdin to Sue Russell for *Star Mothers*, 11/85

97 MUSIA LIVED FOR NATALIE: Constantine Liuzunie to SF, 6/14/99

97 NICK'S LAST-GASP EFFORT: Nina Arrabit to SF

97 NICK'S DREAM: Lana Wood to SF, 8/19/99

97, 98 FAME NEVER WENT TO HER HEAD, WOULDN'T GO IN RIVER, MARIA'S THIRD-DEGREE ON BOYS: Ed Canevari to SF, 5/28/99

97 Natalie Wood Gregson to C. S. Liuzunie, 7/23/70, courtesy of Constantine Liuzunie

98 NATALIE WAS THE QUEEN: Robert Hyatt to SF, 5/10/99

98 MARIA SAID WOMEN WERE CATTY: Randal Malone to SF, 1/25/00

98 FOX SCHOOL WAS EMPTY: "Daisy and Madame X," Harrison Carroll, *Los Angeles Herald-Examiner*, 4/25/65; 7/23/67 *Examiner*

99 *DRIFTWOOD* REVIEW: *Film Daily*, 11/6/47, "Driftwood"

99 FASCINATING DISCOURSE: *Hollywood Reporter*, 3/2/48, "Farm Film Loaded With Fresh Humor"

100 TIERNEY SUSPENDED, CRAIN REPLACED: Academy of Motion Pictures Library file, *Chicken Every Sunday*

100 SYDES' MEMORIES: Ruth Sydes to SF, 5/4/99

101 MARIA'S GRANDIOSITY: Olga Viripaeff to SF; 9/57 *Photoplay*; 11/57 *Movie Show*

101 ACTRESS/DANCER: Randal Malone to SF

101 MARIA TOLD STORIES: Robert Hyatt to SF, 5/10/99

101 MCCARTHY WANTED TO MAKE: "Houston's Term as City of Stars Draws to End," Mildred Stockard, *The Houston Chronicle*, 3/19/49

102 CHAPMAN WAS DIFFICULT: Ted Donaldson to SF, 6/19/99

101, 102 *GREEN PROMISE* INFO: Ted Donaldson to SF; Jeanne LaDuke to SF, 6/21/99; Marguerite Chapman to SF, 1/20/99

106 NATALIE RECALLED HUGE PROPELLERS; MOTHER CRIED "MY CHILD": 1978 *Preview*

106 THEY WERE TELLING HER HURRY: Lana Wood to SF, 8/19/99

106 SOMEBODY PULLED LEVER, DON'T REMEMBER THEM FISHING ME: "Late Actress Was Terrified of the Ocean," Bob Lardine, *New York Daily News*, 12/2/81

106 IT WAS SO TRAUMATIC: Mart Crowley, "Intimate Portrait: Natalie Wood"

106 IT WAS HER SECRET: Jean Hyatt to SF

107 MARIA DIDN'T SUE; THOUGHT DOCTORS WOULD TALK: Olga Viripaeff to SF, 5/7/99 & 5/24/99

107 DIDN'T LIKE DOCTORS: Maria Gurdin to Phyllis Quinn to SF

CHAPTER 9

107 NATALIE HAD NIGHTMARES: Leslie Bricusse to SF, 8/25/99

107, 109 COMBINATION OF INJURY AND FEAR; MARIA READ PALMS: Robert Hyatt to SF, 5/10/99

107 DEDA WOULD TALK: Natalie's eulogy for Nick Gurdin

108 NATALIE BLAMED MOM FOR WRIST: Lana Wood to SF, 8/19/99

108 MARIA'S SUPERSTITIONS: Lana Wood to SF, 8/24/99

109 NATALIE FOUND IT DIFFICULT: *Twinkle Twinkle Little Star*

109 COULDN'T REMEMBER 10 TO 12: 10/84 *McCall's*

109 MISSING OUT, LONELY: "The Natalie Wood Interview," Alis Loewell, *Los Angeles Free Press*, 8/2/74

109 FELT MORE COMFORTABLE WITH GROWN-UPS: Natalie Wood on *Tomorrow*, 2/14/80

110 OLGA'S WEDDING, PICTURE FROM NATALIE: Olga Viripaeff to SF, 7/11/99

110 NATALIE'S NIGHTMARE OF NO IDENTITY: "Natalie Wood's Kiss of Life," Douglas Thompson, *Daily Mail*, 4/7/79

110 NO CLEAR PERCEPTION: Natalie Wood interview excerpt, "Intimate Portrait: Natalie Wood"

111 O'HARA'S *FULLBACK* MEMORIES: Maureen O'Hara to SF

111 MACMURRAY'S COMMENT: KCOP "Tribute to a Very Special Lady"

111 WEARING FALSE EYELASHES: 7/7/56 *Los Angeles Mirror-News*

111, 112 HOUSTON HAD MORE NATIONAL FIGURES; HUGHES PERSUADED ZANUCK: "Torchlight Parade Will Precede 'Green Promise' Premiere," *Houston Chronicle*, 3/18/49

112 BALLYHOO, SCHMALZ: 3/9/49 *The Hollywood Reporter*

112 PLAYS THE ROLE WITH SENSITIVENESS: " 'The Green Promise' Tells American Story," *The Houston Chronicle*, 3/19/49

112, 113 *OUR VERY OWN*: Jane Wyatt to SF, 1/7/99; Ann Blyth to SF, 4/9/99; Joan Evans Weatherly to SF, 6/15/99

115 NOT A CHILD STAR: "The Youngest Veteran," Alexander Walker, *London Standard*, circa 11/30/81; "Natalie Wood," Earl Leaf, *Teen*, 12/61; "A New Year for Natalie Wood," Mike Connolly, *Screen Stories*, February 1962

116 NO FILM STARS: "Time-Check on Natalie," Pauline Peters, *London Sunday Times*, 4/27/80

116 CLIMBED OUT WINDOWS: Lana Wood to SF, 8/19/99

116 ANN DORAN: Ann Doran to SF, 5/26/99

117 MARIA'S PLANS TO LEAVE NICK: Olga Viripaeff to SF, 5/24/99

118 NATALIE SAID CALL THE DOCTOR: "Natalie Wood: Child of Change," Gereon Zimmermann, *Look*, 8/13/63

118 FAMILY DEPENDED ON ME: 10/79 *After Dark*

118 DISCOVERED THE HEARTBREAK: 2/11/79 *New York Daily News*

118 DO ANYTHING FOR PART: Jean Hyatt to SF

118 NATALIE SAID SHE'D DO ANYTHING: Gigi Perreau to SF, 8/6/99

119 GIGI PERREAU'S RECOLLECTIONS: Gigi Perreau to SF, 8/6/99

120, 121 DON ZOUTE'S RECOLLECTIONS: Don Zoute to SF, 8/17/99

121 ROBERT BANAS' RECOLLECTIONS: Robert Banas to SF, 7/6/99

125 EVERYTHING IS COPY: 2/15/97 *Financial Times*

125 NATALIE CRIED DURING JACKPOT: 7/7/56 *Mirror-News*

125 NATALIE TURNED AND STARED: "I Married Bob," Natalie Wood, *American Weekly*, 5/18/58

126 WISHED SHE COULD MARRY HIM: Natalie Wood on *Donahue*, 12/76, Show #11156

126 JUST A STARING KID: "Nat and Bob—Together Again," Joyce Haber, *Los Angeles Times Calendar*, 11/25/73

126 NATALIE WANTED TO GO TO SCHOOL: "Happy Birthday, Natalie," Beverly Linet, *Modern Screen* 8/58; "I'm Not the Girl He Married," Natalie Wood, *Screen Stars*, August 1959

126, 127 WANTED TO BE LIKE OTHER KIDS; BIGGEST SHOCK: 8/59 *Screen Stars*

127 FALSIES; COSTUME CHANGE; DIDN'T BELONG: "Natalie Wood," Arthur Whitman, *Pageant*, June 1967

127 NOTICED HOW MUCH OLDER: "Natalie Wood: Still Shining Bright," Philip Oakes, *London Sunday Times*, 12/28/69

127 LAUGHED AT HER: "Natalie Wood: Symbole 1962 de L'Amour," J. V. Cottom, *Ciné Tele-Révue*, 4/12/62

128 POWDER THREW LANA: Dr. Ted Infuhr to SF; Olga

Viripaeff to SF, 5/24/99; *Natalie: A Memoir by Her Sister*

129 CAN'T GET BILL HOLDEN: Devery Freeman to SF, 9/6/00

129 WORE HER OWN DRESS: Paramount production records, *Dear Brat,* Special Collections, Academy of Motion Picture Arts and Sciences

129 WENT GAGA: Jim Williams to SF, 12/21/99

129 IN AWE; WARM AND SMILING: Leilani Greenwood Overstreet to SF, 9/15/99

129 ALREADY A STAR: Rochelle Donatoni Vukonich to SF, 10/6/99

129 DYING TO DO THEIR THINGS: 6/69 *Screen Parade*

129 THE WAY SHE LOOKED AT YOU: Helen MacNeil Moriarty to SF, 10/18/99

130 MARY ANN MARINKOVICH RECOLLECTIONS: Maryann Marinkovich Brooks to SF, 11/4/99

131 HAD TO ADVANCE HER CAREER: Robert Hyatt to SF, 5/19/99

131 NATALIE LOOKED YOUNGER: Leilani Overstreet to SF

131 NATALIE AT SOCK HOPS: Leilani Overstreet to SF; Helen MacNeil Moriarty to SF, 10/18/99; Rochelle Donatoni Vukonich to SF

132 COULDN'T GO TO BATHROOM: "Natalie Wood and Bob Wagner Get It Together Again," Thomas Thompson, *Cosmopolitan*, August 1975

134, 135 NATALIE WAS INTENSE, MARIA RUTHLESS; FELT SORRY FOR LANA: Gigi Perreau to SF, 8/6/99

134 DIDN'T LIKE IT: "The Recycling of Natalie Wood," Carolyn See, *McCall's* August 1979

134, 135 ACTING WAS DIFFICULT, SELF-CONSCIOUS; LANA HAD A HARD TIME: *Twinkle Twinkle Little Star*

134 STUDIO WANTED HER: 12/28/69 *Sunday Times*

134 LOOKED SAME IN JUNIOR HIGH: Jim Williams to SF, 12/21/99

134 TURN OUT HOMELY: "The Faces Of Love," *Seventeen*, November 1957

134, 135 SHE'D DROWN IT, HAD TO HAVE A SPECIAL CHILD; NATALIE WORRIED HOW PEOPLE PERCEIVED HER; LANA A MUD FENCE; LEFT TO HER OWN DEVICES: Lana Wood to SF, 8/19/99

136, 137 BAD BOY; NATALIE WANTED WHAT SHE COULDN'T HAVE; JIMMY WAS A ROGUE: Jacqueline Eastes Perry to SF, 12/11/99, 3/3/00

136 NATALIE COULDN'T DATE IN JUNIOR HIGH: Jim Williams to SF, 12/21/99

136 PREGNANT IN BOY'S LAP: Olga Viripaeff to SF, 6/12/99; Maryann Marinkovich Brooks to SF, 11/4/99

137 SPENT LIFE IN PIGTAILS: 1/56 *Modern Screen*

138 HER REMARKABLE SINCERITY: " 'Blue Veil,' Wyman Win Human Victory," Edwin Schallert, *Los Angeles Times*, 11/17/51

140, 141 JIMMY'S MEMORIES: Jim Williams to SF, 12/21/99

ACT TWO

CHAPTER 10

145 GAGA WITH JIMMY: Maryann Marinkovich Brooks to SF, 11/4/99

145 MYSTIQUE, JIMMY HAD A TEMPER: Jacqueline Eastes Perry to SF, 12/12/99

145 JIMMY WILLIAMS' MEMORIES: Jim Williams to SF, 11/17/99, 12/21/99, 12/23/99, 1/2/00

146 COULDN'T STAND IT: "Natalie's Teenage World," Barbara Henderson, *Filmland*, July 1956

146 DATED COLLEGE BOY: 7/56 *Filmland*; 8/57 *Photoplay*; "How Natalie Handles Boys and Older Men," *Modern Screen*, February 1957

146 NOBODY TOLD ME WHOM TO DATE: "Knock on Wood," Bridget Byrne, *Women's Wear Daily*, 11/26/79

146 MARY ANN MARINKOVICH'S MEMORIES: Maryann Marinkovich Brooks to SF

146 WENT FOR A COKE: 9/57 *Photoplay*

147 HELD HER SKIRT: Natasha Gregson Wagner, "Intimate Portrait: Natalie Wood"

148 IMPRESSED BY BURR: Faye Nuell Mayo to SF

148 IMPRESSED BY TAYLOR: Robert Blake outtakes

148 CROSBY CHOSE WYMAN: "Leave It to Jane," Hedda Hopper, *Chicago Tribune* syndicate, 1/13/52

148 NATALIE BEAT O'BRIEN: Maria Gurdin to Phyllis Quinn

149 O'BRIEN HAS NO RECOLLECTION: Margaret O'Brien to SF

149 NO MORE RESTRICTIONS ON MAKEUP: Lana Wood to SF, 8/24/99

149 PROUD OF FIRST ROLE IN LIPSTICK: Helen MacNeil Moriarty to SF

149 BOB ARTHAUD'S MEMORIES: Robert Arthaud to SF, 9/29/99

151 ABSOLUTELY ADORABLE: " 'Just For You' Delightful," *Hollywood Reporter*, 7/31/52

152 DORAN RE *ROSE BOWL*: Ann Doran to SF

151 PERCEIVED DARKNESS AS WEAKNESS: Maryann Marinkovich Brooks to SF

152 HAD TO APPEAR A CERTAIN WAY: Lana Wood at Cinematheque

152 CUTEST CUTIE: " 'The Rose Bowl Story' Lively Football Film," *Los Angeles Times*, 8/26/52

153 JIMMY'S YEARBOOK: 1952 Fulton yearbook, furnished to SF, by Jim Williams

153 MUD STILL OPPOSED: Jim Williams to SF

153 NATALIE AND TOM IRISH: Tom Irish to SF, 12/1/99

154 YOU'RE NOT A LITTLE GIRL: 7/56 *Filmland*

154 READ STREET SIGNS: "Be Neat, Try to Please, Natalie's Dating Advice," Lydia Lane, *Los Angeles Times*, 3/16/58

154, 156 DOLLS; SLUMBER PARTY: Maryann Marinkovich Brooks to SF

157 HEDDA'S COLUMN: Hedda Hopper, *Chicago Tribune Syndicate*, 8/2/52

157 THRILLED TO WORK: Natalie Wood, *American Film Institute's Salute to Bette Davis*, broadcast 3/21/77 on CBS, screened at the Museum of Radio and Television, Beverly Hills, California

158 IRISH HAD A PART: Tom Irish to SF

158 SHOT IN 24 DAYS: Dale Eunson to SF, 6/15/99

158 SAILBOAT SCENE SHOT 8/21: 8/21/52 *Daily Variety*

158 SHOT IN SAN PEDRO; HAYDEN'S BOAT: 8/21/52 *Variety*; Dale Eunson to SF; Betty Denoon Hayden to SF, 6/10/99

158 ALL OF A SUDDEN: *AFI Tribute to Bette Davis*

158 FIRST VERSION: *AFI Tribute to Bette Davis*

159 EXPANDED VERSION—A COMPLETE WRECK; FEARED SHARKS: 12/2/81 *New York Daily News*

158 THROWN IN: 11/26/79 *Women's Wear Daily*

159 OLGA BELIEVES: Olga Viripaeff to SF, 5/7/99

159, 160 MARIA'S VERSION: Olga Viripaeff to SF, 5/7/99; Maria Gurdin to Sue Quinn 1/10/87, *Star Mothers*

160 NOT IN SCRIPT: Dale Eunson to SF

160 WAS ON THE BOAT: Betty Denoon Hayden to SF

160 BOTH STOOD UP TO HEISLER: Tom Irish to SF

160 STUDIO MISTREATED HER: 11/26/79 *Women's Wear Daily*

161 TOLD A BOYFRIEND: Scott Marlowe to SF, 6/8/99

161 INVITED FOR A DRINK: Olga Viripaeff to SF, 5/7/99; Maria Gurdin to Phyllis Quinn

161 WHAT A MOUTH; BRACELET: Maryann Marinkovich Brooks to SF, 11/4/99

161 SCENE ON STAIRCASE: Bette Davis, *A Tribute to a Very Special Lady*

162 NATALIE REACHED OUT: Ann Doran to SF

162, 163 WRAP PARTY; BRACELET: Tom Irish to SF

163 DROWNING DREAMS PROPHETIC: Jim Williams to SF

163 FAHD MADE BRACELETS: Natalie's eulogy for Nick Gurdin

164 ARROWHEAD WEEKEND: *Hollywood Reporter* and *Daily Variety*, 9/8/52

164 NATALIE PROFILE: "Divorces Don't Agree with Natalie's Notion," Aline Mosby, UPI "Filmville Fancies," circa September 1952, unsourced, from University of Southern California Archives

165 PRIVATELY CONDONE: Lana Wood to SF, 8/19/99

CHAPTER 11

165 WORST TIME: "Natalie Wood—From Pampered Star to Doting Wife and Mother," Peer J. Oppenheimer, *Family Weekly*, *Hollywood Citizen-News*, 10/18/69

166 LOVED THE FEELING: "Natalie Wood Speaking to John Kobal in New York," *Premiere*, May 1970

166 NO PARTS; WHEN NATALIE WANTED SOMETHING: Jacqueline Eastes Perry to SF, 12/11/99, 3/3/00

166 JIMMY WILLIAMS MEMORIES: Jim Williams to SF, 11/17/99, 12/21/99, 12/23/99, 1/2/00

166 TOOK 2½ YEARS: "It's a Wonderful Whirl," Natalie Wood, *Motion Picture*, August 1956

166 WASN'T IN THE BUSINESS: Maryann Marinkovich Brooks to SF

168 ALL GOOD KIDS; RONNY HOWARD FAMILIES: Rochelle Donatoni Vukonich to SF

168 THE VALLEY IN 1952: Robert Redford to SF, 2/16/00

169 FIRST GENUINE KISS: 8/56 *Motion Picture*

171 ½ OF 9TH GRADE: Natalie Wood's Los Angeles Unified School District official records171

171 ALL A'S: Lana Wood to SF, 8/19/99

173 ROBERT HYATT RECOLLECTIONS: Robert Hyatt to SF

172 IDIOT TEENAGER: 1/56 *Modern Screen*

175 JEAN HYATT RECOLLECTIONS: Jean Hyatt to SF

173 *PRIDE* CONTRACT: *In the Matter of the Contracts Between Revue Productions, Inc., and Natalie Gurdin, a Minor*, Case No. 615141, Los Angeles Superior Court, filed 6/17/53

174 I OBJECTED TO IT: 1/56 *Modern Screen*

177 NEVER FELT GUILTY: Shirley Moore Mann to SF, 2/2/00

177 IN THE SHADOW: Maria Gurdin to Sue Russell, 1/10/87

177 "WAS USUALLY HOME": Lana Wood to SF, 8/19/99

177 SELDOM SAT FOR MEALS: Jim Williams to SF; Jacqueline Eastes Perry to SF

181, 187 GURDINS DETESTED JIMMY; AVOIDED CONFLICT: Lana Wood to SF, 8/19/99

182 STORYBOOK: Maryann Marinkovich Brooks to SF, 1/10/00

183 "WHO WAS THAT GUY," 5000 LETTERS: "Robert Wagner, Heart to Heart," Mark Goodman, GQ, March 1986

183, 184 ILLUSION OF ROMANCE WITH MOORE, SECRETLY INVOLVED WITH HUGHES: Deposition of Terry Moore, Estate of Howard R. Hughes, Jr., Harris County, Texas, Case #139,326

184 OLGA TALKED TO NATALIE ABOUT JIMMY: Olga Viripaeff to SF, 6/12/99

184 WARNED HER SHE'D DIE IF PREGNANT: Robert Hyatt to SF;
Maryann Marinkovich Brooks to SF

185 PUNCTURE INTERNAL ORGANS THROUGH SEX WITH WELL-ENDOWED MALE: Scott Marlowe to SF; Maryann Marinkovich Brooks to SF

185–188 BRIBED MARY ANN; NOT STRONG ENOUGH; BLAMED HERSELF: Maryann Marinkovich Brooks to SF

185 NATALIE ALMOST ELOPED: Olga Viripaeff to SF, 6/12/99

188 NATALIE WAS DEVASTATED: Helen MacNeil Moriarty to SF

188 NEVER DATED HIGH SCHOOL BOYS: 8/13/63 *Look*

CHAPTER 12

189 EACH YEAR WAS THE LAST: 11/57 *Seventeen*

189 DISTURBED THOSE DREAMS: Maryann Marinkovich Brooks to SF, 11/4/99

189 LOATHED HER MOTHER: Scott Marlowe to SF, 6/8/99

189 STAGED A COUP: Margaret O'Brien to SF, 1/26/00; Marie Gurdin to Randal Malone, Malone to SF, 1/14/00 & 1/25/00

190 STARTED TO REBEL: Robert Hyatt to SF, 5/5/00

190 QUIETED HER NERVES: "Those Rebel Years," Natalie Wood, *Motion Picture*, October 1957

190 INSOMNIA: Lana Wood to SF, 8/19/99

190 COULDN'T FUNCTION; BELIEVED IN MOTHERHOOD; PSYCHIATRIST: Maryann Marinkovich Brooks to SF, 11/4/99

191 HEAVY MAKEUP: Robert Hyatt to SF; 3/16/58 *Los Angeles Times*

192 PARSONS REPORTED THE COLLISION: Louella Parsons column, *Los Angeles Herald-Examiner*, 4/5/54

192 MONOTONE: "Glorifying the Scandian Boy," John McCarten,
The New Yorker, 4/10/54

192 BETTE DAVIS LOOK: Robert Wagner on *The Rosie O'Donnell Show*, 1999

194 UNDERLYING RESTLESSNESS: *On the Other Hand, A Life Story*, Fay Wray, St. Martin's Press, New York, 1989

193 DREADFUL: 1/56 *Modern Screen*

194 DELICATE, VULNERABLE QUALITY: "Rick McKay's Night on the Town with Fay Wray," *Scarlet Street* 1998, issue #27

194 SAVILLE CLAIMED TO HAVE SEEN HER: "Natalie's 2nd Childhood," Liza Wilson, *The American Weekly*, 10/31/54

194 ORR CLAIMED TO HAVE SEEN HER: William Orr to SF, 5/29/99

194 DATES OF NATALIE'S TESTS FOR *CHALICE*: Warner's Production Notes for *The Silver Chalice*, the Warners Collection at USC

194, 195 SINATRA ON THE LOT FOR *YOUNG AT HEART*: *Young at Heart* file, Academy Library, Warner's production notes; *Daily Variety* and *The Hollywood Reporter*

195 SINATRA GOT A KICK OUT OF MARIA: Olga Viripaeff to SF, 6/12/99

195 SINATRA INVITED THEM, MARIA ENCOURAGED IT, ETC.: Robert Hyatt to SF, 5/10/99

195 URGED HER TO GET CLOSE TO SINATRA: Robert Hyatt to SF, 5/10/99

195, 198 MARIA WAS A PIMP; EASILY SEDUCED: Scott Marlowe to SF, 6/8/99

195 WOULDN'T SURPRISE HER: Lana Wood to SF, 8/19/99

195, 196, 198 THREW HER TO LIONS; SINATRA AFFAIR; ABORTIONS: Maryann Marinkovich Brooks to SF, 11/4/99

195, 196 CALLED PEOPLE CLYDE: "Why Sinatra Must Hide His Love for Mia," Mike Connolly, *Screen Stories*, October 1965

197 GAVE ME THE FEELING: Frank Sinatra, *A Tribute to a Very Special Lady*

198 WAY OF LYING TO NATALIE: Jean Hyatt to SF, 5/6/99

198 LIKE A GROWN WOMAN: Phoebe Kassebaum to SF, 9/15/99

198 INSCRIPTION: Van Nuys High '54 yearbook belonging to Maryann Marinkovich Brooks

199 PLAY SEXY PARTS; SAID SHE WAS 17; MODELED IN SWIMSUIT: Warner's press releases, *The Silver Chalice* file, Warner's Collection at USC

199 I HAD AMBITIONS: "Little Girl No More," Natalie Wood, unsourced article circa summer 1956, USC Warner's Collection

199 SENSE OF MYSTERY: Paul Newman, *A Tribute to a Very Special Lady*

199 FRIENDS WITH PIER: Jim Williams to SF; 10/31/54 *American Weekly*

200 O'BRIEN MEMORIES: Margaret O'Brien to SF

199, 200 MARGARET WAS SWEET; WORE LEIGH'S DRESS: Jacqueline Eastes Perry to SF, 12/11/99

200 NATALIE HAD PIZZAZZ: Jim Westmoreland to SF, 2/15/99

200, 201 WHISPERS IN THE FAMILY, DESTROYED HIS PAPERS: Aaron Pichel to SF, 4/2/99 & 10/18/99

201 DEVOTED TO MY DAD: Marlowe Pichel to SF, 3/29/99

201 TOLD A PUBLICATION: "The Story of Hollywood's Newest Sister Act," *Calling All Girls*, September 1956

201, 204 18; DATING SOUND MAN BELCHER: Louella Parsons column, *Los Angeles Herald-Examiner*, 6/25/54

201, 202 JACKIE EASTES' MEMORIES: Jacqueline Eastes Perry to SF, 12/11/99, 12/12/99, 12/19/99, 1/4/00, 1/6/00, 3/3/00 & "Conversations with Natalie," notes by Jacqueline Perry

203 PINK ROSES: "She Lives a Teenager's Dream," *Movie Stars*, September 1957

203 CULTIVATED IMAGE: Lana Wood to SF, 8/19/99

204 GOTTEN HER EXPELLED: Phoebe Kassebaum to SF

204 ALL-AMERICAN: Margaret O'Brien to SF

204, 205 RAD FULTON MEMORIES: Jim Westmoreland (AKA Rad Fulton) to SF, 2/14/99, 2/15/99, 3/8/99

205 A "SCENE": Bob Allen as told to Margaret O'Brien, to SF, 1/26/00

206, 207 TOLD DICKIE MOORE; ACCIDENT: *Twinkle Twinkle Little Star*

207 ACCIDENT: "Natalie Wood Unhurt As Her Car Overturned," *Los Angeles Citizen-News*, 8/26/54; Louella Parsons column, *Los Angeles Herald-Examiner*, 8/27/54; *Hollywood Reporter*, 9/1/54

209–10, 212 CONTROLLED FEELINGS, NEVER ALLOWED TO BE HERSELF; SISTER'S DRILL, RECORD PLAYER: Lana Wood to SF, 8/19/99

210 PASSED OUT AT A PARTY: Steffi Skolsky Splaver to SF, 10/1/99

211 SIPPING AT CIRO'S: 6/69 *Screen Parade*

211 5 YEARS BEHIND: Ted Donaldson to SF

211 A FEINT, A LOOK: Randal Malone to SF

212 LONG LINE OF SUITORS: Robert Wagner, as quoted in 8/75 *Cosmopolitan*

213 FRIENDLY, NO SENSE WHAT HE WOULD BECOME: Ed Jubert to SF, September 1999

213 NOT A COOL KID: Phoebe Kassebaum to SF

213 REDFORD MET HER AT REGISTRATION: Robert Redford to SF

215, 216 NOT BRAGGADOCIOUS; SWEET PERSON: Phoebe Kassebaum to SF

216, 217 RELIEVED ABOUT SERIES; ON STRIKE; DIDN'T WANT HER TO MEET WAGNER, WHEN 18: Robert Hyatt to SF

216 *DADDY LONG LEGS*: *Hollywood Reporter*, 10/15/54

216 HEART SHONE THROUGH: "Unforgettable Super-Star Natalie Wood,"
Robert Kendall, *Hollywood Studio Magazine*, March 1982

217 SCHEME TO HIRE WILLSON; MARIA CONCERNED: Robert Hyatt to SF; Jean Hyatt to SF

217 FIRST LOVE SCENE: Interview with Natalie Wood, Jeff Freedman, *Interview*, October 1978

218, 219 STUCK WITH DEAN, NERVOUS, WHAT I EXPECTED, GREASY SPOON, CLASSICAL MUSIC, CHILD ACTOR, READ MOVIE MAGAZINES: *Twinkle Twinkle Little Star*

218 PRODUCER WAS WORRIED; DEAN DIDN'T GET IT: Mort Abrahams as quoted in *James Dean, The Mutant King, A Biography* by David Dalton, St. Martin's Press, 1974, New York

219 DEAN ALMOST OD'D: Maryann Marinkovich Brooks to SF

219 LIKE BEING A GIRL: "The Girl Most Likely To Succeed in 1962," David Lewin, *Express Photo News*, circa 1962, Natalie Wood Collection, British Film Institute

220 PART IN TACEY: Louella Parsons column, *Los Angeles Examiner*, 11/15/54

220 NEVER GROW UP: "Little Girl No More"

CHAPTER 13

220 HUDSON WHISTLED: "Little Girl No More"

221 MINK STOLE: Sheilah Graham column, 12/29/54

221 WORE PRINTS AND PLAIDS: Jacqueline Eastes Perry to SF

221 LOVED CLOTHES: Faye Nuell Mayo to SF, 9/15/99

221 WANTED TO BE GREAT: 7/71 *Pageant*

221 BOBBY CALLED HER: Robert Hyatt to SF

222 NATALIE WEPT, VOICE BUZZING: "Why We Call Natalie 'Tiger,'" Faye Nuell, *Motion Picture*, October 1956

222 FELT EXACTLY THE WAY: 2/11/79 *New York Daily News Sunday Magazine*

222 *REBEL* BACKGROUND: *Nicholas Ray*, An *American Journey*, Bernard Eisenschitz, translated by Tom

Milne, Faber & Faber, London/Boston, 1993; Leonard Rosenman to SF, 3/9/99; Stewart Stern, Los Angeles County Museum of Art 45th anniversary tribute to *Rebel Without A Cause*, 10/26/00

223 FELT AN INSTANT COMMUNICATION: 4/64 *Screen Stories*

223 I'M AN ACTRESS: 11/57 *Seventeen*

223 PREFERRED CHARACTERS WITH WHOM SHE IDENTIFIED: 10/79 *After Dark*

223 MARY ANN'S MEMORIES: Maryann Marinkovich Brooks to SF

223, 243 MARIA WAS SUSPICIOUS; LUCKED OUT, DANGLED: Scott Marlowe to SF

223 JACKIE'S MEMORIES: Jacqueline Eastes Perry to SF

224 FIRST CHOICE WAS O'BRIEN: Margaret O'Brien to SF

224 THREATENED TO RUN AWAY: Natalie Wood interview excerpt, "Intimate Portrait: Natalie Wood"

224 DECIDED TO PLEASE MYSELF: Natalie Wood, as quoted by Gordon Armstrong, National Publicity Director for Twentieth Century Fox, in publicity materials for *Peeper*224

224 NICK THREW UP HIS HANDS: Lana Wood, "Intimate Portrait: Natalie Wood"

224 CRITICAL DECISION: "Mrs. Wagner Not Ms. Wood," Richard Cuskelly, *Los Angeles Herald-Examiner*, 10/13/74

225 WANTED TO BE GREAT: 10/78 *Interview*

255 DONE ANYTHING: *Second Act, An Autobiography*, Joan Collins,
St. Martin's Press, New York, 1997

225 OPERA PUMPS, WORRIED ABOUT RAY: "The Girl Who Grew Up Too Fast," Nick Adams, *Modern Screen*, May 1956; 8/58 *Modern Screen*

225 TOLD SKOLSKY: Sidney Skolsky collection, Academy of Motion Picture Arts & Sciences, Beverly Hills, California

225 KNEES SHAKING: *Modern Screen* circa 10/56

226, 236 WASN'T GOING TO CAST NATALIE; NO FILM IN CAMERA: *James Dean, The Mutant King*

226 CONSIDERED HER FOR JUDY'S FRIEND: *An American Journey*

226 THE ULTIMATE STAR: *Past Imperfect*, Joan Collins, Simon and Schuster, New York, 1978

229 *LITTLE PRINCE* FAVORITE BOOK: 11/68 *Cosmopolitan* et al.

230–42 JAILBAIT; ADAMS GAVE MUD A KISS; SNAPPED BACK: Jacqueline Eastes Perry to SF

230, 231 STAKEOUTS AT THE CHATEAU; DAD ANGRY: Lana Wood to SF, 8/19/99; Lana Wood, "Intimate Portrait: Natalie Wood"

230 MARIA SUPPORTED *REBEL*: Robert Hyatt to SF, 5/10/99; Jean Hyatt to SF, 5/6/99

230, 231 ROMANTICIZED THE RAY AFFAIR; NOT TO GET THE PART: Jacqueline Eastes Perry to SF; Maryann Marinkovich Brooks to SF; Margaret O'Brien to SF

231 OPENED THE DOOR: 10/84 *McCall's*

232–40 FIGURES IN ROMANTIC NOVELS; ASSEMBLY LINE; HATED HER IDOL: Dennis Hopper to SF, 12/21/2000

232 NATALIE ON *WILD BUNCH*: Gigi Perreau to SF

233 HOPPER'S COMMENTS: Dennis Hopper to SF, 12/21/00

234 DENNIS WAS MADLY IN LOVE: Steffi Skolsky Splaver to SF

235 CHORT: 2/57 *Modern Screen*

236 LEANED TO BAKER, REJECTED REMICK: Nicholas Ray notes to Warners, 1/4/55 and 1/5/55, Steve Trilling papers from the Warner Brothers Collection, University of Southern California

236 DATED WINTERS: *Hollywood Reporter*, 2/22/55; Jacqueline Eastes Perry to SF

236 WANTED MANSFIELD: Leonard Rosenman to SF; Faye Nuell Mayo to SF; [Note: Dennis Hopper, who

read with Mansfield, described it as a "serious" screen test (Hopper to SF, 12/21/2000)]

236 TOLD HEDDA: 6/26/55 *Chicago Tribune Magazine*

237 NATALIE'S RAPE: Jacqueline Eastes Perry to SF, 12/11/99; Jacqueline Eastes Perry unpublished manuscript; Dennis Hopper to SF, 12/21/00; Scott Marlowe to SF, 6/8/99 & 8/12/99; Maryann Marinkovich Brooks to SF, 11/4/99; Faye Nuell Mayo to SF, 9/15/99

239 BLACKLISTING WOULD BE HER MOM'S CONCERN: Lana Wood to SF, 8/19/99

239, 240 HATED HER IDOL; MUSTN'T GO TO BED WITH ANYBODY: Scott Marlowe to SF

240 NO WONDER SHE BROKE OUT: 8/75 *Cosmopolitan*

240 SHE WAS IT: Maryann Marinkovich Brooks to SF

240–42 LEFT HER TO DRY; WENT TO GOOGIE'S, DRANK AT VILLA CAPRI, DROVE TO MULHOLLAND, ACCIDENT, NEEDED A SPOKESPERSON: Jacqueline Eastes Perry to SF

241, 242 CAR ACCIDENT; NATALIE KEPT SAYING CALL RAY; TOLD RAY THEY CALLED HER A DELINQUENT: Natalie Wood, *Nicholas Ray: I'm a Stranger Here Myself*, October Films, Inc., produced by James Gutman

241 HOPPER COMMENTS: Dennis Hopper to SF

242 RAY PHONED GURDINS AND NATALIE ASKED TO SEE HIM: Ray, as quoted in *An American Journey* and 7/71 *Pageant*

CHAPTER 14

243–70 LUCKED OUT; LIVE OR DIE; MADE TRAIN NOISES, DISAPPOINTED AT TAUNTS; WENT ALONG WITH THINGS; WANTED TO MARRY RAY: Scott Marlowe to SF

243 ASCRIBED IT TO DIFFERENT PEOPLE: 8/58 *Modern Screen*, 8/59 *Screen Stars;* 7/71 *Pageant* [Natalie at

times said it was a doctor; other times that it was a cop]

243 HOPPER COMMENTS: Dennis Hopper to SF

243 JACKIE'S COMMENTS: Jacqueline Eastes Perry to SF

243 OVERENTHUSIASTIC WANNABE: 2/23/55 *Daily Variety*

243 ALMOST OVER THE EDGE: Phoebe Kassebaum to SF

244 WARNERS WANTED REYNOLDS: Warner Brothers collection, *Rebel Without a Cause*, USC

244 REYNOLDS WASN'T INTERESTED; CAMERA LOVED NATALIE; DEPTH AND SOUL; WOMAN IN A GIRL'S FACE: Debbie Reynolds to SF, 12/21/98

244 LONG'S COMMENTS: Beverly Long to SF, 9/22/99

244, 247 THERE WERE 50 OF US; JIMMY TRUSTED NICK: Natalie Wood, *Nicholas Ray: I'm a Stranger Here Myself*

244 3/1 RAY MEMO: Trilling Warner Brothers collection, USC

245 SEVERAL TESTS: Natalie Wood, excerpted on AMC's *Real to Reel*

245 I SPOILED IT: 10/30/69 *Los Angeles Times*

245 WOULD HAVE SIGNED ANYTHING: 10/84 *McCall's*

245 GAVE HER THE ONLY; SHE WAS INSTINCTUAL: Robert Blake outtakes

245–56 SCARED TO DEATH; MANSFIELD ERA; LOOKING FOR WAYS; POUT; VOICE COACH; SUSAN STRASBERG FIXATION; USED VICKS: Jacqueline Eastes Perry to SF

246 PADDING: Beverly Long to SF; Jacqueline Eastes Perry to SF

246 SPOTTED MINEO IN A LINEUP: Nicholas Ray, as quoted in *The Mutant King*

247–54 FAMILY ATMOSPHERE; TONY WAS AROUND; RAY USED HIS SEXUALITY: Faye Nuell Mayo to SF

247 NO DIRECTOR IMPROVISED: Natalie Wood, "I'm a Stranger Here Myself"

247 LIKED STRUCTURE: Lana Wood to SF

247 COREY ALLEN'S COMMENTS: Corey Allen to SF, 9/22/99

247–62 ALL BUSINESS; THOUGHT NATALIE COULD HANDLE RAY; SHE'D LISTEN FOR HOURS: Maryann Marinkovich Brooks to SF

247 KNEW OF AFFAIR, RAY SEXY, AFFAIR WITH DEAN: Mitzi McCall Brill to SF, 10/3/99

247 ROSENMAN COMMENTS: Leonard Rosenman to SF

248 LOVE TRIANGLE: Jacqueline Eastes Perry to SF; Scott Marlowe to SF; Leonard Rosenman to SF; Faye Nuell Mayo to SF

248 HAD TO LIVE THEIR ROLES: "Natalie Wood Speaks Out: Youth Silly About Dean?" Marilyn Lee, *Los Angeles Examiner*, 7/21/56

248 CRUSH ON DEAN: 10/78 *Interview*

248, 260 DIDN'T HAVE STRONG SENSE; RAY TAUGHT HER ABOUT BOOKS: 7/71 *Pageant*

250–59 WEIRD NIGHT; HENNESSY HAD A MEETING; NEVER SAW HER HUG: Beverly Long to SF

249, 253 THE CAST MUMBLED; COMMITTED TO A PLAY: Marsha Hunt to SF, 7/30/99

250 GREAT DIRECTORS LIKE KAZAN: "Natalie Wood Heralded 'Best' Since Helen Hayes," Ruth Waterbury, *Los Angeles Examiner*, 10/9/55

250, 251 DEAN ALL SHE TALKED ABOUT; TOYED: Sal Mineo, as quoted in *The Unabridged James Dean: His Life and Legacy from A to Z*, Randall Riese, Contemporary Books, Chicago, 1991

250 FLIRTATIOUS: Tom Hennessy to SF, 10/3/99

251 NATALIE WAS SCHOOLED: Ann Doran to SF

251 KEPT HEARING ABOUT METHOD: 12/28/69 *London Sunday Times*

251 TOOK ACTING AS A JOB: Margaret O'Brien to SF

252 FELT INFERIOR TO ANYONE FROM STUDIO: Faye

Nuell Mayo to SF; Jacqueline Eastes Perry to SF; Scott Marlowe to SF; Robert Redford to SF, et al.

253 DORAN COMMENTS: Ann Doran to SF

256 "SPECIAL DISPENSATION" AND HENNESSY COMMENTS: Tom Hennessy to SF, 10/3/99

256 NATALIE MADE UP INTERVIEWS: 8/13/64 *Look*

256 STEFFI SKOLSKY COMMENTS: Steffi Skolsky Splaver to SF

256, 257 FAYE COMMENTS: Faye Nuell Mayo to SF

257–62 QUIET BUZZ; SEEMED STERN; HANG ON TO HER BRA STRAPS: Jack Grinnage to SF, 9/23/99

259 THEY WERE THE GODS: Natalie Wood, quoted in *Elvis*, Albert Goldman, Avon Books, New York, 1981

260 WILD SIDE: Tom Hennessy to SF

260 NATALIE THOUGHT BEING GROWN UP: 5/56 *Modern Screen*

260, 261 UP FOR ANYTHING; BEST DAY OF HIS LIFE: Perry Lopez to SF, 2/9/99

264 COOPER COMMENTS: Ben Cooper to SF, 10/13/99

264 SET-UP DATE: Robert Hyatt to SF

267 TURN THE PAGE: Jim Westmoreland/Rad Fulton to SF, 2/15/99

267 OBSESSED WITH SONG: Steffi Skolsky Splaver to SF; Jacqueline Eastes Perry to SF

267, 268 LYRICS: "When the World Was Young (Ah! the Apple Trees)," Johnny Mercer and M. Philippe Gerard, recorded by Peggy Lee in May 1953, Decca, *Black Coffee* album

269 FAVORITE SCENE FROM *REBEL*: "Natalie Wood to Make First . . ." *The Star*, 10/24/78

271 SAID SHE DATED DEAN: 10/9/55 *Examiner*; Hedda Hopper, *Chicago Tribune* 6/26/55; 8/79 *McCall's*

271 SANG RUSSIAN SONG: Maria Gurdin to Phyllis Quinn

271 OBSESSED WITH DEAN: Lana Wood to SF

271 COMPARED DEAN TO LITTLE PRINCE: "She Grew Up Being a Star!" Seymour Korman, *Chicago Tribune*, 8/18/56

271 TWO PEOPLE: 10/78 *Interview*

CHAPTER 15

272, 273 GAVE HER TIGER; BIG DEAL; PIVOTAL PART: Faye Nuell Mayo to SF

272 BURST IN TEARS: 8/75 *Cosmopolitan*

272, 276 FLOUNCED IN FUR; BLIND DATE WITH HOPPER: Margaret O'Brien to SF

273 TOP 10%: Tom Hennessy to SF

273 DID IT FOR LANA: Jack Grinnage to SF273

273 CHOSE LANA LISA: 8/18/56 *Chicago Tribune*

273, 274 PUSHED ME; SUNBURN; SCARED ON LOCATION; CRUSH ON WAYNE: Lana Wood to SF, 8/24/99

237 TOUGH BUT KIND: "Nat at the NFT," *Photoplay U.K.*, August 1980

274 PATRICK WAYNE COMMENTS; "DUST AND HEAT"; "FRIED" SKIN: Patrick Wayne to SF, 10/6/99

275 GIRL WAS BRILLIANT; WAYNE IMPRESSED BY HER EYES: Vera Miles and Harry Carey, Jr., *A Tribute to a Very Special Lady*

276, 278 LONELY PEOPLE; DON'T LIKE TECHNIQUE; TONGUE-TIED: 1/56 *Modern Screen*

276–85 FREQUENTLY LONELY; KEEPS TIGERS; TAKES TIGERS ON PLANE; STARDOM'S A BY-PRODUCT: "Going Steady with Stardom," Bill Tusher, *Motion Picture*, March 1957

278–87 CUTE AND ECCENTRIC, SCORED FOR EACH OTHER; TURN IT ON AND OFF; DATED BURR, BEARD, GAY PERIOD: Dennis Hopper to SF

276 BURNED TO PLAY SCARLETT: 6/26/55 *Chicago Tribune*

277 BUILT POOL TO MONITOR; HAD TO BE NATALIE WOOD: Robert Hyatt to SF

277 GOT IN, GOT WET: Lana Wood to SF, 8/24/99

278, 287 UPSET AT BILLING; BURR OFFERED HER A WORLD OUTSIDE: Scott Marlowe to SF, 6/8/99

279 BEATNIK PHASE; DINNER IN CHINATOWN: 8/56 *Motion Picture*

281 CRIED HER EYES OUT: "Natalie Wood: It Seemed As If All Was Going Her Way," Roderick Mann, *Los Angeles Times*, 12/1/81

279 DINNER IN CHINATOWN: "Remembrances Of James Dean," Paul Hendrickson, *Los Angeles Times*, 7/22/73

280 VALENTINO; RUNNING AROUND IN: Corey Allen to SF

280 EPIC: Ann Doran to SF

280 GRUESOME THOUGHT: Stanley Kauffman on "Natalie Wood: The Final Days," September Films, United Productions, aired spring 2000

280 LUCKY PICTURE: Natalie Wood, interview excerpt, "Intimate Portrait: Natalie Wood"

281 SINCE HELEN HAYES: 10/9/55 *Los Angeles Examiner*

281 ENDEARING: Ben Cooper to SF

281 HYSTERICAL OVER DEAN: 10/78 *Interview*

281 CAPITALIZING ON FAME: United Press release, Vernon Scott, 4/4/57, USC Warner Brothers Archives

281 BADMOUTHED: Steffi Skolsky Splaver to SF

281 ADAMS SOLD STORIES: Faye Nuell Mayo to SF; Steffi Skolsky Splaver to SF

282, 285 FELT PRESSURE; ANALYZED HER SCRIPT: Lana Wood, American Cinematheque

282 PATS OF JOY: "Actress, 17, Takes Pet to Sign New Contract," *Los Angeles Examiner*, 10/27/55

283 OVERDREW $400: Incomplete Natalie Wood article by Liza Wilson, unsourced newspaper, 8/19/56, from the USC Warner Brothers Archives

284 DORTORT COMMENTS: David Dortort to SF, 6/26/99

285 ANDERSON COMMENTS: Richard Anderson to SF, 4/29/99
286 ESCARGOTS: 2/60 *Coronet*
286 ORSON WELLES MAKEOVER: Maryann Marinkovich Brooks to SF
286 CRAZY ABOUT BURR: Jacqueline Eastes Perry to SF
287 SAFETY NET: Debbie Reynolds to SF
287 CLAIMED TO BE MARRIED: [Note: Burr's sister, Geraldine Fuller, said he was married only once; A&E Biography, *Raymond Burr*, airing 3/2/00]
288 BURR LOVED NATALIE; STUDIO PRESSURED: Robert Benevides to SF, 6/24/99; "Nat Wood–Bob Wagner: Too Much of Everything?" Joan Curtis, *Screen Parade*, November 1958

CHAPTER 16

288 TOP PICKS: "Hedda Hopper Predicts," *Chicago Tribune Magazine*, 1/1/56
288 FIVE LAYOUTS: Warner Brothers publicity files, USC Warners Collection
288–89 DOG PADDLE; PHYSICAL WITH BURR; MORE CONCERNED ABOUT WARDROBE: Judi Meredith Nelson to SF, 6/10/99
289 WANTED PEOPLE TO LIKE HER: 6/69 *Screen Parade*
289 MORE FAN MAIL: 8/19/56 *Los Angeles Examiner*
289 FAN MAGAZINES STRANGE: 12/28/69 *London Sunday Times*
289 COMPARED TO BROOKE SHIELDS: *Twinkle Twinkle Little Star*
290 91 POUNDS, TIME OFF: *A Cry in the Night* file, USC Warners Collection
290–93 BURR SENT FLOWERS; STANDING OVATION; SAW NATALIE THREE TIMES WEEKLY; PHILHARMONIC: *The Burning Hills* file, USC Warners Collection
290 MET AT A PARTY: 1/3/55 *Hollywood Reporter* (in a spin

at Ciro's); 3/86 GQ; "The Love Story of the Year," Patty de Roulf, *Motion Picture*, December 1957; Natalie Wood to Sue Russell

290 RED HEART: Louella Parsons column, *Los Angeles Examiner*, 2/7/56

290 TAB HUNTER COMMENTS: Tab Hunter to SF, 5/3/99

290 COCONUT GROVE: undated *Los Angeles Mirror News*, Natalie Wood Collection, USC Warners Archives; 3/9/55 *Daily Variety*

291 PLAY FEMME FATALE: "Movie Veteran at 17," *People and Places*, March 1956

291 CURTIS RAN INTO NATALIE AT AN OYSTER HOUSE PARTY, SULKING OVER BURR: 11/58 *Screen Parade*; 2/1/56 *Hollywood Reporter*

291 WARNER CHAPERONED: 1/31/56 *Hollywood Reporter*

292, 295 JOKES ABOUT HER LINES; GIRL WITH LEFT BEHIND: Mart Crowley, "Starring Natalie Wood"

292 HEISLER COMPLAINT: Stu Heisler phone call, 2/16/56 memo, *The Burning Hills* folder, Jack L. Warner Collection, USC

294 PLAY CHARACTER PARTS: 7/56 *Filmland*

293 THREW THE BOOK DOWN: Jacqueline Eastes Perry to SF

294 TAYLOR AND BRANDO: 3/5/56 *Daily Variety*

294 EVERY GIRL FALLS: 11/57 *Seventeen*

294, 295 ANNE OF *1000* DAYS; USO TOUR; AN UNDERSTANDING, MARRIAGE: "Hollywood Today," Sheilah Graham, *Hollywood Citizen-News*, 4/5/56

294 REAL HEART IS BURR: Louella Parsons column, *Los Angeles Examiner*, 3/15/56

294 RETRACTED COMMENTS: 2/57 *Modern Screen*

294 BURR SAID LATER: "Little Girl, What Now?" *Dell Hollywood Life Stories*, February 1962; *Raymond Burr*, Ona Hill, McFarland and Company, North Carolina, 1994

295 BURR WAS BITTER: Robert Benevides to SF

289 CUT HER HAIR: Tab Hunter to SF; 3/23/56 *Daily* Variety; 7/56 *Movie Life*; 8/56 *Motion Picture*

289 PLUMAS LOCAS: "S.F. Actress Visits Here," Bob Hall, unsourced San Francisco newspaper, May 1956

289, 290 STARTED A TREND; SCHLOCKY: Tab Hunter to SF

297 MADE HER DO IT: circa 1978 *Preview*

296 UCLA PARTY: Tab Hunter to SF; Ed Tolmas to SF, 10/4/99

296 UNAFFECTED; EVER SEE MARY ANN: Dr. Melvyn Wishan to SF, 10/6/99

297 HONORED US: 7/56 *Modern Screen*; 8/56 *Screen Album*

296 BACKED OFF: Maryann Marinkovich Brooks to SF

296 HUNTER WAS SAFE: Lana Wood to SF

297 TRIP AN INDUCEMENT: "Natalie Wood: Female Rebel Without a Cause," *Exposed*, February 1957

297 SCOTT MARLOWE COMMENTS: Scott Marlowe to SF, 6/8/99 & 8/12/99

299 "EILATAN," NIGHTCLUB TOUR: Warner Brothers publicity, USC Warners Collection

299 PINK PHONE, BREAKFAST IN BED: 8/56 *Screen Album*

299 HAWAII TRIP: "Natalie Wood's Confidential Diary," Natalie Wood, *Movie Parade*, November 1956

299 FELL OFF BOAT; IMPATIENT TO WORK: "Aloha Means Goodbye," *Photoplay*, September 1956

298 READ NIETZSCHE AND WARREN: 2/60 *Coronet*

299 FIRST TIME ON A BOAT: Scott Marlowe to SF

300 PICTURED WITH NEPHEWS: 5/56 unsourced San Francisco paper

300 WONDERS IF OLGA'S HAPPY: 7/56 *Filmland*

301, 302 MADLY IN LOVE; AFRAID OF DOCTORS; MARIA DIDN'T LIKE ANALYSIS, NATALIE DIDN'T LIKE MOM: Lana Wood to SF

303 REALIZED SHE WAS MANIPULATED: Mart Crowley, "Intimate Portrait: Natalie Wood"

303 HYPNOTIZED: "Natalie—And Her Men," *Movie Life*, April 1957

304 REVIEW OF *GIRL*: "The Girl He Left Behind," James Powers, *Hollywood Reporter*, 10/26/56

304 PAID MEDICAL BILLS: Faye Nuell Mayo to SF

305 ADAMS AND BLAIR SPIED: Maryann Marinkovich Brooks to SF

305 TO MARRY MARLOWE: Louella Parsons column, *Los Angeles Examiner*, 7/2/56

305, 310 USING NATALIE; ADAMS PERSUADED NATALIE TO DELAY MARRYING:
"Boy-Crazy Teen-Ager?" *Movieland*, March 1957

307 WORRIED ABOUT FAN MAGS: 3/9/69 *New York Times*

306 WARNERS PRESS RELEASE TO MAKE PICTURE WITH MARLOWE: USC Warners Archives, folder for *The Girl He Left Behind*

307 PRESS PARTY, DESSERT PARTY, 50 STARS: *The Hollywood Reporter*, 7/20/56

309, 316 DATE ARRANGED BY WILLSON; PUSHED PRESLEY: Robert Hyatt to SF

308, 309 STUDIO SET-UP DATE; SENT ONE WITH MANNERS: "Hollywood Can Never Wreck Their Marriage Again!: An Exclusive Interview With Robert Wagner's Mother-in-Law," Stacie Keyes, *TV Radio-Mirror*, January 1976; Joan Curtis, quoted in 11/58 *Screen Parade*

308 CHIFFON DRESS AND TIARA: "I'm Not the Girl He Married," Karen Foster, *Screen Stories*, August 1959

308 HAPPY JACK SQUIRREL: Robert Wagner in an undated, unsourced televised interview excerpted on AMC's *Real to Reel*

308 THOSE EYES, INTELLECT; RUNNING WITH ELITE OF HOLLYWOOD: 3/86 GQ

309 WONDERFUL TALENT, MORE ACCOMPLISHED; SO HONEST: "Now, a New Beginning," Dotson Rader, *Parade Magazine*, 11/17/85

309 PERFECT IMITATIONS, WAITED FOR HIM TO CALL, SENT FLOWERS: "I Married Bob," Natalie Wood, as told to Liza Wilson, *American Weekly*, 5/18/58

309, 311 BURNED AN EFFIGY; PLUNGING NECKLINE, TIGER: 8/58 *Modern Screen*; 3/10/57 Sheilah Graham column

309 ANOTHER DATE: Sidney Skolsky interview with Robert Wagner, 11/21/57, from transcript in Skolsky collection, Academy of Motion Picture Arts and Sciences

310, 315 FIRED WILLSON; PRESLEY NOT WHAT SHE WANTED: Jacqueline Eastes Perry to SF

311 TAB'S A SOFT DRINK: 12/28/69 *London Sunday Times*

311 PLANTED ITEM ABOUT ADAMS: Army Archerd column, *Daily Variety*, 8/15/56; Faye Nuell Mayo to SF; 2/58 *Movie TV* (Natalie said it was a set-up)

311 WOUK'S IMPRESSIONS OF NATALIE: "My Search for Marjorie," Herman Wouk, *The American Weekly*, 5/11/58

313 MET PRESLEY IN MALIBU: Marlowe to SF; "I Got Cold Feet at the Altar: Elvis: Natalie's Fill-in—Or Future?" Irene D. Reich, *Modern Screen*, December 1956; undated, unsourced London newspaper clipping quoting Natalie Wood from the British Film Institute collection on Wood

313 THREESOME: "Natalie Wood: Show-off or Show-Woman?" Louella Parsons, *Los Angeles Examiner*, 12/16/56

314 LONELY ON NY TRIP: "Natalie Wood, the Star Who Beat the Jinx," Peer J. Oppenheimer, *Compact*, February 1957

314 NEEDED SOMEONE AROUND: "Bob, Did You Know?" Judi Meredith, *Photoplay*, March 1958

315 FIKE COMMENTS: Lamar Fike to SF, 2/12/99

315, 317 MUD AND FAHD LIKED PRESLEY; NATALIE CRAZY

ABOUT HIM; CALLED IN "CODE": Maria Gurdin to Phyllis Quinn

315, 318 NATALIE DISCUSSED WITH GOLDMAN; LOOKED THROUGH WINDOWS; HADN'T BEEN AROUND ANYONE RELIGIOUS: *Elvis*

316 *CARNIVAL* REVIEW: *Daily Variety*, 10/11/56

317 PLAYED A REAL RAT: Ben Cooper to SF

317 VAUGHN COMMENTS: Letter from Robert Vaughn to SF, 9/9/99

317 LEFT TOWN ABRUPTLY, SECRETLY: Leonard Hirshan to SF, 5/4/99; Michael Zimring to SF, 7/2/99; Sheilah Graham column, 3/10/57; Louella Parsons column, *Los Angeles Examiner*, 3/10/57

318 WHO SHOULD DRIVE UP: Jerry Schilling to SF, 7/30/97

319 MET BY VAUGHN, TOREADORS: 3/10/57 Sheilah Graham; 11/16/56 *Hollywood Reporter*

ACT THREE

CHAPTER 17

323 GOLDEN GLOBE: information provided by the Hollywood Foreign Press Association [Note: Natalie received the award in January 1957]

323 *MODERN SCREEN* CEREMONY: from video of *The Ed Sullivan Show*, 12/3/56; 11/30/56 *Hollywood Reporter*

323 BEST ACTING AS HER: Dennis Hopper to SF

323 WORRIED LIKED HER BECAUSE NATALIE WOOD: Lana Wood to SF

323 NEUROSES KEPT HER SLIM: "Teenage Dreamboat," *Movieland*, October 1957

324, 325 RJ'S FIRST BOAT; FIRST INTIMACY: 10/79 *Orange Coast*; "Heart To Hart," Jane Ardmore, *San Antonio Light*, 9/27/81

324 FLOATING IN SPACE: "The Very Private Lives of Natalie and Bob Wagner," Leonard Lewis, *Movie World*, March 1959

324 HEAD OVER HEELS: 3/86 GQ

325 STAR JUNKET: 3/10/57 Sheilah Graham column

325 BOYS SWARMING: Karl Malden to SF, 7/29/99

325 NO PICNIC: "Natalie Wood: Bait Enough For Beatty?" Helen Hendricks, *Silver Screen*, October 1962

325, 326 PRIVATE LINE, TALKED ALL NIGHT, BLACK FURNITURE; BURN OUT: 3/57 *Motion Picture*

326 AMBITION OF LIFE: 4/8/57 *Hollywood Reporter*

326 PARTY LINE; LOVE TALK: Dr. Melvyn Wishan to SF

326 TORTURED HER OVER *MARJORIE*: Marlowe to SF

326 HAD TO PLAY THE GAME: Zimring to SF

326, 328 BROOKLYN ACCENT; 3 DATES; TWO-PART SERIES: 8/57 and 9/57 *Photoplay*

326, 327 SWEARING CONTESTS; ACTED AS A BEARD: Judi Meredith Nelson to SF

327 SINATRA WAS COURTING: Faye Nuell Mayo to SF; 4/8/57 *Hollywood Reporter*; 4/30/57 *Daily Variety*

327 TOMORROW WON'T COME: Sheilah Graham column, *Sunday Mirror*, 3/11/57

327 HEADING FOR A FALL: "Natalie Wood: Teenage Tiger," *Look*, 6/25/57

327 SINATRA INCONGRUOUS: "The Night Natalie Wood Can Never Forget," Peer Oppenheimer, *Movieland*, August 1957

327 BOY CRAZY: 3/21/57 *Daily Variety*

328, 334 COULDN'T BE FAITHFUL; LOOKING FOR HAPPINESS; LUNCH WHEN ENGAGED: Jacqueline Eastes Perry to SF

327 CALL IT FASCINATION: 10/62 *Silver Screen*

328 INTENSE ABOUT SOMETHING: "Little Girls Grow Up Fast," *Young Movie Lovers*, 1957 issue

328 COMPARED TO ZELDA: 2/60 *Coronet*

328 HANDS SHAKING: Amanda Duff Dunne to SF

328 SCENES WITH TIERNEY: Anna Lee Nathan to SF

329 NERVOUS HEART: 1/21/57 *Daily Variety*

329 EVERY TIME SHE READS: 3/58 *Photoplay*

329 NO MORE FAN COVERS: "Why Are Men Afraid of Natalie?" Joy Sands, *Movie and TV Spotlight*, October 1957

329 TRIED TO MAKE HER LOOK LIKE FEMME: UP press release by Vernon Scott, 4/4/57

329 MAKING UP MIND BETWEEN R.J. AND NICKY; NICKY WOULDN'T BE BEST THING: Troy Donahue to SF, 5/29/99

330 MET WITH CONRAD HILTON; VERY SERIOUS: Olga Viripaeff to SF;
Lana Wood to SF

330 EVERY 3 MINUTES: "Divorce Without Marriage," *Hollywood's Top 10 Scandals 1963*

330 VIOLENT-TEMPERED HILTON: "Liz, Ms. Taylor Will See You Now," Paul Theroux, *Talk*, October 1999 [Taylor states Hilton "physically abused" her and "kicked a baby out of her stomach"]

330 MINK ON BOAT FOR 19TH BIRTHDAY: 8/58 *Modern Screen*; 7/22/57 *Daily Variety*

330 SHOUP TAUGHT HER; BOOB UPLIFTS: Faye Nuell Mayo to SF; Judi Meredith Nelson to SF

330 CRITICIZED METHOD: "Natalie Wood Heard From: Tells What's Wrong with N.Y. Actors," Joe Hyams, *New York Tribune*, 6/20/57

331 MARRIAGE RUMORS: 8/9/57 *Daily Variety*; 9/8/57 *New York Daily News*

331 CALLS HER BUG; SAME HOTEL: 12/57 *Motion Picture*; Lana Wood to SF
(same hotel)

331 KISSING FOREHEAD; LOVE SEARCH ENDED: 12/57 *Motion Picture*; "Be Careful, Nat . . . It's Your Heart," Natalie Wood, *Screen Stars*, November 1957

331 "MR. WOOD": Louella Parsons column, *Los Angeles Herald-Examiner*, 9/21/57

331, 333 SPEND LIFE IN CRAPPER; SINATRA GAVE HOBOKEN GUIDE: Faye Nuell Mayo to SF

331 RUTA LEE COMMENTS: Ruta Lee to SF

332 "THE NATALIE"; "MY OTHER LADY": Louella Parsons column, *Los Angeles Herald-Examiner*, 10/1/57; 10/9/57 *Hollywood Reporter*

332 NO DAY OFF: 11/57 *Seventeen*

332 SINATRA FROM GREATSVILLE: "Natalie Wood on Love and Marriage," Ruth Schandorff, *Bride & Home*, spring 1958

333 PROPOSAL: 5/18/58 *American Weekly*; Sugar Bates to SF, 8/4/99; 8/57 *Cosmopolitan*; Lana Wood to SF

333 FIRST CALL TO LOUELLA: Louella Parsons column, *Los Angeles Herald-Examiner*, 12/7/57

333 SHOUP GOWN: 12/18/57 *Daily Variety*

333 MARY ANN WAS CONCERNED: Maryann Marinkovich Brooks to SF

333 TOPIC OF SAME STORIES: Jim Westmoreland/Rad Fulton to SF

334 MARRIED TO GET AWAY: Olga Viripaeff to SF

334 MEAL TICKET: Jean Hyatt to SF

335 NO GOOD WILL COME: Robert Hyatt to SF

335 PHOTOGRAPHER ALONG: "Photoplay Was There," *Photoplay*, March 1958 [Note: Bill Avery was the photographer]

CHAPTER 18

336 HONEYMOON: "Natalie and Bob's Hectic Honeymoon," Louella Parsons, *Modern Screen*, April 1958; Louella Parsons column, *Los Angeles Herald-Examiner*, 1/1/58; "Natalie and Bob, Our Wedding," *Photoplay*, April 1958; "Rice and Rings and Wedding

Things," Marcia Borie, *Motion Picture*, April 1958

336 ADAMS ON HONEYMOON: James Bacon, *Los Angeles Herald-Examiner*, 12/3/70; "Their Biggest Problem Is," Walter Crowley, *Photoplay*, June 1962

336 ENTERTAINING GUY: Robert Conrad to SF, 9/7/99

336 CORVETTE, RADIO STATIONS: "Wagner and Wood," Barbara Wilkins, *People*, 12/13/76; "The Way They Were: Natalie Wood," Rochelle Williams, *Rona Barrett's Hollywood*, summer 1979

337 BEST PART CATALINA: "A Famous Author Recalls His Friend Natalie Wood," Thomas Thompson, *People*, 12/14/81; Louella Parsons column, *Los Angeles Herald-Examiner*, 2/14/58; 2/17/58 Sheilah Graham column

337 WROTE 1000 THANK-YOUS: 2/60 *Coronet*; Jack Warner Collection, USC (NWW stationery)

337 TOOK WIFE SERIOUSLY: Lana Wood to SF

337 NATALIE FELT TORMENT: 8/75 *Cosmopolitan*

338 MARIA IN CONTRACTS: contracts and correspondence, Steve Trilling Special Warner Brothers Collection, USC

338 MOVED INTO RJ'S APARTMENT ON DURANT: Thank-you notes, Jack Warner Collection, USC; 1/14/58 Sheilah Graham column; 3/58 Hedda Hopper column; 2/19/58 Sheilah Graham column (no room for clothes)

338 R.J.'S BUTLER: Robert Hyatt to SF; Jean Hyatt to SF

338 NO ROOM FOR BUTLER: "Some Girls Will Do Anything For Publicity," Jason Finchley, *Motion Picture*, August 1962; 8/58 *Modern Screen* (mentions butler); 10/26/58 *Chicago Sunday Tribune Magazine* (names butler, who once worked for Sinatra); Louella Parsons article, *Los Angeles Herald-Examiner*, 5/24/59 (Wagners have "manservant"); 10/60 *Cosmopolitan* (have butler)

339 ECSTATIC OVER R.J.: Ann Doran to SF

339 BALKED AT TOUR: 3/31/58, 7/15/58, 7/21/58 *Daily Variety*; "Which Kind of Marriage Do You Want?" Peer Oppenheimer, *Modern Screen*, July 1958

339 VIRAL INFECTION: 2/60 *Coronet*

339 TUG-OF-WAR WITH WARNERS, TURNED DOWN *SUMMER PLACE* AND *MIRACLE*: Steve Trilling Special Warners Collection, Natalie Wood contracts and correspondence, USC; reports in *Daily Variety* and *Hollywood Reporter*

340 AT HOME ON SOUNDSTAGE: 3/15/59 *Hollywood Citizen-News*

340 LOVEBIRDS IN MONTEREY; GAVE HER PRODUCER'S CHAIR: Jerry Wald memo to Philip Dunne, Twentieth Century Fox archives; "Natalie & Bob: A Return to Paradise," *Screen Album*, November 1958; Louella Parsons column, *Los Angeles Herald-Examiner*, 7/21/58

340 QUEEN OF LOT: 7/14/56 *Los Angeles Herald-Examiner*

340 TURNED DOWN FILM: Faye Nuell Mayo to SF; Scott Marlowe to SF; Steve Trilling Special Warners Collection, USC; trade reports spring/summer 1959

340 DIDN'T SHOW UP FOR *PHILADELPHIAN* MEETING AND SUSPENDED: Steve Trilling Special Warners Collection, USC (memos from Trilling to Warner, telegram sent to Natalie, letter from Warners to Natalie 7/15/59); Mike Zimring to SF; 7/15/59 *Daily Variety* cover

340 REASONS NATALIE GAVE LATER: Natalie Wood interviews, 12/28/69 *London Times*; 6/67 *Pageant*; 5/70 *Premiere*

341 GURDINS OFFERED LAUREL HOUSE: Shirley Mann to SF

341 LEARNED TO LIKE BOATS, WIVES STAYED ABOARD: Prudence Maree to SF, 1/10/00; Andrew Maree III to SF, 1/11/00

342 WAGNERS DISCUSSED THEIR BOAT: "Can They Stay

Happy? They Say YES!" Hedda Hopper, *Chicago Sunday Tribune Magazine*, 10/26/58

342 NOT AFRAID BECAUSE HE'D SAVE HER: "The Very Private Lives of Natalie and Bob Wagner," Leonard Lewis, *Movie World*, March 1959

342 FRINGE CLAN MEMBERS, PLAYED CARDS: 10/6/58 *Hollywood Reporter*; "What Marriage to Natalie Wood Has Taught Robert Wagner," *Young People's Digest*, September 1958

342 SOCIALIZED WITH SINATRA: Louella Parsons column, *Los Angeles Herald-Examiner*, 10/6/58; Sidney Skolsky column, *Hollywood Citizen-News*, 12/31/59

343 SKOLSKY INTERVIEWED WAGNERS: Steffi Skolsky Splaver to SF [see also "Mr. and Mrs. R.J.," Steffi Sidney, *Datebook*, May 1959]

343 NATALIE FIRST CHOICE FOR *SPLENDOR*; PROBLEMS EASING WITH WARNERS LATE '58: see contracts and correspondence, Steve Trilling Special Warners Collection, USC; 12/12/58 *Hollywood Reporter*; 1/26/59 letter from Kazan to Trilling mentions Natalie as first Deanie; Richard Sylbert to SF, 6/17/99; 1/28/59 *Hollywood Reporter* (Natalie for *Splendor*); 5/70 *Premiere* (she went back to Warners for *Splendor*); Billy Rose Theater Collection, Lincoln Center, William Inge Collection (Kazan's notes); 3/79 *Saturday Evening Post* (Kazan kept in mind since *Rebel*)

343 7-MONTH SUSPENSION; NEW TERMS WITH WARNERS: 2/16/59 *Hollywood Reporter*; Trilling Special Warners Collection, Natalie Wood 2/17/59 contract; 2/25/59 *Hollywood Citizen-News*

344 LIVED LIKE STARS, RECKLESS WITH MONEY: 6/59 *Modern Screen*; 11/68 *Cosmopolitan* (ran through her savings in a few months); "Natalie Wood & Bob Wagner to Marry Again!" Alice Random, *Modern*

Screen; Warner Brothers press for *Cash McCall*, Warners Special Collections, USC (matching Jaguars; hired Art Director); Judi Meredith Nelson to SF; Sidney Skolsky column, *Citizen-News*, 12/31/59

344 NEVER THOUGHT ABOUT FURNITURE: *Twinkle Twinkle Little Star*

345 PSYCHOANALYST: Lana Wood to SF; "Intimate Portrait: Natalie Wood" ("just be": Natalie 1980 TV excerpt); 10/79 *After Dark* ("didn't know who the hell")

345 RJ AGAINST THERAPY: 8/75 *Cosmopolitan*; Robert Wagner, "Intimate Portrait: Natalie Wood"

345 NATALIE AFRAID OF PREGNANCY: Robert Hyatt to SF; Scott Marlowe to SF

345 LANA CALLED NATALIE TO MOVE IN, SAME BED: Lana Wood to SF

346 NATALIE PROTECTED LANA: Mike Zimring to SF

346 OBSESSED WITH KEANE; POSED FOR HOURS: Dennis Hopper to SF; Margaret Keane to SF

346 PRESCRIPTION PILLS: Faye Nuell Mayo to SF; Robert Hyatt to SF; (used pills as poker chips) Pat Newcomb, interviewed by Donald Spoto, Academy of Motion Picture Arts & Sciences special collection

347 POCKET FRIENDS: Robert Conrad to SF

347, 350 NAT UPSTAIRS WITH SINATRA; WORRIED WHETHER R.J. COULD HANDLE DRAMATIC ROLE: Robert Hyatt to SF

348 21ST BIRTHDAY WITH SINATRA: Judi Meredith Nelson to SF; 7/20/59 *Daily Variety*

348 CRUSH ON SINATRA: Judi Meredith Nelson to SF

348 PLAYING HOUSE WITH PLAY MONEY: 6/69 *Screen Parade*

349, 350 $150K FOR *CANNIBALS*; KAZAN DIDN'T THINK SHE VIRGINAL: Leonard Hirshan to SF, 5/4/99

349 MOVED DIALECT COACH: Natalie Wood, *Donahue*, December 1976

349 NOSE-PICKING: "Presenting a Happy 'Act': Wagner and Wood," Thomas McDonald, *New York Times*, 6/14/59

349 WANTED *ENTERTAINER*: Judi Meredith Nelson to SF ("desperately"); Warner Brothers Special Collection, *Cash McCall* (couldn't do it because of *Cash* schedule)

350 RESISTED DEANIE BECAUSE IT WOULD OPEN DOORS: *Twinkle Twinkle Little Star*

350 CAREER IN DANGER; LIKE A DOLL: 10/23/61 *Newsweek*

351 DRESSED UP TO MEET KAZAN; NAKED AND GASPING: 2/26/62 *Newsweek*

351, 353 HAS-BEEN; TWINKLE, UNSATISFIED HUNGER; DO ANYTHING BUT WATER SCENE; BEATTY AFFAIR: *Elia Kazan: A Life*, Elia Kazan, Alfred A. Knopf, New York, 1988

351 DISGUSTED WITH HER IMAGE: "What Hollywood Does to Women," Elizabeth Pope, *Good Housekeeping*, June 1962

351 KRANZE COMMENTS: Don Kranze to SF, 9/8/99

352 SUPER CHIEF WITH TAYLOR: "The Fantastic Truth About Those Liz-Bob-Natalie Rumors!" Nell Blythe, *Movie Life*, September 1960; "Heart to Heart With Liz & R.J.," David Wallace, *People*, 10/6/86

352 SUTTON PLACE, R.J. PLAYED PIANO, GOING DOWNHILL: Louella Parsons column, *Los Angeles Herald-Examiner*, 4/23/60; 6/62 *Photoplay*; 11/85 *Parade*

352 RETURN TO GOLDEN WORLD; BE BOLD: *Twinkle Twinkle Little Star*

352 MAKE FOOL; LOVED CRAMPED STAGES: 7/23/81 *Los Angeles Times*; 6/62 *Vogue*

352 JIRAS COMMENTS: Robert Jiras to SF, 9/16/99

353 INGE RECOMMENDED BEATTY: Inge letter to Trilling 6/9/59, Trilling Collection, USC

353 HINGLE COMMENTS: Pat Hingle to SF, 9/7/99

353 NATALIE SAID SHE FOUND BEATTY DIFFICULT: 10/78 *Interview*; 11/68 *Cosmopolitan* (called affair nonsense); 3/9/69 *New York Times*; 2/62 *Screen Stories*
354 TOLD REDFORD: Robert Redford to SF
354 COLLINS DENIES AFFAIR: Joan Collins to SF, by letter
355 NATALIE WAS SERIOUS: Lana Wood to SF
355 PANICKY ABOUT BATHTUB SCENE: Henry Jaglom to SF, 6/23/99; Lana Wood to SF
356 KAZAN COULD CUT AWAY: "Natalie Wouldn't, Necessarily," John Hartl, *San Francisco Times*
357 HAD AUDREY SAY A LINE: "Natalie Wood: Mother, Men, and the Muse," Murray Kempton, *Show*, March 1962
358 LIED ABOUT LEDGE: 12/28/69 *London Times*
358 KAZAN TRICKED NATALIE ABOUT DOUBLE: 2/79 *New York Daily News*
359 KAZAN DENIED: Elia Kazan, AMC's *Hollywood Real to Reel*
359 INTERVIEW ABOUT DOUBLE: "Natalie's Double Couldn't Swim," Frank Quinn, *New York Sunday Mirror*, 6/12/60
360 DOUBLE THREATENED TO SUE: Correspondence file, 8/15/60 letter from attorney Melvin Block to Warner Brothers, Warners Special Collections, USC [states the double could swim]
359 MAGUIRE'S COMMENTS: Charles Maguire to SF, 6/16/99
359 HANCHETT'S COMMENTS: Willis Hanchett to SF, 6/9/99
360 NATALIE ECSTATIC BUT UPSET HOODWINKED: Mart Crowley, AMC's *Hollywood Real to Reel*
360 TALKED ABOUT KAZAN'S MANIPULATION: Dennis Hopper to SF
361 LOCKWOOD'S COMMENTS: Gary Lockwood to SF, 10/7/99
361 KAZAN'S FAVORITE SCENE; BROUGHT HER OWN

PAIN TO IT: Elia Kazan, AMC's *Hollywood Real to Reel*

362 GOT CALL DURING *SPLENDOR*, ODD SITUATION: Natalie Wood, *Donahue*, December 1976

362 FIRST APPROACHED ABOUT MARIA: 7/22/59 *Daily Variety* (Natalie and Elvis Presley for *West Side*); 1/24/60 Hedda Hopper column (offer to Natalie); 12/4/61 *Los Angeles Times* (Natalie said she was considered from the start [Wise confirmed to Army Archerd, 1981])

362 LAWRENCE TOO OLD; WANTED UNKNOWN: Walter Mirisch to SF, January 2001; also Hirshan to SF (wanted unknown who could sing)

362 FAWN IN FOREST: Robert Relyea to SF, 8/16/99; Robert Relyea, *West Side Stories*, MGM-UA Entertainment, produced by Peter Fitzgerald, 1995

362 RELYEA COMMENTS; PANIC SET IN: Robert Relyea to SF, 8/16/99

363 TESTED ALBERGHETTI, ETC.: Warner Brothers Special Collections, *West Side Story* file, USC, handwritten notes of possible Marias

363 NEEDED "NAME": Robert Wise to SF, 7/30/97

363 SAW *SPLENDOR* TEST: Robert Wise, "E True Hollywood Story: Natalie Wood," ("That's our Maria"); Wise, "West Side Stories" documentary

363 IMPRESSED BY DEPTH: Jerome Robbins, AMC's *Hollywood Real to Reel*

363 NOT EAGER TO PLAY INGENUE: 6/30/61 *Daily Variety*

363 SURPRISE 22ND BIRTHDAY: Maria Gurdin to Phyllis Quinn; Louella Parsons column, *Los Angeles Herald-Examiner*, 7/20/61; "Lunch Date With Natalie Wood and Bob Wagner," Lyn Tornabene, *Cosmopolitan*, October 1960 (on-set party, Sinatra at 500 Club)

363 ATTENDED SINATRA'S OPENING: Louella Parsons, *Los Angeles Herald-Examiner*, 8/1/61

364 NEGOTIATED IN ASBURY PARK: Leonard Hirshan to SF; 7/26/61 *Daily Variety*; Natalie Wood, *Donahue*, 12/76 (dance scenes had been shot); Paramount production notes: shooting began in NY on 8/10/61

364 NATALIE TURNED DOWN PERCENTAGE: 3/62 *Show*

365 HARDLY THOUGHT OF MUSICAL ASPECTS: Natalie Wood interview, *Los Angeles Times*, 12/4/60

365 SINGING INTRIGUED HER: Robert Blake outtakes; Olga Viripaeff to SF; Robert Wise to SF; Walter Mirisch to SF

365 AGREEMENT ABOUT HER VOICE: Walter Mirisch to SF; Robert Wise to SF; Saul Chaplin, *West Side Stories* documentary

365 VOICE LESSONS, BELIEVED SHE'D SING: Robert Blake outtakes; Marni Nixon to SF, 10/11/99; Marni Nixon, *West Side Stories*; 12/4/61 *Los Angeles Times* (taking voice lessons and to do own singing)

366 CROWLEY HER BEST GIRLFRIEND: Maria Gurdin to Phyllis Quinn

367 CROWLEY A CARETAKER; HOUSE BEAUTIFUL: Faye Nuell Mayo to SF

367 HOUSE IN DISREPAIR: Louella Parsons column, *Los Angeles Herald-Examiner*, 8/24/61 (on boat); 12/4/61 *Los Angeles Times*; 2/22/62 *Hollywood Reporter* (roof fell in); 9/22/61 *Time*

367 PHONE NOT RINGING: Wagner to *Sunday Express*, 8/5/62

367 MISS HAVISHAM'S MANSION: 11/68 *Cosmopolitan*

367 BEVERLY HOUSE ORNATE: 1/3/60 *Los Angeles Examiner*; 2/60 *Modern Screen*; "Endsville," Louella Parsons, *Modern Screen*, June 1960 (mad young millionaires)

367 BUTLER: 10/60 *Cosmopolitan*; 2/60 *Modern Screen*; Robert Hyatt to SF; Jean Hyatt to SF

368 12-HOUR DAYS; WISE THOUGHT INJURED: "Natalie Wood: Beauty and Violence," Stanley Gordon and

Jack Hamilton, *Look*, 4/11/61; 12/4/60 *Los Angeles Times*

368 MORENO COMMENTS: Rita Moreno to SF, 9/14/99

368 RESENTED NATALIE: Rita Moreno to SF; Tony Mordente to SF

368 EXHAUSTED: Louella Parsons, *Los Angeles Herald-Examiner*, 8/22/61; 9/22/61 *Time*

369 THREATENED NOT TO SHOW UP: Saul Chaplin, "West Side Stories"

369 MORDENTE COMMENTS: Tony Mordente to SF, 9/8/99

369 INSECURE: Lana Wood to SF; Tony Mordente to SF

371 BEATTY NOT AROUND: Bob Jiras to SF

372 NATALIE TOLD HIGH NOTES DUBBED: Marni Nixon, *West Side Stories*; 12/7/61 *Daily Variety* (Wise says Natalie's voice on "borderline"); Marni Nixon to SF

372 NATALIE WAS DECEIVED ABOUT VOICE: Marni Nixon to *Boston Herald*, 9/20/94 (a "conspiracy"); Marni Nixon, *West Side Stories*; Saul Chaplin, *West Side Stories*

372 NATALIE UPSET ABOUT VOICE: Tony Mordente to SF; Olga Viripaeff to SF; Robert Wise to SF; Relyea to SF; Marni Nixon to SF; Morgan Brittany to SF, 8/19/99

373 TONSILLECTOMY: *Daily Variety* 3/23/61, 4/6/61 (scheduled tomorrow), 4/11/61 (complications), 4/13/61 (missed Oscars); 4/6/61 *Hollywood Reporter*; 4/14/61 Louella Parsons (R.J. says "terrible" tonsillectomy); "Why Natalie and Bob Split!" Peter Forbes, *Motion Picture*, September 1961; "The Night Liz Prayed for Natalie," Naomi Katz, *Movie Life*, September 1961 (bled 4 hours); 3/62 *Photoplay* (Maria says Natalie almost died in surgery); "The Story Behind The Split," No. 16, 1961 *Hollywood Romances* (R.J. took adjoining hospital room)

373 PRESSURED TO DO *INSPECTOR*: Correspondence,

Warner Brothers Steve Trilling Special Collection, USC; trade reports

373 NATALIE VISITED R.J. ON SET: 5/4/61 *Hollywood Reporter*; Irving Brecher to SF, 5/29/99; Mother Dolores Hart to SF, 9/23/99

374 WAGNERS TO GO TO EUROPE FOR R.J. TO MEET ZANUCK AND NATALIE TO MAKE *LOVERS*: Louella Parsons column, *Los Angeles Herald-Examiner*, 6/9/61

373 NATALIE SIGNED FOR *LOVERS*: Contracts and correspondence, Trilling Collection, USC; 6/2/61 *Hollywood Reporter* (Natalie signed); Troy Donahue to SF

373 WAGNERS' JUNE SOCIAL SCHEDULE: reports of their attendance in 6/61 trades and Parsons columns (see Parsons: Beatty and Collins just returned from Europe); see also 10/61 *Movie Life* (Wagners and Beatty/Collins foursome); 6/22/61 *Los Angeles Mirror* (hand-in-hand at Jubilee)

374 AFTER *SAIL* WRAPPED: 1961 *Hollywood Romances*; 10/61 *Screen Stories*; 2/62 *Screen Stories*

375 NATALIE'S ACCOUNT OF MARRIAGE ENDING: Robert Hyatt to SF (from Natalie and Maria); Jean Hyatt to SF (from Maria); Lana Wood to SF (from Maria and Natalie); Maryann Marinkovich Brooks to SF (from Natalie)

CHAPTER 19

375 IN HIDING: Robert Hyatt to SF; Jean Hyatt to SF; Maryann Marinkovich Brooks to SF (lost 10 pounds: see also Louella Parsons 6/29/61); 6/61 trade reports and Hollywood columnists; memos and correspondence, Trilling Collection, USC (studio trying to find Natalie); 6/27/61 *Hollywood Reporter*

375 SAW ANALYST EVERY DAY AFTERWARD: Robert

Hyatt to SF; Jean Hyatt to SF; 2/62 *Motion Picture; Twinkle Twinkle Little Star*; 8/75 *Cosmopolitan*; 10/79 *After Dark*; 11/68 *Cosmopolitan*

375 KEPT SECRET: Maryann Marinkovich Brooks to SF; Robert Hyatt to SF; Jean Hyatt to SF; Lana Wood to SF; Roderick Mann to SF, 1/20/00; Faye Nuell Mayo to SF

375 NATALIE DIDN'T WANT DIVORCE: 3/86 GQ

376 R.J. WAS DESTROYED: Prudence Maree to SF

376 SHOULD HAVE HUNG: 11/85 *Parade*

376 STATEMENT: Quoted in newspapers and columns on 6/21/61 across the U.S.; 6/21 *Daily Variety* ("fooled everyone"); 4/62 *Ciné* ("like a bomb"); 6/22 *Los Angeles Mirror* ("baffled"); 8/75 *Cosmopolitan* (Taylor under sedation); 6/27 *Hollywood Reporter* ("come out of hiding")

377 CHECKED IN WITH STUDIO, WHEREABOUTS SECRET, FLU: 6/23 & 6/26 & 6/29/61 Louella Parsons columns, *Los Angeles Herald-Examiner*; William Orr to SF, 5/29/99

377 BEATTY IN NY: 6/29/61 *New York Telegram* (doing retakes and photo shoot); 6/30/61 *Daily Variety;* 10/61 *Movie Life*

377, 378 MIGHT CRACK UP; ALMOST OVER EDGE: 10/79 *After Dark;* "Natalie Wood: Hollywood's Number One Survivor," Thomas Thompson, *Look*, April 1979

378 NEEDED COMPANY AT NIGHT: 10/79 *After Dark*; 11/30/81 *London Sun*; numerous other sources

378 CROWLEY TOOK CARE OF NATALIE: Robert Jiras to SF

378 NATALIE REQUESTED LEAVE FOR EMOTIONAL REASONS: 7/3/61 letter from Warners to Natalie, Correspondence and Contracts, Warners Collection, USC; 2/62 *Screen Stories* (dropped out of *Lovers* because unfit emotionally)

378 TOO MANY MEMORIES: 12/61 *Modern Screen*

378 BUMPED INTO BEATTY AT PARTIES: 7/18/61 *Hollywood Reporter*; 7/25 *Hollywood Reporter*

378 BEATTY'S ROMANCE WITH COLLINS COOLING, AMUSED HER: Joan Collins to SF

379 BEATTY WHAT DR. ORDERED: Maryann Marinkovich Brooks to SF

379 ANALYST DIED: 10/79 *After Dark*; Leonard Rosenman to SF; 6/69 *Screen Parade*

379 FRIENDLY SETTLEMENT: *Natalie Wood Wagner vs. Robert J. Wagner, Jr.*, No. WED 3437, Superior Court, Los Angeles County, 4/16/62; Steve Biegenzahn to SF, 1/8/99; Louella Parsons column, *Los Angeles Herald-Examiner*, 8/17/61; 8/24/61 *Hollywood Reporter*

379 R.J. TO EUROPE; ANALYSIS; LIFE IN TAILSPIN: 10/6/86 *People*; 6/62 *Photoplay;* 10/9/77 *Los Angeles Times Home Magazine;* "Robert Wagner: From 'Heart' In 1952 to 'Hart' in 1980," Ken Ferguson, *Photoplay*, August 1980 (RJ therapy for 6 years); 11/85 *Parade*

379 COLLINS AND WAGNER FRIENDS: Joan Collins to SF; 2/62 *Motion Picture*; 1/30/62 *Los Angeles Times*

380 GOSSIP ABOUT NATALIE AND BEATTY: numerous magazines, columns, etc.

380 NATALIE SUICIDAL: Maryann Marinkovich Brooks to SF

380 GOSSIPS BLAMED MANSION FOR BREAKUP: See such as "Natalie and Bob: What Happened to Their Togetherness?" Mike Connolly, *Screen Stories*, October 1961, et al.

380 NATALIE AS SCARLET WOMAN WITH BEATTY: e.g., three-part series, "The Loves of Natalie," "The Star's Search for True Happiness," and "Running, Running, Running," Jean Bosquet, *Los Angeles Examiner*, 11/12/61, 11/19/61, and 11/26/61

381 BEATTY WASN'T THE CAUSE: Mart Crowley, A&E Biography of Robert Wagner, 7/5/99

381 HASN'T FOUND HAPPINESS: 11/21/61 *Los Angeles Examiner*; 2/62 *Motion Picture*
381 SAME PARIS CINEMA: "The Body Meets the Face," *Hollywood Reporter's 48th Annual*, November 1978
382 COVETED GYPSY 18 MONTHS: 8/9/60 letter from Jule Styne to Trilling, Warners Special Collection, USC (Natalie's lobbying for part); 11/9/60 Louella Parsons column mentions Natalie as Gypsy
382, 383 RUSSELL PLAYED MUD; USED CHILD STAR: Lana Wood to SF
382 MARIE RAVED AGAINST GYPSY: Robert Hyatt to SF; 1/12/62 *Hollywood Reporter*
382 3 UNFLATTERING PROFILES: 4/7/62 *Saturday Evening Post*; 3/62 *Show*; 2/26/62 *Newsweek*
382 CRUSHED BY *NEWSWEEK*: Henry Silva to SF, 12/16/99
383 BRITTANY COMMENTS: Morgan Brittany to SF, 8/19/99
383 ORRY-KELLY AND STRADLING'S TRICKS: "Natalie Wood: How Tricks of the Trade Made Her Sexy," Lloyd Shearer, *Parade*, 12/9/62
384 JILLIAN COMMENTS: Ann Jillian to SF, 10/1/99
385 MALDEN COMMENTS: Karl Malden to SF
385 PHOTOGRAPHER FOLLOWED: Natalie Wood, *Donahue*, December 1976
387 FLYING JARS OF COLD CREAM: 11/68 *Cosmopolitan*
387 TUMULTUOUS WITH BEATTY: Lana Wood, "The Final Days"
388 FALSE REPORT NATALIE IN RUSSIA: "Warren Beatty, Seriously,"Aaron Lathan, *Rolling Stone*, 4/1/82
388 ENCOUNTER IN ROME: 8/75 *Cosmopolitan*; 7/71 *Pageant*; 12/62 *Photoplay*; 1/63 *Photoplay*
389 CONFUSED ABOUT MARRIAGE: "Brash and Rumpled Star," Joseph Laitin, *Saturday Evening Post*, July 1962
389 PARTY WITH MONROE: 11/68 *Cosmopolitan*; 6/69 *Screen Parade*; 6/69 *Movie World*; Shirley Mann to SF

390 THOMPSON COMPARED HER TO MONROE: 4/79 *Look*
390 REJECTED *CHARADE*: 4/64 *Screen Stories*
391, 394 LOVED ANGIE; MORAL CODE; STAYED FRIENDS WITH BEATTY: Lana Wood to SF
392 ROLE TRUTHFUL, MET WITH SCHULMAN: 7/80 *Biarritz*; "Her Family Came Before Her Career," Barbara Glesone, *Orange County Register*, 12/2/81
393 BROKEN UP WITH BEATTY BEFORE: Tom Bosley to SF, 8/4/99; 12/12/62 *Daily Variety* (report of breakup); Hedda Hopper column, 12/16/62; 10/26/76 *San Francisco Times*
393 BOSLEY COMMENTS: Tom Bosley to SF, 8/4/99
392 EDIE ADAMS COMMENTS: Edie Adams to SF, 7/21/99
391 MOST REWARDING; GOOD TOGETHER: 10/26/76 *San Francisco Times*; "Natalie Wood Makes It as an Actress," Bruce Bahrenburg, *Newark Sunday News*, 6/15/69
392 NEILE ADAMS COMMENTS: Neile Adams to SF, 8/18/99
392 IN LOVE WITH MCQUEEN: William Claxton to SF
392 A BEAST: Sugar Bates to SF
394 COULDN'T STOP CRYING: "Hollywood Party," Murray Schumach, *New York Times*, 2/2/64
395 GOT DEPRESSED; QUESTION MARK IN FRAME: Shirley Mann to SF
395 SAW LOEW AT MAY PARTY: 4/64 *Screen Stories*
395 LOEW RESCUED DAMSELS: Janet Leigh to SF; Debbie Reynolds to SF (friend to us); Regina Loew to SF
396 LAUGHED WITH LOEW: Edd Byrnes to SF, 10/15/99; Robert Jiras to SF
396 MARRIAGE RUMORS; SABLE COAT: 10/16/63 *Hollywood Reporter*; 1/64 *Photoplay*; 11/63 *Motion Picture*
396 $200,000; NATALIE OWED A PICTURE, QUINE NEEDED MONEY: Joseph Heller to SF, 9/21/99

397 CONTRACT DEMANDS: Contracts, Warner Brothers Special Collection, USC; David Niven, Jr., to SF, 9/30/99 (2nd to Taylor)

397 DAYS OFF FOR PERIOD: Sugar Bates to SF; Phil Ball to SF, 9/24/99

397 PANIC WITHOUT ENTOURAGE: "Natalie Wood: Hollywood's Child," for *Hollywood and the Stars*, produced by David L. Wolper

397 CURTIS COMMENTS: Tony Curtis to SF, 6/2/99

397, 406 HELL FLYING ALONE; GIFT FOR COMEDY; INTERIM MEN; DAVID LANGE: Robert Jiras to SF

398 PHONED MUD IN MORNING: Maria Gurdin to Phyllis Quinn

398 PHONED OR SAW LINDON AT NOON: various sources

398 MOORE'S COMMENTS: Shirley Mann to SF

398 FAHD HEARTBREAKING: Robert Hyatt to SF

398 PREFERRED DRAMA: Jacqueline Eastes Perry to SF

401 FLIPPED OUT: William Claxton to SF

402–03 SAW R.J. AT LA SCALA; DESPERATE FOR BABY: Lana Wood to SF; 8/75 *Cosmopolitan*

402 MARION A PAYBACK; "FRIENDS": "The Robert Wagners Split!" *Rona Barrett's Hollywood*, September 1970; Katie Wagner, A&E biography of Robert Wagner

403 MOST BEAUTIFUL: "Black and White Ball," Dominick Dunne, *Vanity Fair*, July 1997

403 PROMISED *DAISY*: Contracts and correspondence, Warners Special Collections, USC; Tony Curtis to SF

403 PURSUED THEM RELENTLESSLY: Robert Mulligan, AMC's *Hollywood Real to Reel*

404 ESTRANGED FROM CURTIS: Janet Leigh to SF; Martin and Erin Jurow to SF, 9/19/99

404–05 JUROW COMMENTS: Martin and Erin Jurow to SF, 9/19/99

404 EDWARDS WORSHIPPED SLAPSTICK: Arthur Ross to SF, 9/10/99

405 PARTY ATMOSPHERE, PREFER CLOSED SET: 12/28/69 *London Times*

405 NOT A THRILL: Lana Wood to SF

405 BIRTHDAYS DEPRESSING: 8/75 *Cosmopolitan*

405 STAND-IN DIDN'T SEE TORMENT: Roselle Gordon to SF, 7/19/99

406 A LOT OF FUN: Phil Ball to SF; Jack Cunningham to SF, 10/3/99

406 PLANS WITH COURTENAY: 11/27/64 *Daily Variety*

407 SUICIDE ATTEMPT: Correspondence and memos, Warners Special Collection, *The Great Race* file (sick days); "Intimate Portrait: Natalie Wood"; Robert Jiras to SF; 11/30/64 *Hollywood Reporter* (Cedars as Natasha Gurdin); Mart Crowley, "Intimate Portrait: Natalie Wood" ("deep and complicated"); Olga Viripaeff to SF; David Niven, Jr., to SF; 4/65 *Modern Screen* (upset about *Hawaii*) [note: Walter Mirisch to SF: not aware she was upset]

407 BITTER: 4/27/86 *London Times*

408 ALONE AND EMPTY: 8/79 *McCall's*

408 ANALYST TALKED HER INTO LIVING: 8/75 *Cosmopolitan*

CHAPTER 20

408–09 LEFT U.S. AGAINST ADVICE; CRAZED YUGOSLAVIAN: David Niven, Jr., to SF, 9/30/99

409 NIVEN JR. COMMENTS: David Niven, Jr., to SF

409 BACK TO BABYLAND: 4/65 *Motion Picture*

409 NIGHTCLUB ACT: Tom Mankiewicz, *E True Hollywood Story*

411 BYRNES COMMENTS: Edd Byrnes to SF

411 REACTION ON ONE OTHER THING: "Hollywood's Child" documentary

412 FELT CLOSE TO DAISY: Natalie Wood at San Francisco Film Festival, 10/26/76

412 IDENTIFIED WITH DAISY: Gavin Lambert, American Cinematheque Tribute to Natalie Wood, September 1999

412 NATALIE APPROVED RUTH GORDON: 7/24/69 *Daily Variety*

412 REDFORD COMMENTS: Robert Redford to SF

413 REALLY CREATED A CHARACTER; ENJOYS ACTING ITSELF: 5/1/70 & 12/28/69 *London Times*

415 DISAPPOINTED BY VOICEOVER: Peggy Griffin to SF, 12/9/99; 10/26/76 *San Francisco Times*

415 UPSET AT HALF-SONG: 12/28/69 *London Times*

415 NATALIE DISAPPOINTED BY DAISY: 7/23/67 *Los Angeles Examiner*

416 CLOSEST TO BLANCHE: Rex Reed interview with Natalie Wood, *New York Times*, 1/16/66

416 HUSTON AND LEIGH ATTACHED: *Hollywood Reporter*, 10/2/64, 10/7/64

416 POLLACK COMMENTS: Sydney Pollack to SF, 2/22/99

417 SPIES: Shirley Mann to SF

418 NO IDEA WHY WEDDING CANCELED: Marion Blatnik Picciotto to SF, 10/7/99

418 BETTER LONG ENGAGEMENT: 11/30/65 *Daily Variety*

419 DAISY A FAILURE: 3/25/66 *Life*

420 COSTELLO COMMENTS: Anthony Costello to SF, 4/27/99

421 NORMA A MOTHER FIGURE: Scott Marlowe to SF

421 MONKEYS OFF BACK: 10/79 *After Dark*

422 BANNED MUD PER LINDON: Costello to SF

422 EARLY ASSIGNMENT WAS WORDSWORTH: 7/23/67 *Los Angeles Herald-Examiner*

422 WENT TO EXTREMES: 5/2/66 *Los Angeles Herald-Examiner*; 11/68 *Cosmopolitan*; culture vulture: Joyce Haber

423 DIDN'T KNOW HOW TO BE: Natalie Wood 1980 excerpt, "Intimate Portrait: Natalie Wood"

423 REALIZED SHE WANTED A FAMILY: 10/77 *Los Angeles Times Home Magazine*; 3/79 *Saturday Evening Post*; 8/79 *McCall's*; "How I Did It!" Merrill Shindler, *Los Angeles*, March 1980

423 OLGA'S THE LUCKY ONE: Olga Viripaeff to SF

423 JAGLOM COMMENTS: Henry Jaglom to SF, June 1999

424 *PENELOPE* CONTRACT: Contracts, Warners Special Collection, USC

426 MUD ENCOURAGED HER TO MARRY SINATRA: Robert Hyatt to SF

426 RING-A-DING: Leslie Bricusse to SF, 8/25/99

427 GORTON COMMENTS: David Gorton to SF, 2/22/00

427 HILLER COMMENTS: Arthur Hiller to SF, 2/18/99

428 BEATTY SPOKE FONDLY: 11/68 *Cosmopolitan*; Stuart Whitman to SF, 9/25/99 (Natalie and Beatty were friends)

429 TURNED DOWN BONNIE BECAUSE OF ANALYST: 3/9/69 *New York Times*; 10/26/76 *San Francisco Times*; 8/75 *Cosmopolitan*; 10/13/74 *Los Angeles Herald-Examiner*

429 HIVES: 4/79 *Look*

430 "WORST ACTRESS": 4/21/66 *Daily Variety*; 12/28/69 *London Times* (wrote speech)

430 SUICIDE ATTEMPT; DIDN'T SEEM SUICIDAL: Lana Wood to SF

430 NEVER SAW HER DEPRESSED: Frank Sinatra, *A Tribute to a Very Special Lady*

432 FAHD NAMED HER FIRST: 2/11/79 *New York Daily News*

433 FIRED EVERYONE; SPENT NIGHT ALONE; FLEW ALONE TO NY: Tony Costello to SF; Lana Wood to SF; 4/79 *Look*; 8/75 *Cosmopolitan*; *Twinkle Twinkle Little Star*; 7/71 *Pageant*

ACT FOUR

CHAPTER 21

437 ANGLOPHILE: Tony Costello to SF

437 CRUSH ON FINNEY; SOMEONE TO LOVE HER: Sugar Bates to SF

438 BRICUSSE COMMENTS: Leslie Bricusse to SF

438 COSTELLO COMMENTS: Tony Costello to SF

438 THAT WAS IT: "Natalie Wood – From Pampered Star," Peer J. Oppenheimer, *Family Weekly*, 10/19/69

438, 452 MADE A LIST; SOMETHING ABOUT R.J.: Lana Wood to SF

442 READY TO MARRY AND HAVE CHILDREN: 2/67 *Motion Picture*; 11/9/66 *Daily Variety*; Olga Viripaeff to SF

239, 441 STRONG MAN; FEAR OF FLYING: 7/71 *Pageant*

440 WORKED ON *ROSE GARDEN*: Sydney Pollack to SF; Tony Costello to SF

440 JUST LIVING: 10/30/69 *New York Times*

441 DRESSED LIKE A STAR FOR FLIGHTS: Diane Wells to SF, December 2000

441 NATALIE HIS FIRST BIG CHALLENGE: 8/72 *Photoplay*

441 BOTH HAVE TEMPERS: 7/71 *Pageant*

441 DIDN'T SEE WARMTH: David Niven, Jr., to SF

442 REDFORD COMMENTS: Robert Redford to SF

443 FAINTLY TRAGIC: 11/68 *Cosmopolitan*

444 LIKE BOB SCRIPT: 3/9/69 *New York Times*; 1/70 unsourced U.K. article from British Film Institute Natalie Wood collection; 9/69 *Movie World*

444 KNEW IN 10 SECONDS: Paul Mazursky, *E True Hollywood Story*

444, 445 INSECURE; WOULDN'T DO NUDE: 10/30/69 *Los Angeles Times*; Lana Wood to SF

444 GOULD COMMENTS: Elliott Gould to SF, 10/16/99

445 HAPPY WITH GREGSON: Sugar Bates to SF

445 NO STAR CRAP: Mazursky, "The Final Days"

446 MOCKED STAR IMAGE: 3/9/69 *New York Times*

446 EMBARRASSED AS HELL: Natalie Wood, *Tomorrow*, 2/14/80

447 SCARED TO SKI: 10/30/69 *Los Angeles Times*

447 MAY WEDDINGS: Olga Viripaeff to SF

447–48 RADIATED HAPPINESS, DELAYED CHILDHOOD: 10/18/69 *Family Weekly*

449 FIRST TIME PREGNANT: Natalie Wood, excerpt, AMC's *Hollywood Real to Reel*

449 JUNE '70 DINNER PARTY: Linda Foreman to SF, 9/16/99; *Twinkle Twinkle Little Star*; "Natalie Wood's Real-Life Romantic Comedy," Judy Klemesrud, *New York Times*, 2/10/80; "Happily Ever After," Jon Land, *Saturday Evening Post*, March 1979; 12/76 *People*; 11/74 *Photoplay*; 3/86 *GQ*; 11/85 *Parade*; 12/76 *Donahue*; 8/75 *Cosmopolitan*; Robert Wagner, "Intimate Portrait: Natalie Wood"

452 NATASHA'S BIRTH HAPPIEST MOMENT: 10/79 *Orange Coast*

452 ANOTHER CHANCE AT CHILDHOOD; UPSET AT MUD: Lana Wood to SF

452 NATASHINKA: Natalie Wood's eulogy for Nick Gurdin

452 THOUGHTS ON MOTHERHOOD: 9/72 *Modern Screen*

453 RESTRAINING ORDER: Olga Viripaeff to SF; Maria Gurdin to Phyllis Quinn; Leslie Bricusse to SF; Lana Wood to SF; "Intimate Portrait: Natalie Wood"; 4/79 *Look*; 11/71 *Modern Screen*; 11/71 *Motion Picture*; 8/75 *Cosmopolitan*; 11/71 *Photoplay*; Peggy Griffin to SF; Bob Jiras to SF

CHAPTER 22

454 ISOLATED SELF, TRANQUILIZERS: Lana Wood to SF; 8/17/71 *Daily Variety*; "Natalie Wood Tells," Renee

Haverhill, *Photoplay*, April 1972

454 UPSET, STOPPED EATING, SARDINIA, OLGA COMMENTS: Olga Viripaeff to SF; 4/72 *Photoplay*; Mart Crowley, "Intimate Portrait: Natalie Wood"

455, 456 CALL FROM R.J.; CALLS AGAIN: Natalie Wood, 12/76 *Donahue*; Olga Viripaeff to SF; Maria Gurdin to Phyllis Quinn; Robert Wagner, "Intimate Portrait: Natalie Wood"; 8/11/71 *Daily Variety* (R.J. in town); "New Rules For A Second Marriage," Vernon Scott, *Photoplay*, November 1974; 2/10/80 *New York Times*; 12/76 *People*; *Twinkle Twinkle Little Star*; 11/85 *Parade*

454 TINA CRUSH ON R.J.: 9/70 *Rona Barrett's Hollywood*

455 NOT WHEN; FRANCE: 10/19/71 *Hollywood Reporter*; 10/18/71 *Hollywood Reporter* (villa)

455–8, 456 THOUGHT WORLD; SEPARATE DIRECTIONS; ZIFFREN FINANCES: Peggy Griffin to SF

456 DATED MCQUEEN: Peggy Griffin to SF; Neile Adams to SF; Dennis Roberts to SF (sunglasses); Lana Wood to SF; 10/29 & 12/27/71 *Hollywood Reporter*; "How Steve McQueen Ended Her Heartache," Carol Welles, *Photoplay*, 2/72; "Ali Crushed," June Thayer, *Movie World*, 4/73; "All About Those Dates Between Natalie Wood And Steve McQueen," *Movieland*, 2/72

456 DATED JERRY BROWN: Lana Wood to SF; Peggy Griffin to SF; 2/72 *Photoplay*

457 SMEDLEY NOTICED: "How Bob Makes Natalie Feel Like a Bride Every Night," Marcia Borie, *Photoplay*, 11/72

456, 459 NATASHA PROTECTED HER; R.J. LIKE ROMEO: Natasha Gregson Wagner, "Intimate Portrait: Natalie Wood"

456 PERFECT LOVE: 4/72 *Photoplay*

457 NURSERY RHYMES: "A World of Her Own," Tim de Lisle, *Daily Telegraph Weekend Magazine*, 12/12/98

457 FAVOR FOR REDFORD, LAST CONTACT: Robert Redford to SF

457 MINK AND JEANS, PLAYED LAST SCENE: *Filming "The Candidate,"* Bruce Bahrenburg, Warner Books Inc., New York, 1972

457 PLAINTIVE CALL: Edie Adams to SF

458 HOLIDAY PLANS: 12/28/71 & 1/4/72 *Daily Variety*

458 RECONNECTED AT CHRISTMAS: Peggy Griffin to SF; Lana Wood to SF; 11/74 *Photoplay* (stopped by with gifts; "instant attraction"); 8/72 *Photoplay* (R.J. felt nostalgic, Natalie like a girl again); 12/72 *People* (went on 1/26); "Natalie Wood and Bob Wagner's Baby Girl," Henry Gris, *Photoplay*, 6/74 (together from Palm Springs on); 3/86 GQ (secretly in Palm Springs); 8/75 *Cosmopolitan* (understanding they'd remarry)

458 BAILED R.J. OUT: 3/86 GQ

459 LANA WORRIED; DEVIL YOU KNOW; GOT WHAT WANTED: Lana Wood to SF; Robert Hyatt to SF; "My Sister, Natalie Wood," Sally Ogle Davis, *Ladies Home Journal*, 11/82

460, 464 R.J. NICE; NATALIE WENT OUT OF HER WAY: Sugar Bates to SF

460 TOWNHOUSE FOR GURDINS: "We'd Be Crazy Not to Remarry," Lee Alexander, *Silver Screen*, 8/72

460 NEEDED BODYGUARDS: 4/14/72 *Hollywood Reporter*

460 ZEITENSPRUNG: 8/75 *Cosmopolitan*; Mickey Ziffren, *The Movies*, 10/83

461–63 R.J. SELDOM ON WATER, WANTED BACK; HUNTING "OUR BOAT": 9/27/81 *San Antonio Light*

461 WORST STORMS: "We Almost Died Together," Polly Terry, *Photoplay*, 1/74; 4/24/72 *New York Daily News* (made headlines)

461 TOOK PHOTOGRAPHER ALONG: Michael Childers, "The Final Days"

462 NEITHER RELIGIOUS: Lana Wood to SF; Peggy Griffin to SF; Faye Nuell Mayo to SF; Olga Viripaeff to SF

(used astrologer Carroll Righter); "Pregnant Natalie Wood Cries," *Movie Life*, 1/74 (used Righter)

462 WEDDING: 11/74 *Photoplay*; "Natalie Gives Us Her Wedding Album!" Marcia Borie, *Silver* Screen, October 1972; 10/72 *Modern Screen*; 11/72 *Rona Barrett's Hollywood*

462 SEASICK: 1/76 *TV Radio Mirror*; Maria Gurdin to Phyllis Quinn

463 GRIFFIN COMMENTS: Peggy Griffin to SF

463 TOUGH FOR NATALIE: Lana Wood to SF

464 RETREAT FROM GATSBY: Natalie Wood, 10/76 San Francisco Film Festival; 6/74 *Photoplay*

464 TV LESS PRESTIGE: 11/78 *Hollywood Reporter*

465 CATES COMMENTS: Gilbert Cates to SF, 12/22/99

465 LETTER FROM NATALIE TO RUTH GORDON: courtesy of Barry Redmond

466 GLASS HOUSE, KNIT BLANKET: 1/74 *Photoplay*

467 INTRIGUED WITH IDEA: 6/20/74 *Daily Variety*

467 MOST WANTED BABY: 8/74 *Modern Screen*

467 CRANE'S DEATH: Scott Marlowe to SF

467 SCARED DURING CHILDBIRTH: "Natalie Wood: Save My Baby," *Motion Picture*, 7/74

468 *INFERNO* BORING; CONVINCED R.J. TO MOVE; LOST 50 POUNDS: 8/75 *Cosmopolitan*; 6/20/74 *Daily Variety* (800-calorie diet)

468 A BIT MUCH; NAPOLEON: 8/79 *McCall's*; 4/79 *Look*

468 TOLD TOM SNYDER: 2/14/80 *Tomorrow*

468 MADE A PACT: numerous published interviews with Wood and Wagner

469 RATH COMMENTS: Earl Rath, Jr., to SF, 1/4/00

469 APPEALING WAIF: "Michael Caine Is a 'Peeper,'" Richard Cuskelly, *Los Angeles Herald-Examiner*, 12/3/75

470 GAVE IT THEIR ALL: 3/76 *TV Star Parade*

470, 473 DIDN'T WORK; GREGSON'S KIDS SPENT SUMMERS: Peggy Griffin to SF

470 SEMI-RETIREMENT: 3/76 *Movie World*
470 HOUSE LESS SHOWY; ANALYST FOR GIRLS: Faye Nuell Mayo to SF
470 ZEST FOR LIFE: Natasha Gregson Wagner, "Intimate Portrait: Natalie Wood"
470 ENJOYING THEIR CHILDHOOD: "Natalie Wood: Our Sexual Conscience on the Silver Screen?" *L'Officiel/USA*, August 1980
471 SPOILED ROTTEN: "Out Of The Woods," Claire Lovat, *The Sunday Times*, 12/6/98
471 FACTS OF LIFE AT 4: "Revealing Talent," Jamie Painter, *Back Stage West Drama-Logue*, 1/21/99 (talked about sex); 8/80 *L'Officiel* (not proper)
471 NOT AN OPTION: "Whatever: Natasha Gregson Wagner," Steve Hochman, *Los Angeles Times*, 1/3/99
471 SNIFFED BRANCHES; GUEST COTTAGE WITH SIGNS: Rex Reed, "Remembering Natalie," "Ovation," USA, a Cerberns Production
471 CHRISTMAS OPEN HOUSE: 10/77 *Bon Appetit*; Peggy Griffin to SF; Lana Wood to SF; Gil Cates to SF472
472 HOLLYWOOD COUPLE: Karl Malden to SF
472 PUT NATALIE ON STAGE: Roderick Mann to SF; Lana Wood to SF
472 NORMALCY HAS MYSTIQUE: 10/26/76 *San Francisco Chronicle*
473, 475 GREGSON'S LIFE CHANGED; IRON BUTTERFLY: Leslie Bricusse to SF
474 FOUND *SPLENDOUR*: 9/27/81 *San Antonio Light*
474 WHY DID THEY: Maria Gurdin to Phyllis Quinn
474 THIS LITTLE THING: Mart Crowley, "Intimate Portrait: Natalie Wood"
474 MOORING AT EMERALD BAY: Doug Bombard to SF, 10/10/99
475 REMEMBERS MOMMY AS SOLID: 12/12/98 *Daily Telegraph*
476 DON'T MAKE IT SOUND: 8/75 *Cosmopolitan*

CHAPTER 23

476 GRIFFIN COMMENTS: Peggy Griffin to SF
476 LANA COMMENTS: Lana Wood to SF
477 INSTABILITY NEVER FAR; USED KNIFE AS MIRROR: Leslie Bricusse to SF
477 GIFT THAT FELL: "Raising the Curtain on 'Cat,'" Cecil Smith, *TV Times*; 12/5/76
478 SPENT TIME WITH WILLIAMS: unsourced 7/76 U.K. interview, BFI file on Natalie Wood
478 LISTENED TO FRIENDS: Natalie Wood, 12/76 *Donahue*
478 COMPARED OLIVIER TO DEAN: 10/26/76 *San Francisco Chronicle*
480 STAPLETON COMMENTS: Maureen Stapleton to SF, 2/7/00
480 TINY LITTLE THING: 3/77 *Photoplay*
480 MIXED REVIEWS: "This Tribute Smacks of Exploitation," John J. O'Connor, *The New York Times*, 12/5/76
481 MIDDLE-AGED SQUARES: 10/77 *Los Angeles Times Home Magazine*
481 PARTIES: 10/77 *Bon Appetit*; Lana Wood to SF
481 NEAME COMMENTS: Ronald Neame to SF, 1/9/99
482 CHOSE IT FOR RUSSIAN ACCENT: 10/79 *Orange Coast*
482 TAPED MUD'S VOICE: 2/79 *New York Daily News*; 12/77 *Motion Picture*
482 CHARACTERIZATION: Natalie Wood interview, *Meteor* magazine,
Warren Publishing, 1979
482 BATES COMMENTS: Sugar Bates to SF
482 NEAME COMPLAINED ABOUT MAKEUP: "Film Casting," Jerry Cohen and Ronald L. Soble, *Los Angeles Times*, 7/4/78
483 LOOKED HARD: Robert Werden to SF, 9/20/99
483 MASON COMMENTS; EVIL-LOOKING: Ginger Mason to SF, 8/24/99

484 SYLBERTS' COMMENTS: Richard and Sharmagne Sylbert to SF, 6/17/99
485 ADORED EACH OTHER; ALWAYS DOING THINGS: Roselle Gordon to SF
486 MALDEN COMMENTS: Karl Malden to SF
485 INTERVIEW DURING *METEOR*: 10/78 *Preview*
487 REQUESTED TRAIN: 10/21/79 *Washington Post*
487 I'M AN ACTRESS; NEEDS BALANCE: Natalie Wood interview, "Remembering Natalie;" Natalie to Sue Russell, July 1978
488 I SELL SOAP: Tom Mankiewicz, A&E biography of Robert Wagner
489 BROTHER AND SISTER: Faye Nuell Mayo to SF
489 BURDITT COMMENTS: Joyce Burditt to SF,12/10/99
489 GO ON INSTINCT; IN LOVE WITH *CRACKER*: Natalie Wood, "Remembering Natalie"
490 MARTINELLI COMMENTS: John Martinelli to SF
491 SHAPIRO COMMENTS: Richard Shapiro to SF
491 LEDDING COMMENTS: Ed Ledding to SF
491 MCNALLY COMMENTS: Lola McNally to SF, fall 1999
492 THERE WERE DEMONS: Robert Wagner, "Intimate Portrait: Natalie Wood"
492 CATES COMMENTS: Gilbert Cates to SF
494 RELATED TO *MARRIED*: 2/80 *Tomorrow* show; "My life with the Greatest," Victor Dais, *London Daily Express*, 4/23/80; 3/79 *Saturday Evening Post*
495 RUSSIA TRIP: Peggy Griffin to SF; 2/15/79 *Los Angeles Times*; 4/2/79 *Look*; "Natalie Wood's Sentimental Journey," Thomas Thompson, *TV Guide*, 1/23/82; 7/80 *Biarritz*; 8/79 *McCall's*; 11/26/79 *WWD*; 12/2/81 *Orange County Register*
497 LOOK COVER: 4/2/79 *Look*

ACT FIVE

CHAPTER 24

501 MEMOIRS: Olga Viripaeff to SF; Peggy Griffin to SF; 2/10/80 *New York Times* (chapters in fur closet); 2/11/79 *New York Daily News*; Mart Crowley, "Intimate Portrait: Natalie Wood"

501 TWO TRAGEDIES: from the play *Lady Windermere's Fan*, Oscar Wilde

501 THEME OF WATER FEAR: told to Bob Lardine, as reported 12/2/81 *New York Daily News*

502 WANTED *ORDINARY PEOPLE*: Robert Redford to SF

503 CRITICISM HURTFUL: 11/26/79 *WWD*

503 GRIFFIN COMMENTS: Peggy Griffin to SF

504 ALT COMMENTS: Duane Alt to SF, 10/5/99

504 HYPNOTIZED FOR SCENE; ENACTED DEATH SCENE: "Natalie Wood In 'Eva Ryker,' " Jerry Buck, *Los Angeles Herald-Examiner*, 5/4/80

504 FIRST DEATH SCENE: 12/2/81 *Orange County Register*

504 GRAUMAN COMMENTS: Walter Grauman for SF, 8/10/99

505 HUNT COMMENTS: Grady Hunt for SF, 8/5/99

505 DILLMAN COMMENTS: Bradford Dillman for SF, fall 1999

505 FOXWORTH COMMENTS: Robert Foxworth for SF

506–07 BATES COMMENTS: Sugar Bates to SF

508 NOT HEALTHY: "Natalie Wood on Marriage and Movies," Judy Klemesrud, *Los Angeles Herald-Examiner*, 2/18/80

509 SURPRISE PARTY: 2/7/80 *Daily Variety*; 9/85 *Ladies Home Journal*

509 PRESTIGE PARTNERSHIP; MUSK, LONELY: Roderick Mann to SF

509 LIKE VENTRILOQUISTS: Sue Russell to SF, 4/30/99

509 SECOND RATE: "Reassurances of 'Last Married Couple,' " Vincent Canby, *New York Times*, 2/8/80

510 ONE TYPED ROLE: "Banjo Pickin' with George Segal," Clifford Terry, *Chicago Tribune*, 4/2/98
511 KEPT PROMISE TO FAHD: Shirley Mann to SF
513 EULOGY: written by Natalie and Lana Wood
514 WAGNER PARTY: Gilbert Cates to SF
514 R.J. TOAST: 12/14/81 *People*

CHAPTER 25

515 THE FITS; BEREFT: Maria Gurdin to Phyllis Quinn; Shirley Mann to SF; Lana Wood to SF; Olga Viripaeff to SF
515 MUD STRAINED WAGNER MARRIAGE: Lana Wood to SF; Robert Hyatt to SF; *Natalie: A Memoir by Her Sister*
515 CREATIVE STIRRING: Peggy Griffin to SF; Lana Wood to SF
516 READ *ANASTASIA* IN '80; MORE WONDERFUL: "Natalie Wood Speaks of Her Theater Debut," *Music Center News*, November 1981
516 WANTED TO DO PLAY WITH REDFORD: Robert Redford to SF
516 MUD GAVE HER PHOTOS: Maria Gurdin to Phyllis Quinn
516 FAHD HER INSPIRATION; DON'T BE AFRAID: " 'Anastasia': A Big Steppe For Wood," Roderick Mann, *Los Angeles Times*, 7/23/81
516–17 LANA COMMENTS; NOT "OVERLY THRILLED": Lana Wood to SF
516–17 PRODUCTION COMPANY; BUSINESS SIDE; GOOD TO BE AMBITIOUS: "Natalie!" *Harper's Bazaar*, September 1981
516 GRIFFIN COMMENTS: Peggy Griffin to SF
517 MILFORD COMMENTS: Nancy Milford to SF, 10/15/99

519 MUD PROVOKED ARGUMENTS: Sugar Bates to SF; Lana Wood to SF; Robert Hyatt to SF
520, 526 CALL FROM FOREMAN; INTRIGUED: 7/23/81 *Los Angeles Times*
520 SCREENWRITER'S IDEA: Robert Stitzel to SF, 10/6/98
521 POSED WITH FAN: Diane Wells to SF

CHAPTER 26

521 HAD INPUT; WALKEN WAS FOREMAN'S CHOICE: Robert Stitzel to SF
522 STITZEL COMMENTS: Robert Stitzel to SF
523 FLETCHER COMMENTS: Louise Fletcher to SF, 11/2/99
522 STARTED DIET: 9/30/83 *Los Angeles Times*; Lana Wood to SF; Louise Fletcher to SF
523 GRIFFIN COMMENTS: Peggy Griffin to SF
523 LANA COMMENTS: Lana Wood to SF
523 OLGA COMMENTS: Olga Viripaeff to SF
523 SOMETHING BOTHERING: Betty Bataùsa to SF
527 CORDIAL: Stitzel to SF
527 FINALIZED *ZELDA*: Nancy Milford to SF
527 ANNE SEXTON PROJECT: Allan Folsom, quoted in "The Plot That Made a Wallet Thicken," Bob Sipchen, *Los Angeles Times*, 2/25/93
528 TOOK A LATER FLIGHT: 9/30/83 *Los Angeles Times*
529 MCGIFFERT COMMENTS: David McGiffert to SF, 10/28/99
531 NUELL COMMENTS: Faye Nuell Mayo to SF
532 WASN'T MUCH OF A DRINKER: Christopher Walken's second statement to L.A. Sheriff's Investigators, December 1981
532 R.J. WAS IRRITATED: Margaret (Marti) Rulli to SF, 10/4/99
533 BODY MIKES: David Dukes to SF, 1/4/00

534 MORE EXCITED ABOUT *ANASTASIA*: 11/81 *Music Center News*

535 CROWE COMMENTS: Tonya Crowe for SF

538 TYPICAL TO BRING COSTARS: Marti Rulli to SF, 10/4/99

CHAPTER 27

NOTE: The police statements paraphrased or quoted are from Detectives Duane Rasure and Roy Hamilton's official notes and/or the Natalie Wood file in the L.A. Sheriff's Department Archives

540 DAVERN CLAIMS HE KNOWS: Marti Rulli to SF, 10/4/99; 3/00 *Vanity Fair*

540 DISCLOSE IN A BOOK: Dennis Davern to SF, 2/28/01; Marti Rulli to SF, 10/4/99; 3/00 *Vanity Fair*

540, 549 DAY TO REVEAL; NATALIE BOUGHT HIM A GIFT: Marti Rulli to SF, 10/4/99

541 NOON FRIDAY: police statements of Wagner, Walken and Davern

541 GO A DIFFERENT TIME; CATALINA THEIR FAVORITE; FEELING OF NEGATIVITY; R.J. IRRITATED: Dennis Davern, "The Final Days"

541 WONDERFUL WEEKEND; WORSHIPPED WAGNERS; HELPED RAISE: Marti Rulli to SF, 10/4/99

542 ROUGH CROSSING, WALKEN SEASICK; MOORED NEAR CASINO: police statements of Wagner, Walken and Davern

542 BLOODY MARYS: Walken's 2nd police statement (Detective Roy Hamilton's notes)

542 DRANK AT 2 RESTAURANTS ON AVALON: statements of Walken and Wagner (anniversary at El Galleon); Sharon Milandra and Lee Mead, "The Final Days"; Paul Reynolds' police statement

542 R.J. BOUGHT A NECKLACE: David Stein, "The Final Days"; Wagner's 2nd police statement

542 MANAGER SAW THEM LEAVE AT 10: Paul Reynolds' statement to police

543 NATALIE DIDN'T WANT TO GET INTO DINGHY: Wagner's and Walken's 2nd statements to police

543 MORE DRINKING ON THE BOAT, WENT TO STATEROOM: Walken's 2nd police statement

543 CROSSING TO MAINLAND: Wagner's 2nd police statement

543 NO MENTION OF A NIGHT CROSSING: Davern's and Walken's police statements

543 NATALIE DIDN'T WANT TO GO IN THE DARK; DISAGREEMENT ABOUT MOVING THE BOAT: Duane Rasure to SF, 10/27/99; Wagner's 2nd police statement

544 GRUMPY SEA, NATALIE'S IDEA: Davern's 2nd police statement

544–51 HUBBUB; NEVER GET INVOLVED; BOAT MOVED; STAYED ABOARD SEASICK AND APPARENTLY ASLEEP: Walken's 2nd police statement

544 THOUGHT THE BEST: Davern, "The Final Days"

545 DAVERN TOOK NATALIE ASHORE: Wagner's and Davern's 2nd police statements

545 DISTRESSED, INTOXICATED, WITH DUFFEL BAG AND DAVERN: Police statements of Paul Reynolds, Davern, Ann Laughton

544 REYNOLDS ACCOUNT: Paul Reynolds' police statement

545 NATALIE AND DAVERN CHECKED IN, INTOXICATED; MAID'S RECORDS: Police statement of Ann Laughton; Davern's media accounts

545 WAGNER AND DAVERN LATER ADMITTED NATALIE ASHORE ON FRIDAY: Wagner's and Davern's 2nd police statements; Rasure to SF

546 NATALIE ASKED DAVERN TO STAY: Marti Rulli to SF, 10/4/99; *Vanity Fair* 3/00; Davern's tabloid accounts; Davern requestioned by police per Natalie Wood file

546–47 NATALIE WANTED TO CALL LANA; SHE AND DAVERN WANTED TO RETURN TO L.A.: Marti Rulli to SF, 10/4/99 & 2/28/01

546 WINKLER ACCOUNT: Police statement of Linda Winkler

546 NATALIE ALONE BY THE PIER, CHANGED HER MIND: Marti Rulli to SF, 10/4/99; 3/00 *Vanity Fair*; Diana Magrann to SF, 6/23/99 (Magrann saw Natalie alone, looking "tragically sad")

546–47 NATALIE WOKE WALKEN TO SAY TAKING SEAPLANE; MOOD SHIFTED AND LEFT FOR ISTHMUS: Walken's 2nd police statement

547 EVERYTHING WAS BEAUTIFUL AGAIN: 3/00 *Vanity Fair*

547 FISHING, NICE RIDE, READ SCREENPLAYS, DINGHY RIDE: 2nd police statements of Wagner, Walken, Davern

547 LEFT AVALON AT 11:30: Police statement of Allen Trapp, harbor patrolman

547 #N1: Douglas Oudin to SF, 10/10/99

547 100 YARDS FROM SHORE; 50-75 BOATS: Doug Bombard to SF

547 BLUSTERY; TURNED DRIZZLY: Bombard to SF; Marilyn Wayne to SF, 11/17/99; Walken's 2nd police statement; Laurel Page Bowen to SF, 11/10/99; Marilyn Bowen to SF, 11/1/99; Christina Quinn to SF, 11/1/99

548 NATALIE AND WALKEN LEFT NOTE THEY'D GONE TO SHORE: Wagner's and Davern's 2nd police statements

548 NATALIE'S OUTFIT: Police statements of Christina Quinn, Michelle Mileski, bartender Ted Bauer

548 DOUG'S A PARTY SPOT; ACTION MOVED INSIDE: Michelle Mileski to SF, 10/26/99; Christina Quinn to SF

548 NATALIE AND WALKEN DRANK AT BAR: Christina

Quinn to SF; Michelle Mileski to SF [Mileski thought Wagner and Davern arrived first]; 3/00 *Vanity Fair*; police statement of Ted Bauer [Bauer said all four drank at the bar from 3:30 until 7:30 or 8:00]

548 R.J. AND DAVERN TOOK SHOREBOAT: Wagner's and Davern's 2nd police statements

548 HAVING GOOD TIME; OUT OF IT: Davern, "The Final Days"; 3/00 *Vanity Fair*

548 NATALIE WAS BUZZED: Michelle Mileski to SF

549 WAGNER MADE RESERVATION AND ALL 4 DRANK: 2nd police statements of Wagner, Davern; Mileski and Quinn to SF; police statement of Don Whiting

549 DAVERN NOTICED SIMMERING: Marti Rulli to SF, 10/4/99

549 WALKEN AND DAVERN SMOKED JOINT; HIGHER THAN KITE: 3/00 *Vanity Fair*

549 BROUGHT BACK 2 BOTTLES OF WINE FROM *SPLENDOUR*: Davern's and Wagner's 2nd police statement; Michelle Mileski to SF; Christina Quinn to SF; police statement of Don Whiting

549 ALL FOUR INEBRIATED, WAGNER IRRITATED WITH WIFE: Police statement of Don Whiting

549 SEATING ARRANGEMENTS: Michelle Mileski to SF

550 FROM LIGHT TO DARK, FUSSED ABOUT LIGHTING; NOT BEST MOOD: Christina Quinn to SF; Quinn's police statement

550 SENT MEAL BACK; DRINK HER MEAL: Police statement of Michelle Mileski; Mileski to SF

550 PAIN IN BUTTS, STRANGE VIBRATION, EERIE; R.J. DETACHED: Michelle Mileski to SF

550 ALCOHOL CONSUMED: Michelle Mileski to SF; Christina Quinn to SF; police statements of Mileski and Quinn; police statement of Don Whiting

550 RYAN OBSERVATIONS: John Ryan to SF, 11/15/99 & 2/13/01

551 LAUREL PAGE COMMENTS: Laurel Page Bowen to SF

551 NATALIE WAS MISSING HER DAUGHTERS: Michelle Mileski to SF; Laurel Page Bowen to SF; Christina Quinn to SF

552 NATALIE WITH LITTLE GIRL IN BATHROOM: Christina Quinn to SF; Laurel Page Bowen to SF; Dawn Powers Smith to SF, 9/28/01

552 BRAIDED HAIR AT TABLE: Michelle Mileski to SF; police statement of Susan Bernard

552 ACCORDION PLAYER: Susan Bernard's police statement; Mileski to SF; "More Shock Waves from the Death of Natalie Wood," James Bacon, *Los Angeles Herald-Examiner*, 12/1/81

552–62 FOOLING AROUND, A SPAT; HARD TIME WALKING, PUT HIS COAT AROUND HER: Mileski to SF

553 NATALIE THREW A GLASS: Police statements of Mileski, Quinn, Whiting, Bernard; Quinn and Mileski to SF; Dawn Smith to SF

553 MADE A TOAST: Walken's 2nd police statement; statement of Ted Bauer

553 PROBLEM BETWEEN WAGNER AND WIFE, PRIVATE CONVERSATION; WAGNER WAS IRATE: Rasure's notes of Whiting's statement; Hamilton's notes of Whiting's statement

553 RELUCTANT TO GO BACK: 3/00 *Vanity Fair*

553 HIT TIKI POLE, CALLED AHEAD: Mileski to SF

553 CALLED AHEAD BECAUSE INTOXICATED: Whiting's police statement

553 CALL FROM WHITING, ALL DRUNK, NATALIE UNHAPPY: Police statement of Kurt Craig; Duane Rasure to SF

554 NATALIE YELLED AND STUMBLED: Police statement of William Peterson; Peterson to SF

554 GIGGLING AND R.J. HAD TO EXPLODE: Davern, "The Final Days"

555 ALL IN SALON: Police statements of Wagner, Walken, Davern

554 MORE WINE, SCOTCH, CANDLES: 3/00 *Vanity Fair*; Davern tabloid accounts; Davern to Lana Wood, 3/24/01 (scotch); Davern's statement to R. W. Kroll at 8:30 A.M., 11/30/81 (continued to drink on boat)

555 SMALL BEEF: Walken's 1st police statement

555 DETAILS OF THE BEEF: Walken's 2nd police statement, from Rasure's notes

555 ASSHOLES: Walken's 2nd police statement, from Hamilton's notes

555 DISCUSSION OF NATALIE BEING GONE: Davern's 2nd police statement, from Rasure's notes

556 DISCUSSION OF NATALIE AWAY FROM KIDS: Wagner's 2nd police statement, from Rasure's notes

557 ARCHER RADIOED, HEARD ARGUMENT: From handwritten telephone notepad and from Rasure's notebook in the Natalie Wood file, Sheriff's Department records

557 ARCHER SAW DINGHY: William Peterson's police statement

557 R.J.'S FIRST KNOWN DISTRESS CALL WAS AT 1:30 TO WHITING: Wagner's and Davern's 11/30 statements to Det. Kroll (first call at 1:30); Wagner's 2nd police statement (first search attempt was to radio Isthmus employees); Don Whiting's police statement; Whiting's personal notes

557 WAGNER SOUNDED DRUNK: Police statements of Whiting and Wintler; Whiting and Wintler to SF; Whiting's personal notes

557 THOUGHT SHE TOOK DINGHY TO THE BAR: Whiting and Wintler's statements; Wintler to SF; Whiting's notes; Wagner and Davern's statements to Kroll; Wagner's and Davern's 2nd police statements

557 WHITING'S ACCOUNT: Whiting's private notes

558 WINTLER'S ACCOUNT: Paul Wintler's police statement

558 FIGURED OUT WHICH WAY; R.J. AGITATED, WINTLER

WANTED TO CALL FOR HELP: Paul Wintler to SF
559 NEEDED GUIDANCE, GOT OUDIN, Whiting's and Wintler's police statements; Wintler to SF; Whiting's personal notes
559 OUDIN'S ACCOUNT: Doug Oudin to SF [Note: Rasure never questioned Oudin]
560 DAZED, THOUGHT WENT TO MAINLAND: Whiting's statement to police, from Hamilton's notes
560 COAST GUARD CALLED AT 3:30: Oudin to SF; Sheriff's records
560 CALL TO LIFEGUARDS: Det. Kroll's report; Roger Smith to SF; Jean-Claude Stonier to SF
560 WAGNER'S STATEMENT TO KROLL: Kroll's Complaint Report, Sheriff's records
561 WHITING AND COLEMAN FOUND DINGHY: Whiting's and Coleman's police statements
561 SMITH TOOK DINGHY OUT; SMITH HELPED WITH BODY: Roger Smith to SF
562 BOMBARD'S ACCOUNT: Doug Bombard to SF [Note: Police never questioned Bombard]
562 LOCATION OF BODY: Avalon Sheriff's Detective R.W. Kroll's Complaint Report states that Natalie was found 250 yards north of Blue Cavern Point

CHAPTER 28

563 RASURE COMMENTS AND POLICE STATEMENTS: Duane Rasure to SF, Rasure's notes
563 R.J. ASKED DAVERN TO IDENTIFY THE BODY: Marti Rulli to SF; 3/00 *Vanity Fair*
564 R.J.'S CALLS: Bombard to SF
566 MUD AND LANA HEARD: Maria Gurdin to Phyllis Quinn; Lana Wood to SF
566, 572 OLGA FLEW; R.J. TOTALLY BROKEN: Olga Viripaeff to SF

567 WAGNER'S PRESS RELEASE: Published, among other places, in "Natalie Wood Found Dead Off Catalina," Ted Thackrey, Jr., *Los Angeles Times*, 11/30/81

568 PRESS CONFERENCE: As reported in "Some Drinks, a Fight, a Death," Mark Schorr and Andy Furillo, *Los Angeles Herald-Examiner*, 12/1/81

568 EXTRAORDINARY INTEREST; Dr. Thomas Noguchi to SF, 11/16/99

569 R.J. SEQUESTERED: Olga Viripaeff to SF; Lana Wood to SF; Faye Nuell Mayo to SF; 3/00 *Vanity Fair*; Duane Rasure to SF

569 THERE'S HIS WIFE'S: Katie Wagner, A&E biography of Robert Wagner

569 MUD WENT TO SEE: Maria Gurdin to Phyllis Quinn; Lana Wood to SF

569 TOLD LANA AN ACCIDENT: Lana Wood to SF; *Natalie*, by Lana Wood

570 OUT FOR A SWIM: "The Final Laughter-Filled Night When Natalie Died," Douglas Thompson, *London Daily News*, 12/1/81

570 ARCHERD'S COLUMN: "Just for Variety," Army Archerd, *Daily Variety*, 12/1/81

571 PALLBEARERS: 12/3/81 *Daily Variety*

571 MANULIS COMMENTS: Martin Manulis to SF, 6/10/99

571 NATASHA WAS HYSTERICAL, THEN CALM; WROTE NOTE; COURTNEY IN DENIAL: Peggy Griffin to SF; Evan Smedley Maldonado to SF, 3/2/01

572 WEREN'T WE LUCKY: 9/30/83 *Los Angeles Times*

572 IMPOSTOR NATASHA: Robert Hyatt to SF; George Liuzunie to SF; Lana Wood to SF

572 CARRIED ON CONVERSATIONS: Randal Malone to SF

574 RASURE COMMENTS: Duane Rasure to SF

574 SALERNO COMMENTS: Frank Salerno to SF, 10/26/99

574 DROWNING AND HYPOTHERMIA: Dr. Noguchi to SF; Dr. Joseph Choi to SF, 11/21/99; autopsy report

574 CHOI'S COMMENTS: Dr. Choi to SF

575 NOGUCHI'S COMMENTS: Dr. Noguchi to SF

576 ISAACS' COMMENTS: Godfrey Isaacs to SF, 11/16/99

576 CASE CLOSED: As reported in "Natalie Died by Accident," *London Daily Mirror*, 12/5/81

577 R.J.'S 2ND PRESS STATEMENT: e.g., "Wife Fell Trying to Secure Dinghy, Speculates Wagner," *Daily Variety*, 12/28/81, reporting from a *New York Daily News* copyrighted story

577 NOGUCHI'S MEMOIR VERSION: From *Coroner*, by Noguchi

578–80 MILLER'S COMMENTS: Paul Miller to SF, 2/2/00

578 GRIFFIN'S COMMENTS: Peggy Griffin to SF

580 WOULD HAVE CALLED OUT: Robert Jiras to SF

581 TOLD HOWAR: Christopher Walken to Barbara Howar, *Entertainment Tonight*, 3/2/83

581 GOOD SOUL: Robert Redford to SF

581 LEFT HANGING: "Walken's On-and-Off Career in the Movies," *New York Times*, 11/4/83

581 WHO KNOWS: Olga Viripaeff to SF

582 OOTRA VECHEREEM: Natalie's eulogy for Nick Gurdin

Index